GERARD MANLEY HOPKINS

A Life

ALSO BY PAUL MARIANI

Deaths and Transfigurations: Poems

Thirty Days: On Retreat with the Exercises of St. Ignatius

God and the Imagination: On Poets, Poetry, and the Ineffable

The Broken Tower: A Life of Hart Crane

Lost Puritan: A Life of Robert Lowell

Dream Song: The Life of John Berryman

William Carlos Williams: A New World Naked

Gerard Manley Hopkins, 1874

GERARD MANLEY
HOPKINS

A Life

Paul Mariani

VIKING

VIKING

Published by the Penguin Group

Penguin Group (USA) Inc., 375 Hudson Street,
New York, New York 10014, U.S.A.
Penguin Group (Canada), 90 Eglinton Avenue East, Suite 700, Toronto,
Ontario, Canada M4P 2Y3 (a division of Pearson Penguin Canada Inc.)
Penguin Books Ltd, 80 Strand, London WC2R 0RL, England
Penguin Ireland, 25 St. Stephen's Green, Dublin 2, Ireland
(a division of Penguin Books Ltd)
Penguin Books Australia Ltd, 250 Camberwell Road, Camberwell,
Victoria 3124, Australia (a division of Pearson Australia Group Pty Ltd)
Penguin Books India Pvt Ltd, 11 Community Centre,
Panchsheel Park, New Delhi–110 017, India
Penguin Group (NZ), 67 Apollo Drive, Rosedale, North Shore 0632,
New Zealand (a division of Pearson New Zealand Ltd)
Penguin Books (South Africa) (Pty) Ltd, 24 Sturdee Avenue,
Rosebank, Johannesburg 2196, South Africa

Penguin Books Ltd, Registered Offices: 80 Strand, London WC2R 0RL, England

First published in 2008 by Viking Penguin, a member of Penguin Group (USA) Inc.

3 5 7 9 10 8 6 4 2

Copyright © Paul Mariani, 2008
All rights reserved

Photograph credits: page iv: Harry Ransom Center, The University of Texas at Austin;
page 77: Photograph courtesy of R. K. R. Thornton

"Consule Jones" from *Gerard Manley Hopkins: The Major Works,* edited by Catherine
Phillips. Copyright © the Society of Jesus, 1986, 2002. By permission of Oxford University Press.

LIBRARY OF CONGRESS CATALOGING IN PUBLICATION DATA
Mariani, Paul L.
Gerard Manley Hopkins: a life/Paul Mariani
p. cm.
Includes index.
ISBN-13: 978-0-670-02031-7
ISBN-10: 0-670-02031-1
1. Hopkins, Gerard Manley, 1844–1889. 2. Poets, English—19th century—Biography.
3. Catholics—Great Britain—Biography. 4. Jesuits—Great Britain—Biography. I. Title.
PR4803.H44Z71715   2008
821'.8—dc22
[B]   2008036334

Printed in the United States of America
Set in Kepler
Designed by Francesca Belanger

for our son, Paul Mariani, S.J.

Hopkins in Ireland
for the Jesuit community at Boston College

Above the bluebleak priest the brightblue fisher hovers.
The priest notes the book upon the table, the lamp beside the book.
A towering Babel of papers still to grade, and that faraway look
as once more the mind begins to wander. Ah, to creep beneath the covers

of the belled bed beckoning across the room. He stops, recovers,
takes another sip of bitter tea, then winces as he takes another look
at the questions he has posed his students and the twists they took
to cover up their benighted sense of Latin. The fisher hovers

like a lit match closer to him. The windows have all been shut against
the damp black Dublin night. After all these years, his collar chokes
him still, in spite of which he wears it like some outmoded mark
of honor, remembering how his dear Ignatius must have sensed
the same landlocked frustrations. Again he lifts his pen. His strokes
lash out against the dragon din of error. The fisher incandesces in the dark.

—Paul Mariani

Acknowledgments

First of all, to Oxford University Press, granted on behalf of the Society of Jesus, for permission to quote from the writings of Gerard Manley Hopkins that still remain in copyright. Then those members of the Society who have helped me over the past forty years in my understanding of the poet, especially the tykish, stalwart, generous Father Joseph Feeney, as well as his coworkers in the field, Fathers Philip Endean and Noel Barber. Then the staffs at the Bodleian, Campion Hall, and Lower Leeson Street, Dublin, for their help when I was starting out forty years ago, researching what would become my yeoman's *Commentary on the Complete Poems of Gerard Manley Hopkins*. More recently I would like to thank the staff at the Burns Library at Boston College, where I have been privileged to teach these past eight years.

Then several members of the Hopkins Society, who—outstanding and industrious scholars that they are—form the nexus of much of the most advanced scholarly research on Hopkins, and who have been unfailingly generous with their time and support: those earlier pioneers, Fathers Anthony Bischoff and Robert Boyle, both S.J.s, as well as John Pick, Warren Anderson, and the indefatigable late Norman H. Mackenzie. Then his daughter, who has carried on in his footsteps, Professor Catherine Phillips. Also: Kelsey Thornton, Lesley Higgins, Jude Nixon, Michael Moore, Jerome Bump, Bernadette Waterman Ward, James F. Cotter, and Joaquin Kuhn, among others. A special word of thanks to Father Frederic Schlatter, S.J., whose piece-bright essays on Hopkins's classical scholarship, as well as on Hopkins's friends and associates, have proven models of their kind.

Perhaps my deepest debt of gratitude is to my dear friend Ron Hansen, who led the way in things spiritual years and years ago, when we were both teaching at the Bread Loaf Writers' Conference, when he first surprised me by reading from the manuscript of his then novel-in-progress, *Mariette in*

Ecstasy, to a largely uncomprehending audience, much as Hopkins was misunderstood a century earlier, and I thought, yes, yes, this is what I should like to do as well, work of this dimension and seriousness. A forty-plus-year debt of gratitude to my former mentor and champion at the Graduate Center of New York at Hunter and throughout my teaching career: Allen Mandelbaum, who in my twenty-sixth and twenty-seventh years led me through the havoc and the glory of attempting a commentary on Hopkins's sonnets.

Deep gratitude too to Carolyn Carlson as Executive Editor at Viking, for her astuteness and kind care, and most especially to Beena Kamlani, the one who saw this project—daunting as it so often seemed—through to its successful completion, and who not only step by step oversaw a veritable linguistic maze of data morphed into something like a living presence at the heart of it all, but who watched over this project from its alpha to its omega, once going so far as to toss her varicolored scarf across the editors' table to say that these—these blues and soutane blacks, ivory whites and gold glimmers—were the colors that should serve as paradigm for the forgèd features of this man's life. And to my agent, Tom Grady, a Virgil leading his erstwhile pilgrim through the underbrush and malebolges of publishing the life of a poet who in his own time could publish nothing.

Thanks too to so many of my students over the years, who have accompanied me, often opening new doors to discover glittering gold in the nooks and gewgaw crannies that make up the splendid memory palace of this proto-Modern, amazing Victorian Catholic poet. Colleagues too, on the long journey that seems now, in retrospect, as one stands like some bedazzled Prospero on the shore facing the vast waters of the primordial dark which are but a wink in eternity: Vince DiMarco, John Sitter, Ben Birnbaum, the late Father Bob Barth, S.J., Judith Wilt, Father Joe Marchese, John Mahoney, Joe Quinn, Jack Neuhauser, Bert Garza, Pat Maney, and especially Father Bill Leahy, S.J., who leads as I imagine U. S. Grant led through the vast Wilderness, in this case of higher education. Then those who stood by me through the terrifying, comforting phases of the Long Retreat, through which I came to understand Hopkins in a wholly and holy different light, among them Larry Corcoran and J. J. Bresnahan, both S.J.s.

And, finally, a tender bow to my wife, Eileen, whom I have known for nearly fifty years, life's partner and dearest friend, who has steadied her obsessed husband as he composed and decomposed page after page after page, rings growing by increments into book and book and book, employing first his scratchy pen and pencil, and then his two forefingers on that old Olivetti whose metal teeth he wore down to the bone, and then the generations of computers, so many he has ceased to care to count. A bow too to my three sons, John, Mark, and my oldest, Paul, to whom I dedicate this book, and who to my delight and awe has followed in the footsteps of Fathers Ignatius and Xavier, Ricci and Rodriguez and Hopkins, that little one who stared balefully up at me uncomprehending from his baby's seat in that tiny apartment there on Booth Memorial Boulevard in Flushing all those years ago, while his doting father pored over the poems of the one poet who would most deeply change their lives.

Contents

PART I

WE ARE SO GRAFTED
ON HIS WOOD

1844–1868

Robert Bridges and Gerard Manley Hopkins, 1863.

Chapter 1

In the Breaking of the Bread:
Horsham & Home, 1866, and the Early Years

"The world is chárged wíth the grándeur of God," Hopkins believed. He believed it from his undergraduate years at Oxford as an Anglican seeker. Believed it so strongly that it led in large part to his conversion to the Roman Catholic Church. Believed it as a Jesuit, and called on both Ignatius's *Spiritual Exercises* and the insights of the philosopher Duns Scotus into Christ's Incarnation to formulate a theodicy and a poetics which would articulate and sing what his whole self—head and heart—felt. And the evidence of that grandeur came to be everywhere for him: in the sublime Alps as in violets and running streams and in the ten thousand faces which reflected the very face of God.

All that was wanting, he believed, was the beholder. And when the beheld and the beholder once met, when the essential nature of the thing was instressed upon the eye, ear, tongue, and mind, the heart could not help but rise up as at a sudden unheard symphony, a dance, the heart growing "bold and bolder" as it hurled itself after its Creator, the One who bode there and abided. But to realize this way of seeing into the heart of things would eventually cost him everything, for it would mean giving himself over to this new reality, deeper and more satisfying than anything else he had ever felt, an unbearable lightness everywhere about us, and only the insulation of self-preoccupation keeping the self from feeling its staggering, terrifying sweetness and tenderness.

More, Hopkins's own poetry would come to be charged with incarnating this same reality. It would be his response to the incredible gifts God had lavished on him as on others. His language too would come to be charged with a barbarously refined new energy, but only as he remained true to what he had been charged with doing: singing the earth's praise and bringing news to others of what he had been privileged to see and understand. It would be his overture responding to God's smile. He would not sing of himself, as Whitman was singing of himself there in the New World. Nor would he dwell on himself, as Lucifer had done before his fall. Rather, he would direct himself outwardly toward the sublime Other. At least that was his dream, his reason for uttering his poems, though in time he would plunge deeper into the abyss of the stark self than any poet since Milton.

"Oh, / We lash with the best or worst / Word last!" he would come to understand:

> How a lush-kept, plush-capped sloe
>   Will, mouthed to flesh-burst,
>   Gush!—flush the man, the being with it, sour or sweet
>   Brim, in a flash, full!

That final yes or no to God's universe, of which he realized with honeyed exaltation or salt bitterness he was but a mere spark, a floating mote, would be at the heart of it, and provide for him on his journey—if that was what it was—through its unexpected, protean shiftings. And not only for the years of philosophical inquiry. Not only for the search at Oxford for what remained of Newman and Pusey's movement toward a more integrated Catholic vision. Not only for his search for a religious community to which he could swear fraternal fidelity—whether as a contemplative with the Benedictines, or with the Franciscans, or, as it turned out, with the Jesuits, together with Ignatius's vision of a contemplative order in action, serving wherever it was needed, as needed, like a soldier following Orders.

"I did say yes," he would acknowledge, trembling at the memory of it, when "at lightning and lashed rod" God heard him, "truer than tongue, confess / Thy terror, O Christ, O God." But was that confession a cry of surrender, or the cry of someone unable any longer to hold back the stress of something surging through the very marrow of his soul? It would be the beginning too of his realization that he would have to give up remaining where he was, on ground he understood—the symbolic remembrance of Christ in the Eucharist—because that way of seeing things was no longer enough. He would come to hunger after nothing less than the Real Presence, God actually indwelling in things as simple as bread and wine, and see it as the logical extension of God's indwelling among us, pitching His tent in the desert of ourselves so that He could speak to us as He had with Moses in the tent.

Two look at the world around them. One thinks of oil or gold or another human being and puts a value on it or him or her. Another looks at the world and sees news of God's presence calling. Or two look at a piece of bread or a cup of wine and see bread or wine only—the quotidian, the physical thing itself, while another looks at the same two things and is shaken to the very core by the God-saturated reality brimming in the deepest self. And these ways of seeing come to make all the difference in one's life, one's thoughts, even in the way one comes to taste words.

And so with Hopkins, who for complex reasons needed, he felt, to become a Catholic and (better, worse) a Jesuit priest. Neither choice could possibly lead to preferment or even acceptance in his world, the world of late Victorian England. But they were—those choices—the logical outcome for him of much deep thinking and soul-searching. It would mean going counter to the secular and agnostic cutting-edge thinking of his own day, whether that thinker was Hegel or Lyell, Darwin or Freud. It would mean creating a radically new idiom that would lead to the renewal and possibilities of English, giving it back something of its original Anglo-Saxon force, besides recovering anew the all-but-forgotten beauties of plainchant. It would mean a poetry lettered and saturated with a language shimmering with the possibilities of a sacramental vision of the world around us. It would come to mean the possibility of actually renewing both the world and its words.

So give it a day, a date, a going forth, a crossing over, all in an instant, finally, a yes and a yes again. Call it Wednesday, July 18, 1866. Call it an out-of-the way point somewhere south of London and name it Horsham, on a dull midsummer's day with curds-and-whey clouds faintly appearing and disappearing. Call it what he would with its wondrous, irresistible forces working on him. The instress of it, like the ooze of virgin oil crushed in the press of God's hands, an anointing, a yielding, a yes.

July 18, 1866, Horsham: Hopkins—Gerard Manley (the Manley after his father)—has been hiking the fields and roadways around Horsham now for hours, listlessly observing the oaks and elms of the Sussex countryside a hundred miles to the south of London and his Hampstead home. He is just shy of his twenty-second birthday, five foot four, thin, fair-haired and athletic, with a scrubby thin beard which does not become him. And while he can joke and banter with the best of them, he seems tired, tired beyond his years, tired of standing on the sidelines as the great appetitive world spins on. Isn't that what he himself had written the year before, about the alchemist in the city pining for something, something substantial, something immortal as diamond, beyond the mere cloudlike transitoriness of it all?

Like Moses, preparing to go out into the wilderness calling to him beyond his own too-human concerns? "My window shews the travelling clouds," he had written then,

> Leaves spent, new seasons, alter'd sky,
>   The making and the melting crowds:
>   The whole world passes; I stand by.

Others build. Build massive edifices of one kind or another to crown their days. Even birds build nests. But what of him, watching his life drift away in meaningless activity?

> They do not waste their meted hours,
>   But men and masters plan and build:
>   I see the crowning of their towers,
>   And happy promises fulfilled . . .

And yet something—call it some ineffable mystery—has been calling to him, for he too, like so many of the earnest young starting out, would love to somehow turn the dross of the quotidian to gold. He too would pierce, if only he knew how, "the yellow waxen light" of the phoenix sun, "with free long looking, ere I die." But that would mean surrendering—would it not?—giving up so much: the support of his family, his friends at Oxford, his tutors, his confessor Liddon, the magnetic Dr. Pusey, Urquhart, all those who have counseled him to keep within the Anglican Church into which he was born and raised by caring parents with close connections to that Church.

Nearly all his relatives are Church of England moderates, among them his mother and father and seven siblings, of whom he is the oldest and the one to whom the younger ones look up. If he should go over to the Roman Church, if his imminent "perversion," as his Anglican religionists prefer to name such defections, becomes a fact, it will mean loss of preference, loss of a university professorship at Oxford, loss of prestige among the majority of his countrymen, lookings askance, distrust, and the certain knowledge that his father especially will never understand, certain now that his poor lost prodigal son, with such a promising future ahead of him and who has done so well at Oxford, will have gone mad from too much reading and so gone over to the enemy. And all for what? Out of sheer self-will, to follow a chimerical vision? Or to finally surrender and go over, like his hero, John

Henry Newman, and others before him—to the old Catholic faith, whatever the cost, if he is ever to find rest from his motionable mind?

And yet something like a colossal smile has been drawing him in that very direction. Not only his High Church Anglican teachers and tutors who are still part of this thirty-year-old Oxford Movement which somehow survived even Newman's defection to Rome twenty years before, but churchmen like Pusey and Liddon and his protean, wind-wavering friend Urquhart, along with so many of his own Oxford contemporaries: undergraduates attending Anglican masses where vestments are worn, and incense burned and confession in the form of the writing out of one's sins in exacting detail have become regular practices. Young men quivering like erratic magnets to take that last step of crossing over to Rome, and only waiting for the time when the Spirit will summon them there.

The questions, the pros and cons, the arguments and counterarguments, in short, the logistical nightmare of it all, have been torturing Hopkins for two years now, at least as far back as his telling his friend Ernest Coleridge that he was afraid Coleridge was not very Catholic—he meant Anglo-Catholic then—and warning him against doing what he himself had done when he'd first come up to Oxford: adopting the fashionable attitude of the so-called Liberal and Enlightened Christian. That Laodocian attitude, he had come to see, only led to the loss of one's faith altogether. The truth, the one "great aid to belief and object of belief," the underpinning of it all, came down to the fact of the real presence of God in the Blessed Sacrament. Without that anchor, without that centering and safeguard, Christianity was "sombre, dangerous, illogical." With it, Christianity was not only consistent and grounded in certainty, it was, above all, "loveable," something not only his searching mind but his hungry heart could latch onto. Hold to that, he counseled Coleridge, "and you will gain all Catholic truth."

But it is, he sees, as insects drone and light plays about him on a quiet country road, the very definition of "Catholic" itself which has changed for him in the last two years. Consider John Henry Newman, his hero and spiritual father, a man now in his mid-sixties and a tried veteran of these religious wars, stung into answering his Anglican critics for his abandonment of the Church of England, at last publishing his *Apologia pro Vita Sua.* In a justly memorable passage there, Newman had recalled the day he left his beloved Oxford for the last time. It was the morning of February 22, 1846, and he was then forty-five. After years of arguing with himself and others, he was finally going over to Rome, leaving Trinity, dear Trinity, which had never been unkind to him, behind forever. Twenty years on, and Newman could still see in his mind's eye the lovely "snap-dragon growing on the walls opposite my freshman's rooms there." It was an image he had long taken "as an emblem of my own perpetual residence even unto death in my University." And yet Newman had had no choice then, as he, like other Catholic converts from Anglicanism had seen it, but to leave his university and its environs forever if he was to follow his conscience. He would not see his beloved Oxford again for many years, "excepting its spires," and those only "as they are seen from the railway."

The previous January, Coleridge had come up to Oxford to see how Hopkins was faring amid the gray walls and river meadows of the university. During that time he and Hopkins had had another of their endless peripatetic philosophical talks, the topic this time centering on what seemed the inevitable inconsequentiality and triviality of life. You were born, Coleridge had insisted, you lived, you married (or didn't), had children (or didn't), you toiled, ate, slept, you grew old, you sickened, you died. In the course of the discussion, Coleridge had opined—like so many young men trying on the immense abstractions of an idea—that it seemed a sheer impossibility that God should allow a place like hell to exist in the divine scheme of things. It was Origin's ancient argument for apocatastasis—the final emptying of hell—all over again, Hopkins had realized, only this time fitted out in Darwinian evolutionary dress. How could anything like eternity, Coleridge had argued, depend "on anything so trivial and inadequate as life is"? From a purely scientific perspective, human life did not even amount to a drop in the ocean of eternity.

A week later, still worrying the idea, Hopkins had written him, laying out what he thought being separated from God came down to. He understood Coleridge's point of view, he assured him, but it was equally true that it would be absolutely intolerable to the human mind (and heart) if there was nothing whatsoever—no authority, no touchstone—to "correct and avenge the triviality of this life." Life *had* to have meaning, he had come to believe, just because God had created the universe and held it at every moment in being. True, God's immensity made our "ordinary goings on look more ridiculously trivial than they wd. otherwise." But there was another argument against the triviality of life so prevalent in contemporary thinking, and that was the *fact* of the Incarnation—of God's breaking into the world by taking on human flesh in spite of all its staggering limitations.

Indeed, it was one of the most significant and adorable "aspects of the incredible condescension of the Incarnation . . . that our Lord submitted not only to the pains of life, the fasting, scourging, crucifixion etc. or the insults, as the mocking, blindfolding, spitting etc, but also to the mean and trivial accidents of humanity" that, after making the world, the Creator should "consent to be taught carpentering, and, being the eternal Reason, to be catechised in the theology of the Rabbins." If, therefore, the Incarnation—the Creator's taking on the very stuff of His own Creation—could manifest itself among "trivial men and trivial things," why was it so surprising "that our reception or non-reception of its benefits shd. be also amidst trivialities"? By entering our world and pitching His tent among us, God had lifted everything to an utterly new level of significance.

Trinity Term, mid-April, 1866: An auspicious beginning to Hopkins's third year at Balliol. He has just settled into new lodgings at 18 New Inn Hall Street, in the heart of Oxford, with William Addis, fellow High Church Anglican, who, like himself, is seriously considering going over to the Catholic Church. One afternoon, in fine spring weather, the two walk out together to the Hinkseys, where Hopkins—that inveterate observer of nature—notes the robin's-egg blue spring sky "pied with clouds" while the two discuss religion. On another afternoon, he walks out with his tutor, Walter Pater, Fellow of Brasenose, to discuss Renaissance aesthetics (da Vinci, Botticelli, Pico della Mirandola), the Pre-Raphaelites (among whom Pater has made several friends), John Ruskin, and the work of the German archeologist Johann Winckelmann, though he shies away from speaking of religious matters or anything resembling ascetical practices. Those topics belong rather to the other camp of Liddon and his ilk.

Another afternoon, out walking alone, Hopkins's eye catches swallows "playing over Christ Church meadows with a wavy and hanging flight . . . shewing their white bellies," so that he stops to listen to "the lisp of their wings." Crossing the college cricket grounds, he runs into Tom Case, who tells him about three Christ Church men he caught laughing at a rat whose back had been broken, which kept flying at a bull terrier tormenting it, until Case kicked the dog away and put the rat out of its misery. This too, Hopkins sees, is part of life here at Oxford: baiting a rat the way one smashes an opponent on the field.

Early May. Scholar Gypsy country: Hopkins and Addis stroll across the fields from Bablock Hythe to Cumnor Hill to view the new Anglican church of St. Philip's and St. James', where their friend Edward Urquhart has served as curate for the past two years. How lovely the new-turned earth here, its "vivid green slanting away beyond the skyline," the clouds tinged a pale rose-purple. Oaks, elms, and white poplars in leaf now, and fields of cow-slip, speckled with bluebells and purple orchis, capriciously coloring the meadows "in creamy drifts." He observes the green water on the Upper Isis flowing past the shabbier parts of town and, under the bridges, "swallows shooting, blue and purple above," their "amber-tinged breasts reflected in the water . . . leaning first to one side then the other." How good to be here at Oxford, where a good God can so manifest His Creation. Though already that world is changing in so many ways, spiritually as well as physically. "That landscape the charm of Oxford," he will remember a dozen years later, when he returns here: "green shouldering" the gray of the old build-ings as it has for centuries now, but in so short a time "abridged and soured and . . . soon [to] be put out altogether, the Whytham and Godstow landscape."

Addis is still going on earnestly as they walk, spilling out the elaborate preparations he has taken to prepare for his confession with Henry Liddon, who has advised him to undertake a month-long fast and not read for ex-ams during the whole time. Instead, he has taken to long solitary walks out into the countryside. It was on one of these walks, he tells Hopkins, that he actually fainted from hunger. In fact, Hopkins can't help noticing that his friend keeps breaking out into hysterical laughter. Has Liddon in his Trac-tarian zeal been counseling Addis unwisely? And the fact that he too is be-ing counseled by Liddon in spiritual matters sends a new shiver through him. Strolling by himself along the flower-decked walks of Magdalen Col-lege a week later, he notes the budding green-white leaves of elms and beeches. How beautiful to witness all this, he thinks. And yet something is missing here, some inner music, "the want of the canon" to make the land-scape cohere. It is something he cannot define even to himself. In spite of nature coming into blossom again, there is at the heart of everything he looks upon some deep, indefinable sadness, a fear that nothing matters.

Ascension Thursday: He walks seven miles out to the great Fyfield elm Matthew Arnold had earlier celebrated in *The Scholar Gypsy* and *Thyrsis*. Elms revealing a lightness among the shadows. Chestnut trees and the dis-tinct odor of firs. Rooks cawing near a ruined old country church. Bluebells, primrose and campion, and little children beating the bounds of an old church with white rods. How good it all is. But that very evening he learns of the sudden failure of one London bank after another, the result of fever-ish speculation in the American economy as the defeat of the Confederate South comes home to thousands of British speculators who had made their livings with the now-ruined cotton trade. Then a letter from his father. The Agra and Mastermans, Grandpapa Smith's bank, has been through a crisis—a panic, in fact—in the midst of which Grandpapa, "in a fit of generous impulse, went to them, and instead of withdrawing any of his money paid them in an additional £2500, to shew his confidence, and as a mark of friendship: they having been, he says, very kind to him years ago."

Whit Sunday: He listens as Pusey preaches at St. Mary's, then walks out to Cumnor with another Balliol student, Richard Nettleship. Returning by moonlight, they can hear the cuckoos calling to one other, the back and forth notes overlapping to create "canons of triplets." In the dark he looks hard at the "beautiful blackness and definition of elm tree branches in evening light," what he will call in a poem two decades on, immersed then in a darkness of his own he cannot now even imagine, those "beak-leaved boughs dragonish." A week later, he strolls out into the countryside with Pater, who goes on for two hours railing against Christianity. It is, he tells Hopkins, most unlikely that the "soul"—whatever that is—lives on after death.

In early June, another walk, this one with someone from the other camp: the Reverend Thomas Eaglesim, curate of St. Paul's, during which they are caught in a downpour. Back in his rooms, Hopkins builds a fire to take the chill off, and suddenly decides it is time to burn his private journals. A Sunday afternoon stroll with Alfred William Garrett along Binsey Lane, the willows and poplars yellow now and the buttercups up "and under-reddened with sorrel and . . . oxeyes and puff-balls." And though Garrett goes on about something, he keeps listening for the song of the woodlark, more definite, he suddenly realizes, than even the skylark's *teevo cheevo cheevio chee.* A few days later, he gets up at 3:30 a.m. to watch the sun rise over the Oxford spires and sketches the scene for his sisters, Grace and Katie, "Pilkie" and "Pulkie," as they are affectionately known. He has heard from Papa again. The Agra—alas—has gone belly up, and with it a good part of Grandpapa Smith's fortune, something so painful that no one will talk about it, "as the subject is disagreeable," his father tells him, "and it is to be hoped that part will be recovered."

June 13: Rain and more rain, so that graduation exercises must be held in the Sheldonian Theatre rather than outdoors. He is among the crowd of undergraduates there to send off the graduates. Up on stage is the bewhiskered Matthew Arnold, current holder of Oxford's Chair in Poetry, who has just finished a series of lectures on the Celtic Element in English Poetry, some of which Hopkins has attended. But today Arnold is eulogizing the late John Keble, founder of the Tractarian Movement and former holder of the chair Arnold now holds, as well as the author of the century's most popular book of English verse, *The Christian Year,* which has gone through some 150 editions and sold 350,000 copies.

But Hopkins's mind is elsewhere, trying to locate the inscape in something as shape-shifting as the thronging crowd about him, who seem as bored by Arnold as he is, and are far more interested in heckling some poor devil who has dared to wear a cream-colored coat rather than the traditional graduation black, and who—when he can no longer take their jeers— gets up and stamps out of the auditorium. What, Hopkins wonders, has he just witnessed, this sense of a large crowd moving as one, every head facing in the same direction, intent only on the squirming fellow in the cream-colored coat? Hundreds of "black coats relieved only by white shirt-fronts," he sees, the "short strokes of eyes, nose, mouth, repeated hundreds of times." It is this repeated instress, he realizes, which seems to register the scene's inscape. "Looked at in any one instance," he realizes, "the inscape would be too evanescent to catch," but in the whole design of it, one can catch it, if only for an instant. It is this sudden sense of finding order in randomness, as in the short parallel "cusp-ends of six-foils in the iron tracery of the choir gates" he had gazed so hard at that morning in chapel. News of God, if only one were willing to pay things the attention they ask for.

And now, with the Long Vacation upon him, he prepares to vacate his lodgings. Across the hall from him, another undergraduate has departed, leaving his door open behind him. Hopkins peers in, surprised to discover a painted crucifix in the student's bedroom, along with copies of Benson's *Manual of Intercessory Prayer* and Wilson's *Sacra Privata.* He had not realized until this moment that the fellow was that High Church, but, he sees now, there must be many more like himself up at Oxford now. Then it is off by train to the Somerset countryside for a week-long walking holiday with Addis, most of it in heavy downpours. Actually, it is more of a pilgrimage to visit the remains of pre-Reformation abbeys and cathedrals destroyed by Harry Tudor three centuries before.

Their first stop is the twelfth-century Norman abbey at Glastonbury, where restoration work on the ancient porticoes is underway. Then up to the Tor to oversee the island of Avalon. "Where falls not hail, or rain, or any snow," Tennyson had written in his *Morte d'Arthur,* describing this very place much as Homer had described the Elysian Fields three millennia before,

> Nor ever wind blows loudly; but it lies
> Deep-meadowed, happy, fair with orchard-lawns
> And bowery hollows crowned with summer sea.

They are lines Hopkins himself had already taken by eminent domain two years earlier for his own "Heaven-Haven" (lifting the title from a line by another of his early favorites, the Anglican priest George Herbert), placing his own words in the mouth of a young nun about to take the veil. "I have desired to go / Where springs not fail," the pearl-like poem begins, capturing so poignantly Hopkins's own deepest desires for that most elusive of all gifts, peace:

> To fields where flies no sharp and sided hail
> And a few lilies blow.
>
> And I have asked to be
> Where no storms come,
> Where the green swell is in the havens dumb,
> And out of the swing of the sea.

Later, he and Addis trudge like bent soldiers through heavy rain for six more miles to reach the cathedral at Wells. And though the calendar reads mid-June, it feels more like March. Nothing for it, he knows, but to push on to Bristol, where they stay the night at an inn near St. Raphael's, and there—on the coldest summer day he can remember, with heavy winds and rain—he and Addis attend services and listen with delight to an Anglican choir intone the ancient Gregorian chant. Then the ferry to Chepstow and South Wales, making their way up the Valley of the Wye to Wordsworth's Tintern Abbey, which Hopkins finds to be merely "typical English work." The following day, a lovely steep grass path down to the ferry on the Wye, his eyes taking in the "blue sprays of wych-elm" morphing to green in the strong sunlight.

That evening, a stroll along the Wye by moonlight, the waters "flush, swift, and oily," Addis remarking how the moon has streaked the river with "hairs of light," a phrase which catches Hopkins's attention. That, and the aspens: black, beaklike forms only now, their dapple lost, the darkness throwing "their scarcer leaves into barbs or arrowheads." They have been speaking of friendship, and Addis is explaining that friendship is mere feeling only, remembering a dead friend who once walked these same roads. It is all very sad, these losses, Addis tells him. But not because of those who have gone before. The dead are not dead, he explains. Rather, it is we the living who are lost.

Feet blistered and swollen from the kid boots he has borrowed from a cousin, Hopkins travels to the Abbey Close at Hereford by train, while Addis decides to slog the fourteen miles alone. Later that day, they hike together along the Wye through medieval stands of oak to the Benedictine monastery at Belmont. For both men, this is new territory: an active Roman Catholic religious community recently returned to English soil after centuries abroad. One of the fathers, a kindly man in his mid-thirties, shows them over the grounds. He is Dom Paul Wilfrid Raynal from Mauritius, "probably the first Catholic priest Hopkins ever spoke to," Addis will remember forty years later. When asked directly, Raynal speaks of the "'doubtful validity' of Anglican orders, and says that—until this doubt is cleared by 'competent authority' it is 'unlawful' to participate in the Anglican Communion." Dom Raynal "made a great impression on both of us," Addis will remember, so deep in fact that "from that time our faith in Anglicanism was really gone."

Afterward, Addis hikes another thirty miles to Gloucester, while Hopkins goes on by train. The following day is spent strolling about the cathedral grounds, noting how poorly things here have been restored. Both men, still shaken by their meeting with Dom Raynal, are quiet and sad. Even the morning, which had started out so brightly, has grown dull along with them. Returning home by rail, Hopkins looks out the window at the sodden landscape. Then, just at sundown, a break in the weather, with "soft round curdled clouds bathed with fleshy rose-colour in wedges," before the rains move in again.

From his home at Oak Hill in Hampstead, he takes the train into town to see the Royal Academy exhibition, noting a fine portrait of the celebrated General "Chinese" Gordon in a yellow Mandarin costume. A few days later, he takes in the Water Colour Exhibition, noting Burne Jones's *Cupid Finding Psyche,* as well a painting of Goderich Castle with that green moss on red sandstone he'd noted on his trip up the Wye. Back home he is greeted by the sound of children's laughter and then his sister Millicent improvising on the piano in the main room, so that he is struck by the competence and beauty of her playing as if by a revelation.

At his grandfather's estate at Blunt House a week later, he studies the smoky mist rising from the gravel paths one morning following a heavy downpour, and notes how the scythes have sliced half circles in parallel ranks as far as he can see, and then looks hard at the rows of brilliant red carnations his grandfather so loves, noting "their tongue-shaped petals powdered with spankled red glister." His grandmother is gravely ill now, but still pretty, her skeletal thinness "bringing out the delicacy of her features." Back at Oak Hill, he wanders the fields, studying the oaks and haycocks, then takes in the Belgian art exhibit in London. And then it is off to the south for a few days to view the rural charms of Haslemere and Lavington and Petworth, before boarding the train for the short journey to Horsham, where he is going to try and make up his mind about what has been preoccupying him—silent though he has been about it with his family—since his meeting with that extraordinary Benedictine priest three weeks before.

In fact, he has come to Horsham at the suggestion of none other than Walter Pater. Seductive country, that Sussex, Pater has called it (seductive indeed), where he can read and roam the fields and woods and visit the old Catholic cathedrals and abbey closes. In addition, there is a High Anglican church here with a weekly celebration, which is what Garrett and Macfarlane—who will take Anglican orders in two months' time—have both insisted on. "Oh Macfarlane," Hopkins has twitted him as plans were being made for this summer reading trip. "To think that a rag of popery—for that 'stately' service at Horsham means vestments of course—shd. be leading you and Garrett so palpably by the nose." Have they come all this way to keep up "a thermometer of orthodoxy by an unbending line of talk . . . with regard to almuces, buskins, and apparels, and such anise and cummin?" What kind of Anglicans are they, after all, flirting with Rome like this?

A night at the King's Head in town, and then he and Garrett move into what turns out to be an ugly, run-down farm two and a half miles out in the country, which they have rented from a Mr. Henry Ing for a fortnight at thirty shillings the week. But already the place seems more of a fool's paradise than an ideal setting in which to read and to make as many Anglican services as they can, though the surrounding country is splendid enough. But Hopkins's mind is on other matters. "Love I was shown upon the mountainside," he had written nine months earlier in another poem reminiscent of his beloved George Herbert. He had called it "The Half-way House," the title shifting from its popular Victorian meaning of Herbert's High Church tradition to the Roman Catholic Church he now believes is his own half-way house to heaven. Like every mortal being, he will have only until nightfall if he is ever to find Christ. But if he has only logic and reason to count on, he sees, he will always be snail-like creeping onward while the elusive, ineffable reality of Christ's mystery seems to fly before him like some winged bird. And though he is only twenty-one, he can already feel his own evening coming on, his mind growing darker and darker with a kind of melancholy sadness. And yet he knows that it is up to Christ rather to catch *him* than for him to try and ever catch Christ:

> Love I was shewn upon the mountain-side
> And bid to catch Him ere the drop of day.
> See, Love, I creep and Thou on wings dost ride:
> Love, it is evening now and Thou away;
> Love, it grows darker here and Thou art above;
> Love, come down to me if Thy name be Love.

He has watched his faith in the Tractarian Movement and the Church of England crumble. When Christ walked among us, he realizes, he never or only once—at the institution of the Eucharist the night before he died—partook of Love's proper food. Yet it is that food which Hopkins so sorely wants—the one thing needful for his own well-being: to take God into himself, to consume Love itself. But how is he to do this? There is only one way, and that is—as the disciples on the road to Emmaus that first Easter Sunday came to realize in their hearts—to acknowledge that the risen Christ, who had walked among them, really had been with them "in the breaking of the bread."

And now the reality of that insight has come home to him here, in—of all places—a road leading to Horsham, here and nowhere, accompanied as he is by two friends. And suddenly, there it is, amid the trivialities of the quotidian, as plain as day itself: the impossibility of his remaining any longer in the Church of England. Nothing for it, then, but to surrender and go over to Rome, his best guarantee for the Real Presence in the Eucharist he so much desires now: no symbol but the ineffable thing itself, and there for the asking. In an instant, the interminable struggle of the past three years is over, as now the angel he has wrestled with day in and night out touches his hip and departs. And suddenly he sees what every pilgrim comes to see: that something has been lost even as something greater has been found.

He will say nothing to anyone, he tells himself, until he is back at Oxford in October. Nor will he take any step toward converting until after he takes his degree a year from now, for the simple reason that he will have to find a way to explain all of this to his father, for they both know all too well that the Oxford authorities could—if they wanted—make it difficult for Gerard as a Catholic to take his degree. So, in spite of the deep peace he now feels, he braces himself, like Newman before him, for the long chill of exile about to begin. In the meantime, he can get back to looking for God's complex-but-decipherable designs in everything around him: the clouds, the in-scapes of trees, the shapes of elm and holm and oak leaf, in bluebells, in the radiating lines of river currents. Rose clouds dappled with purple at sunset, darkening oaks, the pale green and blue afterglow on the horizon revealing faint horned rays, the palest crimson spackling the oak leaves. Ruskin would surely applaud all this. Even Pater might nod his approval.

The following afternoon, he and Garrett are at Horsham Station with the spring cart to meet Macfarlane and take him back to the farm. Later that day, as his friends stroll back into town for evensong and compline at St. Mary's, he wanders alone through a grove of trees and open fields, tak-ing in the magnificent views. He has been studying oaks once more, analyz-ing the shape of the leaves as he searches for the underlying design knotting them together, when suddenly the inscape reveals itself. They are like closely packed leaves in a book, he sees, and he has just learned how to read them. "Platter-shaped stars" or bright keys, he notes in his own distinctive idiom not found in any botanist's book, which seem to throw out "long shoots alternately and slimly leaved," the dip and toss of the sprays creat-ing "the wider and less organic articulations of the tree." Next day, he goes back again to study the oaks on the other side of the park, their spare boughs "roughed with lichen, and gracefully and muscularly waved, check-ing each other," the mass "jotted with light and shadow." He has yet to say anything to either of his friends, though both can see that something is troubling their usually playful, fun-loving friend.

July 24: A week after resolving to say nothing to anyone about his deci-sion, as he and Macfarlane are walking along a Sussex country road, Hop-kins suddenly blurts out what has been on his mind. He is going over to Rome, he tells Macfarlane, and tells him why. "I did not attempt to argue with him," Macfarlane notes in his journal that evening, "as his grounds did not admit of argument." In his own journal, Hopkins is short with himself for breaking his self-imposed silence. "Spoke to Macfarlane," he writes, "foolishly."

Instead, his journal will speak metaphorically about what he is feeling. How beautiful wild parsley is, thriving "in clumps by the road side." Or the tree he saw, with "clusters of berries," which turn "glossy black if gath-ered." The tree he has in mind hangs over a stile on its left side, a spray of it standing "forward like a bright blind of leaves drawing and condensing the light." Bushes gathering the wooly darkness, beneath which runs a "dry stoned bed of a streamlet" with "light filtering in." Condensed light filtering through the darkness of a dry streambed. Only later will he remember the name of the tree. It is the white-beam: the cross.

The same day he tells Macfarlane he is going over to Rome, he writes his friend Robert Bridges of Corpus Christi, apologizing for not being in better touch about his summer plans. He has decided not to travel north, and so will not see Bridges before the start of Michaelmas Term. He has no news to share, except to say that Challis of Merton, a member of the High Church Brotherhood at Oxford, has just gone over to Rome. It is his way of preparing Bridges of his own intentions without actually telling him. Next day he walks with Macfarlane into Horsham for late morning services at St. Mary's, after which Macfarlane plays some hymns on the church organ while Hopkins listens from the shadows.

Two days later, the three meet in the enclosed garden behind the local photographer's studio and, after some arranging, Macfarlane, the tallest of the three, is seated, while the other two stand to either side of him. All three are dressed in woolen frock coats, vests, and white shirts. Hopkins, sporting a light mustache, holds a walking stick in his right hand, his derby in his left. He has been experimenting with facial hair for years now, but will in time forego beard and mustache altogether. His hair is short, brushed, and parted high on the left side. What the photograph cannot capture are the sandy-brown highlights of the fine hair and the hazel of his eyes. And though he peers squarely into the camera, there is a look about him as if he were elsewhere. Come tomorrow, he will turn twenty-two and half his life will have been lived.

Wednesday, August 1: The three loaf about in the morning, reading and writing letters, and then after dinner return to the photographer's to decide on a group photo. Macfarlane has been invited to play the organ for the small congregation at St. Mary's. At the post office, Hopkins picks up his mail. There is a letter from Bridges, wondering what on earth Henry Challis's leaving the English Church can possibly mean. On the 2nd, the reading holiday comes to a close. By half past one, each is on his own way: Garrett to London, Macfarlane to Oxford, and Hopkins to the Isle of Wight, where he will spend the next three weeks with his family in comfortable lodgings at Manor Farm in Shanklin.

Settled in at the farm, Hopkins writes Bridges again. He would love to come up to Rochdale (in Lancashire), where Bridges's stepfather, the

Reverend Dr. Molesworth, is vicar, especially as Bridges has said that his strange, fascinating cousin, Digby Dolben, has promised to visit. And though Hopkins has met Dolben only once, and that once through Bridges, the two have taken a liking to each other and have been corresponding and sharing poems. But he has no more time to spare, Hopkins tells Bridges. He means to spend what time he has here at Shanklin and then return home, where he will continue his reading until classes begin. As for Challis, he "never had much belief in the Church of England, and his going over in it-self wd prove as little as any conversion could ever do against it since he never used the same strictness in practices" as Hopkins and Bridges and their friends have done. Still, if Challis's conversion means that he will now become a "strict catholic and . . . destroy his whimsies, that would say something." Of his own decision to do likewise, he says nothing.

Like many comfortable Victorian families, Hopkins's is a large one, with five boys and three girls, a sixth boy, Felix Edward, having died just short of his second birthday on Christmas Day, thirteen years before. Next in line after Gerard is Cyril, twenty now, twenty months younger than Gerard, and slated to follow his father into the marine insurance firm of Manley Hopkins, Son & Cookes. Although it is a lucrative business, none of the others will follow their father into it, most of the children being of a more artistic temperament. Then there is eighteen-year-old Arthur, an inveterate sketcher, better even than Gerard, who is too philosophical and impatient with finish and always in search of some ineluctable inscape, the underlying energy force and deep form holding things like trees and bluebells and concertos and paintings together. In time Arthur will become a well-known illustrator for the *Graphic* and the *Illustrated London News,* and will do the ink drawings for—among other novels—Thomas Hardy's *Return of the Native.*

Then there is the oldest of the girls: Millicent, now sixteen, and already quite accomplished at the piano. Like Gerard, she is of a deeply spiritual nature, and will enter a High Anglican order of nuns in four years; then—at twenty-eight—permanently don a nun's habit at All Saints Convent, St. Albans, where she will live out her long cloistered years until her death in 1946 at the age of ninety-seven. Lionel Charles, next after the gap left by the death of young Felix, is twelve now, ten years Gerard's junior, and the one among all the brothers who most resembles him. He is small, slightly built, plain-spoken, and an inveterate punster and humorist like Gerard and their father. At nineteen he will join the British Consular Service as a student interpreter, and by his mid-twenties will have made himself into a distinguished Chinese linguist with a specialty in ancient Chinese scripts and three-thousand-year-old incised oracle bones, moving up the British bureaucratic chain to become Consul-General in Tientsin by the time he is forty-five. At fifty-four he will retire from the service for reasons of ill health and return to the family home, living on his government pension for another forty-four years, until his death in 1952. Like his three sisters, he will never marry and will outlive all his siblings. Unlike Gerard, he will become—like so many others of his generation—agnostic, never understanding why his brother went the road he did.

Next in line is ten-year-old Katie, cheerful and good-natured, who has already earned a special place in Gerard's heart, and who will in the long years ahead come to preside over the family house, caring for her father and mother, and then—until her death in 1933—living on with Lionel and her younger sister, Grace. Grace is eight, and is already becoming the musical sister. Finally, there is Everard, who has just turned six. Like Gerard and Arthur, he too will show a predilection for drawing, and will in time become a book and magazine illustrator, working for *Punch*.

Manley, the patriarch of the family, is forty-eight. Small, trim, dapper, mustachioed, he has had to struggle to rise into his comfortable middle-class status, his own father, Martin Edward—sometime dealer in glass and indigo—having died at eighty-two, vigorous and importunate until the very end, leaving in his wake six sons and four daughters for his wife, Ann—half his age—to raise in the sprawling environs of London. This branch of the Hopkinses are transplants from Wales and—since the time of Queen Elizabeth and for two centuries afterward—made their livelihood as fishermen and oystermen, clustering around Wivenhoe on the Colne River, northeast of Stratford, Essex, and east of London. Although that world is but a distant memory now, the call of the sea has obviously persisted in Manley's profession as marine adjustor and in Gerard's many drawings of seascapes and even in his once jokingly having signed himself in a letter to his father under the moniker "Arthur Flash De Wyvenhoe."

Eleven at the time of his own father's death, Manley was forced to finally leave school four years later to help support his mother, brothers, and sisters, in short order becoming—unlike his own father—an astute businessman. He is rather like Dickens, who also had to lift himself from poverty in the wake of his father's legacy of financial miscalculations, becoming a specialist in averages—a branch of marine insurance—and eventually publishing a manual on the subject. An autodidact, Manley has mastered French and Latin and studied Greek and Church history. In religious matters, he is a moderate Anglican who admires Jeremy Taylor's tomes, *Holy Living* and *Holy Dying*. Like his siblings, he too has a penchant for painting, sketching, music, and the outdoors, and is the author of several books of poetry, including *The Philosopher's Stone and other Poems,* published a quarter century earlier and dedicated to his friend, the poet Thomas Hood. In the years to come, he will also publish a theory of numbers as well as a history of Hawaii. Austere, clear-eyed, opinionated, he loves telling elaborate jokes and making complicated puns, a mild disease which he has passed on to his children, particularly Gerard.

Twenty-three years before, on August 8, 1843, he and his wife, Kate Smith, were married at St. Mary's in Chigwell, his brother, Charles, and Kate's father, John Simms, serving as witnesses. After a Devonshire honeymoon, the couple moved into the Grove, a three-story late-eighteenth-century brick house in Stratford, Essex, east of London, which Manley had been renting for himself, his mother, sister, and younger brother. Six months later, Manley opened his own Averages Insurance office at 69 Cornhill in the heart of the City, traveling back and forth to the suburbs by commuter rail over the next eight years. There is one glimpse of life at the Grove at this time provided by an American missionary named William Richards, privy councilor to King Kamehameha III of Honolulu, who was in the process of helping Manley's brother, Charles, land a government position there. One evening in February 1844, Richards was an overnight guest at the Grove. He would remember Manley convening family prayers for the household before retiring, then reading aloud a chapter of the Bible the following morning, followed by more prayers and a cold breakfast, then leaving for his London office at nine. Over the next several weeks he was to see the family several more times, and was always favorably impressed.

Sunday, July 28, 1844, 4:15 a.m.: The Hopkinses' first child—Gerard Manley—is born at the Grove and baptized a month later at St. John the Evangelist, an imposing neo-Gothic Anglican church just down the street. Manley's mother and sister, Annie, will help raise the children at the Grove, along with a number of servants. But by then, industrialization—including belching factories and foul-smelling tanneries—banished to the outskirts of London proper, as well as extensive railway heads and docks and overpopulation (Stratford having grown from a modest hamlet to a city of over 20,000), have so disfigured the area that it is time to move. To accommodate his rapidly growing family, Manley has found a new home among the extensive woodlands in Hampstead, just north of London. It is here that baby Felix will die on Christmas Day, 1853, two months short of his second birthday.

Before her marriage to Manley, Kate had lived in a handsome eighteenth-century mansion at 17 Trinity Square, on Tower Hill, within sight of London's infamous Tower. Born in 1821, the same year Keats died, she is the oldest of Maria Hodges's and Dr. John Simm Smith's five boys and two girls. Smith himself had trained as a physician in London with Keats, as Gerard would recall many years later, on one occasion—so the story went—the two of them "snatching" bodies for medical purposes. Unlike Keats, however, Smith managed to thrive and build a lucrative medical practice over time. In 1832, he had the eminent good fortune to become personal physician and guardian to Mrs. Ann Thwaytes, a very wealthy London widow as delusional as she was rich, who had recently convinced herself that Smith was none other than God the Father and she herself the Holy Ghost. From the year Smith began treating her symptoms until her death thirty-four years later, she would settle the princely sum of £2,000 a year on him, in addition to gifts worth some £50,000, all of which good fortune was to come to an end when Mrs. Thwaytes's estranged sister sued in the courts for all rights to her sister's estate, by then worth £500,000.

In fact, it was money from Mrs. Thwaytes's estate which allowed Dr. Smith to provide Kate with a fine education, including a sojourn in Hamburg, where she once lived with a German family in order to learn the language. She also learned enough Italian to read Dante in the original, and enough French to be able to move easily about in that country. She likewise learned to sing and accompany herself on the piano, and to draw and paint in watercolors. She always loved poetry and kept a large commonplace book with excerpts from Shakespeare, Wordsworth, Keats, and eventually her own son's poems. A devoted mother and wife, with a strong attraction to the Anglican Church of her birth, she quickly took to married life, managing her large, happy household.

Years before, her father had begun looking for a summer retreat away from the rigors and summer diseases of London, and had bought Grange Cottage on the edge of Epping Forest in Essex, fourteen miles northeast of London. What hastened this purchase was the cholera epidemic of 1832, which devasted London and claimed the lives of both Dr. Smith's father and brother. Fifteen years later, having by then amassed a sizable fortune, he moved his family to Croydon, a dozen miles to the south of London, into the eighteenth-century Blunt House with its extensive lawns and grounds.

Here Mrs. Smith had overseen balls and elegant dinners at all seasons, and it was to this place that Gerard and his brothers will often come to scramble among the tops of the stately old oaks and elms. In time Lionel will remember the place as a second home for all the Hopkins children.

On Manley's side there is his younger brother, Edward Martin, Gerard's godfather, who presented him with a copy of the King James Bible for his sixth Christmas. Like Manley, Edward has also pulled himself up, taking work first as a Parliamentary reporter, and then, at twenty-one, signing on as secretary to Sir George Simpson, Governor of the Hudson Bay Company, following him to Hawaii, where he served as amanuensis for Simpson's *Journey Round the World,* which Manley himself then saw into publication. Eventually, Edward returned to England via Canada on a special mission for Simpson, one Canadian remembering him as "very dandified . . . in his style of dress and uncommonly nice looking, but with a volubility of speech that I never heard equaled." He has been twice married, first to a young Canadian, Ann Ogden, who died of cholera when Gerard was ten, and then to an Englishwoman, Frances, daughter of Rear Admiral Beechey. An excellent artist, Frances is the only woman who will make the arduous Red River Expedition of 1870 through the Canadian hinterlands, during which she will paint many of the landscapes, as well as a portrait of herself and her heavily bearded husband in a large black hat. Afterward, the couple will return to live in England, first in London and later at Oxford.

Charles Gordon Hopkins, five years younger than Manley, turned out to be something of a con man. Having started out working for a London lawyer, he soon emigrated to Honolulu with the support of Edward and Sir George Simpson, passing himself off there as a lawyer. For a time he edited the government's official newspaper, *The Polynesian,* and in 1845 became a Hawaiian citizen, remaining on the island for the next twenty-three years. By stages he has become private secretary to King Kamehameha III, then Minister for Foreign Affairs, and finally Minister of the Interior. He also managed to acquire extensive ranch lands and to sire at least one son out of wedlock. By 1856, he already had enough influence to procure the General Consulship of Hawaii for Manley, a post Manley worked at assiduously from his home base in London and would for the next twenty years, until Charles's death in 1886 and the unceremonious changing of the guard.

Finally, there is Thomas Marsland Hopkins, seven years Manley's junior and like Manley a poet, who published a collection of pious verse with Manley entitled *Pietas Metrica,* under the pseudonyms "Theophilus" (Loved by God) and "Theophylact" (Watched Over by God). Ordained an Anglican priest, he served as Perpetual Curate at St. Saviour's Paddington in London until his death at thirty-eight four years earlier. He is the one whose example Gerard will follow most closely.

This is Gerard's family, and these are his roots. Now, during the high summer days of August 1866, he walks the bluffs at Shanklin and swims the waters off the coast, as he has done for several summers, thinking his own thoughts and keeping his own council. He sketches trees and flowers and landscapes, and tries to inscape the motion of waves with his brothers, jokes with his sisters, dines with his large family, and attends services at the local Anglican church. What he will not repeat is what he did here at Shanklin years before, and that is to weave a string of sea anemones across his brow in the shape of a sea wreath in imitation of someone in a poem he had written at sixteen. It was an experiment that cost him a good deal of blistering and pain, and from which he learned the hard way that sea anemones, for all their beauty, can—and do—sting, especially when used to make a summer crown.

Chapter 2

The Dense and the Driven Passion:
Oxford & Hampstead, 1866

Oak Hill, Hampstead. Tuesday, August 28, 1866: Tensions, secrecies, hints and leakages. By now Cyril knows something of what has been troubling his brother, and probably Arthur and Millicent suspect something as well. How could they not, knowing him as they do? His mother and father have also been noticing their son's strange, private behavior, but attribute it to Gerard's High Church Tractarianism and his intense preparations for finishing his degree at Oxford. In fact, the family has been back from Shanklin just one day when Gerard decides he can no longer wait, but must write Fr. Newman about his decision. He knows of course what many know: that Dr. Newman—as a leader of the Tractarian Movement of the last generation—has been through all of this himself and has helped many to come over to Rome, as well as advising others to stay where they are in their own faith traditions. Manley and Kate are leaving shortly for Normandy on part two of their holiday, and they are aware that Gerard will be visiting Bridges at Rochdale after all. Gerard also knows, from small hints he has dropped, that his parents will never condone what he plans to do. On the other hand, he is twenty-two now, and feels he must follow his conscience. Yet in spite of such rational gestures, he is being torn apart within.

"Reverend Sir," he writes Newman at the Birmingham Oratory, where Newman has a school. "I address you with great hesitation knowing that you are in the midst of yr. own engagements and because you must be much exposed to applications from all sides." He would like to become a Catholic as soon as possible and wonders if Newman might be able to see him for a few minutes when he passes through Birmingham that Friday. It is not that he needs convincing, for on that score his mind is already made up. Still, "the necessity of becoming a Catholic (although I had long foreseen where the only consistent position wd. lie)" has come upon him rather suddenly and forcefully, so that the question troubling him now is what course of action to take. He sees the inner contradictions of the Tractarian position, and is therefore anxious not to remain a Catholic in desire only. He is a close friend of William Addis, who has recently been to see Newman at the Oratory, and believes it is just a matter of time before Addis declares himself a Catholic. If Newman can see him on Friday, then all well and good. If not, he will be staying for several weeks at Rochdale—a hundred miles to the north—at Dr. Molesworth's vicarage and could come over from there at Fr. Newman's convenience.

Immediately after, Hopkins writes Bridges, asking if Saturday will be soon enough for him to come. If so, he will leave Friday from home and stay over in Birmingham, where he has "some business . . . to do at some time while I am in the north, most conveniently I think then." There is no need for Bridges to meet him at the station; he will find his own way to the vicarage. But—as it turns out—Newman is abroad and will only be returning in mid-September, two weeks into Hopkins's stay at Rochdale. In the meantime, Newman writes Hopkins at Rochdale. Fix a day, he tells Hopkins, and he will be happy to see him.

The time at the Rochdale rectory proves to be awkward. Something is clearly troubling Hopkins, Bridges can see, but his friend keeps deflecting questions, and Bridges leaves it alone. Still, in spite of his anxieties, looking back on this time with Bridges, reading and walking and joking, Hopkins will think of it as the happiest time he has ever known, his heart and mind at last settled on what must be done. Then, on the morning of September 20, he says good-bye to Bridges and the Molesworths and travels south by train for his meeting with Newman. And that too turns out to be even better than he had expected. One of the first things his eye sees is a bird's-eye view of Oxford hanging in Newman's study, where the interview takes place; around the frame is a Latin inscription from Ezekiel: *Fili hominis, putasne vivent ossa ista? Domine Deus, tu nosti—Son of man, shall these bones live? Lord God, you know.* Ah! Rare, dear Oxford, something they both share. Newman is kind and genial, almost in fact "unserious." Best of all, Hopkins is relieved to find that Newman makes so much sense. The sixty-five-year-old priest listens to the young man seated before him. He understands all too well his anxieties about the steps he is about to make, and wants only to be sure that Hopkins is acting deliberately and with knowledge. He listens to Hopkins's earnest arguments, and when Hopkins has given them, saying he can "see no way out," Newman laughs. "Nor can I," he says. "Nor can I."

Except for how things stand at home, he sees no reason why Hopkins could not be received into the Church that very day. Still, there is no need to hurry, Newman tells him. In fact, rather than accept the argument that the learned cannot claim invincible ignorance in religious matters, he remarks offhandedly that in truth it is they of all people who have the greatest excuse, and then goes on to speak kindly of all the Tractarians hold dear. In the meantime, he suggests some books for Hopkins to read and then walks with him over to the football field, where he turns him over to John Walford, who is coaching some of the boys. Walford, Hopkins soon learns, is a former junior master at Eton and a new convert, who means to enter the Jesuit novitiate at Roehampton a year from now. Walford takes him to lunch in the refectory, gives him a tour of the school and the Oratory, and then shows him around St. Chad's Cathedral.

That evening, back home at Oak Hill, he finds a letter waiting for him from his Oxford friend and mentor, the Reverend Edward Urquhart. During his time at Rochdale, Hopkins had written about his decision to become—like Challis—a Catholic, and Urquhart has written back, urging caution. These are difficult issues Hopkins has taken upon himself, and he must be patient. Perhaps in time his religious difficulties will resolve themselves, Urquhart advises him, without Hopkins's having to take any action. But, as Hopkins explains, it is not as if he were some overly scrupulous Anglican. Rather—by God's mercy—he is "a penitent waiting for admission to the Catholic Church."

If he has been reticent before, he means to speak out plainly now. The truth is that for the last two months he has been "a convert to the Church of Christ and am hoping to be received early in next term." Moreover, he hopes that Urquhart—who is responsible in good measure for leading him in this very direction—will stop equivocating and become a Catholic himself. He has just been to see Fr. Newman, who has assured him that Urquhart himself "is at full liberty to believe in" the validity of his own Anglican orders, about which Urquhart had expressed some doubt. In the meantime Hopkins asks Urquhart not to say anything to anyone about his decision until after he has been received into the Church.

Then he writes Bridges, for the first time mentioning his meeting with Newman. He will return to the Oratory, going up from Oxford sometime in October to be received into the Church, and then back to the Oratory again at Christmas to make a retreat. And since Newman has urged him to finish up at Oxford, he plans to be up for the Michaelmas Term at least, and will announce his conversion to his parents by letter once he has actually been received. For the present, he adds, he has "almost ceased to feel anxiety."

But there is another thing he needs to say to his friend, whom he knows has been hurt by his silence at Rochdale. "I was never sorry for one minute," he explains, for it would have been "culpably dishonourable and ungrateful . . . not to have done one's best to conceal it."

And yet what he really wants to share with Bridges is the happiness he feels over his decision, a happiness he could never even have conceived. And for that he owes Bridges a debt of gratitude for his kindness to him during his time at Rochdale. He also hopes Bridges's mother and stepfather will understand, for when he was at Rochdale, he had not planned on becoming a Catholic until after taking his degree. To have said something at that point would have meant Bridges's having to carry the burden of Hopkins's secret and—since Bridges has clearly shown an interest in the High Church movement—thus causing him further anxieties about Bridges's own future. "This will make it plain," Hopkins adds sadly, "that wherever I go I must either do no good or else harm."

He writes Urquhart again, the first to be told of his conversion, he tells him, though at Horsham he let Macfarlane and Garrett know through his own incaution. Now Bridges knows, and he will "perpetually thank God" for Bridges's kindnesses toward him during his stay in Rochdale, when Bridges had no idea what was troubling him. And now Cyril also knows, having forced it from him by his incessant questioning. And of course Newman and one or two other Catholics at the Oratory. But that is all. Not even Addis knows yet. However, he does plan to "let one friend after another hear till the time of my reception." Somehow, he adds, "the silent conviction that I was to become a Catholic has been present to me for a year perhaps, as strongly, in spite of my resistance to it when it formed itself into words, as if I had already determined it." When the actual conversion came, he tells Urquhart, it came "all in a minute." Then he writes Bridges again, who has in the meantime assured Hopkins that he himself never had any intention of going over to Rome and does not now. Hopkins replies that he knows what Bridges must be thinking, after all: that the Church of England has lost Hopkins to the Papists, and that all is with him, Hopkins laughs in capitals, "TRUMPERY, / MUMMERY, AND G. M. HOPKINS FLUMMERY / DESIGNER. / REMOVED TO THE OTHER SIDE OF THE WAY."

Friday, October 12: Hopkins returns to Oxford and his new rooms at 23 New Inn Street for the Michaelmas Term. That same evening, he writes his parents—who are at Dinan in France—with the news that he is going over to the Catholic Church. Garrett has already gone over. Alexander Wood, who has just written him in some confusion about where he stands, on hearing back from Hopkins, has decided to go over on Monday. Then, by sheer coincidence, Wood himself having run into Addis, who had made up his mind to wait at least a year, seeks out a Catholic priest in London that same day and asks to be received at once. Three days later, Hopkins hears back from his parents. Their answers, he writes Newman at once, are terrible, so much so that he "cannot read them twice." They have begged him at least to wait until he takes his degree eight months from now. But that is no longer a viable option. Hopkins is already a Catholic in his heart, "and since it is impossible to wait as long as they wish it seems to me useless to wait at all." He must either "live without Church and sacraments or else, in order to avoid the Catholic Church, to have to attend constantly the services of [the Anglican] Church," which "brings the matter to an absurdity and makes me think that any delay, whatever relief it may be to my parents, is impossible."

Like Garrett, Wood, and Addis, he sees now that "all our minds . . . were ready to go at a touch." Addis's loss especially will be a "deep grief to Dr. Pusey," for they have known each other for years and Addis has even made a retreat with him. As for confession, Hopkins has been accustomed to writing his sins out scrupulously on paper, as Liddon and the Puseyites have encouraged him to do, but Monsignor Eyre—a local Catholic priest— has told him that it is enough for him to confess orally. Then he informs the dean of chapel that he can no longer in good conscience attend chapel or take communion in the Anglican rite.

That same morning, a distraught Manley Hopkins, back home now, writes the Reverend Henry Parry Liddon, who is at the moment away from Oxford in Bristol. "Among those who listened to your Lectures & who were affected by your influence in Oxford," the agitated father begins, the blame for this catastrophe barely concealed, "was my eldest son, Gerard Manley Hopkins, of Balliol." Now, "after a spotless course in the University," his son has just written him and his wife announcing "his determination to join the Church of Rome. This blow is so deadly & great that we have not yet recovered from the first shock of it." True, they had "observed a growing love for asceticism and high ritual" in their son, but they did not want to interfere with his "conscientious views." In fact, they had supposed Gerard was on the point of "taking orders in the English Church." Whatever the case, he is too young and too immature, really, to be allowed to go over to Rome, and he begs Liddon to use whatever influence he can to stop his poor deluded son from ruining his life.

"Our poor boy," he continues, "writes that he has deeply considered the subject, that he has consulted, weighed the grounds, &c. in all which he is mistaken." The truth is that he is acting on impulse and fancy, which Manley blames on his "unremitting reading." Worse, rather than consult the Anglican clergy here in Hampstead or speak with Liddon or his tutors, he has gone to see "a Roman priest in this neighbourhood, possibly others elsewhere and finally, I now discover, Dr. Newman, whose encouragement, I imagine, was curt & cold enough." He begs Liddon to try and talk some sense into his son "before he takes any irrevocable step & shew him all the weight and claim of the English Church over her children." Disabuse him, he pleads, and "save him from throwing a pure life and a somewhat unusual intellect away in the cold limbo which Rome assigns to her English converts."

As soon as Liddon receives Manley's letter, he writes Gerard. He cannot be back at Oxford until the following Monday, he explains, but will try to make his position as plain as possible. Rome's claims on Gerard's allegiance "depend upon the Truth of the Supremacy of the Pope," and that is an historical development subsequent to the Nicene Council. The attempt to impose it upon the East was in fact "the real cause of the great division of the Church." V. S. Coles—who will break with Hopkins over his decision to convert—has already warned Liddon that approaching Hopkins on this matter may be interpreted as an impertinence, and yet, given their friendship, Liddon "cannot bear to be silent," even though Hopkins "should not be willing to listen."

Meanwhile, Hopkins writes his father that he has just learned that the Church "strictly forbids all communion in sacred things with non-Catholics," and so has informed the dean at Balliol that he will no longer be at chapel. Just today the master—Robert Scott—sent for him, telling him he could not grant Hopkins a leave of absence without an application from his father. But this surely cannot be the case, Hopkins knows, as just last term the college "passed a resolution admitting Catholics and took a Catholic into residence," so that it has "no right to alter its principle in my case." He therefore asks his father to ignore Scott's request. After all, he is old enough to make up his own mind on a matter which involves himself alone.

He tries a final time to explain his position to his father. He cannot in all logic suspend his conversion until he graduates, for to wait means he "must either be altogether without services and sacraments . . . or else . . . attend the services of the Church—still being unreceived," which would beggar logic. How can he "fight against God," who calls him to His Church? "If I were to delay and die in the meantime I shd. have no plea why my soul was not forfeit." The truth is that he has "no power . . . to stir a finger: it is God Who makes the decision and not I." Nothing for it then. Doubt the Real Presence in the breaking of the bread—doubt that—and he would "become an atheist the next day." Yet, such a belief would be "gross superstition unless guaranteed by infallibility." One could debate a lifetime, he concedes, whether the Anglican or the Roman Catholic Church had the better claim to be called the Church of Christ. But surely God had to have made His Church attractive and convincing to the unlearned as well as the learned. In any event, Hopkins knows that *he* at least has looked hard at both sides of the controversy.

Nor is he converting for aesthetic reasons, for in that case the Church of England would win hands down. No, he is going over because of the sheer logic of the thing, where the plain reading of a Gospel passage like "Thou art Peter" would be sufficient reason for converting. In fact, the arguments for Peter's primacy "among the Apostles so pursued me that at one time I thought it best to stop thinking of them." Then, too, the more he has studied Catholic doctrine "(at first under the form of Tractarianism, later in its genuine place)," the more he has wanted to embrace it, for it "only wants to be known . . . to be loved—its consolations, its marvellous ideal of holiness, the faith and devotion of its children, its multiplicity, its array of saints and martyrs, its consistency and unity, its glowing prayers, the daring majesty of its claims, etc."

As for the Church of England, it makes no such claims as does the Catholic Church. True, the Tractarians have made them on behalf of the Anglican Church, especially in its liturgical changes, for which they have been long attacked by mainstream members as being too Romish. As for seeking the counsel of other members of the Anglican fold, Liddon has already written asking him to wait. Pusey he means to see tomorrow if at all possible. And as for the Bishop: the man is too busy to listen to individual difficulties, "and those who do apply to him may get such answers as young Mr. Lane Fox did, who gave up £30,000 a year just lately to become a Catholic." When the Bishop did write back, it was to ask about one of Lane's horses, which he "was to put his own price on and ride over for the Bishop to the place of sale." So much for the Bishop's pastoral concerns. No, Pusey and Liddon were his only reasons for remaining an Anglican even this long, "and when their influence gave way everything was gone."

His father has told him he may return home, but only as long as he does not try to convert his brothers and sisters. When they come of age, Gerard tells him, they can make up their own minds about which path they want to follow. And as for the estrangement his conversion is causing between himself and his parents, of course he has thought about it, long and hard, which is why he begs his father to consider for a moment Christ's "last care on the cross," which was to commend "His mother to His Church and His Church to His mother in the person of St. John," so that, even now, warming to it with his newfound zeal, if his parents would but "ask the Mother of sorrows to remember her three hours' compassion at the cross, the piercing of the sword prophecied by Simeon, and her seven dolours, and her spouse Joseph, the lily of chastity, to remember the flight into Egypt, the searching for his Foster-Son at twelve years old, and his last ecstacy with Christ at his death-bed, the prayers of this Holy Family wd. in a few days put an end to estrangements for ever." For once, at least, Gerard pleads with his father, try to "approach Christ in a new way in which you will at all events feel that you are exactly in unison with me. . . . Those who do not pray to Him in His Passion pray to God but scarcely to Christ."

The dense and the driven Passion: it is what he himself has suffered for months now. "What none would have known of it," he will write nine years later, thinking of this time, and of other spiritual crises subsequently. "Only the heart, being hard at bay, / Is out with it! Oh, / We lash with the best or worst / Word last!" But how will his parents ever understand, or anyone else, for that matter, unless they themselves have been where he has been these last difficult months? And now, having written this, he actually feels "lighter-hearted," though he still has not found the words to say what he most deeply feels: that he is—in spite of everything—still his father's loving son.

The following day he adds a postscript. He knows his father is concerned for him, afraid that his boy is closing himself off to any number of professional positions long banned to Catholics in England, and so he assures him not to worry about his future. "It is likely that the positions you wd. like to see me in wd. have no attraction for me," he explains, "and surely the happiness of my prospects depends on the happiness to me and not on intrinsic advantages. It is possible even to be very sad and very happy at once and the time that I was with Bridges, when my anxiety came to its height was I believe the happiest fortnight of my life."

The Reverend William Bright, another Oxford Tractarian, having heard from Urquhart the alarming news of Addis's defection, sends off a note to Liddon. "I wish you could get hold of Hopkins even at this last moment," he pleads, adding that he has heard a rumor (totally unfounded, of course) that Newman himself—*and what rough beast*—is coming to Oxford to "perform the reception." How can young Hopkins have "made himself competent, in so grave & complex a question, to affirm the Roman position? Urquhart spoke as if Addis was acting under what he conceived to be a Call. But does not God call us by the existing knowledge which we have, until He gives us reason to think such knowledge unsound? And how can one believe that these men have gone through a process sufficient to warrant such an assertion as is involved in such a step?" Worse still is that Liberal dons like Jowett, Green, and Pater will enjoy watching the breakup of the movement among the junior ranks. He ends by sneering that Addis was actually supposed to have "longed for an external oracle, & trembled lest, if attacked by cholera, he should die out of the church."

Thursday, October 18: Two letters from two fathers. First from Manley, wondering how all of this began. When Gerard was with Addis that week in June? Or did the catastrophe occur at Horsham? And though Liddon has counseled Gerard to repel all such temptations to convert as not coming from God, Hopkins has not listened. Worse, he has stopped taking communion in the Church of his birth, where God's own Providence has placed him, even though it has been an untold blessing which has allowed him to lead a good and pure life up until now. But now, without the grace of that communion, Manley goes on with his tautological loopings, how can his boy be guided to remain where he really belongs?

Then too there is Hopkins's blatant betrayal of his parents by leaving them "in absolute ignorance of all" until he had already made his decision. Had it not been for Gerard's old friend Edward Bond, who convinced him to tell his parents before he made this catastrophic step, he would have gone over without even telling them ahead of time. And then to have the effrontery to tell his parents that "as we might be Romanists if we pleased the estrangement is not of your doing." At the bottom of the letter, his mother has written a single pleading sentence: *"O Gerard my darling boy are you indeed gone from me?"*

The second letter is from Newman. "My dear Mr. Hopkins," he begins. "It is not wonderful that you should not be able to take so great a step without trouble and pain." He knows, of course, whereof he speaks, having gone this same path himself twenty years before. He has set Sunday, October 21, for Gerard's reception. Nor does he see any difficulty in granting him "leave to continue for a time attendance at the College Chapel," if there is some delay in getting permission to absent himself. In that case he would simply say his own prayers there. But he will explain all this to him when they meet. "Meanwhile," he adds, "you have my best prayers that He who has begun the good work in you may finish it—and I do not doubt He will."

Saturday, October 20: A letter from a flustered Liddon, trying another tack. Gerard's studies, after all, have been in philosophy and the classics, not Church history, so surely he should have come to someone like himself or Pusey to work these things out. Hasn't he always urged him to write out his difficulties so that he or someone else might argue the difficulties step by step? As it is, Gerard has simply closed his mind under the impression that he has had some call from heaven. Really, the very idea that Gerard should be "called" begs the whole question. Does he really think he has been given some "special visitation" by God? How presumptuous to think any such thing.

From the Oxford Union Society building that same morning, Hopkins writes his distraught mother. "Dr. Pusey has not been in Oxford till today," he begins, "so I cd. not go to see him." His friend Coles, concerned over his decision, had already written Pusey, "begging him to come up" and talk with him, to which Pusey wrote back that he has had too many of these converts to Rome petitioning him "for the satisfaction of friends." What these last-minute meetings come down to is Pusey's "listening patiently to arguments for an hour or two hours . . . with a formed intention not to be convinced." So Pusey will not after all see him.

As for his father: he seems to think Gerard is off his head, whereas, in fact, since Horsham, his mind has been "quite cool," so much so that even his parents have taken his letters to them to be "hard and cold." And as for using his own judgment, is it not "all people are inconsistent except those who are all right and those who are all wrong, and those who are most right are most inconsistent if they are a little wrong." Liddon thinks he has been intellectually inconsistent, but is it not Liddon who is inconsistent in not having already become a Catholic? That Pusey, whom he reveres "most of all men in the world"—with "all his learning and genius"—has not become a Catholic makes no sense to him. True, when he was home, he had told Arthur and Cyril he thought Pusey was "puzzle-headed." He did *not* say "muzzle-headed," as his brothers have reported back to them. And, really, who can say why he has been called to take this step? For surely "neither learning, genius, nor holiness nor all three together can bring anyone to the Church and it is as impossible to tell why some are led and not others as why some have any advantage which others have not" or why some should "die early and others old." Besides, what really are his mother's own reasons for not becoming a Catholic? As for communion, he did continue to take it, even when he was at Rochdale. And though he no longer believes in the efficacy of that communion, or even in the legality of Anglicanism, he still continues with his Anglican prayers and fasts, hoping to gain the grace to keep firm in his resolve to follow where he believes he is being led. He had planned to tell his parents about his reception into the Catholic Church, but only at the very last, though in this he sees he was wrong. But in not warning them both months ago he believes he was in the right. Still, if he was wrong there, she must understand that he was trying to ease the pain he knew his decision would inevitably have on her and his father. If they do not believe this, it is useless for him to try and convince them otherwise. He is going up to Birmingham tomorrow to be received into the Catholic Church by Fr. Newman himself. And since he is bent on this course, is it not better to do so as quickly as possible, since "every new letter I get breaks me down afresh?" Does she really think he does not love her? If she really believes his letters are "hard and cold," it is only because he has been trying to show her and his father that he has not gone mad, with the result that he must seem colder than ever. "You might believe," he closes, "that I suffer too."

Later that morning, he receives a hand-delivered letter from Pusey. It would not, Pusey explains, be accurate to say that he has refused to see Hopkins. But he refuses to see him merely to satisfy Gerard's parents, which is simply a way of enabling a pervert to tell his family he has seen Pusey and that Pusey has failed to satisfy him. The truth is that perverts "know very well that they meant *not* to be satisfied" and in fact come "with a fixed purpose not to be satisfied." Such a meeting would be "merely to waste my time, and create the impression that I have nothing to say," which would be a "great abuse of the love I have for all." The fact is that those "who will gain by what you seem determined to do, will be the unbelievers," Pusey insists, and for that Hopkins must bear a heavy responsibility. "Yours faithfully," he signs off. It is the last letter the two men will ever exchange.

In the evening a final note from Liddon, pleading with Hopkins not to see Newman. Suppose he were tempted to become a Deist, Liddon reasons. Would he go to Newman to ask him "whether he considered my objections to the Catholic Creed sufficiently strong to warrant me in announcing my change of belief"? Would it not be better to go rather to that part of Christ's Church in which God had placed him, to give it "every chance of retaining my allegiance"? But, he ends wearily, "you will long ago have been tired of my handwriting." And of course it is too late. Hopkins will be leaving for

Birmingham first thing in the morning to be received into the Catholic Church.

November 4, 1866. The Feast of St. Charles Borromeo: Two weeks later, Hopkins is confirmed—along with Addis and Wood—by Cardinal Manning at St. Mary of the Angels in Bayswater, London. It is a splendid new church served by priests of the Order of St. Charles Borromeo, whose work is among the Irish immigrants who have built Paddington Station, and the order's motto—*Humilitas*—Hopkins cannot help seeing chiseled on the stone walls and transepts above him. It is sad, of course, but inevitable, that not one of his large family is there to wish him well. But these absences—painful as they are—are something he will have to get used to, for he has now effectively distanced himself from the old fold that held them all together.

Then it is back to Oxford and his studies. Still, there is something he needs to clear up with Liddon. He thanks him now for his letters and for the trouble he has taken "to prevent my reception, for of course to you it was the right thing to do." But there is one thing Liddon has said which has clearly rankled. Hopkins knows he can never justify his conversion to his former confessor, but he is anxious "to prevent its being rationalised . . . in such a way as to empty it of any influence" it might have on him and his friends. "You think I lay claim to a personal illumination," he comes to the point, "which dispenses with the need of thought or knowledge on the points at issue." But Hopkins himself never made any such claim. In the sense that he had come at last to see the truth of his position, he had of course been "illuminated." But never for a moment had he claimed that such an illumination was a "supernatural or even unusual access of grace." In fact, he has become a Catholic in the same way that one comes to see that two and two make four. For a long time he tried to resist this conclusion, but when he finally screwed up the courage to actually confront his doubts, "it was not surprising that one minute shd. be enough to answer" the questions that had assailed him for so long. In any event, if Liddon should ever again talk to anyone about his or Addis's or Wood's conversions, he hopes he will not "lay them to any belief in a personal illumination." Then he adds: "Do not trouble yourself to write again: this needs no answer and I know how precious your time is." It will be the last letter between them, except for a hurried and insincere note from Liddon belatedly congratulating his former disciple for actually making it through graduation.

Hopkins writes Macfarlane, telling him the news of the four converts' (himself, Garrett, Wood, and Addis) reception. Perhaps Macfarlane—newly ordained now in the Church of England—will at least remain open to the possibility of coming over to Rome. "Remember," he writes, still in the first flush of conversion *(Our King back, Oh, upon English souls),* "God desires us to believe the truth and not what we for any reason however good, modest, or honourable to ourselves may wish to be the truth." He means to continue praying for Macfarlane as one for "whose conversion there is some reasonable hope, not none at all."

In early December, he writes Newman to say he will not be spending Christmas at the Oratory after all, as he and his parents have reconciled. He does not want to upset them by being away from home at this time of year. In fact, he is happier now than he has been for some time being with them, though he goes alone to mass at the local Catholic church in Hampstead or at old St. Clement's when he is at Oxford. He is looking forward to making his first retreat at the Oratory. And then he lets drop the hint that he is now considering the priesthood.

Newman writes back, advising Hopkins not to hurry a decision as to "whether or not" he has a vocation. "Suffer yourself," he closes, "to be led on by the Grace of God step by step." Ten days later, Newman writes again. Perhaps it might be best if Hopkins made a week-long retreat before Hilary Term begins, for it is always good for a recent convert to spend some time getting "into Catholic ways." And so, come January 1867, Hopkins will head north to the Oratory to get into those Catholic ways. Shortly before Christmas, he writes Bridges asking after his cousin Digby Dolben. Addis is now living with his brother close by at Highgate Hill, and Wood is for the present staying with him at Oak Hill, rather than return home to his father, a Protestant minister who will have no truck with his son's conversion. Wood means to go to Rome as soon as he can, and plans to leave Oxford without taking his degree. Hopkins also promises Bridges to copy out his poem "Summa," which Bridges has asked to see, unfinished though it is, for he has written virtually no poetry in the past year. On Christmas Eve, he attends midnight mass at the nearby Catholic church, while his family celebrates the coming of the Saviour in the festive, well-lit, holly-decked halls of Oak Hill. There will be many such occasions to feel the stranger in the coming years, even among those closest to him. It is only the first indication of what his conversion will come to cost him.

Chapter 3

Towery City and Branchy
Between Towers:
Highgate & Oxford, 1861–1865

A glimpse into the mind of the young Hopkins through a letter he wrote as a boarding student at the Roger Cholmondsley School (usually known as Highgate School) in Hampstead, probably with another student, half serious, half high jinks. He is two months shy of his seventeenth birthday when he addresses Highgate's German instructor, Herr Dr. Müncke, local representative of the Deutschland, asking for advice on how to read Goethe's *Faust*. The letter, dated May 8, 1861, and written from Hopkins's study in Elgin House, asks the good doctor's opinion of Faust's wager with that bored tempter, Mephistopheles. The letter is learned, sophomoric, tongue-in-cheek, and yet earnest. Though it is true he has not yet read *Faust* in the original, he begins, he has read reviews of the work, several translations, and the two-volume critical analysis by George Henry Lewes.

It is Faust's contract with the devil that most concerns young Hopkins: that if Faust ever finds a passing moment in life to be so fair that he should bid it stay, he will surrender his soul to him. Why then, Hopkins wonders, does Mephistopheles introduce Faust, who is after all a philosopher, "to only one of the pleasures . . . able to attract the higher order of intellects?" For surely beer halls and orgies cannot really be serious temptations to someone like Faust. The only real challenge presented to him, then, is Margaret. But what of the pleasures of power, or "the subtle charms of poetry, music, and art," or "the beauties of nature," or the sweetness that comes with greater knowledge? In short, the very things which Hopkins himself finds so attractive.

Worldly power versus its antithesis, the radical emptying of the self, like Christ on the cross: this is the issue which will remain central to Hopkins throughout his life. That, and the question of what one surrenders one's heart to. Love, of course, but an all-consuming love—Eros and Philos and

Agapos like the molten threads of some blowpipe flame—all contained in the trembling frame of a single man. The inscape of a form—a sonnet, a painting, an aria beating against the singer's tongue and teeth as it struggles to free itself and fly into the sun. A German Romantic hero, Faust, versus the fate of five German Franciscan nuns on a doomed ship named the *Deutschland* somewhere in the mist and ice fourteen years down the line. . . .

April 13, 1862: Fast-forward a year to a single diary entry by Hopkins the sixth-former, one which survives only because he troubled to transcribe it in a letter to a classmate. Come June, he will burn the diary itself as too personal, too revelatory of his own youthful anxieties and loyalties and affections for his fellow students. After evening prayers, "Skin"—as he is called affectionately, a replaying of his last name—calls fifteen-year-old Alex Strachey to the dorm rooms which Strachey shares with several other students. One of the formers has confided to him that Alex no longer considers Skin his friend, because he never asks him to walk with him any more. Now Skin confronts Strachey directly to ask if there is any truth to the story. And Strachey answers that indeed there is. But cannot the boy see that he has done this because he had hoped to form a deeper friendship with him, instead of which, during their walks together, Strachey always manages to keep the conversation to the "most trivial subjects"?

Can he not see that he has sacrificed Strachey's company because he finds it pleasurable (and therefore—what he cannot bring himself to say— too dangerous)? And how has the boy responded? "He might find many friends more liberal than I," Skin confesses, "but few indeed who would make the same sacrifice I had." But Strachey seems to have no idea what Hopkins is driving at, and by then the others have come up. At the last moment, he asks Strachey if he has anything to say. No, Strachey answers, and leaves with a crooked smile. "Perhaps," Hopkins sighs, "in my next friendship I may be wiser."

He has been a student at Highgate since the fall of 1854, two months after reaching his tenth birthday. Before that, he was tutored at home by his mother and aunt, and then sent to a local day school for two years. And though it is just possible to walk to Highgate from home, it is a very long trek, so that he and his younger brother Cyril have been boarders since coming here. He has studied mathematics, French, Latin, and Greek, among other subjects, at all of which he excels. In fact, just five days after his diary entry, the Reverend John Bradley Dyne, the school's irascible headmaster for the past thirty years, presents Hopkins with a translation of the *Odyssey*

done in Spenserian stanzas by Philip Worsley, Dyne's former pupil, as a reward for his taking top honors in Greek. Over the years Dyne has sent many
boys on to Oxford and Cambridge, and will send many more. The translation itself is dedicated to Dyne, and the copy Dyne gives Hopkins he in-
scribes with his compliments. But when, a few days later, Skin runs into
trouble with Dyne and refuses to bend to the headmaster's bullying, he inks
Dyne's name out and inserts above it the Hopkins family motto: *Esse quam
videri—To be rather than to seem.*

In early May comes a long letter from his friend Charles Luxmoore, who
left Highgate the year before. He wants to know if Skin is "still cock of the
walk at Elgin." No, Hopkins tells him. In fact, he has just been demoted to a
lowly day boarder. While working for an Exhibition scholarship to Oxford
in the term just ended, he explains, he'd petitioned Dyne "for a private room
to work in, representing to him the great disadvantage I was at compared
with my rivals and indeed the whole sixth [form]," needing not only to
study but to keep order as prefect of the younger students. True, Dyne had
"readily and ungrudgingly" granted him a room, with a fire in the evenings
besides. But shortly after, he was nearly expelled, deprived of a testimonial
from Dyne which would have allowed him to try for the Exhibition, and degraded to the bottom of the prefects "for the most trifling ludicrous little
thing," and then turned out of his rooms. On top of which he had "to make
6 apologies to avoid the other punishments being inflicted."

Tensions have since increased between him and Dyne, so much so that,
"driven out of patience" with him, he cheeked the headmaster wildly, and
Dyne tore into him with his cane. Both the assistant master and the
housemistress in charge of Elgin, seeing the injustice of what Dyne had
done, "soon gave me back my room on their own responsibility, repenting,
I believe, of their shares in my punishment." But a week later, in order to
study at night, Gerard borrowed a candle from the hall after his own had
been taken away, and when the candle was discovered in his room, lost his
room for a second time. Then, before he could get it back, he got into a fight
with Marcus Clarke, another boarder at Elgin. For his part, Clarke had been
"flogged, struck off the confirmation list and fined £1," and he himself had
been deprived of his room for good, "sent to bed at half past nine till further
orders, and ordered to work only in the school room, not even in the school
library." In addition, Dyne has told him in private he hopes Hopkins will no
longer be at the top of the school list after the exams. To top it all, having
arrived late for Highgate's Sunday services for a fifth time simply because

he took the expression, "Sunday as a 'day of rest' too literally," he has now been threatened with expulsion.

Years later, Luxmoore would write Gerard's brother Arthur of his first memory of Skin at Highgate, "coming down the narrow staircase from Dyne's room with the IVth form, when as a new boy I had been put thro my paces," and how Skin and another boy, Karslake, had taken him under their wing, though Luxmoore was the biggest of the three. He would remember too Skin's brilliance in writing elegiacs, at which Luxmoore also excelled, the two squaring off in friendly competitions to see who could compose them faster. And he remembered Skin cheering him on in a fistfight with a day boarder who had unjustly provoked him in chapel. And though never "chums," Skin being too small and too much the scholar, and not one of the roughs like himself, they'd remained good friends during Luxmoore's time at Highgate.

But the thing he most remembered about Skin was his always setting his face to do the right thing, like reading from the New Testament each day to himself, because he'd promised his mother he would. And though at first he'd been singled out for ridicule by the others for this, he'd finally made them understand why he did it, so that eventually the others had come around, making sure he was not hindered from doing what he'd promised her. Skin was popular and respected, "tenacious when duty was concerned," but "full of fun, rippling over with jokes, and chaff, facile with pencil and pen, with rhyming jibe or cartoon; good for his size at games and taking his part, but not as we did placing them first." But let injustice show itself, and the docile Skin could turn "furiously keen for the fray, and only bristled the more, when as was usually the case the authorities tried force and browbeating to silence his arguments and beat him down."

Dyne's approach always seemed to be, "Hold your tongue Sir," Luxmoore remembered. The student was always wrong, and there was always the switch across the backside to make a boy understand his place. Such a conflict occurred once when Skin abstained from liquids of all kinds for three weeks on a bet, "the real reason a conversation on seamen's sufferings and human powers of endurance." Just the other day, in fact, he was talking with some old classmates about Hopkins, and one said "he remembered Gerard showing him his tongue just before the end and it was black." During those three weeks of the wager, "it was the talk of the school, & had the authorities been in touch with their boys, as was of course their duty, they had stopped the whole thing at the outset with a few kindly words."

Instead, Dyne "swooped down on the 22nd day," just after Skin had won the bet, and forced him to return the ten shillings, binding "both by solemn promises and unlimited threats not to pay or receive the bet. In vain your brother pointed out that such a decision really rewarded the other boy, and only punished him, who had endured the suffering and exhaustion of the effort. Dyne was obdurate and Gerard only heaped up to himself further punishment, but of course Dyne was absolutely and altogether in the wrong. . . . [Gerard's] was far away a higher standard than that of his fellows; only there was a still higher law given, 'to suffer wrong patiently.'" At seventeen, Hopkins's essential character is firmly set, as a diamond is set.

Wednesday evening, September 3, 1862: A letter from Hopkins to Ernest Hartley Coleridge, Samuel Taylor Coleridge's grandson, another former Highgate student, enrolled now at King's School, Sherborne. "Dear poet," the eighteen-year-old Hopkins begins. His family is just now visiting relatives at Epsom and Croydon and he is at Oak Hill by himself. During this Long Vacation he has been reading *Prometheus Bound* in the original, and finds it "immensely superior to anything else" in Aeschylus. Too often he finds Greek tragedy to be little more than "stilted nonsense," though Aeschylus, his favorite, is always "full of splendid poetry." He has lately been translating the Greek into octosyllabic couplets. He has also been reading Shelley and finds Tennyson's "St. Simeon Stylites" magnificent, though he has yet to catch the mincing tone of the poet's attack on the extravagances of asceticism. He affixes a cartoon of Simon the cadaverous Stylite atop his column, preparing—like Skin—for his exams.

He has seen Lord Dundreary, the bewhiskered fop in *Our American Cousin,* at the Theatre Royal in the Haymarket. (It is the same play Lincoln will attend at Ford's Theatre in Washington the night he is shot.) Cyril has been studying abroad in Germany, and is now studying in France until Christmas. He still wants madly to join the army, Skin smiles, and "smokes furiously and is utterly unpatriotic." He himself has been at work on a long poem called "Matthew Wakefield," which seems to be going nowhere, and has been composing "descriptions of sunrises, sunsets, sunlight in the trees, flowers, windy skies," as well as an unfinished idyll and a ballad. His long ascetic piece, *Il Mystico,* modeled on *Il Penseroso,* has fared better, though the rich diction evokes Spenser and Keats rather than Milton.

In February 1863, his first poem appears in print. The venue is the national weekly *Once a Week,* and the poem—thirty-two lines of *terza rima* with a concluding couplet—is titled "Winter with the Gulf Stream," which describes in candied Keatsean diction a beautiful winter sunset:

Long beds I see of violets
In beryl lakes which they reef o'er:
A Pactolean river frets

Against its tawny-golden shore:
All ways the molten colours run:
Till, sinking ever more and more

Its brindled wharves and yellow brim,
The waxen colours weep and run,
And slendering to his burning rim

Into an azure mist the sun
Drops down engulf'd, his journey done.

A month later, having finally won his Exhibition to Balliol College, Oxford, he is forced by the Reverend Dyne, that failed "Patriarch of the Old Dispensation," to take Highgate's Easter exams, in which he has "nothing whatever to gain, but my prestige to lose." More seriously, his friend and former sparring partner, Marcus Clarke, is now on the high seas homeward bound for Australia, his father having just suffered a crippling stroke. It is the end of one promising young man's plans for a university education, and the beginning of another's.

Friday, April 17, 1863: Gerard's first day at Oxford, and he and his father are busy getting him settled into his rooms at Balliol on the top floor, beneath a sloped garret, which means much climbing and descending of steps. On the positive side, he has some of the best views of Oxford, and the best scout—or gopher—on his staircase. He has a bedroom, a sitting room, and can use a cellar for storage. And though one Highgate friend is horrified by Hopkins's rooms, he himself finds them comfortable enough. Two fellow students, Secker and Geldart, seem to be vying for Balliol's "palm of ugliness," he tells his mother. But where Secker merely has a "fat, grotesque Chinese look" about him, Geldart has "grey goggle eyes, [a] scared suspicious look as though someone were about to hit him from behind," and a pinched face to boot. No doubt about it: Geldart is bright, but Hopkins would not take "twenty Balliol scholarships to change places with him." On the other hand, there is the strikingly handsome Sir Courtenay Peregrine Ilbert, three years Hopkins's senior and the "cleverest man in Balliol," who lives just one floor below him.

There is all the excitement and uncertainty of any entering freshman on

his arrival at a great university. On Saturday—his first full day at Oxford—
he breakfasts with his tutor, the Reverend Edwin Palmer, thirty-nine, the
external reviewer for the Highgate Easter exams for Oxford, and the one
who had passed on Hopkins. On Sunday, he and his father breakfast with
their Hampstead neighbor Edward Bond, and—after Manley takes the
train back to Hampstead—Hopkins wines with another student. He calls
on Richardson of Magdalen, whom he finds—quoting Oliver Goldsmith—
"remote, unfriended, melancholy, slow," and strolls with him out to the
Christ Church meadows along the Cherwell. In a punt on the river two men
are lolling, one of them Atkinson of Magdalen, who—seeing the two—
minces out mockingly, "Ah! Look away," as if he had caught them at something. Henceforth, Hopkins promises himself, he will have nothing to do
with the scamp.

On Tuesday, he breakfasts with another tutor, the Reverend Benjamin
Jowett, forty-nine, Regius Professor of Greek, who is currently lecturing on
Thucydides. Of him Hopkins confides to his mother that "when you can get
him to talk he is amusing, but when the opposite, it is terribly embarrassing." Among his other tutors are the Reverend James Riddell, forty-one,
who lectures on Aeschylus and Homer and is very popular with the students; Edward Cooper, "a pinch-faced old man, whom everybody likes as
much as they yawn over his divinity lectures"; and the brilliant Henry "Oily"
Smith, Professor of Geometry, the maths master here, who has already assigned Hopkins a paper in algebra to see what he knows. Palmer's lectures
on Aeschines and Virgil have left Hopkins awestruck. A stutterer in private,
in the lecture hall Palmer has learned how to translate long passages from
the Latin "into the most beautiful fluent English." He has assigned Hopkins
an essay a week, to be written in Latin and English alternatively, and Jowett
has warned him to "take great pains" with these, as on them his ultimate
success will depend.

He boats on the Upper Isis with James Strachan-Davidson, first sculling
upriver and then sailing back down under a strong breeze, then canoes
with him on the Cherwell in a wind that nearly sinks Davidson's canoe and
washes his own up on the opposite shore. Still, how delicious these new-
fangled boating contraptions from America are. "It is a long light covered
boat," he explains to his mother, "the same shape both ways, with an opening in the middle where you recline, with your feet against one board, your
back against a cushion on another. . . . The motion is Elysian," the whole
experience "the summit of human happiness."

He thanks his father for the postal order to cover expenses. He has subscribed to the Oxford Union Society, where he can conveniently post and collect his mail, and asks his mother to send up his Exhibition Certificates from Highgate and his chocolate-covered Oxford Pocket Classics edition of *Aeschines and Demosthenes,* which she will find in the bookcase in the Little Room. This is his schedule: Sundays: a university-wide sermon at 10:30 a.m., followed by chapel at four-thirty, and a lecture "on recondite metaphysical subjects." On weekdays, he rises at seven-fifteen and is in chapel by eight. Then breakfast, followed by two or three hour-long lectures. Then lunch in the buttery at one. In the afternoons he walks or goes boating for exercise. Daily chapel—which he doesn't plan to attend—is at five. At seven there is tea, then preparations for the following day's lectures, and so to bed.

He walks often with the man who will become his closest friend at Oxford, William Addis, who has been up at Balliol for a year and a half now. Addis has taken Hopkins under his wing, and today they have gone out to visit Littlemore, the church John Henry Newman's mother built for him thirty years before, and where Newman offered his last sermon before leaving Oxford and the Tractarian Movement behind. Every window in the dark interior "is of the richest stained glass"; the altar and reredos are exquisite; "the decorations . . . on a small scale, but most elaborate and perfect." In fact, everything about Oxford is delightful, and Balliol "the friendliest and snuggest of colleges." The Inner Quad is "delicious and has a grove of fine trees and lawns where [the game of] bowls are the order of the evening." Below the quad level is the Fellows' Garden, "kept very trim, and abutting on it our graceful chapel." True, they have "no choir, organ or music of any kind," but then two of the windows in the chapel "contain the finest old [stained] glass in Oxford," glass which somehow survived the ravages of the Roundheads two hundred years before.

He hears that year's Bampton Lecture, walks with William Brown, hears the crusty, acerbic Reverend Henry Wall, Professor of Logic, give the evening sermon, during which he catches Jowett laughing a mocking laugh. And he has made the acquaintance of many High Churchmen: Gurney, Addis, Hardy, and Brook, who plays the piano gorgeously. He hears Henry Parry Liddon, "Pusey's great *protégé,*" lecture on I Corinthians at St. Edmund's Hall, and is introduced to him after the lecture. And though he had planned to skip out on such religious activities whenever he could, he now plans to attend every Sunday, a fact which will exceed even his mother's "most sanguine expectations." He mentions other friends he has made: "the delightful" Hardy, Dugmore, and Alexander Baillie. How very happy he is here, with "so much liberty to see and do so much."

Monday, June 8: More news of Oxford. He has read in *The Times* that Pusey and other High Church members have managed to prevent Charles Kingsley—recommended by the Prince of Wales himself—from receiving an honorary degree at commencement, and hopes the story is not true. There has also been a petition got up by the undergraduates supporting a bill to abolish mandatory subscription to the Thirty-nine Articles. More than nine hundred—three quarters of the entire undergraduate popula- tion—have signed it, including himself. And though he is "not quite firmly convinced" that the Anglican Articles ought to be eliminated as a require- ment for attendance at Oxford, he still thinks he was right to sign. On a lighter note, he adds that the last time he saw Edward Bond, he and three of his companions had tipped their punt, and Bond was laughing and slosh- ing his way out of the river, looking like "a drowned rat."

Friday, July 10. The Long Vacation: From Manor Farm, Shanklin, Ge- rard begins a long, newsy letter to his Scots friend, Alexander William Mowbray Baillie. "It is impossible to say how much I owe to him," Baillie will sum up his memories of Hopkins years later. "He is the one figure which fills my whole memory of my Oxford life. . . . All my intellectual growth, and a very large proportion of the happiness of those Oxford days, I owe to his companionship. . . . Apart from my own nearest relatives, I never had so strong an affection for anyone." The feeling is in fact mutual. But now, in the summer of '63, Hopkins writes in a bantering, sophistic mood, teasing Baillie for possessing a too-logical mind.

"Dear Baillie," he begins, "Yes. You are a Fool. I can shew it syllogisti- cally. . . . You will allow that he who lies is a fool in the long run, and that he who lies without any object to gain thereby is immediately and directly a fool. Now you are not a fool. But you say you are a fool. Therefore you lie." That is, if his logic is airtight, and he can't be sure it is. The Smalls—exami- nations for new students at Balliol—are over and he, Brown, and Hardy have passed, Hardy becoming "light-headed, light-hearted, light-heeled," and treating them all to drinks at the Mitre afterward. He and Bond have already spent a week back at Hampstead going through Virgil's *Georgics,* and he is now reading Tacitus, who is more complex than any Latin writer he has ever read, almost to the point of hopelessness. He has been to the Royal Academy, and was struck especially by John Everett Millais's *The Eve of St. Agnes,* a work of genius by the greatest living English painter, the art- ist having here arrived "at Nature's self, which is of no school."

He has been pencil sketching here at Shanklin, "a good deal from a Ruskinese point of view," he admits, and is now struck by the ash tree, which he finds here as graceful as anything in Raphael's early manner. That, and barley, "and two shapes of growth in leaves and one in tree boughs and also a conformation of fine-weather cloud." They are his present furies and will consume him until he moves on to some other passion, consigning his past obsessions to his "treasury of explored beauty," acknowledging them "with admiration and interest ever after." A number of these drawings have survived: *Shanklin, Manor Farm, July 19, Buds of the white lily*, elm trees on Lord Yarborough's place on the 22nd, and—the following day—waves breaking at Freshwater Gate seen from above, and a seascape of the Needles blazing against the evening sun. Another day it is the Chine at the head of the Shanklin. And though many of these are left unfinished, there is an energy to all of them. Having once discovered the secret inscape of what he has been observing, he is impatient to move on to the next subject. Shanklin itself is delightful, nor does he for a single moment envy Baillie his Edinburgh. "The sea is brilliantly coloured and always calm, bathing delightful, horses and boats to be obtained, walks wild and beautiful, sketches charming, walking tours and excursions, poetic downs, the lovely Chine [Rock], fine cliffs, everything (except odious Fashionables). My brothers and cousin catch us shrimps, prawns and lobsters, and keep aquariums."

Sunday, September 6: It has been raining now for a solid week. Scots weather, he tells Baillie. Edinburgh weather, for sure. Most of his letter is an attack on contemporary critics and criticism, though he wants to assure Baillie that there really is such a thing as good criticism, as, for example, the work of Schlegel, Coleridge and Charles Lamb, and John Ruskin. How he hates the viciousness of the *Quarterly*, the *Edinburgh*, the *Athenaeum*, and *Blackwood's*, and has "longed for their utter extinction!" Even more, though, he hates feeble criticism, like Forbiger on Lucretius and Virgil, or the late George Brimley on contemporary poetry. The biggest problem with critics is that they are too often theory-driven, cramping in by rules the free movements of genius, the "first requisite for a critic" being "liberality, and the second liberality, and the third, liberality." Yes, he knows how much Baillie dislikes commenting on poetry in manuscript. Still, Hopkins confesses, being one of those "writers of new unnecessary poetry," he needs Baillie to tell him if there is anything at all in his poems because he has nowhere else yet to turn.

Monday, October 19, Oxford: Back at Balliol for Michaelmas Term, he writes his mother. He has new rooms this term on the first staircase in one of the modern neo-Gothic buildings. At least now he can come and go "without climbing a flight of stairs, while my window is too high to be

looked into and yet comfortably placed so as to look and talk out of" onto
the quad. His bedroom windows on the opposite wall look out on St. Giles',
with Magdalen Church on the left. But—alas—they have cut down the
beautiful beech on the quad because it darkened the rooms of two of the
Fellows—Thomas Green being one of them, who teaches moral philosophy
and propounds a "rather offensive style of infidelity," so that it is natural he
would dislike "the beauties of nature." That beech, he laments, had "not its
like in Oxford." The college is also planning to tear down some of the medieval buildings and put up neo-Gothic imitations like the one he is living in
now. Why not have pulled down the old buildings first, and let that majestic beech stand?

Thursday, January 21, 1864, Oxford: Hilary Term. He walks with Addis
out to Cumnor Hall, made famous by Sir Walter Scott's *Kenilworth.* The
hall itself is gone now, except for part of the garden wall and some terrac-
ing, but the old inn still stands, "with the old signboard of the bear and
ragged staff, nearly washed out by rain and dried up by sun." It is authentic
old work, like the Norman tower of the church in the village there, which
calls up the ballad of "Cumnor Hall" Scott had in mind when he wrote his
novel forty years before:

> The dews of summer night did fall;
> The moon (sweet regent of the sky)
>
> Silver'd the walls of Cumnor Hall,
> And many an oak that grew thereby.

But, Hopkins notes sadly, the oaks are gone now. Once again, the social
rounds have begun: breakfast with Gurney of Exeter, and another with his
tutor, Riddell, then with Hardy. He has met Lionel Muirhead of Balliol, a
freshman interested in art. Then there is Alexander Wood, owner of a fine
collection of architectural photographs of abbeys and old churches. He has
also been thinking about joining Liddon's High Church Brotherhood, but
Gurney and Addis have urged him to wait. In March, home between terms,
he tells Baillie how primitive things seem there, after Oxford. There are
only *The Times* and the *Saturday Review* to read, and the local Anglican
Church here is so dreary, and friends talk of Oxford "as if it were Samarkand or Bothnia Felix, and yesterday I was asked if I had given many—I can
hardly bear to write it—many 'parties' yet, that is WINEPARTIES." And
"one of those thoroughly uneducated Aunts one has . . . thought College

Chapels, ours at all events, were places where devotion was impossible on account of the unseemly giggling and so forth."

During the Long Vacation that July, he visits his neighbors, the Gurneys, and is introduced to Christina and Maria Rossetti, Jenny Lind, and the Pre-Raphaelite painter Holman Hunt. He takes in the Junior Water Colours and Old Masters in London, and sheds tears of admiration over a Gainsborough landscape. There is also Luini's *Baptism of Christ* and works by da Vinci, Reynolds, Velasquez, Murillo, Holbein, Hobbemas, Cuyp, Rembrandt, and Guardi, whom he calls a "Caneletto with genius." He is reading Sophocles, with Herrmann's laborious notes, and has been writing a dramatic monologue in the voice of Pontius Pilate, and thinking of writing another in the voice of Judas. Also something called "Floris in Italy," as well as a poetic answer to Christina Rossetti's "Convent Threshold" called "A voice from the world." Also one called "Barnfloor and Winepress" and another called "The Lover's Stars" in the style of Coventry Patmore. And three religious poems of a very Catholic character, which he is sure will not interest Baillie. He has shown his work to no one else but Bond, who spoke encouragingly, something he needs if he is to continue writing, especially now, as he has "a more rational hope than before of doing something in poetry and painting."

At the beginning of August, he travels by rail with Alfred Hardy and Edward Bond to Pen-y-lan, Maentwrog, Merionethshire in North Wales for a two-week walking and reading tour. Trekking across the mountains between Bala and Ffestiniog, the three are caught in a torrential downpour, like something out of a novel, he tells Baillie, mimicking the overblown style in such hackneyed phrasing as "the dry beds of the morning . . . now turned into the channels of swollen torrents," so that they had to take "refuge in a shepherd's hut" where "the shepherd and family gorged me with eggs and bacon and oaten cake and curds and whey." For the first time in his life, he has had to rough it, which has meant "irritating the skin on sharp-textured blankets." Worse, he has had to stop his ears from being contaminated by the bawdy jokes and sexual allusions of his two traveling companions, especially Hardy, who "is always talking of debauching . . . well-dressed girls but when he has introduced himself to them oh then he is very, very sick."

Saturday evening, September 10, 1864: The poet/critic at twenty. By now his ideas of what poetry is and what a poet actually does are beginning to shape themselves. A letter from Baillie reaches him at Blunt House, where he has been reading Cicero's *Philippics* and, for the pleasure of it,

Shakespeare's *Henry IV*. But he has begun to doubt Tennyson, especially now, after reading *Enoch Arden*. He has also been mulling over what he calls the three degrees of poetic language. The highest is inspiration, "a mood of great . . . mental acuteness, either energetic or receptive, according as the thoughts which arise in it seem generated by a stress and action of the brain, or to strike into it unasked." Next is Parnassian, not quite of the highest level, since "it is spoken *on and from the level* of a poet's mind," but not, as with inspiration, where what the poet composes surprises both the reader *and* the poet. Most of what passes for a poet's signature style is Parnassian, so that, if he were Tennyson, he could conceive of himself writing *Enoch Arden*. But this is not the case with a work of real genius, like *Hamlet,* where every new beauty touches the reader and takes him by surprise. When a poet palls, it is because there is too much Parnassian, so that an astute reader as it were has "found out" the poet's secret. Which is why Tennyson has now become merely Tennysonian.

Between these two is Castalian: poetry of a lower order than inspiration but higher than Parnassian. "Beautiful poems may be written wholly in it," but though one can hardly conceive "having written in it, if in the poet's place, yet it is too characteristic of the poet, too so-and-so-all-over-ish, to be quite inspiration." Wordsworth is full of this sort of thing, for example. Finally, there are the lower forms of poetry: the Delphic and the Olympian. Delphic is "the language of verse as distinct from that of prose." As for Olympian: that is the "language of strange masculine genius which suddenly, as it were, forces its way into the domain of poetry, without naturally having a right there." And though Hopkins is hardly ready to write in the higher forms himself, at least he is aware of the work that lies ahead for him if he is ever to become a real poet.

He thinks of himself as a moderate in religious matters, though he dislikes those who hold to all sides of an issue without ever taking a stand themselves. Nor does he care for moderates like Thomas Macaulay, with his "irritating assumption" that "Catholicism or Christianity or whatever it may be is now at last agreed on by thinking men to be an old woman's fable." Better an out-and-out enemy like Carlyle, he insists, who rails against Christianity "in the fiercest way." But he also hates fundamentalist cant, with its "pettiness, irreverence, vulgarity, injustice [and] ignorance" that fills him with humiliation and despair. No wonder he has come to admire more and more "the balance, the heartiness, the sincerity, the *greatness*," of Addis and Pusey, and especially someone like Newman, "the extremist of the extreme" in religious matters, who "went beyond the extremes . . . and took a large faction of his side with him."

Early January 1865: Another long letter to Baillie, who has written Hopkins to congratulate him on taking a first in Mods. He has been reading George Eliot's *Romola,* with its portrait of Savonarola and the bonfire of the vanities, and thinks it a truly great book, though pagan in outlook. Five days later, in bed with a bad cold, and having finished the novel, he is "wretched" over Savonarola's end. Impressed with the monk's being burned at the stake for his beliefs, he tells Urquhart that Savanarola is "the only person in history" about whom he has any real feeling, and can imagine himself following the monk's example like the painters, architects, and other artists of his day. He is the prophet of Christian art, though Eliot herself failed to understand what motivated the man. How strange to think of him paired with Luther, the one "martyred in the Church, the other successful and the admired author of worldwide heresy in schism."

In a paper for one of his tutors that spring, he questions Wordsworth's dictum that the "most interesting parts of the best poems will be found to be strictly the language of prose when prose is well written." But, Hopkins argues, this is simply not so. Rather, "metre, rhythm, rhyme, and all the structure which is called verse both necessitate and engender a difference in diction and in thought" between the two. The underlying structure of all verse, in fact, rests in a continuous or marked "parallelism, ranging from the technical so-called parallelisms of Hebrew poetry and the antiphons of Church music up to the intricacy of Greek or Italian or English verse." Which is why there is a "recurrence of a certain sequence of syllables, in metre, the recurrence of a certain sequence of rhythm, in alliteration, in assonance and in rhyme."

He writes a stunning essay for his tutor, T. H. Green, on "The Position of Plato to the Greek World," drawing parallels with his own times. So with Shakespeare's "complexity and profusion of thought . . . in the revival which ended the Middle Ages," but who simultaneously signaled "the distress given by the loss of unity in the Reformation." Or with Wordsworth, who expresses "the contradiction to the spirit of his times." Or with Plato, who "was able to feel the sadness of complex thought running freely to different conclusions" when the old beliefs disappeared. No wonder Hopkins feels less the poet's "enthusiasm for the new truth" and more his "despair at the multiplicity of phenomena unexplained and unconnected,—*the heavy and the weary weight / Of all this unintelligible world.*" No wonder too that Plato found public opinion worse than any Sophist's reasoning for corrupting young men's minds, his only hope for politics "a far-off, arduous and rigid" ideology "such as must always make its inventor weary and incredulous himself." And yet Plato's own ideals "contained incompatibilities which . . . made the ideals themselves less credible" and left him in a constant state of melancholy. Balance, antithesis, parallelism, along with the tensions of philosophical and theological thought. Indeed, it is his own literary identity Hopkins is discovering. Already he is moving toward a sense of sprung rhythm, with its stressed parallel consonants and assonances and rhetorical forms.

Two months later, he composes a Platonic dialogue on the origins of beauty using three main characters—a Professor of Aesthetics, based in part on Pater, and two aspects of himself: the student of poetry and the young artist. Gradation, variation, bold irregularity, the dapple and balanced asymmetry in the underlying laws of things—of parts to wholes, of sunset skies filled with variegated cloud shapes and colors, the strict parabolic outline of a fine oak, music, and poems, the balancing of masses in a painting, the omega shape of the chestnut leaf revealing hints of the divine.

And then it is on to the structural integrity of the Shakespearean sonnet and the pathos of the final couplets. All beauty is a rhyme, he sums up, a chiming of one thing with another, or of one thing with many things. "On the one hand," Hopkins's fictive Professor of Aesthetics notes, the Shakespearean sonnet "would lose if you put two other lines instead of that couplet at the end, on the other the couplet would lose if quoted apart, so as to be without the emphasis which has been gathering through the sonnet." It is a pathos lost in too many of Wordsworth's casual endings to his own sonnets.

During Lent, Hopkins makes his first confession to Liddon in written form. Even as he writes about nature's beauty, he keeps a record of his failings as matter for confession. On May 16, he notes that he has once again wasted time and has let his temper flare when someone questioned him. He has failed to read two of his lessons and once again stays up later than he should talking. He quarrels with a friend and then cuts him. He spends an evening with Addis talking about nothing. He is troubled by erotic urges. He mocks Urquhart to Addis. He eats too much dessert. He fails to make it to evening lessons, wastes more time. He lets his mind wander during prayer services. When he receives communion on Ascension Day, he admits to himself that he has doubts as to the efficacy of the sacrament and admits to impure thoughts. He draws a crucified arm, which oddly rouses him. He has an erotic dream and wonders if he has sinned in doing so. He feels an erotic charge in drawing a male figure, or in looking at the handsome Fyfe, or in sketching Baillie. He wastes time reading the poems of Edgar Allan Poe. Back home, he mimics to perfection his father's mannerisms to Cyril, who shakes with laughter. Something in the gait or carriage of a stranger troubles him as he is walking about Port Meadow. The mind, the restless mind. . . .

Friday, July 28, 1865: On this, his twenty-first birthday, he arrives at Tiverton Junction in Devonshire on the edge of Dartmoor for a month-long holiday. His father's family is from here, and he can hear on all sides the inflections of his grandmother Manley's speech. He means to explore this landscape in depth and meet relatives he has never seen. Just beyond Halberton he runs into "an old man driving a donkey-cart, who spoke in pure Devonshire" and who talks to him about the Manleys. After some searching, he tracks down the old family farmhouse, still called Manley, though it was long ago sold to someone else, then walks along the canal into Tiverton and calls on his distant cousins, the Misses Barneses.

Then it is on to the cathedral at Exeter. He lunches with his third cousins, Mrs. Patch and her two charming daughters, who play duets on the piano and harp for him, and is struck by their beauty, the one with deep eyes and black hair and "pretty figure all in muslin," the other a "Charles II beauty in character, with cherry lips." He seems overwhelmed by so much beauty, so little of it has he encountered. In late August, he returns home to find a letter from Bridges, asking if he would like to come up to see Coles and Bridges's young, flamboyant eighteen-year-old distant cousin, Digby Dolben, to whom Bridges had introduced him back in February; but Hopkins declines, citing his work.

September 1865: This time he writes an uncharacteristically serious letter to Baillie about the Roman Catholic faith. "You will no doubt understand what I mean by saying that the sordidness of things" is "the most painful thing one knows of: and this is (objectively) intensified and (subjectively) destroyed by Catholicism." Up to now, Hopkins confesses, he has been too much the logician, insisting on the rightness of his own views, and now he wants to advance something without beating Baillie over the head with it. It is a new note in his letters: a seeing into something vast and magnificent, like a river of light into which he feels himself being immersed. How it amuses him "to watch modern science retreating from some of its key assumptions," he explains. Consider, for example, the life of Elizabeth

Seton, an Episcopalian upper-class wife and mother from New York at the turn of the century, who became a Catholic and went on to found the Sisters of Charity. Her example will serve to explain what his own feelings about Catholicism are now. And, though he does not mention it, there is also his "Barnfloor and Winepress," a poem about Christ's Great Sacrifice in the Eucharist. "At morn we found the heavenly Bread," he writes,

> And on a thousand altars laid,
> Christ our Sacrifice is made! . . .
>
> Terrible fruit was on the tree
> In the acre of Gethsemane. . . .
>
> When He has sheaved us in His sheaf,
> When He has made us bear His leaf.—
> We scarcely call that banquet food,
> But even our Saviour's and our blood,
> We are so grafted on His wood.

We are so grafted on His wood. He has seen something, he confesses, has seen into the magnificent mystery of God's love for him and for millions of others like and unlike himself. And though he will try to take matters calmly and wait like Newman and Mother Seton to become a Catholic, he feels from time to time something like a deep joy flooding in on him and overwhelming all his doubts and fears, so that there can be no turning back from what has touched his heart like this.

Chapter 4

Fresh-Firecoal Chestnut-Falls:
Oxford, the Oratory, London, Abroad,
1867–1868

Monday, January 14, 1867: Newman sends a letter to Hopkins at Balliol, which is redirected to Oak Hill, reaching him on Wednesday. "My dear Hopkins," it begins, "Since this severe frost set in a day or two ago, I have wanted to write & tell you that, though rejoiced if you come (as you propose) on Thursday, yet I can hardly ask you to do so at such inconvenience. . . . There are plenty of friends to receive you at the Oratory on *Thursday,* & you will be well taken care of. . . . Yours affect^{ly} in Xt John H. Newman." The week before, Hopkins had taken the train up to Oxford to retrieve his books, among which he had found Cardinal Manning's *The Last Glories of the Holy See Greater Than the First*—three lectures, with a preface, 1861—and sends those on to the wavering Urquhart at Bovey Tracy in Devonshire for his edification, asking him when he has read them to forward them to Addis at Highgate. He promises to send him a copy of "Barnfloor and Winepress," but as for his other poem "Beyond the Cloister," which Urquhart has also asked to see, he has abandoned it "on the score of morality." It is a new and more severe note in Hopkins's critique of his own work, and means that poetry from now on will have to take second place to a higher calling.

He spends Thursday to Thursday (January 17–24) at the Oratory in Birmingham on his first retreat, an exercise meant to familiarize him with two thousand years of Catholic tradition, and to give him the opportunity to talk to the Oratorians and to Newman about many things. Afterward, he goes directly to Oxford to begin the new term. In late February, Newman writes again. Henry Darnell, another convert who left Oxford for the countryside of Aldenham to tutor students for Oxford, taking Addis with him, has offered Hopkins a teaching position after he graduates, and Newman, having heard of the offer, stands ready to match it. "When you said you disliked schooling," Newman begins, "I said not a word. Else, I should have

asked you to come here for *the very purpose* for which Mr. Darnell wishes
for you." Many fresh converts have found teaching positions at the Oratory
over the years, the place serving as a halfway house for those interested in
testing their vocations or finding other professions. Besides, he adds, "I
think you would get on with us, and that we should like you." He will certainly find it more to his liking "to be in a religious house." Hopkins writes
back at once, accepting Newman's offer to teach there beginning in September, and Newman writes back, promising him he will not find the work
hard.

Meanwhile, there is work to be done at Oxford. That March he writes an
essay on "The Probable Future of Metaphysics," noting that the Positivists
have foretold "and many other people begin to fear" that "the end of all
metaphysics is at hand" and that "purely material psychology" will trump
it. But the material explanation of things, he argues, "cannot be refined into
explaining thought and it is all to no purpose to show an organ for each
faculty and a nerve vibrating for each idea, because this only shows in the
last detail . . . that the activities of the spirit are conveyed in those of the
body as scent is conveyed in spirits of wine, remaining still inexplicably
distinct." And how, in any event, can the mind be subsumed "under the
head of the material"?

Worse is to think that psychology and physiology should "withdraw to
themselves everything that is special and detailed in the action of the
mind," with the result that metaphysics will become "mere abstraction"
only, a thing pushed "to the outermost skyline of science." But it is metaphysics itself which holds science together, for it "alone gives meaning to
laws and sequences and causes and developments—things which stand in
a position so peculiar that we can neither say of them they hold in nature
whether the mind sees them or not." There is, however, "a particular . . .
pitch of thought which catches all the most subtle and true influences the
world has to give," and this is orthodoxy in philosophy. But even that lasts
only for a time. "It is like the freshness and strain of thoughts in the morning: materialism follows, the afternoon of thought, in which, just as in the
afternoon poetry is lost on us if we read, so we are blunted to the more abstract and elusive speculation." These movements run in cycles, and the
transcendent mode will in time reassert itself over the material simply because it must, human nature being dissatisfied with any single response to
reality.

There are "three great seasons in the history of philosophy: the first that
of Plato, Aristotle, and the Schoolmen, the second that of Bacon and physi-

cal science and Positivism, the third that of Hegel and the philosophy of development in time." The first is distinguished by the ideas of Form and Matter, so that even its most material matter is still half metaphysical and abstract. The second is distinguished by the ideas of Fact and Law and, even its highest, its most formal expressions are half physical and concrete. The third is led by the ideas of Historical Development, of things express-ing themselves in terms of a time/space continuum. The first "necessarily has a claim to be final and the second makes the claim for its results; as for the third it is in a sort of dilemma that it must contradict itself whether it claims to be final or not." Just now Hegelianism and, by extension, Darwin-ism—the idea of biological and historical evolution, or, put another way, of continuity or flux without fixed points toward which change moves—is in full swing. It is useless to ask if such a development is right or wrong, Hop-kins argues. It *is* simply the current way of seeing things.

But there is also the notion of types or species to contend with. As the prevalent atomistic philosophy sees it, nature is merely "a string, all the differences in which are really chromatic but certain places in it have be-come accidentally fixed and the series of fixed points becomes an arbitrary scale." But the new Realism—Pythagoras *redivivus*—holds that in musical strings the roots of chords are mathematically fixed and give a standard by which to fix all the notes of the appropriate scale. That is, the mind "cannot grasp the notes of the scale and the intermediate sound in one conception." So too with "certain forms which have a great hold on the mind and are al-ways reappearing and seem imperishable." Such fixed points, he argues, are inexplicable, given a "theory of pure chromatism or continuity." So with the development of species along a chain of evolution. It is not a matter of things moving accidentally along a line of development. Rather, the new Realism maintains that the Idea only is given, and it is toward that that the species develops. "A form of atomism . . . seems to hang upon and hamper our speculation," Hopkins closes, like some "overpowering . . . dispropor-tioned sense of personality." But a real sense of self must eventually re-emerge, he believes as strongly as he believes anything, and must work against atomism's insistence on accidental selvings. The problem is that this new sense of what is considered the real is still "too abstract, unpreg-nant, and inefficient." When it is eventually articulated, however, it will probably come round to a rediscovery of the Platonic Idea.

But what of man's duties to himself, given that such a self exists? What of "duty to oneself and self-respect and self-love in a good sense," just as selfishness is opposed to selflessness, and humility to vanity? The Ideal itself flows from the Idea, which "is our thought of a thing as substantive . . . as holding together its own parts and conditions." And don't we measure ourselves by other human beings? "Man comes into relation with other men," though of necessity he brings with him "his properties and his accidents." But man is not a *tabula rasa,* a blank slate, for he brings with him an innate sense of morality. Conscience finds "its first matter in the man himself: a man can compare his today with his yesterday, his aims with his results." Take gluttony or drunkenness. Both are social vices, but that hardly gets at the sense of abhorrence one feels when one considers what these do to a man's self: "they make him not himself; not a natural mind, for he is heavy and sleepy, not a natural body, for he cannot keep his feet." These rob one of oneself, of the gift of consciousness, of that sense of the mystery of self reaching out to the Self of the Other. It is an idea which will preoccupy him for the rest of his life and profoundly shape his mature poems, stamping a sense of selfhood and individuation on everything he says, does, and writes.

In late March, Jowett puts Hopkins through two days of rigorous examinations, "a most trying thing," he writes his mother when term is over. And now, what he feared has come to pass: the outer quad, including Jowett's house, is a wreck. So much of the old medieval work has been destroyed, and the new work pales by comparison. He doubts whether "the fine old groined roof of the gateway, the finest in Oxford, will be kept, and if it is not kept where it is I shd. think it had little chance . . . of being kept for interest anywhere else." Dom Riddell, who cared for such things, would—if he were still alive—have managed things better. In mid-April, he leaves Oxford for the Benedictine priory of St. Michael's in Hereford, on the Welsh border, to make a retreat there during Holy Week and Easter to determine if the monastic way of life is best suited for him, then returns to Oxford to begin his final term. In mid-June, Hopkins takes a first in Classical Greats, graduating once again at the top of his class.

Two weeks later, the handsome and irrepressible nineteen-year-old Digby Mackworth Dolben, Bridges's distant cousin who was so fascinated with the play of Catholic ritual, often to the point of delusion, and who the year before had walked the streets of Birmingham barefoot, dressed in the tattered brown robe of a Franciscan, the young man who at Hopkins's instigation and example had contacted Newman earlier to say he was undergoing a religious crisis and would Dr. Newman see him, and then, talking it all over with his parents, wrote Newman back to say the whole thing had been a mistake—this brilliant, wispy flame who had expected to matriculate at Balliol and then fainted during the examinations and so missed his chance—drowns. The youngest of five in a wealthy family, Digby had spent three years at Eton, and then been privately tutored to prepare for Balliol. After his fainting scene, he returned to his tutor's rectory at St. Luffenham, where his body was discovered floating in the Welland.

Like Gerard a poet of an intense religious turn, Dolben's poems have already been published in the *Union Review* (which has also published Hopkins's "Barnfloor and Winepress"). Forty-four years later, Bridges will edit a volume of his cousin's poems, together with a memoir. Along with Addis and others, Dolben had served as a catalyst in Hopkins's own decision to become a Catholic. And sensing a kindred spirit, at least at first, Hopkins had initiated a correspondence. Initially, the flighty Dolben ignored his letters, but as he considered more seriously becoming a Catholic, he wrote to Hopkins of his intentions. The letters on both sides are gone, though there still remain copies of the poems each sent the other. Dolben's notebook contains his own handwritten copies of Hopkins's "Heaven-Haven" and "For a Picture of S. Dorothea," and Hopkins wrote out at least one of Dolben's poems and kept it all his life. But it is the sense of wasted opportunities Hopkins will most recall in thinking of this distinguished, bright flame too soon extinguished.

Oak Hill, Sunday, July 7, 1867: Hopkins writes Urquhart, thanking him for his letter of congratulations on receiving a first and for sending along his poem, which he likes from a literary point of view, and dismisses from a theological one. He has not sent along "Barnfloor and Winepress," because he has less and less time or inclination these days for "versemaking." That phase is behind him. Early on Wednesday, he and a classmate, Basil Poutiatine, take the train from London down to Newhaven, then board the steamer for Dieppe. On the train to Paris, Hopkins notes flames of mist rising off the brooks and meadows and a peach-colored dawn breaking through the trees "scarcely expressing form," as in any of a number of French Impressionist paintings. Arrived in the Latin Quarter, they check into the Hôtel de Saxe on the rue Jacob, then visit the Universal Exposition. The following day they take in Notre Dame, St. Roch, and the Louvre, Hopkins noting the "silver bright fish-scale-bespattered sunset" over the French capital in the evening. On Friday they walk through the Exposition for a second time, then dine with Poutiatine's father, an admiral in the Russian navy, Hopkins noting the way the waiters lean over to speak confidentially with the great man.

Sunday, July 14. Bastille Day: In rain Hopkins and Poutiatine attend High Mass at St. Eustachez, then ride through the Bois de Boulogne, where

Hopkins notes "the thinness of French foliage" and the "naked shrub-like growth of the oaks." At St. Cloud, it is the smoky foliage of the elms with the branches showing through. Traveling along the Seine back to Paris in the later afternoon, they spot a Nadar balloon high up over the city, the same which in three years will be used to observe the Prussian army's advance on the city. On Monday, it is back to the Exposition yet again, this time to view the paintings of the Belgian artists, all of whom Hopkins notes for their originality. On Wednesday morning, the Admiral departs for St. Petersburg and his son for Normandy and Bayeux to meet up with Baillie and Brown, while Hopkins retraces his steps home, making the Channel crossing in rough weather, standing at the prow to study wave patterns until he finally manages to *see* the waves: "green-blue, flinty sharp, and rucked in straight lines by the wind."

Back home, he accompanies his aunt Kate into London to view the paintings at the French Gallery: rural scenes alongside the grand historical narratives of Alma-Tadema's *Tibullus' Visit to Delia* and Bonnat's *St. Vincent of Paul and the Galley-Slave,* paintings reflecting the renewed interest in Egyptian exotica, and Otto Weber's painting of a woman leading a cow down a country lane, which Hopkins finds "very good, especially the way in which a tree a little way off against the light has its boughs broken into antler-like sprays by the globes of the sunbeams or daylight."

Sunday, July 28: He spends his twenty-third birthday walking through the Hampstead woods, observing the landscape. Then, on Tuesday, he travels with thirteen-year-old Lionel to Harrow, where the boy fails to win a place. On his return, he notices the gross and yellow smog hovering over smoke-sodden London. On August 6, the court finally rules against his grandfather in the case of Mrs. Thwaytes, and the papers have a field day with this one, making Dr. Smith out to be a con man taking advantage of a dotty old woman who believed herself to be the Holy Ghost. It is an embarrassment for the Hopkins family, and a subject they avoid.

August 15, the Feast of the Assumption: Hopkins writes to Urquhart to thank him for sending along a copy of his pamphlet on *The late Oxford University Election,* which he has sent on to Addis. Urquhart's style he finds "ghastly candid, which adds to its literary value but will no doubt exasperate Protestants and most likely put out some Puseyites and make them think it ill-advised." But how will Urquhart's call for intercommunion dialogue with Rome be received by the Pan-Anglican Synod when it meets? he wonders. And yet Urqhuart has not gone far enough. Doesn't he see that "the whole Catholic world is agreed on the infallibility of the Pope in some form or other," and that the Church cannot "retire fr. her claim to be the only Catholic Church and from treating all out of communion with the See of Rome, that is the bishop of Rome, that is the Pope, as *ipso facto* excommunicate fr. the Church?" If Urquhart therefore believes he really is in schism with Rome, "why wait for other schismatics and not do yr. duty at once?" As for the idea of intercommunion, isn't it "enough to say that a claim wh. Rome makes against the Greeks and which it has enforced so long it will never give up for Anglicans with their grounds of yesterday?"

Monday, August 19: An evening thunderstorm with flashes of forked lightning, as he will recall in one of his last poems two decades later. Then a lull, a leaving off, then again lightning and thunder until dawn. It is, he notes, a storm of Aeschylean proportions. On the 22nd, in bright sunlight, he walks to Finchley, where he walks down into a field and sketches an apple tree and some wych-elms. Walking back again, he is struck by "the curves in the clusters" of two ash trees, what he will later call their sonnet-like inscape. The following day, his parents take Millicent and leave for Brittany on holiday, while he walks about Hyde Park and visits the Chapel of the Poor Clares on Notting Hill. It is there, before the chapel's altar and walls and crucifix, that he resolves to give up poetry altogether when he enters the religious life, "if it is better" to do so. Back home the next day, he watches Lionel laying gauze nets on the garden lawn to catch butterflies, noting how the folds of the nets take on a light blue shade on the side facing the sunlight and a dark blue in the shadows. Not merely a *"shadow-modified"* blue, he notes, but a real blue, "as in tapestries and some paintings."

He travels down through the Devonshire countryside to Bovey Tracey to spend two weeks with Urquhart and his family. A Cornish woman from St. Ives in the seat on the train across from him begins a long monologue on the pilchard fishery, reminding him of the Ancient Mariner cornering his audience of one, while the woman's sister merely sneers. Better to commune with the red cliffs out the window, he thinks, better "the copses with slim bare stems." Better the elms, reminding him of a Turner landscape.

Lying in the tall grass one afternoon, he puts his hand up against the sky and sees a "richness and beauty in the blue." A turquoise blue this is, "swarming and blushing round the edge of the hand and in the pieces clipped in by the fingers, the flesh being sometimes sunlit, sometimes glassy with reflected light." That same day he writes Bridges about Dolben's death. What more is there to say? He had looked forward to Dolben's "being a Catholic more than to anything." Still, having met him only that once in

Bridges's rooms at Oxford, it is difficult for him to feel anything much. "You know," he adds, "there can very seldom have happened the loss of so much beauty (in body and mind and life) and of the promise of still more as there has been in his case—seldom I mean, in the whole world, for the conditions wd. not easily come together. At the same time he had gone on in a way wh. was wholly and unhappily irrational." And then he quotes Newman's letter on Dolben. "He had not given up the idea of being a Catholic," Newman had written, "but he thought he had lived on excitement, and felt he must give himself time before he could know whether he was in earnest or not. This does not seem to me a wrong frame of mind. He was up to his death careful in his devotional exercises." On the other hand, Newman never actually met Dolben. Someday, Hopkins adds, he should like to see the place where Dolben drowned, and where he now lies buried. If Bridges has letters from him, those too he should like sometime to see.

Sunday, September 1: He walks to mass at Lord Clifford's place at Ugbrooke, having fasted since the night before, and is relieved when some "kind people offer him breakfast afterwards." On Monday, he drives over the moors thick with furze bloom, stopping to sketch, before going on to Hay Tor. Later, he makes his way down a steep incline into Widecombe to view the pre-Reformation church of St. Pancras with its heavy Somersetshire steeple. There is a mural of *Moses and Aaron* at the east end, but the ceiling is now caving in, and the handsome old painted rood-screen has been cut down and stored in a pew. The local Industrial Exhibition is a washout because the rains soaked through the tents and spoiled many of the exhibits, including some stuffed birds who now look "twice dead."

The following Sunday—the 8th—he misses the train to Newton Abbott and walks the whole way to hear the ascetic twenty-seven-year-old Fr. Kenelm Vaughan say mass. After breakfast, Vaughan drives him "in a little mule-cart to the Augustinian convent of Perpetual Adoration at Abbot's Leigh." He has learned much from the Italian immigrants in these parts, Vaughan tells him. One of them—a woman—upon his asking her to pray for him, told him that she was but a poor sinner, but that she had seen "a great fire on the altar," though she herself was cold. But the story that strikes most home for Hopkins is one the priest tells about himself. He was dying of consumption, and the Sisters were saying a novena for him. Then one Sunday, "he was drinking water from St. Winefred's [sic] well" in Wales and had "crept down to say mass, when, there being no rain, before the consecration a quantity of water fell on him and the altar so that he sent to ask the Canon whether he should consecrate or not he was told to do so and Mass went on: after Mass he was perfectly well." He is a deeply spiritual man, Hopkins can see, who is devoted to the Blessed Sacrament and the Bible, before which he keeps a silver lamp burning, "to make reparation to God for the desecrated use that has been made of it for these 300 years." It is this man who will have such a profound impact on Hopkins's sense of what a priest should be.

September 10th: Hopkins arrives at the Oratory in Birmingham, where he stays for a week to prepare for his teaching duties. At week's end, he hears from Bridges. "My dear Hopkins," Bridges writes, "Without my prolonging this into a schoolgirl's letter . . . did not you think that there was an entire absence of strength in Dolben? It always seemed to me so in spite of his great moral courage . . . in carrying out his 'views.'" Bridges's mother is ill "and has been now for some time. It is a nervous illness which is very distressing to her and to us, but the doctors all assure us that it is not dangerous though tedious and that we shall only have great difficulty in keeping quiet enough after she gets well." Among Bridges's other duties, "not the least tiresome of all being the playing of backgammon every evening" with his cranky stepfather in the little oven called the breakfast room, he has been reading George Eliot's novels and studying Greek and Latin for his Greats. He *must* find time each day to exercise, "which you know is necessary to keep me from deteriorating into some outlandish animal and upsetting all the received theories of species."

The work, Hopkins tells Baillie, seems to be within his abilities, and he hopes to manage his time here well, as he wants to be able "to read almost every thing that has ever been written." But the school day will prove that impossible. "Fancy me getting up at a quarter past six," he tells Urquhart two weeks into the term. "It is however done with a melancholy punctuality nearly every morning." Mass is at seven, followed by preparation and then breakfast in Hall. Then classes from half past nine until noon. Then dinner in Hall at 1:00 p.m., followed by an hour of classes. Then it is time for field sports, called Bosco, after St. John Bosco. Just now it is hockey, though soon it will be football. Tea at 6:00 p.m., followed by an hour and a half more of classes. He has two private pupils whom he sees from 8.45 to 10:00 "on all nights but Saturday and fr. 5 to 6 on the half-holidays Tuesday, Thursday, and Saturday."

All of his time in fact is eaten up reading the books assigned for his classes and in correcting written exercises. But today being a Sunday, "the boys are playing fives like good ones: I wish they wd. play all the other numbers on the clock all the other days of the week." He has the head class—five fifth-formers—plus two special students: one a fellow named Sparrow and the other eighteen-year-old Richard Garnett Bellasis, to whose father Newman has dedicated his *Grammar of Assent.* He likes his students, and thinks of them as his children, "a notion encouraged by their innocence and backwardness. They never swear beyond Confound you, you young fool, and that only one of them." As for the teachers themselves, they are the sweepings of Great Britain, and come from "all quarters indiscriminately." There is even a Dutchman among them. All of them are "nice souls."

But life here in Birmingham is far more primitive than it ever was at Oxford, and Hopkins no longer even sees the newspapers. Has suffrage been extended in the recent elections and democracy thus established? he jokes. And will Benjamin Disraeli, current Prime Minister and saviour of the people, now take the title "of Earl Mount Horeb, Baron Bashan"? He gets no letters anymore, but then he also writes none. The food here is at best Spartan. On the other hand, at least there is music: a violin and violincello quartet made up of the music master, one of his sixth- and one of his fifth-formers, and Newman himself. The country about Edgbaston has turned out to be a blessing, and he walks whenever he can these days. But already he feels overwhelmed by teaching, and wonders if there is anything else he could do—even for less money—which would give him more time for himself. He will think this again a month later, only harder, when one of his charges—"the fattest and biggest" of them—kicks him in the ankle during a football game and nearly lames him.

On November 1, the Feast of All Saints—a school holiday—he writes Bridges, who is busy studying for Greats, and admits that the exams were like "a millstone" around his own neck. Thinking of Dolben, he sees now that there was "a great want of strength" in the boy, and even more of common sense. As for his own boys, though they are taking everything out of him, he still likes working with them. "And as there is nothing but boys visible that is really saying everything there is to be said about the general pleasantness of the place." In imitation of Newman, he has begun learning to play the violin and promises Bridges that if he ever writes a trio or quartet, Bridges will "take the first or second part in it."

The work continues; morphs. When one of the other teachers suddenly leaves, he must take over the second form as well. Then, in mid-November, Henry Challis, another Oxford convert like himself, takes over his classes and he begins working with the fourth- and fifth-formers. He learns that Hugh Francis O'Hanlon, Scholar of Brasenose and Fellow of Lincoln, after taking his degree earlier that year, went down to London and there in his lodgings shot himself. He is only the first of many casualties among Hopkins's classmates. Bridges invites him back to the vicarage again, but he declines, uncomfortable with the thought of having to see Bridges's stepfather once more now that he has defected. Nor is he willing to compromise the intense pleasure he felt during his time at Rochdale. Bridges has now decided to go in for medicine after graduation. "A 2nd is the class I have always imagined you wd. get," he tells Bridges. "Mind it is a good one." And a second is what Bridges gets.

The weather remains wet and mild until December, when it suddenly turns cold and the boys flood the football court to slide and skate on. On the 15th, Poutiatine and another friend come up to the Oratory for a short visit. On the 19th, there are speeches and prizes, and then the boys are gone. Two days later, Hopkins returns home to the pockmarked snows and fogs of Oak Hill. On New Year's Eve, a short note from Newman. If Hopkins is seriously interested in pursuing a religious vocation, Newman writes, it might be best for him to go into retreat at Easter at the Oratory with the students and bring the matter up in that context.

A letter to Urquhart, who has expressed doubts about the Anglican rite of penance. "I am glad you go to confession," Hopkins informs him, "although there is nothing of a Sacrament in the ordinance as you use it, but still it has its value *ex opere operantis* and in some cases the shadow of Peter may cure where the touch of Peter is not to be had." Still, he knows from his own experience with Liddon that this "kind of reasoning is dangerous and likely to mislead." Moreover, it saddens him to think of Urquhart's continued fence-sitting, for "the more frankly you confess the 'ricketiness' of yr. position . . . the less excuse you have yourself for staying in it." Yes, a great work has been going on in the Church of England, and it is precisely "in the restoration of Catholic faith and practice," so that, logically, "the greater the success the [Oxford] movement historically has had the stronger the presumption against the catholicity of the Church of England." On the other hand, both know that the movement toward various forms of Puritanism—the Broad Church schisms—has historically had even greater success in the Anglican Church. So much therefore for numbers alone. But why not bring his concerns up with those who are better informed than he is? If only Urquhart could speak with someone like Father Vaughan, who lives so close to him, and who has such "an extraordinary devotion to the Blessed Sacrament."

New Year's, 1868, Oak Hill: Hopkins attends an evening party at his neighbors', the Hollands, and dines the following evening with the Bonds.

Then a few days with Aunt Kate in London, including a concert at St. James'
Hall to hear selections from Beethoven, Schubert, Bach. On the 8th, he goes
to Blunt House in Croydon with his family to be with his grandparents, and
writes Bridges from there that he will not be able to see him in town before
Bridges and Muirhead leave for Egypt. The year they are away, he confides,
will no doubt "make a great difference in my position though I cannot know
exactly what." For sure, the uncertainty he finds himself in about his future
"is so very unpleasant and so breaks my power of applying to anything that
I am resolved to end it, which I shall do by going into a retreat at Easter at
the latest and deciding whether I have a vocation to the priesthood." He
asks Bridges not to repeat this to anyone, as he has not yet broken the news
to his own family.

Plays, a performance of the Beni Zougzougs, a visit to London's famous
Crystal Palace, rounded off with a trip north to visit relatives. On the 21st,
he is back at the Oratory, holidays over and classes beginning. For the next
few months he has no time to write letters, and certainly no time for poetry,
though he does keep a notebook in which he speculates on the metaphysical nature of inscape in language. "To every word meaning a thing," he
notes in early February, "belongs a passion or prepossession or enthusiasm
which it has the power of suggesting or producing but not always or in everyone." Each word, then, has its own inscape, which "bears a valuable
analogy to the soul, one however which is not complete, because all names
but proper names are general while the soul is individual."

Each word also has three terms or moments: its connotation, or "prepossession of feeling"; its "definition," which is an "abstraction, vocal expression or other utterance"; and its "application, 'extension,' the concrete
things coming under it," i.e., the thing to which the word points. But even
these, he realizes, do not cover everything one means by a word. "For the
word is the expression, uttering of the idea in the mind," and every idea has
two aspects. There is the abstract conception of the word, but there is also
"the image (of sight or sound or scapes of the other senses), which is in fact
physical and a refined energy . . . accenting the nerves, a word to oneself,"
though this image at some level remains inchoate and must escape all
definition.

There are two kinds of mental energy. The first is transitional: the step-
by-step unfolding of a thought or sensation. This is to reason, whether ac-
tively, as in using the critical faculties, or passively, as in reading. The second kind is reserved for the act of contemplation, when the mind is "taken
up by, dwells upon, enjoys, a single thought," as in the act of prayer, poetry,

music, or painting. Art in fact "exacts this energy of contemplation," though it also involves the critical faculties. The two of course are not incompatible, "for even in the successive arts as music, for full enjoyment," both the contemplative and critical faculties are at work. But only the contemplative intellect can approach deep form with its complex inner unity. In other words, "the further in anything, as a work of art, the organisation is carried out, the deeper the form penetrates, the prepossession [or organizing idea] flushes the matter, the more effort will be required in apprehension, the more power of comparison, the more capacity for receiving that synthesis of (either successive or spatially distinct) impressions which gives us the unity with the prepossession conveyed by it."

Some minds will prefer that the prepossession—or inscape—"be conveyed by the least organic, expressive ... most suggestive, way," as with Pater, say, or with the French Impressionists. But by approaching the inscape of a word and its definition in this impressionistic manner, the word becomes bifurcated and unwound, and this, Hopkins sees from experience, is the less useful way of approaching language. What he wants, rather, is to contemplate "that which really is expressed in the object." It is the intellectual attraction "for very sharp and pure dialectic or, in other matter, hard and telling art-forms." Not the fuzzy or suggestive, then, the mere impression, but the sharp-edged brilliance of the thing itself.

But the actual teaching and shepherding of his boys has taken its toll on his ability to concentrate on such ideas. A bare month into the new term and he has had enough. His health has become problematic, he complains to Baillie, and he can find no way to refresh himself. Yes, he still likes the boys, but teaching quickly becomes "very burdensome," especially when one has had as much of it as he has. In short, he is out of his element, trapped, and no longer hears news or sees any of his old friends, except Challis. Otherwise, the place has become "without reservation 'damned, shepherd.'" He means to enter the priesthood soon, it having become for him not only "the happiest and best way," but the only way out he can see for his own peace of mind.

True, he had once wanted to be an artist and a painter, but he sees now that "the higher and more attractive parts of the art put a strain upon the passions which" he believes in his case would be "unsafe to encounter." It is possible that in his priestly life he would still be able to write something from time to time, though of course "not so freely as I shd. have liked, e.g. nothing or little in the verse way, but no doubt what wd. best serve the cause of my religion." The trouble is that his mother has made no secret that his becoming a priest would cause her "great grief," and the thought of disappointing her again preys on his mind "very much and makes the near prospect quite black." He says nothing of his father, who would no doubt support his wife in the matter. And all this, after finally establishing some peace and tranquility on the home front. As a result, he is "reckless about things that I shd. otherwise care about, uncertain as I am whether in a few months I may not be shut up in a cloister." Still, he knows as deeply as he knows anything that once he makes up his mind to follow God's will for him and become a priest, he will have the only "real sense of freedom" he has ever had.

March 1868: Lilac trees budding amid scattered snow showers. Then fretty chervil and wood-sorrel. He visits a convent of the Sisters of Charity at Selly Oak, notes the brightness now night after night of Venus, shining in the evening skies "like an apple of light." Then, at the beginning of April, he learns of the brutal hatchet murders of Bridges's sister's baby and husband, the Reverend Plow. A young man, ejected from Plow's property for taking up with their silly young house servant, has killed them both. Bridges's sister, Harriet, has also been seriously wounded in the attack. But from Bridges, now somewhere in the Middle East, he hears nothing.

On Saturday, April 4, school lets out. The following day—Palm Sunday—the Easter retreat for the boys begins, to end on Maundy Thursday. Giving the retreat is a forty-four-year-old Jesuit priest named Fr. Henry James Coleridge, son of Sir John Taylor Coleridge, Judge of the King's Bench and brother of John Duke, Lord Coleridge, Chief Justice of England. His grandfather, Captain James Coleridge, was Samuel Taylor Coleridge's brother. Fr. Coleridge is a product of Eton and Trinity College, Oxford, having graduated with highest honors in the year Hopkins was born. A staunch member of the Tractarian Movement, he followed Newman until Newman went over to Rome, at which point he became an Anglican priest. Then—with Pusey's condemnation by the Anglican episcopacy and Newman's going over to Rome—he left Oxford to take a curacy near his ancestral home.

In 1852, Coleridge left his curacy, made a retreat with the Redemptorist Fathers, and became a Catholic. That fall, he entered the Accademia dei Nobili in Rome and was ordained four years later. In 1857, he entered the Jesuit novitiate at Beaumont Lodge, Old Windsor, and two years later was sent to St. Beuno's in Wales to teach New Testament Scripture. Six years later, he was reassigned to London to become the first Jesuit editor of *The Month.* A friend of Newman's, he has recently published Newman's "Dream of Gerontius" in one of the first issues of the magazine. He is the first Jesuit Hopkins has ever actually talked to, and it is to Coleridge that Hopkins now confides his wish to become a priest.

On Easter Sunday, Hopkins hears Newman preach. The following day, Addis arrives for a short visit, during which they talk of their respective vocations. Then, on the 14th, Hopkins leaves the Oratory for good and returns home, where life at Oak Hill resumes. He attends a meeting of the Hampstead Conversazione Society to discuss Pre-Raphaelite art, stays with Aunt Kate in London and attends the French and Flemish Exhibit, and visits with Baillie, who is studying law at the Inns of Court. On the 27th, he goes down to Roehampton, southwest of London to stay at Manresa House, the Jesuit novitiate situated on a former eighteenth-century estate, and begins an eight-day retreat arranged by Coleridge. The retreat is meant to aid Hopkins in discerning whether or not he has a vocation to the priesthood, and if he does, to further discern whether it shall be with a contemplative order like the Benedictines, or a more socially active order like the Jesuits. His first night there he reports seeing "a flash of lightning" followed by a terrifying clap of thunder, and in the morning a bright rainbow. On the fifth day of his retreat, he resolves to give up the writing of poetry if he should become a priest and to burn what he has already written.

Sunday, May 3: Bright, hazy, and hot. All day long he hears the cuckoo singing, and now the majestic oaks are in leaf. Walking through Richmond Park adjoining the novitiate the following day, he notes a particular elm, one of its huge limbs "overhanging the sunk fence into the Park." It is like one he remembers at Shanklin, very beautiful looked at from the one side, though from the other the same limb suddenly becomes uninteresting and clumsy. It all depends, after all, on how one sees a thing. Afterward, he writes in his journal that he is now "resolved to be a religious." The following morning, he leaves to return home, his mind made up to become a priest in a religious order, though whether the Benedictines or the Jesuits he does not yet know. Hopkins keeps his own counsel at home, but on May 11 he quietly burns all of the finished copies of his poems he can lay his hands on. He will write no more poems, he resolves, as incompatible with his vocation. In his journal that same day he writes, tersely, "Slaughter of the Innocents."

Then he writes Newman that he means to become a Jesuit, hard as their discipline is, and hopes he has not led Newman into believing that he had ever seriously considered becoming an Oratorian. "My dear Hopkins," Newman writes back at once, gracious as ever, "I am both surprised and glad at your news. . . . I think it is the very thing for you. You are quite out, in thinking that when I offered you a 'home' here, I dreamed of your having a vocation for us. This I clearly saw you had *not*, from the moment you came to us. Don't call the Jesuit discipline hard. It will bring you to heaven." And then he adds: "The Benedictines would not have suited you."

On Tuesday, May 19, Hopkins travels back down to London to the Jesuits' headquarters at Farm Street Church, to be interviewed by Fr. Alfred Weld, forty-five, the current Provincial for the English Jesuits. He holds a B.A. from the University of London and has a reputation as a capable administrator. He is also a Fellow of the Royal Astronomical Society and has already served as Novice Master at Roehampton. After the meeting, Hopkins is assured he will hear shortly about his candidacy. The following day, he visits his grandparents at Croydon. Suburbanization of the area here has continued apace, with the property around Blunt House now being chewed up into lots for private homes. Here, as at Oxford, he realizes, it is only a matter of time before nature's open spaces around will be no more. It is while at Blunt House that he reads in *The Times* that Cardinal d'Andrea has suddenly died in Rome. The reporter has hinted broadly that the Cardinal was poisoned either by the Pope or by the Jesuits. "All I can positively tell you," *The Times* correspondent adds, "is that he did not consider himself altogether safe in the Papal capital." Hopkins's family is sure to be thrilled when they learn that he plans to spend his life with this same order.

Then, on May 28, he takes the train up to Oxford to partake in graduation exercises. Among those he notes in the crowd are Swinburne and the painter Simeon Solomon, to whom he is introduced, and who invites him to visit at his London studio. Afterward, he calls on Liddon at Christ Church, but is told he is not available to see Mr. Hopkins. When he returns home on the 30th, there is a letter waiting for him from Fr. Weld, informing him that he has been accepted into the novitiate come September. Afterwards, Hopkins writes Liddon to say how sorry he was to have missed him at Oxford, for he is afraid now they shall never meet again. "I came a good many times," he tells him, "but your oak was always up. If I had sent you a note in time I shd. have managed better perhaps." But now he must make his farewell in writing. He is going to Switzerland, and after that plans to join the Jesuits, and wants his old confessor to understand how happy he is with his decision. In fact, he cannot think of another prospect "so bright in the world." He signs off: "Ever affectionately yours."

Saturday, June 13: Hopkins writes Urquhart to tell him that he and Bond are shortly leaving for Switzerland and that when he returns he will be leaving for "the Jesuit noviciate [sic] at Roehampton. It is enough to say that the sanctity has not departed fr. the order to have a reason for joining it." Since making his decision, he "has enjoyed the first complete peace of mind I have ever had." He has also been happily surprised at the way his parents, seeing that their son's mind is made up, have accepted his decision. As for Urquhart's ongoing, exasperating vacillations about converting, Hopkins has had enough. It is no longer a matter of intellectual difficulties, he admonishes him, but rather a moral imperative he faces, for his friend is "trying the forbearance of God." Urquhart's fence-sitting, he believes, can only be construed now as either blindness or irony. He understands that with Urquhart's "living a moral life, with the ordinances of religion and yourself a minister of them," it seems "natural to say all things continue as they were and most hard to realise the silence and the severity of God, as Dr. Newman very eloquently and persuasively has said in a passage of the Anglican Difficulties." But the point is that this "way of thinking—all things continuing as they were" constitutes nothing less than an act of infidelity.

Outwardly, the world goes as the world goes, whether one does God's will or shuns it. "Faces, streets, and sunlight look just the same." And this makes vacillating all the "more dangerous and terrible." Will it comfort Urquhart at his death "not to have despaired of the English Church if by not despairing of it" he is "out of the Catholic Church?" And will God thank him for his allegiance or excuse him for it?

> He asks obedience before everything else. Make half an hour's meditation on death and suppose you have received what you call the last sacrament: it will then occur—perhaps this is not a sacrament and if not it is a mockery to me and God; secondly, if it is, perhaps it is received in schism and I have wounded my soul with the "instrument of salvation": this perhaps which gives little trouble on an ordinary Sunday will be very terrible then. Then if you add—but will not God allow for the possible mistake because I cd. not help being deceived? you will be able to answer—certainly not: I always knew there was a doubt.

If Urquhart would but think hard on this final scenario for three minutes he would see this, Hopkins insists. "Above all things say *Domine, quid vis ut faciam?* [Lord, what would you have me do?] Say it and force yourself to mean it. Until you prefer God to the world and yourself you have not made the first step." It is a glimpse no doubt into the searing, cauterizing process Hopkins himself had to face at Manresa House, when he asked these same questions of himself, and which he will render into such passionate lines in "The Wreck of the Deutschland" seven years later, during another existential spiritual crisis:

> I did say yes
>   O at lightning and lashed rod;
>   Thou heardst me truer than tongue confess
>   Thy terror, O Christ, O God;
>   Thou knowest the walls, áltar and hour and night:
>   The swoon of a heart that the sweep and the hurl of thee trod
>   Hard down with a horror of height:
> And the midriff astrain with leaning of, laced with fire of stress.
>
>   The frown of his face
>   Before me, the hurtle of hell
>   Behind, where, where was a, where was a place?—
>   I whirled out wings that spell
>   And fled with a fling of the heart to the heart of the Host.—
>   My heart, but you were dovewinged, I can tell,
>   Carrier-witted, I am bóld to bóast,
> To flash from the flame to the flame then, tower from the grace to
>   the grace.

"You see," he ends, "I do not apologise for this language: it is . . . my right and my duty to use it." And—he adds—"ask our Lady's help."

How beautiful the world about him seems once more, now that he has aligned his will with the Father's. "Honeysuckle at the hedge on the big bank in bloom . . . this is their time of greatest beauty." That same day he notes—with relief—that his father, called in to help his grandfather with the Thwaytes affair, has succeeded in winding matters up. In fact, the plaintiff's solicitor has "highly complimented" Manley on his management of affairs, so that £40,000—or about 10 percent of the estate—will go to Hopkins's grandfather, the rest to Mrs. Thwaytes's sister. The family name has been upheld, and that is the most important thing. The following day, Hopkins lunches with Pater in London, and then visits Simeon Solomon's studio. Afterward, he takes in the Academy exhibit with its paintings by Mason, Millais, and—his favorite—Fred Walker. Saturday evening he watches in awe the prestidigitation of Mademoiselle Vogt playing the finger-glasses, an instrument, he notes, "chromatically more perfect than the violin even" and the tone itself magical. "Ah, to watch her fingers flying . . . like flakes . . . or leaves of white." At the National Gallery on the 27th, he looks hard at a Giotto and suddenly catches the very "instress of loveliness" itself.

Instress: It is an idea he has been thinking about for months now. In some notes on Parmenides written while at the Oratory, he'd noted that the philosopher's central text was "that Being is and Not-being is not— which . . . means that all things are upheld by instress and are meaningless without it." In fact, Parmenides' "feeling for instress, for the flush and fore-drawn, and for inscape is most striking and from this one can understand Plato's reverence for him as the great father of Realism." To be equals Is. "*Esti* may roughly be expressed by *things are* or *there is truth.*" In fact, when he has "been in this mood and felt the depth of an instress or how fast the inscape holds a thing that nothing is so pregnant and straightforward to the truth as simple *yes* and *is*." How pregnant that copula, our ability to say "blood is red," rather than only "this blood is red" or "the last blood I saw was red." It is this ability to recognize that things *are* that so strikes him now, to be able to say that there is a world and that we can say so much about it. "One thing for all men and for every man," and yet "ten thousand men to think and ten thousand things for them to think of . . . are but names given and taken, eye and lip service to the truth, husks and scapes of it: the truth itself, the burl, the fulness, is the thought." For what holds all things together is Being itself, "under its modification or siding of particular one-ness or Being, and Not-being, under its siding of the Many." Truly, Being and its opposite Not-Being "may be called two degrees of siding in the scale of Being," that is, things coming into being or slipping from Being. Being is fire, Non-Being earth, as it were, held in tension by Necessity or Justice, which created the gods, and first of all Love. All this will flame out again and again in his work: slime, mud, dust, the fiery instress of Is.

On the eve of his departure for Switzerland, Hopkins writes Fr. Ignatius Ryder at the Oratory. "I shall be glad to have seen it [Switzerland]," he tells him on July 2, for Bond has told him that Jesuits "are strictly forbidden the country." He wants to review William Morris's *The Earthly Paradise* in the context of the Medieval School of poets writing now in England. But there are difficulties, which will become a characteristic Hamletizing on Hopkins's part. First, he cannot get his hands on the book. Second, what he has written so far is "dull and abstruse." Third, he doesn't have the time to write the essay. And fourth, he lacks perseverance. Still, he should like to sing his "dying-swan-song" before he gives over poetry altogether.

The next morning, early, Hopkins and Bond depart for Switzerland, going by ferry from Dover to Ostend, then on to Brussels by riverboat. Then down the Rhine by boat, with Sunday mass at the cathedral at Cologne, and on to Mainz, the riverbanks along the way edged with poplars. Then by rail to Basel, past walnut and cherry trees and oleanders in bloom, and terraced vineyards. A full moon, and the streets of the city empty, except for one woman at a window holding a candle, and then that too gone. Years later that image too will find its way into a poem.

At the museum in Basel, he notes "a noble dead Christ" by the younger Holbein and a crucifixion. Then, from his train window that afternoon, storks' nests on church roofs and his first view of the Alps. In Lucerne that evening, he watches as bats flit about the pond at the base of Thorvaldsen's statue of the *Dying Lion,* commemorating the Swiss Guard who fell protecting the French King during the French Revolution. Then by steamer to Küssnacht and the Immensee. One morning, early, he glances out his hotel window and is struck by the "noble scape of stars." Finally, in the dawn light: the pink snows of the Alps, morphing to white.

Later, as a guide takes them up the Wylerhorn, he hears two boys coming down the mountain, yodeling. There are flocks of mountain flowers, and tall firs reminding him of the Parthenon. He dons his puggaree, the head scarf falling down behind, and trims it with harebells and "gentians in two rows above like double pan-pipes." How delightful it all is, until, coming down, they lose their way and slide dangerously down "the long wet grass of a steep slope." An all-day hike through the Brunig Pass to Lake Brienz follows, water cascading down the falls like "wax gutterings on a candle," and the *chirr* of mountain grasshoppers, which sound to Bond like "a thousand fairy sewing-machines." The Silberhorn, Hopkins notes, seems "shaped and nippled like the sand in an hourglass," and the two ends of the Jungfrau glacier, reminding him of the "skin of a white tiger or the deep fell of some other animal." He tries sketching the inscape of the mountain, but realizes it would take hours to catch it. Then the Grindlewald and the Faulhorn and—the following day—a glimpse of the Aarhorn, "standing like a high-gabled steeple." On to Meyringen and up the Valley of the Aar to the Grimsel with a French-speaking guide, who bounds up the hillside and brings them back bunches of flowers. At Gelmer Falls, giddy with the play of so many comparisons, Hopkins notes how the falling water looks "like milk chasing round blocks of coal; or a girdle ... of white weighted with irregular black rubies." Or again, "like the skin of a white snake square-pied with black."

Then down the Rhône glacier to explore an ice grotto. At lunch, surrounded by so much beauty, he finds himself repulsed by the face of the Frenchman sitting across from him. Geldart *redivuvus*. The oval face "cut away at the jaws; the eyes . . . big, shallow-set, close to the eyebrow . . . the nostrils prominent; the lips fleshy . . . the nose curved hollow." Down the Rhône Valley to Visp and a Catholic canton, the churches marked by tin-topped, onion-shaped steeples. The Matterhorn reminds him of "a Greek galley stranded" with its "reared-up rostrum." Or seen from the Riffel, where it reminds him of "a sea-lion couchant or a sphinx," or "the hooded-snake frontal worn by the Egyptian kings." Only three years earlier its summit was first reached by seven Englishmen, four of whom perished on the way down. Then Monte Rosa, the Lyskamm, the Jumeaux, the Breithorn, and the Matterhorn itself. Hopkins searches for their inscape, finds it as the sky turns a "dead purple," the snow itself damasking to rose in the last light of day; above the Breithorn, Antares sparkling "like a bright crab-apple tingling in the wind."

At 2:00 a.m. on the 25th, the two men begin the ascent up the Breithorn. "Taurus up," Hopkins notes, and lightning mingling with the dawn. Then the sunrise brightly fleshing the snow of the Breithorn, "the colour changing through metallic shades of yellow recovered to white." They are accompanied by "young Mr. Pease of Darlington, his guide Gasser, and ours Welchen." He notes "the strange rotten-woven clouds," reminding him of the "oozy seaweed" which "lines and hangs from piers and slubbered wood in the sea." At Vevey, there is dancing in the dining room of the Trois Couronnes, while Hopkins goes outside on the balcony to watch the moon silvering the lake, "dinting and tooling it with sparkling holes." On the 28th, his twenty-fourth birthday, he views the dark blues of Lake Geneva, and the cathedral, with its intricate neoclassical capitals and moldings. Their odyssey over, they take the train back to Paris, passing through "a country of pale grey rocky hills of a strong and simple outscape." Then through Paris for the Dieppe–Newhaven crossing, and so by rail home. The long summer drought, he sees, has burned the English countryside white.

On August 4, Hopkins meets Dolben's friend Edgell, a recent convert, in Regents Park, who talks about their dead friend. He writes Bridges to say he will be leaving soon for Roehampton, and hopes Bridges will visit or write him there, warning him that his letters will be read. He also doubts whether he will be able to write back for some time at least. As for his poem, "Summa," he cannot send it, for it was "burnt with my other verses," seeing "they wd. interfere with my state and vocation." He has, however, kept "corrected copies of some things," which Bridges has and promises to send those on. He also hopes that Bridges "will master the peculiar beat" he has introduced into "St. Dorothea." The development is his, he explains, though he discovered it in Shakespeare. It is in fact a foreshadowing of what he will come to call sprung rhythm.

A letter from Frederick Maples, formerly a day student at Highgate with Hopkins, and now an Anglican curate at St. Mary's in Soho. He is having "deep doubts about the Anglican way," and wonders if Roman Catholicism might be the answer. In turn, Hopkins goes to Soho to meet with him. Four days later, at Hopkins's prompting, Maples writes Liddon, telling him that "the temptations to join the Church of Rome are many and appalling." And though, as he did with Hopkins, Liddon urges him to stay put, hoping that this too will pass, Maples will go on to become a Catholic priest.

In late August, Hopkins and Baillie visit the National Portrait Gallery, then trek out to the ancient abbey at St. Alban's, its "great massive Norman tower now impoverished" by bad restoration work in plaster. He notes too the beautiful stained-glass windows in the antechapel, which somehow survived the destruction of the Roundheads. At least the whitewash has been cleared away, and the carvings revived. The abbey itself, he notes, is mostly made up of stonework taken from the Roman walls of Verulamium. A few days later, Bridges comes up to Oak Hill to visit Hopkins and is bitten by Hopkins's dog, Rover, for his troubles. The two men spend an afternoon strolling through London's Hyde Park, catching up on so many things: their families, Bridges's travels, Bridges's new love for things German and his growing distance from Christianity. On the 31st, Hopkins visits Addis, who is about to join the Brompton Oratory—an offshoot of Newman's here in London. Then a trip alone to Ely to visit the ruins of another Benedictine abbey and cathedral. As beautiful as that medieval world was, Hopkins realizes, it is gone now. If the Church is to be rebuilt, it must be on a new model, which is one reason he has chosen the Jesuits.

On Sunday, September 6, he goes down to Croydon to say good-bye to his grandparents, his aunt Annie, and his father's younger brother, Uncle Charles, recently returned from Hawaii after being abroad since the year Gerard was born. His old friend Horace Dugmore visits at Oak Hill to say good-bye. In the evening, suitcase packed, Hopkins bids good-bye to his family, and then, realizing that a settled way of life is ending, walks back to Victoria Road to say a final good-bye to Aunt Annie, who in turn walks back with him to the train station to wave him off. Then it is off to Roehampton and the novitiate, one door closing, as the Jesuit porter, extending a hand in greeting, opens another.

PART II

WALLS, ALTAR AND
HOUR AND NIGHT

1868–1877

St. Beuno's, Wales

Chapter 5

Owner of the Skies & Stars
& Everything Wild: Roehampton, 1868–1870

Thursday, September 10, 1868. Manresa House, Roehampton: Three days into his new life as a Jesuit novice, the twenty-four-year-old Hopkins writes his mother. "There are five novices besides myself now entered and another is expected," he tells her. "The odd thing is that one of them is called Hopkins, so that we must keep our Christian names to avoid confusion and on the other hand I must keep my surname because there is already a brother Jerrard with a J." To distinguish him from the other Hopkins, whose surname is Frederick (also twenty-four and a practicing physician), Gerard will soon acquire the moniker "the gentle Hop" because of his outwardly mild disposition, while his counterpart will become "the genteel Hop."

Two second-year novices have been assigned to the new arrivals to help them adjust to the rules of the house and the ways of the order, one of them being John Walford, whom Hopkins had succeeded at the Oratory the year before. Otherwise, Hopkins adds, "we do not as yet mix with the other [i.e., the second-year] novices." The Long Retreat—thirty days of silence in which the novices will work through the *Spiritual Exercises* of St. Ignatius of Loyola under the guidance of a spiritual director—begins in just a few days, "but will be broken twice or more" by days of repose before the novices plunge once again into the *Exercises*. It is on these days that he may have a chance to write again. In fact, this is all he can write now, he tells his mother, "because of the post and disposition of our times and I thought you wd. rather have a short letter than none." He is not used to having to keep his room so tidy, but that is one of the rules here. For the moment he has his own bedroom, but he is expecting shortly to "move into one of the dormitories or, as they call them, Quarters."

Manresa House, Roehampton—named for the retreat in northern Spain where Ignatius himself underwent the spiritual rigors that formed the basis of the *Spiritual Exercises*—is a classical eighteenth-century structure, which has been done over in the best quasi-military style of the practical English Jesuits. The Jesuit community (novices, novice masters, and other priests assigned here for the formation of new Jesuits) meets in the *aula*, or novices' hall, with its ornate ceiling and Baroque plasterwork, though the fine crystal chandelier has long been removed as out of keeping with the asceticism of the place. The decorative walls with their bas-reliefs sporting nymphs and Pans are paneled over now with pine. The novices sleep in the general Quarters, a room made up of small jerrybuilt cubicles, each with a metal bed, pitcher, basin, and a Charley, or chamberpot. In place of doors, red curtains adorn the cubicle entrances. Upstairs is a tiny chapel for prayer, lit by a skylight and candles.

Communion in Hopkins's time (and until Pope Pius X changed the custom in 1905) is reserved for special occasions and preceded by a strict fast from food and liquids from midnight on. It is normally taken on Sundays, holy days of obligation, the feasts of Jesuit saints, and the feasts of the Blessed Mother and the Apostles, as well as on Maundy Thursday (the institution of the sacrament), the Feast of the Sacred Heart, and about a dozen other feast days, including the first Friday of each month. Catechesis includes the works of Lingard, Hornihold, and Ullathorne, plus works in French by Jean Couturier (Dijon, 1830), *L'Abbé du Clôt* (Lyons, 1843), V. Bluteau (Paris, 1860), and catechisms written in German, Italian, and Spanish. Among those in English are Stephen Keenan's two-volume *Catechism of the Christian Religion* (Glasgow, 1851), Patrick Power's *Catechism: Doctrinal, Moral, Historical, and Liturgical* (1859); James Doyle's *An Abridgment of the Christian Doctrine* (Dublin, 1860) and *The Catechism of the Council of Trent,* translated by J. Donovan the year before.

Among the first-year novices are two seventeen-year-olds: Wilcock and Tom McMullin (whose name Hopkins will consistently misremember as Macmullin), and a young Yorkshireman, Aelred Tempest. Among the larger second-year class of novices are the Kerr brothers, sons of Lord Henry Kerr of Huntleyburn, Rector of Dittisham, Devon, to whom Hopkins is particularly drawn. William, quiet and self-effacing, is thirty-two and has been educated at Harrow and Stonyhurst. He spent ten years in the Madras (India) Civil Service, retiring because of ill health at thirty. Henry, now thirty, joined the Royal Navy at the age of thirteen, then served in the Crimean War, where he rose to the rank of commander at age twenty-eight. But all that glory and advancement is behind him now, having opted for a life of religious service.

Among the other second-year novices are three Irishmen: Ignatius

Gartlan, nineteen, from Northern Ireland, educated at Mount St. Mary's and Stonyhurst Colleges; Daniel Heffernan Considine, also nineteen, from Limerick, educated at Stonyhurst and Lincoln College, Oxford; and the nearsighted Robert Kane, twenty, a Dubliner educated by the Irish Jesuits at Clongowes Wood, who is doing his Juniorate for additional schooling. Then there is Edward Sidgreaves, twenty-eight, from Preston, and Walter Diver Strappini, nineteen, from Guernsey, a recent convert. Finally, there is Francis Edward Bacon, twenty-nine, a Londoner and another convert, who will become one of Hopkins's closest friends in the Society, and one of the few Jesuits to appreciate his poems, copies of some of them being the only ones to survive.

On September 16, the Long Retreat gets underway. "Chestnuts as bright as coals or spots of vermilion," Hopkins notes with delight that first day, as he begins meditating on God's Creation under the guidance of the Ignatian *Exercises.* It is an image which will transform itself in the alembic of his imagination nine years later into "Fresh-firecoal chestnut-falls," a line from a compressed sonnet celebrating the dappled brilliance and design of all Creation. Charged now by the very *Exercises* as by his own Romantic proclivities to see into God's Creation more and more closely, he compares the morning mist condensing over the lawns at Manresa to "water . . . clouded by milk or soda." But of the Long Retreat itself no notes have survived, though we know the general stages through which he would have proceeded.

By the "Spiritual Exercises," Ignatius tells us, "we mean every method of examination of conscience, meditation, contemplation, vocal or mental prayer, and other spiritual activities. . . . For just as taking a walk, traveling on foot, and running are physical exercise, so is the name of spiritual exercises given to any means of preparing and disposing our soul to rid itself of all its disordered affections and then, after their removal, of seeking and finding God's will in the ordering of our life for the salvation of our soul." There are Four Weeks to the *Exercises,* each of more or less seven days' duration, depending on the director's decisions and the response of the exercitants. The First Week is based on the Principle and Foundation of God's Creation, with its Meditations on the First, Second, and Third Sins, as well as a Meditation on Hell. The Second Week includes meditations on the life of Christ, beginning with the Incarnation and the Nativity, a Preamble to Consider the States of Life, and the Two Standards which one may follow ("black, white, right, wrong," as Hopkins will spell it out years later). There are also meditations on how to approach worldly possessions, and another on the Three Manners of Humility, leading up to the making of one's own election or choice. The Third Week is an extended meditation on the Great Sacrifice: the passion and death of Christ, and its complex effect on the one making the *Exercises*. The Fourth Week focuses on the Eastering or Rising of Christ, the Contemplation to Gain Love, and the Three Methods of Prayer.

Since Vatican II, the practice has been for each exercitant to meet with a spiritual director for about forty-five minutes each day, and then pray and meditate in silence for the rest of the day and evening, a routine broken by mass, physical exercises such as long solitary walks, and time in prayer wherever one finds oneself. But in Hopkins's time those making the *Exercises* come together to listen to the director speak, and then disperse each to his own room or quiet space. Little if any news filters in from the outside world during these thirty days, and no visitors are allowed except on the two days of repose, which come at ten-day intervals.

After completion of the Long Retreat, the quotidian duties of the community resume. They are long days, unpunctuated by much rest. There is Rodriguez—the daily reading from Alphonsus Rodriguez, S.J., on *Christian Perfection*, done at the novice's desk. The meals are held in common, usually in silence while spiritual books are read to them. Latin is the language usually spoken, as it is in nearly every Catholic community from London to Rome to Belize, Benarez, Shanghai. There is much to be done in terms of upkeep on the buildings at Roehampton and on the acres and acres of grounds and woods surrounding the community: sweeping the halls, mopping the kitchen floors, taking down dead trees and shaky limbs. Also, communal and private prayers, daily mass (in Latin), recreation outdoors in the afternoons and indoors in the evening.

Even Hopkins's journal notes slip away now into almost complete silence. On October 21, he notes that from the heights of Richmond Park, he could see "trees in the river flat below inscaped in distinctly projected, crisp, and almost hard, rows of leaves, their edges . . . a little fixed and shaped with shadow." September and October are almost idyllic. "A Spanish chestnut and two elms in the grounds seem to fill the air up with an equable clear ochre," he jots down. But two weeks later it is the "brownish paste in the library" he notes, forming big crystals as the weather turns cold. From time to time he is allowed to walk into London, accompanied by a fellow Jesuit. In November, there is a frost, and then days of mild weather with "warm wet winds." So warm that the honeysuckle is already out "and catkins hanging in the thickets." But on the night of December 6, he experiences "the most violent gale" he has ever felt, the force of it snapping a huge elm in half on the grounds.

Two days after Christmas—spent at Roehampton with his fellow Jesuits—two colleagues from his Oxford days, William Holland and Richard Nettleship, visit him on their way back to Oxford after visiting their tutor, Henry Green. Holland finds himself attracted to Hopkins's life here and writes Green, seeking his advice. "I am glad that you and Nettleship saw Hopkins," Green replies on the 29th. "A step such as the one he has taken, though I can't quite admit it to be heroic, must needs be painful, and its pain should not be aggravated—as it is pretty sure to be—by separation from old friends. I never had his intimacy, but always liked him very much. I imagine him—perhaps inevitably—to be one of these, like his ideal J. H. Newman, who instead of simply opening themselves to the revelation of God in the *reasonable* world, are fain to put themselves into an attitude—saintly, it is true, but still an attitude." But, Green is quick to point out to his disciple, "true citizenship 'as unto the Lord' . . . I reckon higher than 'saintliness' in the technical sense. The 'superior young man' of these days, however, does not seem to understand it, but hugs his own refined pleasures or (which is but a higher form of the same) his personal sanctity." In effect, then, Hopkins's joining the Jesuits is merely a more ethereal form of Pater's aestheticism. In any event, Green would prefer not to see any more of his students throw away their lives as poor Hopkins has.

Sunday, February 7, 1869: Finally, Hopkins finds a few moments to write his mother, thanking her for sending a second jersey she has knitted for him. There are hard times in store for his brothers in Spain just now, he tells her. Four months earlier, Spain's revolutionary government issued a decree suppressing the Society, ordering all Jesuit colleges and institutions to be shut down within seventy-two hours, and confiscating all properties—movable *and* immovable—owned by the order. Within the past few days a letter has been received by the novices from their Spanish counterparts, many of whom are now living in exile in the South of France. They had to disguise themselves in order to escape, he tells her. "At Cadiz the Admiral though belonging to the revolution stood their friend and marched them through the town to the fleet. They all had the power of going to their homes but most chose exile and those who did go back seem to have done so against their will and by the advice of their superiors. A boy of 14 who was to be sent home begged with tears to go with the rest into exile and at last his wish was granted. . . . To be persecuted in a tolerant age," Hopkins closes, "is a high distinction."

So far, it has been a very mild winter, with daffodils already in bloom and a weeping willow on the grounds already green now. "The elms have long been in red bloom and yesterday I saw small leaves on the brushwood at their roots," he notes on February 12. Even the primroses are out. But, he will add later, "a penance which I was doing from Jan. 25 to July 25 prevented my seeing much that half-year." Then, in mid-March, the weather turns colder, bringing with it snowstorms. In mid-April it turns warm again, and he hears the cuckoo sing for the first time. From his mother he learns that Bridges's sister, Harriet, has died as a result of the trauma she suffered with the murder of her husband and baby the year before.

On March 29, he finds a few moments to write Bridges about the loss of his sister. "It is nearly a fortnight since my mother gave me the sad news of Mrs. Plow's death," he begins, "but I have not till today had an opportunity of writing to you, as I wished to do. I cannot help thinking that perhaps for her own sake she could not have much wished to live longer with such dreadful grief upon her memory." Indeed, he wonders how Bridges's mother has been able to bear up under the strain. Then he adds that his sister's sufferings should "be looked on as the marks of God's particular love and this is truer the more exceptional they are." He is sorry too to hear that Bridges made the trip out to Roehampton in mid-January, only to be told that he and his fellow novices were just then in the midst of a Triduum.

Mid-May, and another note to himself, observing how the wind tosses the chestnut trees, so that they plunge and cross "one another without losing their inscape." He listens carefully to the speech inflections of his fellow Jesuits. Brother Wells, from the north country, for instance, calls a grindstone a *grindlestone*. And *geet*, he sees, is simply the north country preterite of *get*. Brother Rickaby explains that "*top* is the higher, outer, and lighter wood good for firing only, *lop* the stem and bigger boughs when the rest has been lopped off used for timber." He finds Father Casano's Sicilian pronunciation of Latin instructive. "*Quod* he calls *c'od* and *quae hora* becomes almost *c'ora*." Father Goldie "gives long *e* like short *e* merely lengthened or even opener." And Brother Morris, their forty-one-year-old novice, "gives long *u* very full *(Luca)*." At mass he notices how Fr. Sangalli blunts his m's. And Brother Sidgreaves "has heard the high ridges of a field called *folds* and the hollow between the *drip*." Even the cuckoo's tune seems to have become more distinctive with the listening.

September 8: The annual eight-day retreat ends, after which the second-year novices take First Vows, and Hopkins and his fellow novices graduate to the second year as yet another class of novices arrive. Without any fanfare, one rector—Father Fitzsimon—his health broken with hard work—leaves, and another—Father Gallwey—takes his place. Two new novices leave the novitiate shortly after arriving because of ill health, for this is an order which—given its demands and discipline—prides itself on action. Later that month, another gale force wind tumbles a "fine Spanish oak at the head of the path down the meadow," then a large mulberry tree near where Hopkins and the others were picking berries just hours before. Then a large cedar in St. Aloysius' Walk comes crashing down "into the rye-grass field." Hopkins watches—shaken—the "unending races of leaves . . . leaping and raging along the meadow," and notes the "hangers of smaller but barky branches, reminding him of nothing so much as ship-tackle." Twenty years later this memory will shape shift into the image of "Shivelights and shadowtackle in long lashes," which seem to "lace, lance, and pair" in the "bright wind boisterous."

Monday, October 20: Bridges, now living at 35 Great Ormond Street in London, calls again at Manresa House, and he and Hopkins walk through the grounds speaking of poetry and travel and Oxford. Bridges is studying medicine now, and enrolled at the venerable St. Bartholomew's Hospital, a large complex of some seven hundred beds housed in three buildings, a fourth edifice serving as administration and social center. He is reading physiology, chemistry, and anatomy—after the German and French models—and using the German he learned in his six months in Dresden. Anatomy includes daily lectures on the skeleton as well as attendance in the dissecting rooms, where body parts are distributed for analysis, and he regularly attends postmortems and reviews surgical outpatients. Being in the midst of so much suffering humanity is a far cry from attending classics lectures at Oxford, Bridges assures his friend. It is a good visit, and afterward Hopkins writes home, wondering if his mother might have Bridges up to Oak Hill sometime. "He was," he reminds her, "a great friend of mine and very kind to me and is very nice in himself, as I believe you know." But, he warns her, Bridges has also made it clear that he is so busy these days that he has been refusing all invitations.

From mid-December 1869 until late February 1870, Hopkins is assigned the role of Porter, or Bidellius (Beadle), at Manresa, his duties consisting of keeping notes of the comings and goings of the community. At meals, all the novices listen as one of them reads from the Book of Tobit or St. Bonaventure's *Life of Our Lord.* Too, there are passages from Thomas à Kempis's *Imitation of Christ,* Sister Emmerich's *The Dolorous Passion of Our Lord,* and St. John's Gospel. The first-year novices have made their Long Retreat later this year to coincide with Advent and will finish on Christmas Day. On a Sunday in mid-December the second-year novices, Hopkins among them, hike the eight miles up to Homer Row, in Westminster, to teach catechism. One evening, Father Gallwey stops by as the novices are relaxing in the Recreation Room to tell them that Pio Nono has sent special blessings to them at a benefactor's request. And the great round goes on: care of the grounds, repairs, moppings and sweepings, the emptying of chamberpots. There are studies, of course, and lessons to be learned by heart. On December 21, Brothers Gerard Hopkins, Southern, and Wilcock catechize at Isleworth. Rosaries—beads—are recited weekly while walking. There are also admonitions, during which each novice has a fellow novice appointed to tell him in private of any exterior faults he has noticed in his keeping of the Jesuit rules or customs.

Early on the morning of December 22, Hopkins dreams that he is with one of his Oxford classmates, George Simcox, "and was considering how to get away in time to ring the bells here which as porter I had to ring. I knew that I was dreaming and made this odd dilemma in my dream: either I am not really with Simcox and then it does not matter what I do, or if I am, waking will carry me off without my needing to do anything—and with this I was satisfied." Two months earlier, he'd learned that Edward Bond had been made Fellow of Queen's College, Oxford, where, he told his mother, he would "meet George Simcox constantly, who besides being amiable is the most eccentric and witty man I ever met." And since being with Simcox would mean being in the company of amiability and eccentricity and wit, there is part of him that still pines after an Oxford that lives on in memory only now.

One evening, after recitation of the Litanies, as Father Gallwey is giving the points for meditation, an exhausted Hopkins shuts his eyes and, while still listening to his Rector, begins to dream. Suddenly, he sees one of the Apostles "as if pressed against by a piece of wood about half a yard long and a few inches across, like a long box with two of the long sides cut off . . . used to hold a little heap of cinders against the wall which keep from the frost a piece of earthenware pipe." It is, he realizes, just such objects "which produce dead impressions, which the mind . . . has made nothing of and brought into no scaping, that force themselves up in this way afterwards," so that the connection is "capricious, almost punning." It is an essay into the unconscious and the domain of dream puns, and we are entering the world of Freud here, of the later *Finnegans Wake* and Berryman's *Dream Songs*. "The dream-images," Hopkins continues, "also appear . . . to be flat like pictures" but "coarser and simpler . . . like the spectra made by bright things looked hard at." Like what the last will be left to ponder of our lives after death.

Another phenomenon captures his attention: "One day in the Long Retreat . . . they were reading in the refectory Sister Emmerich's account of the Agony in the Garden and I suddenly began to cry and sob and could not stop. . . . If I had been asked a minute beforehand I should have said that nothing of the sort was going to happen and even when it did I stood in a manner wondering at myself not seeing in my reason the traces of an adequate cause for such strong emotion—the traces of it I say because of course the cause in itself is adequate for the sorrow of a lifetime." And another time when tears unbidden came: on Maundy Thursday eight months earlier, "when the presanctified Host was carried to the sacristy" after mass. Then too he had tried to see himself objectively, wondering what it was about the symbolic action of removing Christ's body from the altar, in preparation for Good Friday. "But neither the weight nor the stress of sorrow . . . by themselves move us or bring the tears as a sharp knife does not cut for being pressed as long as it is pressed without any shaking of the hand." But then there is always some "one touch, something striking sideways and unlooked for, which . . . undoes resistance and pierces." True, people die every day in street accidents or bridge collapses or fires or shipwrecks or at home, yet these hardly affect us or at most "draw slight tears if its matter is not important or not of import to us" because the strong emotion came "from a force which was gathered before it was discharged." "The dense and the driven Passion, and the frightful sweat," he will write six years further on, as the lines coalesce for him into the sudden realization of the sweet face of God revealing itself:

> Thence the discharge of it, there its swelling to be,
>   Though felt before, though in high flood yet—
> What none would have known of it, only the heart, being hard at
>   bay,
>   Is out with it!

Christmas Eve, 1869: Once again, Brothers Hopkins and Wilcock teach catechism at Isleworth, a seven-mile walk from Roehampton. The other second-year novices are free after Rodriguez, except for having to wash basins and prepare the chapel for Christmas. The readings tonight are from the Apocalypse—the Book of Revelations—and Charlevoix's *History of Japan*—the life of the Jesuit Francis Mastrilli, martyred in Japan in the 1630s. Litanies, manual work, beads, spiritual reading, confessions, supper, examen, then bed at 7:45 p.m., to rise again three hours later to prepare for midnight mass, normally not allowed in religious houses for another forty years, but granted by special permission of the Holy Father. Just before midnight, the Long Retreat for first year novices ends and the community sings the *Adeste Fidelis,* followed by communion and the *Te Deum.*

At 1:00 a.m., there is a *haustus* of soup and cocoa in the refectory. Then to bed, to rise again at six-thirty for two more masses in quick succession. Then breakfast, the making of beds, Rodriguez, and a brisk walk to Kensington to hear High Mass at the new pro cathedral of *Our Lady of Victories.* Brother Francis Bacon offers a sermon at the four o'clock dinner, with wine afterward to celebrate the feast day.

And the Christmastide celebrations continue. On the 27th—the Feast of St. John the Evangelist—Brother Considine delivers a tone, or practice sermon, after which there are confessions and Benediction. Following the long Advent fast, the community feasts on turkey, goose, partridge, hare soup, plum pudding, mince pies, and a custard-based cheese cake. After dinner on the 28th—the Feast of the Innocents—the Juniors and novices belt out alternate stanzas of a stirring old glee, "Who's the Fool Now?," which Father Gallwey has found in *The Ballad Literature and Popular Music of the Olden Time,* and to which he adds comic verses poking good-natured fun at the community and himself. Two days later, Hopkins finds a few minutes to write home and send everyone holiday wishes. He thanks his mother for her gift of some new flannel shirts, his old ones having become "very absurd things . . . so small that the waists were somewhere near my shoulders, and they were rotten with age besides," so that he had had to borrow someone else's.

In a Wimbledon churchyard nearby he makes a discovery which will interest his father: the marble tomb of "William Mansel Phillips of Coedgair in Carmarthenshire, second son of Sir Wm. Mansel baronet of Iscoed . . . and of Caroline his wife only child of Benjamin Bond Hopkins Esq." To Hopkins's delight, the discovery underscores the Welsh roots of his lineage, especially as he remembers that he has Mansel cousins, though he cannot remember anything else about them. In another corner of the same churchyard he also found "a tombstone full of Hopkinses beginning with 'John Hopkins familiarly known as Vulture Hopkins.'" How he wishes they had let the nickname die with old Vulture, who, he remembers, has been immortalized in one of Pope's satires. Better oblivion than fame of that sort.

Thursday, January 13, 1870: Another Triduum of Recollection begins. It is a three-day period of prayer prior to the Jesuits' semi-annual renewal of vows. And while the novices will not take vows until the end of their second year, it is also a time for renewing one's fervor. Points for meditation have been given in chapel since the eve of the Epiphany in preparation for this event, along with beads, spiritual reading, Thomas à Kempis, exposition of the Blessed Sacrament, and meditations. For the benefit of the Jesuit lay brothers and some of the young Latin-poor novices, the *Examen Générale* and Bulls are read in English.

By late January, four novices, suffering from severe colds, are brought down to the infirmary to be looked after by a local doctor, and the Mass of St. Martina is offered for the health of the community. Soon after, one of the Jesuit priests leaves, and Hopkins takes over his catechism classes as well. It is all part of what Hopkins will later call the soapsuds impermanency of the Jesuits. On February 5, the community celebrates the feast of the Japanese martyrs, St. Paul Miki, S.J., and his companions, crucified by order of the Taiko at Nagasaki in 1597 and canonized just seven years earlier. It is another reminder of the glory of the Company Hopkins keeps. In early March, he writes his mother for her forty-ninth birthday. They have among them now a "very jolly old gentleman" named Father Baron, one of their own, who "fell on getting out of the train and broke his thigh, and after that . . . passed such a night that he said he never knew there was such pain in the world." He was brought to Manresa "in a spring cart with india-rubber round the wheels" and given "the most wonderful and delightful bed," with "winches and screws to raise or lower or do what you like with. A staff of novices and others always wait on him, read to him, and write his letters, so that anyone might wish to have his thigh broken if you cd. have it broken in the present without having broken it in the past." Father Baron has told Hopkins that he plans "to make use of the 'Alexandrian step' when he can walk, that is the step wh. suddenly became the thing at court when the Princess of Wales got lame with a sore knee."

He and the other novices have just come before the novice master again to ask permission for "little leaves" to keep such things as a watch, razor, pocket knife, or scissors. It is a way of preparing them for the vows of poverty and obedience they will take in September, and so he encloses a duck's feather he found on the property. "I practise at present the evangelical poverty which I soon hope to vow," he tells his mother, "but no one is ever so poor that he is not (without prejudice to all the rest of the world) owner of the skies and stars and everything wild that is to be found on the earth, and out of this immense stock I make over to you my right to one particular."

Mid-March: Hopkins notes an exceptionally fine sunset and records both the source of light and its play along the surfaces of things, prosing it with a new energy and instress in the very observation, as each thing begins to tell itself anew. "Grass cloud," and the light a moist yellow, edged with a pearl white, the purple-brown tufts edged with a "brassy light." Up until this moment, he had "always taken the sunset and the sun as separately from each other." But for the first time he has actually inscaped them together, the sun "all active and tossing out light" like the "boss in the knop of the chalice-stem." It is a telling metaphor, nothing less than a vision of the sacramentality of nature, of all things flowing out and returning to "the true eye and ace," the Alpha and Omega—the cup of the Great Sacrifice from which all things originate and radiate.

And another new instress of language as he records the effects of a late snowfall on the grounds at Roehampton: "It tufted and toed the firs and yews and went on to load them till they were taxed beyond their spring. The limes, elms, and Turkey-oaks it crisped beautifully as with young leaf. Looking at the elms from underneath you saw every wave in every twig" and "the inscapes they had lost." The shimmering form caught for a moment by the eye and our failed attempts to hold on to the quickgold protean beauty of the world, even as the precious particulars of leaf and form vanish away in the great riverine Heraclitean flux of things. How to keep back, he wonders, such beauty from vanishing away?

At the end of the month, he spends a week working in the community kitchen with the brothers, all of whom have taken vows of poverty, chastity, and obedience, though not Holy Orders. Most here are from the Irish working class, and it is among them that Hopkins now washes dishes, scrubs pots and pans, sweeps and mops the floors, takes the garbage out, pares potatoes, grinds the coffee, fixes tea, and in general does whatever tasks the cook assigns him. One Sunday, sitting with the Brentford boys—two Irish blood brothers—he asks them to repeat a ghost story. "At Norris's market gardens by Sion Lane," Hopkins writes in his journal, "there is a place where according to tradition two men . . . were ploughing with four horses: in bringing the plough round at the headland they fell into a covered well which they did not see and were killed. And now if you lean your ear against a wall at the place you can hear the horses going and the men singing at their work." Stories too of ghosts at Sion House, like the image of Our Lady in a stained-glass window, which, they say, "every year is broken by an unseen hand and invisibly mended again."

Then Brother Fitzgerald, who hails from Limerick: there "is a spring hot

in winter" there, "perishingly cold in summer, a sort of Hippocrene, called
Torgha Shesheree . . . the Spring of the Pair, from a pair of plough-horses
which were swallowed up there, the water springing up at the place." But in
checking his notes for accuracy, Hopkins sees that the story has been revised from when he first heard it. When he asks Fitzgerald to account for
the differences in the tellings, Fitzgerald tells him with a wink that there
are two broad stones in the spring, "in one of which is the hoof-mark of one
of the horses, and you may put your arm to the shoulder down it and feel no
bottom."

And now Brother Byrne enters the fray. He tells Hopkins football is very
popular in Ireland, and one football player was going home one Shrove
Tuesday "when in a lonely field a ball came rolling to his feet." The player
kicked it, and it was kicked back in turn, "and soon he found himself playing the game with a field full of fairies and in a place which was strange to
him. The fairies would not let him go but they did their best to amuse him,
they danced and wrestled before him so that he should never want for entertainment." But, Brother Byrne tells him, "they could not get him to eat,
for knowing that if he eat what they gave him they would have a claim upon
him he preferred to starve and they for fear he should die on their hands at
last put him on the right road home. On reaching home he found a pot of
stirabout on the fire and had only had time to taste a ladlefull when the
fairies were in upon him and began to drag him away again. He caught hold
of the doorpost and called on the saints but when he came to our Lady's
name they let go and troubled him no more." There is a lesson here too for
Hopkins, for he too has called on Mary whenever his own troubles have begun to overwhelm him.

These fairies, Brother Byrne explains, are "half-fallen angels who gave a
part-consent to Lucifer's sin and are in probation till the last day here on
earth," and act as they do toward us out of envy. But Hopkins views them
in an even darker way after Byrne tells him about a priest who was out on a
sick call one night and had his whip "snatched from his hand. His servant
got down to look for it and found himself in the midst of the fairies." Only
when the priest began to recite passages from his breviary was the whip
placed back in his hands. Not to be outdone, Fitzgerald tells him that some
of the old Irish forts ("forths," Hopkins hears him pronounce it) belong now
to "witches and fairies," so that "it is very dangerous to cut or take anything
from them." Once, he swears, he saw a man "who had gone to cut a stick in
one . . . come back with his finger hanging off." Another fellow was "ploughing in a field by one of these forths and as he came up the furrow he heard

a clatter of plates and knives and forks by which he guessed that the fairies were at dinner," and that "was enough to make him hungry and he wished for some of that dinner." Then "he saw a plate with knife and fork and a good dinner ready laid on the headland. . . . But when he saw it he repented, for he had heard that if you eat what the fairies give you you will belong to them for good and he would not touch the food. But in an instant before he turned away one of his eyes was thrust out and lay on the plate before him and he was a one-eyed man for life because he had shuffled in dealing with the fairies."

From the larger community, too, Hopkins listens for Irish and Anglo-Saxon turns of phrase. Brother Yates says, "That you mightn't," to express disapproval. "Mend you" or "Sorrow mend you" means "Serves you right." "Soak it" means something like "to lump it." "I haven't got it," meaning "I don't know it." A simpleton is a "crackawly." Seeds of the hip plant are called "Johnny Magoreys." From the mouth of Brother Considine: "Boyo" and "Laddo." And from Brother Wood: "It puts me to the pin of my collar," meaning "It is all I can do to bear it." Two months earlier, while serving as porter, he had written that two of the novices "entered into retreat in the evening," then crossed out the Latinate "entered," substituting for it the Anglo-Saxon "went into." Another time he first writes that several novices have been "appointed to attend Fr. Baron," then replaces "attend" with the words "wait on." He listens harder now to the actual speech of those who make up his community, the Anglo-Saxon and Irish of the language, rather than borrowing only from the literary classics and his Latin and Greek texts, and the lessons he is learning will serve him well in his own prose and poems.

In mid-May, Hopkins sums up his two years of listening and watching carefully at Roehampton. "I do not think I have ever seen anything more beautiful than the bluebell I have been looking at," he writes. "I know the beauty of our Lord by it." And life, lived simply and close to the daily round of the seasons, goes on. Work on the grounds at Roehampton, pruning and chopping wood, cleaning the halls and bathrooms, sewing one's own clothes, working with the brothers in the kitchen, teaching catechism, studying. Then his time at Roehampton draws to a close. On September 8, the Feast of the Nativity of the Blessed Virgin, the final eight-day retreat under Father Gallwey's direction, comes to an end and the remaining four second-year novices—McMullin, Wilcock, and the two Hops—make their First Vows. Until just two years before, renewal of vows had been done in secret, since Jesuits are still officially banned under the insertion of a Penal Code in the Catholic Emancipation Act of 1831. In other words, there has been a kind of general amnesty for all Catholics in England, except the Jesuits. The vows are made in a tiny upstairs chapel, lit by a skylight, the novice master sitting at a small table on which a crucifix has been placed. As if going to confession, each novice enters, and kneels to take their vows in secret, at the end of which the master takes the written formula of the vows from the novice, and the novice withdraws, with a blessing.

But Father Gallwey has done away with all the secrecy, though the law remains on the books. And so he has his novices appear before him in soutanes, birettas, and Roman collars to take their vows. That evening, there is a farewell celebration for the four, and wine is served at dinner. McMullin and Wilcock—not having university degrees—will remain behind for another year as Juniors to undertake additional study in the classics. The genteel Hop is being sent to Mount St. Mary's in Chesterfield to teach, and Gerard, the gentle Hop, will leave for the Scholasticate at Stonyhurst in the north to begin three years of training in philosophy, as mandated by the founder of the order. He has been trained now in the life of a Jesuit, has learned those Catholic ways that were so new to him just two years before, wears his soutane and collar, and has taken his First Vows. But something more has happened, something deeper: a new energy, a new focus, a new way of seeing, different from what Oxford and London have taught him, something more grounded in the earth, the humus, a humility which lets him see others and himself more clearly, as if the world itself in all its humdrum quotidian had been renewed, and this the Eighth Day of Creation.

Chapter 6

The Fine Delight That Fathers Thought: Stonyhurst, 1870–1873

Friday, September 9, 1870: In company with a small group of his fellow Jesuits, Hopkins makes his way north by train some 235 miles, stopping to dine at Holy Name, the Jesuits' new church in Manchester, still under heavy construction. Designed by Joseph Aloysius Hansom, a favorite of the Jesuits and the inventor of the Hansom cab, it is modeled after the typical fourteenth-century French Gothic cathedral, its exterior done in yellow Warwick Bridge stone, and styled after all Jesuit city churches, with its broad central nave, prominent pulpit, short sanctuary without choir stalls (this is not, after all, a monastic order), and its altar in full view of the congregation. The church is almost cathedral-sized, Hopkins can see, and it certainly makes a statement about the growing Jesuit presence here in the old Catholic north. Still, as a piece of architecture, especially when compared with pre-Reformation work, he does not think very highly of it.

Thirty miles farther north the following day they leave the train at Whalley, "a little place in a valley of the moors with an abbey ruin and otherwise worth seeing." At the station they are met by the driver of a team of horses and driven the "four miles over the Hodder and Calder rivers . . . up and down hill," and so to Stonyhurst in Lancashire. He has a lovely view of the light-and-shade-dappled moors from his room, he writes his mother, but it seems to rain here all the time, and "will go on so to the end of the chapter." Summer here is a poor thing, really, though "they say it is mild in winter compared with places more south and I partly believe it; that is I believe it is mild in winter compared with places more north." Three of his fellow Jesuits at Stonyhurst were with him at Roehampton for a year. It is a bright beginning to the three years he will spend here as a Scholastic, and tonight there is "moonlight, supper, and a pleasant sociable bustle."

But by daylight it seems eerily quiet, the second- and third-year Scholastics still on holiday for another two weeks, though he will keep himself busy exploring the area, for it is "excellent country for walks, beauty, and general interest." Yet, what he feels just now is the "strangeness of the place," Roehampton having become—after two years there—a kind of second home. "It made me sad to look at the crucifix and things Fr. Gallwey gave me when I was going," he confesses. "He was very very kind." Still, "the brotherly charity of everyone here can be felt at once: indeed it is always what you take for granted." And now that he has taken First Vows, the twenty-six-year-old Hopkins feels he "can speak more freely . . . because I have bound myself to our Lord for ever to be poor, chaste, and obedient like Him and it delights me to think of it."

Stonyhurst, venerable Stonyhurst: the direct descendant of the college founded by Father Robert Persons, S.J.—one of the Company of Jesus that included Fathers Edmund Campion, Briant, Walpole, Southwell, all martyred for the crime of tending to their Catholic communities in a time when being a Jesuit on English soil was itself a capital offense. Persons too would eventually be captured by government agents—pursuivants—in the reign of James I, tried for treason on trumped-up charges, then drawn and quartered. Back in 1592, he had founded a school for Catholic boys at St. Omer in Artois, all forced to flee to the Continent to be educated in the Catholic tradition. Then, in 1762, driven from St. Omer by the French parliament, the Jesuit college transferred to Bruges, under the protection of the empress Maria Theresa, until the Society was suppressed worldwide by papal edict (with the help of Spanish and Portuguese agents) in 1773. That same year the Jesuits and their students moved to Liège, where the college continued under the protection of the city's prince bishop. Then, in 1794, as French revolutionary forces approached the city, the college again disbursed, to gather this time back on English soil at Stonyhurst, which Thomas Weld of Lulworth, himself educated at the college when it was at Bruges, now placed at the disposal of the Society. From Stonyhurst, the other Jesuit schools have branched out over the past eighty years: to Beaumont, west of London; Mount St. Mary's in Derbyshire; St. Francis Xavier's College in Liverpool; St. Aloysius' College in Glasgow; Wimbledon College near Roehampton; and Clongowes Wood College in Ireland, among others.

Three hundred yards behind Stonyhurst College and to the west lies St. Mary's Hall and the Jesuit seminary, where Hopkins will live for the next three years. It has the look of a substantial military barracks, a no-nonsense three-story yellow sandstone rectangular building, hidden by trees from the Elizabethan aura of Stonyhurst itself. Here some thirty seminarians—Scholastics—live. They study maths, logic, and philosophy (Scholasticism viewed through the lens of the Suarezian interpretation of St. Thomas Aquinas, as sanctioned by the Pope). Each year about ten or so Scholastics arrive and ten go on to do their regency. The quarters themselves are, as always, furnished in Spartan fashion, with a window overlooking the terrace and garden. Each room has a wooden seat with a hinged top in the window embrasure, where coal is stored to keep the fireplace going during the long, wet, cold winters, as there is no central heating. Each room has a small iron bedstead, at the foot of which is a piece of old carpet. Also: a table with two bookshelves on it, a wooden chair at the table, and a Windsor chair by the fireplace to rest a bit more comfortably. To the right of the window: a deal chest of drawers with a small mirror above it. Opposite the fireplace is a washstand with basin. At the foot of the bed is a *prie-dieu*. There are also a few hooks on the back of the door, and a holy picture or two tacked to the wall.

Henry Kerr is here, and Ignatius Gartlan, and twenty-two-year-old Sydney Morgan. There are in all some eighty-five Jesuits at Stonyhurst and St. Mary's, including nineteen priests, fifty-four Scholastics, and twelve brothers, all under the jurisdiction of the rectors. But, in fact, St. Mary's Hall has its own Superior to guide the Jesuits living there: three priests, two brothers, and thirty-five Scholastics, made up of sixteen first-year students, nine each in the second and third years, and one preparing to take the B.A. at London University.

Serving as Rector of Stonyhurst for the past year is the very capable, no-nonsense Father Edward Ignatius Purbrick, forty, another Anglican convert. Born in Birmingham, he was educated at King Edward VI's Grammar School there, and then at Christ Church, Oxford, until his conversion in 1850, when he was forced to leave the university. The following year he entered the Jesuit novitiate (then at Hodder) and has been ordained now for six years. After advanced study in Rome, he served as Superior and Professor of Logic at St. Mary's Hall and was then named Stonyhurst's Rector. He will serve through Hopkins's three years and stay on until 1879, overseeing the massive building projects already underway. Shortly thereafter, Father John Gosford, fifty-two, Spiritual Father for the community, arrives to hear confessions. Then Father Weld—the one who as Provincial had interviewed Hopkins two years before—arrives to take over as Superior at St. Mary's and to teach mathematics.

This will be Hopkins's regular schedule for the next three years: winter and summer, he will rise at 5:30 a.m., recite the Angelus, and then meditate until 6.00. At 7:00 a.m., he will gather with the others for mass, and then have breakfast. From ten until noon, he will attend lectures, wash up, and do his particular examen. Then recitation of the Angelus and dinner at one, followed by recreation until two-thirty. At 3:15 p.m. there will be Circle—discussion—followed by another recreational break until 4:15, when studies resume. At 5:00 p.m. he will say the Angelus for the third time, then return to his studies until 8:10, when he will partake of a light supper. Litanies at 9:30, points for meditation at 9:45, and examen (examination of the day just past) at 10:00 p.m. Then to bed, with gaslights out by ten-thirty. The only change is that on Sundays, Tuesdays, and Thursdays, recreation is extended until half past five.

At the end of the year, trying to highlight the year's events, he jots down some dates from Whitaker's *Almanac:* the opening of the Vatican Council in December 1869; a negro sitting for the first time in the U.S. Congress; Virginia readmitted to the Union. In May 1870, the American yacht *Sappho* has three straight wins; and in June, Charles Dickens dies. Then, in mid-July, the start of the Franco-Prussian War and the siege of Paris. In mid-August, the British Minister of Foreign Affairs tells Parliament that Garibaldi's army, moving on Rome, has an "obligation of not attacking the frontiers of the Papal States and of not allowing them to be attacked." He notes a series of French defeats at the hands of the Prussians in September. On September 7, the British ship, the *Captain,* founders. Thus the great world beyond Stonyhurst in its grinding goes round.

Five months, and almost no letters either to or from Hopkins. On March 2, 1871, he writes his mother to wish her a happy fiftieth. And yet, in spite of all the time that has passed, he can "think of nothing at all" to tell her, everything about Lancashire being "dank as ditchwater." True, there have been a few fine days, but spring seems so far off, and the countryside here seems one long dead winter. On the other hand, "it is not cold, birds are singing, and the garden is full of clumps of snowdrops." He has another cold, but is otherwise faring "better than usual." Evenings, the Scholastics amuse themselves by playing hockey. He notes too that one of the French Scholastics here "preached us a capital sermon in French . . . with such life that everyone [else] must have felt how much he himself came short of it." The truth is, he admits, that the French know how to express themselves better than most Englishmen. So, "one day, when the Professor brought down a thick book to lecture [the French Scholastic] no sooner caught sight of it," Hopkins marvels with that playfulness of his, "than slanting his head like a cannon or a camera being brought into position he gave it one intense wink which the devil might have winked and it wrung his whole body. To one who had seen it it was a thing which could not be passed by: it has become to me a natural division of time and has added a new truth to history." Yes, she may call him "Reverend" if she likes. It is, after all, "a brevet rank given to all religious" of whatever stripe. Alas, he ends, that none of his siblings have written him as they promised they would.

Sunday, March 14, 1871: If for the past three years he has given up writing verse as incompatible with his vocation, certainly his journals have not gotten the message. In fact, they have become a way of writing a prose that captures in its language and rhythms the poetry he has foregone, lifting words to a new level of intensity and precision. "Bright morning, pied skies, hail," he notes. As he walks out into the Lancashire countryside, he observes "water-runs in the sand of unusual delicacy and the broken blots of snow in the dead bents of the hedge-banks," then the inner scaping of the scene, "which helped the eye over another hitherto disordered field of things." Randomness once more resolving itself into order, then, as the inscape is revealed. Looking at Pendle Hill to the south, he observes a new beauty in "the face of snow on it and the tracks or gullies which streaked and parted this," marking "the slow tune of its long shoulder," an idea which will transform itself six years down the line into sibilances such as these:

> And the azurous hung hills are his world-wielding shoulder
> Majestic—as a stallion stalwart, very-violet sweet!

"This is the time to study inscape in the spraying of trees," he notes. "For the swelling buds carry them to a pitch which the eye could not else gather," like "a new world of inscape." "A strange one, that Mr. 'Opkins"— one of the lay brothers will remember him, kneeling on the wet gravel path to better catch the morning light diamonding off the quartz stones. And this: "Take *a few* primroses in a glass and the instress of . . ." Of what—brilliancy? starriness? "I have not the right word," he confesses, the instress "so simple a flower gives is remarkable," and no doubt "due to the strong swell given by the deeper yellow middle." Or recalling Wordsworth's *Ode: Intimations of Immortality*—"The young lambs bound / As to the tabour's sound"—he adds that, oh yes, they do "toss and toss . . . as if it were the earth that flung them, not themselves. . . . Sometimes they rest a little space on the hind legs and the fore-feet drop curling in on the breast, not so liquidly as we see it in the limbs of foals though." And Pendle Hill "dappled with tufted shadow," the dolphin-backed clouds gamboling in the high heavens.

Passion Sunday, April 2: Holy Week and Easter in the community, and a much needed respite from classes. It has been over a year since he last heard from Bridges and he has no one to blame but himself. He does not even know if his friend is still in London, and so addresses his letter to Rochdale. He is now at Stonyhurst reading philosophy and other things, he explains, and expects to be here for another two years. Beyond that the place is "bare and bleak but the rivers are beautiful." And that is all he can think to say. "Please tell me all about yourself," he apologizes. "I am sure I must have behaved unkindly when you came to Roehampton." But Hopkins will have to wait another four months to hear back from Bridges, overwhelmed as his friend is now with medical texts, dissections, and other responsibilities.

A week later, he writes Baillie. "Your letters are always welcome," he begins, "but often or always it is more pleasant to get them than easy to see how they are to be answered." The truth is that he has so little time to read or write except what is required, and when he does have a moment, there seems nothing to say. He should be writing about books with his old friend, as they used to do, but he has no time for literature, no time. He is in fact "going through a hard course of scholastic logic" just now, "which takes all the fair part of the day and leaves one fagged at the end for what remains." The irony of it all is that he has finally learned *how* to read, "at least some books, e.g. the classics," and sees things, so that "now what I read tells." As for Stonyhurst, here "perpetual winter smiles." They have "the highest raingauge in England," at least according to the Observatory here, "and a local rhyme expresses as much." When he asked about May, "they told me they had hail in May. Of June they told me it had one year been so cold that the procession could not be held on Corpus Christi." On top of which, the country is "bare and bleak—what its enemies say of [Baillie's] Scotland."

Still, there is fine scenery all about him: "great hills and 'fells' with noble outline," and "charming effects of light (though I am bound to say that total obscuration is the commonest effect of all), and three beautiful rivers." The clouds here he finds more interesting than any he has seen elsewhere, but "full of soot, for the fleeces of the sheep are quite black with it. We also see the northern lights to advantage at times." He has even found good fishing, which is almost, he jokes, as good as bad fishing, when one can forget oneself in the currents of reverie. He tries to come up with at least one book he can talk about with Baillie, and fails. Then, realizing what a sour letter he has written, he corrects himself by confessing that this life, "though it is hard is God's will for me as I most intimately know, which is more than violets knee-deep." Then, catching himself for having revealed so much of himself, he laughs. "This sprig of rhetoric," he ends, "brings me to a close."

April 25: A letter to his sister and favorite, Katie, now a spunky fifteen, thanking her for writing, though at first he wondered who the letter could be from, "there was such a youngladyship and grownupdom about the address, until I remembered that you were older than you used to be." As for himself, he has prescribed "twenty four hourglasses a day (which I take even during sleep, such is the force of habit) and that even this does not stop the ravages of time." Here it is, five weeks into spring, and it looks and feels like a "whity-greeny January." In the best punning tradition of the Hopkins family, he tells her that the Scholastics have just been vaccinated (from the Latin *vaca* for "cow") against cowpox, a milder form of smallpox, and a Portuguese Scholastic asked him if he felt "the cows in *yewer* arm?" Then the puns begin in earnest. "I told him I felt the horns coming through." He cannot "remember now whether one ought to say the calf of the arm or the calf of the leg." Worse, his shoulder is "like a shoulder of beef," and he dares "not speak above a whisper for fear of bellowing—there now, I was going to say I am obliged to speak low for fear of lowing." At night, he dreams he has "only two of my legs in bed. . . . The long and short of it is that my left forequarter is swollen and painful (I meant to have written arm but I cowld not.)" From cows it is on to lambs. "Our fields are full of them," he tells her. "When they were a little younger and nicer and sillier they wd. come gambolling up to one as if one were their mother. One of them sucked my finger and my companion took another up in his arms. The ewes then came up and walked round us making suspicious sheep's eyes at us, as people say." And when "they are not sucking the breast (to do which they make such terrific butts and digs at the old dam that two of them together will sometimes lift her off her hind legs) they spend their time in bounding and spinning round as if they were tumblers."

Suddenly, his mood darkens. The day they were vaccinated, he tells Katie, he saw something that made him very sad. He was leaving the infirmary where many of the Scholastics were still "laughing and chatting." Then, walking down one of the galleries, he saw one of the young men standing there looking at a picture. "I wondered why he stayed by himself and did not join the rest and then afterwards I remembered that he had had the smallpox and was deeply marked with it and all his good looks gone which he would have had and he did not want to face the others at that time when they were having their fun taking safe precautions against catching what it was too late for him to take any precautions against."

Two days later, Hopkins mesmerizes a duck by holding its beak down on a black table and drawing parallel chalk lines from its beak outwards. The bird is hypnotized, he believes, by "the abiding offscape of the hand grasping her neck," so that she "fancies she is still held down and cannot lift her head as long as she looks at the chalk line, which she associates with the power that holds her." That is one theory. As for him, it is "the fascinating instress of the straight white stroke" that does the trick. Offscapes, inscapes, landscapes, cloudscapes. On May 9, he watches the clouds blowing before a northeast wind, marching "across the sky in regular rank and with equal spaces between." Or it is the crosshatched light on a patch of bluebells as if sketched there, caught in the little wood between the college and the high road and looking like "spots on a snake. " But hold a bunch of them in your hand, and they suddenly lose their inscape. Then, if you draw your fingers through them to awaken them, they refuse, seem "lodged and struggle with a shock of wet heads," so delicate is their living inscape. He even bites into them, hoping to rediscover their inner essence in their "faint honey smell and . . . the sweet gum when you bite them." So, while the distinctive taste of bluebells remains, the inscape is lost, for it is "the eye they baffle."

He stares hard at a peacock, its train spread out to reveal a thousand gorgeous eyes. They lie, he sees, "alternately when the train is shut, like scales or gadroons," but then "fall into irregular rows" when the train is opened, and then it "thins and darkens against the light." But, he notices, it takes on a new splendor when the "outermost eyes, detached and singled, give with their corner fringes the suggestion of that inscape of the flowing cusped trefoil" one finds in paintings. A week later, he discovers an image which will reappear years later as a sign of a much-needed consolation in a weary time. It is a "glowing yellow sunset" over Pendle Hill, "and all the hills rinsed clear" so that the windows of St. Mary's and Stonyhurst, or whatever surface can catch the light, seem to flutter and laugh with the evening blaze. And above the dark shadows between two brows of Pendle Hill he catches "a wedge of light . . . green on the right side, red on the left, as a rainbow would be, leaning to the right and skirting the brow of the hill."

On Whit Monday, May 29, in company with several other Scholastics, he travels the fourteen miles west to Preston to witness the church procession there. And though it is not particularly well done, still the community of faithful flowing through the streets in a great procession out from and back to the church moves him. But the spectacle is broken by news of the murder of the hostages held by the Paris Communards just as French

troops entered the city. Sixty-four are dead, including the Catholic Archbishop, Monsignor Maret, the Bishop of Sura, and the curé of the Made-
leine, along with "Fr. Olivain [sic] with four other of our Fathers. Five
French Jesuits in all executed by the Communists: Fathers Pierre Olivivant,
Leon Ducoudray, Jean Caubert, Alexis Clerc, and Anatole de Bengy. In a
small community like the Jesuits, this is bound to have a profound effect."
Soon memorial cards remembering the martyred priests will appear in sacristies and on bulletin boards and in the Catholic papers, wherever there is
a Jesuit presence, not only at Stonyhurst but in the sacristies at St. Beuno's
and in Liverpool and Roehampton, where Hopkins will meet their faces
again and again, to remind him of the price his fellow Jesuits have paid in
carrying out their duties.

Two weeks later, he gently chastises his mother for not keeping him
better informed about his family, whom he misses. "I suppose you are trying what a minimum of intelligence I can get on upon like the 'one straw a
day' in the story," he jokes, though there is an edge to his bantering, because often he feels the loneliness of not being with his brothers and sisters
and friends. "You give news like odd numbers of the *London Journal*," he
tells her. "You christen people that never were born and cure people that
never were sick. And I ask questions which nobody answers." He wants Arthur to write him about "that American yacht *Sappho* which made [three]
great successes last year." He wants news, news.

Real news—like the infamous Sir Roger Tichborne case in *The Times* of
London, which he and his fellow Jesuits have been following with intense
interest. The young Tichborne had been educated here at Stonybrook thirty
years before. In fact, Hopkins notes, Tichborne's old room is on the very
floor below him where he is now writing. Afterward, Tichborne sailed for
South America, and was returning to England in 1854 when his ship went
down with all hands.

After a year with no sign of his having survived, his estate went to his
younger brother, who died in 1866. Lady Tichborne, half crazed by her double losses, held on to the belief that Roger would some day show up. Enter
Arthur Orton, a fat, light-haired butcher from Wagga Wagga, Australia,
five years Roger's junior, who, on hearing the story, set sail for Paris to see
Lady Tichborne, claiming to be her lost son. Desperate, Lady Tichborne
convinced herself that Orton was indeed her Roger, miraculously restored
to her. That the butcher boy understood not a word of French does not
seem to have troubled her, and she immediately bestowed on him an allowance of £1,000 a year. At that, the guardians of the rightful heir sued to es-

tablish his right to the inheritance and the trial has at last begun. It will last three and a half months.

When the plaintiff's lawyer finally finishes cross-examining Orton, he will be revealed as a fake. Orton will be arrested, convicted of perjury, and sentenced to fourteen years' hard labor, of which he will serve ten, and die penniless. In the years ahead, rumors will circulate that the Jesuits had to be involved, since Sir Roger once attended Stonyhurst. Perhaps, Hopkins puns with his mother, it should be called the Twitchborn case, "because it turns on two people being born with the same twitch—one of them at Wapping, the other at Paris." And then another groaner: "By the bye what shd. you call the claimant's story?—A Whopping Lie." No doubt memories of Grandfather Smith and Mrs. Thwaytes (a.k.a. the Holy Ghost) still burn in his memory. But it is a question, too, of someone stealing one's very identity, the very thing which makes us who we are. Take that away, Hopkins thinks, and what would I have? And how even speak of an *I*?

Holidays begin in late July, and still no summer. And yet how splendid the Hodder, where he can bathe every day now if he likes, "at a beautiful spot . . . between waterfalls and beneath a green meadow and down by the greenwood side O. If you stop swimming to look round you see fairyland pictures up and down the stream." It is this bucolic scene he will remember years later while marking exam books in a hot classroom, worlds from here, while he tries to compose a wedding song for his brother. It rains and rains, swelling the Hodder until it looks like "ropes and hills of melting candy." He watches a massive thunderstorm with "huge rocky clouds lit with livid light" as hail and rain flood the gardens below, "thunder ringing and echoing round like brass," lightning turning "rose-coloured and lilac."

In late July, he finally picks up his pen and writes Bridges, who is still neck-deep examining patients. Bridges had written him just as Hopkins learned of the deaths of his five Jesuit brothers in Paris, but he is still rankling from something Bridges had written supporting the actions of the French Communards. Bridges is beginning to sound too much like Thomas Carlyle for Hopkins's taste, and he wonders "whether you are secretary to the International as you seem to mean me to think nothing too bad for you." He realizes that Bridges was never a supporter of the intelligent artisan. Still, it is only a matter of time before there is a revolution of some kind to rectify the imbalances in capitalist societies, much as he fears the human cost. As a result, Hopkins himself is always "thinking of the Communist future," where the working class will prove master of the situation. It is what Carlyle "has long threatened and foretold. But his writings are, as he might himself say, 'most inefficacious strenuous heaven-protestations, caterwaul, and Cassandra-wailings.' He preaches obedience but I do not think he has done much except to ridicule instead of strengthening the hands of the powers that be."

Then he manages to actually shock Bridges by adding that, from having worked among the lower classes for the past three years, he now sees things in a different light. "Horrible to say," he confesses, he too in a manner is a Communist, for their

> ideal baiting some things is nobler than that professed by any secular statesman I know of (I must own I live in bat-light and shoot at a venture). Besides it is just.—I do not mean the means of getting to it are. But it is a dreadful thing for the greatest and most necessary part of a very rich nation to live a hard life without dignity, knowledge, comforts, delight, or hopes in the midst of plenty—which plenty they make. They profess that they do not care what they wreck and burn, the old civilisation and order must be destroyed.

Yes, it is "a dreadful look out but what has the old civilisation done for them?" After all, England, which destroyed so much of the old Catholic infrastructure, is itself "in great measure founded on wrecking."

He has walked through too many beautiful, irreplaceable abbeys and churches ravaged by those who stood to gain from the breakup of the old lands in the name of change. And yet the vast majority—the workers and artisans—"got none of the spoils, they came in for nothing but harm from it then and thereafter. England has grown hugely wealthy but this wealth has not reached the working classes; I expect it has made their condition worse." Within this modern, "iniquitous order," Hopkins adds, is another order—the pre-Reformation order before Henry VIII, he means—"mostly old and what is new in direct entail from the old, the old religion, learning, law, art, etc and all the history that is preserved in standing monuments." But of all this the working classes "know next to nothing . . . and cannot be expected to care if they destroy it." The more he looks at the matter, the blacker the future looks, and so he means to "write no more." For his part, Bridges is so offended that he writes his radical friend off. It will be two and a half years before Hopkins picks up his pen and—with apologies—tries again.

Early on the morning of August 16, the Scholastics sail from Liverpool for the overnight 250-mile trip to Inellan on the Argyleshire coast and the

Firth of Clyde. The following day, having made their way through the North Channel past the Isle of Arran and the Isle of Bute, they disembark at Greenock, then sail by steamer to Inellan. On Saturday, they take another steamer out to the Isle of Arran and back, Hopkins noting the quiet beauty of Goat Fell and the surrounding mountains. One evening he climbs the brae behind the house where they are staying to watch the sunset, and next day walks deliciously barefoot "over the low-water sands of Holy Loch." Then on to Edinburgh, where he tries to take in the inscape of Castle Rock and Arthur's Seat. At the bottom of the Royal Mile, the Scholastics visit Holyrood Palace with its ruined abbey, where Queen Victoria spends part of each summer. "The so-called Chapel Royal," he notes, "is beautiful transition-work (1170–1175) . . . remarkable among other things for two low arches . . . over the gateway." Afterward they are shown about the castle "by a Mr. Ball a Protestant and a very kind man." But after touring the ramparts, a violent gale catches them as they cross the Firth from Wemyss Bay to Inellan. The rain is so sharp he mistakes it for hail, which "cut one's ears and somebody said was like pebble-stones." On the 28th, the group steams up the Clyde for Glasgow to see the shipbuilding yard there, but so mismanage things that they only reach the cathedral in the evening, after the doors have been locked.

Then it is back to Liverpool by boat and from there by train and carriage to Stonyhurst to begin their annual eight-day retreat under the direction of Father Leslie, a choice which pleases Hopkins very much. When the retreat ends on September 8, Cyril, working now in their father's marine insurance offices in Liverpool, pays Gerard a visit and is a guest at the seminary over the weekend. On Monday, the two brothers travel together as far as Blackburn, where Cyril returns to Liverpool and Gerard heads home to visit his family. His father and Millicent—home from her convent—are both there, the rest of the family having left for a seaside holiday near Southampton. On September 12, he goes down to Croydon to see Aunt Annie and his grandmother, frailer than ever.

The following day, he heads down to Bursledon on the Hamble near Southampton to join his mother and siblings. From the cottage garden here he has a spectacular view of the Hamble itself, with its majestic oaks and elms. One afternoon he goes out to see the ruins of the thirteenth-century Cistercian abbey of St. Mary of Edwards at Netley, built by the same master mason who built Westminster Abbey. Everything about the place is beautiful: the ruins, the grounds, the ivy, the ash trees, even "the bright pieces of evening light." Saturday afternoon he walks into Southampton for confession, and on Sunday hikes to Netley Hospital to hear the Catholic chaplain there say mass. That evening he walks with his mother and Grace "through the stubble fields and wood," all three of them remarking on the clouds. And then it is back to Stonyhurst to begin his second year of studies.

Quid pro quo: One night, a week before Christmas, Hopkins rescues a kitten "perched in the sill of the round window at the sink over the gasjet," that is afraid to come down. He has heard her mewing "a piteous long time till I could bear it no longer," and notes the incident because of "her gratitude after I had taken her down, which made her follow me about and at each turn of the stairs as I went down leading her to the kitchen run back a few steps and try to get up to lick me through the banisters from the flight above." This memory too will find its way into one of his most desolate poems fourteen years later in the image of kissing his Lord's hand, while his heart "lapped strength, stole joy, would laugh, cheer" at the thought of his own rescue from a height he knows only too well he cannot traverse alone.

1872: Four days into the New Year he writes a bantering letter to Baillie, thanking him for writing. "For one thing," he says, "I was sorry to get it, namely that I was then scripturient and quickening towards letter-heat, having something to say which wd. surprise you." While home on holiday, he had come into London to see Baillie in his chambers near the Temple and Law Courts, only to learn he was away. "Your doors were shut like a prison but it was any prison rather than the old Baillie," he can't resist punning. He'd been to Hampstead "to see half my parentage and a proper fraction of my brothers and sisters and was going down to a little place near Southampton to spend the rest of my leave with the complements but the train of omnibuses and so forth which I had laid as far as Waterloo station failed as completely as the Gunpowder Plot."

How much he should have liked to hear Baillie talk about the Tichborne case. "I ask for your professional opinion which I should receive with deep respect," he winks, "just as I should expect you to respect what I might hold *de gratiis gratis datis, de motibus rimoprimis, or de satisfactione et satispassione* (you would be juiced green if you did, for I have not read a word of theology yet, but what you wrote I should truly read with veneration and a pleasant trustful heartfelt incompetence)."

The Christmas holidays are just about over, and the boys at Stonyhurst "have been giving concerts and plays every night," though he has mostly stayed away to husband what little time he has. He did, however, go to see a *Macbeth* they put on, "not to see (for the swan of Avon is very very short of Castalia-water on this stage and would painfully recognise his shadow, especially as women's parts are not given and Lady Macbeth becomes an Uncle Donald)" but rather to hear Matthew Locke's beautiful music played, though he can imagine Baillie shaking his lawyer's bewigged severe white head at him like some Egyptian god. It is Hopkins at his most playful, or— some would say—most eccentric.

In late February 1872, he observes a lunar halo from the upstairs window of the Baddely Library, where he has been reading philosophy. It is not quite round, he notes, pulled as it is by gravitational forces, and he suddenly feels "the odd instress of . . . the moon leaning on her side, as if fallen back." Another night—this time from the gallery window—he catches "a brindled heaven, the moon just marked by a blue spot pushing its way through the darker cloud . . . on the skirts of the rack bold long flakes whitened and swaled like feathers, below the garden with the heads of the trees and shrubs furry grey," and "a broad careless inscape flowing throughout." In early March, he watches sadly as workmen fell ash trees in the grove below. Then a letter from Challis saying he has left the Catholic Church. Another one from that summer of 1866 gone now, like these ash trees, and the news must surely break his heart.

A belated letter to his mother for her birthday, enclosing three primroses, the "firstlings of this mildest of early springs," which "will no doubt look fagged but they must be taken symbolically and they are hedge primroses, not from the garden." And then on to the subject of the Rossettis. First, Maria Francesca, their Hampstead neighbor, whose new book, *A Study of Dante,* has been well received, and to whom he asks to be remembered. Her sister, Christina, also has a new book, *Commonplace and Other Stories,* though he thinks she has been overshadowed by her more famous brother, Dante Gabriel, who also has a new volume of poems out. True, Dante Rossetti has "more range, force, and interest"—masculine traits— "but for pathos and pure beauty of art," Christina has him (and everyone) beat. He promises to write home as time allows, though "no one knows (as Fr. Gallwey said and of me) where I may break out next."

March 13, and still winter. He is in the dining hall as the community listens to an account of de Rancé's conversion. It has been a time of trial and a particularly difficult day for him, he knows. No doubt news of Challis's apostasy and the silence of so many of his old Oxford friends as of his family troubles him here in this flint-backed northern country, so that he does not know now which way to turn. Suddenly he hears the lector read the words *Qui confidunt in Domino sicut mons Sion,* the opening verse of Psalm 125: *Whoever trusts in the Lord is like Mount Sion.* It is the verse which hit home for de Rancé "and resolved him to enter his abbey of La Trappe," and now, on this evening, "by the mercy of God," it comes "strongly home" to Hopkins as well, so that he suddenly finds himself choking back tears and then, there at the table, weeping. *Lord,* he realizes, *to whom shall I turn if not you?*

Letters from Addis and Baillie to say Fletcher of Balliol has died. "He had a house in some very out of the way place" in western Minnesota, Baillie tells him, "and was not very well off. He started off a walk of some 10 or 12 miles to a town to try and get a servant and on returning was caught by a snowstorm. He was found dead only a few hundred yards from his own house. . . . He had only been married a few months." And then Addis's account: "Do you remember Fletcher a Scotch Catholic? He married a young lady of good family whom he had converted from the Scotch Kirk and went out with her to the Red River [in Minnesota]. There he was the great support of the Catholic chapel. One morning he said to his wife 'I have made my meditation this morning on the best way to spend the last day of my life.'" That same day, Addis continues, Fletcher froze to death in the snow. "He had served as a pontifical Zouave shortly before his marriage. The last time I saw him I was commiserating him about his health, which had been shattered by a fall from a horse, and he said quite simply 'No, I think it was a providential accident, for it took me away from Oxford.'" Two very different accounts, Hopkins sees, his heart going out to Fletcher and his poor wife, one account stressing the existential emptiness and isolation of Fletcher's death in a far-off western land, the other seeing in that death God's providential hand. It is precisely the issue he will deal with soon enough when a German steamship is wrecked in another snowstorm.

Late March: A long, comic letter, begun weeks earlier, to his old friend and fellow convert Alfred Garrett, halfway round the world in India, where he has been for the past four years, working with the Indian Education Service in Bengal. "Happy you!" Hopkins begins. "You are in the land of the Vedas," which he himself has never visited but "looked out Dacca in the map and find it lies between the Ganges and Brahmapootra," so that he fears Garrett is "too far east for what is most interesting in India." But do write him, he banters, pleads, for he has "a yearning towards Hindoos; and things even that I could get up from books about them, and do not, have quite another charm when they come by private letter and commended to one's private eye." So, "write about Brahmins," he urges Garrett on, his prose catching fire as he meditates on the stupendous mystery of it all. "Write about Rajpoots, write about Vaisyas, write about Sudras. Be detailed about Benares, be minute about Allahbad. Dwell on Vishnu, enlarge on Juggernaut. Develop caste, describe shuggee. Be long, be lengthy, be voluminous, be tedious." He wants to know anything and everything about this exotic world. "If you tell me that you know Sanscrit I go April-green with envy, if you say the Mahabharata is your toast-crumb ordinary breakfast book, I am jaundiced all marigold under the eyes. . . . The Vedas and Hindoo philosophy are what I should hugely like to go in for." And, most of all, does Garrett "like India and in particular the banks of the Brahmapootra? (refreshing billowy majestic name! the next best thing to bathing in it)."

As for himself, he has been studiously studying philosophy and maths and logic and will be at Stonyhurst for another year and a half. Then he will probably be sent somewhere to teach, and after that "sent to my theology for three or four years and meanwhile ordained." Things are well at home, in fact "pleasanter than they have ever been since my conversion, which is a great comfort." Cyril and Arthur are engaged to two sisters, "very charming girls." Cyril will be married later this year, and Arthur has become—not without some struggle—an artist and illustrator. Addis is at the London Oratory, and will become a subdeacon in another week. Wood is studying medicine and then going out to Tasmania, where his brother has land. He mentions the sad news about Fletcher and Challis. And dear Baillie writes "a kind of pleasant wail of despair from the midst of waist-deep comfort and plenty." He asks for prayers for himself, but especially for Challis.

Further diminishments: "Mr. Kennedy left us," Hopkins notes. "He offered himself to Fr. de Smet for the American mission." Then Sweetman leaves. In mid-June, members of his community travel "to see a poor bedridden factory girl at Preston who has been for years living on no food but the Blessed Sacrament, which she receives once a week." On July 5, he notes that "in Germany, Bismarck's law expelling [the Jesuits] was signed by Emperor Wilhelm." He steps into "a great shadowy barn, where the hay had been stacked on either side, and looking at the great rudely arched timber-frames . . . and tie-beams, which make them look like bold big *A*s with the cross-bar high up—I thought how sadly beauty of inscape was unknown and buried away from simple people and yet how near at hand it was if they had eyes to see it."

And expansions: On July 28, his twenty-eighth birthday comes and goes. Studying for his exams in the Baddely, he comes across the medieval Franciscan, Duns Scotus's, *Sentences*—in Latin—in the stacks and is "flush with a new stroke of enthusiasm. It may come to nothing or it may be a mercy from God. But just then when I took in any inscape of the sky or sea I thought of Scotus." *Haeceittas,* thisness, individuation—that which makes this oak tree this oak tree only, or this rose this rose only, or this person this person only, and not another—something unique and separate, God's infinite and incredible freshness of Creation every nanosecond of every day, world without end. Thomism is fine for understanding the unity of all things—being, species, and so forth. But *haeceittas*—thisness—the dappled distinctiveness of everything kept in Creation. With that he can certainly identify.

A week later, exams over, the Scholastics leave for Douglas and the Isle of Man on holiday. On August 4, he visits Onchan Kirk. Most of the work is poor, he sees, but "the steeple is so strongly and boldly designed that it quite deceived me and I took it for old work well preserved." One day, hiking to Laxey, he hears a little girl singing "a Manx song, though indeed it was but four lines, a rhyming couplet and the third line repeated, and she recited it only. It sounded just like English words done into nonsense verses: thus the third and fourth lines or burden seemed 'The brow shall loose, the brow shall loose.'" And Manx, being a Celtic language, "can be understood by a speaker of Irish." Even better, the people here are "the most good-natured . . . I have ever met."

From a cliff he catches the inscape of the sea roiling the shore, how it "toes the inlets, now with a push and flow, now slacking, returning to stress and pulling back." He goes mackerel-fishing with some of the others in a smack off the coast and sees cormorants—"Black Divers—flying by the boat and screaming." He baits a line with mackerel skin and watches as the blue-silver forms gather a few feet down. Then he notices that the boat has pulled away with the outgoing tide, so that he and the others cannot get into the bay again and must row for all they are worth under the cliffs to get back in. And as he pulls at his oar, he looks up and his eye catches a sheep "hanging in one of the softly fluted green channels running down between the rocks of the cliff."

August 8: He and the others hike to the Laxey waterwheel, seventy-two feet in diameter, the biggest in the world, he notes. "The water is delivered a little below its highest point and turns the wheel towards itself, acting . . . by its weight in the buckets . . . [and] geared by a long timber shaft . . . running by little wheels on a rail to an oscillating head." It is used to pump water from the lead mine and the great wheel turns "once in 25 seconds." Two days later, he looks hard again for the scaping of the waves, but the shoreline is all milky surf, so that he cannot "unpack the huddling and gnarls of the water and law out the shapes and the sequence of the running," though he does manage to catch "the looped or forked wisp made by every big pebble the backwater runs over." The foam, he notes with Ruskinese precision, seems to dwindle and twitch "into long chains of suds, while the strength of the back-draught shrugged the stones together and clocked them one against another." Years before, he had studied the action of waves like these on the Isle of Wight: the foamlaps and halfmoons of the thing, the "dance and swagging of the light green tongues . . . in a place locked between rocks." Like the wild freedom of words locked into form.

Monday, August 12: He visits the churchyard at Kirk Braddan, as beautiful as any he has seen—"fine and beautiful ashes and a wychelm with big glossy happy and shapely leaves, spanish chestnuts," the ground sloping "down to the road with tier upon tier of thick black gravestones." He notes especially the Viking crosses among the stones, "with runes engraved and curious work containing dragons and monsters, more odd than pretty and a little Japanese in look." Then on to the Tynevald mound, "from which the Manx laws are published," and the red sandstone ruins of Peel Castle and St. German's Cathedral and a round tower "ascribed to St. Patrick." Still, it is the sway and raw force of the sea which most holds his attention, breaking "under the strong rocks below the outer side of the castle . . . blown up and plunging down and bursting upwards . . . in spews of foam."

On August 20, the community returns to Stonyhurst via Liverpool, where Hopkins visits with Cyril. Then the train north to Blackburn, where he gets out to walk the last seven miles back to Stonyhurst, the Lancashire landscape looking more beautiful than ever. After the sharp winds on the Isle of Douglas, he thinks, the inland breeze feels "warm and velvety." At supper, the Rector waits on the community, a gesture of Christ-like humility that touches him deeply. Then, two days later, the shattering news that his fellow Jesuits have just been expelled from Germany as part of Bismarck's *Külturkampf.*

He writes his mother to thank her for sending the latest *Illustrated London News* with Arthur's illustration, "The Paddling Season." It is a drawing of two little girls dressed up and seen from the back and a little boy with a toy yacht on a string facing them. Arthur's best drawing yet, he thinks, having heard others also admiring it. Still, the artist in him can't help pointing out how it might have been bettered. "The boy's face is poor in expression and if Arthur can refer to one of Keene's drawings in a late *Punch* [Aug. 10, 1872] . . . and look at the boy on the steps, who is in all respects a parallel to his boy" and like enough to what Everard, now twelve, looks like, "he will see the difference." Still, if Arthur "can keep up illustrating in this way . . . his monetary success is assured, for the drawing is a firstrate article," which will command "its own price and is not to be got elsewhere except in the recognised first hands, Du Maurier etc."

At the beginning of September, the Scholastics undertake their annual retreat, this one directed by Father James Jones. He learns from Sib Splaine, who tells him through tears that Win Stanton, one of the cleverest boys at Stonyhurst, has hung himself. "He had been reading a novel of Trollope's in which a hanging is described," Hopkins notes, shaken himself, "and it was believed he was trying to act it. His body was naked except that his shoes were on. He was not throttled but died by some shock to the spine." Cyril and Uncle John come over from Liverpool to spend the weekend visiting at Stonyhurst. Afterward, he and another Scholastic wander over Pendle Hill, famous for its witches in James I's time, lore on which Shakespeare drew for *Macbeth.* They can still make out several "black scalped places on it that look made for a witches' Sabbath." You can almost "fancy them dancing" there, he imagines, "higher and higher at each round and then flinging off at last one after the other each on her broomstick clear over the flat of country below." A boy guides them across the fields to Clitheroe, speaking of a *felly* as a *felk,* and rhyming *nave* with *have.* Then downhill to Little Mearley Hall, "where they were marking a sea of sheep and the farmer . . . showed us the front of the house" built with stone taken from the abbey nearby.

Saturday night, October 5: A golden-crested wren gets into his room and circles about, "dazzled by the gaslight on the white ceiling." He catches it gently and lets it out through the window. But in it comes again. He catches it again and ruffles its crest, smoothing "the little orange and yellow feathers . . . hidden in it." Next morning, he finds many of the feathers about his room and includes them in a letter to Cyril for his wedding day. Three weeks later, in bed with a fever brought about by swollen hemorrhoids and an alarming loss of blood—his old complaint—Father Gallwey comes up to sit beside him, taking his hand to comfort him. Hopkins will have to return to London at Christmas to see a physician about this.

In mid-October, he witnesses "a great fall of stars, identified with Biela's comet," radiating "from Perseus or Andromeda," and falling slantwise to the left. And soon the kitchen boys are "running with a great to do to say something red hot had struck the meat safe over the scullery door with a great noise and falling into the yard gone into several pieces." One of the brothers has seen burn marks on the safe "and the slightest of dints as if made by a soft body." If anything did fall, Father Perry, Stonyhurst's astronomer, surmises, "it was probably a body of gas."

"They are having at me with ethics and mechanics," he writes Baillie in early December, and though today is "a whole holiday," he has spent "a miserable morning over formulas for the lever." He is teaching himself to play the piano, but very slowly. The new Bishop of Salford, Dr. Herbert Vaughan, a Stonyhurst alumnus, was at the college two weeks ago, and the school held a literary reception in his honor. "Congratulatory addresses in prose and verse in all sorts of languages [were read] by the masters at the College, the boys, and us Seminarians," he explains, and the "half-English half-Italian young sucking Mezzofanti among us who could have written in seven languages . . . and had several if not all of his irons" ended up producing "a hermaphrodite French Alexandrine Bucephalus and a five-footed Italian sonnet." Hopkins himself was asked to write some Greek verses "and shed twenty-four iambics with much ado," but at least, he adds, "it raised a blister in my dry and shrunken Greek and led me to begin reading the beautiful *Iphigenia among the Tauri.*"

And then back to Baillie's account of the death of Miles Fletcher, "American-outward-bound," who died in that Minnesota snowstorm. There is also Addis's account, which throws another light altogether on his death. Fletcher "had been leading a devout life," he explains, "and on the morning of his death said to his wife that he had been making his meditation on the way he should like to spend the last day of his life." In fact, then, Fletcher's "was a happy and providential, not an untimely end." "Lovely-felicitous Providence / Finger of a ténder of, O of a féathery delicacy," Hopkins will write three years on, meditating on the wreck of a German steamship during a whiteout. "Thou art above, thou Orion of light," he will address the Lord of winter, summer, and all seasons between in the *Deutschland*:

> Thy unchancelling poising palms were weighing the worth,
>   Thou martyr-master: in thý sight
> Storm flakes were scroll-leaved flowers, lily showers—sweet heaven
>   was astrew in them.

December 12, and a blandyke or monthly holiday: "Hard frost, bright sun, a sky of blue 'water.'" In the afternoon, he hikes out to the fells with Herbert Lucas. Pheasants and grouse flicker up before them, the ferns under the trees ginger-colored above the snow, Parlick Pike "sheeted with taut tattered streaks of crisp gritty snow. Green-white tufts of long bleached grass like heads of hair," the inscape like running water or waves breaking against a seabeach, "as if my eye were still growing," though when he is out with someone else, "the eye and the ear are for the most part shut and instress cannot come." And a week later: "Under a dark sky walking by the river at Brockennook," everything "sad-coloured," the "red and blue stones in the river beaches brought out by patches of white-blue snow." Silvered snow damasking the fields, the snowline gilded now "with an arch brightness," reminding him of the Caravaggio-like flaming "taper Tommy was screening with his hand the other morning in the dark refectory," and how it "struck out the . . . shells of the eyes and the cleft of the nostrils and flat of the chin and tufts on the cheeks in gay leaves of gold."

Two days before Christmas he returns home. "Remainders of snow on the hills as far as Macclesfield, as on Pendle and Whalley Nab," he notes from the train window crossing the Lancashire countryside, and floodwaters to the south. "Great rains and gales . . . everywhere." On Christmas Day at Oak Hill, Cyril and his new bride, Harriet, arrive for dinner, along with Aunt Kate and her children, and all is as it has been for many Christmases past.

At year's end, Hopkins is operated on by two doctors—Mr. Gay and Mr. Prance—for hemorrhoids. The operation lasts only half an hour, but he spends the next two weeks in bed recovering, during which time he has visitors. Campbell and another young Jesuit, Henry Marchant, come over from Roehampton. Then Addis—newly ordained—comes up from Brompton, in Kent. Then Baillie, Bond, and Alexander Wood, who fills him in with the particulars of Basil Poutiatine's death the previous summer. Basil had wanted to marry a Greek girl, the daughter of a physician, but his father— the Russian Admiral—had disapproved "because of the inequality of rank," though that had been got over. Basil's doctor had weighed in, saying "the marriage was impossible on the score of his health. The girl's father . . . treated this as a shift to get off the match, the girl herself seems to have fallen in with her family, and they gave Poutiatine who was in the same hotel in Paris, so much annoyance that he took to flight for Strasburg [sic] where the Admiral was, leaving even his luggage." He tried to throw the family off the trail by taking the train north, thinking to switch trains and head for Strasbourg, but began walking the wrong way. His body "was found in a pool or horse- or cattle-trough by the roadside only a few feet deep," Hopkins notes, trying to reenact his friend's final moments. "His hat was on the bank" as if he had "stooped to drink, been seized with a fit, and fallen in—or fallen in and been seized with a fit." Wood thinks the death was not a suicide, but Hopkins is not so sure. In fact, as the list of his lost classmates grows, Hopkins will come to believe that most are suicides. Ah, dear Oxford, what it has done to its children.

By mid-January 1873, he is up and about again. Except for some gale winds, the weather remains mild, the elms "hung and beaded with round buds and many trees," revealing a "smoky claret colour." On the 20th, he visits the Old Masters Exhibition in London, and then goes down to Roehampton to stay with his community for the next two weeks, before returning to Stonyhurst and the annual Triduum in early February. Late in the month it begins snowing heavily again, and he finds himself studying the "flat-topped hillocks and shoulders" of snow. Snow waves, he thinks. And so there it is again: a world "full of inscape," and what we mistakenly call chance "falls into an order as well as purpose." As in "the random clods and broken heaps of snow made by the cast of a broom" forming circles, and again in footprints left in the "ankledeep snow across the fields leading to Hodder wood."

Monday, March 3: A letter to his mother for her fifty-second birthday. Lent has begun, but—she will be relieved to hear—once again he is not to fast. In fact, his Rector has forbidden it. His work this term has also been lightened. He is sending Lionel an article which will explain why "we feel wind colder than still air when a thermometer marks no difference," and he promises to write Arthur soon, for he wants to know more about the painter Fred Walker, whose work he so admires. Read Edward Lear's *More Nonsense*, he tells her, which is something like Lewis Carroll's *Alice in Wonderland* but far better. There she will learn how to make Gosky Patties and see flowers that never were, especially the Manypeeplia Upsidownia. "But the stories are the best," for there she can read "how the Four Little People who went round the world 'continued their journey with the utmost delight and apathy,'" and above all "the parting scene with the Bluebottle Flies, the strains of whose Evening song 'over the heads of the transitory Titmice lit up the intervening and verdant mountains with a serene and sickly suavity known only to the truly virtuous.'" Lear has managed to nail the inanities of comfortable Victorian middle-class expectations, which Hopkins himself has come to so deeply distrust.

April 8, Tuesday in Holy Week: He is reading in his room, when suddenly he hears the sound of axes and looks out the window to see the beautiful ash tree in the corner of the garden being lopped and cut down. With a few strokes a beautiful thing like that maimed and destroyed, so that "there came at that moment a great pang and I wished to die and not to see the inscapes of the world destroyed any more." Nine days later, he walks with Clarke to Whitewell, ten miles to the north. Crossing the river, they catch sight of a shoal of salmon and—on the open hills—a warren of hares. Under a stone hedge, he spots a dying ram, "a thick flesh-coloured ooze, scarlet in places, coiling and roping its way down" its nose, "so thick that it looked like fat." Even in death, there is the fascination of looking hard. Then a late snowstorm, the birds clucking and scurrying away under bushes. After which, finally, the spring rains.

That May, "Bluebells in Hodder wood, all hanging their heads one way. I caught as well as I could while my companions talked the Greek rightness of their beauty." It is a blue light they give off, he sees, "beating up from so many glassy heads," and so floating "their deeper instress in upon the mind." On the 15th, Arthur marries his sister-in-law Harriet Bockett's sister, Rebecca, and soon after Hopkins hears from the newlyweds in "a two-handed letter." In late May it is the cry of corncrakes at night, "and swifts rounding and scurling under the clouds." And the studies and preparations for examinations continue. On a June Sunday, a group of seminarians—including Hopkins—walk to nearby Billington to join in a church procession. Another day he notes "shadows sharp in the quarry and on the shoulders of our two young white pigeons. There is some charm about a thing such as these pigeons or trees when they dapple their boles in wearing its own shadow." Even the fells are "melled and painted with colour and full of roaming scents" now. Lying on the grass by the quarry at Kemble End in the company of Brother Strappini, he watches a cuckoo fly by with a small bird after it. Returning to St. Mary's, he stops at the stables to observe a nest of peacocks. A stablehand is eager to show him a newly hatched brood of peafowl and—though they cannot be found—Hopkins is touched by the man's kindness. Thunder-colored pigeons in the kitchen yard "like little gay jugs . . . strutting and jodjodding with their heads," one "up on the eaves of the roof" with a satin green head shimmering like moist flame.

Then renewal of vows on the 20th, the Feast of the Sacred Heart. On the 23rd, he is successfully examined by the Fathers *de universa philosophia*—on all of philosophy—and a week later goes over to the college to teach rhetoric for a week in the absence of the regular teacher. "A high wind," he notes on July 18, the music of inscape "blowing the crests of the trees before the sun" and "ruffling the leaves which came out in their triplets threaded round," and the sun "sitting at one end of the branch in a pash of soap-sud-coloured gummy bimbeams rowing over the leaves." Or the high water at

Hodder Roughs, "lit from within . . . looking like pale gold" or ginger syrup. Below the rocks he catches a "bubblejestled skirt of foam jumping back against the fall, which cuts its way clean and will not let it through," or "looping watersprigs that lace and dance and jockey in the air . . . like bubbles in a quill." At the base of the falls, "a sour yellow light . . . like smoke kindling all along the rock, with a sullen noise . . . come bumping to the top in troubled water."

And this on the 22nd: "Very hot, though the wind, which was south, dappled very sweetly on one's face" and "rippled and fluttered like light linen." Or the terrifying Sublime of lightning again: "Thunderstorm . . . booming in gong-sounds, as at Aosta, as if high up and so not reechoed from the hills; the lightning very slender and nimble," in which several people are killed. Two days later, another blandyke. "Mr. Colley and I crossed the river at Hacking Boat, went up the fell opposite near the Nab, walked some way, and coming down at Billington recrossed at the Troughs." A farmer points at the driver of his mower "peerkin' on the seat" (perched on the seat), explaining that the hay has to be "shaked." And the ferryman at the Troughs tells them "how in the hot days working in the hay he had 'Supped [sipped] beer till' he 'could sup no more.'"

On July 29, the day after Gerard's twenty-ninth birthday, Arthur and Rebecca arrive at the college, and he shows them over the grounds. The next day he takes them to Ree Deep, with its "beautiful long outlook," and then to Lambing Clough with its waterfalls, where it begins to rain heavily. "Somehow," he tells his mother, "we did not make so much of our time as we should but we enjoyed it very much, at least I did." That same morning one of the Scholastics, Brother Scriven, wasted with consumption, at whose sickbed he'd sat the week before, dies. "In the night he had a great struggle," Hopkins notes, "in which he started up in bed and caught hold of the Rector with both hands. Afterwards he was calm."

Early August and another holiday: again the Scholastics travel to Liverpool and then by boat to the Isle of Man, staying at Derby Castle in Douglas. Come September, he tells his mother, he is going to teach "one of the higher classes in one of our schools," though he does not yet know where. The year's teaching has been given him "as a rest," and he thinks it "as good an arrangement as could have been made." After that he will go on to theology, "a four year's business." He writes Bond, now a barrister in London. The talk turns to the poetry of Matthew Arnold, whose *Empedocles upon Etna* Hopkins has brought with him to Douglas. He has, he confesses, read the poems "with more interest than rapture . . . for they seem to have all the ingredients of poetry without quite being it." What he misses is a certain ease, though they "do not leave off of being, as the French say, very beautiful." The truth is that Arnold "seems a very earnest man," sees "the difference between jest and earnest," and is a master of both. "But then very unhappily he jokes at the wrong things."

He has also been reading Newman's *The Grammar of Assent* and finds it heavy going, though "the justice and candour and gravity and rightness of mind" is there in all Newman writes. Still, what dissatisfies Hopkins in Newman "is a narrow circle of instance and quotation—in a man too of great learning and of general reading quite like the papers in the *Spectator*," plus a lack of brilliancy, "which foolish people think every scribbler possesses, but it is no such thing." In spite of which he thinks Newman remains "our greatest living master of style . . . and widest mind." He himself would write more carefully, he jokes, but all about him he notices that everyone else seems immersed in the *Manx Sun* or Mrs. Brown's popular novels.

On Saturday, August 16, the Scholastics rise at 4:00 a.m. in the midst of a storm to catch the boat back to the mainland, dun-colored waves leaving "trailing hoods of white breaking on the beach." He stares hard at the breakers one last time, "wanting to make out how the comb is morselled so fine into string and tassel,"and discerns "big smooth flinty waves, carved and scuppled in shallow grooves" bursting against "the rocky spurs of the cliff." And though it is by then only eight in the morning, a young man is already drunk aboard the boat, singing "I want to go home to Mamma," the foam "exploding and smouldering under water" in accompaniment.

At Blackburn he leaves the train with some of the others to hike back to Stonyhurst, passing "infinite stiles and sloppy fields" after so much rain. Then a bright sunset, the sky "lamping with tipsy bufflight, the colour of yellow roses." But the group walks too fast, and by the time they reach Stonyhurst, he is knocked up. They will be staying at the college for a week, as St. Mary's is being used just now for the secular priests' retreat. Worse, all the gas jets are out at the college, so that the Scholastics have to get about in the dark with candles in bottles. "Things not ready," he laments, and suddenly everything seems thrown into "darkness and despair." He is tired and depressed, even as "nature in all her parcels and faculties gaped and fell apart . . . like a clod cleaving and holding only by strings of root." But, he knows, such things "must often be" in his life as a religious. It rings as a new and darker note, which will in the years ahead become a burden and refrain.

On Sunday morning he learns that a group of German Jesuits, expelled by the Falck Laws the year before and housed now at Ditton Hall outside Liverpool, are at Stonyhurst for their annual Villa, or holiday. That evening they provide the English community with a concert, and again on Tuesday, to which the English community reciprocates by providing an evening of skits and farces. Then, the secular priests' retreat over, Hopkins and the rest of the seminarians return to St. Mary's. On the 27th, the German Jesuits return to give a farewell concert before returning to Ditton. "They were kind, amiable, and edifying people," Hopkins notes, and a group of Scholastics—himself among them—respond by hiking down to Whalley Station to see them off. Afterward, he goes for a walk with Herbert Lucas along the river, discussing Scotism with him for the last time. That same evening he receives his new assignment. He is being sent back to Roehampton to teach rhetoric to the Juniors. In the morning, he will leave for London with Vaughan and Considine, who are going to teach at Beaumont, all three bound for "fresh woods and pastures new."

Chapter 7

Of Realty the Rarest-Veinèd Unraveller: Roehampton, 1873–1874

Late on the afternoon of August 28, 1873, a scraggly-bearded Hopkins in black soutane, his hair parted neatly down the center, reaches South London and Roehampton with his bags, not as a novice this time, but as Professor of Rhetoric, whose charge will be teaching eleven Jesuit Juniors. They are unlike any other students he has had or will ever have: all very tractable, responding to their teachers' assignments and lectures with the seriousness of those who have taken a vow of obedience. Nearly all have been educated at Stonyhurst, among whom are several converts. Compared to the other Scholastics who have been assigned work in the British Province, this is a plum of a job, given to him because his superiors have noticed how physically exhausted he gets, and because—given his Oxford education and penchant for literature—he would seem to be ideally suited for teaching classical rhetoric. That first evening at Manresa he just manages to catch Father Gallwey, the newly appointed English Provincial, who—as always—speaks to him "most kindly and encouragingly," assuring him that Gerard is going to do just fine now that he is back in London.

On Saturday, the community begins its annual eight-day retreat, during which Hopkins receives what he takes to be "a great mercy" about the ultimate judgment on Digby Dolben. (Although he makes extensive meditations of his time in retreat, the notes themselves have disappeared.) In the two remaining weeks before classes begin, he writes up some of his lectures and attends several art shows in London. On September 8, he talks with Brother Duffy on the grounds at Roehampton about ploughing, something which has always fascinated him, and Duffy names the ploughing tools for him: "the cross, side-plate, muzzle, regulator, and short chain." He listens intently to the man's language: "spraying out" for "splaying out" and of "*combing* the ground." He watches a beautiful sunrise from the hall window, and at night the full moon "in a palecoloured heartsease made of clouds." Then "toadstool rings in the big pasture before the house, some very big," the grass "fagged, drained, and baked."

At the Kensington Museum he notes the "bold masterly rudeness" of della Robbia's blue plates, Pisano's pulpits, the bronze gilt doors for the Duomo with their representation of the Transfiguration, and copies of Michelangelo's paintings at the Vatican, and is struck by their simplicity, force, and "masterly realism." He notes too "the instress of expression in the faces" of two sisters in a portrait by G. F. Watts, something he has also remarked in the work of Burne-Jones and Fred Walker. He studies a display of classical musical instruments—harpsichords, spinets, virginals, dulcimers—comparing them to what the music theorist, François-Joseph Fetis, has to say about these beautiful if silent instruments before him.

That night, back in his room at Roehampton, he records a terrifying nightmare. In it "something or someone," some incubus, seems to leap on him and hold him down, startling him awake. It is like the sort of nervous collapse one has when "one is very tired and holding oneself at stress not to sleep yet suddenly goes slack and seems to fall and wakes, only on a greater scale and with a loss of muscular control reaching more or less deep." The force of this, Hopkins notes, was to his chest, so that he could only whisper at first, his voice gradually becoming louder. If only I can recover myself, he thinks. If only I can move a finger, an arm, my body. "The feeling is terrible, the body no longer swayed as a piece by the nervous and muscular instress, seems to fall in and hang like a dead weight on the chest. I cried on the holy name and by degrees recovered myself."

So this is what hell is like, he shudders, this is what perhaps lies ahead for me: the soul imprisoned forever in its dead body. It is the inchoate fear of being buried alive in oneself and knowing it. It is a sense of utter helplessness he felt on leaving Stonyhurst, a deep anxiety he will experience more and more in the years to come, and which has descended upon him as he prepares to teach again. The sense of not being up to the demands of the work assigned him, a wrestling with forces larger than himself, and not knowing whether these forces mean him harm or are merely testing his mettle. "But ah, but O thou terrible," he will write a dozen years on,

Why wouldst thou rude on me
Thy wring-world right foot rock? Lay a lionlimb against me? Scan
With darksome devouring eyes my bruisèd bones? And fan
O in turns of tempest, me heaped there; me frantic to avoid thee
        and flee?

On September 22 classes begin, and he meets with his students to explain the elements of classical and modern rhetoric. "I have paid a good deal of attention to Milton's versification and collected his later rhythms," he will tell a friend four years later. "I did it when I had to lecture on rhetoric some years since. I found [Milton's] most advanced effects in the *Paradise Regained* and, lyrically, in the *Agonistes*. I have often thought of writing on them, indeed on rhythm in general; I think the subject is little understood." From the abundant but scattered notes of his that have survived, it is clear just how deeply Hopkins thought about these things during his year at Roehampton. Not only is Milton on his mind, but the whole range of Greek and Latin prosody, as well as French, German, Italian, Irish, Icelandic, Anglo-Saxon, Middle English—*Piers Plowman*, and Chaucer especially—indeed the whole history of English poetry up to his own time.

One senses that his learning is so advanced, so esoteric, that he must often have overwhelmed the novices, though his self-deprecating humor may often have saved the day. A few fragments, then, to give a sense of what he taught them. "The accent of a word means its strongest accent," he explains, "and this is of two kinds: pitch (tonic) and stress (emphasis). Words like bodies have both centers of gravity and centers of illumination (highspots)." In English, stress or accent is strong, the pitch weak. "The Greek name for accent is *prosodia*, that is the tune sung to a word, the note or pitch of a syllable. The Latin for this is *accentus*."

Rhythm is the "repetition of feet, the same or mixed, without regard to how long." And meter "is the grouping of a certain number of 'feet.'" Prose may have rhythm, but it does not employ meter. "In modern verse a verse means a complete metrical figure, a metrical unit, for as the foot is the rhythmic unit, which it repeats, so a verse is the metrical unit of repetition," whether it be a line or couplet or triplet or stanza. A poetic line "is an intermediate division between foot and verse, like a clause and marked off by rhyme or other means," which "we must judge by the ear."

Verse he defines as "the recasting of speech into sound-words, sound-clauses and sound-sentences of uniform commensurable lengths and accentuations." The music of poetry is a "recasting of speech used in a wide sense, of vocal utterance, into words, clauses, and sentences of pitched sounds. . . . The musical syllable is the note, the musical foot or word the bar. . . . Feet give their names to the rhythms that are made out of them." Moreover, each foot and rhythm has a particular character. With the iamb or the anapest, "the rhythm is forward and expresses present action. With the trochee or dactyl, a sense of succession is implied, which is why the

form suits narrative." In time he will reveal his brilliance in prosodic matters, creating a revolution not only in his own poetry but in the poetry of
generations to come. We are still unpacking the lessons Hopkins gave us a
hundred and twenty-five years ago, for he initiated a music whose rhythmic echoes continue to challenge our own sense of what can be done with
the poetic line. But it was with these unpromising beginnings, in a modest
Jesuit classroom in Roehampton, that the ideas for the revolution were first
tried on. The poetry itself will take another two years to break into
blossom.

Autumn 1873: "This morning, blue mist breathing with wind across the
garden after mass," he writes, everything looking "less and nearer, not bigger and spacious in the fog. Tops of the trees hidden almost or where seen
grey, till the sun threw a moist red light through them." And this: "Woodpigeons come in flock into our field and on our trees. . . . A doe comes to our
sunken fence to be fed: she eats acorns and chestnuts and stands on the
bank, a pretty tri-ped, forefeet together and hind set apart. The bucks grunt
all night . . . and fight often: it is their season." At the end of October come
the first hard frosts. "Wonderful downpour of leaf: when the morning sun
began to melt the frost they fell at one touch and in a few minutes a whole
tree was flung of them; they lay masking and papering the ground at the
foot. Then the tree seems to be looking down on its cast self." And again:
"Elmleaves very crisp and chalky and yellow, a scarlet brightness against
the blue. Sparks of falling leaves streaming down." On December 1, he notes
the "frosting on trees and cobwebs like fairyland." And a week before
Christmas, the felling of more trees "going on sadly at Roehampton."

At Christmas, he is given permission to visit with his family for a week.
He goes with Arthur to view the Winter Exhibition of Water Colours and is
struck by Fred Walker's exquisite *Harbour of Refuge*, a watercolor repro-
duction of the oil painting shown the year before. The execution, he decides, is rough, the "sunset sky and boughs of trees against it most rude, yet
true and effective enough." On the other hand, the young man mowing is "a
great stroke, a figure quite made up of dew and grace and strong fire: the
sweep of the scythe and swing and sway of the whole body even to the rising of the one foot on tiptoe . . . was as if such a thing had never been painted
before, so fresh and so very strong." Against which there is the image of an
elderly woman being supported by a young girl "with an enforced languor
in her," the girl's face "pensive and delicate and sweet; auburn hair; beautiful, rather full hands crossed; a pretty clever halo of a cap." Youth and age
and the essential poverty of life, in tension with the figure of the young man

scything the grass. It is an image that will resonate for him down the years, perhaps no more so than in these lines from the *Deutschland:*

> But wé dréam we are rooted in earth—Dust!
> Flesh falls within sight of us, we, though our flower the same,
> Wave with the meadow, forget that there must
> The sour scythe cringe, and the blear share come.

January 22, 1874: With Bridges just miles away on the other side of London practicing medicine at St. Bartholomew's, and not having heard from him now in two and a half years, Hopkins at last picks up pen, consumes his pound of crow, and tries again. "My dear Bridges," he begins. "My last letter to you was from Stonyhurst. It was not answered, so that perhaps it did not reach you. If it did I supposed then and do not know what else to suppose now that you were disgusted with the red opinions it expressed, being a conservative." But Hopkins has "little reason to be red; it was the red Commune that murdered five of our Fathers." Besides, he protests, he said nothing in his letter "that might not fairly be said. If this was your reason for not answering it seems to shew a greater keenness about politics than is common."

He recently ran into one of Bridges's Oxford connections, who told him that "so and so . . . breeds fowls and Bridges writes—but nothing distinct." But in the *Academy* for January 17, he came across Andrew Lang's "appreciative review of a Mr. Bridges' poems, Robert Bridges the title shewed." (Reading the *Academy* these days, he will write Edward Bond, allows him "to pretend to know what is going on in literature and so on and, as Confucius said to his son in advising him to read the classical ballads of China, I shall be worth conversing with.") The characteristics Lang describes in the poems sound like what Bridges would write if indeed he did write poetry, he guesses. And so he writes now to ask if he is the Bridges in the review. But his real reason for writing is to renew their old friendship. "I think, my dear Bridges, to be so much offended about that red letter was excessive."

March 1: A visit from his fellow convert, Alexander Wood, who has just published his *Ecclesiastical Antiquities of London and its Suburbs,* which is doing briskly. He is getting married right after Easter, he tells Hopkins. On the 2nd—the same day his brother Lionel sets sail for Peking—he writes his mother for her birthday. He is allowed to take wine during Lent to keep up his strength and because he is teaching, so that one of the Jesuit wits has taken to referring to the exception as Gerard's "Lenten Festivities." Bond's sister is getting married to a Mr. Pooley (what a name! he once told Bond, but then he also remembers how one whole night he lay in bed contemplating the ugliness of his own name, "till I was so mortified that even now it is a cure to vainglory to recall the thought").

On the day after Easter, he walks out to Wimbledon Common, hoping to catch a sham fight made up of some seven thousand volunteers, but is too early. Instead, his attention turns to a magnificent steed, and he suddenly catches its inscape. It is very like the inscape of the horse in the "bas reliefs of the Parthenon" seen in the British Museum, the very thing Sophocles seems to have felt and which he expresses in two choruses of *Oedipus at Colonus* of the "likeness of a horse to a breaker, a wave of the sea curling over." Focusing his attention on the horse's flank, he notes how "the set of the hair symmetrically flowed outwards from it to all parts of the body, so that, following that one may inscape the whole beast very simply."

Three days later, he takes Mr. Tournade—a young French Jesuit bound for the China missions—to the Kensington Museum, where he makes a further study of the folds of a Greek gown as they fall from the bosom of a Greco-Roman Melpomene. Then some modern Japanese work: a night hawk in combat with a dragon on a gilded platter, and a suit of Japanese armor. On the 11th, Cyril's wife, Rebecca, gives birth to a daughter, Beatrice Muriel, the first of the next generation of Hopkinses. At the same time, his uncle James—his mother's younger sister's husband—is dying at sixty. On the 19th he writes Bond, delighted that he is coming out to visit. Bond wants to know if they can go for a walk in Richmond Park. Of course, he tells him, "even to Ham common, and so on by Berkshire to Caerleon, Lyoness, Avilion, and the great Atalantis. Be pregnant, bring thoughts, news, strokes, touches . . . butts, bulls, blunders," even to a discussion of the pros and cons of whether or not the British Empire should have burned Coomassie two months before, thus bringing to an end the African Ashanti war. After all, he jokes, the natives "could put it up again in the afternoon," seeing as equatorial metropolises consist merely "of bamboos and a high temperature." In time he will learn what else empires are capable of doing to their subjects, but not yet. Not yet.

On June 12, he goes into London with Mr. Bampton to see the Academy exhibit, then to study Butterfield's design for All Saints' Church on Margaret Street. "I wanted to see if my old enthusiasm was a mistake," he writes, and now understands better Butterfield's "want of rhetoric . . . and even of enthusiasm and zest in his work." Still, there *is* genius in the "rich nobility of the tracery in the open arches of the sanctuary and the touching and passionate curves of the lilyings in the ironwork under the baptistery." At the Academy, he stands before Holman Hunt's seven-foot-long *Shadow of Death.* There is about it, he notes, a "true sunset effect—that is the sunset light lodged as the natural light and only detected by its heightening the existing reds, especially in the golden-bronze skin he has given to our Lord's figure." And though he finds Christ's face "beautiful, sweet and human," it is not pleasing, mainly because there is "no inscape of composition whatever" in it. But the gem of the exhibition is Alma-Tadema's *Old Damascus: Jews' Quarter,* with its renderings of architectural detail, like the inlay of the blue-paneled door, the roundels, arch mosaics, and stripes on the pillars and pavement. It is in the attention to detail, he knows, that a work of art— whether a painting or a poem—succeeds or fails.

In early July, Hopkins attends a session of the House of Lords and hears the Lord Chancellor address the House. He walks over to Wimbledon to watch another stirring military exercise and to see the flags of the Empire "folding and rolling on the wind." He attends a session of the House of Commons as it debates a Schools Endowment bill, and spots Gladstone "preparing to speak and writing fast," but must hurry back to Roehampton. On the 23rd, he goes out with the novices to Beaumont for Rector's Day and observes the "shires-long of pearled cloud under cloud," then the "beautiful blushing yellow in the straw of the uncut rye fields" waving in the July breeze. All this, he confesses, he "would have looked at again in returning but during dinner I talked *too* freely and unkindly and had to do penance going home." On the 29th—the day after he turns thirty—he administers final exams to his novices. He is very tired now, and depressed, so that Father Gallwey tries to cheer him up with some kind words. But he can't help feeling that he has "never been so burdened and cast down as this year," the tax on his strength being greater than anything he has ever felt before. And yet, "in all this our Lord goes His own way."

August 5: To Beaumont for Speech Day, then afterward up the hillside to study the beeches overlooking Windsor and the Valley of the Thames. The following day he joins a group of Jesuits departing for Villa at Teignmouth on the Devonshire coast. Teignmouth is dull, a place of red sandstone cliffs and beach sands continually blowing and stinging. One evening, alone, he climbs the hills toward Bishopsteignton, "by a place a little girl called . . . Ku-am, perhaps she meant Coomb." All this west country, he sees, has these "rosy cocoa-dust-coloured handkerchiefs of ploughfields, sometimes delicately combed with rows of green." On the 14th, the community travels to Exeter to visit the great cathedral, which is under restoration, the quality of the work being such that "you cannot well tell what is old and what new." The most beautiful thing he sees is a tomb on the north side of the choir wall dating from 1206, the flow of the tracery enclosing the panels, all of them "original, flush, sweet, and tender, and truly classical, as befits and marks a flush and hopeful age." At Chudleigh Rocks, a view from a clifftop into "a deep and beautiful cleave," where he sees the remains "of a Danish Camp used in Alfred's war with the Danes." Riding home in a wagon afterward, he looks up at the stars, at all the fire-folk in the air. "I leant back to look at them and my heart opening more than usual praised our Lord to and in whom all that beauty comes home."

August 18: Calm seas. He watches a great seine floating and covering watery acres of ocean. "The fish landed are mostly dead," he realizes. "They kill one another with their weight and crowding: only those at top are alive." Then he walks out with John Lynch to visit Butterfield's church at Babbicombe, as he had seven years before, but is less impressed by it. The following evening he dines with John Tozer, a convert, and brother to the Anglican Bishop of Central Africa. Other guests include Bishop William Vaughan and Miss Betts, "a convert [and] a simple-minded young lady," whom he immediately takes to. She had, he learns, "tried her vocation for 7 months in the Benedictine convent here and given up because it was so 'prim' and no words could say what she had suffered there."

On August 20, the group heads for Bristol and St. Raphael's, which he'd once visited with Addis. The following day, they walk the recently completed Clifton Suspension Bridge, spanning the dizzying Avon Gorge hundreds of feet below. How odd to see people walking so far below him like ants. Our modern world, he thinks, with its towers and high-vaulting suspension bridges and railroads connecting the entire country. Then back to Beaumont by train. Approaching Windsor in the early evening, the group runs into smog "rolling up the valley of the Thames" from modern London. How splendid by contrast Old Windsor is with its "eye-greeting burl of the Round Tower; all the crownlike medley of lower towers warping round," and the red and white houses at the base "gabled and irregularly" jut-jotting against them. He stays at Beaumont for the weekend, bathing in a willowy, still section of the Thames along Runnymede, then taking a drive through Windsor Great Park before finally returning to Roehampton.

On August 26, he receives his orders. To his surprise, he will not be staying on a second year at Roehampton, but will leave at once for St. Beuno's in North Wales to begin his course in theology. He has one day to pack. On Friday morning, the 28th, one year to the day after his arrival, he rises at 5:00 a.m. to catch the early train to Wales. Looking out his bedroom window, he glimpses the full moon waiting to greet him, big and brass-colored "and beautifully dappled," "hanging a little above the clump in the pasture," as if to say hello or good-bye.

Chapter 8

A Pastoral Forehead of Wales:
St. Beuno's, 1874–1875

Friday afternoon, August 28, 1874: He is met at the small cathedral town of St. Asaph by Henry Kerr and Louis Bodoano, who escort him back through wooded, flower-laced lanes by trap to the imposing neo-Gothic gray buildings that make up the Jesuit theologate at St. Beuno's. In his sparsely furnished room he finds a jar of scarlet geraniums placed there by Francis Bacon. The following day he writes his father. Everyone here, he notes with relief, has been "very kind and hospitable." All in all, it has been an auspicious beginning to his time in "wild Wales." And while he had been expecting "another year's teaching at Roehampton," now his ordination and profession will be a whole year earlier. St. Beuno's—named for a medieval Welsh bishop—"stands on a steep hillside," commanding "the long-drawn valley of the Clwyd to the sea, a vast prospect, and opposite is Snowdon and its range, just now it being bright visible but coming and going with the weather." Besides, the very air, after his time in London, seems to him "very fresh and wholesome." Snowdon: Wordsworth's Snowdon, which the poet had climbed seventy years before, writing of his ascent up the imposing mountainside in darkness until, suddenly, the rays of the morning sun surprised him with what Hopkins will call—looking at this same range—"warm breast and with, ah! bright wings!"

Holidays will continue for another five weeks, until October 2, when the current group of seminarians is ordained and sent on their way to various schools, parishes, and foreign missions. Then those remaining will get down to the business of theology, and the hours will be filled with "lectures in dogmatic theology, moral ditto, canon law, church history, scripture, Hebrew and what not." In spite of which, he is already toying with the idea of "getting up a little Welsh," as all his neighbors around here speak the language. The house itself "is built of limestone, decent outside, skimpin within, Gothic, like Lancing College done worse. The staircases, galleries, and bopeeps are inexpressible: it takes a fortnight to learn them. Pipes of affliction convey lukewarm water of affliction to some of the rooms," though "others more fortunate have fires. The garden is all heights, terraces, Excelsiors, misty mountain tops, seats up trees called Crows' Nests, flights of steps seemingly up to heaven lined with burning aspiration upon aspiration of scarlet geraniums: it is very pretty and airy but it gives you the impression that if you took a step farther you would find yourself somewhere on Plenlimmon, Conway Castle, or Salisbury Craig."

The Rector here is Father James Jones, forty-six, of Welsh-Irish descent, whose family hails from Sligo. Jones's older brother is also a Jesuit, but with the Irish Province. Educated at Clongowes Wood College, James Jones entered the English Province in 1850 at twenty-two, doing his theology at the old Jesuit university in Palermo. He has worked in the West Indian missions and Rome, and has been at St. Beuno's for the past three years teaching moral theology. He has served as Rector now for the past year. There are forty-one seminarians at St. Beuno's, and ten professors, and all have been required by Father Jones to daily "mount"—wear—the Roman collar as well as their black soutanes, a departure from past practice, when clerical garb would have brought on deep suspicion among the neighbors. Hopkins is one of fourteen first-year students, eleven of whom are from the English Province; one—a Frenchman, Albert Wagner, from the Province headquartered at Lyons; and two—Charles Morrogh and George Kelly—on loan from the Irish Province. Nearly all the men are about thirty, the age when most Jesuits have been forged enough to begin advanced studies in theology. Six were born in 1843, three in 1844. The genteel Hop is here again, alongside the gentle Hop. Then there are the Splaine brothers—Cyprian and William—from Liverpool. Cyprian, educated at Stonyhurst, has taught seniors there for the past five years, preparing them for their London B.A. entrance exams. Conscientious and assiduous in his teaching and studies, he has taught Latin and moral theology and is now learning Hebrew. William, who joined the order two years before Hopkins, has already spent several years teaching at Beaumont and Stonyhurst.

William Dubberley, educated at Stonyhurst, has taught for the past five years at Beaumont. Hugh Ryan is from Limerick, though a member of the English Province. Educated at Oscott, he studied at Trinity College, Oxford, but left without taking a degree, and has been teaching high school students in the Jesuits' Liverpool schools for the past several years. Joe Rickaby, a year younger than Hopkins, is the son of the butler to Baron Herries, who paid for Joe's and his younger brother, John's, education at Stonyhurst.

Both are now Jesuits. Four years before, armed with an M.A. in philosophy from the University of London, where he distinguished himself in maths, logic, and philosophy, Joe began preparing Jesuit seminarians and lay philosophers at Stonyhurst for the London University B.A. Then there is Stephen Hayes, an Irishman educated at Stonyhurst, and a Jesuit for the past eleven years. Having earned his B.A. from the University of London, he too has taught at Beaumont and Stonyhurst. Sydney Smith, thirty-one, is the son of an Evangelical Anglican clergyman. In 1864, he was received into the Catholic Church at the Jesuit's Farm Street Church and two years later joined the order. He has come to St. Beuno's from teaching at Stonyhurst. Clement Barraud, a convert from French Huguenot Protestantism, studied at Stonyhurst before becoming a stained-glass artist. At nineteen, he joined the Jesuits and has taught at various Jesuit schools. Finally, there is Austin Marchant, thirty-one, a Londoner, who has taught at Stonyhurst and Liverpool.

Hopkins loves the Welsh language—"all vowels," which "run off the tongue like oil by diphthongs and by triphthongs"—as much as he loves the Welsh landscape, and hikes whenever he can about the countryside, through fields and cow paths and into the small country villages he finds everywhere. One Sunday, he strolls with William Kerr out past Maenefa, the high hill rising directly behind St. Beuno's, on to the next hill. It is all furze and heath, and from here one can "look round the whole country, up the valley towards Ruthin and down to the sea." The sky this day is leaden and "roped with cloud, and the earth in dead colours," and there's Snowdon, though once more clouds cover the top from view. In spite of which, all about him, here for the asking, he can feel the very "instress and charm" of this beautiful country.

One day, walking with Henry Kerr, he visits Brynbella and St. Asaph with its cathedral, looking more like a sizable parish church with its choir stalls and massive tower. He hears talk of Tremeirchion Cows and Cwm Calves, of Denbigh Cats and Caerwys Crows. With Bacon he visits the Cwm churchyard and the tiny gray knoll-top limestone chapel in the fields behind St. Beuno's, built by the Jesuits twenty-five years before. This is the Rock, "a great resort of hawks and owls," and one fine May day three years from now he will inscape a small hawk called a windhover circling the fields, capturing the mastery of the thing striding high there above him in stressed lines of rare and exquisite delicacy.

Another afternoon he walks with James Purbrick to Trefnant, "where we went into a pretty little new church built of the same limestone as St.

Beuno's" but adorned with mottled gray marble pillars. It is good work, also done by Hansom, who designed St. Beuno's itself a quarter of a century before, along with that massive new Jesuit church at Manchester he visited once en route to Stonyhurst. It is the same Hansom who—alas—seems to be less successfully restoring the cathedral at St. Asaph. James Purbrick, forty-six, and one year shy of ordination, is the elder brother of Edward Purbrick, the current Rector of Stonyhurst. The Purbricks are converts and retain much of their old Calvinist zeal and businesslike manner. It is Edward who will become the English Provincial who will have such a profound impact on the lives of hundreds of Jesuits, including Hopkins himself.

On September 11, the annual eight-day retreat begins. This year it is directed by Father Henry Coleridge, the first Jesuit Hopkins ever met. Hopkins begins by speaking with his Rector, the kindly, solicitous Father Jones, trying to discern if his vocation is to spend his days here, "laboring among the Welsh." He has already begun learning the language with an eye toward that goal, he explains, but with Father Jones's help, he sees soon enough that the real reason for wanting to stay is that he has found a home here in Wales. But, he realizes, working among the Welsh is not his primary reason for wanting to remain, and so he gives up the idea. He will, however, continue to learn the language, but for its own sake, and in spare moments. Yet even as he comes to this new resolve, the sense of a new music that has been welling up in him since his arrival likewise ceases, and suddenly he finds himself shedding "many tears, perhaps not wholly into the breast of God but with some unmanliness in them too."

Then, Hopkins thinks, maybe his life's work *should* be the conversion of Wales. But after weighing this decision by St. Ignatius's Rules of Election—in other words, taking the matter directly before God as his judge and what his purity of motive really is—he drops the matter. It is a fantasy, he realizes, a beautiful fantasy, of the priest/poet working among the Welsh country folk, administering poems and sacraments, but it is just that: a fantasy, unworkable, shallow, infantile even, and he breaks it. The work his Master has called him to lies elsewhere, he knows, though where has yet to be revealed to him. Still, his love of the Welsh landscape and its people and their melodious language will bear fruit in the new rhythms and vibrant possibilities he can feel being grafted to the English stock he has mastered in his life in London and at Oxford, along with his reading of Milton, Wordsworth, Keats, and Tennyson.

With the retreat over, three days of ordination ceremonies begin. On Friday and Saturday, minor orders are conferred, and on Sunday morning,

September 20, sixteen priests prostrate themselves before the altar to be ordained by the Bishop. These include five of their own along with eleven German Jesuits, exiles under the Falck Laws who have been preparing at Ditton for this day, among them many of the same men he had met at Stonyhurst the year before. As the choir sings the *Veni Creator Spiritus* and Holy Orders are administered, Hopkins breaks down again and weeps at what he is seeing. It is all, he understands, part of God's great mercy shown to him in these sixteen men being consecrated to God. The day before, he himself was one of seven who "received the tonsure and the four minor orders," the tonsure consisting of "five little snips but the bishop must have found even that a hard job." Not to be outdone, he has cut his own hair down to the scalp to show he takes this tonsuring seriously. The minor orders, he explains to his mother, "are those of Doorkeepers [Porters], Readers, Exorcists, and Acolytes: their use is almost obsolete." Now he will prepare himself for the three major steps—subdeacon, deacon, and priest—which he hopes to take in three years' time.

How he would have loved to labor for the conversion of Wales, he tells her. For, though he has vowed obedience to his order, "if people among us shew a zeal and aptitude for a particular work, say foreign missions, they can commonly get employed on them." The Welsh "are very civil and respectful but do not much come to us and those who are converted are for the most part not very stanch," for they are "much swayed by ridicule," and so keep their beliefs to themselves. Methodism is the popular religion here, and though they have "a turn for religion, especially what excites outward fervour, and more refinement and pious feeling than the English peasantry," they also have "less steadfastness and sincerity." Hopkins warms to these Celts, as he does to the Irish, and has always looked on himself as half Welsh. Besides which, there is the "great charm" of the landscape and the majesty of Snowdon and the surrounding mountains, which lift his spirits whenever he gazes on them. Yes, he knows what she and Papa will say: that the Welsh "have the reputation also of being covetous and immoral." No matter. He loves them, and would spend his days here if it was simply up to him.

He has given up the piano now, both because he fears he may be "musically deficient somewhere" and because the closest thing to a piano at St. Beuno's is "a grunting harmonium" in the church, badly out of tune. Just before leaving Roehampton, he'd read in the *Academy* John Tyndall's address to the British Association and found it both "interesting and eloquent, though it made me 'most mad.' It is not only that [Tyndall] looks back to an obscure origin, he looks forward with the same content to an obscure future—to be lost 'in the infinite azure of the past' (fine phrase by the by)." It is all of a piece with Darwinism, though he cannot bring himself to believe "that man is descended from any ape or ascidian or maggot or what not but only from the common ancestor of apes, the common ancestor of ascidians, the common ancestor of maggots," and that "these common ancestors, if lower animals, need not have been repulsive animals," though what "Darwin himself says about this," he admits, he does not know.

One of the six to receive minor orders with him is Brother Magri, "a Maltese, who has an interesting history," Hopkins notes. "It is said he was to be married, when he broke off the match, gave his property over to his brother, and fled to our noviceship." In any case, Hopkins is anxious to learn all he can about the Maltese language. It is mainly Arabic, Magri tells him, its roots going back to the Phoenician incursions into the region half a millennium and more before Christ. Another fascinating linguistic system for Hopkins to probe, then. But on a more somber note, he has just learned that one of his former pupils, Brother Richard O'Neill, has died at Stonyhurst of typhoid fever brought with him from Roehampton. There was, Hopkins remembers, "a sad wistful look" about poor Richard, "a sort of mark of early death stamped upon him," though he may simply be interpreting after the event.

Thursday, September 24: In the late afternoon, he walks with Joe Rickaby up the hill behind St. Beuno's. There is over the entire landscape what he calls "a beautiful liquid cast of blue," though in the valley below he can see the effects of modern industrialization in the "yellow and lurid" smoke rising from the Denbigh limekilns. He watches the early autumn sun set in a mix of "rosy juices and creams" among mare's-tail clouds turning slowly to gold, the ploughed fields resembling maroon-gray diamonds in the sodden afterglow.

And then—with the beginning of October—the school year begins. Father Luigi Tosi, a specialist in dogmatic theology, gives an inaugural address in Latin to the assembled theologians. "An interesting talk," Hopkins notes, but "a little amusing, shewing that the present persecution [of the Church] was *'omnium taeterrima.'*" The phrase, he remembers, means something like "the worst of all offenses," and is Horace's, who used it to describe Helen of Troy's erotic preferences, which led to the Trojan War. It is the sort of wordplay to delight a Latin scholar like Hopkins.

Each school morning, Monday to Saturday, begins with back-to-back classes, followed by an additional three classes on Monday, Wednesday, and Friday afternoons. Thursdays and Sundays are *ad libitum*—free days.

All lectures are given in medieval Church Latin. Each morning from now on, the community will rise at five-thirty to meditate for an hour on passages from the Bible or on points such as alms, humility, or obedience, as suggested by Father Jones. At seven there is mass, with communion reserved for Sundays and holy days of obligation. All meals are eaten in silence. During breakfast, the beadle announces the activities of the day, followed by readings from the Roman martyrology. The main meal is served at 1:00 p.m., with readings from either the *Lectio Divina* or the lives of saints. Then classes, followed at five by teas and cakes, and at five-thirty the theological disputations called Circles. At seven-thirty there is a light repast made up of leftovers, with readings from the Menology—narratives recording the heroism of those English and Continental religious men and women who suffered martyrdom, persecution, or exile since the time of Henry VIII. Monday nights there are tones—cadenced recitals of mock sermons to keep the Scholastics toned and ready. Otherwise, the men play cards, shoot billiards, read the newspapers or a book, or carry on light conversation until 9:00 p.m., when there are litanies and Benediction in chapel. By ten everyone is in bed, and candles and gaslights snuffed out. Because there is only one old, eagle-clawed bathtub in the entire house, and because there is a general lack of dependable hot water, only one hot bath per person per month is permitted.

Thursday, October 8. An ad libitum: A beautiful fall day, with snow on the mountain crests in the distance, including—most impressively—Mount Snowdon. Hopkins walks with Barraud the twelve miles to Holywell to bathe in the stone pool at St. Winefred's Well, after which they return to St. Beuno's filled with a deep joy. "The water in the well," Hopkins writes, is "as clear as *glass,* greenish like beryl or aquamarine, trembling at the surface with the force of the springs." And in fact he is almost mesmerized by the strength of the spring waters rising and steadying there like strands of rope. What is this, if not an image of God's grace flowing on and on, without end, there for the asking? "I steady as a water in a well," he will write the following year,

> to a poise, to a pane,
> But roped with, always, all the way down from the tall
> Fells or flanks of the voel, a vein
> Of the gospel proffer, a pressure, a principle, Christ's gift.

St. Winefred's Well is the most important of the many holy wells or pools to be found throughout all of Wales, in a tradition predating Christianity itself. In the Middle Ages this was already an important center for pilgrimages, a place where England's kings came to ask for special favors, a place so important to the popular imagination as to be left undamaged by the Puritan Roundheads, intent on destroying anything that smacked of Romanist superstition. The legend surrounding the well is one to which Hopkins will pay homage in several of his poems and dramatic pieces in the years to come, and goes like this: St. Beuno, who brought monasticism to northern Wales in the seventh century, restored his niece, St. Winefred, to life after she was decapitated by Caradoc, a psychopathic suitor whom she had rejected. The shrine itself is first mentioned as a place of pilgrimage as early as 1115, and from 1240 to the time of Henry VIII was part of Basingwerk Abbey. Henry V himself made a pilgrimage here before his victory at Agincourt, as did Edward IV before the Battle of Towton Moor. It is also likely that Henry VII made a secret visit to the site before the Battle of Bosworth in 1485. In fact, the stone building which roofs the well and which Hopkins has come to visit goes back to the 1480s, and was built for Henry VII's mother. Looking up, Hopkins can clearly see the King's coat of arms in bas-relief on the ceiling work.

Father Di Pietro, the pastor of the church attached to St. Winefred's Well, tells Hopkins that not long before "a young man from Liverpool, Arthur Kent . . . was cured of rupture in the water." No wonder "the strong unfailing flow of the water and the chain of cures from year to year all these centuries" should take hold of his imagination, then, and that he should feel a sense of wonder "at the bounty of God in one of His saints, the sensible thing so naturally and gracefully uttering the spiritual reason of its being . . . and the spring in place leading back the thoughts by its spring in time to its spring in eternity," so that back in his room at St. Beuno's, he can still feel "the stress and buoyancy and abundance of the water."

One Sunday in early November he walks out with William Splaine and catches sight of a "vast multitude of starlings making an unspeakable jangle." They have settled in the trees, and now row by row they rise as at a signal, looking "like a cloud of specks of black snuff or powder struck up from a brush or broom or shaken from a wig." Then round and round in sweeps like a whirlwind, "narrow black flakes hurling round," falling and rising again and again. All he needs is a gun, Splaine jokes, and it would surely "rain meat." But Hopkins's thoughts are elsewhere. How "full of enthusiasm and delight" the starlings must be, he thinks, each hearing the cries of the others "and stirring and cheering one another" on.

Baillie writes to tell him he has come down with consumption and has been spitting blood, so that he has had to leave his London law practice and has decided to recuperate by a leisurely sailing up the Nile and studying Egyptian hieroglyphs and archeology. It will be two years before Hopkins hears from him again. Then there are the actions of Prime Minister Gladstone, who has published his Expostulation with Catholics upon the Pope's Syllabus of Errors, themselves meant to combat the excesses of Modernism. In turn, Father Jones sees to it that time is taken at meals to have some of the responses to Gladstone read out, including those by Newman and Cardinal Manning.

By late November the weather has turned so cold, and the heating pipes have proved so useless, that the frugal Rector gives in and allows hearth fires in the Recreation Room and the new wing. There is also much rain and flooding in the Clwyd Valley, followed by heavy snow and frost through Christmas and New Year's. Then it grows milder again. There is even skating, though several of the seminarians manage to fall through the ice on the lake at Ilyn Helyg. In mid-January 1875, he writes his mother, thanking her for sending along clippings from the London newspapers, including two drawings by Arthur from the *Graphic*, though he finds fault with both of them.

Early in February, while taking his Welsh lesson with the elderly Susannah Jones—he is at the moment trying to translate *Cinderella* into Welsh— he asks her for the Welsh word for "fairy." *Cipenaper*, she tells him. Ah! *Kidnapper*, he realizes, "moulded . . . to give it a Welsh etymology." He tells her what he thinks fairies look like. About this high, he says, holding his hand out and his palm down. After all, he has been through all this before with the Brentford boys at Roehampton. But, Susannah insists, she really did see them once on the Holywell Road, on her way to her grandparents' farm. It was haymaking season, very early in the morning, when she caught sight of three little men wearing black frock coats and odd black caps, all dancing before her. "'Why she has seen the kippernappers,'" her grandmother says. And there—midsentence—Hopkins's journals come to an abrupt stop, and a window into his world is curtained forever.

But another opened. On February 20 he writes Bridges, who has finally written to him. "My dearest Bridges," he begins, "the above address [St. Beuno's] shews how impossible it is for me to execute your kind and welcome wish by calling at Maddox Street. There was never any moral difficulty, I could have got leave to spend more than an hour and a half with you, but a long crow-flight is between us." If only the invitation had come earlier, when he *was* at Roehampton, "what a pleasure it would have been and what a break in the routine of rhetoric, which I taught so badly and so painfully!" But now he is here, fenced in by waist-high snow drifts, "under the sign of Sts. Beuno and Asaph studying theology. . . ." And so, the correspondence with Bridges is up and going once again, after a year-long hiatus.

Hegel is what he has been reading, Bridges explains, in the original German—a language he mastered in his time in Dresden years before—and though Hopkins says he finds what the philosopher has to say interesting, he admits that much of it is beyond him. Besides, he has no time these days "to read even the English books about Hegel, much less the original." And he has very little German himself. Still, he could read Hegel if he wanted to. On the other hand, "it was with sorrow I put back Aristotle's *Metaphysics* in the library [at Stonyhurst] some time ago feeling that I could not read them now and so probably should never." And then there is Duns Scotus, whom he cares for "more even than Aristotle and more *pace tua* than a dozen Hegels." But that is his own predilection, not Bridges's. He is glad too to hear that Bridges is "nearer the top than the bottom of Hegel's . . . bottomless pit." He would have written sooner, he explains, but the pressure of his theological studies leaves him time for nothing else, in spite of which he has been trying to learn a little Welsh. Then there is Hebrew, which is another part of his curriculum. But at least the two men are speaking again.

There has been a flurry of attacks on the Jesuits featured in the *Quarterly Review,* stemming from those by a Dr. J. Huber writing from Berlin *(Der Jesuiten-Orden),* and these have caused Hopkins's mother some concern. And so he writes to assure her not to worry. The Jesuit *Month,* in fact, has picked up the gauntlet and has been responding with a number of essays, though the most recent article is rather "vague and dull," and so she can skip that one. Still, he is glad she has not "such an altogether unfavourable opinion of the Society" anymore. And if those "'very bad things' done by [the Jesuits] . . . are historical actions, such as the iniquitous charges of instigating the Gunpowder Plot, murdering Cardinal I forget who in China, or introducing brandy among the Canadian Indians, incredible and well shewn up as such charges are," he cannot speak to them, for he has "no time for the history of the Society or any other history." But if they are doctrines and moral teaching, she can rest easy, for he lives "in the midst of all that and I know or can easily ascertain what we do and have taught." Moreover, one of his fellow Jesuits here, "who furnished some of the matter for the *Month*'s reply, told me that it was impossible to believe in one writer's good faith, the misrepresentations and mistranslations were so flagrant."

So far there has been no real spring here in Wales, though now "things begin to look greener and the cuckoo may be heard." The latest of his colds is gone and he is fine except for his daily indigestion, "which makes study much harder and our shadowless glaring walks to my eyes very painful." He has also followed through on that "alleged cure of a case of rupture at St. Winefred's well," as he promised his father he would. In fact, he wrote the fellow, "enclosing a set of searching questions. . . . He answered the letters and promised answers to the questions in a week or so when he should have been able to tell more certainly the permanence of the cure." But the answers never came, and so the case itself cannot be deemed satisfactory. In the meantime, he has "heard of another cure having just been worked in London by the moss or water" of St. Winefred's, and promises to inquire into that case. And now, he adds, there are new religious persecutions going on, this time in Poland, though one would never know it from the papers, "worse than anything that wd. have been thought possible in this century." Cossacks have stormed into the villages, where the peasantry "are driven by the knout to the Greek Orthodox Church churches," and when they refuse, "they are scourged to blood, then put into the hospital till their wounds are healed sufficiently for them to be flogged again." It is another instance of the persecution of the Church going on continually round the world.

Six weeks later, he writes his mother again to thank her for the bottled medicine, "which came packed in so much sawdust that it will serve to sweep my room for weeks." The medicine, which tastes like "death and cremation," he is sure must therefore prove effective. Examinations are almost upon him now. He also asks to be remembered to Mr. Manley and to Watson—these are the Watsons of Shooter's Hill, whom he will remember in a poem two years on—"and all Christen soules." In July, he passes his examinations in moral and dogmatic theology, and then the holidays are upon them.

July 22, 1875: Provincial's Day, and Father Gallwey comes up from London to look in on his theologians. Following dinner, the community gathers at the Little Rock on the hill behind St. Beuno's to spend an evening singing and listening to songs. For the occasion, Hopkins composes a comic song called "Consule Jones," modeling it after a Welsh air named for another Jones—"Sweet Jenny Jones," or (in Welsh) "Cader Idris." Traditional music, then, a mixture of Irish and Welsh (like Father Jones himself), and Hopkins writes the lyrics to be sung in the person and voice of the beadle at Beuno's, Peter Prestage, gifted with a fine tenor voice. There is a tradition among the

Jesuits of taking off on popular tunes and then adding their own lyrics in order to make palpable hits on their own, as Father Gallwey had done at Roehampton several years earlier. And so Hopkins chooses a rollicking four-beat measure in 3/4 time, with some wonderfully wild rhymes—*Beuno's* and *my nose, merits* and *ferrets, Sisyphus / busy fuss, turban'd / serpent, promise I'll / domicile.* And of course there are the outrageous Latin puns, endemic to the Hopkins clan: *sinecure* with *sine qua non,* along with assorted inside jokes about graces and merits and tones.

Of the thirty-eight theologians at St. Beuno's at the moment—English, Irish, Scots, and North American—Hopkins manages to cram in twenty of them in the poem's forty-eight lines. As beadle, the speaker in the poem notes, he has made a point of watching the goings and comings of those under his charge. There's Barraud, warbling snatches of tunes as well as trying out practice sermons before the community in his French accent, and Reeve, out hunting rabbits with his ferrets, and Bacon, checkmating his American chess mate while others read the papers or novels, or banter with each other before litanies begin. And Scoles, who hands out scones and cakes to the Welsh children in the neighborhood—locally known as *Taffies*—as he teaches them catechism. And Clayton, already a capable administrator (he will be named English Provincial in the last year of Hopkins's life), a Sisyphus forever overseeing the construction of paths through the property in a project seemingly without end, while others do the actual backbreaking spadework.

Murphy, too, who has already acquired a reputation for his hell and damnation sermons. And Hayes, who seems forever to be scribbling in one of his diaries. And Lund, in protective netting, gathering sweet honey from the beehives for the community. And the gentle Lapasteur, who would rather die than gossip, rendered comically here as the serpent in St. Beuno's garden, dropping calumnies left and right. And capable Tom Rigby from Preston, who will be ordained in September, then do his Tertianship, and return to St. Beuno's in the autumn of '77 as the new Rector, just as Hopkins is leaving. And of course the Kerr and Splaine brothers, Hopkins switching their identities, the two retiring brothers reinvented now as swaggering cavalrymen strutting about the fields as they read their breviaries or tell their beads.

Some fun, too, at the expense of the heating system at St. Beuno's, with those "pipes of affliction" conveying "lukewarm water of affliction" to some of the rooms (especially those in the Tower Hamlets, where, when the west wind howls, the heat climbs to a balmy 46° Fahrenheit), while the more fortunate souls have working fireplaces in their rooms. And, finally, a gentle poke at Father Jones, who had thought to save money by forbidding fires in the Recreation Room, until the genteel Hop, with his medical knowledge, pointed out to him how much more expensive it would be if the community came down with colds, chilblains, or worse. "Such are my thoughts of our folk and our domicile," he ends,

> Couched in plain language not meant to be rude;
> And having thus been as good as my promise I'll
> Keep you no longer, and here I'll conclude.

"He was perhaps the most popular man in the house," Joe Rickaby would remember forty years after Hopkins was gone. "Superiors and equals, everybody liked him. We laughed at him a good deal, but he took it good-humouredly, and joined in the amusement."

In early August, a week after Hopkins turns thirty-one, the seminarians head out for their Villa at Barmouth in the first of two groups, Hopkins being among those in the latter, scheduled from August 16 to the 30th. But his vacation is cut short, and he is required to stay behind to help Father Jones, so that he arrives at Barmouth a week late. In mid-September, the annual eight-day retreat is held, followed again by ordinations. There are twenty-five this year, with a group of Capuchins from the monastery at Pantasaph joining the Jesuits, and it turns out to be the largest number of Roman Catholic priests ordained together in Great Britain since the Reformation. And then it is good-bye to many of those he has grown fond of, including the Kerrs and the Splaines and Rigby, as they begin new assignments, and yet another group of Jesuits arrives to begin their theology studies in the great unending round, and Hopkins is appointed Beadle of Moral Theology. At the beginning of October, classes again, mornings and afternoons, with fires once more allowed in those rooms that can accommodate them, and the whining of afflicted steampipes, and heavy snows and cold rains from early November on, as another long hard winter moves in.

On Friday evening, December 3, the Feast of St. Francis Xavier—one of the original Company of Jesus and a missionary to the Far East—Hopkins gives a sermon at dinner. Perhaps included in it is a recitation of two occasional pieces, translations he has made of *O Deus, Ego amo te*, a Latin poem attributed then to Xavier himself. "Nid, am I Ti fy ngwared i," Hopkins's Welsh translation begins,

> *Y'th garaf, Duw, yn lan,*
> *Nac, am mai'r rhai na'th garant Di,*
> *Y berni am fyth I dan . . .*

And his English version:

> O God, I love thee, I love thee—
> Not out of hope of heaven for me
> Nor fearing not to love and be
> In the everlasting burning.
> Thou, thou, my Jesus, after me
> Didst reach thine arms out dying,
> For my sake sufferedst nails and lance,
> Mocked and marred countenance,
> Sorrows passing number,
> Sweat and care and cumber,
> Yes and death, and this for me,
> And thou couldst see me sinning . . .

"Ad lib[itum] sermon at dinner by Mr. G. Hopkins," the beadle notes. Then—by way of a quiet joke: *"Sermon purely Ab Lib."* What no one yet sees, not even Hopkins, is that the iron is hot, and that after all this time of quiet preparation—the journals, the classes he has given in rhetoric at Roehampton, the years of study and prayer and meditation—he is at last ready to strike the iron in the forging fire. The Spirit, that "arch and original Breath," the "strong spur, live and lancing like the blowpipe flame," is about to descend in darkness and breathe mercifully on a young Jesuit, and English poetry will never after be the same for it.

Wednesday evening, December 8: Hopkins picks up a copy of *The Times* and on page five learns that the day before—the eve of the Feast of the Immaculate Conception—a half-swamped lifeboat carrying three men had come ashore from the North German steamer *Deutschland,* sailing from Bremen bound for New York. After thirty-eight hours in the flint-flaked icy waters off the Kentish coast, two of the three are dead, and the third—Quartermaster Beck August or August Beck, it is not clear—is half frozen and nearly incoherent after his ordeal. About one hundred fifty passengers were aboard the steamship when it ran aground on the Kentish Knock, and he thinks the boat may have already split in half. Everyone out there, in fact, may already be dead.

Beneath that story, further news, this time from a correspondent at the Harwich rescue station. The *Deutschland,* under Captain Brickenstein, with a boatload of emigrants, set sail from the North German port of Bremen on Sunday evening, December 5, in good weather, but, having been caught in a blinding northeaster, grounded itself off the English coast the following morning around 5:00 a.m. Hopkins knows this storm, knows what it is capable of, because St. Beuno's has already felt its punishing force all day Monday as it traveled east across England, making it almost impossible to get about his part of Wales as well. Some of the crew and passengers have come ashore at Harwich aboard the tug *Liverpool* and are now under the care of a Mr. Oliver John Williams, the North German Consul at Harwich. Already some fifty crew and passengers are known to have drowned. Among the cabin passengers missing are Ludwig Heerman, J. Grossmann, Maria Forster, Emil Hack, Bertha Fundling, five nuns, Procoopi Kadolkoff, and O. Lundgren. Five nuns—all nameless.

Then more information in the papers as the hours tick by, the names, like the victims themselves, scattered and mangled. On the night of December 6, after no sign of rescue boats coming to their aid, many—at the captain's urging—took to the ship's rigging (the *Deutschland* being a combination steamship and sailing vessel) and lost consciousness, or finally gave up and let go the ropes, to hit the deck below or be pulled out to sea. Others chose to stay below deck in their cabins or in the dining room, and were drowned there as the waves poured into the hold. Among the missing are Barbara Hilkenschmidt, Henrico Tassbender, Lorbela Reenkober, Aurea Radjura, and Brigella Dambard. In time these will metamorphose into the five lost nuns: Barbara Hultenschmidt, Henrica Fassbender, Norberta Reinkober, Aurea Badziura, and Brigitta Damhorst.

Saturday, December 11: On page seven of *The Times,* the following passage catches Hopkins's eye: "The bodies of the four German nuns were removed today for interment at a convent of the Franciscan order, to which they belonged, near Stratford." Stratford: where Hopkins was born, the place he calls his first home. Five nuns lost from a convent in Westphalia. And then, further down the page, this:

Five German nuns, [four of] whose bodies are now in the dead-house here, clasped hands and were drowned together, the chief sister, a gaunt woman 6 ft. high, calling out loudly and often "O Christ, come quickly!" till the end came. The shrieks and sobbing of women and children are described by the survivors as agonizing. One brave sailor, who was safe in the rigging, went down to try and save a child or woman who was drowning on deck. He was secured by a rope to the rigging, but a wave dashed him against the bulwarks, and when daylight dawned his head- less body, detained by the rope, was seen swaying to and fro with the waves. In the dreadful excitement of these hours one man hung himself behind the wheelhouse, another hacked at his wrist with a knife, hoping to die a comparatively painless death by bleeding. It was nearly eight o'clock before the tide and sea abated, and the survivors could venture to go on deck. At half past ten o'clock [Tuesday morning, December 7] the tugboat [*Liverpool*] from Harwich came alongside and brought all away without further accident.

The following Monday, the four Franciscan Sisters whose bodies have been reclaimed, Daughters of the Sacred Hearts of Jesus and Mary, from the convent at Salzkotten, Germany, exiled by Bismarck's anti-Catholic Falck Laws, and laid out in white habits, are waked in Stratford. Then, fol- lowing a solemn Requiem Mass officiated over by Cardinal Manning, who also gives the eulogy, they are buried side by side in St. Patrick's Catholic Cemetery, Leytonstone, Sister Fassbender's body having been irrevocably claimed by the sea.

"You ask, do I write verse myself," Hopkins will explain three years later, when the poem he begins writing now has long been composed and won- dered at and rejected:

What I had written I burnt before I became a Jesuit and resolved to write no more, as not belonging to my profession, unless it were by the wish of my superiors; so for seven years I wrote nothing but two or three little presentation pieces which occasion called for. But when in the winter of '75 the *Deutschland* was wrecked in the mouth of the Thames and five Franciscan nuns, exiles from Germany by the Falck Laws, aboard of her were drowned I was affected by the account and happening to say so to my rector he said that he wished someone would write a poem on the subject. On this hint I set to work and, though my hand was out at first, produced one.

For several years, he has had "the echo of a new rhythm" haunting his ear, which now he realizes "on paper." It is sprung rhythm he is speaking of here, a rhythm generated by "scanning by accents or stresses alone, without any account of the number of syllables, so that a foot may be one strong syllable or it may be many light and one strong."

Perhaps it was on the evening of December 11 that Father Jones saw Hopkins reading the account of the *Deutschland* disaster and, seeing how moved he was by what he'd read there (and knowing that Hopkins had composed "Consule Jones" and other occasional pieces), did mention in passing—and to comfort the man—that it might be nice if someone wrote a poem on the subject, especially in light of the witness the tall nun had given in her extremity. Whatever hint Jones did drop, it is enough for Hopkins, who has been chaffing for years now for just such a chance to release himself from his self-imposed exile and begin composing again.

And so he begins writing about the disaster itself, which he will soon cross-hybridize with the celebratory odes reminiscent of Pindar and Wordsworth's *Intimations Ode* and the pastoral elegy in the tradition of Milton's *Lycidas*. The *Deutschland* "would be more generally interesting if there were more wreck and less discourse," he will later tell Bridges to appease him, "but still it is an ode and not primarily a narrative. There is some narrative in Pindar but the principal business is lyrical." And so with the *Deutschland*. Thirty-five eight-line stanzas of varying line length, the poem divided into two parts: Part the First, ten stanzas long, focusing on the self's encounter with the mystery of God's workings; Part the Second, two and a half times as long again, focusing on the nuns' encounter with that same mystery: Christ, *Ipse*, the only One. A cry on the part of one witness (the tall nun in her extremity) to another witness (a thirty-one-year-old Catholic convert and Jesuit, preparing for the priesthood) pleading with Christ to come and take possession once again of his and all English hearts, including the hearts of those who hear his voice in these lines.

The stanzas themselves, with their triple rhymes—*ababcbca*—form a movement out from the Creator in the unfolding of the Great Procession, and then back in the great return, transfigured now, the same and yet different, alpha to alpha, *aaa: Bremen / women / them in.* Like Dante at the beginning of the *Divine Comedy,* feeling his way, but eager to announce a new idiom and rhythm and instress in the accentual stress of the lines, the stress of his heart, the electrical charge of the compound epithets and the verbs—*sailed, bound, tell, drowned, vault, reeve, sweeps, hurling, spins, unchilding, unfathering:* a heart in hiding addressing the Almighty, the Father, Christ, the Pentecostal Spirit, the outriding stress and the mercy. Where has this tapped energy come from? How long has it lain dormant, waiting for this moment to be released, like a spring shower after a long winter?

And so he begins with *The Times* shipping news and the account—with illustrations—in the *Illustrated London News,* informed now by the stress and inscape of what he can discern from the shock and chaos of the disaster:

> Into the snows she sweeps,
>   Hurling the haven behind,
> The Deutschland, on Sunday; and so the sky keeps,
>   For the infinite air is unkind,
> And the sea flint-flake, black-backed in the regular blow,
> Sitting Eastnortheast, in cursed quarter, the wind;
>   Wiry and white-fiery and whirlwind-swivellèd snow
> Spins to the widow-making unchilding unfathering deeps.

What was it like, Hopkins wonders, evoking the waves of that shock night, as if Fate itself had taken possession of the ship's course? What was it like to feel the ship grind to a halt on a smother of sand, the propeller sheering off in the darkness, leaving the stunned passengers to the whims of the waves?

> ... Hope was twelve hours gone;
>   And frightful a nightfall folded rueful a day
> Nor rescue, only rocket and lightship, shone,
>   And lives at last were washing away:
> To the shrouds they took,—they shook in the hurling and horrible
>   airs.

What can any of us do in the extremity of such situations, when even the bravest perish, like that sailor in the safe rigging above, like Perseus looking down on Andromeda, like the hero in ten thousand novels who risks all to save women and children in distress, roping himself and rappelling down, down ... only to be smashed against the ship's hull in a split second, end of story, for all his "dreadnought breast and braids of thew"? No match finally for the fury of such a storm, the sailor's headless body will dangle like a cat's plaything from a string, like a bell swinging helplessly back and forth in the cobbled foam-fleece, ticking off the meaningless minutes and hours. And if the self-reliant hero of literature can be snuffed out like that, amid the cries and confusion of women and children, so of course can any of us:

> One stirred from the rigging to save
>   The wild woman-kind below,
>   With a rope's end round the man, handy and brave—
>   He was pitched to his death at a blow,
> For all his dreadnought breast and braids of thew:
> They could tell him for hours, dandled the to and the fro
>   Through the cobbled foam-fleece. . . .

> . . . Night roared, with the heart-break hearing a heart-broke
>   rabble,
> The woman's wailing, the crying of child without check—
>   Till a lioness arose breasting the babble,
> A prophetess towered in the tumult, a virginal tongue told.

A virginal tongue told. It is not only the cry in the wilderness storm of the tall nun, but Hopkins's cry too in the uttering of these lines—the male and female of it—a voice calling out above the chaos, startling passenger and reader alike. *O Christ, Christ, come quickly!* Were the words a prayer, he asks, or a cry of terror and helplessness? A sudden seeing into the heart of the meaning of the storm, or an oath uttered in extremity? What in God's name did she mean? How read the storm, the reality, you, here, "Away in the loveable west, / On a pastoral forehead of Wales" at St. Beuno's, reading dogmatic theology and Christology and the rest, not even aware of the suffering these people and this lioness fronting forked lightning endured, until the ordeal was over, Christ's passion and death—and rebirth—enacted once again down the long history of the ages:

> I was under a roof here, I was at rest,
>   And they the prey of the gales;
>   She to the black-about air, to the breaker, the thickly
> Falling flakes, to the throng that catches and quails
>   Was calling "O Chríst, Chríst, come quíckly" . . .

None escapes death, we know, we know. And yet, don't we put off that realization again and again? In spite of which—one way or the other—

swiftly or by a long-drawn-out process, whether by sword or railroad accident, flame or fang or flood, death the horseman, death on drum must
come. Fred Walker's mower is here, scything through the summer grass
cringing and falling away, much as our own blear share must come. "Thou
mastering me / God!" Part the First begins, with the emphasis where Hopkins
knows it needs to be—not on the self, but on the Creator, the Master, *Ipse*,

> giver of breath and bread;
>   World's strand, sway of the sea;
>   Lord of living and dead;
>   Thou hast bóund bónes and véins in me, fástened me flésh,
>   And áfter it álmost únmade, what with dréad,
>   Thy doing: and dost thou touch me afresh?
>   Óver agáin I feél thy finger and fínd thée.

Again and again we are created and re-created and so touched afresh
and yet again afresh. As at Horsham, or on that first retreat with Father
Coleridge, or again at Roehampton when he wondered if indeed he had a
religious calling. And now, here again, tears falling as he meditates on the
deaths of his sisters in faith, exiles like the Jesuits at Ditton or in southern
France, exiles like himself from his own family, from friends, from his own
first world. "I did say yes," he acknowledges again now in the prelude to his
ode, the shipwreck of himself, barely standing on the foundering deck of
himself, the terror of it, the sense of falling as from a great height. Say it, say
now what you said then in the chaos of your own wrestling with God:

> I did say yes
>   O at líghtning and láshed ród;
>   Thou heardst me truer than tongue confess
>   Thy terror, O Christ, O God;
>   Thou knówest the wálls, áltar and hóur and níght:
>   The swoon of a heart that the sweep and the hurl of thee trod
>   Hárd dówn with a horror of height:
>   And the midriff astrain with leaning of, laced with fire of stress.

The terror of holding back, of equivocating, of pretending not to hear
when it becomes clear what one must do, in spite of the cost, in spite of
knowing that peace will come for him in no other way, of the heart's fleeing
not *from* but *into* the heart of the Host: the total surrender of self as Christ

surrendered himself in that splendid kenotic gesture of his suffering and death, the King become Servant of Servants for mankind. And the freedom and peace that came with that surrender, as he came home like the carrier pigeon, like the dove, at last. To flash, then, from the torment of separation and the hell within to the flame of Love itself. What, after all, am I, he asks, but "soft sift / In an hourglass," a smother of sand falling away toward my inevitable end, the restless mind forever shuttling, mined with a motion that runs out and out and out? And yet that other image of St. Winefred's Well, the clear waters flowing up like unstinting grace year after year after year from the depths of the surrounding Welsh voels continually feeding the thirsty, refreshing them, God's great, unstinting, ever fresh bounty. And the self,

> at the wall
> Fast, but mined with a motion, a drift,
> And it crowds and it combs to the fall;
> I stéady as a wáter in a wéll, to a poíse, to a páne,
> But roped with, always, all the way down from the tall
> Fells or flanks of the voel, a vein
> Of the góspel próffer, a préssure, a prínciple, Chríst's gíft.

And for a long moment we are outside the stress of history and in another rhythm altogether—God's time, aeonic time, the time of the stars, of the sublimity of thunder, the beauty of the "dappled-with-damson west," God's infinitely pied beauty, kept constantly in being, and constantly refreshed. God there for the asking, if we will but ask, His mystery instressed and stressed upon us, if we will but look hard enough:

> I kiss my hand
> To the stars, lovely-asunder
> Starlight, wafting him out of it; and
> Glow, glory in thunder;
> Kiss my hand to the dappled-with-damson west:
> Since, thóugh he is únder the wórld's spléndour and wónder,
> His mýstery múst be instréssed, stressed;
> For I greet him the days I meet him, and bless when I understand.

The theology of it, the Incarnational insight, stressed in upon the poet as now, in this renewal of Christ's emptying of himself for his beloved, wounded human creatures. "Not out of his bliss / Springs the stress felt," Hopkins has come to understand, but with the realization of our own contingency, our radical creatureliness, where every intake of air is—finally—a gift. The truth is that when we are comfortable we look elsewhere, to this world, to our well-laid plans for our own futures, as if those futures were assured us. "Nor first from heaven (and few know this) / Swings the stroke dealt," by some special intervention, some *Deus ex machina*. No, the fact is that God's infinite instress "rides time like riding a river / (And here the faithful waver, the faithless fable and miss)." It is the Word made flesh, entering into and redeeming time, Christ's Great Sacrifice, the ramifications of his radical self-emptying and humility, not grasping after what was his by right, but returning everything to the Father in an act of total self-emptying, even unto a criminal's death on a cross. But only to those who have been there, only to those who have experienced what it means to suffer, to be stripped naked, to be at bay, like the hart/heart dogged by doubts, despair, and hard at bay. The bay. Yes, the ocean, but the baying of the hounds of hell closing in on us, as must happen to each of us at some point in our lives:

> We lash with the best or worst
> Word last! How a lush-kept plush-capped sloe
> Will, mouthed to flesh-burst,
> Gush!—flush the man, the being with it, sour or sweet,
> Brim, in a flásh, fúll!—Híther then, lást or fírst,
> To hero of Calvary, Christ's feet—
> Never ask if méaning it, wánting it, wárned of it—mén gó.

"The lush-kept, plush-capped sloe," fruit of the blackthorn, strange fruit indeed, sweetness eked out from thorns, like the thorns that crowned the head of the Messiah King. It all comes down to that final yes or no, he has learned. Christ as comfort or Christ as curse, Christ as our bitterness or Christ as our sweetness, then, at the hour of our death: a no or a yes in acknowledging the rude rood, the cross. Death as annihilation, or death as our return to God, whether we mean to, or want to. For we have been warned of it, as the nun seems to have realized in the hour of her death, calling for Christ to come, and come quickly. "Wring thy rebel," Hopkins cries out, and ring thy rebel with the bell of the nun's cry tolling, with the ringing of these lines wrung from him, rebellious at heart like all human beings, but "dogged in den" too, trapped, cornered, with no way out, with a stark yes or no at the end. Yes, I will. Or no, *non serviam*. But he has said yes, at what cost only he and God know. And yet, with the surrendering of his own will, his own way of doing things, comes too a great relief, "Beyond saying sweet, past telling of tongue." For, he has learned, God is both

> lightning and love, I found it, a winter and warm;
>   Father and fondler of heart thou hast wrung:
> Hast thy dark descending and most art merciful then.

And whether You come, Lord, at once, like a lightning flash or a trumpet crash, unmistakably, in the unshapeable shock night of it, as you came to Paul on the road to Damascus, murder in his heart, sure that what he was doing was right, or whether you come as you did to St. Augustine (Make me yours, O Lord . . . but, ah!, not yet), melting the heart with "a lingering-out sweet skill," however you come, Lord, come—*maranatha*—"Make mercy in all of us, out of us all / Mastery, but be adored, but be adored King."

Midway through *The Wreck of the Deutschland*, in the 18th stanza, the very heart of the poem, there is a striking confessional moment as the meaning of the nun's cry comes home to the poet. Ah, to be caught weeping like this in the midst of his song, he chides himself. But if he has addressed himself to God, he turns now to his own self-willed heart, this once at least uttering the truth:

> Ah, touched in your bower of bone
>   Are you! turned for an exquisite smart,
> Have you! make words break from me here all alone,
>   Do you!—móther of béing in me, héart.
> O unteachably after evil, but uttering truth,
>   Why, tears! is it? tears; such a melting, a madrigal start!
>   Never-eldering revel and river of youth,
> What can it be, this glee? the good you have there of your own?

And who has called him to himself like this? Why, a woman, a nun, a Sister *and our sister*, of all those on board the only one who cried out in the darkness as the seas crashed over the decks, freezing and blinding her along with the others, this virginal tongue calling after her Master, seeing in the midst of the terror the same Christ who once, in a fishing boat on the Sea of Galilee, awoke to calm the raging tempest.

Ah, who was this woman, this prophet, this lioness braving the storm?

he wonders. One of five German nuns, exiled by Bismarck's Second Reich. From Eisleben in the Deutschland, near where St. Gertrude, the Benedictine nun and mystic, died, and where Martin Luther, leading voice of the Protestant Reformation and beast of Dante's waste wood, was born:

> She was first of a five and came
> Of a coifèd sisterhood.
> (O Deutschland, double a desperate name!
> O wórld wíde of its góod! . . .
>
> Loathed for a love men knew in them,
> Banned by the land of their birth,
> Rhíne refúsed them, Thámes would ruín them;
> Surf, snow, river and earth
> Gnashed: but thou art above, thou Orion of light;
> Thy unchancelling poising palms were weighing the worth,
> Thou mártyr-máster: in thý síght
> Storm flákes were scróll-leaved flówers, lily shówers—sweet héaven
> was astréw in them.

Five nuns, all daughters of Francis of Assisi, the first to bear the stigmata, the marks of Christ's wounds, in his own hands and feet and breast, manifesting in their own deaths the reality of Christ's passion and death all over again, here, now, in England, those nail and lance marks etched into Love itself, marks freely chosen and accepted by the Lamb of God, the perfect sacrifice, our lovescape, "Before-time-taken, dearest prizèd and priced," stressed in upon Hopkins and—he would have it—on the reader as well.

"The majesty! what did she mean?" he wonders. And so he calls on the Spirit for inspiration, begging him to "Breathe, arch and original Breath." Was it love in her for Christ, the desire to imitate his sufferings? No, not at that moment facing the sublime terror of it all. "Or is it that she críed for the crówn thén, / The keener to come at the comfort for feeling the combating keen?" Again, no. Rather, we ask for relief, even death, when we most feel like tired draft horses repeating endlessly the daily grind of things. But let the "electrical horror" of imminent death ambush us, and we would willingly go back to the Sisyphean "jading and jar of the cart." Anything rather than death. It is one thing to meditate on the passion in our rooms or in a church pew, and quite another to suddenly feel the roiling deck going under in the burl "and beat of endragonèd seas." Then what was it? he asks, as now the very syntax itself, under the strain, breaks down:

> But how shall I . . . make me room there;
> Reach me a . . . Fancy, come faster—
> Strike you the sight of it? look at it loom there,
>   Thing that she . . .

And then the answer in the consoling presence of "the Master / *Ipse*, the only one, Christ, King, Head." For only he can "cure the extremity where he had cast her," as Christ had cured his own extremity only in surrendering to Him. Enough. The rest is residuary, cast-off, the shucked seed:

> Do, deal, lord it with living and dead;
> Let him ride, her pride, in his triumph, despatch and have done
>   with his doom there.

A full-blown beacon of light, then, in the midst of the storm, comforting passenger and crew alike, comforting Hopkins, who in turn wishes to comfort his readers with news of this "lovely-felicitous Providence," this God who so passionately cares, this

> . . . Fínger of a ténder of, O of a féathery délicacy, the bréast of the
>   Maiden could obey so, be a bell to, ring óf it, and
> Stártle the poor shéep back!

And is the shipwreck then a harvest? Has it all turned out a divine comedy after all, as in Shakespeare's *Tempest*, where the poet-magician Prospero turns the tempest-tossed ship into a harvest of grain, where all manner of thing shall be well? How subtle this Craftsman is after all, Hopkins sees, how extraordinary this "master of the tides, / Of the Yore-flood, of the year's fall," quenching the ever restive, ever-searching "motionable mind," the buzzing brain "mined with a motion," at rest for a moment now in the very "Ground of being, and granite of it." Ah, You, You "past all / Grasp God," You "throned behind / Death with a sovereignty that heeds but hides, bodes but abides"—and the rhyming goes on right into the next stanza—

> With a mércy that oútrídes
> The all of water, an ark

> For the lístener; for the língerer with a lóve glídes
>   Lówer than déath and the dárk;
> A véin for the vísiting of the pást-prayer, pént in príson,
> The-last-breath penitent spirits—the uttermost mark
>   Our passion-plungèd giant risen,
> The Christ of the Father compassionate, fetched in the storm of his
>   strides.

The all-merciful eastering Christ, "Our passion-plungèd giant risen," whom the nun and the poet and so many others have called upon in their extremity—waiting for anyone, even in the very last moment of life, who asks for mercy to be shown her or him, as Christ, the harrower of hell, reaches out now to take them by the hand, like the thief on the cross stealing heaven at the last moment with a simple word: Christ, Master, the only One, "fetched in the storm of his strides." Burn now, the poet begs Christ, each day born anew to the world, this "Miracle-in-Mary-of-flame" conceived and reconceived again and again, come back once more, "royally reclaiming his own," like the spring rains which harbinge each year's eastering. And then, at the last, he addresses the nun herself, England's saint, England's *genius loci*, "at our door / Drowned, and among our shoals," asking her to remember us as we go our individual journeys toward "the heaven-haven of the reward."

Finally, Hopkins turns to us his audience, his congregation: "Our King back," he pleads, "Oh, upon English souls!" For, really, that is what he hopes for from his poem more than anything, for poetry *does* make something happen: Christ's Real Presence in Liverpool and Manchester and Oxford, London and Wales, our Pentecostal Fire, our King, our Lord:

> . . . Let him éaster in us, be a dáyspring to the dímness of us, be
>   a crímson-cresseted east,
> More bríghtening her, ráre-dear Brítain, as his réign rólls,
>   Príde, rose, prínce, hero of us, hígh-príest,
> Our héarts' charity's héarth's fíre, our thóughts' chivalry's thróng's
>   Lórd.

Christmas Eve: Alone in his room, Hopkins writes his mother in the hours leading up to midnight mass and the coming of the King into the world once more. He thanks her first for sending him the newspaper clippings, though he mildly chides her for two oversights: for sending two duplicates and for forgetting to include "the most interesting piece of all, the account of the actual shipwreck." He is already at work "writing something on this wreck," he tells her, "which may perhaps appear [in print] but it depends on how I am speeded." For reasons he does not go into—that will be the poem's domain and its *raison d'être*—the account of the disaster "made a deep impression on me, more than any other wreck or accident I ever read of."

Christmas night, the community gathers in the Recreation Room to play the latest fad coming out of the United States: a spelling bee. That night Clarke wins, when his nearest opponent mistakes "ingenious" for "ingenuous." Other words which fell the scholastics are: "hiccough," "chrisom cloth," "yolk" (not yoke), "ate" (not eight), "rosery" (a bed of roses, and not the word for beads), and—lastly—"allegiance," the word by which Hopkins himself was "disgracefully felled." *Allegiance.* But then a word like "ceiling," which all his life he will insist on spelling "cieling," would have done the trick as well. The gaslight in his frigid room has been guttering and flickering the whole time he has been writing, until he has almost ceased noticing it anymore. True, the fellow in the next room has a new gaslight, "lucky for him: it does not perceptibly lessen my light." On the other hand, the poor man has also "lost eight teeth." A wry note in a dark time filled with inexorable graces, including the sudden, unexplained, hundredfold resurrection of his precious, long-silenced poetic gift.

Chapter 9

The Grandeur of God:
Wales, 1876–1877

Shrove Tuesday, February 22, 1876: A late winter's blandyke, and Hopkins sets out with a group of scholastics for Moel Fammau—Mother of Mountains—"the highest of the hills bounding the valley," he tells his mother, "and distant as the crow flies about nine miles. There stands on it what remains of the Jubilee Tower erected in honour of George III's 50th year of royalty [1810], an ugly and trumpery construction, makebelievemassive but so frail that it was blown over by the gale that wrecked the *Royal Charter*"—he is thinking of another shipwreck, this one a vessel off the Anglesey coast on her way to Liverpool in October 1859, with the loss of all four hundred and fifty aboard. Man will build his Babels, by whatever name he calls them, each trying to outdo the last. And now the remains of a dead king's make-believe tower merely "cumbers the hilltop and interrupts the view." But as he hikes along the hills toward the moel, he thinks: nothing can beat God's grandeur, as here, in the Vale of Clwyd, for charm. Ah, nothing!

Even on a day like today, with the sky overcast and threatening. Look, look at the sea, he thinks, and the "distant hills brimmed with purple, clouds trailing low, the landscape clear but sober, the valley . . . so verdant," and yet highlighted with a "pale blush-colour from the many red sandstone fresh-ploughed fields." He and Clarke, along with two other Jesuits, all strong hikers, are the only ones to actually make it to the top. Coming down, the day turns clear and blue and beautiful. "Looking up along a white churchtower," he notes, "I caught a lovely sight—a flock of seagulls wheeling and sailing high up in the air, sparkles of white as bright as snowballs in the vivid blue." As later he will catch in the morning's eastering spring light a windhover, "morning's minion" a veritable "king/dom of daylight's dauphin," drawn by the dappled dawn, and etched out damascenelike against a kaleidoscopic shower of rose-purple lights.

But now, on that same winter's evening, the community gathers in the

Recreation Room to merrily mouth glees and listen to excerpts from Shakespeare, Dickens, and George Eliot, and then match wits for round two of
the new-fangled spelling bee. This time Hopkins manages to hold his own.
"I am proud to say that I am the winner of a spellingbee," he writes his
mother. "We sat down some dozen or score [theologians] and my last rival
was despatched by *meddler*," when the homonym *medlar* was meant. Ho-
mophonic puns run riot wherever Jesuits are gathered, it seems, especially
in spelling bees. To make things more interesting, Father Jones has offered
a prize of five shillings—with which prize money Hopkins plans to buy the
Complete Works of Goronwy Owen "or some other great Welsh poet." The
spelling bee, after all, "was conducted on a good principle: short and, usually,
common words were asked and this was found sufficient to behead any ordinary man in a few rounds, taking confusion and slips into account, for the
spellingbee," he can't help punning, "puts a bee into most people's bonnet."

Monday, June 12: He is one of two defendants in one of the practice disputations carried out each term by the theologians. The subject this time is
taken from the *De Sacramentis:* on the Nature of the Sacraments. Like the
other contenders, he must explain and defend his thesis, and then answer
objections anyone may posit—all of this in Latin. A week later, in the pre-
dawn light of one of the longest days of the year, as he wakes from sleep, he
looks out the window from his room in "The Mansions" and catches sight
of the waning moon. Low over "dark Maenefa the mountain," the lunar
sliver seems to hook and clasp the earth, as if it might lift it and him with it.
A gift, this moment, "unsought, presented so easily," parting him "leaf and
leaf," so delicately, like grace itself.

On the 26th, he begins another letter to his mother to say he has heard
from Lionel, who is now in Peking. A difficult fraternal relationship, this
one, for though the two brothers most resemble each other physically, they
are continents apart on the subject of religion, Lionel having already settled
into an adamantine kind of agnosticism. As for the fate of the *Deutschland,*
he tells her, the Jesuits publish a magazine called *The Month,* and he has
asked its editor, Father Coleridge, his "oldest friend in the Society," if he
will take it, though he knows Coleridge's tastes in poetry run very much
counter to his own, more so than Coleridge's famous ancestor, with whom
he feels a close kinship. The fact is that he already knows Father Coleridge
will "personally dislike it very much," but has asked him "to consider not
his tastes but those of *The Month*'s readers." For his part, Coleridge has told
Hopkins that he is aware that there is "a new sort of poetry" now being
written in America by a fellow named Walt Whitman, which does "not

rhyme or scan or construe." But if Hopkins's poem at least rhymes, scans, and construes, and does not (like Whitman) "make nonsense or bad morality," he does not see why Hopkins's ode "shd. not do" for *The Month*. But though Hopkins sent the poem off some time ago, he has yet to hear back, a sign that his ode "cannot appear in the July number but otherwise seems to shew he means to take it."

Two days later, he adds a postscript to his letter. He has just heard back from Coleridge. The *Deutschland* is to appear, but in the August number, anonymously, though the editor has asked him to first "do away with the accents which mark the scanning." He would have done without the accents gladly, he explains, *if* he thought his readers could "scan right unaided, though he knows they will not," and if the lines "are not rightly scanned they are ruined." He means to humor his editor, but still, "some lines . . . will have to be marked." And since the poem is to appear anonymously, he warns his mother that she "must never say that the poem is mine."

Friday, July 28: Hopkins's thirty-second birthday. The difficult annual examinations in moral theology are over and he has passed, and now it is time for the Scholastics to celebrate. At the request of Father Jones, he has written an occasional piece which will be printed along with Father John Morris's sermon for the Silver Jubilee of Dr. James Brown's installation as Bishop of Shrewsbury. "That event came off on my birthday," he tells his father afterward, though the Bishop did not arrive until the day after, and "on Sunday [July 30] we presented him with an album containing a prose address and compositions, chiefly verse, in many languages, among which were Chinese and Manchoo, all by our people, those who had been or were to be ordained by his lordship. The Chinese and Manchoo (and perhaps there may have been some others) were by a little German very very learned, with a beaky nose like a bugle horn, and they were beautifully penned by himself." The Welsh piece he himself wrote, he adds, "for, sad to say, no one else in the house knows anything about it." He has also written something in Latin and English. "After mass the Bishop sat on a throne and received the address and album and a cheque for £100 with it," after which there was "a high dinner and music at dessert," his own poem—"The Silver Jubilee"—having been "set effectively by a very musical and very noisy member of the community and was sung as a glee by the choir."

His Latin poem—alas—has been radically reworked by others, he adds, because the opening nine couplets proved to be too metaphysical and complex for his learned audience. "His mihi post tantas, immania saecula, clades," he had written in the voice of his beloved England, unburdening himself of the sense of repression the Catholic Church has been under since Henry VIII's schism: "His mihi, prisca, viris tu recidiva, fides." *After so many great disasters, after so many degrading generations, with the help of men like this* [the Bishop], *you, ancient Faith, have been revived for me.* The English poem, on the other hand, written in five crisp quatrains, rings out with jubilee. An opening octosyllabic couplet is followed by a third line chiming on its second and fourth foot, and the Jubilee refrain echoes in each fourth line at a time when the event itself is being met by public silence everywhere in Wales. But at least not here at St. Beuno's, as Hopkins pulls out all the stops to ring out the high-hung bells and braggart bugles, made all the more conspicuous by their absence:

> Not today we need lament
> Your wealth of life is some way spent:
> Toil has shed round your head
> Silver but for Jubilee.
>
> Then for her whose velvet vales
> Should have pealed with welcome, Wales,
> Let the chime of a rhyme
> Utter Silver Jubilee.

The *Deutschland,* on the other hand, has not yet appeared, and "whether it will be in the September number or in any I cannot find out," he adds with a hint of exasperation. "Altogether it has cost me a good deal of trouble." In the meantime, the community is enjoying a summer holiday, and half the St. Beuno's community is already on its annual Villa at Barmouth on the Welsh coast. The others, including himself, are to follow on the 16th, when the rest return. And, yes, he is aware that there is a problem with the drainage there at Barmouth, as his mother noted with alarm in her last letter, because "the town empties its sewage, like other well-watered shores, into Neptune's salt wash, and bathers have sometimes 'gone nigh to suspecting it.'" It is the price of modern progress, and these ecological insults and wounds to nature will soon find a way into his poems.

Early one morning during his Welsh holiday, Hopkins and a group of Scholastics scull up the brackish Mawddach to an old inn dubbed the George III. There they breakfast, relax in the sun, and return downriver on the ebb tide late in the afternoon. At the inn, he leaves behind some lines for the Visitors' Book, titled "Penmaen Pool." Ten quatrains, all ending with a refrain echoing the title. Ten rhymes therefore chiming off Penmaen Pool: *school, tool, stool, rule, wool, full, cool, Yule, who'll,* and *school* again. (*Renewal*—another rhyme he uses in his first draft, he sees is a freak and changes.) Place names, too: *Cadair cliff* and *Grizzled Dyphwys dim, the triple-hummocked Giant's stool,* and—further afield—*Charles's Wain* and *sheep-flock clouds,* and the River Mawddach itself:

> how she trips! though throttled
> If floodtide teeming thrills her full,
> And mazy sands all water-wattled
> Waylay her at ebb, past Penmaen Pool.

And to top it off: a glass of good ale quaffed at the inn, all "goldy foam / That frocks an oar in Penmaen Pool." Come winter, he imagines, there would be innocent pleasures to be found here as well, though of a starker variety: "Furred snows, charged tuft above tuft" towering (that word again) "From darksome darksome Penmaen Pool." Occasional pieces, then, in the aftermath of his brilliant and massively symphonic ode, which he learns now has been rejected by his own.

September 1876 and the start of his third year of theology. "Changes in the Province are like Puss in the Corner and the September ones are sometimes called General Post," he explains to his mother. "I find them . . . 'very fatiguing,' but those of Provincial and Rector of the house one cannot help knowing and liking to know." Change, of course, "is inevitable, for every year so many people must begin and so many more must have ended their studies and it is plain that these can seldom step into the shoes left by those, so there is an almost universal shift. Then besides there are offices of fixed term, like Lord-mayoralties or Septennates. Add deaths, sicknesses, leavings, foreign missions, and what not and you will see that ours can never be an abiding city nor any one of us know what a day may bring forth." And anyway, "it is our pride to be ready for instant despatch." And so, on his return to St. Beuno's fresh from his Welsh holiday, he learns that Father Jones has been appointed Provincial and will leave for London and Mount Street at once, with Father Gallwey, whose term as Provincial has just concluded, replacing him.

Under Gallwey, there will be a tightening of administrative reins. Permission will be required from a professor or superior "on the advisability of reading" a particular author or text. There will also be a stricter enforcement of the rule of silence and of speaking Latin at the appointed times.

Moreover, explicit permission will be needed before a Scholastic may visit another in his room, and only if business cannot be conducted *obiter ad perpaucis—in passing, and with as few words as necessary*. Moreover, Scholastics will no longer walk in the garden after dark. Toward Hopkins, however, Gallwey remains his old, kindly, caring self, brooding over his charge with affection as before, allowing the Muse in the months ahead to settle its fiery wing once more on Hopkins's shoulder.

On Saturday, September 23, the community's annual eight-day retreat ends. Hopkins's anxious mother has once again written to ask him about the fate of the *Deutschland,* and at last he writes to tell her to "sigh no more" over his foundering wreck of a poem. In fact, he is "glad now it has not appeared," though why he should be glad he does not explain. He also commissions Grace to purchase a large photograph of Pope Pius IX for the "good woman" who has been teaching him Welsh and to have it framed. "The sort of thing I have in my mind's eye," he explains, "are those nice glazed table-portraits you have at Oak Hill with a strut to keep them standing on the slant," though "a hanging picture would also do." He also makes it clear that he does not want one of those "smutty smirking old-woman presentments of him." Those his sister is to shun as she would a rattlesnake. After all, Pio Nono is "a very fine looking man," and portraits of him should be as common to procure at shops as those of Bismarck or Disraeli.

Early 1877. Another hard winter: Snow and bitter wind work their way once more into the crevices of the Scholastics' rooms, especially those in the Tower, so that some of the rooms become unusable. Those whining heating pipes of affliction Hopkins had complained of two years before still refuse to do their job, so that by the end of February "the boiler supplying the hot water pipes," even when "heated as much as possible," cannot raise the temperature in the new rooms facing east (and west) above 46° Fahrenheit. Fires must be kept going in the Provincial's and visitors' rooms, where the shivering Scholastics gather to keep warm.

January 6. Epiphany: Hopkins warms his inkwell to answer a letter he has just received from Baillie, now back in London after a year in Egypt regaining his strength after his long bout with pneumonia. He is answering at once, Hopkins explains, that he may not be like "my blackguardly aunts and other kinsfolk and friends, to whom I wrote without any necessity interesting letters of Well-wish . . . at Christmas and have not got a line of answer from any one of them." Baillie has mentioned meeting one of Hopkins's sisters in town, and Hopkins—trying to figure out which of the three it might be—makes some telling comments about the eldest, Millicent. Now twenty-seven, she has given herself over (as once he did) to Puseyism, and has been an out-sister of the Margaret Street convent in London for the past three years. "Consequently she will be directed by some Ritualist," he adds with knowing contempt from his own experiences with Liddon and Pusey. Their hands, he tells Baillie, who had wisely avoided contact with them at Oxford, are the worst "she could fall into: these men are imperious, uncommissioned, without common sense, and without knowledge of moral theology."

Baillie's travels through the Middle East have led him to a study of Arabic, which Hopkins—that philologist par excellence—admits he finds quite difficult, though "rich and voluminous." He knows he will never master Hebrew, which he needs for his study of Scriptures, far less Arabic, though he, like Baillie, finds the study of Egyptian hieroglyphs fascinating. A French Jesuit who was at St. Beuno's last year encouraged him to study Coptic before taking on ancient Egyptian. "The hieroglyphics of themselves attract," Hopkins explains, and "have the originality and quaintness of Chinese without the grotesqueness and ugliness." Moreover, there have been so many fresh finds lately, adding to the store of ancient Egyptian literature and culture.

But what he has done instead is to study Welsh, so that now he can at least "read easy prose and . . . speak stumblingly." His "greatest difficulty, amounting mostly to total failure," remains understanding the spoken word. Moreover, Welsh poetry "is quite as hard [to master] as the choruses in a [Greek] play," especially given the small and inadequate dictionary he has at his disposal. Then, in a postscript added two weeks later, he tells Baillie what has been on his mind for some years now: how kind Baillie always was toward him, "much kinder than I deserved, and that as I am of a blackguardly nature and behaviour (I believe it from my heart and clearly see it) so as compared with you in particular I appear to myself in the light of a blackguard." *Blackguard.* "It is the word that hits my meaning," he insists, "and I must employ it."

Friday, February 23: Six months after learning that his *Deutschland* has been rejected, Hopkins begins writing a series of experimental Italian sonnets in counterpoint and sprung rhythm. He composes the first nine days into the Lenten season, at a time when he is preparing for his examinations in moral theology *ad audiendas confessiones*—to see if he is fit to hear confessions—and the poem is in counterpoint. It is called "God's Grandeur," and it is by any standards an extraordinary achievement. "The world is chárged wíth the grandeur of God," he begins, stressing both the moral imperative—that the world is charged with the duty of praising God—and the electric metaphor of a world charged with a boundless energy. It is a world, he has come to see, alive and flush with meaning, with an instress capable of surging through human beings, something it would do so much more often if only the beholder paid more attention to what is there for the asking. This grandeur can either flame out like the zigzag of light from a piece of gold foil when it strikes the eye, or gather in us, incrementally but inevitably, like the greengold ooze of oil dripping from freshly pressed olives. It is a grandeur which can wake us to the presence of God, as Paul was struck on the road to Damascus: as something overwhelming, earthshaking, unmistakable. Or it arrives slowly over a matter of years, as grace finally enwombed Augustine. One way or the other, the luminous mystery of the universe will at last make itself felt in us.

Why is it then that we humans habitually refuse to respond to all that glory? Why is it that

> Generations have trod, have trod, have trod;
>> And all is seared with trade; bleared, smeared with toil;
>> And wears man's smudge and shares man's smell: the soil
> Is bare now, nor can foot feel, being shod.

St. Ignatius begins the *Spiritual Exercises* by asking many of these same questions, and Hopkins will come back to this strange, sleepwalking inability of humans to respond to what is there before them every waking moment. Worse are the terrible inroads we humans have made on the world itself, holding it more and more in disdain and captive with our strip mining and drilling for oil, the furious felling of forests and old trees, ruining the very water we drink and the very air we breathe, the smear and smudge we leave on everything we touch like some patina of cloacal pâté. And so we grow deaf and blind early, insulating ourselves from the freshness of the world about us, hardly ever allowing ourselves to come in direct contact with the earth beneath our very feet. Instead, we turn inward on our petty self-concerns, shod like some great gray drayhorse plodding round and round in an ever-narrowing circle, as if getting and spending were all we were capable of understanding.

And yet, the poet-prophet reminds us, for all this indifference and malice aforethought, nature is never spent, never exhausted or bought up, for if we crucify the world as we crucified Christ—the hints are there in the crushed oil of Gethsemane, which served as prologue to the Great Sacrifice, and the final eastering image of morning springing after all seems lost—still, the Creator/Spirit is continually renewing our world and us. But how?

(And here the very rhythms of the poem soften.) Much as a mother bird broods over the great, bent, broken nest of the world with its warm heart and breast and with—ah! (that exclamation of sudden discovery) bright wings, the way the sun each day rises again, as if on the first day of a new Creation:

> . . . There lives the dearest freshness deep down things;
> And though the last lights off the black West went
>   Oh, morning, at the brown brink eastward, springs—
> Because the Holy Ghost óver the bent
>   World broods with warm breast and with ah! bright wings.

And the very next day another sonnet, "The Starlight Night." If "God's Grandeur" is an announcement of a new voice in the lyric, taking the form of a pastoral homily on duty, this poem is sheer celebration and gratitude. "Look at the stars! look, look up at the skies!" the poem begins, fifteen exclamation points underlining the ecstatic nature of the poem, as metaphor morphs into metaphor, despite the frigid rooms and the long cold and an important examination coming up in another week. Look, he says, there it is for the asking: the late winter/early spring sky, there for the taking, the heavens filled with fire-folk sitting there, the constellations forming bright boroughs and circle-citadels, earth echoing sky or sky earth with its elves'-eyes and quicksilver quickgold.

As for the stars: to what shall we compare them? They are like . . . like whitebeams rippling in the winds, or like the leaves of airy abeles torn free and flying here and there. Or they are flocks of doves scattering from a barn at a sudden scare, flake doves, like Dante's vision of the saints rising like embers from a burning log suddenly struck with a poker—*smarrita!*—or like flame or fiery-white snowflakes, the underlying instress after all being the same in each example. A "May-mess," he calls it, here, now, in the dark of winter, an infinity of stars in an exploding galaxy on a clear crispcold night like a thousand thousand white blossoms on pear and apple and cherry tree. Or—closer—like March-bloom and the early yellowing of willow trees. If the day before he had pondered the essential economy of things—the cost, the bottom line—here he supplies an answer. How does one come to own the infinite riches one sees everywhere above one, this infinity of promise which has so lifted his heart? Not with money, no, but with counter-coin, with "Prayer, patience, alms, vows," the currency all of us have always for the asking.

And yet, beautiful as this heavenly display is, all of this is but the barn, the outer shell, like so many bright pieces of gold, storing within an infi-nitely greater spiritual bounty: the shocks of wheat, the shock of a won-drous reality beyond all guessing, beyond anything we might have hoped for, where Christ waits, and his mother, and all his saints, there for the ask-ing, there as his Master said he would always be:

> These are indeed the barn; withindoors house
> The shocks. This piece-bright paling shuts the spouse
>> Christ home, Christ and his mother and all his hallows.

That same day he writes Bridges, reminding him that the place where he has lived these past two and a half years is called St. Beuno's and not Bruno's, and the town St. Asaph, not Asaph's. Again he thanks his friend for his offer to visit him in London, something which is out of the question now that he is here in Wales, a fact which Bridges also seems to have for-gotten. "You have forgotten or else you never got a letter I wrote *from this place* a year or so ago," he reminds him. "It was in answer to one of yours about Henry [Heinrich] Heine and other things [forgetful himself, he means Hegel, not Heine] and there too you, with the same kindness and futility as now, proposed to come and see me at Roehampton hundreds of miles away." He wants Bridges to write that long and interesting letter he has for so long promised to write. As for Bridges's letters being opened, Hopkins reminds him once again that

> it is quite unreasonable and superstitious to let it make any difference. To be sure they are torn half open—and so for the most part as that one can see the letter has never been out of the envelope—but how can a superior have the time or the wish to read the flood of correspondence from peo-ple he knows nothing of which is brought in by the post? No doubt if you were offering me a wife, a legacy, or a bishopric on condition of leaving my present life, and someone were to get wind of the purpose of the cor-respondence, *then* our letters would be well read or indeed intercepted.

He thanks Bridges for his two poetry pamphlets—*The Growth of Love*, made up of twenty-four sonnets and published the previous year, and *Car-men Elegiacum*, a gathering of Latin elegiacs just out. But he is going to have to wait to read them until after he takes his examination in moral theology in a few days. Moral theology, as he has told Baillie, "covers the whole of life and to know it it is best to begin by knowing everything, as medicine, law, history, banking." Still, it is law that Hopkins "should most like to know . . . knowledge of law [being] very advantageous. *Emphyteusis, laudemium, mohatra, antichresis, hypotheca, servitus activa et passiva.*" These he has lifted from a Latin treatise on contracts he is reading, all of which terms he must master come March 3, going over the subject again and again "and in a hurry [which] is the most wearisome work and tonight at all events I am so tired I am good for nothing," as he writes his mother on March 1.

There has been "sharp frost with bitter north winds," he tells her, "but today the wind is changed." Worse was missing the total eclipse of the moon the evening before. "I saw it only when it was three parts over, the moon being dazzling bright and the shadow brown." And he has just written Arthur "a long letter with criticisms about his Xmas drawings," which appeared in the *Illustrated London News,* but has had no answer. "I suppose he must be huffed," Gerard surmises. "At least I pretend to think so." And now, for her fifty-sixth birthday, he is sending along "two sonnets I wrote in a freak the other day. . . . They are not so very queer, but have a few metrical effects, mostly after Milton," by which he indicates his having mounted a counterpointed trochaic rhythm on an iambic meter, the falling meter clashing with the rising. Such rhythms, he tells her, "are not commonly understood but do what nothing else can in their contexts." And so he sends her his earliest drafts, the first pressings, replete with the awkwardness of his initial attempts at the sonnet after a ten-year hiatus. They are worth reading to see just how quickly he caught such errors and replaced them with something far better. The offending words and phrases are in italics and almost all are confined to the octave of each poem.

"God's Grandeur" he first titled—simply—"Sonnet," and it runs as follows:

> The world is charged with the grandeur of God.
>> It will flame out, like shining from shook foil;
>> It gathers to a greatness, like *an oozing oil*
> *Pressed.* Why do men then now not *fear* His rod?—
> Generations have *hard* trod, have *hard* trod;
>> And all is seared with trade; bleared, smeared with toil;
>> And bears man's smudge and wears man's smell. The soil
> Is *barren;* nor can foot feel, being shod.
> And, for all this, nature is never spent;
>> There lives the dearest freshness deep down things;
>> And though the last lights *from* the black West went

O morning, *on* the brown brink eastwards, springs—
Because the Holy Ghost over the bent
World broods with warm breast and with ah! bright wings.

"The Starlight Night," too, will undergo revisions in the interest of neo-plasms, alliteration, and instress, a removal of any phrase that drags down or hinders the forward motion and tired Keatseanisms imbedded in the poem like vestigial remnants of his Parnassian Oxford work. Here is the poem he sent his mother, the words that will be transformed into quick-gold italicized, and the too-special *parclose*—an ecclesiastical architectural term for the screen that separates the inner sanctuary from the main part of a church—replaced with the special coinage, "piece-bright paling," with its complex punning on *piece-bright* (money) with *peace-bright* and *pal-ing*—in its sense of within the pale or community or area fenced in, but also a world which pales in relation to the spiritual splendor lying beneath:

Look at the stars! look, look up at the skies!
   O look at all the fire-folk sitting in the air!
   The bright boroughs, the *glimmering* citadels there!
Look, the elf-rings! look at the out-round earnest eyes!
The grey lawns cold where *quaking gold-dew* lies!
   Wind-beat *white-beam,* airy abeles *all on* flare!
   Flake-doves sent floating *out* at a farmyard scare!
Ah well! it is a purchase and a prize.

Buy then! Bid then!—What?—Prayer, patience, alms, vows.
Look, look—a May-mess, like on orchard-boughs!
Look—March-bloom, like on mealed-with-yellow sallows!—
These are *the barn, indeed:* withindoors house
The shocks. This *pale and parclose hides* the spouse
Christ *and the Mother of Christ* and all His Hallows.

March 11. Eight days after taking (and passing) his examination, Hop-kins offers the assembled community at St. Beuno's a Dominical or prac-tice sermon in the refectory during dinner. He climbs the stairs to the second floor, opens a small door, and stands in the doorway in a pulpitlike enclosure above the assembled Scholastics and faculty dining in silence in the hall below. It is the fourth Sunday in Lent, and he has taken for his text a passage from John 6:10: *Dixit ergo Jesus: Facite homines discumbere*—And

Jesus said, Make the men sit down. "And now, brethren," he begins, "you have heard the Gospel of Christ feeding 5000 men with five loaves in the wilderness and how they would have made Him king." Then he proceeds to compose the scene: Let us turn the story over in our imaginations, and "go in mind to that time and in spirit to that place, admire what Christ says as if we heard it, and what He does as if we saw it, until the heart perhaps may swell with pride for Jesus Christ the king of glory."

A rhetorical flourish in the best manner of the Victorian Jesuits, seventy or more of whom *are* sitting at long tables below him, sipping their soup and munching their bread: a composition within a composition, a scene within a scene. *Make the men sit down,* he thinks. That will be his motif, his mantra. "Lend me your ears," he exhorts, "and go along with me . . . for you are as when Our Lord said: make the men sit down; and at the end of all we will crown Christ king . . . in our hearts and souls. . . . Listen for what is to come." And when was the *time* of this miracle? he asks. Near Easter, as now, the world turning again toward springtime, the time of day toward evening.

And where was the place? Then he is off, the earnest scholar on a tear, offering them far more information than any of them would have thought to ask for. "It was beside the sea of Galilee . . . which lake is 12 miles long and 7 wide at the broadest, and the Jordan running through it with a strong stream; so that if it were in this valley it would stretch from . . . St Asaph to Ruthin . . . and would fill the valley from hill to hill." Except, he is quick to explain, that the Jordan "runs from north to south, not like the Clwyd from south to north." As for the Sea of Galilee, it is "shaped something like a bean or . . . a man's left ear; the Jordan enters at the top of the upper rim, it runs out at the end of the lobe or drop of the ear." Then there is Bethsaida. Bethsaida Julias, he explains, which "stands by the Jordan as it were above the ear in the hair." Capharnaum, on the other hand, is situated "on the bow or rim nearer the cheek." Then there is the other Bethsaida, "where Peter and Andrew and Philip lived, against the cheek where the bow of the ear ends." And Tiberius is lower, "on the tongue of flesh that stands out from the cheek into the hollow of the ear." To make this all clearer, he adds, think of the Clwyd Valley. "St Asaph would be where the Jordan enters the valley . . . Chorozain might be Bodfari; and the place of the miracle seems to have been at the north end of the lake, on the east side of the Jordan, as it might be at this very spot where we are now upon the slope of Maenefa." And on with this unconscious parody of the Ignatian composition of place, until he has explained himself blue.

And who are the people in the Gospel story? Christ and his Apostles and disciples up on the mountain, the crowd below. The Apostles have been busy spreading the word, and now Christ tells them to "come apart to a lonely place and rest awhile." But, like his brother Jesuits who have their duties to perform, they will not get that rest. "For the apostles had done their work too well and all the country was astir about Jesus. So now they lift up their eyes from the mountain side where they are resting and lo they are not alone even here!" Men and women and children have followed them in large numbers, including the sick and lame, he explains. Then Christ turns to Philip and asks how they are to feed such a crowd. "Here, brethren, remark a mystery," Hopkins's voice rings through the refectory: Christ would give Philip, "instead of the contemplation of this world's studs and steeds and splendour, its chivalry and chariots and chargers, an eye to dwell on the glory of the kingdom of heaven." Christ wishes to test Philip, as he has tested Hopkins and each of these men here in the refectory. For if we are sad, "we think we shall never be happy more, though the same thing has happened to us times and times; if we are sick we despair of being ever well, though human nature every day is in some one or other sickening and re-covering; if in poverty we despair of being ever better off, though the times keep turning and changing; if tired we complain as if no sleep or rest would ever refresh us; if the winter is cold we make believe it will never be summer again." He speaks of what he knows in himself, he tells his fellow Jesuits, "and it may be something of the same is true in you. Whereas *they that trust in the Lord are as Mount Sion.*" They are the same words that changed De Rancé's life forever, he knows, the very words of the Psalmist which once brought Hopkins to tears in this very same room.

To what shall he compare the feeding of the five thousand? he asks. To "a sheet of white rain coming from the sea," which "blots out first the Orms' Heads on Moel Hiraddug, then spreads mile after mile, from hill to hill, from square to square of the fields, along the Vale of Clwyd." Just so, he ex-plains, the barley bread was multiplied through that crowd of five thou-sand. It is the same Christ who deals "me out my life, my voice, my breath, my being," and He may withdraw it if it is his will. Otherwise, he begs Christ to help him "employ it much better than heretofore to His glory." Crown him, then, king of your hearts, he prays now, for just as "His hand created you once, now it deals out to you your being and the bread and all things that keep you alive." "Thou mastering me/God," he had begun his great ode, "giver of breath and bread."

But in fact he does not get this far in his homily, for, as he exhorts the men repeatedly to sit down, he notices that several of them are trying to stifle their laughter. But it is too much, and soon some of those listening are laughing so hard they are nearly rolling in their chairs. "This made me lose the thread," a flustered Hopkins notes after the ordeal is over, "so that I did not deliver the last two paragraphs right but mixed things up." The repeated phrase, *Make the men sit down,* "far from having a good effect," has made his listeners laugh uproariously, which is not exactly what Jesuit sermons are meant to do. As for the Jesuit Fathers, they must certainly be wondering if homiletics is, after all, young Hopkins's strong point.

Early in April, Hopkins sends Bridges a postcard warning him that "a junk of a letter is under weigh laden to her gunwales with judicious remarks" on Bridges's two poetry pamphlets. For now that Easter week is here, he can write that long letter he has promised for the past six weeks. "You have no call to complain of my delay in writing," he chides his friend. "I could not help it." After all, he is not like Bridges some "consulting physician," which shows how little he understands the pressures Bridges has been under working in a very large public hospital. And besides, Hopkins adds, he has so little free time anymore, and finds himself always so "very very tired, yes 'a thousand times and yet a thousand times' and 'scarce can go or creep.'" It is a note that was there from his days at the Oratory, and it will return with increasing frequency in his correspondence and in his journals: the sense of ennui, of physical exhaustion, making him unfit to do the very duties he has committed himself to performing.

As for Bridges's Latin elegiacs, he finds them "elegant" and "full of happinesses." And yet, they are too damned obscure and crabbed. Besides, the subject matter would interest no one. He also dislikes Bridges's "foolish sneer at Rome" about the uselessness of making pilgrimages, which, he reminds Bridges, all people make, not just Catholics. And though he does not "remember to have read so much good Latin verse together," he also believes such performances are "a waste of time and money." On the other hand, the sonnets are "truly beautiful, breathing a grave and feeling genius, and make me proud of you (which by the by is not the same as for you to be proud of yourself)." Still, there is room for improvement: "words might be chosen with more point and propriety, images might be more brilliant etc."

But Bridges's Miltonic counterpointings and reversed feet—which Hopkins himself has "paid much attention to"—these Bridges has yet to master. The fact is that Milton's "achievements are quite beyond any other English poet's, perhaps any modern poet's." But then Bridges's sonnets remind him more of Shakespeare than Milton for sheer tenderness. They are certainly not like Wordsworth's, "for beautiful as those are they have an odious goodiness and neckcloth about them which half throttles their beauty." And those with "a Tennysonian touch about them" he likes least, "not for want of admiring Tennyson . . . but because it gives them a degree of neckcloth too." No, it is a manly tenderness and music he most admires in his friend's sonnets.

Besides, Hopkins insists, Milton was "a very bad man: those who . . . break themselves and . . . consent to those who break the sacred bond of marriage, like Luther and Milton, fall with eyes open into the terrible judgment of God. And crying up great names, as for instance the reviews do now Swinburne and Hugo, those plagues of mankind, is often wicked" and reveals "a blackguard and unspiritual mind." Coincidentally, he adds, he has written two sonnets of his own, quite independently of Bridges's writing him on the matter, "with rhythmical experiments of the [same] sort," and will send them on. "How our wits jump! Not but what I have long been on metrical experiments more advanced than these," by which he means his *Deutschland* ode. "You will," he adds, "see that my rhythms go further than yours do in the way of irregularity. The chiming of consonants I got in part from the Welsh, which is very rich in sound and imagery." But to his mother he will say simply that Bridges's sonnets are beautiful, "designedly written in Miltonic rhythms but not violent like mine," and that he is "quite proud of them."

And then a word on something Bridges has told him: that Richard Benson, a Puseyite and now an Anglo-Catholic Cowley Father, had said to him that when Hopkins left the Anglican fold, he in fact became a "vert" (i.e., a pervert). The comment, Hopkins says, "throws light . . . on what the Epistles say of the avarice of the Gnostic heresiarchs," in which company he places Benson. But he is surprised Bridges should take the word "pervert" to heart, for no doubt "every sect and party employs them of its renegades: they seem made to hand. Nevertheless it is particularly stupid of the Puseyites to do so," he adds, "since according to them 'verts,' as they sillily call them, do no more than if a bird built her nest first in one, then in another bough of the same bush."

And who is this Beuno? Bridges wants to know. Is he dead? Yes, Hopkins tells him. "He did that much 1200 years ago. . . . He was St. Winefred's uncle and raised her to life when she died in defence of her chastity and at the same time he called out her famous spring which fills me with devotion every time I see it and wd. fill anyone that has eyes with admiration, the flow of *aglaon hudor* [bright water] is so lavish and so beautiful." St. Winefred's Well, whose waters have been such a boon to him, and will remain so all his life. But he is also aware that Beuno is in fact "a mythological centre to the Welsh and crystallises superstitions or till lately did, as for instance odd marks on cattle were called Beuno's marks." As for Bridges's parting shot that he really does not like Jesuits, Hopkins asks him if he has ever actually met one.

Two weeks later, at Father Gallwey's suggestion, Hopkins writes a 38-line presentation poem (in Latin) for the renowned Dominican preacher and staunch Irishman Thomas Burke, who recently spent three years in America spreading the Gospel and—in a series of lectures published five years earlier—defending the Irish against the attacks of the English historian J. A. Froude. At the moment, the white-haired Burke, dressed in the white robes of his order, walks among the crowblack-clad Jesuits at St. Beuno's. He is only forty-seven, but already his health has been broken by his labors. And now it has been given to Hopkins—that staunch Englishman, and on St. George's Day, to boot—to host this Irish dove among Maenefa's crows. And if the poem Hopkins writes is a good-natured send-up, it is also reverential, revealing the gentlemanly wit Gallwey so much likes about Hopkins.

And another thing. While Burke is a staunch supporter of Aquinas, Hopkins is known for being one of a half dozen Scotists in all of England at the moment. Still, he will give Burke and Aquinas and the other disciples of Aquinas their due, in lines which are comic whether read in Latin or translated into English:

> *Doctus Aquinatis reserare oracular Thomae,*
> *Sit amen est illo nunc quod in ore latet,*
> *Quem tam Gudinus, Godatus, tamque Gonetus,*
> *Tam Cajetanus perspicuum esse jubent . . .*

Which means:

> One skilled in interpreting the oracles of Thomas Aquinas,
>   If in fact there is still anything at all obscure
> In the words of him whom Godinus, Godatus, yes, and Gonetus,
>   And even Cajetanus work to make a model of clarity . . .

This Englishman would praise this Irishman (whose name is so difficult to render in Latin), if he would let him—though he has a well-deserved reputation for having laid low Hopkins's countrymen here and in the United States. Besides, it is St. Winefred, a Celtic saint, who has healed Hopkins and will—he hopes—heal him again. And may she also soften Burke's heart with love toward Hopkins's countrymen, for the Irish are and have been a faithful people, he graciously acknowledges. And may the good Dominican father offer as a gift from his heart fidelity to this Welsh soil on which they have both met. It is a theme—the tensions between the Irish and the English—that Hopkins will come back to with increasing tensions in the years ahead.

A paper Hopkins presents on Saturday evening, April 28, is for the last meeting of the St. Beuno's Academy, and is presented to Father Gallwey and fifteen Scholastics and faculty. It is entitled "On the Composition of Place in the Spiritual Exercises," and it makes three important points for Hopkins's own poetics. First: that composition of place must always be of a real and never of a fictitious place. Second: that such compositions of place are *not* intended to keep the mind from wandering or merely to assist the passive imagination. And third: that the true object of such compositions is to make the one undertaking the *Spiritual Exercises* "present in spirit at the scenes, persons, etc. so that they may really act on him and he on them." And though its primary import is spiritual and directed toward the *Exercises,* composition of place has already had a profound impact on the persons and places Hopkins has evoked in his *Deutschland* and will in nearly every poem (and sermon) he writes henceforth.

As in the four new sonnets he composes that April and May: "As kingfishers catch fire, dragonflies draw flame," "Spring," "The Sea and the Skylark," and "In the Valley of the Elwy." The kingfishers sonnet is about the Scotist individuation of things, where once again the opening lines flame out, and where things reveal themselves—kingfishers, dragonflies, falling stones ringing out as they plash into the well water below, as well as the sounds of violin and guitar and piano string, and the distinctive chime of a bell. But more: it is about Christ playing—acting in all seriousness, at the same time delighting in the never-again-to be-repeated distinctiveness of human beings in ten thousand separate places and revealed in the faces of those who keep God's graces:

> Each mortal thing does one thing and the same:
>> Deals out that being indoors each one dwells;
>> Selves—goes itself; *myself* it speaks and spells,
> Crying *What I do is me: for that I came.*
>
> Í say more: the just man justices;
>> Keeps gráce: thát keeps all his goings graces;
> Ácts in God's eye what in God's eye he is—

> Chríst. For Christ plays in ten thousand places,
> Lovely in limbs, and lovely in eyes not his
> To the Father through the features of men's faces.

In early May, he writes a sonnet celebrating the coming of Wales's long-deferred spring. Spring: that musical echo, that hint and "strain of the earth's sweet being in the beginning/In Eden garden." For nothing, Hopkins fairly sings, "Nothing is so beautiful as Spring." Even weeds, furled in on themselves like little wheels, begin to "shoot long and lovely and lush." And thrushes' eggs, with their rich deep skyblue color, "look little low heavens," and the song of the thrush itself rinses and wrings and rings off the echoing timber, creating a rich musical timbre, striking the ear like little lightnings. And "glassy peartree leaves and blooms": how they brush

> The descending blue; that blue is all in a rush
> With richness; the racing lambs too have fair their fling.

Ah, "what is all this juice and all this joy?" he asks, but a glimpse, a musical strain of earth's sweet being in the beginning, there "In Eden garden," when God walked in the garden in the cool of the evening with a man and a woman, before sin and pride and self-will destroyed all that, and left us with what we have: an echo only, a strain, of that original fullness. But worst is to see innocence lost in children, to see it cloy and cloud as inevitably it does as self-bent sin curdles and sours everything. And so he turns to Christ and begs him to take that youthful springtime goodness for his own, that Scotistic sense of the world before the Fall, before it all began to unravel, in all but one human being, and that a woman, a maid and a mother, the quintessence of springtime and Maytime, born without sin as Adam and Eve had been, which we get glimpses of whenever we hear the laughter of little children. That is the gift surely "most . . . worthy the winning."

But halfway through Mary's month, Hopkins's deep fatigue returns, and he travels by horse—with the blessing of the minister at St. Beuno's—to the working class resort town and rail station at Rhyl, eight miles north, along the northern coast of Wales. As he walks along the beach there, he begins composing yet another sonnet as he hears again two timeless sounds. On his right, the ocean tide lapping up against the shore and then receding, as it has for thousands of years. And on his left, the song of a bird—a skylark this time—ascending into the heavens, its "rash-fresh" score rewinding and replaying with delicate modulations as it has also done for millennia.

These things, being pure, go themselves, as kingfishers do, for they enact what they were meant to do, unlike the human inhabitants of Rhyl, "this shallow and frail town," sign of "our sordid turbid time." And we, "life's pride and cared-for crown," the Omega point of Creation, expelled long ago from that sweet Eden and the promise of that prime? Though we may speak of progress and social evolution, we too, like these tawdry, weathered, boarded-up seaside buildings—our makings—are "breaking down / To man's last dust" and draining "fast towards man's first slime."

"Dear Sir," he had written William Butterfield three weeks earlier, commending the architect's work in the medieval pointed style he so admired, "I hope you will long continue to work out yr beautiful and original style," though he does not think the present generation "will ever much admire it," for the simple reason that most people simply do not know how to look at medieval architecture "as a whole having a single form governing it throughout, which they would perhaps see in a Greek temple." For them, old work means a farmyard with a "medley of ricks and roofs and dove-cots," and they could care less about anything like a "pure beauty of line, at least till they are taught to." And in its place, what? Modern brickwork, the same red rectangle repeated ad infinitum: brickish skirts—as at Oxford and in the London suburbs: shoddy work, all of it, and so "out of keeping with nature." Such buildings and designs are for him, as for Ruskin, a bitter reminder of what Victorian society really thinks of itself. And so, a bare three months after the uplift of "God's Grandeur" and "The Starlight Night," in a time of exhaustion, Hopkins looks—as he increasingly will in his life as a Jesuit—at that other reality which cannot be avoided: a world of poverty, economic stagnation, decay, the logical implications of Darwin and Huxley's downward spiraling evolutionary model. In short, at what a life modeled on entropy and self-imprisonment and death has come to look like.

And then another sonnet to the skylark, like and unlike Shelley's Ode, also written that spring, this one likening the human condition to a caged songbird. "As a dare-gale skylark scanted in a dull cage," the poem begins, just so, "Man's mounting spirit in his bone-house, mean house, dwells." Surely the skylark, like the thrush, remembers how once it dared the winds and gales in its free fells, among trees and valleys and uncumbered air—like those hawks soaring over the fields at St. Beuno's? Or like most of his contemporaries, treading out their hobnail-booted daily grind, "in drudgery, day-labouring-out life's age." Elation and depression: bordering on the bipolar in Hopkins's mood swings. For if he is capable of composing a poem like "God's Grandeur," of singing "sometimes the sweetest, sweetest spells," his spirit can also droop as much as any caged songbird, "deadly sómetimes in their cells," or even wringing (and ringing) "their barriers in bursts of fear or rage." Rest, sweet rest, surcease, freedom: man and bird both need these, God knows:

> Not that the sweet-fowl, song-fowl, needs no rest—
> Why, hear him, hear him babble and drop down to his nest,
>   But his ówn nést, wíld nést, no prison.

But Hopkins is no Gnostic, no Neo-Platonist ready to shuck the bone-house of the body. No, we are humans, made of flesh and spirit, and "Man's spirit will be flesh-bound when found at best." And when will that be? In the resurrection, when the body will sing at ease with the mind and spirit, unencumbered, "úncúmberèd," much as Christ rose from the dead, much as "meadow-dówn is nót distréssed / For a ráinbow fóoting it nor hé for his bónes rísen." *Son of man, shall these bones rise?* Yes, and again, yes, Hopkins answers, in spite of being driven to the extremity of exhaustion by study, work, and physical weakness.

Wednesday, May 23: The close of the Whitsun holidays, and the day on which Hopkins composes "In the Valley of the Elwy," praising in song the Welsh landscape he has so loved. The poem is very much the twin of "The Sea and the Skylark," written shortly before. He remembers a house, he writes, where all were good to him, where the comforting smell and cordial air of the place seemed to reflect the goodness of its inhabitants like some protective hood, like a mothering wing over its bevy of eggs, an image he had used in "God's Grandeur" as well. But it is not Wales he is thinking of here. Rather, it is the hospitality of the Watsons of Shooter's Hill in South London (though he does not name them).

Yes, the air here in Wales, in this valley, is likewise lovely and sweet. Only here, he has come to see, "inmate does not correspond" to the place. And so he prays to God, who loves all souls and holds all in balance, to complete these Welsh people where they fail, "Being mighty a master, being a father and fond." It is a prayer similar to the one he had uttered at the close of the *Deutschland* the year before: that Christ the King might return, might yet be "a crimson-cresseted east" to the world and to Wales, that the convert in his newfound fire might witness the great change hinted at in the dramatic conversions of his Oxford companions in the waning days of the Oxford Movement, a change he is coming to realize will not be visiting the majority of his countrymen—English *or* Welsh—any time soon.

"Vanity of vanities, and all is vanity": Hopkins's meditation on Ecclesiastes and a translation—both vivid and idiomatic—composed that spring based on a homily by St. John Chrysostom—John the Golden-tongued—on the fall of Eutropius, Byzantine eunuch, former slave, and upwardly-mobile consul, put to death by order of the Eastern Emperor once he had fallen from grace. "Where now are the bright keepings of the consulship?" Hopkins's Englishing of the Greek has it. "Where is the gay torchlight now? Where are the clapping hands and the dances and the assemblies and the festivals?" Gone, all gone. A wind blew and "cast the leaves and shewed us the tree bare and all that was left of it from the root upwards shaking." And now where are all those friends, those "make-believes, followers of the fashion? Where are the suppers and feasts? . . . They were all night and dreaming: now it is day and they are vanished. They were spring flowers, and, spring over, they all are faded together. . . . They were bubbles, and are broken. They were cobweb, and are swept away." And so this spiritual refrain is left us to sing, coming in again and again: "Vanity of vanities and all is vanity."

Bismarck, Disraeli, Gladstone, the French Communard, all Caesars and Kaisers and Czars, all Imperators and Emperors, all the powers of this world, listen! Listen to what the Church, the very Church "you yourself made war on once has opened her breast and welcomed you in," while the theaters that "courted you . . . have betrayed and undone you. . . . You are making havoc of the Church, and it is yourself you are hurrying over the cliff's edge—but you pushed by me, not to hear. . . . And all this I say now . . . not to sink the boat the seas break over but to signal those who scud before the wind, that they may never feel the waters rolling overhead." The theme of shipwreck again: the ancient motif of the Church, sounded by Hopkins in a troubled time, here, as he had in the *Deutschland:* "You . . . that wear *the pride and plume* of wealth make your gain by [this man's] misfortune: for nothing, no nothing has so little strength to stay as the things of man."

The pride and plume of wealth. A hint into what Hopkins himself thought the best poem he ever wrote, "The Windhover." The sonnet is dated precisely: May 30, 1877, a Wednesday. The company of Scholastics walk out the west doors of St. Beuno's and across the fields and the hawk-haunted valley to the raised Rock with the small chapel on its height, where each weekday in May they come to attend mass. *To Christ Our Lord,* he will formally dedicate the poem years later, though surely it is to Christ Lord, Christ King, that he has already dedicated his entire life, and now he is only four months from ordination. All those years of preparation, all the study, all the exams taken and passed, leading to this. He is both elated and awed at the prospect of houselling and unhouselling Christ each day in the

Blessed Sacrament, taking the Eucharist from the locked tabernacle to distribute it to one and all. It is a gift which has cost him not less than everything: the prospect of marriage and family, of wealth, of a sense of independence (however delusional), of being ready at a day's notice to go where he is sent by his superiors, to serve wherever there is a need.

"Bran Maenefa, the Crow of Maenefa," he has taken to styling himself, with his collar and ankle-length black soutane, its free-hanging pieces at shoulder level, modeled after the gowns of the Oxford dons. Crow he is, and neither skylark nor thrush nor one of those high-flying hawks he can see circling in the wind currents above him, mastering the big wind so effortlessly as he treads the swirled grass beneath his feet. The inscape, the achieve of, the mastery of unself-conscious nature, doing what it does so gracefully: "I caught this mórning morning's mínion, king-/dom of daylight's dauphin, dapple-dáwn-drawn Falcon," he begins, breathlessly, taking in the whole inscape of the small hawk above him

> in his riding
> Of the rólling level únderneath him steady aír, and stríding
> Hígh there, how he rung upon the rein of a wimpling wing
> In his écstasy! then off, off forth on swing,
>> As a skate's heel sweeps smooth on a bow-bend: the hurl and
>> gliding
>> Rebuffed the bíg wínd. My heart in hiding
> Stírred for a bird,—the achieve of, the mástery of the thing!

Like Eutropius, or Napoleon, or any prime minister or minor courtier for that matter, like any of us, really, who would go our own way. But that was not Christ the King's way, who surrendered and emptied himself in a radical kenosis, a man who attracted all sorts of people by his very presence, a natural teacher, poet, miracleworker, healer, high priest, breaking himself for others as he is broken each day now in the breaking of the bread. Not a grasping after, but rather a spending of himself for the asking. And in that descent into humanity, yes, in that buckling of his broken body on the cross, on which he died that others might have life and that abundantly, in that self-emptying Hopkins finds a beauty "a billion/Times told lovelier" than anything that had come before in Christ's time on earth.

But dangerous, too, for it would draw untold others to try and emulate a reality which flew directly in the face of the world's ancient, haggard lies that pass for wisdom. The fire that breaks from Thee then, he thinks, the

fire that will fire him to act. *Oh, our king back upon English soil,* Hopkins
had prayed in the *Deutschland* ode the year before. That sense of *king* making up the linguistic inscape of the poem, where the first line ends with the
word itself, chiming eight times in the octave's rhyme words, masculine and
feminine, rising and falling rhythms both: *king, riding, striding, wing* then
swing, riding, hiding, thing. The hidden king ringing out news of himself in
the things of this world, emptying himself for us, the brilliancy of that kenotic
act that would pull billions of souls after him, "the achieve of, the mastery of
the thing!" King/thing: the *king* circling out in the great procession from the
Godhead, and entering into the *things* of this dappled, variegated world.

But why should all this be so difficult to understand? Hopkins asks in
the poem's final lines. After all, the menial task of the ploughman cutting
through any of these fields before him will turn up the humus, the soil, so
that the morning light flames out in the millions of tiny specks of diamond-
edged sillion, until the very earth itself seems to take fire. Or consider the
way blue-bleak embers in a grating seem dead, until they fall and break themselves to reveal the gold-red flame within. Like Christ on the cross, this chevalier going before and leading by example, the bloody wounds in his soldier's
hands and feet and side a gift of his very self, a ransom worth more than gold,
a redeeming, a buying of a fallen race back by showing what a human being
could do if only he spent himself in the service of the Creator/Father:

> Brute beauty and valour and act, oh, air, pride, plúme, here
> > Buckle! AND the fire that breaks from thee then, a billion
> Tímes told lovelier, more dangerous, O my chevalier!
>
> > No wónder of it: shéer plód makes plóugh down síllion
> Shíne, and blue-bleak embers, ah my dear,
> > Fall, gáll themsélves, and gásh góld-vermílion.

Ah yes, a king's ransom in the gashed blood gushing from the Crucified
One, who came to give his all to buy us back with the only sacrifice large
enough to be acceptable to the Father, the new Adam redeeming the first,
and all his progeny.

Midsummer and Yet Another Gem: "Pied Beauty," a poem of pure praise
for nature's splendid variety, a curtal sonnet, three fourths the size of a regular one, ten and a half lines long, a form Hopkins himself has invented, the
two parts in Pythagorean mathematical harmony with each other, composed at nearby Tremerchion in the Welsh countryside. "Glory be to God

for dappled things," the poem rings out, for skies pied as brindled cows, as for the detail of rose-moles stippled upon swimming trout, spots too quickly dimmed when taken from their waterworld, as Hopkins, that avid fisherman, has seen with his own eyes. These rose-moles chiming with freshfallen chestnuts revealing their inner rose red, chiming with those fresh fire coals in the closing lines of "The Windhover."

Or the pied beauty of finches' wings—yellow and black and gray and white. And then panning out again to take in the Welsh landscape, with its variegated shades of greens and browns and blues. And all trades as well, with their gear and tackle and trim, adding to God's variegated abundance. All things opposite and different and unique, as Scotus would have noticed— all of this fathered forth by a Creator who contains all perfection in himself, a Creator therefore past all change. And what shall we do in the face of all this splendor and grandeur and goodness? What do? What do, but praise Him:

> Glóry be to God for dappled things,
>   For skies of couple-colour as a brinded cow;
>   For rose-moles all in stipple upon trout that swim;
> Fresh-firecoal chestnut-fálls; fínches' wings;
>   Lándscape plotted and pieced—fold, fallow, and plough;
>   And áll trádes, their gear and tackle and trim.
>
> Áll things counter, original, spáre, stránge;
>   Whatever is fickle, frecklèd (who knows how?)
>   With swíft, slów; sweet, sóur; adázzle, dím;
> He fathers-forth whose beauty is pást chánge:
>   Práise hím.

On June 27 and again on the 30th, Hopkins travels back up to Rhyl, the second time to discuss Welsh etymology and things Celtic with the Welsh scholar John Rhys at his home on Conwy Street. In between, on the 28th— along with Father Minister and two others—he starts for Pant y Coed in the community trap driven by a new horse named Bob. Along the road, the shaft suddenly collapses and the horse goes down. Hopkins and the others are left shaken but unhurt, unlike poor Bob, who must be put down because of his suffering.

Bridges writes to discuss the topic of Miltonic rhythm, but Hopkins is forced to put him off. "Having both work here to do and serious letters to write I shrank from the 'distressing subject' of rhythm on which I knew I must enter," he finally writes in mid-June. "I could not even promise to write often or answer promptly, our correspondence lying upon unprofessional matter." The letter is short and to the point. Even now he has time only to acknowledge the death of Bridges's stepfather, Dr. Molesworth, for whom there does not seem to be much love lost on either Hopkins's or Bridges's part. But he is relieved to hear that Bridges's mother—whom Hopkins does like—will be coming now to live with Bridges at 52 Bedford Square. It is yet another reason Hopkins should like to visit if and when he gets down to London.

Then the dreaded exams, which Hopkins passes, but not sufficiently well to warrant his going on for the Long Course, that is, the fourth year that would allow him to become a Professed Jesuit. Come September and ordination, he is told, he will be sent out to work, though where that will be, and what kind of work he will be given, he will not know until September. Not going on for a fourth year in theology means he will never be able to serve in an administrative capacity, as either Rector or Provincial. It is an embarrassing episode for a scholarship student who graduated with a first from Oxford, and it will leave a long, sad, and bitter taste in the man.

But why did he fail? How could this have happened to him? Since the examiners have long since gone to their own respective rewards, the answer remains problematic. Still, three things should be considered. First, Hopkins already had a reputation for reading Suarezian Scholasticism through the eyes of Duns Scotus, which made him appear both odd and certainly out of the mainstream of the received Jesuit theology of his time. If the Thomistic way of understanding was via the species, Scotus was for individuation, the *haeceittas* or one-of-a kindness of experience. Not its sense of belonging to a general type or category—tree, woman, man, love, virtue, kindness, face—but rather the sense that this experience—here, now, at this particular moment—was special and could never be exactly repeated or duplicated, thousands of unique encounters therefore capable of changing the beholder as well. The mind held, yes, but the heart as well, in the electric exchange. All this was possible because God, that subtle Maker, is at every moment making things anew and fresh and forever themselves.

The trouble with this radical view was that, while he and the other Scholastics had been encouraged by Father Gallwey to question their professors, something Hopkins had done repeatedly not only in his classes but in the debates held on Saturday evenings, and though the Scholastics throve on such probing inquiries, knowing they would surely be coming up against religious and philosophical antipathies once they hit the ground running, the thought of questioning theological assumptions in the final exam would have earned him no high marks from his examiners. And if he did try to persuade them to accept a Scotist interpretation of Aquinas, he chose the wrong forum. "As a theologian," his fellow Jesuits who knew him then and later assert, "his undoubted brilliance was dimmed by a some-what obstinate love of Scotist doctrine, in which he traced the influence of Platonist philosophy." And it was this idiosyncrasy which "got him into dif-ficulties with his Jesuit preceptors who followed [the more scientific model of] Aquinas and Aristotle. The strain of controversy added to bad health . . . marred his earlier years."

The second factor would indeed have been Hopkins's problematic health, the stress he seemed often to be under, the loss of weight, the re-peated head colds, the fatigue, the digestive and enteric problems, the need to get as much rest as he could, in spite of his willingness to soldier on. Three years of hard theology seemed to have almost undone him again and again, and increasingly so in the past year, so why add the burden of a fourth year of intense study to the man?

Third, the Jesuits would need strong administrators for their schools and colleges and foreign missions in England and British Guiana, Africa and India, and whatever Hopkins's strengths, they did not lie in that direc-tion. True, this was an examination in theology, but it is a factor which may have entered into the equation, especially given his Scotist eccentricities and his insistence on going his own way. Perhaps in time he would make a good preacher. He certainly had the intelligence and the knowledge, but at this point he also had a pronounced tendency to overelaborate, to go on at too great length and so lose his audience. Yes, he had a minor reputation for versemaking, but what the Jesuits needed far more than poems was manpower: teachers to teach and preachers to preach, to get the work done that must be done to care for a burgeoning Catholic population. In any case, he was not going on for a fourth year of theology.

And though he is heartsick over the news, he will keep this to himself like the good soldier he is and serve wherever he is sent. It is only when he makes his Final Vows five years later that he will confess to his fellow Jesu-its that there was a time when he "had hoped to be professed" and the fact that he never would be remained "a sad heartache" for him. But now, the day after his exams, he is going home and will have to break the news some-how to his family. He knows what his father will probably think about that, both with regard to himself and to those Jesuits who have ruined his oldest boy's chances for advancement in the world, even if only the world of Jesuits.

·   ·   ·

Hopkins spends the next three weeks—from July 25 until August 13—at home with his family, managing to get over to London to dine with Bridges, Woodridge, and Mrs. Molesworth and talk poetry, and even stay the night at 52 Bedford Square. On August 8, he writes Bridges to say that his bag has finally shown up, together with the manuscript of the *Deutschland* of which he spoke, which he is now sending on to him. He asks his friend to spend special care on the accentual marks he has been at pains to provide, and to return the poem as soon as he can, as it is his only copy. He also sends along a corrected version of one of his sonnets, asks Bridges to correct something in "The Caged Skylark," and encloses an article by E. W. Gosse from the July *Cornhill*—"A Plea for Certain Exotic Forms of Verse"—which quotes one of Bridges's triolets as perhaps the first example of the French form successfully transplanted to England.

The topic of religion having inevitably come up in their talks, Bridges has let drop one of his snide comments to Hopkins, who is still smarting from its fallout. Moreover, Bridges seems to have made it plain that whatever religious feelings he once had at Oxford are pretty much gone, and that he has settled into a comfortable sort of fashionable skepticism and indifference about the whole matter. "It seems," Hopkins adds sardonically now, "that triolets and rondels and rondeaus and chants royal and what not and anything but serving God are all the fashion."

Two days later, he writes Bridges again. He has just heard from his Provincial and must leave Monday morning to return to Wales. Bridges in turn asks him—wryly—who this mysterious Provincial is that Hopkins should run at his beck and call. "What mystery is there about the Provincial?" Hopkins answers testily. "He is head of our province and as he wants to see me on Sunday [at Farm Street] there is no longer any reason for my not going away on Monday, as I meant at first." And then, still smarting at what he knows is coming: "Much against my inclination I shall have to leave Wales."

Two days after returning to St. Beuno's, he writes his father to thank him for his unexpected kindness during his visit home. "No sooner," he adds wistfully, "were we among the Welsh hills than I saw the hawks flying and other pleasant sights soon to be seen no more." Then he provides a window into the freedom of a tramp's life. "I found my bag from Bodfari heavy enough," he writes, "nevertheless I was merrily jaunting along with it on my shoulder when I overtook a tall Lancashire man on the tramp for work, who offered to carry it; I agreed and paid him handsomely, for I could afford to throw my money about," Hopkins being very conscious about the allowance he has been given for his holiday, most of it still unspent. "He told me he had long been a sailor but had left the sea for a settled life on land; if so he must have made all his voyages in a storm, for that is the only way in which a tramp's life cd. look a comparatively settled one." Hopkins has brought the man "to our farm, where I think he got work." Then he adds, "I have heard no appointments yet."

A week later, he answers another of Bridges's letters, with its new load of snide comments about Hopkins's Provincial opening his correspondence and reading it. His letter would hardly amuse Father Jones, Hopkins retorts, and then quotes his own *Deutschland* ode to the effect that the Provincial is at the moment "on the unfathering deeps outward bound to Jamaica." In fact, he adds, "I shd. not think of telling you anything about his reverence's goings and comings if it were not that I know this fact has been chronicled in the Catholic papers." Enough that Bridges's joking about Provincials and poems amuses him. And so to business. Bridges has read the *Deutschland,* read it once only, and refuses for any amount of money to read it again. In fact, he includes a parody of it in his letter. "Your parody reassures me about your understanding the metre," Hopkins answers now. "Only remark, as you say that there is no conceivable licence I shd. not be able to justify, that with all my licences, or rather laws, I am stricter than you and I might say than anybody I know. With the exception of the *Bremen* stanza [Stanza 12], which was, I think, the first written after 10 years' interval of silence, and before I had fixed my principles, my rhymes are rigidly good—to the ear. . . . In fact all English verse, except Milton's, almost, offends me as 'licentious.' Remember this."

And, no, he did not "invent sprung rhythms but only sprung rhythm." He knows from his year lecturing at Roehampton that "single lines and single instances of it are not uncommon in English." Milton has them, and Shakespeare, and Campbell and Moore, "not to speak of . . . Nursery Rhymes, Weather Saws, and Refrains." What he *has* done—and is the first to have done—"is to enfranchise them as a regular and permanent principle of scansion." And, he insists, even those "long, e.g. seven-syllabled, feet of the *Deutschland,* are strictly metrical." Nor is the *Deutschland* counterpointed, for counterpoint depends on a regular meter, and so is de facto excluded by sprung rhythm. In a few of his sonnets he has mingled the two systems, a "most delicate and difficult business," for sprung rhythm depends solely on the number of stresses in a line, like the underlying accentual beat in Anglo-Saxon verse, whether there are one, two, three, or even more unstressed syllables between accents. Or none.

But why use sprung rhythm at all? Because, Hopkins stresses, "it is the nearest to the rhythm of prose, that is the native and natural rhythm of speech, the least forced, the most rhetorical and emphatic of all possible rhythms, combining . . . opposite and . . . incompatible excellences, markedness of rhythm—that is rhythm's self—and, naturalness of expression." The rhythms of speech itself, he means, because those rhythms are in and of themselves musical, and separated from a slavish reliance on traditional meters. In the long run, his verse is "less to be read than heard. It is oratorical, that is the rhythm is so. . . . I cannot think of altering anything." Why should he? He is not writing for the public. Bridges is his public, and it is Bridges he hopes to convert—in more ways than one.

As to Bridges's saying he would not for any amount of money read the *Deutschland* again, he nevertheless begs him to do so. "Besides money, you know, there is love." And if the poem seems obscure in places, he advises one of his first readers, he is not to bother "with the meaning but pay attention to the best and most intelligible stanzas, as the two last of each part and the narrative of the wreck. If you had done this you wd. have liked it better and sent me some serviceable criticisms, but now your criticism is of no use, being only a protest memorialising me against my whole policy and proceedings." And, he adds, "for your greater interest and edification . . . what refers to myself in the poem is all strictly true and did all occur; nothing is added for poetical padding." The poem is in its deepest sense, then, a naked confession of his own deeply held religious feelings.

But Bridges will never take to the *Deutschland*. Forty years on, long after Hopkins is gone and he himself an old man, he will try as his friend's first editor to warn Hopkins's audience that "the labour spent on this great metrical experiment must have served to establish the poet's prosody and perhaps his diction: therefore the poem stands logically as well as chronologically [first] . . . like a great dragon folded in the gate to forbid all entrance, and confident in his strength from past success." But, he adds, he himself "advises the reader to circumvent him and attack him later in the rear," having been "shamefully worsted in a brave frontal assault, the more easily perhaps because both subject and treatment were distasteful to him." But this says more about Bridges than it does about Hopkins.

Saturday, September 1: Back in his beloved Wales, Hopkins composes another sonnet, this one titled "Hurrahing in Harvest." It is the outcome, he tells Bridges, "of half an hour of extreme enthusiasm as I walked home alone one day from fishing in the Elwy." "Summer ends now," the poem begins, celebrating the harvest—a harvest for the eyes in both the gathered stooks of wheat and the "meal-drift" of clouds. A celebration, then, but an elegy too for wild Wales in the weeks before he will have to leave this beautiful landscape:

> now, bárbarous in béauty, the stóoks ríse
> Around; up above, what wind-walks! what lovely behaviour
> Of silk-sack clóuds! has wilder, wilful-wávier
> Méal-drift moulded ever and melted acróss skíes?

But, as in "The Starlight Night"—his celebratory poem of six months before—he is looking for something deeper, some sign that Christ can indeed be gleaned from the beauty all about him:

> I wálk, I líft up, Í lift úp heart, éyes,
> Down all that glory in the heavens to glean our Saviour;
> And, éyes, heárt, what looks, what lips yet gáve you á
> Rápturous love's greeting of realer, of rounder replies?

Is what he is looking for there, then, in "the azurous hung hills" of the Clwyd Valley, blue melding with blue? Do they make up Christ's "world-wielding shoulder / Majestic—as a stallion stalwart, very-violet-sweet!"? Christ *pantokrator*, Christ the King, the World-wielder, Christ the Wheat, the Host and the Harvest, upholding his servant even now, on a Saturday at the beginning of September, as he walks back from fishing in a Welsh river. Well, "These things, these things were here," he sees, and are always there for the taking,

> and but the beholder
> Wánting; whích two whén they ónce méet,
> The heárt réars wíngs bóld and bolder
> And hurls for him, O half hurls earth for him off under his feet.

But whose feet? the poem's syntax teases us. Christ's, at whose feet Hopkins offers this act of praise? Or is it he himself who has been swept off his feet in an ecstasy of realization of Christ's sacramental presence in the world around him? But isn't it both beholder and beheld, the thing being looked hard at looking hard back at the stunned beholder?

Saturday, September 15: Hopkins and the other Scholastics—all four tiers of them—begin their annual retreat. The following Friday, he and his class receive the order of subdeacon, followed the next day by the order of deacon, and then—on Sunday, September 23—the order of priest bestowed on them by Bishop James Brown, the same Hopkins had celebrated in his poem the year before. This is the day Hopkins has been waiting nine long years for, and now it is here. He and the others sleep in until eight. Then ordinations from ten until noon. There are sixteen new priests being ordained, including Hopkins, followed by a sumptuous dinner with seating for fifty guests—though no one is there from his own family. Roast mutton, soup, ham, chicken, turkey, beef tongue, peas, French beans. Then a stroll about the gardens, followed by an impromptu concert by the Scholastics in the Recreation Room. Later the *Te Deum* is sung, followed by the Benediction. After the guests depart, there is a light repast, at which the senior priests propose the Bishop's health, and the Bishop in turn proposes the Rector's, who in turn toasts the newly ordained priests.

Then it is back to business, as classes once again get underway. Rooms are changed, texts distributed, a new choirmaster chosen. But none of this affects Hopkins, for six days after ordination he takes to his bed. Dr. Turnour from the village comes to see him, accompanied by the house surgeon from Denbigh Hospital, so that they can circumcise him. The operation is successful, but Hopkins is confined to his bed for the next ten days. On October 9, he is finally able to get up and move about. He has his new assignment. He will be going to Spinkhill, Mount St. Mary's College, in Chesterfield, Derbyshire, to teach and serve as the school's assistant bursar. "The work is nondescript," he tells his mother. "Examining, teaching . . . with occasional mission work and preaching or giving retreats." He expects to know more once he gets there. "The number of scholars is about 150, the community moderately small and family-like, the country round not very interesting but at a little distance is fine country, Sheffield is the nearest great town."

He also commiserates with her over the death of her father, Dr. John Smith, just days before. He is glad his "dear grandfather's end was peaceful and that all his children could be present to witness the last moments of an affectionate and generous father," he tells her. But there is something more he wants to say. "I had for years been accustomed every day to recommend him very earnestly to the Blessed Virgin's protection; so that I could say, if such a thing can ever be said without presumption, If I am disappointed who can hope? As his end drew near I had asked some people to pray for him and said to someone in a letter that I should take it as a happy token if he died on Sunday the Feast of the Holy Rosary. It is a day signalised by our Lady's overruling aid asked for and given at the victory of Lepanto." Hopkins takes it as a sign, then, that his prayers have been heard, "and that the queen of heaven has saved a Christian soul from enemies more terrible than a fleet of infidels." He asks his mother not to make light of what he has told her, "for it is perhaps the seventh time that I think I have had some token from heaven in connection with the death of people in whom I am interested."

In the week before his departure, Hopkins is gifted with a final sonnet: "The Lantern out of Doors." It is certainly the saddest and loneliest of his Welsh sonnets, filled as it is with a sense of loss: loss by death or loss by distance. As he looks out the window of his room, he sees a lantern swinging in the dark. Someone is out there, either someone from the community, or some farmer perhaps. He does not know. It is an image for each of us, he realizes, for "Men go by me whom either beauty bright / In mould or mind or what not else makes rare." Consider Dolben and Challis and his Highgate friends. Or Urquhart, Pusey, Baillie, and Bridges. Or his Oxford friends already gone, like his grandfather now. "They rain against our much-thick and marsh air," he laments, like that figure out there in the misted night, all of them "Rich beams, till death or distance buys them quite." And then a second time the refrain: "Déath or distance soon consumes them." Let the eye wind after as it tries to follow the lantern light flickering and growing dimmer, still, none of us can be in at the end for anyone, and worse, as the saying goes, once "out of sight is out of mind." Death has done its work, and the light that stood in for our life is inevitably swallowed up in dark.

But no. There is one who can wind after, who does mind, who is interested because we are the interest paid out on his Great Sacrifice. He is the one who can be in at the end as we ourselves never can, the one who broods over us, is haunted with care for us, his foot kindly following his kind, this God who deigned to take on our flesh and our human condition even unto death:

> Christ minds: Christ's interest, what to avow or amend
> There, éyes them, heart wánts, care haúnts, foot fóllows kínd,
> Their ránsom, théir rescue, ánd first, fást, last friénd.

More than ever he will need such a friend, as he begins his journey as patchwork priest filling in here and there, going where he is sent, as now, to work with fifth- and sixth-formers at Spinkhill, the least lovely place he has been sent to in his nine years as a Jesuit. On Friday, October 19, 1877, at half past nine in the morning, Hopkins bids farewell to his fellow Jesuits at St. Beuno's, then rides off in the community trap with his bags and few belongings for the rail station at Rhyl and the new, diminished world beyond that is more or less awaiting his arrival.

PART III

IN HARNESS

1877–1884

*Gerard Manley Hopkins
at Oxford, October 1879.*

Chapter 10

Father Hopkins: Mount St. Mary's, Stonyhurst, & Farm Street, 1877–1878

Toward evening on October 19, 1877, Father Hopkins, thirty-three, arrives at Mount St. Mary's College, a school founded by the Jesuits as long ago as 1620. But that was in the time of the draconian Penal Laws, and the school has since undergone many transmutations before opening in 1842 at Spinkhill under the leadership of Father Randall Lythgoe, then Provincial of the reestablished English Jesuits. The core buildings here date back to the sixteenth and seventeenth centuries, with the chapel being the oldest. When troops under Charles II raided the Jesuit college at Holbeck, the Jesuits brought what they could salvage to this place. Two centuries later, it was Hansom—here as at St. Beuno's—who saw to the construction of the new college buildings, beginning in 1840. Construction on the New College is in progress even as Hopkins arrives, and will continue for the next thirty-five years. Sent here to teach Latin to fifth and sixth formers, he soon finds the work as overwhelming as that he encountered at the Oratory ten years earlier. On top of which, one of the other masters—Mr. Hepburne—takes ill, and for several weeks Hopkins must teach the fifth-form syntax students as well as his own.

W. F. Lee, one of Hepburne's students, and now Father Hopkins's, will remember Father Hopkins with affection long after. He had "a well-deserved reputation for scholarship," Lee will recall, and was a much gentler and more trusting master than Hepburne, who knew his charges. On one occasion, Hopkins gave them "that hoary chestnut, 'The Assyrian came down' to turn into Latin elegiacs." The students were delighted, because they already had a Latin crib of the poem. Even Lee borrowed a few verses of the crib, fitting them seamlessly in with his own poor attempts. "Fr. Hopkins's lead pencil had been very busy" with his own botched translation, he will recall, "but when he came to the cribbed lines," he penciled in some "firm wavy strokes of commendation and the side note, 'extraordinarily good.'" He never seems to have suspected that his boys might cheat like that, and—even though many of them used the same crib—he does not seem to have caught on.

Even on Sundays he gets no rest, for then he must help out the local parish priest at mass. And though the weather remains mild into late January, the Yorkshire skies are overcast and cloudy for weeks. How he misses being able to see great vistas, as he could at St. Beuno's and Oak Hill. Nor is there any surcease from his duties at Christmas, for the boys do not go home for vacation but instead present plays and musical concerts each night. But this diversion, at least, gives him some enjoyment. "Their acting," he tells his mother, "was creditable and Berkeley my particular pupil is a born actor, a very amusing low comedian and still better in tragedy; his Lady Macbeth, in spite of being turned into 'Fergus' Macbeth's younger brother, was quite a 'creation.'" Hopkins himself provides the comic prologue for the schoolboys' production: a farce consisting in the speaker's seeming to forget all his lines. But Berkeley, he warms himself, "did it so naturally that he overshot the mark and most part of the audience thought he had forgotten in earnest and that his strange behaviour was due to 'refreshments' behind the scenes."

On Twelfth Night—January 6, 1878—the schoolboys perform a "mumming," dressing "in red and yellow paper clothes" to give "two performances in aid of the poor schools," to which the country folk came, "laughed prodigiously at the jokes and sometimes at the wrong places and wept freely at the pathetic scenes." Even Mr. Hepburne's charges are a source of amusement. Asked to write an account of the 1755 earthquake at Lisbon, they have provided such gems as: "It was a fine bright day when at ten o'clock a picture of extreme suddenness came on." And: "After the earthquake 'an old ruffian of a mob ran about killing everyone he met.'" And: "this catastrophe has left many a mark on the minds of learned men." But then there are the interminable student copybook essays to pore over, "with no doubt more of the same sort on the Earl of Nithsdale's escape" from an English prison dressed in women's clothes.

In late February, he sends word to Bridges for the first time in nearly half a year, asking him to return the *Deutschland* manuscript before it is irreparably lost, as in fact in time it will be. He is both "pleased and flattered to hear" that Bridges and his mother have twice called at Oak Hill to pay a visit. "Write me an interesting letter," he pleads. "I cannot do so. Life here is as dank as ditch-water and has some of the other qualities of ditch-water: at least I know that I am reduced to great weakness by diarrhea, which lasts too, as if I were poisoned." In fact, it is only because the school has called a holiday in honor of the election of the new Pope, or even "this note would have lain still longer." Two weeks earlier, on February 7, Pio Nono had died after thirty-two years as pontiff. Then, after a week of secret meetings, word of the election of a new Pope: Gioacchino Luigi, Pope Leo XIII, who will serve for the next twenty-five years. Virtually all of Hopkins's life will be lived, then, under just two popes. Pius IX's loss is especially felt by the Jesuits, for he had been their champion. When one of his cardinals expressed surprise that he was so attached to an order against which even bishops and cardinals had brought serious charges, he is said to have replied, "You have to be pope to know the worth of the Society."

March 5th: For Shrove Tuesday, Hopkins's fifth- and sixth-formers put on a one-act burlesque called *A Model Kingdom,* based on Henry Carey's eighteenth-century *Chrononhotonthologos.* Ten-year-old Jimmy Broadbent, playing the herald, struts on stage, announcing that "Your faithful Gen'ral, Bombardinion / Sends you his Tongue, transplanted in my Mouth, / To pour his Soul out in your Royal Ears." To which the boy king replies, "Then use thy Master's Tongue with Reverence." But while the verbal wit unfolds on stage, Hopkins's attention is drawn to Jimmy's eleven-year-old brother, Henry, tortured that Jimmy is going to forget his lines. And that for Hopkins is where the real drama lies. Two years later Hopkins will recall this moment, when young Harry, having asked Hopkins to stand near him while Jimmy was on stage, broke into tears of relief upon hearing his younger brother proclaim his lines, unaware of the drama of his older brother fretting over him. "Brothers" is a tender poem, the conflicting emotions of a play within a play remembered, written in a bold sprung rhythm and trimeter couplets and tercets as a fitting form for this modest drama so far removed from the *Deutschland* tragedy of two years before. "How lovely" that memory, when "the elder brother's / Life" seemed love-laced in the younger's, and

> Smiled, blushed, and bit his lip;
> Or drove, with a diver's dip,
> Clutched hands down through claspèd knees;
> And many a mark like these,
> Told tales with what heart's stress
> He hung on the imp's success . . .

Jack, that imp, belting out his lines with such "bráss-bóld élan," and Harry, crying for love, at the same time—like any eleven-year-old—embarrassed by his weeping before the other boys, his "tear-tricked cheeks" flaming "For fond love and for shame." Knowing what he knows of human nature, of what ten- and eleven-year-olds are capable of in terms of Hobbesian self-interest, Hopkins has been likewise moved by this inherent capacity of the human heart for kindness:

> . . . Nature, bad, base, and blind,
> Dearly thou canst be kind;
> There déarly thén, deárly,
> Dearly thou canst be kind.

Still, in his six months since leaving Wales, Hopkins has written no poetry whatsoever. "My muse turned utterly sullen in the Sheffield smoke-ridden air," he confesses to Bridges at the beginning of April. But all that is about to change with the news of yet another shipwreck: the foundering of the HMS *Eurydice* on Sunday afternoon, March 24, off the Isle of Wight. A refitted training ship returning from six months in Bermuda with some 327 sailors aboard, most of them young men not much older than his own students, the *Eurydice* is caught in a freak gale-force spring snowstorm hidden by a landmass until too late, and sinks within eight minutes, taking all but two of those on board with her. The catastrophe, Hopkins confesses, "worked on me and I am making a poem—in my own rhythm but in a measure something like Tennyson's *Violet* (bound with *Maud*)," and also using what he calls overreeving, "where the rhyme is completed by the first letter of the next line to complete the rhyme in the line before it." He is relieved to have the *Deutschland* back from Bridges, and admits that, yes, it "would be more generally interesting if there were more wreck and less discourse . . . but still it is an ode and not primarily a narrative." His model there was Pindar, he explains, where "the principal business is lyrical." However, this new poem is almost all narrative and is a tribute to the lost youth of England. *The Loss of the Eurydice* is less than half as long as his *Deutschland*—thirty quatrains of four-stress lines, with three stresses to the third line, each stanza conceived of as one long line "rhymed in passage." He wants narrative speed for this poem, he explains, rather than the meditative sweep of the *Deutschland,* in part to please Bridges who had demanded more narrative for the *Deutschland* ode.

"It is with deep concern that we have to announce the loss of one of Her Majesty's ships," Hopkins would have read in *The Times* on the 25th, the day after the disaster:

Yesterday afternoon [the *Eurydice*] was observed passing Ventnor [on the Isle of Wight] under full sail on her voyage up the Channel, when a sudden snow-storm came on, accompanied by heavy squalls of wind. When the storm cleared away the *Eurydice* was nowhere to be seen. . . . A passing schooner picked up five men, among them the first lieutenant, who survived only a short time; two only of those who were rescued are now alive, and there seems little or no hope that the lives of any others of the crew can have been saved. The weather cleared almost as suddenly as it had become foul, but nothing could be seen from Ventnor but a few large boxes rapidly carried away by a strong ebb tide.

The tragedy has hit home. First, there is the shipwreck itself, with all of its existential and psychological resonances for Hopkins. Then the crew, made up of young men just starting out. And then the fact that the ship sank so near the Isle of Wight, where he and his family had spent so many summer holidays, on whose hills and roads he had walked and sketched, and on whose waters he had fished, boated, and swum.

"It would be premature to attempt to divine the causes of this disaster, and very likely we shall never know much more about it than we do at present," *The Times* has opined. But once again—like Milton and Wordsworth before him—that is exactly what Hopkins opts to do, in a poem he hopes will sit better with a Victorian audience, or—barring that—a Catholic audience, or, barring that, with his fellow Jesuits. "The *Eurydice*—it concerned thee, O Lord," he begins, addressing the only One who could have been in at the end, as he had written in his last poem before leaving Wales. Six times the number of those who perished in the *Deutschland* disaster. Again, as in Milton's *Lycidas,* which the poem echoes in many of its details, Hopkins evokes the flockbells of sheep grazing on the cliffs at Ventnor, four miles south of Shanklin, knelling the dead. And the narrative, much like the *Deutschland*'s Bremen stanzas, detailing the storm, this one sweeping north to south on a promising blue March day, with the *Eurydice* within sight of home after so many months away. "Hailropes hustle and grind their / Heavengravel," he describes the hailstorm. "Wolfsnow, worlds of it."

Within minutes, the storm, hurtling along at forty miles an hour, passes over the ship, capsizing her, and sucking the crew down with her, death coming in the form of frigid seawater pouring through the ship's open gun portals, gulping "messes of mortals." This time, at least, he will not repeat the mistake he realizes he made in the *Deutschland* in not naming the victims, as now he gives to man after man their living names. Captain Marcus Hare, going down with his ship, a model to follow even to the brackish end. "It is even seen," Hopkins comments, that those who would swerve from doing their duty, can and will—in the moment of crisis, "At downright 'No or yes?'"—doff all and drive "full for righteousness," as Hare did. Or Sydney Fletcher of Bristol, one of the two survivors, taking "to the seas and snows / As sheer down the ship goes," pulled down in the afterdraught of the ship's sinking, but managing to rise from the terrifying pull of the sea to gasp air. And in lines which evoke something of Whitman's elegies for his Civil War dead, he evokes now the dead Christ in the figure of a handsome sea corpse:

> Look, foot to forelock, how all things suit! he
> Is strung by duty, is strained to beauty,
>   And brown-as-dawning-skinned
> With brine and shine and whirling wind.

> O his nimble finger, his gnarled grip!
> Leagues, leagues of seamanship
>   Slumber in these forsaken
> Bones, this sinew, and will not waken.

And then the ostensible reason for the poem, the analogy made here as in the *Deutschland* and at least half of the sonnets of '77: that the wreck is a sign of the impending loss of Hopkins's beloved England itself. For England too is like Eurydice gone down to hell, the poet's own "people and born own nation, / Fast foundering own generation." Oh, he "might let bygones be," might overlook the curse attendant on those under the Tudors who took possession of the abbey closes and monasteries and grand cathedrals, or simply left these sacred places to crumble under the elements, the "hoar-hallowèd shrines unvisited." But greater temples than these perished in the loss of the *Eurydice*: "These daredeaths, ay this crew, in / Unchrist, all rolled in ruin."

Why, he wonders, did Christ allow it, the "riving off that race" of English, a people once so "at home" with the Catholic faith, time was, so at home with Catholic truth and grace that a pilgrim could find his way to the now dismantled shrine of Our Lady of Walsingham by simply following the Milky Way, a faith that nurtured then as it might do once more if his countrymen would but open their hearts to the possibility? For one of our own did see into the deep sacramental nature of things, he reminds his readers, the Scotsman, Duns Scotus, the unnamed "one."

Well, no matter. Let be, for there is surely more of the same coming as the world goes its appetitive ways. Weep for your dead, he warns, as Christ warned those in Jerusalem as he was led to his own death. Ah, mothers, weep for your dead sons. Wives weep for your husbands, sweethearts for your lovers. Not that grief of itself will yield you any good. Still: "shed what tears sad truelove should." No, the only one who can reach the drowned men now is "Christ lord of thunder." Better for the poet, then, to kneel in supplication and pray, pray to the merciful Master for help for these man boys in their final agonizing moments, since for God time is infinitely malleable, and he will have heard what the poet (and the reader) asks even now, a month or a century on:

> the prayer thou hearst me making
> Have, at the awful overtaking,
>   Heard; have heard and granted
> Grace that day grace was wanted . . .

It is all one can do. As for those precious souls, those "last-breath-penitents": only God can be in at the end, only the Father can help there.

Once again he sends a shipwreck poem off to Father Coleridge at *The Month* to await his decision. This year, he tells his mother—though the news can hardly leave her feeling the better for it—he has kept the strict Lenten fast, as his superiors had forbade him from doing while he was in training. However, the regimen, he assures her, has left him no worse, though "thinner than I ever saw myself in the face, with my cheeks like two harp-frames." He also has some good news. After six months spent teaching the young at Spinkhill, he is leaving for Stonyhurst, where he will remain until July, coaching advanced students for their London University degrees, after which he is to be sent to Farm Street in London. His dear old supporter, Father Gallwey, has finally been able to get him stationed there, where his main work will be preaching.

And so he is leaving Lancashire just when the neighborhood "is gayest and prettiest, as vermilion tiles and orchard blossoms make it," and just when he had finally become adjusted to the place. In fact, he has become very fond of his boys here and believes "they lead a very happy life with us, though the discipline is strict." He is especially proud of his pupil Herbert Berkeley, who has "carried off an 'Intercollegiate' prize, for which several of our schools compete." Hopkins is more pleased than he "should have thought possible," and does not think he will "easily have so good a pupil

again," for Herbert is always "eager to take down everything I say and repeats it with minute accuracy long afterwards." He has even taken a group
of boys about the countryside to show them some of the local landmarks.
And two days before—on Easter Monday—he took them "to Clumber Park
the Duke of Newcastle's seat," where they had "a very pleasant day; also the
next day a party of ourselves went there driving and managed to see Steetly
chapel, the most beautiful little Norman ruin you can imagine." And then
there was Creswell Crags, "a cleft between cliffs with water between," though
"both days were murky and did no justice to trees, buildings, or pictures."
Still, there are many places in South Yorkshire he has not had time to visit,
like Chatsworth and Haddon Hall and Hardwick Hall. And now he is leaving
for Stonyhurst and the Lancashire landscapes of his philosophical years.

Monday, May 13, 1878: Two weeks after settling in at Stonyhurst, he
writes Bridges, enclosing his *Eurydice,* which *The Month* has just refused.
"It is my only copy," he tells Bridges, warning him to "write no bilgewater
about it: I will presently tell you what that is and till then excuse the term."
He is still smarting that Bridges steadfastly refuses to have anything more
to do with his *Deutschland.* "Granted that it needs study and is obscure, for
indeed I was not over-desirous that the meaning of all should be quite clear,
at least unmistakeable," he explains, "you might, without the effort that to
make it all out would seem to have required, have nevertheless read it so
that lines and stanzas should be left in the memory and superficial impressions deepened, and have liked some without exhausting all. I am sure I
have read and enjoyed pages of poetry that way." Including, Hopkins might
add, Bridges's own poems. Sometimes we enjoy and admire "the very lines
one cannot understand, as for instance [Shakespeare's] 'If it were done
when 'tis done' sqq., which is all obscure and disputed, though how fine it
is everybody sees and nobody disputes." Besides, he adds, "you would have
got more weathered to the style and its features," which, he insists, are—
after all—"not really odd."

And what exactly does Hopkins mean by "bilgewater" criticism? This:
"vessels sailing from the port of London . . . used once to take Thames water
for the voyage: it was foul and stunk at first as the ship worked but by degrees casting its filth was in a few days very pure and sweet and wholesomer
and better than any water in the world." Just so, when a poem like the
Deutschland "is presented us our first criticisms are not our truest, best,
most homefelt, or most lasting but what come easiest on the instant. They
are barbarous and like what the ignorant and the ruck say." Like Bridges's
criticisms. "The *Deutschland* on her first run," delighting in the run now of

his own imagination, "worked very much and unsettled you, thickening and clouding your mind with vulgar mudbottom and common sewage . . . and just then unhappily you drew off your criticisms all stinking . . . and bilgy, whereas if you had let your thoughts cast themselves they would have been clearer in themselves and more to my taste too."

And so he refuses to pay any attention to Bridges's comments on the *Deutschland*, "perceiving they were a first drawing-off." Similarly with his new poem, "which being short and easy please read more than once." And, in a postscript eight days later, he offers Bridges the same advice he had given when he sent off the *Deutschland*: that he must not read the poem quickly and "slovenly with the eyes but with your ears, as if the paper were declaiming it at you. For instance the line 'she had come from a cruise training seamen' read without stress and declaim is mere Lloyd's Shipping Intelligence; properly read it is quite a different thing. Stress is the life of it." Stress: a voice under pressure, in the higher, vatic registers. A voice. A living and impassioned voice.

This time Bridges responds with close criticism. "It gave me of course great comfort to read your words of praise," Hopkins writes back. "But however, praise or blame, never mingle with your criticisms monstrous and indecent spiritual compliments like something you have said there." And then on to Bridges's questions. As for the double stress on "lúrch fórward," it is "imitative as usual." Yes, he dislikes having rhymed "foot he" with "duty" and "beauty" so much that he has already changed the rhyme to "suit! he": "how all things suit! he / Is strung by duty, is strained to beauty." Obscurity he will always try to "avoid so far as is consistent with excellences higher than clearness at a first reading." And if "mere novelty and boldness" strikes Bridges as affectation, his criticism remains merely bilgewater.

Hopkins knows more than ever now that in the kind of life he lives, he "shall never have leisure or desire to write much," though he should at least like to finish an ode on the Vale of Clwyd which he began in Wales. "It would be a curious work if done," he thinks, and contains even more advanced "metrical attempts . . . something like Greek choruses, a peculiar eleven-footed line for instance." Among his surviving poems, the closest poem to fit this description is *The Leaden Echo and the Golden Echo*, with its chorus of Welsh maidens at a place that sums up the holiness and beauty of Wales for him: St. Winefred's Well. It is a poem which begins with a line exploding with Welsh *cyngnedd*—consonantal chiming: "How to kéep—is there ány any, is there none such, nowhere known some, bow or brooch or braid or brace, láce, latch or catch or key to keep. . . ." As for those poems of his which Bridges has made copies of: he may do as he likes about showing them. But even so simple a gesture as this will have repercussions for Hopkins.

Within days of arriving at Stonyhurst, Hopkins tries his hand at a May month poem for the Virgin Mary, hoping to display it—along with other poems—before Mary's statue in the inner alcove of the main building. Like the *Eurydice, The May Magnificat* is composed of quatrains, this time twelve of them, based on Andrew Marvell's brilliant *Horatian Ode Upon Cromwell's Return from Ireland,* with this variation: that, whereas Marvell uses octosyllabic couplets throughout, each quatrain of Hopkins's poem is made up of a four-stress couplet followed by a three-stress couplet. As severe and tight as the collar of the form is, it also uses sprung rhythm and a series of compound epithets, things not seen before among the community. It proves so novel, in fact, that it does not pass muster with the Jesuit in charge of May month selections. But by now there is for Hopkins what must be a bittersweet sardonic bite to such refusals.

The poem begins mildly enough, opening with the question why May is Mary's month. Why not ask Mary herself, Hopkins suggests, who might answer by saying that spring means "Growth in every thing":

> Flesh and fleece, fur and feather,
> Grass and greenworld all together;
> Star-eyed strawberry-breasted
> Throstle above her nested
>
> Cluster of bugle blue eggs thin
> Forms and warms the life within;

Mary and Nature, then, as two examples of motherhood, he stresses, punning on Mary's own song of praise, the *Magnificat:*

> Their magnifying of each its kind
> With delight calls to mind
> How she did in her stored
> Magnify the Lord.

But then May is as fitting a symbol for Mary as Mary is for May, as now the poem lifts into its roll and rise, its carol and creation, one compound epithet folding into another, and all ending in a final couplet which returns the poem to something closer to the medieval Catholic origins of the Marian genre and to Duns Scotus's reading of nature:

> When drop-of-blood-and-foam-dapple
> Bloom lights the orchard-apple
>   And thicket and thorp are merry
>   With silver-surfèd cherry
>
> And azuring-over greybell makes
> Wood banks and brakes wash wet like lakes
>   And magic cuckoocall
>   Caps, clears, and clinches all—
>
> This ecstasy all through mothering earth
> Tells Mary her mirth till Christ's birth
>   To remember and exultation
>   In God who was her salvation.

Not only have both his poems been rejected by his fellow Jesuits at *The Month*, but now even his May poem for Mary. And even Bridges, who understands something of his poetry, does not understand it nearly enough. Still there is one thing he can do, at least, and that is to write someone else the kind of letter he should like to have had, if even from a stranger. That, at least, is within his power. And so, on June 4, he picks up his pen and writes one of his former (younger) masters at Highgate, an Anglican priest who had once been a member of the Pre-Raphaelite Brotherhood, but who has since dropped into the obscurity of a country vicarage. This is Richard Watson Dixon, now forty-five, and destined, it would appear, for an obscurity almost as deep as Hopkins's own.

"I take a liberty as a stranger in addressing you," Hopkins begins. "Nevertheless I did once have some slight acquaintance with you. You will not remember me but you will remember taking a mastership for some months at Highgate School, Cholmondeley, where I then was." This was back in the early 1860s, and when Dixon left, he gave a copy of his book of poems, *Christ's Company*, to one of the other masters, a Mr. Lobb. It was the title of the book that initially attracted Hopkins, he explains, and when he went up to Oxford in 1863, he read it, "surprised at it, then pleased," and at last becoming "so fond of it that I made it, so far as that could be, a part of my own mind." Then he read Dixon's *Historical Odes and Other Poems* and his prize essay too, *The*

Close of the Tenth Century of the Christian Era. Later, he introduced Dixon's poems to his friends and, "if they did not share my own enthusiasm, made them at all events admire." Even when he entered the Jesuits, "in which I knew I could have no books of my own and was unlikely to meet with your works in the libraries I should have access to, I copied out *St. Paul, St. John, Love's Consolation,* and others from both volumes and keep them by me."

True, he might have written any time these past dozen years, but he was not even sure Dixon was still alive. But in the February number of the *Athenaeum,* he read a review of the first volume of a *History of the Church of England from the Abolition of the Roman Jurisdiction* by a Richard Watson Dixon, and since then has been meaning to write, since he has long felt he owed Dixon "something or a great deal." Hopkins also knows what it means to have "written and published works the extreme beauty of which the author himself the most keenly feels," only to have them fall "out of sight at once" and to be "almost wholly unknown." If the roles were reversed, he realizes, he should certainly find comfort in knowing that at least one reader somewhere—some stranger—"deeply appreciated" what he had tried to do, so that he would not have "published quite in vain."

How many beautiful works "have been almost unknown and then have gained fame at last," he surmises, though no doubt "many more must have been lost sight of altogether." That work like Dixon's is due for a revival is unlikely, he admits, no matter that it is excellent in itself, and when such a thing happens, "it is an evil in itself and a thing which ought not to be and that I deplore, for the good work's sake rather than the author's." He remembers that Dixon's poems had "a medieval colouring like Wm. Morris's and the Rossetti's [sic] and others but none seemed to me to have it so unaffectedly." More, Dixon's *Ode to Summer* should be placed beside Keats's Odes to Autumn and the Nightingale and on a Grecian Urn. "The extreme delight I felt when I read the line 'Her eyes like lilies shaken by the bees' was more than any single line in poetry ever gave me and now that I am older I could not be so strongly moved by it if I were to read it for the first time." It is a duty in charity that he has written so, he ends, and is meant to "make up, so far as one voice can do, for the disappointment" Dixon must often have felt over his "rich and exquisite work almost thrown away." He signs himself: "Gerard M. Hopkins, S.J.," and adds that he too is a member of " 'Christ's Company.' "

The Reverend Richard Watson Dixon opens this letter on June 6 there in his country vicarage, and is so touched by it that it takes him two days before he can respond. "You cannot but know that I must be deeply moved," he begins. "Nay shaken to the very centre, by such a letter as that which you have sent me: for which I thank you from my inmost heart. . . . I can in truth hardly realise that what I have written, which has been generally, almost universally, neglected, should have been so much valued and treasured. This is more than fame: and I may truly say that when I read your Letter, and whenever I take it out of my pocket to look at it, I feel that I prefer to have been so known & prized by one, than to have had the ordinary appreciation of many."

He was talking with his friend, the painter Burne Jones, recently, who said to him that "One only works in reality for the one man who may rise to understand one, it may be ages hence." Hopkins, Dixon is happy to say, is that very man. He even thinks he remembers him from his days of teaching at Highgate: "a pale young boy, very light and active, with a very meditative & intellectual face," who "got a prize for English poetry. I may be deceived in this identification: but, if you have time to write again, I should like to know. I little thought that my gift to Mr. Lobb, which I had quite forgotten, would bear such fruit."

About fame, or the loss thereof, he agrees with Hopkins: "It is often a disadvantage to rise into fame, at least immediate fame; it leads a man to try to excell himself, or strike out something new incessantly, or at least not to work so naturally and easily as he would if he did not know that the world was watching to see what he will do next." Three years before, he had from his friend Dante Gabriel Rossetti (even the Canon is not adverse to a little name-dropping, it appears), "a letter of warm & high approbation & criticism . . . when he read my poems," which he had not seen before. "You are one of the most subtle as well as varied of our poets," Rossetti had written then, "and the neglect of such work as yours on all hands is an incomprehensible accident." Now, besides Rossetti's letter, Dixon can place Hopkins's. Courteously, beautifully, he notes "with admiration the arduous and self-denying career which is modestly indicated in your Letter & signature: and which places you so much higher in 'Christ's Company' than I am."

And so a much needed correspondence for both men gets underway. On June 13, Hopkins writes back. "Pax Christi," he begins. It is the same salutation that he uses when he writes to his fellow Jesuits. *The peace of Christ be with you.* He is very glad that he wrote Dixon, especially as his writing that letter could affect Dixon "so much and draw out so kind an answer." Yes, he was the boy Dixon remembers: "I did get a prize for an English poem, I do not well remember when; it may have been while you were there." He means *The Escorial,* written at Easter 1860, when he was fifteen. And he knew the poet, poor Philip Worsley, another Highgate student, who went on to become a scholar of Corpus Christi College and translated the

Odyssey and part of the *Iliad* into Spenserian stanzas, before consumption took him at the age of thirty-one. He remembers too that Worsley told him once how Dixon used to "praise Keats by the hour—which might well be: Keats' genius was so astonishing, unequalled at his age and scarcely surpassed at any, that one may surmise whether if he had lived he would not have rivalled Shakspere."

As for fame, he was "not thinking of the harm it does to men as artists: it may do them harm . . . but so . . . may the want of it," if—and here he quotes *Lycidas*—"Fame is the spur that the clear spirit doth raise / To shun delights and live laborious days." Besides, it is "a spur very hard to find a substitute for or to do without," as he too well knows. But he means something more: that fame is by its very nature dangerous, "as dangerous as wealth every bit . . . and as hard to enter the kingdom of heaven with. And even if it does not lead men to break the divine law, yet it gives them 'itching ears' and makes them live on public breath." The poet Coventry Patmore, "whose fame again is very deeply below his great merit," has also "said something very finely about the loss of fame" recently in *The Hidden Eros*. But what Hopkins regrets most "is the loss of recognition belonging to the work itself."

He also recommends his friend Bridges's pamphlet, *The Growth of Love*. The sonnets "are strict in form and affect Miltonic rhythms (which are caviar to the general)" and are "both manly and tender." If Bridges is not rich in imagery, he does excel in poetic phrasing. Two days later, Hopkins returns to the question of fame again. The truth is that fame "is a thing which lies in the award of a random, reckless, incompetent, and unjust judge, the public, the multitude. The only just judge, the only just literary critic, is Christ, who prizes, is proud of, and admires, more than any man, more than the receiver himself can, the gifts of his own making." And the real value of fame "is to convey to us . . . some token of the judgment which a perfectly just, heedful, and wise mind, namely Christ's, passes upon our doings." Since that can be done "as well by one as by many," and since he feels competent to pass fair judgment, "it seemed in the circumstances a charity to tell you what I thought. For disappointment and humiliations"—such as he himself has felt, though he is too much of a gentleman to ever say so—"embitter the heart and make an aching in the very bones."

At the beginning of July—after two months spent tutoring B.A. candidates at Stonyhurst—Hopkins takes up his new duties at Farm Street in London, where he has been brought as select preacher. On the 11th, two weeks short of his thirty-fourth birthday, he hands over his will, customary among all Jesuits who have taken vows of poverty, bequeathing "all my real and personal estate and effects whatsoever and wheresoever of which I may be seized or possessed" to the then-Provincial Father James Jones, resident at Farm Street. Father Tom Rigby and the two Kerr brothers, who witnessed the signing at St. Beuno's, serve as Hopkins's executors. It is all pro forma, but binding under English law, and the will is registered in the Public Record Office in London two days later.

In London, finally, he is able to see Bridges again, telling him that he plans to be at his apartments on the 15th at two in the afternoon. Just now he is busy preparing three sermons which he will preach in August, and has been spending the days making up his theology, though he knows his work as preacher "will soon thicken." He has been assigned here, "but permanence with us is ginger-bread permanence; cobweb, soapsud, and frost-feather permanence." He tries Bridges's place on the chance of finding him in, but misses him. "You will learn that I have just called at Bedford Sq.," he writes, having brought with him "a basket of clean linen"—new poems—"but did not deliver it," and sends the laundry now between the sheets of his letter. Among the poems he is including are "Hurrahing in Harvest," a corrected version of "The Windhover," and "Pied Beauty," his experimental curtal sonnet. He also encloses a poem of his father's that Manley is anxious for a published poet like Bridges to comment on.

On August 4, Hopkins delivers the first of his sermons at the small, neo-Gothic Farm Street Church, with Bridges in one of the pews listening. It is the mass for the tenth Sunday after Pentecost, and Hopkins preaches on Christ's Parable of the Pharisee and Publican. Standing at the pulpit, he explains to his small congregation what Pharisees are and what Publicans. They are not pubkeepers, as the word is commonly used in England, but rather tax collectors. Then he outlines the moral distinctions of good and bad behavior as a part of the work each person does, so that he who touches pitch will be defiled, as "he who handles flour will be whitened." Then on to an explanation of what pride really is. For, though the Pharisee upholds the law, "he said nothing of his sins or sorrow for them, he only spoke of the sins of others, and for them he did not ask God's pardon." In acting so, he showed himself to be "presumptuous towards God, uncharitable and contemptuous towards men." And this thought too will shortly find its way into one of his sonnets.

Charity means doing one's duty, Hopkins insists. The Pharisee injured the Publican's honor, and robbed God of His Honor as well, "and after that what does God care for tithes of potherbs? In all this we are not told that the man committed a mortal sin, we are only told the Publican was justified *rather than* he; but the proud and pitiless man will sin mortally when the occasion comes." Perhaps there is a quick glance toward Bridges. But the Publican "threw his whole self, body, voice, and soul, into his acknowledgment of his sins and such humility was pleasing to God and he was justified." Afterward, Bridges tells Hopkins that he liked neither the music *nor* the mass. And so it will continue between the two friends.

"Next Sunday's sermon must be learnt better than last's," he confesses to Bridges. "I was very little nervous at the beginning and not at all after. It was pure forgetting and flurry. The delivery was not good, but I hope to get a good one in time." He is also open to "any criticisms which are not controversy." And then: "I am glad you did not like the music and sorry you did not like the mass." Edgell of Oxford, he adds, the same fellow who converted back in '68, "lives in the street and comes to church here regularly."

Two days later, Bridges writes Muirhead what he apparently won't say to Hopkins, that "Gerard Hopkins is in town preaching & confessing at Farm St. I went to hear him [last Sunday]. He is good. He calls here: and we have sweet laughter, and pleasant chats. He is not at all the worse for being a Jesuit; as far as one can judge without knowing what he would have been otherwise. His poetry is magnificent but 'caviare [sic] to the general.'" Their Anglican friend Stuckey, on the other hand, is now preaching at venerable St. Paul's. "He is very fat—as ever—and his left eyebrow has gone a snowy white, which embarrasses one a little one gets used to it."

In September, his preaching for the time finished, Hopkins is sent off to do mission work in the north. Late that month, he hears back from Dixon, apologizing for his silence, due in part to a carriage accident, but mostly because he remains overwhelmed by Hopkins's charity in writing him as he has. But what has been most consoling to him is the passage in which Hopkins wrote of Christ as "the great critic, the unfailing judge of the gifts which he has given. I have drawn deep consolation from that: it came upon me with the force of a revelation." Yes, he does remember Hopkins at Highgate: "we used to dine together in the Boarding House; & that Mr. Lobb and I have often talked of you. He knew more of you than I did: & repeatedly expressed his great opinion of your ability. I remember that we once laughed together over some not very laudatory criticism which you passed at table upon 'Father Prout.'" And has Hopkins "continued to cultivate the poetic faculty"?

"A visit to Great Yarmouth"—140 miles to the northeast—"and pressure of work have kept me from answering before yr. very kind letter," Hopkins writes back in early October. He hopes Dixon has recovered from his carriage accident. He himself "escaped from such a one with very little hurt not long ago in Wales," though he "witnessed a terrible and fatal coach-accident years ago in the Vale of Maentwrog." He does not remember what he said now about Father Prout—the pseudonym of Francis Sylvester Mahony (1804–66), an Irish Jesuit expelled from the order who went on to become a leading contributor to *Fraser's Magazine* as a humorist. But he does remember that he himself "was a very conceited boy." As for Lobb, he doesn't even know if the man is alive or dead. "The truth is," he confesses, that he has little love for his Highgate schooldays, "and wished to banish the remembrance of them, even, I am ashamed to say, to the degree of neglecting some people who had been very kind to me." Of Oxford on the other hand he is very fond, having become a Catholic there. "But I have not visited it, except once for three quarters of an hour, since I took my degree." And now the Jesuits actually have a house and church not far from the university.

As for Milton, of whom Dixon had offered some astute criticism in his last, Hopkins finds his verse both "necessary and eternal," like Purcell's music. In truth, Milton's verse is the finest not only that English has to offer, but Latin and Greek as well. His "rhythm and metrical system" is so extraordinary, in fact, that he cannot understand how "so great a writer as Newman should have fallen into the blunder of comparing the first chorus of the [*Samson*] *Agonistes*" with the opening of Southey's *Thalaba the Destroyer*, "as instancing the gain in smoothness and correctness of versification made since Milton's time." The truth is that Milton was "ahead of his own time as well as all aftertimes in verse-structure," and those choruses in the *Agonistes* are Milton's "own highwater mark," so that to compare Milton to Southey is like comparing "the Panathenaic frieze and a teaboard and deciding in the teaboard's favour." Indeed, when he taught rhetoric at Roehampton, Hopkins paid "a good deal of attention to Milton's versification and collected his later rhythms," finding "his most advanced effects in the *Paradise Regained* and, lyrically, in the *Agonistes*." He has often "thought of writing on them, indeed on rhythm in general," for it is a subject little understood.

As for himself, he burned his early work shortly before he became a Jesuit, resolving to write no more verse unless prompted by his superiors, and so "for seven years I wrote nothing but two or three little presentation pieces which occasion called for." And then came the *Deutschland* disaster, which so deeply touched him, and said so to his Rector, who hoped "someone would write a poem on the subject. On this hint I set to work and, though my hand was out at first, produced one. I had long had haunting my ear the echo of a new rhythm which now I realised on paper."

And then he is off, having found a new audience, to explain sprung rhythm, condensing much of what he had tried to teach his Juniors at Roe-hampton five years earlier. "To speak shortly, it consists in scanning by ac-cents or stresses alone, without any account of the number of syllables, so that a foot may be one strong syllable or it may be many light and one strong." There are "hints of it in music, in nursery rhymes and popular jin-gles, in the poets themselves," and as a topic several critics have mentioned it. He provides instances of the rhythm: "Díng, dóng, béll; Pússy's ín the wéll; Whó pút her ín? Líttle Jóhnny Thín. Whó púlled her óut? Líttle Jóhnny Stóut." But no one, as far as Hopkins knows, "has professedly used it and made it the principle throughout," even though he is convinced that it is "a better and more natural principle than the ordinary system, much more flexible, and capable of much greater effects." But when he submitted the poem to *The Month,* he had "to mark the stresses in blue chalk, and this and my rhymes carried on from one line into another and certain chimes suggested by the Welsh poetry I had been reading . . . and a great many more oddnesses could not but dismay an editor's eye," so that the ode was ultimately rejected.

Since then, he adds, he has "held myself free to compose, but cannot find it in my conscience to spend time upon it; so I have done little and shall do less." Months earlier, he composed "a shorter piece on the *Eurydice,* also in 'sprung rhythm,' as I call it, but simpler, shorter, and without marks, and offered the *Month* that too, but they did not like it either." Beyond that, he has written "some sonnets and a few other little things; some in sprung rhythm, with various other experiments," like outriders and counterpoint. But, he adds, "even the impulse to write is wanting, for I have no thought of publishing." And then there are his pastoral duties to perform, for he must "hear confessions, preach, and so forth." To be honest, even with these done, he has "a good deal of time to myself, but . . . can do very little with it."

In late October, after just three months in London, Hopkins learns that he is to be transferred once again. It is now clear that his sermons have not had the desired effect on his Jesuit superiors, and that he will have to be tried elsewhere. On Sunday evening, November 3, he sends Bridges a note. He is at the moment at Beaumont Lodge, Old Windsor, to the west of London, an-other eighteenth-century estate purchased by the Jesuits twenty years before, which formerly served as their novitiate until that was transferred to Roe-hampton. He is beginning his annual eight-day retreat here tomorrow. After that, he will return to Farm Street to pack up and leave for his new assign-ment, wherever that may be. No doubt the news that he cannot be used at Farm Street hurts, but on this subject he remains silent. "I daresay," he tells Bridges with his customary resignation, "we may not meet again for years."

Chapter 11

Quaint Moonmarks, Pelted Plumage:
Oxford & Bedford Leigh, 1878–1879

Thursday afternoon, November 21, 1878: Father Hopkins arrives at the parish of St. Aloysius Gonzaga at 25 Woodstock Road in the working-class section of Oxford. He is here to serve as assistant curate to stately, plump Father Parkinson, S.J., a product of Cambridge and another convert from Anglicanism. St. Aloysius is a new church, built just three years before for the Jesuits—again by Hansom—and designed in the fourteenth-century imitation French Gothic tradition, replete with lively Italianate highlights and flourishes. It has been built to make the statement that, after two hundred years, the Jesuits have returned to Oxford, and have built close to the university. From the 1580s and for the next hundred years, Jesuits from Oxford were hounded and persecuted by Elizabeth's and then James I's secret agents, the very houses sheltering them pulled down piecemeal around them, so that they might be sniffed out, caught, chained, imprisoned, tried, and then—in each case—hung, drawn, and quartered.

And though centuries have passed, this contemporary Oxfordian, Gerard Manley Hopkins, will either be held in suspicion by the Oxford dons as attempting to seduce young men over to Rome or largely ignored, even by his own working-class parishioners. Still, he does have friends here—people ready to welcome him warmly, among them Pater, now under a shadow cast by none other than the powerful Benjamin Jowett, who has evidence of Pater's homosexual leanings (though of this academic blackmail Hopkins himself is not aware). There are also Francis Paravicini, a don at Oxford and former classmate of Hopkins's, and his wife, Frances, sister of Robert Williams, one of Hopkins's tutors, herself a convert, a woman Hopkins considers "a very sweet good creature." Both will solace and comfort him in the difficult times ahead.

It would be useless trying to say where Hopkins is these days, Bridges writes Muirhead in December, because by the time he finds out, Hopkins

will no doubt be somewhere else. "When last I heard of him he was converting Pater at Oxford," he quips. "Whether he is actually sent to undermine
undergraduates steadily I cannot say." Three weeks after his arrival, Hopkins at last signals Bridges that he is at St. Aloysius' Church "(or Presbytery
or 'something churchy')," and apologizes for not saying good-bye in person
before hurriedly packing up and leaving for Oxford. More of his "acquaintances are up" than he had expected, and he sees that the Puseyites are still
up to their "very dirty jesuitical tricks." He asks Bridges to send the *Deutschland* on to one of his fellow Jesuits, Father Cyprian Splaine, now at Beaumont Lodge, who has asked to see both of his "almost famous Rejected Addresses."

1879: Three weeks into the New Year: Hopkins writes Bridges again to
say that something has been preying on his mind. "When we met in London," he begins, "we never but once, and then only for a few minutes before
parting, spoke on any important subject, but always on literature. This I regret very much. If it had ended in nothing or consisted in nothing but your
letting me know your thoughts . . . it would have been a great advantage to
me. And if now by pen and ink you choose to communicate anything I shall
be very glad." But there is another thing he needs to say to him. "You understand of course," he confesses, "that I desire to see you a Catholic or, if not
that, a Christian or, if not that, at least a believer in the true God (for you
told me something of your views about the deity, which were not as they
should be)." Most likely Bridges believes that his "already being or your ever
coming to be any of these things turns on the working of your own mind,
influenced or uninfluenced by the minds and reasonings of others as the
case may be, and on that only. You might on reflection expect me to suggest that it also might and ought to turn on something further, in fact on
prayer, and that suggestion I believe I did once make."

But he knows too well the illogicality of asking an agnostic to ask God
for guidance. And so he offers another suggestion: that Bridges make some
sensible sacrifice of himself, to strain himself, to see if he might be something more. If he can't pray, then at least do something for those in need, as
any humanitarian might do. He is sure Bridges already gives alms. Still, he
might give more. Indeed, do it, Hopkins pleads, give "up to the point of sensible inconvenience. . . . The difference of mind and being between the man
who finds comfort all round him unbroken unless by constraints which are
none of his own seeking and the man who is pinched by his own charity is
too great for forecasting, it must be felt." It is in fact "the difference between paying heavily for a virtue and not paying at all," and it "changes the

whole man, if anything can; not his mind only but the will and everything." He is talking not only "pure Christianity" now, but pure common sense as well. For Bridges "may have done much good, but yet it may not be enough: I will say, it is not enough." Nor would he presume to judge from "particular knowledge," which would in any case "be very wrong and indiscreet."

Miffed and sardonically amused both, Bridges fires off three letters in succession, taking his Jesuit friend to task for suggesting that he should undergo mortifications, wear a hair shirt, act the fanatic, etc., all of which leaves Hopkins shaken. "You so misunderstand my words," a hurt Hopkins fires back. He has been made, in fact, "to appear a downright fool." Does Bridges really think he would send someone like Pater "a discipline wrapped up in a sonnet 'with my best love'?" Still, how can Bridges "object to doing good and call it 'miserable' to be generous? All the world . . . approves of charity and of the corporal works of mercy, though all the world does not practise what it approves of." Why, even a scoundrel like Walt Whitman "nurses the sick." No, what he was suggesting was that Bridges try giving alms to the needy, "whether in money or in medical or other aid." And when he spoke of "sensible inconvenience," he meant digging deep, for Bridges "might know of someone needing and deserving an alms," which would force him "to buy no books till next quarter day or to make some equivalent sacrifice of time."

He certainly did not ask Bridges to "derweesh" himself, that is, flagellate himself. But he did speak of putting himself out "for charity's sake (or one might say for truth's sake, for honour's sake, for chastity's sake, for any virtue's sake)." Everyone knows or can guess "how it feels to be short of money, but everybody may not know, and if not cannot well guess, how it feels to be short of money for charity's sake." He has put the matter as plainly as he can, and if what he has written reads like some preacher's "blustering bread-and-cheese style," it is to defend what he had counseled.

And why did he write as he did in the first place? Because, he explains, as if addressing a third person, he believes Bridges has his priorities all wrong, and yet "it will do no good to reason with him nor even to ask him to pray." There was only one thing then to offer by way of counsel: get Bridges to give alms, which Scripture says enables one "to resist sins" and "will not let the soul go out into darkness, to give which Daniel advised Nabuchodonosor and Christ the Pharisees, the one a heathen, the other antichristians, and the whole scripture in short so much recommends." Hopkins has in fact heard from a man whom he trusts "that there is for every one a fixed sum at which he will ensure his salvation, though for those who have sinned greatly it may be a very high sum and very distressing to them to give—or keep giving."

It was only "with hesitation and fear" that he wrote Bridges at all about this. But now that he has explained himself, he hopes Bridges sees clearly what was on his mind, and that when he answers, he will make his "objections, if any, to the practice of almsgiving, not to the use of hairshirts. " For even Bridges must see "that it is a noble thing . . . to give alms and help the needy and stint ourselves for the sake of the unhappy and deserving." At any rate, he is relieved that Bridges did not stop writing altogether, as he did when Hopkins wrote his "red letter" years before. At least there has been an advance there. But the attempt to bring his friend over, if it is done, will have to be through other means than suggesting that Bridges change in any significant manner. And Hopkins knows better than most from his time in the confessional and counseling others how slim the chances are of anyone changing unless they themselves want to change.

Back at Oxford now not as a scholar but as a parish priest, Hopkins cannot help but see the place he loves through different eyes. His work is among the Irish working class and the influx of Italian immigrants, as well as Irish and Anglo-Irish troops stationed at the Cowley Barracks outside of town. He has also been made chaplain to the poor and destitute—old men, women, and orphans—at Nazareth House, in a private residence converted for the purposes, at the junction of Cowley and Rectory Roads. There are a handful of Catholic students now in attendance at Oxford, including a number of converts. But there are also old acquaintances, including former tutors and classmates teaching here, as he might have done had he remained an Anglican. And so that winter he calls on his former tutor in moral philosophy, Thomas Green, Fellow of Balliol, whose wife, Susan—whom Hopkins thinks a dear woman—is the critic John Addington Symonds's sister. And then there are Pater and his wife. From time to time Hopkins shows visitors about Oxford. There are also modest concerts put on by his church, which no doubt have the effect of humanizing the congregation, though he finds neither the church choir nor the choice of music very good.

The Young Men's Association has sponsored one such concert. Shopkeepers, mostly, "a fine wellmannered set of young men," Hopkins notes, "but their peculiarity and all our congregation's (excepting the University men and some of the gentry) is that they have a stiff respectful stand-off air which we can scarcely make our way through nor explain, but we believe it to be a growth of a University, where Gown holds itself above and aloof from Town and Town is partly cowed by, partly stands on its dignity against

Gown." On the one side, he sees, they "rally to us, . . . take parts in our ceremonies, meet a good deal in the parishroom, and so on, but seem as if a joke from us would put them to deep and lasting pain." As no doubt Hopkins has already found out when he has tried joking with them.

He is also learning a great deal about how local politics play out here. At a meeting held at the Town Hall on the subject of "Private Charity & Poor Law Relief" at which Hopkins is present, Alsager Hill, vice chairman of the London Charity Organization, a liberal lawyer with strong sympathies for the working class, speaks at length, though Hopkins is unable to follow the man's drift. Then one of the Gown, Thorold Rogers, Professor of Political Economy, stands up and rebuts Hill in what Hopkins perceives as "a vigorous and trenchant style," with the result that "no resolutions were made nor anything done," in part because "there is not much distress at Oxford and plenty of people to relieve it." He notices too that Hill went on and on, "combating the kind of objections which nobody in the room wanted to make." Then one of the local businessmen attacked his friend Henry "Silver" Spooner, Fellow of Balliol and now Vicar of Boughton, "for saying that employers ought to support their aged workmen." Such a notion, the pro-workhouse businessman thinks, is simply utter nonsense.

In mid-February, he writes Bridges, asking him not to let his friend Edmund Gosse the critic mention Hopkins's poems or his theory of sprung rhythm in an article Gosse is writing on Bridges's new book, called, simply, *Poems*. After all, since he has no intention of publishing, he just wants to be left alone. And even if he did publish someday, Gosse's mention would merely be "'puff preliminary,' which it wd. be dishonourable of me to allow." He is not being coy or modest now, for he has taken no step to publish beyond the attempt he made "to print my two wrecks in the *Month*." If his superiors knew of his having "some poems printable and suggested my doing it I shd. not refuse," he admits. "I should be partly, though not altogether, glad." But such an eventuality is very unlikely. What he will do is try to keep his verses, even in their uncorrected state, together in one place, so that "if anyone shd. like, they might be published after my death." Although that too "is unlikely, as well as remote."

Besides, if he really did mean to publish, shouldn't he have more poems to show, and follow up with even more? But how can such a thing be? He "cannot in conscience spend time on poetry, neither have I the inducements and inspirations that make others compose. Feeling, love in particular, is the great moving power and spring of verse and the only person that I am in love with seldom, especially now, stirs my heart sensibly and when

he does I cannot always 'make capital' of it, it would be a sacrilege to do so."
Then, again, he has made writing verse "so laborious." It is a strange way of
phrasing it, but it is Bridges he is writing to, and the subject of what is most
deeply on Hopkins's own mind—Christ and Christ's example of hiding
oneself—would make little sense to Bridges or to almost anyone anyway.
Besides, the sensible closeness to Christ he felt in Wales, when he could
glean his Beloved in the very clouds and vales, seems to have abandoned
him here at Oxford.

The fact is that he is in harness now and has work to do—Christ's
work—but it takes the shape these days of ministering to the poor, or
preaching, or teaching catechism, of hearing confession, or—most trying
of all—living in close proximity to his superior, Father Parkinson. As for his
poems: yes, they are odd, though he could defend every so-called oddness if
need be. In truth, he would eventually like to achieve "a more balanced and
Miltonic style." Still, good Scotist that he is, he knows that just "as air, melody, is what strikes me most of all in music and design in painting, so design, pattern or what I am in the habit of calling 'inscape' is what I above all
aim at in poetry." The difficulty is that "it is the virtue of design, pattern, or
inscape to be distinctive and it is the vice of distinctiveness to become
queer." And this vice, he admits, he "cannot have escaped."

In late February, a copy of Bridges's *Poems* arrives at St. Aloysius' and
Hopkins writes him at once: "Your precious little volume is to hand—also
to head and heart, breathing genius everywhere, like sweet-herbs." One
poem especially—"Hymn to Nature"—has much "impressed the mind of
my chief, Fr. Parkinson, the Parkinsonian mind, I shd. prefer to say; who
read it murmuringly out over tea, with comments and butter." But hearing
Parkinson read it, he was suddenly "struck with a certain failure in the
blank verse. The verse-paragraphs drag; they are not perfectly achieved."
There are also lines that echo passages in Milton and Tennyson. Then too
he finds Bridges's *Elegy* unequal because, as he had already warned him
when he read the piece in manuscript at Bedford Square, two lines in it
echo Gray's *Elegy in a Country Churchyard.* "They [the lines] do it," Hopkins insists, and "they will do it to every ear, it is a great fault to do it, and
they do it. They are not at all the best lines and they can be easily changed
and yet they echo lines which are held to be of faultless and canonical
beauty." Gray's poem "may be outdone but, if you understand, it cannot be
equalled." Other than that, and the fact that the meaning is bad, he finds
the piece "beautiful and full of music." As for the pieces Bridges has attempted in sprung rhythm, the rhythms there have actually distorted the

thought of the poem. Overall, though, he admires the "freshness and buoy-ancy and independence" of the poems, "marked with character throughout and human nature and not 'arrangements in vowel sounds,'" like Swin-burne's work. He wants Bridges to tell him when the reviews appear, for he can always walk over to the Union at the university and read them there, as he did as an undergraduate. "As I am criticising you," he ends, remarking what he said earlier to Dixon, "so does Christ, only more correctly and more affectionately, both as a poet and as a man; and he is a judge *qui potest et animam et corpus perdere in gehennam* [*who can hurl the body and soul into hell*]."

He now has two new sonnets of his own "soaking": "Duns Scotus's Ox-ford" and "Henry Purcell," "which if they shd. come to anything you shall have, and something, if I cd. only seize it, on the decline of wild nature." He encloses six tentative lines, which he will likewise let soak for another two years, until they coalesce into the lyric "Inversnaid." But the other two are soon ready. "Duns Scotus's Oxford" is a paean to Hopkins's beloved Oxford, fast disappearing, the Oxford that was and in places still is: medieval Ox-ford without the utilitarian ugliness. "Towery city and branchy between towers," he begins, the tree-lined streets and fields that for centuries blended so beautifully with the gray stone of old Oxford, when nature was balanced against human nature, those "coped and poisèd powers, the intel-lectual and religious imagination reconciled, the sound of bird and bell, the Cherwell and the Isis:

> Cuckoo-echoing, bell-swarmèd, lark-charmèd, rook-racked, river-
> rounded;
> The dapple-eared lily below thee; that country and town did
> Ónce encounter in, here coped and poisèd powers . . .

Country and town, the need for open spaces and the unchecked real es-tate development already apparent as nature is churned under. All this Hopkins sees here in his beloved England—in London and Oxford, as in Manchester and Glasgow, encroaching even on his beloved Wales. New growth in the suburbs, spreading like a cancer, as Oxford expands outward and things fall apart: yellow brick tract buildings without imagination de-stroying the fields and open spaces and tree-bowered ways at a price, as real estate—that other realty and reality—has come to dominate the eco-nomic imagination. It is all graceless growth in any way one cares to take the word:

> Thou hast a base and brickish skirt there, sours
> That neighbour-nature thy grey beauty is grounded
> Bést in; graceless growth, thou hast confounded
> Rúral rural keeping—folk, flocks, and flowers.

And yet, something remains, something in the air, the atmosphere, the music of the place, the same that Duns Scotus lived on six hundred years earlier when he was a dominus, a don, a duns. He too knew these weeds and woods and rivers and many of these same stone groined walls. It is *his* spirit Hopkins can feel still haunting this place, he "who of all men most sways my spirits to peace." And because Oxford nurtured him—as it has nurtured Hopkins and thousands of others—with its landscapes and real estate—its *real* estate—it provided the necessary conditions for the Franciscan priest and philosopher to see more deeply into the inscape of reality and unravel it the way one might probe the inscapes of elm trees or oaks or cloudscapes or the currents of moving water or, say, bluebells, in order to come at the metaphysical reality of God's amazing gift in preparing one human being—Mary—to be a fitting temple for the incarnate Word of God. It was "a not / Rívalled insight" on Scotus's part, Hopkins realizes, whether one considers the Greek Platonists *or* the Italian Neo-Platonists, his defending the fact of the Immaculate Conception against the best medieval philosophers the University of Paris could muster against him:

> Of realty the rarest-veinèd unraveller; a not
> Rívalled insight, be rival Italy or Greece;
> Who fíred Fránce for Máry withoút spót.

The Immaculate Conception, defined as dogma by Pius IX when Hopkins was ten years old, and celebrated each year since by Catholics on December 8. The following December, which will mark the twenty-fifth anniversary of the proclamation of the feast, Hopkins will tell his little working-class congregation in the smoky industrial town of Bedford Leigh about the dogma, "known and believed by almost all Catholics long before," as "told by our Lord to his apostles," and so "found in the Scriptures, in the works of the Holy Fathers and of great divines." Of course, there were those who denied it back in 1854. Nevertheless, when the Pope spoke, they too submitted and "made an act of belief like other Catholics." It is a comfort, then, to think that Duns Scotus, "the greatest of the divines and doctors of the Church who have spoken and written in favour of this truth[,] came from England: between 500 and 600 years ago he was sent for to go to Paris to dispute in its favour. The disputation or debate was held in public and someone who was there says that this wise and happy man by his answers broke the objections brought against him as Samson broke the thongs and withies with which his enemies tried to bind him."

And yet, how many of Hopkins's fellow Catholics or fellow Englishmen know about Scotus? "And so I used to feel of Duns Scotus," he will write another friend years later, "when I used to read him with delight: he saw too far, he knew too much; his subtlety overshot his interests; a kind of feud arose between genius and talent, and the ruck of talent in the Schools finding itself, as his age passed by, less and less able to understand him, voted that there was nothing important to understand and so first misquoted and then refuted him." Worse, in time they took his name and, with a kind of savage stupidity, turned it into *Dunce*. Against that kind of misunderstanding, who or what shall stand?

The second Scotist sonnet he has let soak is "Henry Purcell," a poem—in stressed alexandrines—for his favorite composer, and for which he provides a short headnote: "The poet wishes well to the divine genius of Purcell and praises him that, whereas other musicians have given utterance to the moods of man's mind, he has, beyond that, uttered in notes the very make and species of man as created both in him and in all men generally." *Haeceittas:* individuation in both the make of the artist and the artist's makings. With Scotus, he was working with someone in the Catholic tradition. Not so now. Nevertheless, there is something so special about Purcell that—more than fame—he wishes Purcell's spirit to be at peace, that this heavenly composer *be* in heaven. And so, he begins this way, praying—as he did in the *Eurydice*—that God will have heard his prayer in that multidimensional all time/no time centuries before Hopkins was even born.

> Have fáir fállen, O fáir, fáir have fállen, so déar
> To me, so arch-especial a spirit as heaves in Henry Purcell,
> An age is now since passed, since parted; with the reversal
> Of the outward sentence low lays him, listed to a heresy, here.

"Henry Purcell" is a metapoem, a poem on the theme of what is distinctive not only about Purcell, but about Hopkins and about genius wherever it is found. Any good poet or painter or composer will suggest a dark or light or sentimental or elegiac or satiric mood, and a meaning—whether narrative, meditative, or even abstract. But there is something more that Hopkins is after: the inscape or distinctive pattern of a poem. As he had said to Bridges: it is air and melody that he most looks for in music as it is design in painting, and it is design or inscape that he aims for in his own poetry. He wants the forgèd feature, the abrúpt sélf that breaks through the poem, and which gives one a sense that a poem is distinctively, unmistakably, one's own:

> Not mood in him nor meaning, proud fire or sacred fear,
> Or love or pity or all that sweet notes not his might nursle:
> It is the forgèd feature finds me; it is the rehearsal
> Of own, of abrúpt sélf there so thrusts on, so thróngs the ear.

Yes, he wants his spirit to be lifted by the composer's angelic air. But he wants more: an eye for the sakes of him, for those distinctive markings flashed off the poet unself-consciously, while his whole attention is on the lilt and lift of his poem. Just as some great stormfowl, waddling along a winter seashore and then gathering speed and lifting into flight like Baudelaire's albatross, will, for us watching below, flash a "colossal smile / Óff him," and in doing so delights and surprises us a second time. It is the sense that we have not only understood a fine poem but have somehow caught a glimpse of the poet, an inscape, within and behind the words as well. And so the poem lifts into a roll, a rise, a carol and creation in the magnificent assonantal lettering of "thunder-purple seabeach plumèd purple-of-thunder," thus capturing something of Homer's *polyphlosboios*—his sound for purple storm waves crashing against the shore—and renders the insight into a Baroque English to out-Milton Milton, before the language settles back into a middle register once more. That colossal smile—a metaphor for God's grace—will return exponentially six years down the line, when the poet most needs it, and a mountainside breaks into a great grin, lighting his way. But here, now, these lines:

> Let him oh! with his air of angels then lift me, lay me! only I'll
> Have an eye to the sakes of him, quaint moonmarks, to his pelted
>   plumage under
> Wíngs: so some great stormfowl, whenever he has walked his while
>
> The thunder-purple seabeach plumèd purple-of-thunder,
> If a wuthering of his palmy snow-pinions scatter a colossal smile
> Óff him, but meaning motion fans fresh our wits with wonder.

In late February he signals Dixon that he has returned to his alma mater, where he can see with his own eyes Dixon's "little-headed willows two and two." Sadly, he adds, the Oxford landscape, with its distinctive "green shouldering grey," has already been "abridged and soured and perhaps will soon be put out altogether." It has been a bitter winter here at Oxford, with much flooding along the rivers, and Oxford a mere skeleton of itself. Besides, there is too much to do here, so that he is constantly "called one way and another, and can find little time to write." As for Dixon's poetry, he tells Bridges, too much of it is obscure, so that "from remarkably clear speaking he will lapse into a gibberish. But the imagery, colouring especially, is rich in the extreme, as like Keats as anyone that has since succeeded in being. Pathos very real and touching. Curious weirdness, rather morbid. Very fine metaphysical touches here and there," though, he agrees, too often these touches are "lost in wildernesses."

Then back to Dixon again to try to explain sprung rhythm. Hopkins says that Bridges has three poems in the new volume Bridges has sent Dixon, composed in "a mitigated sprung rhythm"; but to show Dixon what sprung rhythm is really capable of, he will send him both the *Deutschland* and the *Eurydice* as soon as he can get them back from another reader, Sib Splaine. Also some sonnets, as soon as he can write them out. On March 13, three weeks after beginning this letter, he sends it off, apologizing for its length. "I have been up to Godstow this afternoon," he adds, and is "sorry to say that the aspens that lined the river are everyone felled." But that loss has evoked one of Hopkins's most touching elegies for wounded nature. "My aspens dear, whose airy cages quelled, / Quélled or quenched in leaves the leaping sun," he writes in lines he will call, simply, "Binsey Poplars," are felled, felled, and not one spared that used to dandle "a sandalled / Shádow that swam or sank / On meadow and river and wínd-wándering weed-winding bank."

It is a poem in two stanzas, the second doubling the first in length, eight and sixteen lines respectively. All it takes is ten or twelve strokes of the ax to havoc a tree that took decades to make up part of a beloved landscape. In an hour or less, nothing is left but the echoing memory of what will be lost for at least another generation. If only we knew what havoc we do when we "Háck and rack the growing green!" It is like the sharp pinprick that in a moment can "make no eye at all," he cries, so that we can feel the wound to ourselves even if we cannot or will not feel the wound to the aspens. And once gone, "Áfter-comers cannot guess the beauty been," the loss felt in the poem's final lines, like Rachel calling after her children who are no more:

> The sweet especial scene,
> Rúral scene, a rural scene,
> Swéet especial rural scene . . .

On March 29, he finally sends off his two "almost famous" wreck pieces to Dixon, asking him to return them when he is finished as he has no other copies. Better to tackle the *Eurydice* first, he advises, "which is in plain sprung rhythm and will possess you with the run of it. The *Deutschland*, earlier written, has more variety but less mastery of the rhythm and some of the sonnets are much bolder and more licentious." A week later, a stunned Dixon replies, having read Hopkins's poems with more "delight, astonishment, & admiration" than he can easily say. "They are among the most extraordinary I ever read & amazingly original," he gasps, and they must—must—be published. Perhaps he could insert a footnote in the next volume of his *Church History,* where he treats of the Jesuits, though Hopkins may "think it odd for me to propose to introduce you into the year 1540, but I know how to do it. My object would be to awaken public interest & expectation in your as yet unpublished poems." Ah, how very beautiful and useless such sentiments are, Hopkins must surely think: to be introduced to the world via a footnote in an Anglican canon's history of the suppression of the Church in the time of Henry VIII. But so overburdened is he with work that it takes him six weeks to answer. And when he does, it is to tell Dixon that he has absolutely "no thought of publishing until all circumstances favour, which . . . shd. come from one of our own people." True, the life he now leads "is liable to many mortifications, but the want of fame as a poet is the least of them."

On Shrove Tuesday, Hopkins writes Bridges. "The reason you have not heard from me sooner," he explains after a five-week silence, "is that my chief Rev. T.B.P. has thought well to break his collarbone and be laid up in a charming country house commanding the White Horse Vale, throwing the whole of the work at the hardest time of the year on his underling." Nevertheless, he has just read the current *Academy,* which contains a short, unsigned, but positive review of Bridges's *Poems (Some very remarkable work, undeniable beauties, original, but not yet completely achieved).* It is a good review, he thinks, and wonders why Bridges should take umbrage at the reviewer's saying that the poet will get even better. Certainly, Bridges must feel the truth of that. "Otherwise it is no hardship to anyone to say he will do better yet and be more master of himself than even now." For example, he might get rid of those vulgar poems with their sexual innuendoes, "horn-jokes, Benedicks, and all that kind of thing, tedious when not odious." Could his friend not grow up?

In the meantime, Bridges has shown some of Hopkins's poems to his old Oxford friend and companion during those eight months in Germany, the man in whom Bridges will come to confide his own growing religious doubts, the Reverend William Sanday, destined to become Dean Ireland Professor at Oxford. And what does the good Reverend think of them, Hopkins muses. "Genial admiration? I hope so. Not read my writing? Alas, how far from the path of salvation must that man be that endeavours to persuade his conscience he cannot read my writing!" Then, warming to it, he adds Lear to the equation: "Will he not make his generation messes to gorge his appetite?" As for Bridges using his suggestions for revising his poems, Hopkins answers directly: Why else make them? "Rather look upon them as shoelasts on which to shape your final handiwork." Shoelasts: the form the workman uses to give the shoe its best appearance.

When he writes Bridges again, nine days after Easter, it is to remonstrate with him for showing his poems to Bridges's friend Andrew Lang, who has already expressed a distaste for Hopkins's work. "I think I have seen nothing of Lang's but in some magazine," he writes. "That and a sonnet prefixed to his translation of the *Odyssey*. I liked what I read, but not so that it left a deep impression. It is in the Swinburnian kind, is it not?" Hopkins knows too well that not everyone will like his poems. "Moreover the oddness may make them repulsive at first." Still, Lang might have at least given them a second reading and liked something in them. Indeed, he admits, "when, on somebody [Fr. Splaine] returning me the *Eurydice,* I opened and read some lines, reading, as one commonly reads whether prose or verse, with the eyes, so to say, only, it struck me aghast with a kind of raw nakedness and unmitigated violence I was unprepared for." But, he insists, "take breath and read it with the ears, as I always wish to be read, and my verse becomes all right. I do warm to that good Mr. Gosse for liking and, you say, 'taking' my pieces: I may then have contributed fuel to his Habitual Joy."

How can he best acknowledge Hopkins's influence on his own work? Bridges has asked, especially his experiments in sprung rhythm. And now Hopkins assures him that he has done quite enough by mentioning in print that the poems in sprung rhythm owe something to a friend "whose poems remain, he regrets to say, in manuscript." Besides, why should he and Bridges not be influenced by each other's work? "One ought to be independent but not unimpressionable," he points out. "That wd. be to refuse education." Meanwhile, he is sending along three more poems for Bridges's edification: "Duns Scotus's Oxford," "Henry Purcell," and "Binsey Poplars." In fact, the last owes the phrase "wind-wandering" to Bridges's "wind-wavering," though he is aware that Bridges himself borrowed the epithet from Robert Burns.

And what, he wonders, will Bridges think of his experimenting with six-stress lines in the Purcell sonnet? It is a meter, he thinks, that, "unless much broken, as I do by outrides, is very tedious." But Hopkins can see that Bridges still does not understand how sprung rhythm works. And so, two weeks later, he tries again. Bridges is thinking only in terms of classical quantity in measuring the line. But "since the syllables in sprung rhythm are not counted, time or equality in strength is of more importance than in common counted rhythm," and Bridges's "times or strengths" are not equal enough.

On top of everything else—including doing the work of two priests—Hopkins is also suffering from dysentery, which the doctor has assured him is merely "an irritation due to the remains left by the operation for piles, though that was some years ago. He gave me a comforting prescription, which did the required work and rather more," so that he is somewhat better now, "barring fatigue," which, he admits "easily comes over me." He encloses a slightly amended copy of "The Windhover," which he still thinks "the best thing I ever wrote," and two new sonnets, both "capable of further finish." They are "The Candle Indoors" and "The Handsome Heart," the first a companion to "The Lantern out of Doors." And though he had not at all meant it to be, it soon "fell in." "The Handsome Heart: at a Gracious Answer," on the other hand, is "historical, autobiographical, as you would say, or biographical," and was conceived during the heavy work of the Lenten Triduum, April 10–12, while Father Parkinson was laid up in the country and "two boys of our congregation gave me much help in the sacristy in Holy Week. I offered them money for their services, which the elder refused, but being pressed consented to take it laid out in a book. The younger followed suit; then when some days after I asked him what I shd. buy answered as in the sonnet." He notes that the boy's father, an Italian immigrant, has been reduced to selling ices. "'But tell me, child, your choice; what shall I buy / You?'" the poem begins. To which the boy answers, "'Father, what you buy me I like best.'" Ah, Hopkins remembers, "With the sweetest air that said," and though

still plied and pressed,
He swung to his first poised purport of reply.

What the heart is! which, like cárriers let fly—
Doff darkness, homing nature knows the rest—
To its function fine it, wild and self-instressed,
Falls light as ten years long taught what and why.

The youthful heart as carrier pigeon, doffing darkness and swinging naturally to its true homing in grace, its first instress: "'Father, what you buy me I like best.'" And Hopkins thinking, ah! if I could only buy you heaven, or safety from the devils who roam. A handsome face, yes, but better: a handsome heart. Brace sterner that strain of goodness, he prays here, knowing how innocence in a ten-year-old is almost always—perhaps always—lost as one grows older. Innocence: that inner strain that trembles like a compass needle toward its true north naturally:

Mánnerly-hearted! more than handsome face—
Beauty's béaring or muse of mounting vein,
All, in this case, bathed in high hallowing grace . . .

Of heaven what boon to buy you, boy, or gain
Not granted?—Only . . . O on that path you pace
Run your race, O brace sturdier that young strain!

"The Candle Indoors" reverses the situation of his earlier "The Lantern out of Doors." Now it is the poet who is outdoors walking at night, deep in thought, alone, his eyes filled with tears. "Some candle clear burns somewhere I come by," he begins, musing how even that small light can put "blissful back / With yellowy moisture mild night's blear-all black," and muses too why "to-fro tender trambeams truckle at the eye." How his heart wishes that whatever Jessy or Jack should be moving about indoors, busy at whatever work, might likewise be busy at the work of glorifying God. It is a natural wish for Hopkins the Jesuit, who understands praise for the Creator to be the essential reason why any of us exist at all. But with eighteen months behind him now as a priest, and working among Town as well as Gown, he also knows that such expectations are unrealistic if not naïve, and that the dogged world goes its own appetitive way, brooking nothing, no matter how many hours he logs in.

Then, suddenly, he sees that he has it all wrong. The human instinct when things go awry is to expect things themselves to change. But that is not going to happen any time soon, he knows. Better then to change one's

own outlook and spirit, where one does at least have some control. And so
he chides himself to come "indoors, come home; your fading fire / Mend
first and vital candle in close heart's vault," for there at least he *might* be
master. Summoning two passages from Matthew's account of Christ's
Sermon on the Mount, he ends by focusing on his own Pharisaical self-
righteousness. "What hinders?" he asks, "Are you beam-blind," blind to the
beam of wood in your own eye as you are to the real significance of that isolated beam of light caught in the darkness, which has once again called him
to himself? So, you would remove the speck of a fault from your neighbor's
eye? And who are you, after all, Father Hopkins? "That liar / And, cast by
conscience out, spendsavour salt?"

     "You are the salt of the earth," Christ had said. "But if the salt loses its
savor, with what shall it be salted? It is no longer good for anything but to
be thrown out and trodden under men's feet." Since therefore Hopkins is
well aware of the human tendency to point to "the sots and thralls of lust"
when his own life—given over to Christ's cause—seems to be one massive
failure, he will have to go over this territory again and again and again in
whatever time he has left to change his own too critical judgment of others.
A lesson gleaned on the lonely back streets and alleys of Oxford, then, as
Hopkins goes about his duties visiting the sick or dying or returns from his
work at the Cowley Barracks. It is Oxford's other face, the Town side rather
than the Gown, seen by night, and it is as good a place as any to learn
humility.

     Everything he sees now, in fact, he sees through the prism of his faith.
Indeed, so deeply embedded are the *Spiritual Exercises* in everything he
does that he can scarcely see anything without also seeing God's hand in it.
The downside is that others do not see what is so clearly there for him, and
that has inevitably led to disappointment after disappointment for him in
the daily round of things. But unexpected graces too. And so, in August, he
tells Bridges pointedly that he finds within his work as a priest "a good deal
of matter to write on." One of his duties has been to serve as chaplain to the
Catholic troops at the Cowley Barracks, and so—in line with "The Handsome Heart"—he begins composing yet another narrative on a Sunday afternoon in late July. It is "The Bugler's First Communion," made up of
twelve quatrains, the lines heavily run-on and enjambed, and rhyming
abba. The poem centers on a bugler boy—half English, half Irish (and sharing his parents' "best gifts surely")—who came in his regimental red that
very day to receive his first communion. A simple gesture, but one fraught
with high drama for Hopkins: going to the tabernacle—Christ's own cup-

board—to fetch "Low-latched in leaf-light housel his [Christ's] too huge godhead." The very God of the universe, present in such a small white wafer. How can such things be?

And now he prays for God's blessings on this boy, pleading that the lad's guardian angel—"Frowning and forefending angel-warder"—might "Squander the hell-rook ranks sally to molest him," for this good priest surely fears that the boy might be molested by one of the more seasoned soldiers. "How it dóes my heart good, visiting at that bleak hill," to see these "slips of soldiery ... tender as a pushed peach," listen to his words. It is this which gives his heart such joy, and makes the sacrifice of his own life as a priest worth it all. This is the heart of it, the unselfish giving to others, to see them awaken to the God-saturated world about them and respond from the heart and acknowledge Christ king over them:

> Nothing élse is like it, no, not all so strains
> Us: freshyouth fretted in a bloomfall all portending
>   That sweet's sweeter ending;
> Realm both Christ is heir to and thére réigns.

But he knows too well what happened to the harmony of Eden with the dissonant entrance of evil, what happens to spring, what happens to anything beautiful: how it is marred, scarred, tarred with the world's thick pitch. And so he prays not to see the boy again, that he or the boy might be called away rather than that he should have to witness the innocence of "God's own Galahad" lost, or that the boy should ever become indifferent to the gift of the Eucharist Hopkins has proffered him there before the altar at St. Aloysius'. Enough! As a priest he has done what he can and now he will have to leave the boy's future to the Lord. All he can do is leave behind this poem, this record of his plea for a boy soldier. That, and his heartfelt prayers that

> Would brandle adamantine heaven with ride and jar, did
>   Prayer go disregarded:
> Forward-like, but however, and like favourable heaven heard these.

That is Hopkins's prayer, *his* sacrifice, itself a pale shadow of Christ's emptying of himself. Weeks earlier, he had preached to his congregation of Christ's ultimate sacrifice. Christ's blood "beat and sympathised with the feelings of his heart, performing nobler offices than any other blood can ever do," he had reminded them. Now, self-sacrifice is of its very nature the highest act of religion, he had explained, and the purest charity. It is, in fact, what he has most wanted to emulate in his own life. All his life Christ kept up this offer of himself until he spilled his own blood in his suffering and death, a gift so very precious in his Father's eyes that it was enough to buy back every lost soul that ever was or would be.

On Tuesday, August 12, yet another sonnet, this one in a "more Miltonic plainness and severity than" anything else he has yet written. He sees that there is something in the poems he has been writing—about altar boys and bugler boys—that has been verging on the sentimental, and so he turns now to try his hand at something closer to Bridges's chastened style, trying his own hand at the classical mythology Bridges employs. Frankly, he thinks the gods and goddesses a frigid and unworkable subject, but perhaps they might be salvaged by using them as an analogue for Christ and his Church. He cannot say the sonnet "has turned out severe," he tells Bridges, much less plain, but at least "it seems almost free from quaintness and in aiming at one excellence I may have hit another."

"Andromeda" is a poem whose subject he has already treated in the *Deutschland* and *Eurydice:* God's brooding care for His people. That very morning, perhaps over breakfast, Hopkins would have read in *The Times* that Leo XIII had remarked that most of the evils afflicting society at present were due to the widespread teaching of false philosophy. To attain its true end, Leo has insisted, philosophy must be made subject to faith if it is to remain free of error. And so he is instructing Catholic institutions to adhere to the norms of Scholastic philosophy, especially the writings of Aquinas, whose doctrines had been "followed by religious orders and approved by Popes and by Councils."

What, then, of poor Duns Scotus? That will come, eventually. But for now, the Pope's call for a return to Scholasticism makes sense, especially given the free-thinking heresies of the day. And so he composes "Andromeda" as an allegory of rescue, the Church once more being assaulted, not this time from the East, as in Spain and France and Germany, but, in a kind of pincer movement, by some novel and worse threat from the West. Perhaps he is thinking of the new self-divinization he hears about in the United States especially, the kind of Transcendental philosophy rampant in Carlyle's American disciple Emerson, and Emerson's child, Whitman. Whatever form such liberalism takes, as Newman himself has been careful to point out, it always subjugates religious orthodoxy to the offspring of a radical, freewheeling Protestantism.

"Now Time's Andromeda on this rock rude," the poem begins, with Andromeda—the Church—bound to the rock rude—the rood, the cross, the Rock—the Church with its shepherd, the successor to Peter, bound in time. "On this Rock I will build my Church," Christ had said, pointing to Peter, Cephas, the Rock, with perhaps a touch of sadness and irony, and yet ultimate trust in the one he was leaving to feed his flock. But this is Hopkins's Church, continually assaulted on all sides, and

> With not her either beauty's equal or
> Her injury's, looks off by both horns of shore,
> Her flower, her piece of being, doomed dragon food.

And what does the long history of the Church teach? That "Time past she has been attempted and pursued / By many blows and banes." And yet worse lies ahead, Hopkins suspects, in an even "wilder beast from West than all were, more / Rife in her wrongs, more lawless, and more lewd." *More lawless, and more lewd.* Is Hopkins punning on Wilde's name in evoking that "wilder beast"? And is Wilde's spiritual father, Walt Whitman, the anarchic succubus? Whitman, singing not to God but rather of and for himself. Like Lucifer rebelling against his Creator as he turned to listen instead to his own voice. It is a new strain of radical selfishness and self-love Hopkins fears, and it makes Pater and Swinburne and Wilde's examples pale by comparison. Meanwhile, the Church waits patiently, "forsaken as she seems," even as the poet tries on patience for the Church's sake as well as for his own, knowing that Christ/Perseus will in his own good time come "to alight disarming," this time as Christ Victor, "With Gorgon's gear and barebill / thongs and fangs."

August 17, 1879: Hopkins preaches at St. Clement's in Oxford on Mark's account of the cure of the deaf and dumb man. "The man," he begins, "that says to himself as he walks: Christ is my king, Christ is my hero, I am at Christ's orders, I am his to command, / that man is a child of light." Then what are we to do? The answer is simple: do one's daily duties for the greater glory of God. Those who witnessed Christ's cure of the man born deaf and dumb, Hopkins reminds his congregation, "admired the completeness and delicacy of the cure. Much more should we admire what Christ has done for us—made us deaf hear, if we will hear, not with a touch of his fingertips but with his hands . . . stretched on the cross; made us dumb speak in praise and prayer to God . . . [in] the shedding of all his precious blood."

At the end of the month, he is missioned to St. Joseph's, on Trenchard

Street in the port city of Bristol, seventy-five miles west of Oxford. It is the very church where the remains of Bishop Walmesley are interred, the same man who sent Catholic bishops to the New World and who withstood the No Popery riots a hundred years earlier at the cost of the destruction of his own church and library. Hopkins ministers here for a few days, then travels north to Worcester to preach. There, on the 31st, he delivers a sermon on the ten lepers. "They call him . . . teacher, a word not common in the Gospel," he explains, "as much as to say / Heavenly physician, give us a prescription for our leprosy; learned doctor in the Law, tell us of something that will do us good; he gave them such a prescription, it was seemingly nothing but what had always been in the Law laid down for the recovered leper, but in his mouth it had the power of a miracle." And suddenly they were cured. But, like most people, "they thought no more of their benefactor," but went off somewhere else. Still, "the man or woman, the boy or girl, that in their bloom and heyday, in their strength and health . . . and with the fresh body and joyously beating blood give [God] glory, how near he will be to them in age and sickness and wall their weakness round in the hour of death!"

"Have, get before it cloy," Hopkins had ended his sonnet, "Spring," two years earlier, on a similar note:

> Before it cloud, Christ, lord, and sour with sinning,
> Innocent mind and Mayday in girl and boy,
> Most, O maid's child, thy choice and worthy the winning.

Only one leper returned, and he a Samaritan and enemy of the Jewish nation, who "cast himself down on his face at the feet of this prophet of the Jews." But where are the other nine? Christ asks. Like children, upon whom our love and pains and thought without end are lavished, they take little notice. Or like the sick, who "cease to think of those who nurse them, are exacting and discontented." Or even—as he has learned for himself—the poor, who think "you are bound to do what you do freely; grasp, having one thing at once ask for another."

On September 7, he preaches at St. Aloysius' on Christ's Sermon on the Mount. You cannot serve two masters, Mammon and God, he tells his congregation. But why not just say money or wealth? Why say Mammon, "as if it were someone's name?" "Watch someone who 'hastens to be rich,' goes to work early, works hard, returns late, spares his purse, scants his pleasures, and ask for whose sake he lives thus, *slaves* thus?" Certainly not for

God. Nor does such a one even pretend to do so. But he does not even slave so for his own sake, for he seeks peace neither here nor hereafter. Money is his master, his idol, his god. And so Hopkins advises what Ignatius advises in the *Spiritual Exercises:* if a man would obey God's commandments but aim at nothing higher, then he "may take as much care of money as will not make him break the commandments and fall into mortal sin." But what if you wish to aim higher and follow Christ? Then "provide for necessities and leave the rest to God." Having followed this advice himself, Hopkins knows that this burden at least has been lifted from him, and that in exchange he has been given the wild earth and the night skies for the asking.

The following Sunday he is at St. Clement's again, this time to preach on the necessity of attending mass on Sundays and holy days. "*This* is the house of God," he tells his little congregation. And none but they and "the congregation at St. Aloysius' can say this." Look at the beautiful old churches, he tells them, all of them once Catholic but long ago usurped, "temples of God turned to dens of thieves." True, the present owners are pious according to their lights. Still, are they not the children of those who stoned the prophets and persecuted the people of God? No, it is *this* church, this modest building where God truly comes, as much as he loves the old churches with their bare, ruined choirs. *Here* and here only is the key which can unlock heaven and bring Christ to them in the Eucharist. And this key, he explains, is in his lips as a priest. It is the power given him by Christ himself through his Church. We are "a holy nation, a royal priesthood. In the streets, the shops, the market you go about [with] the special care of angels, the special assault of devils because Catholics. *But here you are met for your holiest duty* . . . to see the slaying of the spotless lamb" once more. And if he as priest is the principal minister, all of the worshippers join in the offering. "This is why you are here," he reminds them, "to be at the slaying of the spotless lamb," the tremendous sacrifice, the holy mass.

September 21, and his last sermon at Oxford. Today he preaches on the calling of Matthew as a model of the religious calling. God "calls the infidel, heathen, heretic to his Catholic faith," he tells them, as well as converts like himself. And while he "draws all more or less on," he calls some more strongly than others. True, many are called to the faith, "but few are chosen to accept it." Then, again, some accept the call only to leave, "become Catholics and apostatize." He knows from his own experience that converts feel they have been led by God's will, and that not to follow would be denying God's gift and sinning. "We who are converts have all heard that voice which others . . . say they cannot hear." Which is why he is here at Oxford again, standing before them, exhorting them, having himself followed that call and the tortuous road that has brought him here, this time in a black soutane and collar, a million miles from his beloved Balliol.

And then, just as the Michaelmas Term begins and the Oxford undergraduates return, he is missioned to the parish of St. Joseph's, Bedford Leigh, 160 miles to the north, where he will fill in for three months before going on to Liverpool. On October 1, two days before he leaves, he goes to Foreshaw's to have his portrait taken, the image serving as his *carte de visite*. The following day—his last full day in Oxford—he composes "Peace," a sad poem he will share with no one, not even Bridges, for another five years. It is another curtal sonnet, this one in long, plaintive alexandrines: "When will you ever, Peace, wild wooddove, shy wings shut," he begins, "Your round me roaming end, and under be my boughs? / When, when, Peace, will you, Peace? . . ."

Oh, he knows that peace does sometimes come, and that he is not without God's consolations. But the world's "piecemeal peace is poor peace," for what "pure peace allows / Alarms of wars, the daunting wars, the death of it?" Well, then, if the peace he pines for will not settle on him, what does his Lord offer in its place? Patience. "Patience exquisite, / That plumes to Peace thereafter." For when peace does finally come, he realizes, it will come "with work to do," and not merely to coo. We are given Christ / Perseus' peace, he has come to see, for a reason: so that we can do the work Christ has called us to do, just as in "God's Grandeur" the dovelike Spirit comes each day to brood and hatch new life. Off, then, to do the work he has promised his Master he would do. And about that special call he has said yes to and which he had preached on just two weeks before, all he can think is: may God hear him. May God graciously hear him.

"I have left Oxford," he tells Bridges five days after his arrival at Bedford Leigh. For the next three months he will serve as supply priest to Father James Fanning, S.J., at the large dark sandstone church in this northern industrial town on the outskirts of Manchester. It is called St. Joseph's, and it was built a quarter of a century before to serve the English and Irish working-class Catholics, thus replacing a small chapel that had been there since the seventeenth century, and which has been staffed from the beginning by Jesuits. He does not yet know what the work will entail, though he will surely say mass, preach, and hear confessions. The town itself is "smaller and with less dignity than Rochdale and [lies] in a flat; the houses red, mean, and two storied; there are a dozen mills or so, and coalpits also; the

air is charged with smoke as well as damp." But—and this makes all the difference for him—the people here "are hearty" and he has already taken to them. At Oxford, on the other hand, "every prospect pleases and only man is vile, I mean unsatisfactory to a Catholic missioner." Yesterday he was at St. Helen's, "probably the most repulsive place in Lancashire or out of the Black Country. The stench of sulphuretted hydrogen [with its rotten egg smell] rolls in the air and films of the same gas form on railing and pavement." Welcome to industrial Britain.

"The little hero of the Handsome Heart," which poem he is finally sending, "has gone to school at Boulogne to be bred for a priest and he is bent on being a Jesuit." As for the bugler boy of his other Oxford poem, he has been "ordered to Mooltan in the Punjaub," and was set to sail just before Hopkins left Oxford. In truth, he is "half inclined to hope the Hero of it may be killed in Afghanistan" before he loses that beautiful innocence of his. He is also at work on two tragedies: one about St. Winefred and the other about Margaret Clitheroe: two women—one Welsh, one English, both martyrs, who have fascinated Hopkins for years. "The first," he tells Bridges, "has made some way and, since it will no doubt be long before it is finished, if ever, I can only send you some sample scenes." Both tragedies will be short, "3 or even 2 acts; the characters few." They are in alexandrines and sprung rhythm, a form "which lends itself to expressing passion," and while he finds himself "equal to the more stirring and critical parts of the action"—the core of the drama—"about the filling in and minor parts" he is less sure, since he has had so little dramatic experience. And then of course, as with every English dramatist, there is the shadow of Shakespeare to contend with, whose "scope and richness of . . . gifts, equal to everything," leaves him in despair. There was a man who—unlike himself—had "sufficient experience of life and, of course, practical knowledge of the theatre."

On September 21, he officiates at a church wedding and afterward composes the lyric "At the Wedding March" in triple rhymes. In the first two stanzas, he addresses the groom and bride, then, in the last stanza turns inward, in tears, to his own "wonder wedlock" with the only one who can fill up his heart, the one who "Déals tríumph and immortal years":

> Gód with honour hang your head,
> Gróom, and grace you, bride, your bed
> With lissome scions, swéet scíons,
> Out of hallowed bodies bred.

Eách be other's comfort kind:
Déep, déeper than divined,
Divíne chárity, déar chárity,
Fast you ever, fast bind.

Then let the Márch tréad our ears:
Í to hím túrn with tears
Whó to wedlock, his wónder wedlock,
Déals tríumph and immortal years.

Then comes a letter from a downcast Bridges, asking him whether in fact there is anything in his poems to warrant his going on. Yes, of course, Hopkins answers, though he sees he will have to answer carefully and fully before sending his letter on. First of all, he begins, Bridges should remember that he sees his work at its "very least advantage when it comes to me on purpose to be criticised. It is at once an unfinished thing, in my eyes, and any shortcoming or blemish that in print I should either not notice or else easily digest with the excellence of the context becomes a rawness and a blot." It is just as if he had written it himself, then, "and were dissatisfied, as you know that in the process of composition one almost always is, before things reach their final form." If he did not at first care for the manuscript poems Bridges showed him in London, he saw them in a new light once they had been printed, and liked them a great deal more. Before that, they were "too near the eye." So too with his new book, where "almost everything seems perfect and final and exercises its due effect and the exceptions prove the rule, such as the pieces in sprung rhythm."

The following day, after visiting the local workhouse, he picks up his pen again to continue. He knows he is not Bridges's best judge, "being biased by love." But on the other hand, perhaps he is. Different as the two men are—Bridges a confirmed agnostic, his identity only nominally tied up with the English Church, Hopkins a former Anglican and convert, one of those rare individuals who has tried to give over his entire life to an ideal which sometimes startles by its immanent beauty, but too often seems so elusive as to be an infinity away—there is nevertheless a strong attraction between them.

And now Hopkins is out with his feelings. "I think," he says, that "no one can admire beauty of the body more than I do, and it is of course a comfort to find beauty in a friend or a friend in beauty. But this kind of beauty is dangerous." Bridges the athlete, Bridges the manliest of men, six feet tall, bearded, tough, ironic, who has seen his full of tragedy, who serves the poor as a city doctor now, but whose deepest desire is to write. So, the mortal beauty side of it noted, Hopkins moves quickly on. "Then comes the beauty of the mind, such as genius, and this is greater than the beauty of the body and not to call dangerous." But more beautiful even "than the beauty of the mind is beauty of character, the 'handsome heart.'" And now to the heart of the matter. The truth is, he tells Bridges, that "if I were not your friend I shd. wish to be the friend of the man that wrote your poems. They shew the eye for pure beauty and they shew, my dearest, besides, the character which is much more rare and precious." But since he must not "flatter or exagger- ate I do not claim that you have such a volume of imagery as Tennyson, Swinburne, or Morris, though the feeling for beauty you have seems to me pure and exquisite." Still, when it comes to questions "of character, of sin- cerity or earnestness, of manliness, of tenderness, of humour, melancholy, human feeling, you have what they have not and seem scarcely to think worth having."

And then he addresses something Bridges has heard about Hopkins's effectiveness as a priest when Bridges was recently up at Oxford. "I hardly know what you allude to," Hopkins fires back. And perhaps it is better he should not. The truth is that when Hopkins went up to Oxford a year ago, he did fear that people "wd. repeat against me what they remembered to my disadvantage," though what that is, he does not expand upon. But, he adds, "if they did I never heard of it." In truth, he saw little of the university crowd, except once when Bridges came up and they dined with some of their old tutors and friends, for his work lay at St. Aloysius' and St. Clem- ent's and the barracks.

Still, "it is perhaps well" he is gone now, for he never really "hit it off with Fr. Parkinson," and he was not happy at Oxford. Yes, he liked the people he worked with—his people—"but they had not as a body the charming and cheering heartiness of these Lancashire Catholics, which is so deeply com- forting." And besides, at Oxford "people criticised what went on in our church a great deal too freely," which was damned "impertinence of the sheep towards the shepherd, and if it had come markedly before me I shd. have given them my mind." This—where an injustice or slight is per- ceived—is the side of Hopkins it would be better after all not to rouse.

With Dixon, there is another problem, for the Canon is so convinced of the brilliance and originality of what he has seen of Hopkins's work that he keeps urging Hopkins to publish. But, as right as Dixon is, it is something Hopkins will not allow himself to do. It is almost as if this were his special temptation in the wilderness, the allure of that very fame he keeps saying he despises. After all, fame does not suit the life of a Jesuit, which is the hidden life, where the only reward that matters is inward, intimate, between oneself and one's God. To do otherwise is to too closely follow the lead of Lucifer, whose song became a song of self-praise and self-adulation. But for him, the emphasis must be on God, on the Other who masters the self so that it may become more Christ-like. And that means the emptying of the self to be filled with God, as Christ showed, in buckling under so that he might better reveal the Father's life and shine in harmony with Him. But who will understand this, if even the good Canon, a fellow Christian, cannot?

And so, when Hopkins learns that Dixon has sent a section of *The Loss of the Eurydice* to one of the local Carlisle newspapers, giving Hopkins's name and "a line or two of introduction" from himself, a visibly upset Hopkins writes back at once. It is *precisely* what he had asked Dixon *not* to do and hopes he has not actually sent the poem out, though if he has, he doesn't think it would garner much notice outside Carlisle. Yes, he could explain the situation to his Provincial, as he is bound to do, but it might not be so easy to guard himself "against what others might say." He knows that his friend "acted out of pure kindness, but publication of my lines except by the ordinary channels" can never serve him. So the matter, he hopes, is closed.

But two weeks later, troubled with his own possible impurity of motives—that through some fault of his own, his poem did make it into print—he tells Dixon to withdraw the piece, if it is not too late. "I cannot consent to, I forbid its publication," he says as plainly as possible. "You must see that to publish my manuscript against my expressed wish is a breach of trust." Whoever heard of fame being won by publication in a local newspaper, he explains. After all, if everything of its own intrinsic goodness gravitated to fame, Dixon's own poems "wd. long since have been famous." Consider this: if Tennyson himself, "putting aside marks of style by which he might be recognised, were to send something to the *Nineteenth Century* or best circulated London magazine without his name it wd. be forgotten in a month." And "no name and an unknown name is all one."

Yes, it is true, what Dixon has said, that the Jesuits have traditionally supported literary excellence. And if so, "it may be left to look to its own interests. It could not approve of unauthorised publication, for all that we publish must be seen by censors first." Besides, if the paper were to publish it, people would be at a loss to appreciate its sprung rhythm. And so Dixon writes back to say that, reluctantly, he has withdrawn the poem. "You are very welcome to shew my poems to anyone you like so long as nothing gets into print," Hopkins assures him a few days later. And the temptation to bugle his name abroad for the moment passes.

Each Sunday—often in the morning and again in the evening—throughout November and much of December he preaches. Once on the healing of Jairus' daughter and the woman with the issue of blood. Another time on the mustard seed and the leaven. On vocations. On Christ as hero. On scandal in the Church. "There will be black sheep among the white," he acknowledges, "there will be even bad shepherds, I mean priests, the pastors of Christ's flock." Scandals must come, he quotes his Master's words, "only woe to him." For, just as the Church was once a tiny mustard plant, "all in one little infant frame in [Mary's] womb," now, in the year of Our Lord 1879, there are over two hundred million Catholics worldwide and—he can only hope—the branches of the faith will continue to grow, though he is painfully aware that England's 350-year-old apostasy has left it, "alas, part withered."

For one Sunday evening in late November, he chooses a subject dear to his heart: Christ as Hero. "You know how books of tales are written," he reminds his congregation, how "mothers make a hero of a son; girls of a sweetheart and good wives of a husband." Or how "soldiers make a hero of a great general, a party of its leader, a nation of any great man that brings it glory." Just so, Christ is a hero: the hero of the Gospels. More, he is a warrior, a conqueror, and especially a king, "though when he came to his own kingdom his own did not receive him, and now . . . we Gentiles are his inheritance." More, he is "a statesman, that drew up the New Testament in his blood and founded the Roman Catholic Church that cannot fail." A thinker, too, who "taught us divine mysteries. He is an orator and poet, as in his eloquent words and parables appears." He is, in fact, "all the world's hero, the desire of nations," the hero "of single souls and his mother's hero." Even those who "do not follow him . . . look wistfully after him, own him a hero, and wish they dared answer to his call." In the nature of things, he adds, "it is at the father's or the mother's mouth first the little one should learn." But, alas, he knows too well, "the parents may be gossiping or drinking and the children have not heard of their lord and saviour."

It is one of Hopkins's most passionate sermons, and it tells us quite explicitly who his heart was wedded to, who he tried to follow, the only one who could ever quiet his mind and fill his heart. "There met in Jesus Christ all things that can make man lovely and loveable. In his body he was most beautiful, . . . moderately tall, well built and tender in frame, his features straight and beautiful, his hair inclining to auburn, parted in the midst, curling and clustering about the ears and neck as the leaves of a filbert. . . ." And the best proof? "His body was framed directly from heaven by the power of the Holy Ghost, of whom it would be unworthy to leave any the least botch or failing in his work." Moreover—as he had stressed in "The Wind-hover"—"in his Passion all this strength was spent, this lissomness crippled, this beauty wrecked, this majesty beaten down." But now, in his resurrec-tion, all that beauty has been more than restored. Make him your hero, then, he urges his little congregation. For himself, he will make no secret of it: he looks forward "with eager desire" to someday "seeing the matchless beauty of Christ's body in the heavenly light."

November 30: The first Sunday in Advent and a time of reflection. "Life and time are always losing," he warns his congregation. "Always spending, always running down and running out," with death always there, waiting in the wings. "Age is a warning, sickness is a warning, and the deaths of others that go before us are a great warning." And while none has seen the last day, "all men have seen death." It is what he has witnessed firsthand in comfort-ing the sick and dying or in listening for long hours in the confessional, that "more than ever is there riotous company, drunkenness, lewdness, strife, brawling, even bloodshed." It begins with "rioting or revelry" and bad com-pany. Oh, they "seem hearty friends, goodnatured companions and such," and shouldn't a man have a friend to "unbend from his work at times, see company and life? Must he sit mum? must he mope at home?"

But look closer, he warns. A real friend "loves you, he thinks of you and not only of his own pleasure." On the other hand, "a rout of drinking com-panions do not love one another, they are selfish, they do not love their own, how can you think they care for strangers? Their own children may be hungry, their mothers or their wives in tears, their homes desolate and they are so good as to spend their time, their money, and their health with you." So then what? "You treat them or they you. If you treat them you like a fool spend your money on the worthless; if they treat you often you are eating their children's bread, you are draining the blood of their little ones."

Unruly company leads inevitably to drunkenness and turns a man into a beast, he explains, as if taking his cue from Hogarth or Falstaff and his friends. "It drowns noble reason, their eyes swim, they hiccup in their talk, they gabble and blur their words, they stagger and fall and deal themselves dishonourable wounds, their faces grow blotched and bloated, scorpions are in their mind, they see devils and frightful sights." Worse is drunken-ness itself, "confirmed and incurable," creating "a world of woe. It defiles and dishonours the fresh blooming roses of youth, the strength of manhood, the grey hairs of age. It corrupts the children yet unborn, it gives convulsions to the poor sucking child. It is ugly in man, but in woman it is hideous beyond what words can say."

It "lays waste a home. There is no peace, there is no reverence or honour. The children are scandalised and taught to sin. Nay, it breaks home quite up," so that "wife runs from drunken husband or husband from drunken wife. . . . Feet may go bare and hearth be cold but the fire in the throat must be quenched with liquor. . . . The family cannot go to mass, obey the Church's commandment, worship God on his holy day in his holy place and be present at the great sacrifice; though it should cost not a penny they cannot do it, because the clothes are pawned." Still, there is a remedy for all this, he reminds them, and that is to beg God's forgiveness. For though temptation is everywhere, yet the confessional "is a place . . . where those who will be good can be. Here the young woman can grow up, live, and die in maidenly or in motherly innocence; here the young man can make and keep his strength and manhood sacred to God. And if you have fallen, if you have fouled your white robe and stained your lightsome armour, you can with ease recover all again." But this nightmare is, in fact, too often his workaday world, what he sees, in spite of the good cheer of his flock, in the tenements all about him.

And though the people here—including a large influx of Irish laborers—have made him feel at home, there is trouble brewing as well in the vexing issue of Home Rule for the Irish, which has made itself felt more and more. It is something the Liberals keep bringing up until it has wearied him. To think, he tells Baillie, that "I could ever have called myself a Liberal! Why, the Devil himself 'was the first Whig.'" And how has the British government responded? By "arresting Irish agitators that will do far more harm in prison than on the stump." On the other hand, the economy seems finally to be undergoing a revival. In fact, this very day he saw "two barge-loads of some salt-'chemicals'—going to one of the mills." He can only hope that Disraeli is right in saying that the economy is on the upswing. Yes, he is still "cut off . . . from all modern and all classical books here," but at least he can read Shakespeare and Boswell, whose *Life of Dr. Johnson* is, with the exception of St. Augustine's *Confessions* "and some other spiritual works the most interesting book" he has ever read.

On Gaudete Sunday, December 14, Hopkins preaches his last sermon at Bedford Leigh. In spite of everything, he tells his congregation, it is a time of rejoicing, for the Lord is coming again as an infant among them, with a joy no one can take from them. Otherwise, how many would ever be able to re-joice? "One might say: I am in such want that I am not sure of my next meal: how can I have any joy? Another says: I have just lost a child, a wife or a hus-band: how can I rejoice? Another is in sickness or pain or ill-used or slan-dered by unkind tongues." Yes, these are surely "sorrows so great that for a time they may take from the world all comfort." But there is still "your heav-enly hope," and of that no one can rob you. And "if we feel the comfort little," that is "our fault and want of faith; we must put a stress on ourselves and make ourselves find comfort where we know the comfort is to be found," for "cheerfulness has ever been a mark of saints and good people. The Apostles went rejoicing . . . the martyrs were cheerful," and when Christians being led to execution were "mingled, through their persecutors' malice, with common convicts / all would not do, the martyrs by their joyous looks could easily be told from those who were to suffer the just reward of their crimes."

Then he turns to one of their own, the martyr, his beloved Margaret Clith-eroe, who, paraded through the streets of York, "to be pressed to death on Ouse Bridge, all along the road as best she could with her pinioned hands deal-ing out alms to the poor." But how "marvellously cheerful and happy she looked," so that "her murderers . . . had nothing for it but to pretend she was possessed by 'a merry devil.'" Rejoice then and be happy in the thought of Christ's coming among them, he urges his flock. It is his farewell message to them.

The following day, he leaves for St. Beuno's and wild Wales to make his eight-day retreat. The day after Christmas, he walks to his beloved St. Winefred's Well to bathe again in the warm waters, smoking now in the frosty air. "Many thanks for your kind Christmas boxes," he writes his mother on the 27th. "The comforter I shall employ, but to give away [to the poor]; the gloves and mittens however I shall wear." The Vale of Clwyd looks very beautiful in the winter air and is as always a great comfort to him. There has even been fine skating weather, though he has let the chance slip. "Do you know," he tells her, "if you cared to have it, there is a pleasing photograph of me taken the day before I left Oxford by Foreshaw of St. Giles's. I have no copy myself, but I have seen one. I do not like portraits in shopwindows, but as I was going away I let it be." It is this very image, ironi-cally, by which millions will come to know Hopkins. Then, on the 29th, he returns to Bedford Leigh to pack up his few belongings and leave for his next assignment in Liverpool, that teeming port city with its poor Irish working-class families and its sprawling slums. Bad as he has had it, he has yet to live and work in the midst of so much poverty and misery.

Chapter 12

Of All Places the Most Museless:
Liverpool & Glasgow, 1880–1881

In nomine Patris, et Filii, et Spiritus Sancti. Amen. Intoibo ad altare Dei. I will go up to the altar of God. Father Hopkins, in alb, stole, and chasuble, facing the altar, hands his black biretta to the altar boy on his right, and then, his back to the congregation, ascends the steps to the tabernacle, as if leading them into the Holy of Holies, where he places the paten and chalice, then descends the steps again to begin the prayers at the foot of the altar.

Ad Deum qui laetificat juventutem meum, he intones, to which the altar boy, an Irish lad of ten, responds, speaking for the congregation, few of whom know Latin, including the altar boys themselves. *To God,* the boy mouths, *who gives joy to my youth.*

Judica me, Deus, Hopkins half-chants, following the *Ordo Missae,* as now he recites the Vulgate Latin for the 42nd Psalm. *Et discerne causam meam de gente non sancta: ab homine iniquo et doloso erue me. Judge me, O God, and distinguish my cause against an ungodly nation: deliver me from the unjust and deceitful man.*

Quia tu es, Deus, comes the response of the people in the high voice of the small boy, *fortitudo mea. Quare me repulisti. Et quare tristis incedo, dum affligit me inimicus? For Thou, O God, art my strength. Why have you cast me from Thee, and why do I go about sorrowful while the enemy afflicts me?*

And so the pattern, repeated day after day, week after week, year after year, in an endless round of giving praise back to God in the eternal reenactment of Christ's sacrifice on Calvary. . . .

Tuesday, December 30, 1879: Thirty-five-year-old Father Hopkins in black coat, soutane, and biretta arrives by rail and tram into the bustling heart of coalsmoke-soaked Liverpool and is deposited at the rectory of St. Francis Xavier on Salisbury Street. The church is a huge stone neo-Gothic structure, built by the Jesuits in the mid-1840s, and is the largest Catholic parish in all of England, with the care of some thirteen thousand souls. The

Jesuits here have a reputation for magnificent preaching before large numbers at both the morning and evening masses and the other services. There are also various ongoing lecture series, for which tickets must be purchased to guarantee a place in the pews or along the back of the church. Perhaps here, his superiors think, Hopkins can finally shine as a preacher, what with his Oxford education and mastery of rhetoric. In any event, he knows he will certainly be kept busy hearing confessions, attending weekly or monthly meetings of various sodalities and other organizations, and tending to the poor and sick. On Friday, January 2, 1880, he signals Bridges by postcard that he is at last settled, but—alas—cannot write more now "and shall have less time than ever." Decades later, Bridges will remember that it was Hopkins's time here in Liverpool that nearly killed him.

That Sunday evening, Hopkins delivers his first sermon to the mostly working-class faithful Irish who inhabit the slum tenements of "Jenkinson Street and Gomer Street and Back Queen Ann Street and Torbock Street and Bidder Street and Birchfield Street and Bickerstaffe Street," the ones who labor on the docks, drive the trams, repair the cobblestone streets, shovel the oat-speckled horse dung droppings which are everywhere, or light the streetlamps, clerk in the shops, yes, inhabit the local pubs, and all in all try to feed their large families.

Hopkins has decided to focus on the Our Father and the sentence "Thy will be done" this first Sunday, as next week he will dwell on what comes just before: "Thy kingdom come." His first sermon, then, will be on Christian duty, Victorian civic duty, and he tells his congregation that they and he have a solemn responsibility to love God or risk being lost. Recalling their patron saint Francis Xavier's hymn (one of his favorites, which he has translated), he reminds them they could do worse than to utter, "'*O Deus, ego amo te: Non amo te ut salves me / Aut quia non amantes te / Aeterno punis igne*' / 'O God, I love thee, I love thee—Not out of hope of heaven for me / Nor fearing not to love and be / In the everlasting burning.'" The question then is this: "Do I feel for God love enough to be saved?" For he knows too well—it is a thought that keeps nagging at him—that even those who serve God "to the best of their power; whose sins have been by penance forgiven; who do their daily, weekly, and yearly duties; who thought, and with reason, that they were in God's grace—in the hearts of such persons the fear may nevertheless stir . . . that they have been thinking about and doing small duties and overlooked and left undone the great one, that they do not love God and for want of love will be lost at the last." Under every yes, then, a no, a no, and again a no. He knows this, fears it, and wonders if—in the great accounting which is surely coming—he will himself be among the lost. To have searched one's conscience, told one's sins, have heard the absolution at the priest's lips spoken, to have done the penance enjoined, and still to have no peace, that it has all been for nothing, "that my repentance is hypocrisy and my sacrament sacrilege." And all "because I was not in my heart sorry for my sins."

Peace, poor peace. . . . he had written just before he left Oxford. Well, then, at least let him solace his flock. With God's help he means tonight to put their minds at rest, for there may be some out there listening "to whom it will be comforting and serve to put an end to their distressing thoughts." To love God is to wish His will be done, "and, when God's will is against ours, to wish His will done rather than ours because God is God and we are only men." *This*, he tells them, is to be on the path to salvation. "I do not care how cold his love may be," he assures them, "he may never have shed a tear over Christ's passion, heaved a sigh for his own sins, felt his heart kindle at anything holy." The fact remains that that person loves God and that is enough. True, he adds, "there is a sweeter, tenderer love," but of that he does not mean to speak tonight. Yet to obey God's commandments: that "is better than sacrifice," and "seas of tears and sighs to fill the firmament are waste of water and loss of breath where duty is not done." Duty, in short, is everything.

The following Sunday, standing on a stool behind the lectern now because he is that much shorter than the other preachers, he describes Eden, God's First Kingdom, and reminds his congregation that they are God's adopted children. True, "we cannot father ourselves on God, for we have neither the power nor the right." But we are part of a covenant, a commonwealth, duty-bound to obey their king. As with England, so with God.

On the 18th, he picks up his theme again. In God's commonwealth, he explains, there were but two estates: God's and man's. First the one man, then the man and the woman, and many more promised. And God walked with Adam and Eve in Paradise, then, taking the afternoon air with them, much as Her Majesty, Queen Victoria, he reminds his Anglo-Irish congregation, "is seen at the opening of Parliament, as she drives in her Parks in the sight of her subjects." And what was the nature of this commonweal? "That God should be glorified in man and man glorified in God." God would make the laws and man would obey, for his own happiness. All he had to do was care for Paradise, and "increase and multiply and fill the earth and subdue it." Keep it, that is, against the Devil.

But man "did not keep it and so . . . was cast from Paradise out into the waste wilderness." There was only one commandment to keep: they were not to eat of the Tree of Knowledge. To eat of it would mean death, and death would end all. God "had staked his honour and authority on that one law and to break it was to . . . undo the commonwealth." Hopkins looks down at his watch and sees that his time is up. He had hoped "to speak of God's second kingdom, . . . of the new City of God . . . the Catholic Church," but that is too much for one sermon, for "the heavenly Jerusalem will not be huddled in a corner."

But like a professor who has gone over the time allotted and must re-configure what to leave in and what to leave out, he decides to stay with the melancholy business of the Fall. On January 25, 1880, Septuagesima Sunday, he delivers his fourth sermon. It is titled "On the Fall of God's First Kingdom." But before he can deliver it, his superior forbids him to use the title, fearing it will be misunderstood by the more literal-minded members of the congregation. And because it is too late to change the printed bills which have been posted advertising Hopkins's sermon, blank slips of paper must be pasted over the title. He is also charged with either leaving out or rephrasing "all passages speaking of God's kingdom as falling."

And so he begins by taking his congregation back into a time before human time. "Before God was king of man," he explains, "he was king of angels and before man fell angels had fallen. Then man was made that he might fill the place of angels. But Satan, who had fallen through pride and selflove," resolved that man should fall in the same way, and that, "whereas a breach had been made" in God's heavenly kingdom, God's earthly kingdom should be broken utterly to pieces, something Satan could accomplish only by fraud. And then—in true Victorian fashion—he explains that Satan attacked "the weakest spot and tempted the woman."

Like many of his co-religionists in 1880, Hopkins takes the Genesis story as historical narrative rather than as sacred myth. Satan "chose his disguise" and "spoke by the serpent's mouth; he watched his time, he found Eve alone." And now he warms to it, evoking Milton's *Paradise Lost* with its drama and panoply, playing out for them the temptation scene. Fancy "that rich tree all laden with its shining fragrant fruit and swaying down from one of its boughs, as the pythons and great snakes of the East do now, waiting for their prey to pass and then to crush it, swaying like a long spray of vine, . . . not terrible but beauteous, lissome, marked with quaint streaks and eyes or flushed with rainbow colours, the Old Serpent." And now the serpent offers Eve the fruit in mock homage, a brute's tribute to man, presenting it with his mouth or sweeping it from the boughs down before her feet; and she at first declines it.

Then came those studied words of double meaning the Scripture tells us of: What! and has God forbidden you to eat of the fruit of Paradise? Was God then a tyrant? A sullen lawgiver? A rackrent? And what was this thing called death, after all? No, the serpent tells her, "you will not die. . . . God knows, on the day you eat of it your eyes will be opened and you will be as gods, knowing good and evil." And so, Hopkins laments, "she fell and . . . drew her husband after her. Most dearly he loved her, and she stood before him now lovely and her beauty heightened by distress, a thing never seen before in Paradise, herself a Tree of Knowledge of Good and Evil and offering him its fruit." And so in turn Adam ate and fell. Then followed "the first and most terrible of evictions, when Cherubim swayed the fiery sword and man was turned from Paradise." And if his Irish congregation is thinking of those back home who have been evicted by their landlords for disobeying the law and refusing to pay rent, his message will have hit home that much harder.

Expulsions and explosions: Thursday morning, February 5, the eve of the Liverpool elections. Hopkins boards the train at Lydiate, north of Liverpool, having said mass that morning at Rose Hill, a private chapel belonging to the Randall Lightbound family, one of the old Catholic families, and now he is returning to Liverpool. "Every week one of our community goes to Lydiate," he will explain to his mother, "to a Catholic country house, so as to say mass next morning and return." So he was returning with John Lightbound, "the only unmarried son," when "there entered the railway carriage a tall fine venerable-looking old gentleman with a benevolent air and silvery beautiful locks and beard, Mr. Musgrove, in whose office John Lightbound is and considers as the greatest being in the world 'under the deity.'"

Musgrove, being a Radical, begins handing out portraits of Lord Ramsay, pointing to the future member for Liverpool. "I hope," Hopkins retorts, "that this is not the portrait of the future member for Liverpool." And from there "we fell, pleasantly at first, into politics, but I talked so outrageously against Liberals and worse that Mr. Musgrove was shocked and hurt and in a beautiful but alarming and no-joke-ative way, began addressing himself in such Noachian and Abramitical Methusalem-like strains to two little lads in the carriage, about their living to see something or other and marking his words, that it was very touching and brought on a creeping in the midriff. On alighting Mr. Musgrove made off ahead and my host and the lads', the two infant Samuels', father told me how dangerous it was to broach politics to strangers." So it is, Hopkins admits, "and I was compunctious enough all that day."

For his part, Hopkins has supported the Conservative candidate, Mr. Whitley, in what turns out to be a hotly contested election, Whitley finally winning by a plurality of only 2,000 votes. "The deities of the parliamentary Olympus intervened," *The Times* reports on February 6, in language which Hopkins picks up to describe the events, "and threw their protection around their favourites. Lord Hartington assured the electors that Lord Ramsay's opinions and pledges on Irish affairs did not deprive him of the cordial support of his leader, and at the last moment Sir William Harcourt went to Liverpool and exerted some of his usual eloquence in Lord Ramsay's support." But the Irish "form a very large body in Liverpool"—some ten thousand—and are "disposed to give their votes simply in the interest of Home Rule."

For the moment, however, the perceived crisis has been averted, and the Conservative candidate declared the victor. As for the misunderstanding between Hopkins and his hosts, Hopkins tells his mother, "I wrote John Lightbound a letter to make my apologies to Mr. Musgrove and said how wrong I had been. I got an answer to say that Mr. Musgrove had been hurt indeed but now wd. think no more of the matter." In spite of which, on February 26th, as he again boards the train at Lydiate for Liverpool, "Mr. Musgrove got in and sat in the same corner, looking all sacred and silvery, and I was in my corner, but he wd. make me no sign of recognition. He had not forgiven me." Left to himself, Hopkins explains, he would "have accosted him and humbled myself till he had given in, but John Lightbound, as a kind of priest who had studied his theology and knew more than I cd. be supposed to do about the deity and propitiatory rites and ceremonies, wd. not have anything more said. I am very sorry, for Mr. Musgrove appeared, at the very time I was outraging him, a kind and good man and a gentleman; but what more could I do? I think it was for him to speak and shew he bore no malice."

But he cannot let the matter go until peace has been restored. And so, the next time he goes to Lydiate, he means to set matters right. And how deliciously he does so, with that playfulness he can summon in almost any situation. "A friendly scene of reconciliation between Mr. Musgrove and me," he reports back to his mother, "which I had determined to bring about next time we shd. meet, and luckily I was with the more genial Randal [sic]

Lightbound, not with Mr. Musgrove's highpriest John. It took place on a bitter cold morning by a glowing waiting-room fire at Town Green station. I advanced and eat humblepie ravenously, Mr. M. was very goodnatured and himself finished the dish. He must, as you say, be radiant now." As for the younger son, John, he "has never since alluded to my affair: it stirs memories too sacred and terrible."

"By great good luck," he also tells his mother, "for we seldom have the opportunity of applying the mass to our own intentions, I was able to say mass for you this morning." He has "handselled" that handsome stole she made him "on a poor consumptive girl" the day before, for he has vowed to keep nothing beyond the barest minimum of possessions and is forever giving away what extra clothing he has to the poor. He writes to Cardinal Newman, now seventy-nine, as he does each year for his birthday, and receives in return "a pretty little card of a spray of dogwood leaves, one green, two red and withered, symbolical perhaps of age."

April 25: Fourth Sunday after Easter. Hopkins only jots down notes for his sermon, for writing out sermons seems to do no good. Still, his Rector urges him to write so that he can go over what Hopkins means to say *before* Hopkins says it, though he will pooh-pooh the whole idea of scrutinizing Hopkins like some errant schoolboy when the time comes for him to show him what he has written. So far, Hopkins has not had much luck with his homilies here in Liverpool. Phrases like "The Loss of God's First Kingdom" and the word "sweetheart" in another have already gotten him in trouble. So today he plans to focus on Christ's discourses—his Last Will and Testament, as it were—which St. John gives in such detail as taking place at the Last Supper. Hopkins knows these are "out of their season" now that Easter has come and gone, but it is difficult to give these their "proper attention when engrossed with the Passion." Now, then, is the time to remember what Christ asked of his followers before his crucifixion. Christ's last instructions, he explains, are "reckoned by writers on Holy Scripture to be among the very darkest and most mysterious that the sacred page contains." And so he exhorts his brethren to pay close attention to the words he has to say, and not "to stare or sleep over them but to heed them," for it is both "contemptible and unmanly . . . for men whose minds are naturally clear, to give up at the first hearing of a hard passage in the Scripture . . . to care to know no more than children know." And for today, the mysterious passage he wants to focus on is this: *And when he, that is the Holy Ghost, whom our Lord in this place calls the Paraclete, has come he will convince the world of sin and of justice and of judgment.*

What exactly is a Paraclete? "One who comforts, who cheers, who encourages, who persuades, who exhorts, who stirs up, who urges forward, who calls on." And he brings the idea home with a sports analogy: "You have seen at cricket how when one of the batsmen at the wicket has made a hit and wants to score a run, the other doubts, hangs back, or is ready to run in again, how eagerly the first will cry / Come on, come on." That is what a Paraclete is: "something that cheers the spirit of man, with signals and with cries, all zealous that he should do something and full of assurance that if he will he can, calling him on, springing to meet him half way, crying to his ears or to his heart: This way to do God's will, this way to save your soul, come on, come on!"

Christ too is a Paraclete, he explains, for he cheered men on by his own example. "He led the way, went before his troops [and] bore the brunt of battle alone, died upon the field, on Calvary hill, and bought the victory by his blood. He cried men on; he said to his disciples . . . Follow me; they did so." He told his followers to deny themselves and take up his cross and follow him. And "when they would not follow he let them go and took all the war upon himself. . . . For though Christ cheered them on they feared to follow, though the Captain led the way the soldiers fell back; he was not for that time a successful Paraclete: all, it says, they all forsook him and fled." How hard it is to do good in this world. "The flesh is against it, the world is against it, the Devil is against it." But with Christ's ultimate victory, "the hellish head was crushed," though "the earthly members were not aware of a wound." And then, once more, his time is up. Yes, he would have liked to have shown them "how the Holy Ghost has followed and will follow up this first beginning, convincing and converting nation after nation and age after age till the whole earth is hereafter to be covered." He would have liked to have shown them "the thousand thousand tongues" by which the Spirit works. But there is no time.

No time. At that same mass, he reads off the names of those who have recently died. Among them is Felix Spencer, a blacksmith from Birchfield Street, who died of pulmonary tuberculosis on April 21, age thirty-one. A week later, Hopkins composes one of the few poems he will write during his time at Liverpool, this one for an unknown workman, dead in his prime. "Félix Rándal the fárrier, O is he déad then?" he begins, as if surprised to learn that Felix should be gone so soon. And is his "dúty all énded" now,

Who have watched his mould of man, big-bóned and hardy-
          handsome

Pining, píning, till time when reason rámbled in it, and some
Fatal four disorders, fléshed there, all contended?

And so it is with death, no matter how many of the dying he has watched
over. He remembers how "Sickness broke him," and how Felix had cursed
at first, unwilling to believe that someone as strong as himself could suc-
cumb to a wasting consumption. But Hopkins had also seen Felix change
under his ministering, his anointing him with the oil of the sick, offering
the "sweet reprieve" of confession, and the "ransom" of holy communion
"Téndered to him": Christ's gift of himself as payment, as legal tender offered most tenderly. And then the Lancashire blessing and farewell: "Áh
well, God rést him áll road éver he offénded!" Life as a journey—the age-old
metaphor—a plodding on of our days, like workhorses in the daily grinding
going round. And then the surprising, transfiguring end, as Felix's "more
boisterous years" give way to suffering, and suffering to a new creation,
"When thou at the random grím fórge, pówerful amídst péers / Didst fettle
for the great grey drayhorse his bright & battering sandal!"

The reverence of that "thou," the address at the end as Felix enters the
great mystery. And so, what Felix did for his great grey drayhorses drumming the cobbled streets of Liverpool, Hopkins has been privileged to do
for Felix. In its closing lines, the poem circles back to Felix's prime, at the
same time crossing the threshold of a mystery as Felix enters his new life
with bright and battering sandals, his sacramental armor, the image of the
horseshoe signaling the Omega, the true end point, and Felix, like his name,
truly blessed now, going forth to meet his God.

No doubt Hopkins feels very much like a drayhorse himself these many
months, exhaustion setting in, his daily round to be at the beck and call of
his superiors, his congregation, the sick, those in the workhouses, the demands of the Lightbounds and other Catholic families. That same week he
tells his mother he is "knocked up" with work and illness, "the work of Easter week (worse than Holy Week)" being especially hard, on top of which he
has been suffering "with a bad cold, which led to earache and deafness."
Even now he has no strength, and as long as he remains in Liverpool he
does not see how he will ever fully regain his strength.

Here too, as at Oxford, there are so many poor Italian families, where
the men eke out livings as "organ grinders" or selling ices, that he wonders
how those who have known the Neapolitan or Tuscan sun can bear this
awful, wintry, smog-laden Liverpool air. So far, he has seen nothing of
spring "but some leaves in streets and squares. It is good, and all advise it,

to get out of town and breathe fresh air at New Brighton"—the seaside beaches six miles off—"or somewhere else," but he has had no time yet to get away. He is still gloomy over the recent elections, which have ended with Disraeli being defeated for his run as Prime Minister, and Gladstone—Hopkins's old enemy—now in control. Besides, he has had to remind himself, he really "ought to have no politics," and he has burned his fingers, "not only with Mr. Musgrove, where I was to blame, but elsewhere too, where I was not."

Two months earlier, Dixon had returned Hopkins's poems and enclosed a short letter in the same envelope, explaining that he had copied out some of the poems, and has read them all "many times with the greatest admiration." The *Eurydice,* he feels, "no one could read without the deepest & most ennobling emotion." The sonnets he finds "truly wonderful," his favorites being "The Starlight Night," "The Skylark," "Duns Scotus's Oxford," and "The Windhover." The *Deutschland* he finds "enormously powerful," though there are "such elements of deep distress in it that one reads it with less excited delight though not with less interest than the others." But it takes Hopkins ten weeks to realize that Dixon has enclosed a letter in his packet. Now he tells Dixon that his praise has been "deeply kind and cheering" to him, especially when parish work has proven so "very wearying to mind and body and leaves me nothing but odds and ends of time." There may be merit in what he does for Christ's sake, but very little in the way of Muse.

Saturday evening, May 22: During a lull in hearing confessions, he begins a long-delayed letter to Baillie, speaking of how fagged and harried he is with work. He has just been told by his Rector that another priest will be coming to preach for his two new missions and so Hopkins will not be delivering the sermon he has been preparing after all. And Baillie has taken him to task for not speaking more highly of his Oxford experience. But that is not how Hopkins sees it. After all, he insists, "not to love my University would be to undo the very buttons of my being and as for the Oxford townspeople I found them in my 10 months' stay among them very deserving of affection—though somewhat stiff, stand-off, and depressed." And though he saw "very little of the University," he could not "but feel how alien [that world] was, how chilling, and deeply to be distrusted. I could have wished, and yet I could not, that there had been no one that had known me there. As a fact there were many and those friendly, some cordially so, but with others I cd. not feel at home." To be so close to the world that had shaped him, including the very Puseyites who had once led him by their logical arguments right into the Catholic Church, and who—on his return after a dozen years—would have nothing to do with him. And his Catholic community, standoffish, inherently distrusting him both as a convert and as a former member of the enemy: the Gown. With the folks at Bedford Leigh, on the other hand, he felt as if he had been "born to deal with them." Religion, he confesses, "is the deepest impression I have in speaking to people, that they are or that they are not of my religion. And then it is sweet to be a little flattered and I can truly say that except in the most transparently cringing way I seldom am." The truth is that "these Lancashire people of low degree or not of high degree are those who most have seemed to me to welcome me and make much of me."

He hopes Baillie translates some of his ancient Egyptian hieroglyphics, for he is sure to do a better job than what the Biblical Archaeological Society has done. He found the translations in the first Egyptian volume "a very bad business" indeed. The most curious thing there was something called *Travels of an Egyptian.* The ancient text was, in reality, "a sarcastic criticism, and meant to be published too, on a journal or account of his Syrian travels by a man calling himself and laying a great stress on being, a Mohar, whatever a Mohar is. . . . Altogether [the text] is condemned [as too] modern in spirit and levels all up or all down surprisingly." It is the beginning of an interest Hopkins will share with Baillie over the next decade.

Two weeks later, he picks up where he had left off. He does not see how he can be long here, he tells Baillie. In fact, since his ordination, he has "been long nowhere yet." But here among the tenements of Liverpool he is constantly being "brought face to face with the deepest poverty and misery." On this he could write a great deal, he adds, "but it would do no good." Besides, "when you have a parish you can no longer read nor have intellectual interests." Still, he has heard some concert music and some Wagner, which did not impress him, but then Wagner in concert rather than on stage was bound to lose greatly. "The Germans call him the Master of Masters and Hartmann the greatest of philosophers and the last new thing everywhere the greatest that ever was." But he is tired of fads, of this "barbarous business of greatest this and supreme that. . . . What is the thing that has been? The same that shall be." For is not everything finally "vanity and vexation of spirit"?

"I wish I could pursue music," he writes Bridges in mid-June, "for I have invented a new style, something standing to ordinary music as sprung rhythm to common rhythm: it employs quarter tones." At the moment, he is working on an air for his own sonnet, "Hurrahing in Harvest." He also encloses "Felix Randal" and "At the Wedding March," the only things he has written in nine months. And is it true that Bridges is to be married? It has been "a great comfort," he adds, to have had Bridges and his mother take such an interest in his own family, and he hopes that Bridges's marriage "will not lessen this intimacy." Who else is out there that he could talk poetry with if not with Bridges? It is one of the last links with his old, familiar world.

He prepares several more sermons, but is prevented from giving them for one reason or another. Then, on Friday evening, July 16, at half an hour's notice, he must reformulate a sermon he formerly gave at Bedford Leigh. "I thought people must be quite touched," he notes, "and that I even saw some wiping their tears, but when the same thing happened" the following week, he realizes that it was merely sweat his parishioners were wiping away. One evening he preaches on Mary Magdalen. It is the Victorian image of the fallen woman, her history conflated with several other women in the Gospels. "Bad as she was," he says, "she would not be blinded," and "she came to the light though she was . . . to be shewn a sinner by it." What courage that took, he urges his flock on, for "how many a heretic loves his heresy, how many a bad Catholic loves his impurity or his fraud better than the light of truth and virtue! keeps from the church, the mass, the priest, wants to live in peace, that is in sin, even sometimes to die in peace, that is in calm despair and damnation." Afterward, a member of the congregation comes up to him to tell him, "with great simplicity, that I was not to be named in the same week" with Father Clare. "'Well' I said 'and I will not be named in the same week. But did you hear it all?' He said he did, only that he was sleeping for parts of it."

In early August, he returns home on vacation for some much needed rest, and finally completes "Brothers," the poem commemorating his time at Mount St. Mary's two years before. When he visits Bridges in London, he gives him a copy of the poem, and also shows him something else he has been working on for the past several years. It is "The Leaden Echo and the Golden Echo," and Bridges is much struck by its musicality. "The reason . . . why you feel it carry the reader along with it," he explains to Bridges, "is that it is dramatic and meant to be popular. It is a song for St. Winefred's maidens to sing." He has also composed some speeches for the play, but the work is still in its "roughest first thoughts," "too lyrical" and not yet dramatic enough. *That* will need time and the pitch of tortured instress to create. Then it is back to Liverpool to make his annual retreat.

On Friday, August 20, the first full day of the retreat, he makes extensive notes on the Ignatian *Principle and Foundation,* meditating in depth now on Being and Nothingness. Alone once more with his God, he finds himself at a deeper cleave of thought than he can allow himself when preaching, since most of his congregation would be confused, bored, or scandalized by the depths of his probing. But thinking deeply about it now, in the sacred space allotted him, Hopkins has to admit that he finds the self—himself— to be "more distinctive and higher pitched than anything else I see; I find myself with my pleasures and pains, my powers and my experiences, my deserts and guilt, my shame and sense of beauty, my dangers, hopes, fears, and all my fate, more important to myself than anything I see." But where does "all this throng and stack of being, so rich, so distinctive, so important, come from?" For nothing he can see answers him, "and this whether I speak of human nature or of my individuality, my selfbeing. For human nature, being more highly pitched, selved, and distinctive than anything in the world, can have been developed, evolved, condensed, from the vastness of the world not anyhow . . . but only by one of finer or higher pitch and determination than itself and certainly than any that elsewhere we see, for this power had to force forward the starting or stubborn elements to the one pitch required."

It is frankly impossible for Hopkins to believe that human life could really have evolved by random chance, for when he considers his selfbeing, his "consciousness and feeling of myself, that taste of myself," he continues, he finds it "more distinctive than the taste of ale or alum, more distinctive than the smell of walnutleaf or camphor, and is incommunicable by any means to another man. . . . Nothing else in nature comes near this unspeakable stress of . . . distinctiveness . . . this selfbeing of my own." Nothing, he sees now, "explains it or resembles it, except so far as this, that other men to themselves have the same feeling. But this only multiplies the phenomena to be explained so far as the cases are like and do resemble." Yet when he searches nature, he can find no resemblance. He can taste the self "but at one tankard, that of my own being. . . . When I compare my self, my being—myself, with anything else whatever, all things alike, all in the same degree, rebuff me with blank unlikeness; so that my knowledge of it, which is so intense, is from itself alone."

This is Hopkins the speculative theologian, Hopkins the Cartesian and Scotist, playing on the idea of *haeceittas,* thisness, radical individuation, with himself his only audience, and the difference between this language and the language he must use for his working-class congregation is vast and profound. Where does this taste of selfbeing come from, then? he asks.

Is it from chance? Myself? Or some extrinsic power? "Chance in name no one acknowledges as a cause or principle or explanation of being," he reasons, and certainly the Positivists have not explained the existence of things, but have left it to what they call chance, without explaining what chance is. His way of proceeding, on the other hand, is by the laws of logic and reasoning, its bedrock Aristotelian and Scholastic. "Chance applies only to things possible; what must be does not come by chance and what cannot be by no chance comes. Chance then is the *energeia*, the stress, of the intrinsic possibility which things have." No one else "can taste *my* shame, *my* guilt, or *my* fate. This is that selftaste that nothing else in the world can match." This, then, is what hell is: to be locked forever into one's own self, to taste one's sweating self. "God's self is outside my self, his *I am* is not my *I am*. And so the self subsists, created and upheld by God, but distinct from God's own universal self."

In the years remaining him, these core insights will inform his poetics as profoundly as his theology, until the two become fully realized aspects of the man. Yes, there is deep joy in discovering in all things that they are "counter, original, spare, strange." But as he looks deeper, there is also the potential, he realizes, for becoming so fascinated by the song of oneself that one will give over looking for the source and turn inward on the imagination as that sole source. And if that is what we most desire—to dwell forever on ourselves, as Lucifer does—then God will give us what we have most deeply wished for, and its name is hell.

His retreat over, it is back into the heart of the city to preach, visit the sick, bury the dead, say mass, daily read his breviary, and hear confessions. On Saturday, September 4, the hottest day of the year, he spends all afternoon and evening in the confessional box, the smell of alcohol and sour sweat drifting through the curtained screen separating him from those who have come to confess their sins and go home feeling for the moment clean. When he picks up a "languid pen" the next day to write Bridges, he is once again suffering from diarrhea and vomiting, though at least it has rained and cooled the air a bit. There has been so much work, he complains, that he has not been able to get to Bridges's *Poems* or *The Growth of Love* pamphlet until now. He is happy that Bridges and his friend Woolrych like his musical settings for Bridges's poems, though he is still waiting for his sister Grace to finish them. "If I could make my own harmonies, much of the expression of the piece could be conveyed in the accompaniments," he explains. As for his poem "The Brothers," it does, he confesses, owe much to Wordsworth, and was in fact "first written in stanzas in Wordsworth's manner, but when I compared it with his inimitable simplicity and gravity I was disgusted and meant to destroy it, till the thought struck me of changing the metre, which made it do."

The topic turns next to the Renaissance lyric and Wyatt and Surrey. Hopkins thinks the latter the greater of the two, though he thinks Bridges—like others of their generation—has misread Surrey. As for *Piers Plowman*, he has not studied it enough "and so cannot pronounce how far triple time is boldly employed in it." He thinks "it arose from a simple misunderstanding or misreading of Chaucer," who wrote when the language was fast changing and soon "became obsolete, and they being much read and not rightly scanned thus came to suggest rhythms which they never thought of." Something like that, he believes, has "happened often in the history of verse."

Finally, he encloses "a little piece composed" since beginning this letter, "not founded on any real incident." Nor is he "well satisfied with it." The piece, written while at Lydiate with the Lightbounds on September 7, is "Spring and Fall: to a Young Child," in four-stress couplets, with a central tercet. It is about the size of a miniature sonnet, a kind of compressed *Intimations of Mortality*. The time is early autumn, with the first hints of oncoming winter and the death of the year. A small girl weeps over the unleaving of her first world, her Eden and her Goldengrove. Yes, you weep now, little one, he tells her, but in time you will become accustomed to these losses, though "worlds of wanwood leafmeal lie":

> Márgarét, áre you gríeving
> Over Goldengrove unleaving?
> Leáves, líke the thíngs of mán, you
> With your fresh thoughts care for, can you?
> Áh! ás the héart grows ólder
> It will come to such sights colder
> By and by, nor spare a sigh
> Though worlds of wanwood leafmeal lie;
> And yet you *will* weep and know why.

Loss, tears, death: no matter the name. All being, alas, devolves into non-being. It is a bold thing Hopkins does in this poem, paraphrasing a passage from St. Paul's First Letter to the Corinthians (2:9): "Eye hath not seen, nor ear heard, neither has it entered into the heart of man, what things God hath prepared for them that love him," for Hopkins's lines swing two ways at once. They can mean that what Margaret experiences now is but an intimation of the reality of death—the blight that comes with the unfolding of life and that comes home to all of us in time. But the lines can also mean that there is another intimation, a heavenly one, that also waits for those who search for it, something beyond death. Still, the second reading is there only by intimation, the stress here being on the early realization that Margaret shall one day be no more. It is a poetic extension of the notes Hopkins had written two weeks earlier on Being and Nothingness, this time in the form of an adult addressing a child, as sorrow's springs, which both share, are revealed in the inevitable loss of one's first world:

> Now no matter, child, the name:
> Sórrow's spríngs áre the sáme.
> Nor mouth had, no nor mind, expressed
> What héart héard of, ghóst guéssed:
> It ís the blíght mán was bórn for,
> It is Margaret you mourn for.

That is the one way. But the other is the counterconsolation of Divine Providence, which he preaches on in late October. The Lord, he reminds his Liverpool congregation, "takes more interest in a merchant's business than the merchant, in a vessel's steering than the pilot, in a lover's sweetheart than the lover, in a sick man's pain than the sufferer, in our salvation than we ourselves." But therein lies the rub: in the word "sweetheart," uttered within the sacred confines of the church. "In consequence, I was in a manner suspended" from preaching, he notes drily, "and at all events was forbidden (it was some time after) to preach without having my sermon revised. However when I was going to take the next sermon I had to give after this regulation came into force to Fr. Clare for revision he poohpoohed the matter and would not look at it." But that evening—before the strictures are in place—he goes on, warming to it. Can they not see that everything in Creation is "made and provided for us, the sun, moon, and other heavenly bodies to light us, warm us, and be measures to us of time; coal and rockoil for artificial light and heat; animals and vegetables for our food and clothing; rain, wind, and snow again to make these bear and yield their tribute to us; water and the juices of plants for our drink; air for our breathing; stone and timber for our lodging; metals for our tools and traffic; the songs of birds, flowers and their smells and colours, fruits and their taste for our enjoyment"? It is all a million-fold contrivance of Providence planned for our use and patterned for our admiration.

And yet we know that Providence seems imperfect. "The sun shines too long and withers the harvest, the rain is too heavy and rots it . . . the air and water carry in their currents the poison of disease; there are poison plants, venomous snakes and scorpions; the beasts our subjects rebel . . . the coal-pits and oilwells are full of explosions, fires, and outbreaks of sudden death, the sea of storms and wrecks, the snow has avalanches, the earth landslips; we contend with cold, want, weakness, hunger, disease, death . . . every-thing is full of fault, flaw, imperfection, shortcoming."

But why should such things be, he asks, who had once found God's Providence in the wreck of the *Deutschland* and again in the *Eurydice*? Because "if we were not forced from time to time to feel our need of God and our dependence on him, we should most of us cease to pray to him and to thank him." And so, to make up for the fissures in His Providence, God has given each of us a guardian angel, "to keep thee in all thy ways." How much does God make of us, then, when He will have His very courtiers, those who gather about His throne, to look after us? Courtiers, his congregation thinks. Aye, courtiers, indeed. Ah, that dreamy Father Hopkins. And does Hopkins himself feel this consolation now, or is he simply urging others on in the face of his own growing desolation?

Tuesday evening, October 26: Back at Rose Hill to say mass next morn-ing, he picks up his pen and writes Bridges. "I never could write," he ex-plains, for "one is so fagged, so harried and gallied up and down. And the drunkards go on drinking, the filthy, as the scripture says, are filthy still: human nature is so inveterate. Would that I had seen the last of it." That, it seems, is his life now, ministering to such as these. But seven years later, af-ter the memory has been rubbed smooth by the river of time, he will recall another drunken incident from his time in Liverpool, when the church or-ganist there dismissed as inferior a hymn of his sister Grace's he had given him to play. And "see what became of him: he got drunk at the organ (I have now twice had this experience: it is distressing, alarming, agitating, but above all delicately comic; it brings together the bestial and the angelic elements in such a quaint entanglement as nothing else can; for musicians never play such clever descants as under those circumstances and in an in-stant everybody is thrilled with the insight of the situation) and was dis-missed. He was a clever young fellow and thoroughly understood the properties of narrow-necked tubes."

"What fun if you were a classic!" he tells Bridges. "So few people have style, except individual style or manner—not Tennyson nor Swinburne nor Morris, not to name the scarecrow misbegotten Browning crew." "London Snow" he thinks "a most beautiful and successful piece," though he does not much care for the cold clinical detachment of his "On a Dead Child." Moreover, Bridges still has too many echoes of Hopkins's own lines in his poems, especially phrases and rhythms lifted from the *Deutschland,* which, since it is the "longest piece extant in sprung rhythm . . . could not help haunting your memory." In the meantime, he has been trying his hand at some humorous verse—it being all the rage just now—and promises to send Bridges some examples soon.

Mid-December: He preaches on Jesus and the Samaritan woman at the well, focusing on how Jesus refused to eat while God's work was still to be done. "First the soul's good looked to," he sums up, "then the body's. This rule our Lord laid down in the Sermon on the Mount. Seek first the kingdom of God and his justice, and the rest—such as food and clothing and our other needs of this life—shall be added to you." And did not his Master practice what he preached, putting "God's work before his own comfort"? For he was hungry, but "made it his meat . . . to do the will of God who sent him [to] finish that work." So may he, he prays, find the strength to do likewise.

"My parish work has been very wearisome; of late especially," he confesses to Dixon three days before Christmas. He does not believe he has overrated Dixon's poems. Yes, there are faults, but against these he would set "their extreme beauties—imagery inheriting Keats's mantle, the other-world of imagination . . . the 'instress' of feeling, and a pathos the deepest, I think, that I have anywhere found." He has been particularly struck by Dixon's *Ode on Conflicting Aims,* "on the pleasures of learning and the sorrows of sympathy," with its theme of "the loss of taste, of relish for what once charmed us."

It is a theme he understands too well, one which used "to dismay and dishearten me deeply, it made the best of things seem empty." There are reasons for this, Hopkins knows. First, disenchantment, as an untrained taste is replaced by a maturer one. Or, again, how "the mind after a certain number of shocks or stimuli, as the physiologists would say, is spent and flags." It is why jokes become stale. But another reason is that "insight is more perfect earlier in life . . . especially towards elementary impressions." There was a time, he can remember, when "crimson and pure blues seemed to me spiritual and heavenly sights fit to draw tears." Now he can barely see what he saw then, though he hardly cares to dwell on the fact anymore. So with his youthful feelings about Tennyson, whose poems enchanted him when he was young. Ah, yes, "as the héart grows ólder / It will come to such sights colder / By and by . . ."

January 18, 1881: A record snowstorm and gale sweeps through England, shutting down London and cutting it off from the rest of the country. Two days later, Hopkins writes Bridges that he has just walked out of town "by frost and starlight" to Gill Moss, deep snowdrifts "frozen as hard as ice." He even managed to lose his way, until "two children fetching milk led me," telling him, "'you must follow ooz,'" until he found his way again. On the 26th, he walks down to the Mersey to see with his own eyes the ice "coated with dirty yellow . . . floating down stream with the ebb tide." It "everywhere covered the water," and was continually "ploughed up" by the steam ferry-boats chuffing under great strain back and forth between shores. Huge flocks of gulls were constantly being pampered by "throngs of people . . . chucking them bread." Nor were they "quick to sight it and when they did they dipped towards it with infinite lightness, touched the ice, and rose again, but generally missed the bread: they seem to fancy they cannot or ought not to rest on ground." He hears that the Thames too is now frozen so solid that an ox was roasted whole on it. Just today there has been "a thaw, and the frostings, which have been a lovely fairyland on the publicans' windows, are vanished from the panes."

In the meantime, he has been busy setting "Spring and Fall" to plainchant. And thinking of his *Deutschland,* he considers it a far better poem than the *Eurydice,* though there are "immaturities in it I should never be guilty of now." He also refuses to go along with Bridges's self-assessment that "The Dead Child" is the best thing Bridges has written. No, the rhythm and thought falter, and the diction is not exquisite enough. Take phrases like "'wise, sad head'" and "'firm, pale hands,'" for example, which belong rather "to a familiar commonplace about 'Reader, have you never hung over the pillow of . . . pallid cheek, clammy brow . . . long, long night-watches . . . surely, Sir Josiah Bickerstaff, there is some hope! O say not all is over. It cannot be'—You know."

Nor does he appreciate Bridges's saying he takes delight in not caring what people think of his work. It is the sort of comment he finds in Bridges which "opens out a wide vein of to me saddening thoughts," and which he will not go into just now. Both his parents have been very sick, he adds, but have now recovered. And then he speaks of a small miracle he has just witnessed, "a case of [a] remarkably rapid recovery from typhus in a little lad whom I anointed," and which he attributes to the effects of the sacrament itself. The doctor, who had given the boy up, "brought another one today or yesterday to see the phenomenon." And now he is off—"with heigh ho, the wind and the rain"—to Rose Hill and Lydiate to say mass.

February 26: News reaches England of the disaster at Majuba Hill in the region adjoining the Transvaal, where General Colley and three hundred of his British soldiers, comprising two companies of the 58th, two of the 60th Rifles, three of the 92nd Highlanders, and fifty men attached to the Naval Brigade have been killed or wounded by a much smaller number of Boers who sent the British flying. Hopkins, devastated by the news, blames the defeat on Gladstone, that "truckler to Russia," and the Freemasons. It is "a deep disgrace," he tells his mother, and "a stain upon our arms; which indeed have not shone of late," and the effect is bound to "be felt all over the empire." The Transvaal, he will tell Bridges months later, the defeat still rankling him, "is an unredeemed disgrace. And people do not seem to mind. You know that our troops ('our gallant fellows,' as the reporter had it) ran." He hopes that this will not result in the British surrendering Kandahar, which would deal a serious blow to the Pax Britannica his countrymen are trying to maintain around the world.

In late March, Dante Gabriel Rossetti writes Hall Caine about Caine's forthcoming anthology, *Sonnets of Three Centuries.* "There is an admirable but totally unknown living poet named Dixon," Rossetti tells Caine. "I will send you two small vols. of his which he gave me long ago. . . . I forgot till today that he had written any sonnets, but I see there are three in one vol. and one in another. . . . If I live, I mean to write something about him. . . . His finest passages are as fine as any living man can do." Caine might want to ask Dixon for an original sonnet. "Mention my name," he closes, "and address him at Carlisle. . . . Of course he is a Rev." In turn, Dixon writes Hopkins that Caine "has written for my consent to reprint a couple of my Sonnets in a large collection of Sonnets . . . he is publishing. It is a very important undertaking & he is evidently a man of very high poetical insight & ability." And since Caine has asked for any "sonnet treasure" he might be aware of, Dixon has sent him two of Hopkins's—"Starlight Night" and "Skylark"—for "inspection; to gratify him." Would he be willing to see one of those published? In turn, Hopkins sends off three old sonnets for Caine to choose from, if he so wishes.

For the fact is, he tells Bridges, that as long as he remains in Liverpool, he can write nothing. "Every impulse and spring of art seems to have died in me, except for music, and that I pursue under almost an impossibility of getting on." Nor does he believe he will stay much longer in Liverpool. Meanwhile, he keeps groping with musical harmony (via Gregorian chant), trying to harmonize some of his own airs. By May he believes, in fact, that he has "become very musical of late," but is afraid it is God who is unwilling to help him get on with things, for if he "could conscientiously spend even a little time every day on [poetry] I could make great progress." In truth, "the only Muse that does not stifle in this horrible place" is Music itself.

As for Bridges's remarks about his so-called rhythmic eccentricities, he can only reply that he has "heard so much about and suffered so much for and in fact been so completely ruined for life by my alleged singularities that they are a sore subject." His failure to take a fourth year of theology, his being shunted about from Stonyhurst to Farm Street to Oxford to Bedford Leigh and now here, where he has failed as a select preacher. How jaded he feels these days. In the meantime, he is sending Bridges those comic verses he promised earlier. One of these, he warns, pokes fun at Gladstone. Another at the Anglican Church.

Hall Caine writes to say that he will not be able to use any of Hopkins's sonnets, the purpose of his book being to "demonstrate the impossibility of improving upon the acknowledged structure [of the sonnet] whether as to rhyme-scheme or measure." Poor soul, Hopkins notes sardonically. He writes "to me as to a she bear robbed of her cubs. I am replying now and reassuring him and smoothing down. To support himself he shewed some of my sonnets he had . . . to 'a critic of utmost eminence'; who thought with him. . . . However he had Andromeda and one cannot say there is any novelty in rhythm there." And now, to add insult to injury, Caine plans to refute Hopkins "in a special paragraph" in his preface, unless of course Hopkins objects. This of course Hopkins will have to do, "for otherwise some reply seems called for, and it will be equally vexatious to reply and not to reply." Worse still, the eminent critic George Saintsbury seems to have refuted Hopkins's sonnets without naming him in an article in the *Academy,* where he speaks of some minor poet's too-ready willingness "to break his rhythms without sufficient cause." So this is what it means to be a nihilist, he sighs, "an influence at once baneful and unknown."

Two weeks later, having read one of those "omnium gatherum" anonymous reviews in the *Academy* he is sure is by Saintsbury, Hopkins reads a notice of Bridges's work, reproving him for continuing to print his work anonymously in "furtive pamphlets," even as Saintsbury professes his "very high admiration for this mysterious and yet well-known author's work." On the other hand, Saintsbury does not like Bridges's experiments in sprung rhythm, even if they do contain "the elements of some fine poetry. . . . When the new prosody is worth much, it seems to us to be reducible with advantage to the old." This, Hopkins adds, "is not an unfriendly notice and expresses real admiration," though it is, to be sure, impertinent, in Saintsbury's usual manner.

As for Bridges's refusing to allow his own sonnets to be published in Caine's anthology because Hopkins's poems have been rejected, though his own worst "malignant nature is pleased by hearing you or others call people rogues and damfools and egregious asses, yet it is not right." What good can come of insulting people and making enemies? And now Caine may go after *him* to get back at Bridges. Besides, Bridges's poems "would have graced the book," for "there would have been nothing in it so good." And then there are those comic poems Hopkins has sent, which will sicken Bridges with their vulgarity, especially the one about the Church of England (which single copy Bridges has already destroyed). The truth is, Hopkins admits, he knows he has in him "a great vein of blackguardry" and is certainly "no gentleman; though I had rather say this than have it said."

May 15: The fourth Sunday after Easter: An old sermon refitted. Hopkins ascends the pulpit at St. Francis Xavier and begins with a brilliant parallel construction: "After they had eaten the Paschal Lamb, after they had partaken of the Agape . . . , after he had washed their feet, after he had set on foot the Sacrament of the Holy Eucharist, offered in a bloodless shape the Sacrifice of his Body and Blood . . . and given them their first communion, after all these he delivered a long, solemn, and mysterious discourse, which . . . fills four chapters of St. John." Christ was leaving them, but in his place he would send another Paraclete—the Holy Ghost. After all, like all of us, Christ was time- and space-bound, and "in some seventy years . . . he must at any rate have died and in fact his enemies made an end of him long before that time." And what would that mean for those millions and millions to come? Moreover, "he came to the Jews . . . a very small part of the whole world," and "what was this to the millions of gentiles?" Happy those who knew Christ "in the flesh, but it was for the good of mankind at large . . . that he should go away and another Paraclete should come." For it is the Spirit that "makes of every Christian another Christ, an After Christ; lives a million lives in every age . . . is breathed into each at baptism" and "passes like a restless breath from heart to heart." Christ, who plays in ten thousand faces not his. . . .

Three days later, he reads on page twelve of *The Times* that there has been an audacious robbery at the home of the Hopkins family's neighbor

Mrs. Dudley Baxter on the same Sunday evening he had preached on the blessed coming of the Holy Spirit. Alone while her family was at church, Mrs. Baxter had gone upstairs and found a shoeless, well-dressed man. He has a pistol, he tells her, and means to use it if she does not comply with his demands. And so she gives him between £4 and £5 and is then told to show him to the front door, where he puts on his boots, walks off, and waves, after which Mrs. Baxter faints. Knowing the house, Hopkins writes his mother, "the account made the more impression on me. I am afraid the scoundrel cannot well be caught, or not this time. Perhaps the thing will grow too, which is not pleasant." Even Oak Hill, then, his first haven, is no longer safe from such incursions.

In the meantime, his parish here has been holding a bazaar, the Holy Bazaar having lately become "the eighth sacrament," and yesterday he and some of his fellow priests went over "to spend money at it." A friend of theirs, "a very good and uproarious old fellow, Mr. Derby, who told me with shouts of glee once that if I would go out with him he wd. 'make my lip curl like a bee's knee in a gale of wind,' drove us over and treated us royally." Lunch at a halfway house, "dinner at St. Helen's, and more drinks at the halfwayhouse returning. The horse reared with excitement to see a pony start from the innyard before him, which made the rosy young ostler open his mouth, which so much pleased Mr. Derby that he chuckled on the way home and said he should remember 'that ostler' to the day of his death."

A terse note from Bridges to say he has destroyed all of Hopkins's comic verses and begs him to send no more. "I am sure that they are not natural to you," he adds, and "will do you no credit." Hopkins, hurt by Bridges's action, promises to send no more. Still, he adds, he does not feel ashamed of what he sent, "unless for a certain blackguardry, but will not defend them." As for his quips at Gladstone, he believes the current state of politics "is indeed sad," in fact, "heartbreaking, for I am a very great patriot. Lamentable as the condition of Ireland is there is hope of things mending, but the Transvaal is an unredeemed disgrace. And people do not seem to mind." In spite of himself, he asks Bridges to persuade Caine "to put in my 'Andromeda,'" then catches himself. *Absit.* Enough. "It is my fixed principle never to quarrel."

Sunday, June 26: A sermon on the Sacred Heart of Jesus, verging on the Gothic in its insistence on the physical aspects of the human heart, but Hopkins pushes through on this muggy morning in late June. Is not poetry "full of mention of the heart?" How often we speak of "a great heart, a narrow heart, a warm heart, a cold heart, a tender heart, a hard heart, a heart of stone, a lion heart, a craven heart, a poor heart, a sad heart, a heavy heart, a broken heart, a willing heart, a full heart, of heart's ease, heartache, heartscald, of thinking in one's heart, of loving from one's heart, of the heart sinking, of taking heart, of losing heart, of giving the heart away, of being heartwhole." In every one of these cases, he explains, we do not mean the piece of flesh we call the heart, "but the thoughts of the mind that vessel seems to harbour and the feelings of the soul to which it beats."

Since the great divide of the Reformation that pitted Protestant against Catholic, what has happened? A New World has been "discovered and peopled from Europe; the means of travelling and the speed of it have increased prodigiously; communication between men . . . has been made easy in a still more extraordinary degree; the realm of nature has been laid bare and our knowledge of it widened beyond measure." But though "we write to one another a hundred times as fast and often as our forefathers could," we have not advanced in communicating with one another. For is it not true that it is the deeper things which need heeding to? Like the mystery of God's great heart, of His infinite love and care for us. But, he wonders, is anyone out there listening?

At the beginning of July, a penciled note from Bridges apologizing for destroying those comic verses, explaining that he has since come down with pneumonia, no doubt contracted from his work at St. Bartholomew's. Deeply shaken, Hopkins replies at once. "I am afraid you must be very sick," he writes. Still, he has "attended people in pneumonia and anointed them, they recovered. I shall visit you, I cannot anoint you, but I hope nevertheless that by the time I come you will [be] on the highroad of recovery." He will be there just as soon as he can get away. In the meantime, back to those comic verses, the only copies of which Bridges destroyed, which really were pretty funny.

Two days later, he makes the trip down to London, only to find Bridges so sick that he is able to see him for only a few minutes. And when he returns a second time, he is told that Bridges is too sick to see anyone just now. In fact, the pneumonia will bring an abrupt end to Bridges's medical practice altogether, a practice that had once meant seeing and diagnosing over thirty thousand patients a year, or one patient from the depressingly long queues at St. Bartholomew's every ninety seconds for hours on end. True, Bridges had long thought of retiring at forty, but now the pneumonia has only hastened those plans.

Throughout the dog days of July and August, Hopkins makes his Liverpool rounds, saying mass, hearing confession, visiting the sick and those in the workhouses, serving as chaplain to various Catholic organizations including the St. Vincent's de Paul Society, and setting up poorboxes in the Catholic churches for their relief. He has even tried to get annulments for questionable marriages. Alms have been distributed to over five hundred poor families, and there have been some three thousand four hundred visits to these families by members of the congregation over the past year. And thanks to Hopkins, a Penny Savings Bank has now been started at St. Francis Xavier's to help the destitute. But all in all, he will tell Dixon afterward, "my Liverpool . . . experience laid upon my mind . . . a truly crushing conviction of the misery of town life to the poor and more than to the poor, of the misery of the poor in general, of the degradation even of our race, of the hollowness of this century's civilisation: it made even life a burden to me to have daily thrust upon me the things I saw." Then, suddenly, his time there is over, and on August 10th, Hopkins finds himself two hundred miles to the north at St. Joseph's Church, 40 North Woodside Road, Glasgow, where he has been sent to fill in for two weeks, though in fact he will stay on for the next two months. "Dearest Bridges," he writes five weeks into his Glasgow stay. "How is it you do not know I am here? On Oct. 10 I am to be at Roehampton (Manresa House, as of old) to begin my 'tertianship,' the third year . . . of noviceship which we undergo before taking our last vows. Till then I expect to be here mostly, but must go to Liverpool to pack; for I came for a fortnight or so only and left my things: indeed I am going to pieces as I stand." And though Glasgow is a wretched place, he likes it better than Liverpool and gets on "better here, though bad is the best of my getting on." How he longs for his Tertianship to begin, when he shall "have been made more spiritual minded."

He has already decided to write no poetry for the ten months he is in Tertianship, in order that he may *vacare Deo*—empty his mind for the things of God—as he did in his noviceship thirteen years before. And so he would love to finish several long poems before then, though he fears he shall not. One is an ode on his fellow Jesuit Edmund Campion "for the 1st of December next is the 300th anniversary of his, Sherwin's and Bryant's martyrdom, from which I expect of heaven some . . . great conversion or other blessing to the Church in England. Thinking over this matter my vein began to flow and I have by me a few scattered stanzas, something between the *Deutschland* and [Dryden's] *Alexander's Feast,* in sprung rhythm of irregular metre." The problem of course is that "the vein urged by any country sight or feeling of freedom or leisure (you cannot tell what a slavery of mind or heart it is to live my life in a great town) soon dried and I do not know if I can coax it to run again."

How slowly and laboriously poetry comes to him now, he confesses to his friend, whereas musical composition continues to come easily, for I can make tunes almost at all times and places and could harmonise them as easily if only I could play or could read music at sight." If he could only play the piano or get at one, he thinks he might be able to improvise on it. He is even sure he can counterpoint without actually having a piano to practice on. This evening, for example, he got a young lady "to play me over some of my pieces, but was not well pleased with them. What had sounded rich seemed thin." As for his own poetry, he confesses, he can't help feeling about it now what he feels toward Browning's work: he can admire "the touches and the details, but the general effect, the whole . . . I think it repulsive." On the upside, he has been promised two days to see something of the Scottish Highlands before he leaves Glasgow.

Then he writes Dixon, asking if it would be possible to meet him at Carlisle on his way back to Liverpool. Dixon answers at once, inviting him to be his guest at the parsonage. But, not being able to say mass there, Hopkins declines, explaining that since becoming a priest, he has "never missed doing so except when I could not help it." It is not a practice he is willing to give up, even to see Dixon. What he would like to do, though, is this: arrive at Carlisle by half past twelve and leave by the eight o' clock train and be in Preston that same evening, where Father Goldie, "a good friend of mine and very hospitable," could put him up. In that time they could either see Carlisle Cathedral or go down to Hayton.

Then, on the morning of September 26, he sends a telegram off to Dixon to say his plans have changed and that he will not be able to meet his friend after all. Two days later, he heads to Loch Lomond by train, and then by boat to Inversnaid, following in Wordsworth's footsteps. And here, in this wilderness, Hopkins's Muse awakens once more, and he writes his first serious poem in over a year. It is called "Inversnaid," and in its four-stress quatrains has about it that strain of musicality he finds easier to write these days than any other verse. Here in the Scottish Highlands his heart opens to the lightsome fawn-froth of the beadbonny stream twindling over the dark waters below:

> This dárksome búrn, hórseback brówn,
> His rollrock highroad roaring down,

In coop and in comb the fleece of his foam
Flutes and low to the lake falls home.

A wíndpuff-bónnet of fáwn-fróth
Turns and twindles over the broth
Of a póol so pítchblack, féll-frówning,
It rounds and rounds Despair to drowning.

Degged with dew, dappled with dew
Are the groins of the braes that the brook treads through,
Wiry heathpacks, flitches of fern,
And the beadbonny ash that sits over the burn.

Ah, "What would the world be, once bereft / Of wet and of wildness?" And then a prayer that this place be left in peace, as a sign of God's presence. "Let them be left," he pleads, "O let them be left, wildness and wet; / Long live the weeds and the wilderness yet." Then back by rail to gloomy Glasgow and the teeming city masses, and his unending duties among the wretched poor.

Chapter 13

Aeonian Time:
Roehampton & Tertianship, 1881–1882

Saturday afternoon, October 8, 1881: Bags in hand, Father Hopkins arrives back at Roehampton to begin his Tertianship. There are some one hundred fellow Jesuits now at Manresa House, including an upper community of seven priests, headed by the Rector and novice master, Father John Morris, who is, like Canon Dixon, a scholar of the Reformation. In addition there are nine Tertians, including Hopkins, and the Tertian Master, Father Robert Whitty (familiarly known among his fellow Jesuits as "Viewy Bob"), who will guide the nine through the third year of their novitiate. Then there are twenty-four Juniors, post novices taking classes to make up deficiencies in their formal education, fifty novices in their first or second year, and eleven lay brothers to do much of the manual work about the former manor and estate grounds.

No sooner are the Tertians settled in than they are assigned their chores: sweeping and dusting the rooms and hallways, chopping wood, washing dishes and scrubbing pots and pans, and mending their own clothes. In addition, there is the daily round of spiritual reading, studying the Institutes of the Society, public confessing of faults once a week in the refectory and asking penances of the minister, daily mass, and meditations, at which one of their number reads aloud in the refectory during meals. Within weeks, they will begin making the Thirty Days for a second time, and then—in the time leading up to Lent—they will prepare sermons, which they will offer during the Lenten season, as they take part in the missions offered in various parish churches throughout the country.

"I am a novice again," Hopkins explains to Dixon as soon as he has settled in. "This second probation lasts ten months, ending on St. Ignatius' feast July 31. We see no newspapers nor read any but spiritual books. In Lent we go out to give retreats and so on; beyond that in *eremo sumus* [we are hermits]." He had hoped to have finished his remarks on Dixon's poems by now, but he has some things to add in the time he still has free. The truth is, he was so jaded in his parish work that he "kept putting things off." But now, "in this retirement the mind becomes both fresh and keen."

Dixon replies on the 11th. He has had a note from Bridges, who is now at Torquay in Devonshire, slowly recovering from his bout with pneumonia. And he supposes Hopkins is determined to go on with the religious life, though it must be a severe trial, and ends: "I will say no more." The following day, Hopkins writes back. He wonders if Dixon knows Disraeli's novel *Lothair,* because Manresa House "is the divine Theodora's" and "some of the scenes are laid here." Then on to a discussion of the sonnet, of which he recognizes "stricter and looser forms," though only the Italian sonnet is a sonnet proper, the Shakespearean form, such as Dixon employs, being "a very beautiful and effective species of composition in the kind." Still, the real characteristic of the sonnet is its division into eight and six, and "what is not so marked off and moreover has not the octet again divided into quatrains is not to be called a sonnet at all." It is a brilliant form in its mathematical subdivisions of four and three, because it "pairs off even or symmetrical members with symmetrical (the quatrains) and uneven or unsymmetrical with uneven (the tercets)." Even the rhymes "are founded on a principle of nature and cannot be altered without loss of effect," so that if one tries to run "the rhymes of the octet into the sestet a downright prolapsus or hernia takes place and the sonnet is crippled for life."

Hopkins means to cease writing literary criticism as well as poetry during his time here. But for now he offers these nuggets: Browning is all frigid bluster. In fact, the man has "too much of what came in with Kingsley and the Broad Church school, a way of talking (and making his people talk) with the air and spirit of a man bouncing up from table with his mouth full of bread and cheese and saying that he meant to stand no blasted nonsense." Tennyson, too, has picked up this tone. But what *he* looks for in a poet is "a true humanity of spirit, neither mawkish on the one hand nor blustering on the other," something he prizes in both Dixon and Bridges. What he finds in Browning too often are "pointless photographs of still life" and "minute upholstery description" that lends nothing to the heart of the poem. Like Balzac, except that Balzac's descriptions at least tell. The fact is that "Browning is not really a poet, that he has all the gifts but the one needful and the pearls without the string."

And then it is on to the question of his future with the Jesuits. "I see you do not understand my position in the Society," he explains. "This Tertianship . . . is not really a noviceship at all in the sense of a time during which a candidate or probationer makes trial of our life and is free to withdraw."

At the end of the second year in the novitiate, in fact, all Jesuits "take vows which are perpetually binding and renew them every six months (not for every six months but for life) till we are professed or take the final degree we are to hold, of which in the Society there are several. It is in preparation for these last vows that we make the tertianship; which is called a *schola affectus* [a schooling of the heart] and is meant to enable us to recover that fervour which may have cooled through application to study and contact with the world." The pattern—including making the Long Retreat again— is "nearly the same as those of the first noviceship."

As for himself, personally, he has not only made his vows "publicly some two and twenty times," but renews them every day to himself, "so that I should be black with perjury if I drew back now. And beyond that I can say with St. Peter: To whom shall I go?" And besides, here his mind is "more at peace than it has ever been and I would gladly live all my life, if it were so to be, in as great or a greater seclusion from the world and be busied only with God. But in the midst of outward occupations not only the mind is drawn away from God, which may be at the call of duty and be God's will, but un- happily the will too is entangled, worldly interests freshen, and worldly am- bitions revive. The man who in the world is as dead to the world as if he were buried in the cloister is already a saint. But this is our ideal."

Two weeks into his time at Roehampton, he writes Bridges to ask again about his health. "I hear on two hands that you are mending," he notes, "but, as before, very slowly. . . . I shd. have written before, but it is no easy task meeting one's out of door liabilities (any how writing letters is what I mean) with a day so sliced up into the duties of a noviceship as this life is. I see no newspapers, read none but spiritual books." Although just now it is "raining very heavily, thro' a white fog," the weather here has been mostly "bright and frosty," and "the look of nature (whose face I had almost forgot- ten) was very sonsy, as the Glasgow people say."

The great gale of October 14, which swept through much of southern England, and which Bridges "must have felt at Torquay, was here terrible, nearly killed two of us, left a scene of havoc, and knocked all round our neighbourhood tall trees down like ninepins." The two nearly done in were fellow Tertians, working in a woodshed just outside his window, when the top half of a tall cedar broke off and smashed the shed, battering and bruis- ing the men "with a rain of tiles." Still, this blessed spot, "though it has suf- fered much from decay of nature and more from the hand of man, is . . . beautiful. It is besides a great rest to be here and I am in a very contented frame of mind." One of the schoolboys who used to come to him for confession at Mount St. Mary's is now a novice at Manresa. Many years later, that novice will remember Hopkins from this time trying to rake leaves with a group of Jesuits on a windy day, and repeating over and over in mock despair, *"Ventus dissipat omnem meum laborem. The wind scatters all I have labored over."*

But there is always time for horseplay, and Hopkins hurts his wrist wrestling with another Jesuit. The two had clasped hands, he tells Bridges, "crossfingered," with both thrusting forward, when suddenly the fellow "brought my left arm down, which is not allowed, and twisted it so hard that something is wrong at the wrist and within these three days, weeks after the event, it has become more painful." Is it a broken ligament, like the one he sustained years before in a fall? "And will it take a year and more to mend? and will it at last be as strong as before?" He hopes Bridges is recovering, and that his mind "will recover its vigour soon, your vein glow, and your muse sing."

"I can understand that your present position, seclusion and exercises would give to your writings a rare charm," Dixon writes Hopkins, hoping that he will go on writing more poems with their "terrible pathos." There is about his work, he feels, "a right temper which goes to the point of the terrible; the terrible crystal. Milton is the only one else who has anything like it: & he has it . . . through indignation, through injured majesty, which is an inferior thing." *A terrible crystal:* Dixon has indeed seen in Hopkins's poems a radical humility and passion, a "terrible pathos." It is nothing less than the sense of a man speaking directly into the intense fire surrounding the face of God, in praise as in anguish, without flinching or drawing back, as Ezekiel and Jeremiah and Job and the Psalmist did.

In the time left before his Long Retreat begins, Hopkins tries to finish his literary business with Dixon. He speaks at length on the English, French, and Italian sonnet form, of proportion, lightness, and gravity achieved by metrical adjustments, line breaks, monosyllables, pauses, and outriders, the last of which he employs liberally, "for they more than equal the Italian elisions and make the whole sonnet . . . longer, if anything, than the Italian." But he is "ashamed . . . to talk of English or any literature, of which I was always very ignorant and which I have ceased to read."

Several days later, he adds an important postscript. *This* is why he is a Jesuit, and why he is here, he tells Dixon as plainly as he knows how. "My vocation puts before me a standard so high that a higher can be found nowhere else," so that the real question for him "is not whether I am willing (if I may guess what is in your mind) to make a sacrifice of hopes of fame . . . but whether I am not to undergo a severe judgment from God for the lothness I have shewn in making it, for the reserves I may have in my heart made, for the backward glances I have given with my hand upon the plough, for the waste of time the very compositions you admire may have caused and their preoccupation of the mind which belonged to more sacred or more binding duties, for the disquiet and the thoughts of vainglory they have given rise to. A purpose may look smooth and perfect from without but be frayed and faltering from within." In sum, he adds, he has never wavered in his vocation. But, he adds, "I have not lived up to it." In any case, he has foresworn all literary composition while he is here. "The time is precious and will not return again and I know I shall not regret my forbearance."

Monday evening, November 7, Day 1: The First Week: The Long Retreat begins under the direction of Father Robert Whitty, former Provincial, now in his mid-sixties. Whitty is a man known for his simplicity, wisdom, and holiness, and for encouraging those he is directing to get up in the middle of the night to meditate and pray. He is especially wary of any signs in his Tertians of spiritual tepidity. He is a good choice, and so—in the sacred time now allotted him—Hopkins begins to think and pray deeply on the matters closest to his heart. He begins, as he will end, with a meditation on the nature of Christ's sacrifice. In the beginning, before time itself, he imagines, the "first outstress of God's power was Christ," the Logos, the Word.

Q. But why did Christ go forth from the Father at all, "not only in the eternal and intrinsic procession of the Trinity but also by an extrinsic and less than eternal, let us say Aeonian one?"

A. Out of love, so that the Logos, the Son, might give God glory by giving himself over to "the barren wilderness outside of God, as the children of Israel were led into the wilderness to offer sacrifice." So, then, the outward procession of the Son in the Incarnation is a continuation of God the Son's full sacrifice of Himself to the Father: "a consequence and shadow of the procession of the Trinity.... It is as if the blissful agony or stress of selving in [the Trinitarian] God had forced out drops of sweat or blood," and these drops were the instantaneous creation in time of the entire universe.

It seems clear here that Hopkins is reading Aeonian time in light of the Book of Revelation. Thus, in going forth to offer his sacrifice, "Christ created angels to be his company ... first to the hill of sacrifice" at Calvary, and afterward "back to God." Humankind would likewise partake in the sacrifice and the Son would redeem everyone. And so the Father "for the sake of the Lamb of God ... would accept the whole flock and for the sake of one ear or grape the whole sheaf or cluster; for redeem may be said not only of the recovering from sin to grace or perdition to salvation but also of the raising from worthlessness before God [to] the meriting of God himself. . . . But when Satan saw the mystery and the humiliation proposed [by God's taking on matter] he turned back . . . to seize [Creation] of his own right and merit and by his own strength, and so he fell, with his following." Satan, that *kosmokrator* and world wielder (ironically, it is the same epithet Hopkins had used to describe Christ himself four years earlier), demanded sovereignty over Creation, but was finally "left master only of the material world." Satan: the glittering serpent in the garden, the dragon who mesmerizes with the things of this world, the monster who gathers up "the attributes of many creatures," the one who insists on singing his self-hymn of praise, his song of himself, and who, by "aiming at every perfection ends by being a monster, a 'fright.'"

Eight days into his retreat, Hopkins is still meditating on the ideal of service to the Lord. The angels, like Adam, he reasons, must have been "created in sanctifying grace" and so invited to enter into a covenant with their Creator. As in a commonwealth each angel was to contribute toward the Great Sacrifice. The most fitting metaphor he can think of to grasp this immensity is the idea of a symphony, the music of the spheres, each angel like a note "of a scale and a harmonic series."

Q. But what is it in us that keeps on saying no, when it is a yes we want? What, really, was behind Satan's *non serviam*?

A. It was that Lucifer chose to dwell on his own power and beauty, as if he had created himself, thus insisting on instressing his own inscape, "like a performance on the organ and instrument of his own being . . . a hymn in his own praise." And so the heavenly kingdom began to implode in upon itself. Other angels were drawn in by Lucifer's example. "It became a concert of voices, a concerting of selfpraise, an enchantment, a magic, by which they were dizzied, dazzled, and bewitched. They would not listen to the note which summoned each to his own place . . . and distributed them here and there in the liturgy of the sacrifice; they gathered rather closer and closer home under Lucifer's lead and drowned it, raising . . . a counterpoint of dissonance and not of harmony." What followed then was "a kind of suicide": sin itself assuming the insane "loveliness of heroism," the destruction of the commonwealth, the revolutionary cry of freedom at all costs, the very grasping after the godhead itself. And so followed the fall as the angelic hordes "from their selfraised . . . tower of eminence flung themselves" like lemmings down into the abyss.

Once again, Hopkins is at a crossroads. There is his own deeply held belief and celebration of the self, of all things going themselves, but always in harmony with their Creator. But where there is self-consciousness, where there is a consciousness of the self, there is a danger as well: that the self may reject its Maker to dwell instead on itself. This kind of focus on the song of oneself (*pace* Whitman) leads inevitably to the deepest selfishness, apartness, being out of the commonwealth, the community, the heavenly choir. And that, Hopkins knows, means radical isolation, means hell, means cutting oneself off from the living waters of the Creator and falling back on one's sweating self.

And so, on Day 9 of the First Week, he turns to consider what it means to give oneself over to God, to Christ, and take up one's cross, as Christ promised to do from before time itself, "when none but himself could know that he was to die a violent death." Nor did he, as the Gnostics would insist, "entrap Pilate, Caiaphas, and Satan into crucifying him, as though without that he could not redeem man. . . . He had all his plans ready, matured during his hidden life, and adapted for every case." And then Christ's time on earth was up. Of the sacraments, the graces he would leave behind for humankind, only baptism was instituted before his death. The Eucharist itself "was . . . hurried forward, forestalled perhaps by the suddenness of that event." The other sacraments, "which he had always meant to institute, were put off till after he rose again." He claimed to be "king and would in his own time have come to the throne: but everything was to be in its right time and natural order, which there was wanting. The Eucharistic Sacrifice was the great purpose of his life and his own chosen redemption." He knew too that he would die early, "because he was sent to overthrow Satan's empire, who would certainly, if he were allowed, as he was, have his adversary's life." Those called to follow Christ most closely, he knows, are therefore called on to follow him in a life of self-emptying, of hardship, even as others are called to follow him in the example of his passion and death. Hopkins knows he has tried to model his own life after his Master's in exactly these ways, though he is aware that even now there is more of himself he might give his Beloved, and that thought must surely terrify as well as comfort.

He turns to meditate on Christ's words, that *Whoever wishes to come after me must deny himself, take up his cross, and follow me.* It is the King's call to those "who have already committed themselves to something." Such disciples are, as "The Windhover" had stressed, instressed, Christ's "knights," his officer soldiers, his lieutenants, as it were, bound "to live up to a standard of courage above the civilian and even above the private soldier." It would be cowardly, therefore," to decline a glorious campaign from dislike of the hardships to be borne in securing its success, dislike of being obliged to share

[Christ] his general's lot." True disciples offer themselves "without reserve to all laborious DUTY," that is, to "do all, however laborious, that it involves."

It is really a matter of justice, then, of the just man justicing. Like the good general he was, Christ led the way in sacrificing himself, facing into the terror of "his own scourging, crucifixion and death," even as he was "betrayed, abandoned, and—it seemed—[left] alone." So, too, with Hopkins. Did he not long ago sign on to follow Christ's standard in the necessary warfare of the Christian life? And so he will have to steel himself with God's help to continue to go wherever he is called. Nor can there be any "holding back out of personal dislike for the campaign, or indecision, or— worse—out of fear."

Peace, poor peace. That is what he needs more than anything, to quiet his busy mind. And in fact, Father Whitty has told his Tertians "that consolation should be our normal state, and that when God withdraws it he wishes us to strive to recover it." But, Hopkins argues, even "natural 'consolation' or good spirits come and go without any discoverable reason and certainly God could make us most happy without our knowing what we were happy about, though of course the mind would then turn with pleasure to any, the first pious thought that came, as its object." Yet—as he has learned from his own experience, and from what spiritual wisdom has taught him—"the greater the disproportion the greater the likelihood of the consolation being from God."

And now he forces himself deeper, into a prolonged meditation on Hell. Ignatius "speaks of the present condition of the lost," he writes. And, since the lost are now without bodies, Ignatius "mingles . . . things like brimstone and tears (which the disembodied soul cannot shed) and the worm of conscience." For, just as it is by the imagination that we realize these things, so it is "by the imagination that the lost suffer them and that as intensely as by the senses. This simple explanation," Hopkins has come to see, "will never strike our scholastics, because they do not see that there is an intellectual imagination." What happens is this: we commit an evil act willingly, which, on remembering it, makes us feel shame, regret, or even disgust, and which "leaves in our minds scapes or species, the extreme 'intention' or instressing of which would be painful and the pain would be that of fire, supposing fire to be the condition of a body . . . texturally at stress . . . from without, and . . . this is expressed by" those tremendous flames Ignatius mentions, in the same way that a current of air in a blowpipe "casts or addresses a jet of flame this way or that." Then the understanding, "open wide like an eye . . . is confronted by that scape, that act of its own which blotted out God and

so put blackness in the place of light," so that now "the lost spirit dashes itself like a caged bear . . . violently instresses [those scapes] and burns, stares
into them and is the deeper darkened." The keener the consciousness, then,
the greater the pain. Three years on, and Hopkins will turn these theological speculations into one of his most powerful sonnets—the longest, he will
insist, ever composed, both in length and in length of time to complete, a
dies irae of a plainchant he will aptly call "Spelt from Sybil's Leaves."

On the evening of November 18, Father Whitty gives his Tertians some
points on Christ's hidden life, the years spent in Nazareth before beginning
his public mission. "It is the great help to faith for us who must live more or
less an obscure, constrained, and unsuccessful life," Hopkins writes. His life,
in fact. And "what of all possible ways of spending 30 years could have
seemed so ineffective? What might not Christ have done at Rome or Athens,
Antioch or Alexandria! And sacrificing, as he did, all to obedience his very
obedience was unknown." The repulsiveness of spending year after year in a
backwater like Nazareth, he thinks, out of the mainstream altogether: a burden in itself. He will have reason to remember this in the time he has left.

Spiritual tepidity is not a matter of being between hot and cold, Father
Whitty tells his Tertians, but the going from hotter to colder, the being in
God's grace, but being content to live according to habit. So that "while we
strive, though we commit faults, we are not lukewarm." It is "when we give
up struggling and let ourselves drift" that tepidity begins. Fervor means "being
on the boil, the shewing the stir of life, of a life not shared by all other things,
and the being ready to pass, by evaporation, into a wholly spiritual condition."
Freezing, on the other hand, "is the earthly blockish insensible condition of a
soul which may indeed be melted by warm breath but must first be so melted
before it can sway to it." Ice, ice at the black heart of it, then.

Thursday, December 1, Day 23: Third Day of Repose: "Our retreat is
still in hand," Hopkins writes his old friend and former student at the Oratory, Edward Bellasis. "But today we rest and I get my letters,—my bro-
chures, my music, my banknotes, my offer of a cardinal's hat (you will
understand presently) and so forth," he says in a bantering mood. He thanks
Edward for sending along the music to Newman's poems, but wonders how
long it will take before he can hear it performed. A cello accompaniment is
out of the question, he knows, but he might get the songs sung and played
on the piano. And though there is a piano here, it is "out of tune and several
singers on it, besides pianists: the difficulty is to get at them. We 'tertians'
or novices in our dotage dare no more speak to a novice proper, to a scholastic (or student), or to almost anybody."

On the envelope, Bellasis has written "The Reverend, Etc. Hopkins," and now Hopkins tweaks him. It is the "Etc" which "finds me out," he answers, "which gets me (in Yankee phrase).... *Etc* may conceal anything—M.R.I.A., F.R.I.B.A., A.P.U.C. [a group of random abbreviations standing for Member of the Royal Irish Academy, Fellow of the Royal Institute of British Architects, *Anno Post Urbem Condita*] and probably conceals S.R.E."—Sua Reverente Eminenza, employed in addressing a cardinal. But he has not yet—like Newman—been made a cardinal. In truth, though he does not say so, come August, he will take his final vows as Spiritual Coadjutor only and not as a Professed Jesuit, which means that—despite his Oxford credentials—he will never be able to hold any major office as a Jesuit. And all because of one exam on a September afternoon in Wales four years before.

Thursday morning, December 8: The Feast of the Immaculate Conception, the Final Day of the Long Retreat: A meditation on Ignatius's great "Contemplation for Obtaining Love": "This last exercise of the book corresponds to the Foundation," Hopkins notes, except that when he began these *Exercises,* there was "no mention of love." There everything was couched in terms of duty. But here, now, at the end, it all opens up. Now "everything is of love, the love and duty of a grateful friend. . . . All God gives us or does for us He gives and does in love and therefore . . . all we do towards God we should do in love." And so, on thinking on the Holy Spirit, he is privileged to see that, yes, "all things therefore are charged with love, are charged with God and if we know how to touch them give off sparks and take fire, yield drops and flow, ring and tell of him." It is a fitting close, this paean to God's love, to the unfolding of the Thirty Days. Finally, after the long fast and praying, the Tertians are allowed *two* glasses of claret with the other Fathers after dinner. In the evening there is a solemn Benediction, and the *Te Deum* is sung in thanksgiving.

Enriched and renewed by his Long Retreat, he responds now to Dixon, whose letter has been sitting unanswered on his desk for the past month. And so, to Dixon's fervent hope that he "will pursue poetry still," he writes back that "when a man has given himself to God's service, when he has denied himself and followed Christ, he has fitted himself to receive and does receive from God a special guidance, a more particular providence." There is in his reply a new clarity and insight into his thinking, a rinsing away of what is non-essential in the eyes of God. As for the fate of his poetry, he explains now, if Dixon values what he writes—as he does himself—"much more does our Lord. And if he chooses to avail himself of what I leave at his disposal he can do so with a felicity and with a success which I could never command. And if he does not, then two things follow; one that the reward I shall nevertheless receive from him will be all the greater; the other that then I shall know how much a thing contrary to his will and even to my own best interests I should have done if I had taken things into my own hands and forced on publication." This has been Hopkins's principle and "in the main" his practice, and leading the sort of life he does here now at Roehampton, it seems easy. But "when one mixes with the world and meets on every side its secret solicitations, to live by faith is harder, is very hard; nevertheless by God's help I shall always do so."

Then a letter to Bridges, scolding him for not having written. "Why did you not reply to my last addressed to you at Torquay and ricocheting off Bedford Square? as this too must do. What plea, what flimsiest pretext have you got? You are well and strong or fast getting so, so Mrs. Molesworth says . . . and having nothing to do." He on the other hand is kept busy, so that he refuses to waste time on Bridges now. And with his little community of Tertians already being broken up to be sent here and there to fill in, he adds that he does "not expect to be much longer here." By Christmas Eve, he tells his mother, his community has already been "much diminished," some "called off altogether and others . . . despatched for Christmas duty." Still, things "have a general topsyturvy cheerful air," and now that Christmas is here, it is "being hung everywhere." Father Morris's novices end their retreat tomorrow, he notes. They "bear his impress and are staid. We used to roar with laughter if anything happened, his never do."

Christmas he spends at Manresa with his community. Concerts are got up by the Juniors and novices, and a grand dinner with three glasses of wine, dessert, apples, oranges, and biscuits. On the 28th, the Feast of the Holy Innocents, there is another feast—fowl, turkey, ham, jellies, and blancmange—with the Tertians invited to the Fathers' room afterward for coffee. On New Year's Eve, he says mass at St. John the Evangelist, where—as a second-year novice a dozen years before—he had opened a catechism center.

New Year's Day, January 1882: He is distressed to learn that his mother is ill, especially as he is "hourly expecting orders to return to Liverpool. One of our Fathers [William Hilton, S.J.] who was for the best part of two years my yokemate on that laborious mission, died there yesterday night after a short sickness"—he had contacted typhoid from his work in the slums—"in harness and in his prime. I am saddened by this death, for he was particularly good to me; he used to come up to me and say 'Gerard, you are a good soul' and that I was a comfort to him in his troubles. His place must now be supplied and it must be by one of two, both in this house." Mercifully, and this once, Hopkins is spared from having to return to Liverpool.

During January and midway through February, the lull time in the Tertianship between the Long Retreat and the beginning of Lent, the Tertians have been kept busy preparing sermons for a series of retreats they will give during Lent. Hopkins, assigned to preach at Preston and Maryport, will cover the standard topics for working-class congregations: God's Creation and Plan, the Four Last Things (the Art of Dying), and Hell. During this time, he immerses himself once more in the central tenets of his faith, but—inevitably—through a poet's eye. He begins by evoking the splendor of dappled Creation where once there was nothing. In a flash, he will tell his congregation, where there was darkness and the void, suddenly there is a universe. Look at the size of the world, he tells them, then consider the speed of light, which flies "six or seven times round the earth while the clock ticks once." And yet it takes thousands of years for this same light "to reach us from the Milky Way, which is made up of stars swarming together, . . . running into one, and looking like a soft mist, and each of them a million times as big as the earth." And all of this, he reminds them, all of this "arose at a word! So that . . . the world itself was easier made than the least little thing that man or any other creature makes in the world."

Q. And why did God create?

A. To give Him glory. "It is like a garden, a field he sows: what should it bear him? praise, reverence, and service; it should yield him glory." Birds sing for God, the thunder reveals his terror. All things "tell of him" and "give him glory." But, he adds, not having self-consciousness, "they do not know him." This, then, makes "poor praise, faint reverence, slight service, dull glory." But man was created "to praise, reverence, and serve God; to give him glory." It is a prosing of his magnificent "As kingfishers catch fire" composed five years before in wild Wales, that same enthusiasm for the moment recovered.

Q. But does man then reck His rod?

A. No, for though we are God's vineyard, "we have yielded rotten fruit, sour grapes, or none." Still, it is Lent, a time for renewal. "We can change; we can repent and BEGIN TO GIVE GOD GLORY. . . . Any day, any minute we bless God for our being or for anything, for food, for sunlight, we do and are what we were meant for, made for—things that give and mean to give God glory." But it is "not only prayer that gives God glory but work," Hopkins understands more fully now, laboring as he has among the working-class poor. "Smiting on an anvil, sawing a beam, whitewashing a wall, driving horses, sweeping, scouring, everything gives God some glory if being in his grace you do it as your duty. . . . To lift up the hands in prayer gives God glory, but a man with a dungfork in his hand, a woman with a sloppail, give him glory too. He is so great that all things give him glory if you mean they should."

And then it is on to a reflection of the end of our short lives.

Q. Do you love sunshine, starlight, fresh air, flowers, fieldsports?

A. Then be beginning to despair, "for you will see them no more. . . . Do you love townlife, homelife, the cheerful hearth, the sparkling fire, company, the social glass, laughter, frolic among friends?—Despair then: you will have no more of them for ever, the churchyards are full of such men as you are now, that feasted once and now worms feast on." For that last and shortest day "is coming," and then it will all be a matter of "rottenness and dust and utterly to be forgotten." Though you love wife or husband, child or friend, despair.

> Do you love money?—Despair then: death shall make you drop it, death shall wring it from you; though your funeral were costly, yet poor shall you lie. Do you love fame . . . and to make yourself felt, to play your part somewhere in the world? do you take an interest in politics and watch how the world goes?—Despair then: the world will do without you and you must do without the world, for you shall be where you cannot stir hand or foot to make it worse or better. Do you love what is better than all these, to do God's work, to do good to others, to give alms, to pray, to make God's kingdom come? Make haste then, work while it is day.

Then on to death and the last sacraments, of which he had written so poignantly in "Felix Randal." That spring, he will tell his Preston congregation something of what he has witnessed as a priest among the reeking slums and pubs and "dens of shame" he has had to visit, where members of his congregation lay dying of heart attacks or beatings or stabbings. "If things like this should happen to any of you make an act of sorrow for your sins," he pleads with them, "earnestly asking God to give you the grace, which he will: do this and you will be saved," for it is "a wretched wretched thing to die in fear, without the sacraments."

In any event, there is no escaping death. "Most of you," he knows, "will not die suddenly, but some few of you will. . . . There are dangers by land and sea, wrecks, railway accidents, lightning, mischances with machinery, fires, falls; there are murders." How often has he had to console "widows and the orphaned children of suddenly murdered men?" How many go on living in mortal sin, "who if they died suddenly must therefore die in mortal sin." Still, God has provided us with "the last sacraments, the grace of contrition, and holy hope." Send for the priest, he urges them, "while the sick man has his senses, that he may make his confession duly." But even if it is too late for that, if there is "some sorrow for sin," even that might be enough. Beg for this sorrow, he tells them, plead for it "with inward tears at least. . . . Summon your last strength for that. God knows our need." Still, "the better you serve God the better and more special will his providence be over your death," for as "you live so you will die."

Lastly, he prepares his sermon on Hell, meant to change his listeners' lives in the hour or less allotted him. Think of hell as a prison and a place of torment, he exhorts them. If the devils wander, still, they carry their torment with them wherever they go, as he too well knows. And do not believe that hell is merely a myth, for just as "shutting our eyes will not do away with a steeple or a sign-post," so not believing in hell does not "put it out of being." Hell means losing God, he stresses, but if that isn't enough to move us, think of the pain of that unquenchable fire. Conjure up in the mind's eye "those huge flames" and the lost, suffering "a torment as of bodily fire" afflicting "the indestructible mind." Think of a glassblower breathing on a flame. "At once it darts out into a jet taper as a lance-head and as piercing too," where "sinners are themselves the flames of hell." Hear, then, the wailings and blasphemies against Christ our Lord and all his saints "because they are in heaven and they lost in hell." True, not all blaspheme, for there are those, he fears, like himself, under whose stalwart yes there remained that final no, in which case, there will be rather "a sullen dreadful silence of despair," knowing "their chastisement is just."

And the stench, revealed as only a poet or a James Joyce, who will learn how to craft his own hell sermon from Hopkins's contemporaries, could reveal it: "the brimstone, the dregs and bilgewater of that pit, all that is foul and loathsome." Too, "the blinding stifling . . . remembrance of a crowd of sins . . . like smoke; stinging remorse" like "biting brimstone." The lust they once so loved will now revolt them "like vomit and like dung," and yet they will never be able to rid themselves of those images. Worse still will be the bitter taste of it all: the tears, the grief, "the worm of conscience, which is the mind gnawing and feeding on its own most miserable self." Agenbit inwit.

And then the turn, the hope, the hand of God extended: "By God's mercy we shall never see that place at all." And now he imagines a sea of bowed heads. He has called a spade a spade, which he so dearly loves to do. So he will join with them in prayer before the mystery of God as Holy Week approaches: We are sorry Lord. Forgive us. "Lamb of God that takest away the sins of the world, spare us. . . . Lamb of God, have mercy on us." And then he will commend them to the Blessed Mother before he genuflects before the cross and walks back into the sacristy to prepare for confessions.

Late January 1882: He hears from Bridges that his friend is finally on the mend. Hopkins has been preparing sermons and instructions, he tells Bridges, and at the beginning of Lent will travel north to St. Ignatius at Preston in Lancashire, and then from March 19—the fourth Sunday in Lent—until April 2—Palm Sunday—conduct Lenten mission-services at Maryport on the Cumberland coast. He expects then to return to Roehampton, but could be called off anywhere at any time. He is still "like a novice," and since his arrival here months earlier has been to town only to see the dentist, "and could not hope to visit you." On the other hand, Bridges could come to see him, "and the place is worth seeing." The calm of mind he has daily felt here has been delightful. But he also knows that when he leaves, he will have to leave his hard-won peace behind as well.

"Bridges struck the truth long ago," Dixon prophetically tells Hopkins in late January, "when he said to me that your poems more carried him out of himself than those of any one. I have again and again felt the same: & am certain that as a means of serving . . . religion, you cannot have a more powerful instrument than your own verses." To this, Hopkins answers by explaining that his "mind is much employed at present on the subject of Sacrifice, about which I am getting together some materials, with a view possibly to write about it some day." Which of course is the gist of the matter, even if he himself does not realize what Dixon has, for there is something in Hopkins that keeps fighting his own extraordinary creativity, keeping it under an adamantine compression so intense that it has even affected his physical well-being. Sacrifice is all, he keeps telling himself. Making of oneself an acceptable sacrifice. But in his self-immolation, he has provided a space for an intense flame, which will burn away the dross to leave behind a scattering of diamonds to be lifted by others from the ashes of time.

On Monday, February 20, with Lent two days off, he leaves for Preston. There he remains for three weeks, when he and another Jesuit, Father Alfred White, fifty-two, begin directing their two-week Lenten mission at Our Lady and St. Patrick's, Maryport, on the Cumberland coast. It is—again—a mostly Irish population that have come here with their families to work on building the new docks. The Lenten mission begins at ten on Sunday morning, March 12th, with Hopkins singing High Mass and preaching to a congregation of some seven hundred and fifty. The following Sunday he sings the 11:00 a.m. mass and delivers another sermon, and in the evening presides over the initiation of forty-five little girls into the Society of the Children of Mary, greeting them in their pure white veils as they gather in Lady Chapel for prayer. The sweet Maybloom of innocence, he must surely be thinking. How indescribably beautiful . . . and passing.

March 26. Passion Sunday: The two weeks come to a close—the sermons, confessions, private talks, along with the mission itself ending that evening. Then he writes a hurried note to Dixon. Perhaps now they can spend a few hours together before he returns to Preston to hear Lenten confessions. "I mean to be at Carlisle tomorrow by the train which reaches there at 12.25 and to leave it for Preston at about 4: could I hope to meet you?" The chance, he adds, "may never occur again." And if the Canon missed him at the station, he might find him at the cathedral. And so, for a few hours, the two finally see each other after a hiatus of twenty years.

How he wishes their meeting might have been longer, he writes Dixon on Palm Sunday. He could see that Dixon was shy and that time would be "needed for this to wear off." As for himself, there is "very little shyness left" in him, though he also knows it is not easy for him to show his real feelings to another. "How very glad I am to have seen you & to have a full knowledge what you are like," Dixon writes two weeks later. "So far as I can remember, you are very like the boy of Highgate." Yes, he did seem shy, and knows he is quiet and retiring, Dixon admits. "I have often tried to overcome it," he adds. "But the effort is always apparent to those with whom I am, & never succeeds. You must therefore forgive it: it is not from want of feeling or affection." At the moment he feels "most acutely" the death of another poet, Dante Rossetti, for he was "one of my dearest friends. . . . It leaves an awful blank."

April 3. Hopkins writes Bridges from Preston: "I hope, my dear heart," he begins, "you are now really better; not better, well; strong, vigorous, lusty, beefish, as apt to pull an oar [as Bridges had at Oxford fifteen years before] as to turn a sonnet with the best in either kind." He has been to Maryport "to take part in a Mission, which is something like a Revival without the hysteria and the heresy, and it had the effect of bringing me out and making me speak very plainly and strongly (I enjoyed that, for I dearly like calling a spade a spade)." It was, he remarks, "the first thing of the sort I had been employed in."

And he has finally met Dixon. "We spent some hours together, and he gave me dinner and shewed me the Cathedral. Partly through this sightseeing and more through shyness on his part (not on mine) we did not get much intimate or even interesting talk. I was amused when his hat twice blew off in English Street to watch his behaviour. I wish I could have been with him longer." On Wednesday he takes the train back to Roehampton, only to learn that he is needed at St. Elizabeth's in Richmond, where the parish priest has taken ill at the busiest time of the Church year. And so, from Holy Thursday through Easter, he finds himself carrying out the greater part of the Holy Week liturgy for the first time as a substitute parish priest.

At the end of April he directs a Mr. Plant, an elderly businessman who has come to Manresa House for a private eight-day retreat, in the midst of which another gale tears through Roehampton, ripping up still more of the old trees on the grounds. Then, on May 6, the forty-six-year-old Chief Secretary Lord Frederick Cavendish, newly arrived in Dublin, and his Under Secretary Thomas Burke, fifty-three, are slashed to death in Phoenix Park by four members of the Invincibles, an extreme wing of the Fenians. The weapon of choice is a surgical knife, wielded by a man going by the moniker "Skin-the-Goat." It is the dawn of a new phenomenon in Great Britain, urban terrorism, and the ripples from this event will shortly have a profound impact on Hopkins, though of course he has no way yet of knowing this.

That same day he writes Baillie, whom he has not seen in two years, though he knows he is practicing law now just across the Thames. Glasgow, he tells his Scots friend, was "repulsive to live in," and yet there were "alleviations: the streets and buildings are fine and the people lively. The poor Irish, among whom my duties lay, are mostly from the North of Ireland, scarcely distinguishable in tongue from the Scotch and at Glasgow still further Scoticised." And though they seem always "very drunken and at present very Fenian, they are warmhearted and give a far heartier welcome than those of Liverpool," so that Hopkins found himself "very much at home with them" during his time there. Then too how delicious to daily hear English spoken with a Scots accent. He hopes Baillie will make his way down to Manresa for a visit.

In mid-May, Hopkins invites Bridges out for Ascension Thursday, the 18th. "Come in the afternoon, the earlier the better," he advises. "But if it rains I should say put it off," for he should like Bridges to see the grounds to their best advantage. And though the late gale has withered many of the lime trees, still, "the buttercups this year are remarkable." And so, for the first time in over a year, Bridges sees Hopkins again, bringing with him his sister, Maria's, eldest boy, young Bertie Molesworth, which means that anything like a real talk between himself and Hopkins will be out of the question.

Worse, Bridges is, as always, out to disconcert his friend, so that, as they stroll about the impressive grounds, he spies some peach trees cared for by Davis the gardener and insists on pocketing some fruit. Seeing Hopkins's discomfort, Bridges taunts him by offering him one, which Hopkins refuses. All right, Bridges says, he'll *buy* the damned things if he has to. But Bridges misunderstands the point of the theft, and Hopkins—embarrassed—tries to brush off the matter. "My heart warmed towards that little Bertie Molesworth . . . so that if you were to bring him again I shd. be glad to see him," he writes Bridges two weeks later, trying to put the best face on things. "But I am afraid he felt dull. He is shy I dare say." Still, he adds, "it cannot be denied . . . that the presence of a third person is a restraint upon confidential talk." As for Davis, he adds, he "wd. have let you have [those peaches] on reasonable terms."

Then a letter from Bridges, conciliatory, bantering, bullying. How goes Gerard's poetry? he asks. Since coming here, Hopkins reminds him, he has written nothing, though he would still like to get on with that ode to Campion. "It is dithyrambic or what they used to call Pindaric," that is, "in variable stanzas . . . like [Dryden's] *Alexander's Feast* or *Lycidas* [and] has some new rhythmical effects." As for Bridges's *Prometheus the Firegiver*, if he must write about it during his Tertianship, then he will shortly say "how beautiful and masterly it is, what a sense of style, unknown in our age, in the phrasing and the verse, how vigorous the thought, and how Greek . . . the choruses, and yet so fresh." He has in the meantime gone through some poems of Bridges's and revised them twice through. "The worst is that one seasons over a thing and one's first verjuice flattens into slobber and sweet syllabub. Or one ripens; yet there is something"—he quotes Dryden here— "in 'the first sprightly runnings.'" The underlying metaphor has something, of course, to do with the lushness of stolen peaches about it.

For the episode of the stolen fruit, small as it seems, signifies everything in the dealings between the two men, so that neither will soon forget it. Certainly not Bridges, who will recall that spring afternoon fifty years on as if it were yesterday. By then it will entail nothing less than a revisioning of Genesis and *The Nicomachean Ethics,* appearing as it does in Bridges's final *Testament of Beauty* under the heading "Ethick" and the repudiation of pleasure, pleasure being something Bridges himself, he admits, learned to enjoy only by degrees and then only after his parson stepfather's demise:

> when the young poet my companion in study
> and friend of my heart refused a peach at my hands,
> he being then a housecarl in Loyola's menie,
> 'twas that he fear'd the savor of it, and when he waived
> his scruple to my banter, 'twas to avoid offence.

Such sublimation as Gerard practiced, Bridges will believe to his dying day, was nothing less than "a self-holocaust," justified in Hopkins's case by a "delicacy of sense," one of those for whom the slightest temptation will "distract them wholly from their high pursuit," so that "they flee God's garden, whose forbidden fruit / (seemeth to them) was sweeten'd by a fiend's desire / to make them fond and foolish." Ah! Bridges the tempter.

June 8. The Feast of Corpus Christi: It is the annual procession, symbolizing Christ's movement out from the Father and back in glory, and it is, to Hopkins's dismay—especially as Bridges is once again present, this time without his nephew—a large and shambling affair. It begins with the *O Salutaris* being sung, and a cross-bearer leading the way out from the sanctuary with the Blessed Sacrament, followed by twelve novices and a choir of twenty-two Juniors and novices dressed in cottas, followed by four Juniors in copes and another four in dalmatics, six priests in chasubles, and a deacon and subdeacon, also in dalmatics. At the end of the procession Father Whitty follows in cope and white vestments, surrounded by four Juniors carrying a canopy that covers the Sacred Host and himself. The procession winds its way along the cedar-lined walk, the choir singing the *Pange Lingua* and other hymns, then enters St. George's Hall, where the host is elevated and the *Adoro te devote* sung. After Benediction, the procession returns to chapel for a second Benediction, this one for the visitors in the back pews, Bridges among them.

But there is another procession that same day—this one at the train station for those off to the Ascot Day Races—the passenger cars around London packed with spectators and gamblers. In the midst of this bustle Hopkins has come with Bridges to see him off, watching him climb up the train steps into one of the cars. He sees someone he takes for Bridges seated by a window, then waves and murmurs from the platform, until he realizes that he is waving at some cardsharp on his way to the races. "It was a needless and tedious frenzy," in which there ensued "a lovely and passionate scene . . . between me and a tallish gentleman. . . . I smiled, I murmured with my lips at him, I waved farewells, but he would not give in, till with burning shame (though the whole thing was, as I say, like the duels of archangels) I saw suddenly what I was doing."

Then Hopkins tries to explain the real significance of Corpus Christi, a feast different "from all other feasts in this: that its . . . occasion is present. The first Christmas Day, the first Palm Sunday, Holy Thursday . . . Easter, Whitsunday, and so on were to those who took part in them festivities *de praesenti*, but now, to us, they are anniversaries and commemorations only. But Corpus Christi," being "the feast of the Real Presence . . . is the most purely joyous of solemnities." And then he is back in the first week of the Long Retreat and Aeonian time transposed to London. The great procession, he explains, "represents the process of the Incarnation and the world's redemption." For just as Christ went forth from "the Father as the Lamb of God and eucharistic victim to die upon the altar of the cross for the world's ransom; then rising returned leading the procession of the flock redeemed / so in this ceremony his body," as victim, "is carried to the Altar of Repose" and then "back to the tabernacle at the high altar, which will represent the bosom of the godhead. The procession out may represent the cooperation of the angels, or of the patriarchs and prophets, the return the Church Catholic from Christ's death to the end of time. If these things are mismanaged, as they mostly are, it is not for want of significance in the ceremony." *This* is his reality, then, not Ascot Day and the races, but the world seen fittingly through the transfiguring and transcendent lens of faith.

Soon after he learns that he is one of eight who will be allowed to take Final Vows, though only at the level of Spiritual Coadjutor. He is also one of three who are to be cautioned. It is a standard formula for the time, and it means that something is to be brought to the Jesuit's attention. In all likelihood, it is his "eccentricity" and singularity the Provincial wishes to caution him about. But it is also likely that the Provincial wants to ask Hopkins about his frequent weariness and bouts of depression. In short, he may simply want to tell him to go a bit easier on himself.

June gives way to July and July to August. Beginning on August 7, Hopkins makes his annual eight-day retreat along with the others. During this week, he manages to write sixteen pages of a rough draft on the *Spiritual Exercises* with the idea of eventually writing a commentary on them. Praise of God, he notes, must always take precedence, even before "reverence and service." On the morning of the 15th, the Feast of the Assumption, mass is celebrated at St. Joseph's by Father Purbrick, and Hopkins—along with the other Tertians—makes his Final Vows. They are the same ones made on the same day that Ignatius and his companions pledged themselves to perpetual poverty, chastity, and obedience on Montmartre—The Hill of Martyrs—in Paris three hundred years earlier. Sometime that afternoon

Hopkins speaks briefly with Father Purbrick, who tells him he will let him know shortly where he is being sent.

Two days later, he writes to his fellow Jesuits at Preston, thanking them for sending him a letter of congratulations. They are Fathers Shapter, Lapasteur, and Goldie. "Pax Christi. My hearties," he begins. "I am to call to yez on my way to Glasgow so very shortly," though "this is to know more than the Provincial knows." As for Final Vows, the ceremony "was thought striking and edifying by those who witnessed it," but then he was one of the performers. But his own feelings are mixed, he confesses. "Sometimes I thought last vows were an *eventus nullus* [non-event] and made no difference. Then too I remembered that once I had hoped to be professed and that is always a sad heartache to me. Then again and finally I thought the other thing was better, because our Lord says: *Nonne qui recumbit? Ego autem in medio vestrum sum sicut qui ministrat* [*For who is greater, he that sits at table or he that serves? Is it not he that sits at table? But I am in the midst of you as one who serves*—Luke 22:27]."

He will be sorry to leave, for his heart is still very much here. "At least I shall never be so happy, I am afraid, again as I have been under 'Viewy Bob.'" After the ceremony, the Tertians visited with the novices. "Charming boys they are," he jokes. "One of them is 68 years of age. There was an entertainment in the evening, in the society's wellknown style of gingerbread jokes and a rococo gilding of piety and tears and fond farewells, but still the general effect very nice." And then there is poor Harry Bellamy, he adds, who has just "lost his father by an accident and is very anxious to get prayers for him. He died a Protestant; still prayers may do much, all that is necessary in fact: in these cases I always pray backwards, if you understand, and God allows discount. It is really a great light. You ask him to have granted the grace and the difference of tense is only to you." And so Aeonian time again. "By the tenor of this letter," he ends, "I gather I must be in good spirits—a thing never to be granted if I can help it, it saps sympathy and importance."

Shortly after, Purbrick calls Hopkins in. After consultation, he has decided to send Hopkins not back to Glasgow but to Stonyhurst, where he will teach Greek and Latin to those Jesuits preparing for the external intermediate and degree exams at the University of London. He will leave on Tuesday morning, August 22. The ten happy months are over. Time now to descend Mount Tabor and get back into harness and teach the young again. He is thirty-eight.

Chapter 14

Metaphysician of Sunsets & Snowflakes:
Stonyhurst Again, 1882–1884

September 1, 1882: Since his Provincial has given him "leave to go to any one of our houses I liked" till term begins in October, he tells Bridges, he opts to stay at St. Francis Xavier's in Worcester, Herefordshire. It is an imposing mid-nineteenth-century edifice in the Greek Doric style, and he stays a week, in his free time viewing an exhibition of paintings he has wanted to see. He likes it here, considers prolonging his visit, but then thinks better of it and goes on to Stonyhurst to prepare for his teaching assignment. And though Purbrick has told him that if he wants to visit elsewhere during the month, he has only to ask, he decides against asking. "He would no doubt readily have given me leave to visit you," he tells Bridges afterward, and "had there been the possibility of saying mass, I might therefore have seen Yattendon. But it was not to be." But now he is back at Stonyhurst. How he would love to show Bridges around the place with its fine old buildings, along with the new work going up under a dizzying swirl of construction. It is all "worth seeing," he adds. "The new college," though not a thing of beauty, is at least "imposing and the furniture and fittings are a joy to see. There is always a stirring scene, contractors, builders, masons, bricklayers, carpenters, stonecutters and carvers, all on the spot."

He is here to teach Latin and Greek, "and perhaps hereafter English (when I know more about it) for the London B.A. degree." Moreover, Purbrick has told him that what time is "left over I might employ in writing one or other of the books I had named to him. But very little time will be left over and I cd. never make time. Indeed now," he adds in a gesture of defeat, "with nothing to do but prepare, I cannot get forward with my ode [on Campion]. But one must hope against hope."

He has been preparing by reading the Greek tragic poets again, though he has made very slow progress. At the moment it is "the *Agamemnon* and *Supplices* (Aeschylus's, I mean). How noble is the style!" The going is slow, because in reading he has been correcting the Greek and making emendations "which seem to be great improvements," paying especially close attention to "the art of the choric parts." The inscape or deep form of the Greek lyric poets, including the lyric sections of the dramatic poets, is in fact one of the subjects on which Hopkins has told Purbrick he would like to write, especially as it will tie in with his teaching here. He has already made one significant discovery. It has to do with what he calls the underthought of Greek lyrics: that there are *two* strains of thought running concurrently through them. There is of course "the logical meaning, which everyone sees," but "beneath that like a subterranean river another line of thought revealed in the images the poet employs." It is a major discovery, which he has already adapted to his own lyrics.

There is also the Lancashire landscape, which he describes in a stunning single-sentence catalogue. "Acres of flat roof," he begins, if one takes into account all the buildings at the college, "which, when the air is not thick, as unhappily it mostly is, commands a noble view" of "Pendle Hill, Ribblesdale, the fells, and all round, bleakish but solemn and beautiful." Then there is a garden with a bowling green, walled in by massive yew hedges, a bowered yew walk, two real Queen Anne summerhouses, "observatories under government [contract], orchards, vineries, greenhouses, workshops, a plungebath, fivescourts, a mill, a farm, a fine cricketfield besides a huge playground." There is "the old mansion" itself, as well as "ponds, towers, quadrangles, fine ceilings, chapels, a church, a fine library, museums, MSS illuminated and otherwise, coins, works of art; then two other dependent establishment[s], one a furlong, the other a mile off." And what else?

> The river Hodder with lovely fairyland views, especially at the bathing-place, the Ribble too, the Calder, Whalley with an abbey, Clitheroe with a castle, Ribchester with a strange old chapel and Roman remains; schoolboys and animation, philosophers and foppery (not to be taken too seriously), a jackdaw, a rookery, goldfish, a clough with waterfalls, fishing, grouse, an anemometer, a sunshine gauge, a sundial, an icosihedron, statuary, magnetic instruments, a laboratory, gymnasium, ambulacrum, studio, fine engravings, Arundel chromos, Lancashire talked with naïveté on the premises (Hoo said this and hoo did that).

And, he adds pointedly, if he were showing this place to Bridges, as he showed him about Roehampton, "as I hope to do (I have to shew it too often: it takes from an hour and a half to three hours: I do it with more pride than pleasure) you could not make me wretched now by either stealing or buying fruit."

But if the new college is booming, it is at the expense of the pollution and blight he has already witnessed in Liverpool and Bedford Leigh, Manchester and Glasgow: trees denuded, sweet salmon-bearing rivers blackened with industrial waste, air clouded with soot, so that—soon after his arrival at Stonyhurst, and looking out over the vast expanse of Ribblesdale and its environs—he begins his first sonnet in over two years. It is called "Ribblesdale," and it is a fitting twin of several of the ecological sonnets he had written in Wales, especially "In the Valley of the Elwy." *"Nam expectatio creaturae revelationem filiorum Dei expectat,"* the headnote reads. *"Vanitati enim creatura subjecta est, non volens sed propter eum qui subjecit eam in spe."* It is from St. Paul's Letter to the Romans: *"For the whole of creation is waiting eagerly for the children of God to be revealed. It is not for its own purposes that creation has been frustrated, but for the purposes of him who imposed it, so that all of creation itself might be freed from its slavery to corruption and brought into the same glorious freedom as the children of God."*

"Earth, sweet Earth, sweet landscape," he begins, meditating on the Lancashire landscape calling out to him, here, now, in late summer, to be witness:

> with leavès throng
> And louchèd low grass, heaven that dost appeal
> To, with no tongue to plead, no heart to feel;
> That canst but only be, but dost that long—

But already a dissonance has wormed its way into the poem in words like "throng" and "louchèd low," suggesting overcrowding and slouching, as in the way crowds move past one in Liverpool and Glasgow and elsewhere.

> Thou canst but be, but that thou well dost; strong
> Thy plea with him who dealt, nay does now deal,
> Thy lovely dale down thus and thus bids reel
> Thy river, and o'er gives all to rack or wrong.

Now even the beautiful Ribblesdale, drunk with pollutants, seems to reel and stagger about like a drunk on a city street, and—unable to speak out—can only *show* the damage inflicted upon it by the industrial age. And man? Dear and dogged man? Heir since the Fall from Paradise to "his own selfbent . . . bound," in his endless going round and round like an ox or horse turning a wheel, and all the while stripping the earth bare—"a traction engine twice a day fetches stone from a quarry on the fells; engines of all sorts send their gross and foulsmelling smoke all over us; cranes keep swinging"—with no one to consider what the world will be hereafter. All this "bids wear / Earth brows of such care, care and dear concern." The brows of hills fresh-quarried, abandoned strip mines defacing the earth long after this generation shall have trod on into oblivion. But the brows too of the disfigured earth frowning against this radical defacement. The poem staggers into some yaw-pitched half-recognized form, but refuses to fully reveal itself yet. It will need another six months before it can lift its shattered face.

October 13: Having heard nothing from Bridges, he tries again. "You are in the infinite leisure of Yattendon and you do not write," he chides. In the meantime, he has managed to complete a version of *The Leaden Echo and the Golden Echo,* "meant for a maidens' song" for *St. Winefred's Well,* and sends it off now for Bridges's perusal. It is an exquisite, highly wrought lyric in two parts, the first—*The Leaden Echo*—sixteen lines of varying length, followed by the second—*The Golden Echo*—doubled to thirty-two lines. Both parts are brilliantly interlaced with consonantal Welsh chimings—*The Leaden Echo* containing the following in the first line alone: *bow, brooch, braid, brace,* morphing to *lace, latch, catch,* and *key.* There are also rhyme echoes throughout: *keep/deep, none/done/none, away/grey/may/bay/decay,* as well as *fair/despair/hair/despair/despair/despair,* a word echoed throughout and then repeated five times running at the close, like Lear's *Never, never, never, never, never!*

Is there any way to keep back beauty?, Winefred's maidens ask despairingly, and the answer comes back: no, no there isn't, for we all move inexorably toward our own deaths and annihilations. It is "Spring and Fall" writ large:

> How to kéep—is there ány any, is there none such, nowhere known
> 　　　some, bow or brooch or braid or brace, láce, latch or
> 　　　catch or key to keep
> Back beauty, keep it, beauty, beauty, beauty . . . from vanishing
> 　　　away?
> Ó is there no frowning of these wrinkles, rankèd wrinkles deep,

Down? no waving off of these most mournful méssengers, still
   méssengers, sad and stealing messengers of grey?—
No there's none, there's none, O nó there's none,
Nor can you long be, what you now are, called fáir,
Do what you may do, what, do whát you may,
And wisdom is éarly to despair:
Be beginning; since, no, nóthing can be done
To keep at báy
Age and age's evils, hoar hair,
Ruck and wrinkle, drooping, dying, death's worst, wíndingsheets,
   tombs and worms and tumbling to decay;
So be begínning, be begínning to despair.
O there 's none; no no no there 's none:
Be begínning to despáir, to despáir,
Despair, despair, despair, despair.

And the Golden Echo answers, halving the final word, *despair,* and re-
versing direction: *Spare! Cease! Quiet now!* And then a veritable upflowing
river of rhymings: *Spare/there/air/hair/care/where,* then *sun/sun/one/
undone,* and *place/face/grace/girlgrace,* interlaced with six doublings—
*sweet/fleet, truth/youth, breath/death, deliver/giver, slept/kept, mould/
fold*—followed by a series of triplets: *numbered/slumbered/cumbered,
fonder/yonder/Yonder.* There *is* such a key, the Echo answers, and it consists—paradoxically—in freely giving back one's beauty—the whole incredible catalogue of things (maiden gear, gallantry and gaiety and grace,/
Winning ways, airs innocent, sweet looks, lovelocks, gaygear, girlgrace)—
into the Father's care, who will keep it far better than we ourselves ever
could by trying to hold on to it. "Spare!" the chorus of maidens begins:

 ... Resign them, sign them, seal them, send them, motion them
   with breath,
 And with sighs soaring, sóaring sighs, deliver
 Them; beauty-in-the-ghost, delíver it, early now, long before déath
 Give beauty back, beauty, beauty, béauty, back to God ...

Much taken by the extraordinary music of the poem, Bridges answers
Hopkins at once, noting that—to his ear—the lyric, with its fluctuating line
lengths, has strong echoes of Whitman in it. But no, Hopkins answers. "I
have read of Whitman's (I) Pete [*Come Up from the Fields Father*] in the

library at Bedford Square [Bridges's personal library] (and perhaps something else; if so I forget), which you pointed out," he begins defensively.
Also, "two pieces in the . . . *Academy*" the year before, one on the "Man-of-
War Bird," the other beginning "Spirit that formed this scene," as well as
short extracts of Whitman's poetry in a review of *Leaves of Grass* by Saintsbury in the *Academy* eight years earlier, when Hopkins was teaching rhetoric at Roehampton.

This is all he can remember, and in any event, he has not read more
than half a dozen pieces. Still, he realizes that even this modest a selection
has been "quite enough to give a strong impression of [Whitman's] marked
and original manner and way of thought and in particular of his rhythm. It
might be even enough, I shall not deny, to originate or, much more, influence another's style." And then he adds the reason why he is reluctant to
make the association with Whitman: "I may as well say what I should not
otherwise have said, that I always knew in my heart Walt Whitman's mind
to be more like my own than any other man's living. As he is a very great
scoundrel this is not a pleasant confession. And this also makes me the
more desirous to read him and the more determined that I will not."

But he and Whitman are two altogether different kinds of poet. Whitman's is all irregular rhythmic prose, a rugged and savage art, to quote
Whitman himself, whereas his own rhythms are all "weighed and timed,"
like the rhythms of those Greek tragic choruses he so much admires, or
Pindar. He urges Bridges to read his lines "till you have settled the true
places of the stress, mark these, then read it aloud, and you will see. Without this these choruses are prose bewitched; with it they are sprung rhythm
like that piece of mine."

In fact, *Echoes* is an advance on what he did three years before in "Binsey Poplars." Both poems, he points out, are composed of two stanzas in a
1:2 ratio. Eight to sixteen for the first, sixteen to thirty-two for the second,
with the lines in the *Echoes* correspondingly longer. It is what he has been
doing and will do with the sonnet form as well: lengthening his lines first to
six stresses and eventually to eight, and then adding tails. He does not
mean to run down Whitman, for his prosaic style has its own advantages.
"But you cannot eat your cake and keep it: he eats his offhand, I keep
mine. . . . Neither do I deny all resemblance." If Whitman has a preference
for the alexandrine, so does he. But he came to that by degrees. He did not
take it from Whitman. Besides, the *Echoes* is not even in his own voice but
in the voice "of a good but lively girl and not at all like—not at all like Walt
Whitman." A week later, he adds a final note: "My de-Whitmaniser . . . was

stern and a bit of a mouther," he admits. Still, he hopes he has made his point. Clearly, Bridges has touched on a sensitive issue, which goes deeper than mere prosody, but touches the question of selfhood and the kenotic emptying of the self he both desires and fears.

It takes only a month of teaching before Hopkins is once again worn down. In early October, he returns Bridges's *Prometheus*, explaining that his mind is "dull and museless and I shd. do no good by keeping it longer and delaying you. The opening is now richer than before," he adds, but the four first lines—

> From high Olympus and the domeless courts,
> Where mighty Zeus our angry king confirms
> The Fates' decrees and bends the will of the gods,
> I come: and on the earth step with glad foot

—seem to him "perhaps the worst in the play," whereas, as Pindar says, the opening lines "*chre themen telauges* [*over our work's beginning we should set a front that shines afar*], though the second line . . . is Miltonic and fine." To his ear, too much of the poem seems written in Bridges's style of Parnassian. Moreover, "the blotching of the [manuscript] copy with countless corrections"—his and Dixon's—"is a heavy toll on its charm in reading" and he wants "to see it in plain print." Yes, the action of the play is good and the unities observed, but how will the thing play? For it has little in the way of bidding, by which he means the art "of saying everything right to or at the hearer, interesting him . . . and of discarding everything" else. How hard it is, he knows, to combine this speaking directly to a reader with such a monumental style as Bridges uses here. In any event, that word "domeless" will have to go, for it makes no sense.

What is wrong with "domeless"? Bridges demands to know. "It is not archaeologically right," Hopkins writes back, and conveys little in the way of a clear image. Again Bridges writes back, asking him if he should just replace the whole four lines. If there is some reason for "domeless," Hopkins responds, just tell him. Courts are seldom domed anyway, so why "tell us that those on Olympus are domeless." And then he is off on a roll. "No: better to say the kamptuliconless courts," if he is so inclined, *Kamptulicon* being a floorcloth made up of cork and india rubber, for surely Mount Olympus has none of those amenities either. Or better still: "Minton's-encaustic-tileless courts," for surely the floors of the Capitol buildings in Washington have not yet found their way to those airy heights where angry Zeus doth reign. Or, maybe, "vulcanized-india-rubberless courts," for that phrase would surely call attention to itself. And if the critics should say such things do not belong to the period, he "would have (as you have now with *domeless*) the overwhelming answer, that you never said they did but the contrary, and that Prometheus, who was at once a prophet and as a mechanician more than equal to Edison and the Jablochkoff candle and the Moc-main Patent Lever Truss with self-adjusting duplex gear and attachments meant to say that emphatically they had not got those improvements on Olympus and he did not intend that they should." But if Bridges cannot see his way to a more straightforward approach, he closes, "remember that that fault is found *in your first line*." It is Hopkins at his most playful and griggish, a mad hatter's sort of humor which cheers him even in the most difficult of times.

The same week that Hopkins is playing with "domeless," Father William Eyre, S.J., Rector at Stonyhurst, reports to Father Purbrick that the new arrival, Father Hopkins, was seen getting "into his room publicly through the window, lately, in order to save time by not having to go round by the corridor." And two days before, he was seen in the swimming bath *with his clothes on*. One month at Stonyhurst and already Hopkins has made a name for himself for outlandish if innocent behavior. The astronomer Father Perry's pet monkey climbs out onto the steep roof of one of the buildings and refuses to come back in, so Hopkins climbs out after him, creeps along the dizzying roof's edge, and carries it back inside while the community below watch in amazement at the black-robed figure dangling above them in pursuit of a monkey.

Even the students note Hopkins's unorthodox play. Young Alban Goodier—who will later become a Jesuit priest and an archbishop—will remember one day that autumn coming down with a severe toothache and being told to walk about the playground to distract himself. Father Hopkins, on his way through the gardens, sees the boy is in pain and tries to distract him. He puts his books down and shimmies to the top of one of the twenty-foot football goalposts. Then he slides back down, dusts himself off, and continues on his way. Young Alban can hardly believe what he has just seen and for the moment his toothache is indeed forgotten.

Father William Delany, S.J., president-elect of the new University College, Dublin, is busy searching for some top Jesuits to staff his college, which is now in the hands of the Irish Jesuits. Delany sees the school as a training ground for a revived Catholic Ireland, something separate from Trinity College, with its Anglican and more secular training. There is the feeling in Ireland that it is only a matter of time before Home Rule becomes law here, and the Jesuits want the Catholic majority to have a voice in the new Ireland. And though there are several laymen on the staff of the college—holdovers from the old Catholic University—it is far cheaper to find Jesuits to fill the positions, since their £400 per annum salary can be folded back into the running expenses for the new university.

Already, though, the Irish Provincial, Fr. Tuite, has warned Delany against bringing professors in from England, since he sees Newman's selection of English professors and officials as the main reason the old Catholic University failed years before, and now he is afraid the same might "happen with regard to us." It is of paramount importance, he sees, especially with the rise of Irish national feeling, that we "not hurt national *prejudices* on any account," and so Tuite is especially wary of bringing Englishmen into Ireland just now. He is particularly adamant that Delany not bring over English converts— former Anglicans and Methodists and Presbyterians—who are, to put it bluntly, "unsuited to this country and its thoroughly Catholic people."

But Delany needs an international group of Jesuits to teach in Dublin if the university is ever to succeed, and so he writes to the English Province— among others—outlining his plans and seeking recruits. On November 5, George Porter, S.J., English Assistant to the Jesuit General in Rome, writes Delany that there is only one Jesuit he can think of who might fit the bill: Father Hopkins. "I think Fr. Purbrick might be induced to let you have Hopkins or [J. T.] Walford: I do not think he would part with [Joseph] Rickaby or [Herbert] Lucas. Hopkins is clever, well-trained, teaches well but has never succeeded well: his mind runs in eccentric ways."

Five days later, Purbrick himself writes Delany that—of the seven men he has named as possible candidates for the Irish university—six are "the cream of the [English] province" and cannot be spared. The only possibility would be Hopkins. But he also warns Delany that, while Hopkins "is very clever and a good scholar . . . I should be doing you no kindness in sending you a man so eccentric. I am trying him this year in coaching B.A.s at Stonyhurst, but with fear and trembling." And so Hopkins's name is thrown into the tiny ring for a professorship in Dublin, a situation of which he himself knows nothing.

In the meantime, Bridges returns to an old sore point. It is the question of just how earnest Hopkins really is about remaining a priest and a Jesuit, in spite of every indication that the experiment has proved a failure. Forget it, Hopkins tells him now. It was "the injustice to myself I was thinking then," he says, and he meant only to mildly rebuke Bridges for "being so unreasonable" toward him in thinking Hopkins was merely playacting in a charade. The truth is that someone "who is deeply in earnest is not very eager to assert his earnestness, as they say when a man is really certain he no longer disputes but is indifferent. And that is all I say now, that to think a man in my position is not in earnest is unreasonable and is to make difficulties."

New Year's, 1883: Since his holidays began, he writes Bridges four days into the New Year, "I have been in a wretched state of weakness and weariness, I can't tell why, always drowzy and incapable of reading or thinking to any effect." He is also dismayed by Bridges's *Prometheus* being published by Henry Daniel's private press in a limited edition of 100, all on handmade Dutch paper, at 10s 6d the copy. He himself would much prefer getting the word out to as wide an audience and as cheaply as possible. "I cd. not venture to ask that our library should subscribe half a sovereign for an *édition de luxe* of a new book by an almost unknown author," he remonstrates, "still less could I expect, nor shd. I like, you to present me, that is our library, with a copy. Here then is a downright deadlock and there is nothing for it but for me to wait for the second edition."

Then he moves on to a discussion of the true nature of a gentleman, and his belief that a true gentleman is a higher calling even than the poet/artist or the philosopher. And yet "to be a gentleman is but on the brim of morals and rather a thing of manners." How much more, therefore, "must art and philosophy and manners and breeding and everything else in the world be below the least degree of true virtue." This is "that chastity of mind" which lies "at the very heart . . . of all other good, the seeing at once what is best, the holding to that, and the not allowing anything else whatever to be even heard pleading to the contrary." And so, while "Christ's life and character are such as appeal to all the world's admiration," there is "one insight St. Paul gives us of it which is very secret" and seems to him "more touching and constraining than everything else is." He means Paul's insight in Philippians 2. 5–11 into Christ's emptying of himself out of love for the Father and the human race. But more, it is his own deepest secret about how to live. For Christ, finding "his human nature informed by the godhead— thought it nevertheless no snatching-matter for him to be equal with God, but annihilated himself, taking the form of servant; that is, he could not but see what he was, God, but he would see it as if he did not see it, and be it as if he were not and instead of snatching at once at what all the time was his, or was himself, he emptied or exhausted himself so far as that was possible, of godhead and behaved only as God's slave, as his creature, as man, [and] humbled himself to . . . the death of the cross. It is this holding of himself back," Hopkins sees, which is "the root of all [Christ's] holiness and the imitation of this the root of all moral good in other men."

As for the English ideal of the gentleman which Bridges has evoked: the notion itself, Hopkins agrees, has been a great service to mankind. It is also true that a real gentleman "is in the position to despise the poet, were he Dante or Shakspere, and the painter, were he Angelo or Apelles, for anything in him that shewed him not to be a gentleman." But if he is a gentleman, this is something he will not do. And yet "the quality of a gentleman is so very fine a thing that . . . one should not be at all hasty in concluding that one possesses it. People assume that they have it, take it quite for granted, and claim the acknowledgment from others." But this virtue is "'no snatching-matter.' The more a man feels what it means and is—and to feel this is certainly some part of it—the more backward he will be to think he can have realised in himself anything so perfect."

A true gentleman, then, will feel that he is anything but. The truth is that most poets and artists are not gentlemen, for gentlemen "do not pander to lust or other basenesses nor . . . give themselves airs and affectations nor do other things to be found in modern works." If you want an example of a real gentleman, he argues, look at Dixon. In everything he writes, "You feel he is a gentleman and thinks like one." Of course Bridges, having someone else in mind for the model of the perfect gentleman, tells Hopkins that he feels offended by not being included in Hopkins's short list.

In mid-February, Hopkins writes his annual birthday wishes to Newman, and broaches the topic of writing a commentary on the Cardinal's *Grammar of Assent.* "Dear Fr. Hopkins," Newman answers on the 27th, "Thank you very much . . . for the complimentary proposal you make in behalf of my *Grammar of Assent.* But I cannot accept it, because I do not feel the need of it, and I could not, as a matter of conscience, allow you to undertake a work which I could not but consider at once onerous and unnecessary." After all, the book has reached five editions in the twelve years since its publication, is even being translated into various subcontinental Indian dialects, and is "frequently referred to in periodical home publications." Yes, it has been subjected to misreadings by those who have not bothered to read it carefully, and if it turns out to be worthless, "a comment, however brilliant, will not do more than gain for it a short galvanic life, which has no charms for me." When Hopkins writes back to say that he had not meant to pay Newman a compliment, but rather to comment on his *Grammar,* Newman tweaks him by insisting that Hopkins did indeed pay him "a very kind compliment. You seem to think compliments must be insincere: is it so?" And the matter drops.

During Holy Week, with the students on vacation, Hopkins goes down to St. Wilfrid's, Preston, to help out Father Goldie and the others, and then, on the Tuesday after Easter, takes the train down to Oak Hill for a visit with his family. While at Preston, he hurriedly answers Bridges. No, he reassures him, he was not implying that Bridges was not a gentleman. Actually, if he had wanted to name "a conspicuous instance" of a blackguard, he should have taken himself, "as I was going to do and to tell a good story too thereanent, but refrained because I thought it might look as if I wanted to draw a faint protest from you and because humility is such a very sensitive thing the least touch smutches it and well meant attempts to keep it from jolting, like the Ark when the cattle shook it, do more harm than good; but all the same I shd. have been sadly sincere and sadly truthful."

And then he says what has long been on his mind: "How many many times must you have misunderstood me not in my sonnets only but in moral, social, personal matters! It must be so, I see now. But it would embitter life if we knew of the misunderstandings put upon us." In the seven months he has been at Stonyhurst, he sighs, he has managed one sonnet— "Ribblesdale"—"and three triolets, which have been published in the local *Stonyhurst Magazine*." But as "they have the taint of jest" they dare not meet Bridges's eye, and since Bridges destroyed his other comic attempts, he refrains from sending the triolets on.

The beginning of May—Mary's Month: Hopkins begins a lengthy poem to be hung on the statue of Our Lady. He calls it "Mary Mother of Divine Grace compared to the Air we Breathe," a title he will later shorten to "The Blessed Virgin compared to the Air we Breathe." "We hang up polyglot poems in honour of the Blessed Virgin this month," he tells Bridges. "I am on one in English in three-foot couplets." But because it is long, he does not think he will "find it either convenient or desirable" to send him a copy, especially as it is on a subject Bridges is sure to misunderstand. "It is partly a compromise with popular taste, and it is too true that the highest subjects are not those on which it is easy to reach one's highest." And yet, how the lines rise. "Wild air, world-mothering air," he begins, in full control of his beautifully articulated metaphor of Mary's transparent presence in the world, air and grace

> Nestling me everywhere,
> That each eyelash or hair
> Girdles; goes home betwixt
> The fleeciest, frailest-flixed
> Snowflake; that's fairly mixed

> With, riddles, and is rife
> In every least thing's life . . .
> Mary Immaculate,
> Merely a woman, yet
> Whose presence, power is
> Great as no goddess's
> Was deemèd, dreamèd; who
> This one work has to do—
> Let all God's glory through,
> God's glory which would go
> Through her and from her flow . . .

The poem owes something to his modernization of the medieval *Angelus ad Virginem* of the year before and much to Scotus's insights into the nature and effects of the Immaculate Conception. But this is poetry; this is all energy and light, a joyful hullabaloo, praise fully, lovingly given to Mary in this most Marian of hymns:

> Of her flesh he took flesh:
> He does take fresh and fresh,
> Though much the mystery how,
> Not flesh but spirit now
> And makes, O marvellous!
> New Nazareths in us . . .

See how the sky is azured, he says. Now, raise your hand, and look how that blue "laps / Round the four fingergaps." And yet the ever present sky in no way stains the light. No more does Mary by her presence, except to make the world that much fairer. Consider too what effect sunlight would have, he argues, if there were no atmosphere to soften and diffuse its intensity:

> the sun would shake,
> A blear and blinding ball
> With blackness bound, and all
> The thick stars round him roll
> Flashing like flecks of coal,
> Quartz-fret, or sparks of salt,
> In grimy vasty vault . . .
> Through her we may see him

> Made sweeter, not made dim,
> And her hand leaves his light
> Sifted to suit our sight.

And then a final prayer that Mary, "thou dear / Mother" and his very "atmosphere," may

> round me lie
> Fronting my froward eye
> With sweet and scarless sky . . .
> World-mothering air, air wild,
> Wound with thee, in thee isled,
> Fold home, fast fold thy child.

Soon enough he will come to such sights colder, when that comforting, mothering mantle of May blue will have withdrawn, and he will have to face night after night—alone—those "Quartz-fret . . . sparks of salt" in the "grimy vasty vault," in that earnest, earthless evening overhead, where dawn seems infinities away.

Thursday, June 7. Oak Hill: Hopkins's cousin Magdalen, daughter of his deceased uncle, the Reverend Marsland Hopkins of Oxford, marries Archibald Commeline, formerly of Magdalen College, Oxford. He knew Commeline at Oxford, Hopkins tells Bridges, but barely. Both Kate, twenty-seven, and Grace, twenty-six, are among the bridesmaids, but on the day of the wedding a distraught Grace keeps to her room to mourn the death of her own fiancé. The previous summer, when his parents and Grace were on holiday in Switzerland—Hopkins tells Bridges—they met at Lake Geneva "a young man Henry Weber son to a doctor at Sensburg in East Prussia. He was attracted by Grace's playing and, the weather keeping them in, was constantly at her piano: when they parted, though they had known each other for less than a fortnight, they were both deeply in love." And though Weber was in frail health and had very uncertain prospects, Hopkins's parents allowed the engagement. Then, "after some illusory rallies, just when Grace and he had persuaded themselves that he was to recover and all would be well . . . he died. The news reached Grace on the very eve of Magdalen's wedding. It was an overwhelming blow. Magdalen wished the wedding to be put off, but that was neither possible nor desirable; but a gloom was cast over the day."

And now Hopkins writes to console his sister. "My dearest Grace," he tells her, "Once more death shows its power suddenly to darken our hopes and disenchant us. But the firmest and most fruitful ground of comfort is to look on everything that has happened, your meeting with Henry Weber, your engagement, the months that have since past, and his death, as things providential, always meant (more than permitted) by God to be and their times and circumstances appointed." Of course he cannot know for sure, but he believes Weber's love for her was "a steadying and purifying thing rather than otherwise. If so, then for your . . . happiness . . . to end for him in death and for you in a deep disappointment marks it as a sorrow more especially of God's sending and of which he undertakes to be the comforter."

Suppose, on the other hand, they "had married and lived a long happy prosperous life together and reared your children, would not this be of God's giving and would you not have returned and been bound to return him thanks for the blessings bestowed?" But now all of this has been swept away. Is it not plain, then, that "our Lord knows what he does and in striking so hard pities your poor heart and means for you something far better, the brighter that seeming future was the better this real one?" And so, he exhorts his sister to patience, so that her grief "shall not make you exacting or selfish or . . . unfit you for ordinary duty." For he knows too well that it can have this effect on some, making "mere wrecks of them."

Blessed are they who mourn, he reminds her, *for they shall be comforted.* He is going to say mass for Henry's repose tomorrow and hopes "it may avail him and if so, whatever you may think, he will be grateful to his betrothed's brother for it. . . . I have not written this without tears. Good-bye, dearest child, and believe me your loving brother Gerard." The following day, after mass, he adds a postscript: "During the mass I felt strongly those motions from God (as I believe them to be) which I have often before now received touching the condition of the departed, by which was signified that it was well with him." For the next sixty-two years, until her death in 1945 at the age of eighty-eight, twice what her brother will live to see, Grace will remain unmarried.

On July 26, at the request of Mrs. Waterhouse, Bridges's soon-to-be mother-in-law, he sends a too-long Prayer for Protestants for inclusion in her *Book of Prayers* anthology, as requested, but which she will reject as not non-sectarian enough. "Almighty and Everlasting God," Hopkins begins,

we appear before thee humbly to acknowledge that thou art the one true God . . . the maker of all things made, the watchful witness and just judge of all things done. We . . . firmly believe those secrets of thy being which man could never know of till thou didst of thyself reveal them, sending into the world thy only begotten son Jesus Christ our Lord, who being God is thy equal and being made man became thy servant and for our salvation died upon the cross. With thee and with him . . . we acknowledge the Holy Ghost, three equal persons in one nature and godhead. . . . We wish to love thee as . . . thou dost deserve to be loved and hast commanded us to love thee. . . . For thy sake [we] love our neighbours . . . wishing them well, not ill; purposing to do them good, not evil; forgiving also all who have offended us, as we by thee hope to be forgiven.

But even this is too dogmatic, and—in fact—too overtly Christian for the readership Mrs. Waterhouse has in mind.

The Jesuit appointments for Stonyhurst will be made public very soon, he tells Bridges in late July, and "it seems likely that I shall be removed; where I have no notion. But I have long been Fortune's football and am blowing up the bladder [soccer ball] of resolution big and buxom for another kick of her foot. I shall be sorry to leave Stonyhurst; but go or stay, there is no likelihood of my ever doing anything to last. And I do not know how it is, I have no disease, but I am . . . always jaded, though work is not heavy, and the impulse to do anything fails me or has in it no continuance." As it turns out, he will be assigned to Stonyhurst for another year, but in a deeper sense he is right: Dame Fortune and his superiors do indeed have other plans for him.

On Sunday, July 29, during Speech Day activities at the college, he is asked by Father Eyre to escort the white-haired sixty-year-old English Catholic poet and critic Coventry Patmore about the campus. Friend of the Pre-Raphaelites, of Rossetti and Holman Hunt, Patmore has spent nearly twenty years as an assistant librarian in the British Museum, writing poetry in his spare time. In 1854, at thirty-one, he published his best known poem, "The Angel in the House," dedicated to his wife. Eight years later, he lost his wife and that same year converted to Catholicism. In 1865, now forty-five, he married again, and the following year became a landed gentleman, purchasing an estate in East Grinstead. A dozen years later he published *The Unknown Eros* and then *Amelia,* together with his essay on *English Metrical Law,* followed by *Principle in Art* in 1879. After eleven years of marriage, his second wife also died, and five years later, in 1881, now fifty-eight, he has married for a third time. Eros, and a form of Christianity verging on Gnosticism, have served him for his major themes, and made his name known in England.

Yes, there are faults in Patmore, Hopkins has already told Bridges, who does not care for Patmore's work. "Bad rhymes; continued obscurity; and, the most serious, a certain frigidity when . . . the feeling does not flush and fuse the language." And yet "for insight," Patmore beats all living poets—Tennyson, Browning, Arnold, the Rossettis, and certainly Swinburne. His insight is "really profound," and he has "an exquisiteness, farfetchedness, of imagery worthy of the best things of the Caroline age." For twenty years and more, Hopkins has been reading and quoting from Patmore, and now he finally has the chance to spend several days with the poet.

"The holidays are come," he writes Bridges in early August, "and from the height of buzz and bustle we have been suddenly steeped in the dankness of ditchwater. I have leave of absence and . . . am going to Hampstead and presently to Holland for a few days with my people" to meet Grace, who has insisted on visiting her dead fiancé's grave in Germany. "An escort was found for her as far as Berlin and at the station nearest Sensburg Mrs. Weber met her. Now she is with them and they treat her like one of themselves." He has had a letter from her written from there, and now he and his parents are "going to fetch her home and that is how I am to go to Holland." He has also spent several days hosting Coventry Patmore, who he knows Bridges does not care for. Still, upon Hopkins's mentioning Bridges to Patmore, "he expressed at once his admiration of your poetry but knew it only from reviews and had tried without success to get it from his bookseller . . . I wish you would let me know in what form it now is obtainable: the titles I mean, for I have had the books but they are not here." He also showed Patmore all of Dixon's poetic manuscripts in his possession "and made an enthusiastic convert of him." He has even asked Hopkins to look over his manuscripts for suggestions. "I do not know but it was bragging to mention this," he confesses, "however now there it is, all blubbering in wet ink."

He goes down to Holy Name parish in Preston to help out his fellow Jesuits there for the Feast of the Assumption, and then, just before heading for home, writes Patmore to say he has just received a copy of Dixon's *Mano: a Poetical History of the Time of the Close of the Tenth Century Concerning the Adventures of a Norman Knight*. The long poem is written in *terza rima*, Dixon explains, and "an address to the Reader in the same measure draws attention to the measure itself." It was Bridges, in fact—to whom Dixon has dedicated the book—who got Dixon to rewrite the poem according to his understanding of the form. But Hopkins has found the style too archaic, and therefore blighted. Still, "it is a better one than Swinburne's or Morris's" in that mode, and at least Dixon has made it his own: "a style and not a trick."

Three days after returning to Oak Park, he crosses the North Sea to Holland with his parents, his sister, Kate, and their cousin Magdalen for a week-long vacation before meeting Grace to escort her back home. In late 1928, Kate, approaching seventy, will recall her brother hearing her and Magdalen laughing in their hotel room in Ghent one evening and suddenly standing at the door smiling, asking what all the laughter was about. Eager to join them, he spends a half hour leaning out their window and pointing out the bats "flitting to & fro, hearing their tiny voices," and showing them how to throw "little bits of plaster" from the flaking walls and ceiling "into the air to cheat them into diving at it believing it food."

Monday, September 3: With Grace now safely back home, he bids good-bye, trusting that his sister will eventually "settle down and be happy." For she is "too sweetnatured to let herself be soured or enfeebled by a grief," he tells Bridges. In time, he thinks, "she may even come to care for someone else, though no doubt she does not believe she ever could." And then he is off to Beaumont, west of London, for his annual retreat. Father George Renorden Kingdon, S.J., sixty-two, a Trinity College, Cambridge, convert who ten years before had been Hopkins's colleague at Stonyhurst, will be his spiritual director this time round. He is a good soul with a spirit of joy about him, and a good match for Hopkins. And so Hopkins begins his retreat with notes on the affective and elective wills—what his natural inclinations (desires of the flesh, desires of the eyes, physical and intellectual) lead him to do, and what his *arbitrium,* his conscious will—formed by his priestly vocation—urges him on to do, even when it goes counter—as it often does—to his natural inclinations. But in meditating on the *Processu Peccatorum* (the catalogue of sins), "an old and terribly afflicting thought and disgust," which he does not name, moves him to seek Father Kingdon's guidance. *Remember,* his spiritual director tells him, *that we are always in God's presence, and it is He who with infinite love and mercy watches over us.* For Hopkins the advice comforts, and, advised "not further to dwell on" what is troubling him, he leaves off such black thoughts awhile.

But what is evil, after all? Evil means corruption, and corruption leads to temptation and sin. Which brings him back to Adam and Eve, and the "false standard of right and wrong" they established. "For Eve was deceived into thinking there was something morally beautiful in disobeying, that God had really meant her to disobey." Adam too was "deceived so far as to think God would admire the generosity of his self-sacrifice," for it is the nature of malice to provoke temptation, "then with consent sin and from sin damnation." The sinner banishes God, "and dying finds himself from God banished . . . which is what he wanted but not the way he wanted it." And banishment means the "infinite removal of good," which in effect is an "infinite evil."

And the hours drag on. "There is a way of thinking of past sin such that the thought numbs and kills the heart," he knows too well, "as all this Week of the Exercises will do if care is not taken in giving it." But this is not, he knows, how we should approach our sins, but rather as "our Lady felt or would feel when sins were presented to her and shrunk from them instantaneously and which our Lord feels" and who means us "to put on His mind according to our measure." For the holy ones "turn from sin by nature . . . and finding it embodied with a thing they love find it infinitely piteous: 'O the pity of it!' and why should it ever have been?" Pity yourself, he thinks, "that such a thing as sin should ever have got hold of us," for this "pure pity and disavowal of our past selves is the state of mind of one whose sins are perfectly forgiven." But then there is that nagging caveat which has so often sapped him of peace: that we should "not wholly get rid of the shame of sin, for it is a part of penance." And so he licks his old wounds and admonishes himself once again to be on guard against the Tempter, who is always out there waiting.

Wednesday, September 5: A meditation on Death, which, when it comes, as indeed it must, means the soul will be thrown back on itself "with only the scapes and species of its past life; which being . . . undisplaced by a fresh continual current of experience, absorb and press upon its consciousness." Then it will know at last whether God "is pleased or displeased." So, it will come down to a final yes or no, and on each scape, each action, God has set a stamp or seal or instress which says "*right, good,* or . . . *bad, wrong.* Now the sinner who has preferred his own good, as revenge, drunkenness, to God's good, true good . . . by his attachment to which and God's rejection of it" will be "carried and swept away to an infinite distance from God; and the stress and strain of his removal is his eternity of punishment." Hopkins will come back to this terrible realization with greater and greater frequency in the time ahead, where, "wáre of a wórld where bút these twó tell, éach off the óther," the soul will be tied to the rack of its own instressed inscape, "Where, selfwrung, selfstrung, sheathe- and shelterless, thóughts agaínst thoughts ín groans grínd." In groan . . . ingrown, like an ingrown toenail, a cancer, the corrupt self grown inward forever, that sweating self.

September 7: Halfway through his retreat, he insists on going on with his meditation on Hell. The stress of removal forever from God applies to the very core of oneself, and its name is Pride. And what else is Pride but "the matching of the sinner's self with God's and for himself preferring it"? But when the hour of death comes, when the "self is set face to face with God's self, the true position of things between man and God will in a terrible instant make itself known." So it is *we* who condemn ourselves to a hell where we will be forever left alone to dwell on ourselves, the terrible memories played over and over and over and over.

The following evening, after five days of it, a weary Hopkins begins at last to move toward the chink of light called consolation. Meditating on Christ's baptism and starting out on his own life's work, he realizes that Christ must have turned to his mother to ask her blessing on it and on him. He too must remember to ask her blessing on whatever he undertakes henceforth. Wasn't it Father Whitty who told him on the Long Retreat that the greatest "part of life to the holiest of men consists in the well performance . . . of ordinary duties"? Nor has he been called, as others have, to a life of deprivation and heroic sacrifice. His work lies merely in the daily grind of teaching or preaching, he reminds himself. Nor has he been called to witness with his life. And so he admonishes himself to stop bewailing his "cowardice or nonperformance" in great things, and to remember that he has an obligation "to fulfil all justice." And more: "since God gives me at present no great humiliations and I am not worthy of them and did not accept them well when they came, to welcome the small ones whenever such shall occur."

That same evening, the fifteenth anniversary of his entering the Society of Jesus, Hopkins makes a solemn promise to offer up the rest of his life as a sacrifice in imitation of Christ. It is what his life has been tending toward all these years in any event, and this is the logical next step: to give himself up as an immolation, to pick up his own cross, follow Christ to Calvary, and nail his writhing self to Christ's. There is a fine line between pride and the radical emptying of the self as an act of love, he knows, and Hopkins has tried with everything he has to give himself in love. "During this retreat I have much and earnestly prayed that God will lift me above myself to a higher state of grace, in which I may have more union with him, be more zealous to do his will, and freer from sin."

After meditating on Christ's Temptation in the Wilderness that evening, he begs once more to be lifted up, "acknowledging it was a great grace even to have the desire." He has tested himself, and believes this desire "is a pure one and it is long since I have had so strong and spiritual a one and so persistent." Then he turns to think of his fellow Jesuits: those just entering the order, as he did all those years ago, and those others "who should this morning have taken their vows." And then he turns to the vexing question of his poems, languishing as they are in manuscript, and "earnestly asked our Lord to watch over my compositions, not to preserve them from being lost or coming to nothing, for that I am very willing they should be, but that they might not do me harm through the enmity or imprudence of any man or my own." He will not destroy them, he decides, but give them to his Beloved as a love offering, that "he should have them as his own and employ or not employ them as he should see fit." This prayer, he adds with relief, "I believe is heard." But the following morning, it dawns on him what it is he has just prayed for. "In meditating on the Crucifixion," he realizes that what he has just done is to ask "to be raised to a higher degree of grace," which also means being "lifted on a higher cross." So be it, then. So be it. "Then I took it that our Lord recommended me to our Lady and her to me."

On Monday, September 10, the last day of his retreat, he mediates on the risen Christ on the road to Emmaus alongside two of his disciples. "This morning in Thanksgiving after mass," he confesses, he could only feel "a deep residue of bitterness in his mind." True, he has a new "insight in[to] things." But while he meditates on Christ's presence in the midst of his disciples like some rising sun, he realizes with a start that he himself feels only desolation. Well, Christ never promised it would be easy. And then, suddenly, he finds himself comforted by the very comfort Christ "gave those two men, taking that for a sample of his comfort and them for representatives of all men comforted." If not comfort for himself, then at least the comfort of a priest knowing that he has tried to comfort others.

And so back to Stonyhurst via Oxford. He had wanted to spend a few hours with Bridges at Yattendon, but he takes the wrong train at Reading and is whirled past the village where Bridges now lives. "The worst of it," he writes Bridges that evening, is that he does not "even see how another opportunity is ever to occur." Back at Stonyhurst, he writes Patmore to thank him—on behalf of the college—for the four-volume set of poems he has so graciously sent. Since yesterday he has reread a great part of the *Angel in the House,* and with pleasure. But now, more than ever, he feels the task he has undertaken—to comment on Patmore's poems for a revised edition of his poetry—"is a dangerous and an over-honourable one and perhaps it was presumptuous to accept it," though accept it he has. And as his business now will be "to find faults, not beauties," he wants Patmore to understand first of all how much he admires his poems. A week later, blushing at his own boldness, he sends Patmore his remarks. Hopkins has "one serious fault to find and on that I lay so much stress that I could even wish you were put to some inconvenience and delay rather than that [*The Angel in the House*] should go down to posterity with it."

Here is the rub: why is it that we so often find evil beautiful? Not, he answers, "by any freak of nature," for "nature is incapable of producing beautiful evil." No, the explanation is old, simple, and undeniable. "It comes from wicked will, freedom of choice, abusing the beauty, the good of its nature." And that is why he has such difficulty with Patmore's statement that "Women *should* be vain." What Patmore has managed to do is to "introduce a vice . . . and make the highest relish of pure love come from the base 'smell of mortality.'" Everyone has at least one cherished fault, he points out. "We do this ourselves, but when another does it towards another vice not our own favourite . . . we are disgusted." Recently, the *Saturday Review* contrasted "the Catholic and Protestant ideal of a schoolboy" and "looked on chastity as a feminine virtue (= lewdness a masculine one: it was not quite so raw as I put it, but this was the meaning)." Even the historian Mommsen believes "great nations should break treaties." But to Hopkins personally, "we shd. in everything side with virtue, even if we do not feel its charm, because good is good."

Still, how "can anyone admire . . . vanity in women?" Is it not "vanity makes them first publish, then prostitute their charms? In Leonardo's famous picture 'Modesty and Vanity,' is it not almost taken for granted that the one figure is that of a virgin, the other that of a courtezan? If modesty in women means two things at once, purity and humility, must not the pair of opposites be no great way apart, vanity from impurity? Who can think of the Blessed Virgin and of vanity?" In his own experience, "nothing in good women is more beautiful than just the absence of vanity and an earnestness of look and character which is better than beauty." Not having a wife, he must turn for examples to his sisters and the modesty with which they show him "their compositions in music or painting, which I, with a brother's biased judgment but still sincerely, admire, they seem to be altogether without vanity—yet they might be with reason vainer of these than of their looks, and towards a brother not be ashamed to shew it." But now, alas, as one of the fruits of that "wilder beast from West" he had warned against in "Andromeda," "pernicious doctrines and practice are abroad and the other day the papers said a wretched being refused in church to say the words 'and obey': if it had been a Catholic wedding and I the priest I would have let the sacrilege go no further."

Fearing he has "'done it' this time," Hopkins is relieved when Patmore writes back, thanking him for his trenchant and honest criticism. Still, if

Patmore agrees that others might fall "into the same misunderstanding" as Hopkins himself, "we ought not to fire a forest . . . in lighting a pastille." Yes, he knows that patching up old poems is extremely difficult. "For a time," Hopkins admits, "we keep the connection with our past feelings open." But eventually those feelings recede, though we still "have an insight into them; then something comes between and a long while after looking back, like the tail of a train going round a sharp curve, you see your own self quite from outside." One cannot rework poems that have entered into history, he explains, for you are no longer the same poet who wrote those poems.

At last Bridges writes to tell Hopkins that the Protestant prayer Hopkins wrote for Mrs. Waterhouse is too specific in its Christian formulations and might damage the sales of the book if it is included. How sad, Hopkins writes back, that the general public "can no longer be trusted to bear, to stomach, the clear expression of or the taking for granted even very elementary Christian doctrines." But there is another thing he wants to say. Even a doctrine like the Incarnation may be believed by people like himself, Bridges has underscored. That is, as a mystery. But once the doctrine has been formulated and reduced to the world of pros and cons, its mystery evaporates, and so does its hold on the mind.

But, Hopkins objects, Bridges does not mean by "mystery" what a Catholic does. "You mean an interesting uncertainty: the uncertainty ceasing interest ceases also." But a mystery to a Catholic means "an incomprehensible certainty." Yet mystery is more than "a curiosity only; curiosity satisfied, the trick found out (to be a little profane), the answer heard, it vanishes at once." If a doctrine like the Trinity "is to be explained by grammar and by tropes, why then [one] could furnish explanations for [one]self." But then, Hopkins asks, "where wd. be the mystery? the true mystery, the incomprehensible one?" Now, in the Trinity, "there are three persons, each God and each . . . the only God." To many this is merely a dogma, "an equation in theology, the dull algebra of schoolmen." But to others "it is news of their dearest friend or friends, leaving them all their lives balancing whether they have three heavenly friends or one . . . their knowledge leaves their minds swinging; poised, but on the quiver."

He had not meant Patmore to know that he wrote poetry, "but since it has come naturally and unavoidably about there is no more to be said." And so he asks Bridges to send him the manuscript book Bridges has been putting together containing his handwritten copies of Hopkins's poems. Hopkins would like to make corrections to these, and then send the book on to Patmore. "You were right to leave out the [accent and other] marks," he adds. "They were not consistent for one thing and are always offensive. Still there must be some. Either I must invent a notation applied throughout as in music or else I must only mark where the reader is likely to mistake, and for the present this is what I shall do."

Then he writes Patmore with comments on his *Amelia*. The problem is this, though Hopkins does not say so directly: that, while Patmore is a Catholic, there is something of the Gnostic about him, for too often he finds Patmore's poems deviating from basic Catholic doctrine. "Those who accuse themselves of sinning in hope," he tries explaining to the freewheeling Patmore, "mean that they sinned in presumption; mocking God, as good as telling him they know best what matters and what does not matter and making themselves and not him, by a hideous perversion, the standard and fountain of morality." As for Patmore's "The Kiss," though "this is a little gem of execution and will be a favourite, yet there is something about it that offends me . . . I cannot help having a wish that Victor and Amanda might both once be well whipped."

On November 7, in another long letter to Patmore, this one on sprung rhythm as the basis of good English poetry, he explains why so much modern poetry bores him. The sprung rhythm he employs, it is important for Patmore to understand, "is the making a thing more, or making it markedly, what it already is; it is the bringing out its nature." And though he has done so himself, "it is a radically bad principle to call English feet iambs and trochees. . . . Cicero says there are only three sounds in music, the turn, the rise, and the fall," and even modern "musical notation arose from a complicated system of accents, rising, falling, and so on."

November 15: A letter is published in *Nature* from the Reverend Hopkins on the phenomenon of shadow-beams in the east at sunset. The phenomenon, he writes, "was beautifully witnessed here today and yesterday," when "the sky was striped with cirrus cloud like swaths of a hayfield; only in the east there was a bay or reach of clear blue sky, and in this the shadowbeams appeared, slender, colourless, and radiating every way like a fan wide open." And today he saw in the east "alternate broad bands of rose colour and blue, slightly fringed." All of this, he explains, "is merely an effect of perspective, but a strange and beautiful one." Perspective. Doesn't it all come down to a question of perspective, he has often asked himself, as in his dealings even with those closest to him, like Bridges?

On December 6, he sends Patmore a batch of comments on the first part of *The Unknown Eros*. What especially troubles him is Patmore's anti-Semitism, particularly in his labeling the late Disraeli the party's Jew. "This is a hard saying, all politics apart," Hopkins remonstrates. He knows that many Englishmen "speak so, but I cannot see how they can be justified. For *Jew* must be a reproach either for religion or for race. It cannot be for religion here, for Disraeli was not by religion a Jew: he had been baptised young and had always professed Christianity. His Christianity was a shadowy thing, I know, but so is that of thousands. If he believed in anyone I suppose that was Christ and did not, as Jews do, 'look for another.'" Therefore, Patmore must be condemning Disraeli for his race. But, Hopkins remonstrates, "that is no reproach but a glory, for Christ was a Jew. You will I know say that this dilemma is as fallacious as most dilemmas are and that Jew is a reproach because [you think] the Jews have corrupted their race and nature, so that it is their vices and their free acts we stigmatise when we call cheating Jewing—and that you mean that Disraeli in 1871 overreached and jewed his constituents. But what you say is wider than that and . . . will sound unjust and passionate, the more as time goes on." And even Disraeli's enemies will admit that he, "of all eminent statesmen, was truly devoted to and truly promoted the honour of England."

But, like a dog with a bone, Patmore will not let the issue go. "My dear Sir," he writes Hopkins on December 9. "The political action and inaction of England—her ministers & her people—during the last twenty years or more fill me with an actual thirst for vengeance—I sometimes long for some hideous catastrophe—though I & mine should be involved in it—which should wake the country from its more hideous sleep." For his part, he hates Disraeli "more, if possible, than I hate Gladstone, and 'Jew' or *any* stone seemed good enough to throw at such a dog." Does not Father Hopkins "remember the details of the passage of his Reform Bill in 1867? . . . How it ended—rather than Mr. Disraeli should go out of office—in actually consummating the revolution wh. the Radicals were only dreaming of?" It is the vicious underside of Victorian civilization, such talk, and its acids burn.

In mid-November, a year after approaching Father Purbrick about Hopkins's coming over to Ireland, Father Delany tries again. Again Purbrick writes Father Eyre at Stonyhurst for his opinion. On the 20th, Eyre—with a wink in his eye—informs Purbrick that "Father Gerard Hopkins may, at any time, go stark-staring mad, and as (1) it would be well to take him out of himself, and as (2) it is better the denouement should not be when [poor, mad] George the third is King, alias, when I am in charge, I should strongly recommend his being handed over to Father William Delany, S.J." On the 28th, Purbrick brings up Hopkins's case with his *consultors* in London. It would of course be a good thing to have a Jesuit university somewhere in the British Isles, they believe. Likewise, it is possible that "Fr. Hopkins could be spared from his present employment and that we ought to try to help the Irish University to this extent."

With this go-ahead, Purbrick signals Delany the following day: "I have no objection to your inviting Fr. Gerald [sic] Hopkins to stand as a Candidate for a Fellowship." In fact, he is "the only man *possible*. You know him. I have the highest opinion of his scholarship and abilities—I fancy also that University work would be more in his line than anything else. Sometimes what we in community deem oddities are the very qualities which outside are appreciated as original and valuable." He has said nothing to Hopkins about all this, because he thinks an invitation direct from Delany with Purbrick's sanction would be "more complimentary and appetizing to him." And so, while Father Hopkins gazes at sunsets over Ribblesdale, the inexorable wheels of destiny are put into motion.

At Stonyhurst, on several evenings that December, he notes that the afterglow created by the eruption of the volcano Krakatoa in Indonesia months earlier appears lusterless, giving "to objects . . . the peculiar illumination which may be seen in studios and other well-lit rooms, and which itself affects the practice of painters," especially Rembrandt. These afterglows are like inflamed flesh, he thinks, or like reflections from a great fire, apocalyptic in size. And soon enough, these minute Victorian observations of sunlight and shadow will transform themselves into poetry of an extraordinary beauty and sublimity in what he will call the longest sonnet ever written.

Just after Christmas, Father Delany crosses over from Dublin to Stonyhurst to speak directly with Hopkins about his accepting one of the new professorships at University College, then invites him, with Father Eyre's permission, to return with him to visit the new Jesuit college in Dublin for himself. University College is actually two town houses—Nos. 85 and 86—facing onto St. Stephen's Green, the largest common in Europe, and situated next to the small Byzantine-style chapel marking the site of Newman's university founded there thirty years before. The college has been given thirteen Catholic fellowships by the government, each worth £400 a year. This will be Hopkins's salary, should he accept the double position of Professor of Greek and Examiner in Classics, though the salary itself will be poured back into the school to help keep it afloat. And while the Irish Provincial himself considers the two eighteenth-century buildings—both in deep disrepair—merely "dingy old barracks," Father Delany has won the day and will be allowed to refurbish them on the cheap for his new university.

The stakes here are high, the struggle being for the right of the majority Irish Catholic population to a university of its own. As the old teaching staff dating back to Newman's tenure dies off or retires, Delany plans to replace them with as many Jesuits as he can lure to Dublin. He proposes two Jesuits, Brother Robert Curtis in mathematics, a graduate of Trinity College, Dublin, and Father Hopkins in classics, both of whom he will report on at the end of January as being "the most qualified of the candidates" interviewed. Besides teaching, Hopkins will have the added responsibility of examining hundreds of students for matriculation six times a year in Greek and Latin. Then, after visiting the school, it is off to Clongowes Wood with Delany for a short visit with the Jesuits there. There is a photograph of Hopkins taken on the grounds late in December, with one of the ivy-laced main buildings as backdrop. Hopkins, in buttoned black soutane and biretta, looks very uncomfortable, his body imploding inward, as if he wished he were anywhere but here.

January 3, 1884: "I have to wish you a happy and a fruitful new year and to add my last comments, on the second *Book of the Unknown Eros*," Hopkins, now back at Stonyhurst, writes Patmore. He apologizes for not getting his comments off sooner, but—in an amazing feat of understatement—explains that his "time at the end of the year has been quite broken." There was, he writes, "a competitive examination held . . . the other day, with a prize for the best arrangement of living English writers in prose and verse: the winning selection and several others were printed in the *Spectator*. I think the prizewinner put Browning at the head of his list. In most lists Tennyson, Ruskin, Newman, Matthew Arnold, and Browning got high places." But, alas, Patmore's name he has seen nowhere. "Indeed I believe you were not in the running. And when I read *Remembered Grace, The Child's Purchase, Legem Tuam Dilexi* and others of this volume I sigh to think that it is all one . . . to see very deep and not to see at all, for nothing so profound as these can be found in the poets of this age, scarcely of any."

No doubt thinking of his own fate as he prepares to leave for Ireland, deemed dispensable for his perceived eccentricities, he notes that real excellence is too often overlooked. So it was with his dear "Duns Scotus when I . . . read him with delight: he saw too far, he knew too much; his subtlety overshot his interests; a kind of feud arose between genius and talent, and the ruck of talent in the Schools finding itself, as his age passed by, less and less able to understand him, voted that there was nothing important to understand and so first misquoted and then refuted him." Four months earlier, he had earnestly prayed to be lifted into a higher union with God, to be—in a sense—crucified like his Master. But Ireland? Who would have thought that Ireland would be his proving ground?

Saturday, January 5, 1884: Father Alexander Charnley, S.J., secretary to the General Provincial in Rome, writes Purbrick in London that "Fr. Hopkins is going to be a fellow of the new Royal University. He may be a success in the native city of Oscar Wilde, but I should rather be afraid that his appointment may be considered a fraud. However Fr. Delany is acting with open eyes. Even in his Oxford days," Charnley has heard, Hopkins's "future usefulness was questioned," a fact confirmed for him by an old friend of Hopkins's, Paravicini of Balliol.

There have been, in fact, two candidates for the Chair in Classics. One is Father Hopkins, the other Father Reffé, Prefect of Studies at Blackrock College, and Dr. Walsh, president of Maynooth, has been an outspoken and tireless champion of Reffé. On the other hand, Delany has the support of the Senate of the Royal University and has opposed Reffé on the principle that unless Catholic teaching is concentrated in a single institution—i.e., University College—there will be no chance at all of there being a real flagship Catholic university presence. Delany carries the day and Walsh's proposal is overwhelmingly rejected, and Hopkins is appointed to the position. But Walsh, who will soon become Archbishop, will not soon forget the perceived slight. The thought of having yet another Englishman teaching classics to Irish undergraduates is and will remain a sensitive issue with him.

Besides his having been a scholarship student at Balliol, and subsequently taking a first in Classics under Jowett, Hopkins is Delany's choice because he will be able to hold his own against the classics fellows at Trinity. So Delany explains to Dublin's Cardinal McCabe on January 23. This is especially important since old Trinity "prides itself on its [Latin and Greek] verse writers." To cap his argument, he explains that writing classical verse is Hopkins's strong suit. And so, on January 30, 1884, the University Senate votes to accept Hopkins, who in truth does not want the job, though he will of course in obedience do as he is bidden. Eyre for one knows just how disappointed Hopkins must be at having to leave Stonyhurst for Dublin, but there it is. Fiat, done, approved by his fellow Jesuits in England and Ireland and Rome. Ah well, Eyre writes Purbrick just after Hopkins has packed his things and left for Ireland. In poor Father Hopkins "we had a man of fine classical learning and perhaps overly gentle teaching methods." And some—who will go unnamed—having "stoned the prophet," will now "want to build him a monument!"

PART IV

DUBLIN

1884–1889

Robert Bridges and Gerard Manley Hopkins, 1888.

Chapter 15

Spelt from Sybil's Leaves:
Dublin, 1884–1885

Monday, February 18, 1884: A reluctant and apprehensive Father Hopkins, five months shy of his fortieth birthday, arrives by boat in rough weather at Kingstown and then is taken by tram with his few belongings to 85–86 St. Stephen's Green, Dublin, to begin his duties as Professor of Greek and Examiner in Classics for the Royal University of Ireland. Because he has arrived midway through the college's first academic year, he will not begin lecturing until November, though he will find himself soon enough inundated in the work of preparing and grading endless university examinations. The university itself consists of two adjacent Georgian houses that have now been yoked together. No. 85, the former Clanwilliam House, is the earlier of the two, built in 1738 and once an architectural jewel of Georgian Dublin. Designed by Richard Castle, architect for the rich and famous of Swift, Goldsmith, and Burke's Dublin, it has an imposing façade of Wicklow granite and a winged Palladian window facing onto the thoroughfare below. The large central hall—the Apollo Room—is decorated with stuccowork depicting the Sun God and his Muses, and the magnificent Salon—one of the finest examples of the Baroque style in all of Dublin—is crowned with an exuberant ceiling revealing a world of classical gods and cupids, the creation of the Lafranchini Brothers, the finest plasterworkers in Enlightenment Dublin, a far happier time for the Anglo-Irish Protestant ascendancy. Now, however, the rooms have been sectioned off or added to and all that neoclassical glory painted over in dark brown as befitting a Jesuit residence. The back of the building faces the Iveagh Gardens with their statues and sunken gardens, part of the newly rich Guinness estate.

No. 86, the adjoining building, built a quarter of a century later, features a staircase with pastel walls in Rococo, replete with floral swags and musical instruments once highlighted in a cake-frosting white, but painted over now in the same tundish brown. It was here, some thirty years earlier, that a Catholic university was first established, with John Henry Newman as its first Rector. And while—in the best of all possible worlds—Newman's *Idea of a University* had called for a kind of transplanted Oxford to rise up here in Catholic Ireland, the reality began falling far short of the ideal from the start.

"Your Eminence and dearest Father," Hopkins writes the octogenarian Cardinal for his birthday two days after his arrival at St. Stephen's. "Pax Christi—I wish you a very bright tomorrow and health and happiness and the abundance of God's grace for the ensuing year." He is writing, if Newman can believe him, "from where I never thought to be, in a University for Catholic Ireland begun under your leadership, which has since those days indeed long and unhappily languished, but for which we now with God's help hope a continuation or restoration of success," he whistles in the dark. "In the events which have brought me here I recognise the hand of providence, but nevertheless have felt and feel an unfitness which led me at first to try to decline the offer made me and now does not yet allow my spirits to rise to the level of the position and its duties. But perhaps the things of most promise with God begin with weakness and fear."

Sadly, however, he must report that "the buildings since you knew them have fallen into a deep dilapidation." They were already "a sort of wreck or ruin when our Fathers some months since came in and the costly last century ornamentation of flutes and festoons and Muses on the walls is still much in contrast with the dinginess and dismantlement all round." The only thing which still looks bright—"and that no longer belongs to the College"—is "the little Church of your building, the Byzantine style of which reminds me of the Oratory and bears your impress clearly enough."

And though living conditions here are Spartan at best, and though Bishop Walsh, as a sign of his disapproval of the Jesuit experiment in education, has had what remains of the old university library dismantled and shipped off to Blackrock College, Delany has still managed, with his unbounded energy, to gather under one roof an impressive array of scholarship from all over England and Europe. Besides Hopkins, who will teach Greek and Latin, and serve on the board of community *consultors* advising Delaney, there are a number of other Jesuits. First, there is the Frenchman, Father Jacques Mallac, whom Hopkins seems to have taken to right from the beginning, perhaps because they are both exiles here. Mallac, a former freethinker and lawyer who once practiced at the French bar before entering the Society, will lecture in philosophy until 1890, and then return to France. There is also the German, Father Kieffer, who lectures in the new electrical sciences, as well as four Irishmen—Father John J. O'Carroll, fluent in eighteen European languages; Father Denis Murphy, who teaches history; Father Edmund Hogan, who is pioneering in Irish language and history; and Brother Robert Curtis in mathematics, a brilliant young Jesuit from a distinguished Dublin family, who, because he suffers from epilepsy, may not be ordained.

Dublin itself, which a century earlier had been Britannia's greatest city after London, has since slid precariously into a cultural and economic backwater surrounded by slums. Other cities—Manchester and Glasgow and Liverpool—have met the challenge of rapid industrialization, but not so Dublin, which can boast only of its whiskey distilleries, Guinness's brewery, and Jacob's biscuit factory. And while there is a large professional class in the city—lawyers, doctors, judges, academics, university students, and bureaucrats—there is also a great deal of poverty, with women and children begging everywhere, and alcoholism among the ravaged poor endemic. The Act of Union and the subsequent end of the Irish Parliament earlier in the century means that many of the Anglo-Irish Protestant landed gentry now spend more time in London than in Dublin. And most of the last-century large town houses around St. Stephen's Green have been let to rent by absentee landlords. Many of the buildings look crestfallen and bedraggled, some having been turned into apartments in which whole families occupy a single room each. Mostly St. Stephen's Green has been spared the worst ravages of this new reality, but even here only one of the old houses—occupied by the Church of Ireland's Archbishop—still serves as a private dwelling.

Where the upper floors of the stately old houses have been turned into apartments, the lower have been converted into offices inhabited by lawyers, doctors, house furnishers, auctioneers, and the owners of small private schools. Only a few doors down from Hopkins's room is a temperance hotel, as well as the St. Stephen's Green Turkish, Electric, Russian and Medicated Baths, and the St. Stephen's Green Bazaar, where people can save a few pennies buying candles, deal furniture, and pots.

Off nearby Merrion Square are the gasworks and railway lines, and to the west of the Green—in the direction of St. Patrick's Cathedral (where Swift's bones lie) are the Liberties, dangerous even in daylight to walk through. Adjoining the cathedral itself is Bull Alley, with its slaughterhouses and dens of prostitution and endless pubs servicing the uniformed British garrison stationed at Dublin Castle. On the Green itself, a scattering of the city's poorest children play side by side with well-dressed middle-class children supervised by governesses talking with nurses rocking prams. That is, except when unemployment explodes, and then hundreds of the poor—squalid and hungry—exit the Liberties to erupt on the streets around St. Stephen's, especially on the north side, begging for scraps and pennies, or for anything to survive.

Like any city suffering from economic deterioration, Dublin has been steadily losing population, and with it the city's tax base, even as the numbers of the poor continue to grow. Disease has become more and more widespread, so that people from the country now fear even coming into the city. And though there has been some progress in making potable water available, efforts to modernize the public drainage system have foundered for lack of money, so that the River Liffey, which empties directly into the sea, continues to serve as the major sewer line, those living in the old stately buildings along its banks so defeated by the stench that they have abandoned the city for the countryside if and when they can.

Worse still are the private drainage systems and subsoils of the houses themselves, including the ones at 85–86 St. Stephen's Green. Scarlet fever, bronchitis, and tuberculosis are only some of the diseases that continue to claim the lives of the middle and professional classes as well as the poor, and typhoid, carried by infected milk and diseased drainage, is far more prevalent here than in London, Edinburgh, or even Liverpool. Within the city limits alone thousands of cattle have been crowded into unsanitary dairy yards, capable of spreading tuberculosis and anthrax.

And then there is the problem of underrepresentation in a city where Catholics make up 80 percent of the population but less than 40 percent of Dublin's professional class—its doctors and lawyers and professors. Even at that, the Irish Catholic professional class clings mostly to the lower rungs of the social ladder, due in part to the difficulty of moving upward, and to the fact of centuries of discrimination. Naturally, there are increasing sectarian and political tensions in the city, and to be counted an Irish Catholic is to be counted, with few exceptions, a Nationalist. Given who he is, Hopkins inevitably finds his closest sympathies with the Anglo-Irish professional class, Protestant and Catholic, though the latter have been branded "Castle Catholics"—that is, Catholics sympathetic to the crown—regarded as traitors by the Nationalists.

In the meantime, Anglo-Irish Protestants continue their retreat to the city's southern suburbs, where the only significant Catholic presence is among the domestic servants. So too with Trinity College, which has closed in on itself, avoiding unnecessary contact with the surrounding working-class Catholic population, although Catholics are now allowed to attend the university. Enter Hopkins, sent to Dublin to teach what is perceived as two all-but-dead languages to an Irish Catholic population far more interested in gaining what has been so long denied them: positions of economic and political power. For most of them—from the Catholic clergy on down through his own students—Hopkins, with his Oxford background and moreover an English convert to Catholicism, will remain under suspicion and an anomaly at best.

On the Friday after Ash Wednesday, February 29, Hopkins, here now two weeks, meditates on the crowning of Christ the King with thorns by the Roman garrison stationed in Jerusalem, king, that is, "not only . . . over the Jews but also born of the Jews to be king over others, the Gentiles." Of course the Romans have crowned him "in mockery, mocking both . . . at the Jews and him, at him for claiming to be a king and at the Jews for claiming to have one." Still, he sees, what the soldiers did "was mystical and both the crown and the adorations were types of his true rights and royalty." Just so, he prays now, as the long night descends over him, to "crown him king over yourself," and then "of English hearts and of Ireland and all Christendom and all the world." Consider, he adds poignantly, his hero's "mental pain: the humiliation, the terrible sense of having been abandoned even by one's own."

Sunday, March 2: As Christ "was led by the spirit into the wilderness," Hopkins prays now to be "guided by the Holy Ghost in everything." And five days later: "Seeing Christ's body nailed consider the attachment of his will to God's will." Then, once more, he prays what he had prayed for on his retreat six months before: to be "bound to God's will in all things, in the attachment of your mind and attention to prayer and the duty in hand; the attachment of your affections to Christ our Lord" over anything the world has to offer. *That* must come first.

March 7: "Remark the above address," he writes Bridges three weeks into his time in Dublin. "It is a new departure or a new arrival and at all events a new abode. I dare say you know nothing of it, but the fact is that, though unworthy of and unfit for the post, I have been elected Fellow of the Royal University of Ireland in the department of classics." He now has "a salary of £400 a year," but contemplating "the six examinations I have yearly to conduct, five of them running, and to the Matriculation there came up last year 750 candidates, I thought that Stephen's Green . . . paved with gold would not pay for it." True, "it is an honour and an opening and has many bright sides, but at present it has also some dark ones and this in particular that I am not at all strong ... and do not see at all how I am to become so. But to talk of weather or health and especially to complain of them is poor work."

The college itself is little more than "a ruin and for purposes of study very nearly naked." In fact, he has "more money to buy books than room to put them in." True, he has "been warmly welcomed and most kindly treated" by Father Delany and the staff, but nothing in his experience, including his time in Liverpool, has prepared him for the bleak reality of Dublin. The city, he has to confess, is joyless and "as smoky as London is," though he "had fancied it quite different." The generous open expanses of Phoenix Park are the one place where he can walk and meditate, but it is far off and takes planning to get out there and back. Yes, he can force himself each day to fulfill his duties, to say mass and lecture and grade a nation, but his spiritual life has always been sustained by the vital beauties of nature, as at Oxford and Wales, and all that seems sadly lacking here.

March 8: A meditation on the Transfiguration of Christ. It is good to think of the purity of Christ's body transfigured, he thinks, especially as a remedy against sexual temptation. And then to consider "the thought of [Christ's] mind and genius" as a hedge "against vainglory." Then he remembers something he had learned during his Tertianship: to try and enter "into the joy of our Lord, not his joys but the joys" he felt in being able to help others. Words to remember, to be warmed by, warned by. Two weeks later another meditation, this one on Christ's Five Wounds—his crucified hands and feet, and the lance wound that tore his heart to pieces. How important it is to keep focused on Christ in spite of feeling no consolation, as he tries to let himself fall into the waiting hands of God.

Meditating on the piercing of Christ's side, he sees it in a new and terrifying light: "the sacred body and the sacred heart" waiting all these millennia for the opportunity to discharge themselves and testify to "their total devotion ... to the cause of man." "The dense and the driven Passion, and frightful sweat," he had written eight years before as he composed *The Wreck of the Deutschland* in wild Wales, but felt now with a new intensity. "Thence the discharge of it, there its swelling to be." Six days later, he meditates on the agony of Christ's mother as she too joins her son in the ineffable darkness. A mother's fears, he thinks, her "discomfort, care, helpless grief, bereavement." Then, for a bare moment, he sees a splinter of light in the distance: "Christ's joy in spite of his sorrows," he thinks. Consolations in the midst of travail. Wish, he tells himself, "to enter into this joy."

It takes Patmore several weeks to read through Hopkins's poems, and when he reports back, it is only to say that he has been defeated by them. "The thought and feeling" of the poems, even "without any obscuring novelty of mode, are such as . . . require the whole attention to apprehend and digest them; and are therefore of a kind to appeal only to the few." In spite of which Hopkins has raised the bar even higher by "following several entirely novel and simultaneous experiments in versification and construction, together with an altogether unprecedented system of alliteration and compound words." Any of these novelties, let alone all of them, would be enough to produce a startled sense "of distraction from the poetic matter to be expressed."

The truth is that Patmore finds it as hard to follow him as it is to follow Browning, that prince of obscurity. And while "The Blessed Virgin compared to the Air we Breathe" and a few other pieces are exquisite, like Bridges he does not believe he "could ever become sufficiently accustomed to your favourite Poem, 'The Wreck of the Deutschland,' to reconcile me to its strangenesses." So there it is: of all his readers, not one of them has understood, much less appreciated, the first pressings of his mature work. When Hopkins answers Patmore, it is to tell him that his poems are not written according to theory, but according to feeling, that they are in the popular vein, and in "the native earth and real potato" style, "potato style," having come from Bridges's defining Hopkins's work as *perittotatos,* Greek for unusual, remarkable, and over-subtle, a word Hopkins has reworked for his own amusement. Better a joke than to laugh in total exasperation.

April 16. Wednesday in Easter Week: A reprieve. From Clongowes Wood College, where he has come for some well-deserved rest, he tells Bridges that he has not been able to get to his new plays, *Nero* and *The Return of Ulysses,* what with preparing and grading Greek and Latin exams. How he wishes he could get on with his own play, and hopes reading Bridges's work will spur him on in that direction. Patmore, he confesses, "did not on the whole like my poems, was unconverted to them, though he did express admiration for 'The Blessed Virgin compared to the Air we Breathe.'" The amusing thing is that he had copied out only a third of that long poem for him. He also notes that Dixon, now relocated to a new parsonage in Warkworth, has sent him a little volume printed by Bridges's small press publisher, Daniel, entitled *Odes and Eclogues.* He likes "the get-up" better than what Daniel did for Bridges's *Prometheus,* he says, and is even willing to admit that there may be some arcane advantage in publishing in limited editions of a mere hundred, "but it would be tedious to explain how." And then, suddenly, in capitals, he shouts: "AND WHAT DOES ANYTHING AT ALL MATTER?"

The truth is that he does not like the idea of Bridges publishing in limited editions, and would rather he came "before the public in the usual manner," that is, in inexpensive trade editions. Life here in Dublin is at an ebb, he adds. And—to make matters worse—a strong east wind is blowing, something far worse than anything he ever remembers in England. And then, feeling he may be spiraling into a depression, he adds: "I am in a great weakness. I cannot spend more time writing now."

A week later, Bridges writes to say that he is engaged to his lovely young neighbor, Monica Waterhouse, daughter of the architect. On the 30th, Hopkins writes back to say that the secret is out: that, yes, he too is engaged. That is, as Bridges turns the page to read on: "on examination papers." He is not at all surprised that Bridges should be getting married. In fact, nothing about marriage surprises him, having officiated at the marriages of many couples over the years. He is glad too because he thinks everyone "should marry, and do not see why" Bridges did not do so "years ago, except that" he was "waiting for Miss Waterhouse to turn up, indeed to be born, which having happened and being to complete your happiness I am very glad of it and feel sure she must be both good and charming." Of course he wishes both of them "great joy and am your (the both of yiz) affectionate friend." But the way he phrases his happiness suggests that he is also worried he may lose Bridges's friendship once he is married. As for himself, he is just now "recovering from a deep fit of nervous prostration. . . . I did not know but I was dying."

In early May, Patmore writes Bridges that for him Hopkins's poems are a vein of "pure gold imbedded in masses of unpracticable quartz." But he cannot bring himself to believe that the poems were not written from a preconceived theory, though Hopkins insists they are not. Still, Hopkins's genius is "unmistakable, and is lovely and unique in its effects whenever he approximates to the ordinary rules of composition." He wishes he had not "had to tell Hopkins of my objections," but it was either that or say nothing, "and silence would have implied more difference" than he felt. Seldom has he "felt so much attracted towards any man as I have been towards him, and I shall be more sorry than I can say if my criticisms have hurt him." A month later, Bridges tells Dixon quite baldly that Patmore has "seen Gerard's poems and has disliked them, admitting the genius." It is as Hopkins himself had feared would happen with most readers, even those disposed to like them.

Saturday, July 5: After five months in Ireland and correcting many many exams, Hopkins begins an Irish holiday, at the end of which he will travel to Clongowes Wood to make his annual retreat. And so he starts out for the west country: Castlebar, Letterfrack, Connemara, Galway, and Killarney, staying at Jesuit houses as he makes the circuit by train, trap, cart, boat, or on foot. His first evening out, he writes his father a birthday letter from Castlebar in County Mayo. He has bought "a circular ticket which will take me over [a] great part of Ireland," though being at Castlebar was not on the original agenda. Still, "fortune does and should play a great part in travel," as his father no doubt knows, randomness and chance being topics close to Manley's own heart, who recently published a book on the subject. "More by token I have written a paper on Statistics," Gerard adds, "from another point of view than yours." So, having "left Dublin this morning meaning to go to Westport on the coast," he "fell in with a clergyman [Father Blake] who, finding me to be a friend of a friend of his invited me to stay with him, which I gladly did." Tomorrow he will continue west in a trap with a driver he has just hired, taking in Ireland's west country along the way.

Two weeks later, he writes Bridges from Furbough House in Galway, a Jesuit residence. He has just passed through the rugged mountainscapes of Connemara, he explains, "the fine scenery of which is less known than it should be," and just yesterday "went to see the cliffs of Moher on the coast of Clare, which to describe would be long and difficult." And then he adds, almost as an afterthought, that "in returning across [Galway] Bay we were in some considerable danger of our lives." He does not elaborate on the sudden storm which nearly capsized their boat and which would have smashed it against the dizzying cliffs of Moher, though the image of such looming, disorienting mountains will soon enough work its way into one of his darkest poems. The house where he is staying is quite charming, he notes, and "stands amidst beautiful woods, an Eden in a wilderness of rocks and treeless waste." Indeed, he finds "the whole neighbourhood . . . most singular."

And now that Dixon has agreed to officiate at his wedding in September, Bridges wants Hopkins there to serve as his best man. "I ought to have answered you before," Hopkins begins, "but indeed I hardly thought you were in earnest . . . pleasant and honourable as the position would be." But what a strange position to put him in as a priest, and besides, he tells his

friend, the time is "most unpropitious," since he will have just begun another round of examinations, including coming up with questions, having
them printed, and then grading each and every one down to the last quarter and eighth of a point.

As for the debilitating weakness of which he had complained, it is a
nervous condition that will not let up, and that he sees "no ground for
thinking I can, for a long time to come, get notably better of it," though holidays ameliorate its effects at least for a while. There is no reason for alarm,
he assures Bridges, "though weakness is a very painful trial in itself." If only
he could get regular hard exercise. Turning to Bridges's query why he—a
celibate—wants to see Bridges married, Hopkins explains that the "single
life is a difficult, not altogether a natural life; to make it easily manageable
special provision, such as we have, is needed, and most people cannot have
this." Meanwhile, Patmore is still holding on to his poems, as if to give him
"the opportunity of repentance for not admiring all the poems," he jokes.
Strange that such a plain-spoken man should feel such "guilt and . . . repro-
bation" for not liking his poems. But it will be to no avail. "Like Esau and
Antiochus [Maccabee]," Patmore is not going to get the grace he needs to
admire the poems, and so seems now to be "in a fair way to die in his
sins."

On Tuesday, July 22, his annual eight-day retreat begins. He is at Clongowes Wood College and again begins with a meditation on praise of God
as man's essential reason for being. Praise by reciting the Daily Office, by
saying mass, especially proclaiming the *Gloria*. "Take it that weakness, ill
health, every cross is a help," he writes. *Calix quem Pater meus dedit mihi
non bibam illum?* the Latin has it. *Shall I not drink the cup which my father
has given me?* Consider, too, the necessity of remaining indifferent as to
where we are placed or to what work we are assigned, work which must be
done by "the elective will, not the affective essentially." What we should do,
and not what we would like to do. Strive to do God's will, he urges himself
on, and the affective will follow after. Once again he reminds himself to
spend time examining his days and asking God to strengthen his faith. Otherwise, he knows he will never keep this resolve. "Say the stations [of the
Cross] for this intention," he urges. Dwell especially on "how the Blessed Virgin praised God" and "rejoice in her glory" in having lived her life for him.

Father Denis Murphy, S.J., fifty-one, librarian and Lecturer in Religion,
Modern Languages, and Physics at University College, is his director this
year, and he finds himself dwelling especially on what Murphy has said
about "peace, contentment, a good conscience." Man "was created CRE-

ATED." He tries again: CR. . . . Again: CREA . . . Consider that "Christ was *created* [sic] to praise etc and so to save his soul, that is / enter into his glory." And while Christ's "sacrifice might have been unbloody," as Duns Scotus had come to understand, "by the Fall it became a bloody one." But if man was essentially created to give praise to the Creator for His illimitable gifts and graces, then why does he still not reck His rod? And what has that primal and constant refusal done to the very way we read the world around us? It would take a lifetime to even begin unraveling this mystery, and time is growing shorter. On the sixth day of his retreat, he turns forty.

Even as Hopkins ponders these questions, Patmore is visiting Bridges at Yattendon, and the visit goes well. "I am extremely glad to hear from both of you that you and Mr. Patmore were so well pleased with one another," Hopkins writes Bridges from St. Stephen's Green in early August. Bridges has offered to write out all of Hopkins's poems in a book and send it to him so that he can at least have his work between two covers, and for this Hopkins is grateful. "That book could be the greatest boon to me," he says, "if you are so good as to offer it—a godsend and might lead to my doing more. And if you were to complete 'Wild air,'" of which Bridges has the only full copy to be had, "that would be the *comble*. The former copy you made of it I must have, but it got mislaid in moving to Ireland."

He has added his 1877 curtal sonnet, "Pied Beauty," to the collection, and now encloses a copy of "St. Patrick's Hymn," something he thinks both "very beautiful and almost unique." In fact, he is thinking of publishing "a new and critical edition of St. Patrick's 'Confession,' a work worthy to rank (except for length) with St. Augustine's *Confessions* and the *Imitation* [*of Christ*] and more like St. Paul and the Catholic Epistles than anything else I know, unless perhaps St. Clement of Rome." He is actually "better and fresher for my holiday," he adds, though "how long this improvement will last" is anyone's guess, and he can only say with St. Patrick, "Salvation is the Lord's."

Three weeks later, he thanks Bridges for sending the manuscript book with his poems. As for "the piece of a new garment" he also found in the package, he concludes that it must be a cut of Bridges's wedding trousers. "Circumstances," he jokes, "may drive me to use my piece as a penwiper." And then he turns to Bridges's condemnation of his fellow Jesuits for not realizing that they have a poet in their midst. Surely the Society "cannot be blamed for not valuing what it never knew of," he explains. After all, how many people have ever seen his work? There were the editor and subeditor of *The Month*, to whom he offered the *Deutschland* and the *Eurydice*. Then his parents and two of his sisters, as well as Dixon, Patmore, and Bridges himself. Years ago, Father Cyprian Splaine—now teaching at Stonyhurst— wrote asking to see the *Deutschland* and a few other things, and Splaine in turn showed them to several other Jesuits. "They perhaps read it, but he afterwards acknowledged to me that in my handwriting he found it unreadable; I do not think he meant illegible." And, finally, there is Father Francis Bacon, stationed at St. Aloysius' in Glasgow, "a fellownovice of mine, and an admirer of my sermons [who] saw all and expressed a strong admiration for them which was certainly sincere." And that is all. But, then, "poetry is unprofessional. . . . No doubt if I kept producing I should have to ask myself what I meant to do with it all; but I have long been at a standstill, and so the things lie."

On the eve of Bridges's wedding, and deep in the midst of another round of exams, Hopkins sends off a note to the Bridgeses to wish them "the happiest of days tomorrow, and all the blessings of heaven on that and all the days of your wedded life. I did not consider the mails; the consequence is that these wishes must, like the old shoe, be sent *after* you; but there is no harm in that if when they overtake you they ever after attend you." A month later, he is still wallowing in papers. "Consider the services to God of men and angels," he begins, focusing on the necessity of performing in justice the duties assigned him, much as he hates them. "Consider your own misery and try as best you can to rise above it, by punctuality, and the particular examen; by fervour at office, mass, and litanies," he reminds himself once more, as well as "by good scholastic work" and "by charity if you get opportunities."

Then, with the nights growing longer and darker, he begins a sonnet on his winter world and his sense of self-wreckage and helplessness. It is unlike anything he has written before, darker and bleaker by far. "The times are nightfall, look, their light grows less," he begins, the lines recalling "The Candle Indoors" and the "Andromeda" of five years before, but darker, darker. Now he watches as his dappled world unwinds, like the British Isles themselves, their western third withering in a smoldering revolt:

> The times are nightfall, look, their light grows less;
> They waste, they wither worse; they as they run
> More bring or baser blazon man's distress.
> And I not help. No word now of success:
> All is from wreck, here, there, to rescue one—
> Work which to see scarce so much as begun

. Makes welcome death, does dear forgetfulness.
Or what else? There is your world within.
There rid the dragons, root out there the sin.
Your will is law in that small commonweal. . . .

The lines are tentative, shattered, raw. Not even work can help him anymore, for even that seems empty now of significance. Better, then, the death
of consciousness itself, better death. And then the turn: if you can't change
the world, try changing yourself, for God's sake and your own. It is what
Hopkins has been warning himself he must do in his self-examinations for
years, with mixed results. And now it is as clear as night that he will have to
descend deeper yet into the terrifying cosmos of the self before he can hope
to rise.

At the same time, he begins composing "Spelt from Sybil's Leaves," his
own *Dies irae*. It is a sonnet in eight-stress lines with strong medial caesu-
rae (the longest sonnet and the longest making, he will later quip) and it
will take two years before he can find the right ending, but he begins it now,
with the star-gazer looking upon the dark heavens. "Earnest, earthless,
equal, attuneable, vaulty, voluminous, . . . stupendous / Evening, dealing
the dark down, time's drone, sullen hulk-of-all, hearse-of-all night." Then a
revising of the second line: "dealing the drone-dark down, hollow hulk-of-
all, home-of-all, hearse-of-all night." And eventually something like this,
stopping halfway through the tenth line for the next two years:

Earnest, earthless, equal, attuneable, | vaulty, voluminous . . .
        stupendous
Evening strains to be tíme's vást, | womb-of-all, home-of-all,
        hearse-of-all night.
Her fond yellow hornlight wound to the west, | her wild hollow
        hoarlight hung to the height
Waste; her earliest stars, earl-stars, | stárs principal, overbend us,
Fíre-féaturing heaven. For éarth | her béing has unbóund, her
        dápple is at an énd, as-
Tray or aswarm, all throughther, in throngs; | self ín self stéepèd
        and páshed—qúite
Disremembering, dísmémbering | áll now. Heart, you round me
        right
With: Óur évening is óver us; óur night | whélms, whélms, ánd will
        énd us . . .

The cold winter sunset as prelude, then, to his own last and shortest day, when darkness shall cover his world, when the moral imperative and not the exquisite development of one's aesthetic sensibility will become the sole standard for judging the self's worth.

Preparing to lecture to his undergraduates that autumn, he pores over Cicero's *De Officiis (On Duty)* with them, stressing that duty is what "we are bound to in conduct, what we must do . . . if we would obey the sovereign lawgiver God." For, "just as the eye recognises light, colour, illumination; the ear / sound; the understanding / meaning / so the conscience recognises a proper object of its own," and that is "an imperative voice bidding and forbidding." More, God alone determines right and wrong. And so "we recognise the rightness of right" and "the wrongness of wrong . . . by an ordinary exercise of thought, just as we recognise that a line is straight or crooked, . . . a sheet of linen clean or spotted . . . by applying some standard, rule, or principle." It is the stress of conscience which "bids or forbids us," so that "we feel that self-preservation is right and so a duty, self-destruction wrong and so a sin, the sin of suicide, a case of murder." It is an odd and unsettling thought, Hopkins's preoccupation with suicide. "If there were not a power outside of us forbidding it," he explains to his students, "if the Eternal, as Hamlet says, *had not fixed his canon gainst self slaughter,* it might be unreasonable, wrong in the sense of perverse or crooked, to take our own lives, but who could forbid it?" Only the self, legislating its own extinction or refusing to give in to such carrion comfort. "But as it is," he adds, "we feel a higher will than our own forbidding the unreasonable deed." Cicero saw that there could be no "derivation of duty from one eternal unchangeable divine law binding all." But it is not Cicero who is foremost on his mind just now.

Of the vast variety of human pleasures, he explains, Cicero "takes no notice, seemingly because pleasure is not moral good." But, Hopkins demurs, there *is* such a thing as moral pleasure, which comes down to peace, pure peace, the "peace of conscience," and that is our real happiness, "for if pleasure be extended to all time or beyond this life and to our highest . . . faculties it will not differ from happiness." But what if we have failed in the duties assigned us? Well, we have the winter trees outside the darkening classroom windows, spelling out the scapes of the damned on the damascened darkness: wrong, right, right, wrong, tick tock:

> Only the beak-leaved boughs dragonish | damask the tool-smooth
> bleak light; black,

Ever so black on it. Óur tale, O óur oracle! | Lét life, wáned, ah lét
    life wínd
Off hér once skéined stained véined varíety | upon, áll on twó
    spools; párt, pen, páck
Now her áll in twó flocks, twó folds—bláck, white; | ríght, wrong;
    réckon but, réck but, mínd
But thése two; wáre of a wórld where bút these | twó tell, éach off
    the óther; of a ráck
Where, selfwrung, selfstrung, sheathe- and shelterless, | thóughts
    agaínst thoughts ín groans grínd.

One's duty writ large on the stars. This extraordinary poetic meditation on hell likewise follows the *Exercises:* what he had noted in his Thirty Day retreat and in his sermons on the last things—how the world of pied beauty must give way at last to a world where only the moral imperative tells. That, and the despair of the naked self knowing it has not measured up as now, like a broken tower, it begins to buckle and collapse in on itself, the mind alone remaining to torture itself with what it has chosen in place of God.

And this, also composed during that first fall in Dublin: thirty lines of a soliloquy by St. Winefred's killer, the psychotic Caradoc, from the second act of Hopkins's stalled play begun five years before. Act II—*Scene, a wood, ending in a steep bank over a dry dean. Winefred having been murdered within, re-enter Caradoc with a bloody sword.* He has never written anything remotely like this before, nothing nearly so dark, except in his meditations on the fall of Satan or his Ignatian sermon detailing the luminous depravity of the serpent seducing Eve. At last he has allowed himself the freedom to imagine what crossing the dark divide into pure evil might be like: the headiness of it, the momentary disbelief of actually having cut the head from the body of the one dearest to him out of lustful rage. One thinks here of Macbeth surrounded by his enemies, of Othello tortured by his own jealousy, of poor mad Lear on the heath. And so, "Heart, you round me right with," becomes now:

My héart, where have we been? | What have we séen, my mind?
What stroke has Caradoc's right arm dealt? | what done? Head of a
    rebel
Struck óff it has; written | upon lovely limbs,
In bloody letters, lessons | of earnest, of revenge;
Mónuments of my earnest, | récords of my revenge

On one that went against me | whéreas I had warned her—
Wárned her! well she knew. | I warned her of this work.

But did he actually murder innocence in cold blood like this? Surely, this must be a terrible dream, except . . . except for the bloody sword he holds in his hand:

> . . . here, here is a workman | from his day's task swéats.
> Wiped I am sure this was; | it seems not well; for still,
> Still the scarlet swings | and dances on the blade.
> So be it. Thou steel, thou butcher,
> I cán scour thee, fresh burnish thee, | sheathe thee in thy dark lair;
>   these drops
> Never, never, never | in their blue banks again.
> The wóeful, Cradock, O | the woeful word! Then what,
> What have we seen? Her head, | sheared from her shoulders. . . .

A disembodied head rolling over and over in the blood-smeared grass. This is darker than anything Hopkins has ever allowed himself to dwell upon in his poetry, and it tells us something of where the man has been these last months.

"I have been & am distressed by the news of your illness," Dixon had written him back in July, "& have had you almost constantly in my mind. . . . Will you let me know how you are?" But in spite of the urgency of the letter, it takes Hopkins three months to get back to him. Finally, in late October, from Milltown Park, he raises his head over the top of his infernal ditch to answer: "I am heartily ashamed of myself that I never answered your most kind and comforting letter received on Galway Bay in the summer." Nor has he time even now to answer, except to say that he is, "thank God, much better since then and now drowned in the last and worst of five examinations. I have 557 papers on hand: let those who have been thro' the like say what that means." Then it is back into the sulfurous ditch once more.

"I have had no time for unnecessary letterwriting and am just over a bout of severe work which leaves me jaded," he confides to Grace a week later. And now lectures are about to begin, to call them by too grand a name. Actually, these amount to giving lessons in Greek and Latin, and he is relieved to have the change, for they say that "public speaking, acting, preaching, and so on prolongs life." The weather so far this autumn has been very mild, so that he has not needed a fire in his room, and can still "sit in the open air." This is due, he suspects, "to the volcanic dust [from Krakatoa], which still floats and cannot come down; and for the same reason I believe the winter will be mild."

And then a word of consolation for Grace's still-fresh loss, and mention of the Webers, who "no doubt . . . love you," as she deserves "to be loved. And in the thought of your loss, mingled of sweet and bitter, I should think the sweetness would by degrees gain upon the bitterness." If he cannot find the consolation he so sorely needs, at least he can offer comfort to others. He has been to a concert here recently and encloses the bill, "with notes made on the spot," and hopes to hear more music soon. He has also made "the acquaintance of our two musical examiners here in Dublin: Sir Robert Stewart, who has a pleasant hearty undisguised snubbing way and has lent me his lectures," and the other Dr. Joseph Smith, from Worcester. He met Stewart—"we were intimate in about you could count forty"—at the Royal University "as the degrees were being conferred, including nine lady bachelors, 'girlgraduates,' one of them also a bachelor in music, Miss Taylor by name."

On Monday, November 3, he begins lecturing, and it will not be long before the myths start circulating about his scrupulosity in teaching. Stories such as: to make sure students in his classes do not have an advantage over other students, he assures them that nothing he teaches will be material for the final examinations, the upshot being that only a few of the more serious students continue to attend his classes after that, the others dropping in from time to time to find out what they can safely count on *not* having to study for. Stories too about his odd teaching practices, as in demonstrating how Achilles actually hooked Hector's bloodied corpse through the feet and dragged it around Troy's walls behind his war chariot, Hopkins lay on his back and had a student drag him around the floor. Or—in another version—dragged the student around the floor himself.

Some of his students will even learn that he writes poetry, for two of them—George O'Neill and Martin Maher—will recall his reading some of it to them, though Maher will admit he never had a clue what Father Hopkins was talking about. Maher will also remember Hopkins teaching Latin to a class of fifteen, in which he illustrated his points by drawing beautifully detailed sketches on the board, then erased them as if they were nothing. He was "a very good religious," and very devout and absorbed when he said mass.

A week into his teaching, Hopkins thanks Bridges for sending him some details about his life as a married man, and only wishes he had written more. "I have a kind of spooniness and delight over married people," he confesses, "especially if they say 'my wife,' 'my husband,' or shew the wedding ring." He looks forward to reading Bridges's *Eros and Psyche,* and is now awaiting civilization's executing "its daily eggtrick over the book with the usual adroitness as far as the south side of Stephen's Green," by which comic circumlocution he means the postman's punctual delivering of said book to him. He also mentions that he has written a short notice of Dixon for the fifth edition of Tom Arnold's *A Manual of English Literature Historical and Critical.*

He has also had "a great light on the matter of harmony," and has had the temerity to send a harmony for one of Patmore's lyrics on to Sir Frederick Gore Ousely, Professor of Music at Oxford, and is now eagerly awaiting his censure. At Stonyhurst, he had begun writing plainchant for Collins's *Ode to Evening,* for, "quickened by the heavenly beauty of that poem," he jokes, "I groped in my soul's very viscera for the tune and thrummed the sweetest and most secret catgut of the mind. What came out was very strange and wild and (I thought) very good." Later, here in Dublin, he "began to harmonise it, and the effect of harmony," well in keeping with the plainchant, seems to have created "a new world of musical enjoyment as in this old world we could hope to be." It is the same modified plainchant he has used to harmonize his still-unfinished "Spelt from Sybil's Leaves."

But the giddiness of that letter gives way to edginess a few weeks later when he tells his mother that he will not be coming home for Christmas this year, for if he came now he could not reasonably visit the following summer. Besides, traveling long distances in wintertime "is harder, more tiring, and the broken sleeps are a great trial to me." And then "it is so soon after coming to Ireland; it does not look so well." If he knew Millicent's convent address he would write her, "for what is gained in a world in which one scarcely ever meets one's family by not at least writing?" Nor has he ever written Lionel since his return to China, and that too weighs heavily on him. Alas that "letter writing, so pleasant in doing," should become a "most harassing duty to set to with other work on hand." And then there is Ireland, where he knows too well that their countrymen clearly "have enemies," both open and secret.

Life here at the college is "like living at a temporary Junction and everybody knowing and shewing as much," though he believes the university will weather the difficulties "for no other reason than that Fr. Delany has such a buoyant and unshaken trust in God and wholly lives for the success of the place." Bless him, he adds, for continuing to be "as generous, cheering, and openhearted a man as I ever lived with." In fact, the whole community here gives him "almost as much happiness, but in particular Robert Curtis, elected Fellow with me, whom I wish . . . you could someday see, for he is my comfort beyond what I can say and a kind of godsend I never expected to have." Curtis's parents live here in Dublin and he has often been to their home for a meal and some cheer.

Christmas in Dublin: On the 20th, a meditation on the Great O's of Advent: *O Sapientia. O Wisdom, who came out of the mouth of the Most High.* "Desire this heavenly wisdom," he exhorts himself. "Consider how the Scripture sets it above gold and all earthly goods, precious stones, by which you may understand gifts of mind. . . . Wish to see by its light." On Christmas Eve, his thoughts turn to Mary and Joseph. "Poor, strangers, travellers, married. . . . Their trials were hurry, discomfort, cold, inhospitality, dishonour. Their comfort was Christ's birth." Try at least for now to forget "your own trials, rejoicing over Christ's birth. Wish a happy Christmas and all its blessings to all your friends."

Writing to Bridges on New Year's Day, 1885, he admits that it would have been better for him to have gone home, rather than spend his holidays in Dublin. Besides, it "would have been the world of pleasant to have seen" the Bridgeses. One bright spot is that he has composed a harmony to the tune he made years ago to Thomas Campbell's *Battle of the Baltic,* which is at least intelligible, and he means to send it on to Parry to look at. "There is a bold thing in it," he explains: "in the second verse a long ground bass, a chime of fourteen notes, repeated ten times running, with the treble moving freely above it. It is to illustrate 'It was ten of April morn by the chime.'" And "if Parry should approve it I am made, musically, and Sir Frederick may wallow and choke in his own Oozeley Gore."

He is now sending Bridges what he has of *St. Winefred's Well.* "I do not believe you will succeed in producing a 12 syllable or 6 foot line which shall not, as you say, be an Alexandrine," he warns Bridges, who is experimenting in that direction in his *Feast of Bacchus.* He himself has had to grapple with this problem in his own play, and finds the meter "smooth, natural, and easy to work in broken dialogue, so much so that it produces nearly the effect of 5 foot blank verse; but in continuous passages it is a very different thing." In the more passionate passages—such as Caradoc's soliloquy—he has used sprung rhythm to good effect. "But it is strange," he adds, "that you should select for comedy" what he himself has employed for tragedy.

The following day, he is off to Clongowes Wood to make a much needed retreat under the direction of Father Peter Foley, longtime spiritual director at the college. As it is Christmas time, he meditates on the Coming of the Magi and prays "to be on the watch for God's providence, not determining where or when but only sure that it will come." The following night—January 6—he reminds himself to pray "according to Fr. Foley's instructions . . . for the spirit of love in all your doings. For indeed it seems a spirit of fear I live by." On the 19th, back at St. Stephen's, he meditates on Christ's cure of a demoniac. "Pray," he tells himself, "not to be tormented," consoled with the thought that at least the poor man did not kill himself, "because the devils were not allowed to drive him to that." Ah, he thinks, so even infernal tormentors are limited in the damage they can do.

The college is momentarily expecting "as a student and boarder AN IM-PERIAL PRINCE or at least a prince from the Austrian Empire," he writes his mother in late January 1885. "He has four names tied together with hyphens besides Christian names." He means Prince Maximilian Waldburg Wolfegg, who will be joined by his younger brother, Joseph, in April. Their father—a member of the royal house—has agreed to pay the princely sum of £500 for their two terms at the college. Then, in the midst of his letter, he hears the paperboys on the street below crying up the news of a series of explosions that have just rocked London. On top of which, if she could hear him sneezing with his infernal cold, she would "think it a dynamite counterblast to the explosions planted by Irish-Americans at the Houses of Parliament and the Tower."

And now the Prince's younger sister "wants to read some good English story books." Accordingly, Father Mallac, the force behind the two princes' coming to Dublin, went to his bookseller's to get some Catholic children's books, only to learn "that children were born in the first chapters of both of them." Now, this is not "a bad thing to do," he acknowledges in his deadpan manner, "and must be allowed also to the characters in fiction," though in one of them the child was stillborn. This, for a young countess, Father Mallac found too strong. So Mallac has asked him to name some books "which shd. be interesting and in which the personages should have got their birth completely over before the story begins." For his part, Hopkins mentioned *Alice in Wonderland*—a book he has never admired because it is not funny, as well as the stories of Mrs. Molesworth, Mrs. Ewing, and Miss Thackeray (modernized), and *Ruth and her Friends*, all highly praised, though he has read none of them. But Mallac doesn't want love stories either, which "is a great difficulty," for even "the most highly proper English stories have love in them." And so he wants her "to name some good books (1) in good English (2) in which the characters shall be born behind the scenes and come on the stage alive, (3) with no or the least possible lovemaking in them." Expense of course is "no great object to the princely exchequer."

January 26, 1885: News that the British garrison at Khartoum in the Sudan has fallen after a long siege, and General "Chinese" Gordon and most of the troops killed. For this national disaster Hopkins lays the blame squarely on Gladstone. The story leading up to this catastrophe has been in the papers since Gordon's arrival in Khartoum on the same day Hopkins arrived in Dublin, the General having been sent to the Sudan to oversee the evacuation of some two thousand women and children and six hundred troops. On top of which, the English consul-general to Egypt had begged the British to see to the evacuation of an additional fifteen thousand Europeans out of Khartoum and into Cairo. To do this, Gordon had tried to negotiate with Mohammed Ahmet, leader of the Mahdi, from Khartoum, but had been refused. In the months following, as Gordon found his own forces surrounded, he promised to make Ahmet a Sultan in return for his help, only to have Ahmet remind him that he already had the imperial powers of the Mahdi, and to demand that Gordon himself become a Muslim.

In turn, Gordon had telegraphed the British to say he needed only a few thousand Turkish troops to flush the rebels, but no help was sent. Then— for months after—only silence from the trapped garrison. In November, British forces sent to relieve Gordon were routed. Finally, on the evening of January 26, one of the pashas inside the city opened the city gates to the Mahdi. At the last moment, Gordon tried to make his way to the Austrian consulate, only to be shot dead and his severed head stuck on a pike and carried through the city amid wild celebrations. For Hopkins as for the English, it is a defeat for the British Empire beside which even Majuba Hill pales.

But there is trouble closer to home. On Sunday, March 1, a crowd of some eight thousand, together with a dozen bands, gathers in Phoenix Park to protest the expulsion of the Irish member of Parliament, Bill O'Brien, by the British Speaker a week before. On the fringe of the huge crowd in their black soutanes stand Fathers Mallac and Hopkins, alternately peering through a shared pair of opera glasses at the distant figure of the bareheaded O'Brien speaking from the back of a dray. With a cold east wind blowing, and at this distance, it is difficult to make out what O'Brien is saying. But there is cheering, and the sounds from time to time of a dozen Irish bands, their music intermittently squealing and thrumming as the wind rises and falls.

Then the Lord Mayor, presiding over the "monster meeting," makes a motion to great cheering and the waving of Irish and American flags as he condemns the expulsion. *When they struck at the most insignificant repre-sentative of the Irish people,* O'Brien shouts into the wind, *millions of Irish hearts felt the blow, and were only burning for an opportunity of returning it.* All of Europe is watching and have now seen that *in the heart of the British Empire, there is in unison with them a nation of Irishmen all over the globe, whose relations with England are simply the relations of civil war, tempered by scarcity of firearms.* True, there *were half-a-dozen Englishmen in the Commons for whom he . . . had a deep respect . . . and he had no hesitation in placing Mr. Gladstone first in the list.* But such men are *only as rain drops in the ocean of English cant and ignorance.* For the truth is that *the Irish heart would rather claim kinship with the Russian or Frenchman* (then a voice from the crowd shouting, "Or with the Mahdi"), *Aye, or the Arab of the des-ert, than with the English.* (More cheers)

Nor will it do for the English Ministry to insult the Irish people to-day and send over the Prince and Princess of Wales to-morrow. He means no slight to the Prince, for he is—as princes go—a good enough fellow, *and he should be sorry that the Irish people should treat an English Prince as disgracefully as the English have treated an Irish representative.* But it would behoove the British to remember that *there was no part of the world where England's Army was not confronted with dangerous foes.* So, if the English really want to send Prince Edward over, let them first raze Dublin Castle, empty the jails of political prisoners, disband the police, and change the administra-tion of the country. In fact, O'Brien closes, he has always kept the civic flag flying. But the day the Prince of Wales lands at Kingstown, he has vowed to take it down.

"Yesterday Mr. O'Brien M.P. held his monster meeting in the Phoenix Park to protest against his suspension," Hopkins writes his mother the fol-lowing day. As excitable as the Irish are, he says to calm her fears, "they are far less so than from some things you would think and ever so much froths off in words." Nor was Father Mallac, who was nineteen when he witnessed the revolution of '48 in Paris, much impressed. In Paris, he told Hopkins, "the motions of the crowd were themselves majestic and . . . organized themselves as with a military instinct." Not so here, where things seem so much more chaotic. Alas, "the grief of mind I go through over politics," he ends, "over what I read and hear and see in Ireland about Ireland and about England, is such that I can neither express it nor bear to speak of it." Just now, as he writes, the newsboys are "crying some bad news in the streets." But then, he sighs, "all news is bad."

Chapter 16

We Hear Our Hearts Grate
on Themselves: Dublin, 1885

A number of truly extraordinary sonnets, several with alternate lines attached, some left unfinished, like his other work, for years. Cries which have burned their way into the minds and hearts of hundreds of thousands of readers since. A hodgepodge, bitter spelt not from leaves of grass but from scattered leaves rustling across the floor to be read by some Sybil, syllables leaving the indelible impression of someone having been to hell and partway back. Pieces of cloth and flesh left behind for others to somehow reassemble. Among them, a sonnet written sometime between late 1884 and the spring of '85 , beginning with the complaint: "To seem the stranger lies my lot, my life / Among strangers."

A stranger to his old school now, to most Englishmen, to many of his friends, to his own Jesuit colleagues often, to his own family. And a stranger now even to himself here in Ireland, this lover of England, wife to his "creating thought," dismissed as an eccentric on both sides of the Irish Sea. And all—finally—because he has tried to do God's will and follow in the footsteps of Christ in deed and word. Christ, his peace and parting, his sword and strife, as Christ had warned would happen to those who followed him:

> England, whose honour O all my heart woos, wife
> To my creating thought, would neither hear
> Me, were I pleading, plead nor do I: I wéar-
> Y of idle a being but by where wars are rife.
> I am in Ireland now; now Í am at a thírd
> Remove . . .

And yet, he knows, from the friends he has made here in Ireland, "Not but in all removes I can / Kind love both give and get." Only there is this to consider: that a dark God should have hidden Himself from him, so that He is heard neither in his poems, nor in his classes (for he can see it, surely, on the yawning faces of his students), nor even in his letters home or to Bridges. "Cassandra wailings," his enemy Thomas Carlyle would have called them: a voice crying in the desert. Still, he believes, he holds in his heart a secret worth everything: Christ, his Word/Wisest. And like the good Jesuit he is, would get that news out to others. "But how? For Christ's own sake, how!?"

> Only what word
> Wisest my heart breeds dark heaven's baffling ban
> Bars or hell's spell thwarts. This to hoard unheard,
> Heard unhéeded, leaves me a lonely began.

"And there they lie . . . [the] beginnings of things, ever so many, which it seems to me might well have been done, ruins and wrecks," he will confess come May. And what word wisest—whether this be the unaccountable loss of his easy intimacy with Christ or the strain he feels in not being able to get on even with his own work, much less his poems, scattered here and there and piling up unpublished, or, when read in manuscript, misunderstood or rejected by his friends, Catholic, Anglican, *or* agnostic: all this leaves him always scrambling to defend his style, his meaning, his music. Always to be beginning again, beginning again, at forty a eunuch, a lonely began.

"To hunger and not have, yét hope ón for," Hopkins's dark doppelganger Caradoc sings in an ecstasy of despair, knowing that, yes, yes, he has finally given over the struggle and consigned himself to self-damnation, so that now he can settle on the sad scapes of his own self-preoccupations, and watch that self as if on some ill-lit stage "storm and strive and / Be at every assault fresh foiled, worse flung, deeper disappointed." Such turmoil and torment has, he swears, "a sweetness, / Keeps a kind of joy in it, a zest, an edge, an ecstasy, / Next after sweet success."

If you can't succeed, there is at least the perverse pleasure, as Milton's Satan knows, in going about, head unbowed, in a very special hell of one's own making, thinking: at least *I made this.* The heady wine of day-in, day-out failure. The rage and zest of knowing that, whatever else you do, you will fail again each done damned day. But is this Caradoc speaking, or himself? And if himself, how avoid the carrion comfort of such despair, of the sick self feeding vulturelike on the bones of the self? How find fresh water to revive the parched soul, the sweating self?

March 12, 1885. The Feast of St. Gregory the Great: Hopkins meditates on Pope Gregory's coming upon a cluster of Anglo-Saxon slaves being sold in the Roman marketplace, and thinking: But these are *Angeli—These are Angels, not Anglos*—and deciding to send missionaries to barbarous England to raise these tribes into the full humanity of Christ. A blessing, then, this coming of Christ to the English twelve centuries before. Ponder, he tells himself, "the best you know of England," then "the worst," and then, once more, his hopes for his beloved England's conversion. After everything, after every failure, even to bring his own family over with him, he will not give up on the dream of what England might be again.

Three days later, he meditates on the woman taken in adultery and on Christ's saving her from being stoned to death. Jesus' stooping to write "on the ground has something to do with [Moses'] writing of the tables of the law," he thinks. But the crowd will have to wait until this new lawgiver has drawn up the new law. Be careful not to pass judgment too easily, Christ warns them. "Let him that is without sin throw the first stone." Pray, Hopkins warns himself, "pray to keep to this spirit and as far as possible rule in speaking of Mr. Gladstone for instance." For it is just possible that the man might have some redeeming qualities.

March 16: A meditation on Christ's feeding of the five thousand with the pitiful little at hand. Remember, he tells himself, that "*every* effort is good," every effort counts with God, whatever the outcome, even for those whose days and nights are spent in grading a nation. The following day—the Feast of St. Patrick—he thanks God for the gift of the saint, and for the way Patrick was glorified in God, for he too—like Hopkins—experienced exile from England and suffering, struggling to maintain both his piety and his patience. Consider too the saint's "selfsacrifice and zeal; his miracles and success." And thank Patrick for his *Confession,* which Hopkins loves so deeply, breathing as it does "an enthusiasm which as far as feeling goes I feel but my action does not answer to this." He ends his meditation by begging for the saint's "help for Ireland in all its needs" and then for himself in his role as teacher and examiner. Two days later, on the Feast of St. Joseph, he meditates on the saint's "holiness and his humility," especially "in having to accept being thought Christ's father when he was not. Pray to him, then, as the patron of the hidden life." Pray to him for those "suffering in mind . . . as I do."

Five days later, he tells Bridges that he is, as always, "in a low way of health . . . especially now in Lent." Not that he is fasting, but still, "the restriction of diet" does make a difference. In fact, "the delightful old French Father [Mallac] who teaches Logic here . . . will have it that I am dying—of anaemia. I am not, except at the rate that we all are." Still, how he could do with a little more zest. He has been rereading Bridges's *Nero* "carefully for two months now," and finds that it breathes a "true dramatic life." Yet, he warns him, for a play to be acted, not only must there be the requisite stir of action but that action must be seen. So, if the death of Nero's mother is the climax of the story, "it shd. then be the climax of the stage business." You cannot trust the audience to get it, he explains, for "there is no depth of stupidity and gape a race could not fall to on the stage that in real life gapes on while Gladstone negotiates his surrenders of the empire." So much for Hopkins's nine days' resolve to henceforth think more kindly of the Prime Minister.

He is sending Bridges all he has of *St. Winefred's Well:* "the first lines of the first scene, a dozen lines of dialogue or less, as well as the beginning of another soliloquy," and—at the heart of the endeavor—Caradoc's "soliloquy after the murder, 71 lines," which has cost him "a very great effort." The writing of that, he confesses, has been "laborious, yet it seems to me a success," and "the unities will be much closer than in modern plays." But a bare week later he confesses that, though he "once thought well of the pieces," he no longer knows what he feels. Still, he hopes Bridges will see how, as the emotions become more intense in Caradoc's soliloquy, the rhythm too "becomes freer and more sprung." The truth is, he adds, that he has "written nothing stronger than some of those lines." Nothing that catches the zest, the heady wine of knowing that, whatever you do, no matter how hard you strive, you are powerless over the fact that you have not only lost what is most dear to you, but damned yourself in the process.

He has been setting Dixon's *Ode to Evening* to a new kind of music. This is a radical experiment, and "like a new art," the effect unlike anything he has ever heard. "The air is plain chant where plain chant most departs from modern music," though the harmonies "are a kind of advance on advanced modern music." The very old, then, welded to the most technically advanced. The combination of the two Hopkins finds "most singular" but also the "most solemn," and hopes he has "something very good in hand." He is thankful for Bridges's friend, Parry's, comments on his new harmonies, and though Parry's remarks are not encouraging, still "they are instructive and if I could manage it I should attend Sir Robert Stewart's or somebody else's course, as he advises." Besides, his own understanding of music is diametrically opposed to Parry's, for "what he calls variety I call sameness, because modulation reduces all the rich diatonic keyboard with its six or seven authentic ... modes to one dead level of major." He hopes Bridges will find the ode "slow and easy to play," but if he does not like it, it will be because he sees something Bridges has not. In fact, "if the whole world agreed to condemn it or see nothing in it I should only tell them to take a generation and come to me again."

What he has discovered in the old music are the grounds for a melodic line with "an infinite expressiveness and dramatic richness," so that "putting in or leaving out . . . a single note in an 'alphabetic' passage changes the emotional meaning." Anyone who knows and loves plainchant feels this, he adds, though "the rest of the world (and I expect this includes Parry), do not," for modern music with its tyranny of the bar falls far short of what music could express about human emotions if it were allowed to. Listening, for instance, to "one of Chopin's fragmentary airs struggling and tossing on a surf of accompaniment what does it matter whether one or even half a dozen notes are left out of it? Its being and meaning lies outside itself in the harmonies; they give the tonality, modality, feeling, and all." And so the human voice is drowned out by a complex of notes, which instead become the *raison d'être* for the music. Such music, then, is rather like Lucifer's falling in love with the sound of his own voice. But, he adds with a sardonic chill, if he should ever compose anything, it will probably be his "own requiem, like Mozart, but in plain chant." In any event, the music he speaks of here chimes eerily with both his unfinished "Spelt from Sybil's Leaves" and Caradoc's paean to despair.

Wednesday morning, April 8, 1885: The long-anticipated, long-dreaded visit by Edward, Prince of Wales (future King of England), and his wife, Alexandra, Princess of Wales and daughter of the King of Denmark, is "now an accomplished fact," *The Times* notes. The royal couple has "once more landed upon these still friendly though neglected shores, and have received an enthusiastic welcome." Seventeen years "have passed since the illustrious visitors were last here," during which time Ireland has experienced its share of adversities, "and generations have come and gone like passing waves." Still, those loyal to the crown, while challenged "by the ungracious action of a disloyal section, shook off their apathy," preparing "to give the Royal visitors such a reception as would efface any unfavourable impression . . . produced by the perverse action" of the Dublin Corporation "in refusing to greet the royal couple."

Still, the memory of the Phoenix Park murders remains fresh, so that police and military security for the visit have been high. "The Prince and Princess of Wales have been and gone," Hopkins will write his mother six weeks later. "They were well received all things considered: most people wanted to be civil and respectful, on the other hand it was felt with reason that to the royal family Ireland owes little gratitude. The Queen, who spends months every year in Scotland . . . has only thrice in all her [fifty-year] reign visited Ireland and never lived there." And Hopkins, having been on Irish soil for the past year and more, begins to soften in his opposition to Home Rule.

On April 20, he picks up a copy of the *Pall Mall Gazette* and reads of the death by drowning of Martin Geldart, his old Oxford companion of twenty years before. Geldart had been on the Newhaven ferry bound for Dieppe ten days earlier when he apparently pitched overboard into rough seas. It is the same Geldart Hopkins had described in a letter to his mother in his salad days as being the ugliest man he had ever laid eyes on. Still, they had become friends, and Hopkins had once stayed with Geldart and his family for a week in the Long Vacation. After Oxford, Geldart had gone on to become an Anglican curate, then, dissatisfied, left to become a Unitarian minister, losing more and more of his faith until even his liberal Liverpool congregation had dismissed him.

Three years earlier, he had published—in Oxford-blue cloth covers, and under the pseudonym Nitram Tradleg, his own name cleverly written backwards—a memoir describing the hell of his undergraduate years, calling it *A Son of Belial*, for which one was to read Balliol. A nervous, edgy, and strange figure, Geldart had recalled the uneasy religious ambiance of his time at Oxford, satirizing under other names Jowett, Liddon, and Coles, with Hopkins appearing as Gerontius Manley, Geldart's "ritualistic friend," the first name borrowed from Newman's poem of the same title. It was a reminder that, unlike himself, Hopkins had followed Newman over to Rome. "Gerontius Manley and I had many talks on religion," Geldart had written. "He was quite at one with me on the hollowness of Protestant Orthodoxy, but he had a simple remedy—the authority of the church," while Geldart himself had opted for Rationalism. "Gerontius Manley, with four or five of my [Anglo] Catholic friends at Belial besides," had "practically confessed by joining the Church of Rome to the disgust of Canon [Liddon]." As for their mutual friend, V. S. Coles, "logic was never his strong point; gushing was his forte. Gerontius gushed as well, but then he meant it." Just weeks earlier, Geldart had sent Hopkins a copy of his memoir, which he had since read. Ironically, he was in the midst of writing Geldart when word of his death came.

"I wake and feel the fell of dark, not day," Hopkins begins a sonnet written about this time:

> What hours, O what black hoürs we have spent
> This night! what sights you, heart, saw; ways you went!
> And more must, in yet longer light's delay.
> With witness I speak this. But where I say
> Hours I mean years, mean life. And my lament
> Is cries countless, cries like dead letters sent
> To dearest him that lives alas! away.

In the interstices of the long nights, alone, he has had all the time in the world (it seems) to dwell on his own bouts of near madness, melancholy, darkness, despair, even thoughts of suicide. Never-ending nights, years-long nights. The *Ow! Ow! Ow!* of those dead-end *hours* fermenting at last to *sours,* the serpent's hissing sibilants rustling through the poem. Darkness like a fell of woods—Dante's *selva oscura*—or the fell of an animal's pelt smothering him. To pray, to call out for comfort to dearest him, Christ, *Ipse,* the only One—only to learn at last that his prayers are like so many dead letters, sent into the insolid Void to an address and an addressee Unknown. To hunger after the Other, only to taste oneself, to *be* gall, *be* heartburn, to be thrown back on the pitiful self, in this reenactment of the close of "Spelt from Sybil's Leaves," to taste what the damned taste, their sweating selves, where the waters of the Spirit which should feed one have dried up in the long years' drought. And then to realize—for that brilliant final semicolon carries a nearly infinite weight—that bad as he has it here, the eternally dammed experience far worse, that his hell, bad as it is, is not at least that hell:

> I am gall, I am heartburn. God's most deep decree
> Bitter would have me taste: my taste was me;
> Bones built in me, flesh filled, blood brimmed the curse.
> Selfyeast of spirit a dull dough sours. I see
> The lost are like this, and their scourge to be
> As I am mine, their sweating selves; but worse.

Then *worse* giving way in another agonized sonnet to *worst:* "No worst, there is none," he writes, the monosyllables piling up and drumming their way home. A pitch of grief so intense as to become almost diabolically exquisite: "Pitched past pitch of grief, / More pangs will, schooled at forepangs, wilder wring." Wring, ring, rung, wrong. . . . To turn toward his

Comforter, Christ and the Holy Spirit, those unfailing Advocates, as he had
preached at Oxford and Liverpool to give others succor and consolation. Or
to Mary, sweet mother and comforter. Only to find they have all vanished,
leaving a terrifying emptiness behind:

> Comforter, where, where is your comforting?
> Mary, mother of us, where is your relief?
> My cries heave, herds-long; huddle in a main, a chief-
> woe, wórld-sorrow; on an áge-old anvil wínce and síng—
> Then lull, then leave off. Fury had shrieked "No ling-
> Ering! Let me be fell: force I must be brief."
> O the mind, mind has mountains; cliffs of fall
> Frightful, sheer, no-man-fathomed. Hold them cheap
> May who ne'er hung there. Nor does long our small
> Durance deal with that steep or deep. Here! creep,
> Wretch, under a comfort serves in a whirlwind: all
> Life death does end and each day dies with sleep.

How measure our own descent into the dizzying depths of the self?
What metaphor shall we use against those interior yawing sublimities? The
pain of separation from God, like an incessant throbbing in the brain, and
nothing for it. And what is left, what remedy against such a radical, unmap-
ping disjuncture—to name what is by its inchoate nature nameless—except
by the death of consciousness, and if not death, death's sister, sleep? "Tomorrow, and to-morrow, and to-morrow," Macbeth utters in exhaustion,

> Creeps in this petty pace from day to day,
> To the last syllable of recorded time;
> And all our yesterdays have lighted fools
> The way to dusty death.

The only comfort Hopkins can find in this Job-like, Lear-like whirlwind, try
as he may, is this: that all life—*all / Life*—"death does end and each day dies
with sleep." That, and the rough comforter he can pull over his head there
in his bleak upper-story room on dank St. Stephen's Green, a stranger in an
alien place far from the comfort of home.

"Mortal my mate, bearing my rock-a-heart," he writes in another unfinished sonnet from this time. It is addressed "To his Watch," its cold tick a
counterpoint to his warm heart's tock. Which of the two will fail first, he

wonders, "and lie / The ruins of, rifled, once a world of art?" But here's the difference, he sees: each man and woman has an allotted time, and no more, and then, as in "Spelt from Sybil's Leaves," comes "comfort's carol of all or woe's worst smart." Day gives way to day, and there is no recovering time. It has always been so.

"I will this evening begin writing to you," he signals Baillie in late April, "and God grant it may not be with this as it was with the last letter I wrote to an Oxford friend, that the should-be receiver was dead before it was ended." He means "poor Geldart, whose death, as it was in Monday last's *Pall Mall*," Baillie must have heard about. "I suppose it was suicide, his mind, for he was a selftormentor, having been unhinged, as it had been once or twice before, by a struggle he had gone through." And this on top of the suicide of Tom Nash a month before Geldart's. Nash: another Oxford classmate and friend of Geldart's, and a lawyer, like Baillie. That death too was most certainly a suicide, Hopkins believes, "and certainly too done in insanity, for he had been sleepless for ten nights: of this too you will have heard." It is a comfort to Hopkins—of such strange comforts can he count on now—and even "seems providential that I had renewed my friendship with Geldart some weeks before it was too late. I yesterday wrote to his widow." And so, at forty, he tallies up the losses: "Three of my intimate friends at Oxford have thus drowned themselves, a good many more of my acquaintances and contemporaries have died by their own hands in other ways: it must be, and the fact brings it home to me, a dreadful feature of our days."

Two weeks pass. He picks up the letter and resumes. In the past few months he has been going through old letters, he confesses to Baillie, "accumulations of actually ever since I was at school, destroying all but a very few, and growing ever lother to destroy, but also to read, so that at last I left off reading; and there they lie and my old notebooks and beginnings of things, ever so many, which it seems to me might well have been done, ruins and wrecks." Beginnings, only beginnings, leaving him "a lonely began." But among those old letters he has found comfort in Baillie's, overflowing as always with kindness. Once, twenty-five years before, Baillie had caught him staring intently at a watering hose on the Outer Quad and commented on it. But what was it, what was it Baillie had said then? Something like "Busy curious thirsting fly"? Or was it "The dying Christian to his soul"? Either way, there was a comment. That he remembers, even if the actual words escape him now. Or perhaps it was someone else who made the comments. And what is the nature of memory, after all, that we can reshape our pasts like this? Or is it that memory, which makes up so much of who we are, has begun to distort and disremember all now?

Surely Baillie must be wondering why it has taken him all this time to write a simple letter. Because it is a symptom of his "disease, so to call it," he explains, that "the melancholy I have all my life been subject to has become of late years not indeed more intense in its fits but rather more distributed, constant, and crippling. One, the lightest but a very inconvenient form of it, is daily anxiety about work to be done, which makes me break off or never finish all that lies outside that work." But it is useless to write on the subject of depression, for even when "I am at the worst, though my judgment is never affected, my state is much like madness." Worse, he sees "no ground for thinking I shall ever get over it or ever succeed in doing anything that is not forced on me to do of any consequence."

Sunday, May 17, and "still winter." Today he begins another sonnet cursing the long winter and the cheerless east wind, gets the first quatrain down, then lets it spin off into the world of lonely begans:

> Strike, churl; hurl, cheerless wind, then; heltering hail
> May's beauty massacre and wisped wild clouds grow
> Out on the giant air; tell Summer No,
> Bid joy back, have at the harvest, keep Hope pale.

Hail is covering the streets, he tells his mother that same day, "like pailfuls of coarse rice" spilled. He is still languishing, but manages to hobble on. How he would love to go to sea for six months, or see Epping Forest with Everard come summer.

Still later that same day, he begins a letter to Bridges, once again apologizing for his silence, due solely "to work, worry, and languishment of body and mind—which must be and will be," his fits of melancholy at their worst resembling madness. He needs change, but that he cannot often get. Bridges's *Ulysses* is a fine play, Hopkins acknowledges, but the most he can summon is "a dry admiration." Its worst fault is its unreality, the bringing in "a goddess among the characters," a dramatic strategy which revolts him. "Believe me," he adds, "the Greek gods are a totally unworkable material; the merest frigidity," and they will "chill and kill every living work of art they are brought into."

For, besides the hideous, unspeakable stories told of them, they are neither ladies nor gentlemen but cowards only: "loungers, without majesty, without awe, antiquity, foresight, character; old bucks, young bucks, and

Biddy Buckskins. What did Athene do after leaving Ulysses? Lounged back to Olympus to afternoon nectar." Such images have their effect on the psyche, he knows, long after the stories in which they are imbedded are forgotten. They are dangerous, for they gnaw at one's peace of mind and serenity. Then too Bridges's archaisms destroy the play's earnestness. Five months later, Hopkins will have to explain himself to Dixon as well. No doubt, he will tell Dixon, the Greek myths are more beautiful "than other mythologies as Homer's epic is [superior to] other epics," free as it is "from that cumber of meaningless and childish rubbish which interrupts and annoys one even in the midst of fine invention in for instance the Irish legends."

But since mythology is the historical part of religion, he can only feel loathing and horror when he thinks "of man setting up the work of his own hands." The Indian gods at least are imposing, but the Greek gods remind him of "some company of beaux and fashionable world at Bath in its palmy days or Tunbridge Wells or what not." Still, they are "susceptible of fine treatment, allegorical treatment for instance," and handled in this way give "rise to the most beautiful results," since "the moral evil is got rid of and the pure art, morally neutral and artistically so rich, remains and can be even turned to moral uses." So with his own Perseus/Christ and Andromeda. But how can "the heathen gods . . . be taken seriously on our stage," or even humorously, for that matter? Still, he knows he must have "damped and damned and . . . hurt Bridges" in telling him so, and for that he is sorry.

But as for *St. Winefred's Well,* how could Bridges think he would "in cold blood write 'fragments of a dramatic poem'?" For him, "a completed fragment, above all of a play, is the same unreality as a prepared impromptu." He sent what he had because he hoped Bridges might encourage him to continue. For "in matters of any size" he "must absolutely have encouragement as much as crops rain." And then he mentions that he has "after long silence written two sonnets, which I am touching: if ever anything was written in blood one of these was." Exactly which two of the sonnets of desolation he is referring to he does not say, but lines like "I am gall, I am heartburn. God's most deep decree / Bitter would have me taste: my taste was me; / Bones built in me, flesh filled, blood brimmed the curse" and "My cries heave, herds-long; huddle in a main, a chief- / Woe, world-sorrow; on an áge-old ánvil wínce and síng" are surely strong contenders. But these Hopkins cannot bring himself now to show to anyone, not even Bridges. Or especially Bridges, who would diagnose them as signs that his friend's life is as much a failure as poor Geldart's was, if all were known.

He has been seventeen months in Ireland now, without seeing his family once. How he thirsts to be back on English soil. And so he writes Addis to say he would love to see him when he gets back to London. How good it would be to talk over their lives as converts and now as priests. Addis sends him a short note from his parish in Sydenham in South London to say a bed is at his service there and he will be most welcome. At the beginning of August, Hopkins is back at Oak Hill, and the following day takes the train down to Addis's parish, Our Lady and St. Philip Neri, to celebrate mass and to preach. It is a new church, just three years old, and it will serve the parish for the next fifty-five years until it is obliterated by German bombers in 1940. On this particular Sunday in the summer of 1885, though, Hopkins preaches on the Pharisee and the Publican, a sermon he has now used three times. He has a particular reason for wanting to preach on the topic of self-righteousness, for Addis has told him that he is being carefully watched by one of his parishioners: a busybody of a woman who finds Addis's sermons too unorthodox and so has been taking notes in order to present evidence against him to the Bishop.

"Two men went to the Temple to pray," Hopkins tells Addis's congregation. "When they went home after their prayer one . . . was made just, and the other was not." What he is most anxious to do today, then, is to advise both himself and the congregation "against the sin of pride," for in a few minutes' time, "one man [was] put into the way of salvation; the other . . . of eternal ruin." There is a suddenness about the story, Hopkins stresses, "as if the way of God were full of incalculable hurricanes and reverses, in an instant building up and in the same casting down, making it seem better . . . to live recklessly and trust to a single hearty act of sorrow than to toil at prayers and mortifications which a breath of pride may in one fatal instant shatter and bring to nothing." Let him (or her) who has ears to hear hear.

He spends a week at Oak Hill with his family, and then joins them for their summer holiday in Midhurst in West Sussex, twenty-five miles west of Horsham. On August 17, he leaves to spend two days with the Patmores at Hastings in East Sussex, seventy miles to the southeast. Then, on the evening of the 19th, he takes the train to Holyhead and the overnight ferry back to Kingstown and Dublin. His holidays are over. The Patmores, he writes his mother the following day, were very kind and the current Mrs. Patmore he found to be "a very sweet lady." There were also two daughters there by Patmore's first wife, "very nice, not handsome, one [Bertha] sadly lame since a child but a most gifted artist, a true genius," who "draws butterflies, birds, dormice, vegetation, in a truly marvellous manner; also illuminates." And then there was little Piffy by the present Mrs. Patmore: Francis Joseph Mary Epiphanius Patmore, "a very interesting and indeed alarming little two-year-old born on Twelfth-night," of "such a strange sensibility and imagination that it beats anything I ever saw or heard of. He treats flowers as animated things, animals as human, and cries—howls—if he thinks they are hurt or even hears of their being hurt." Such behavior, he confesses, he "should not like . . . in a brother of mine."

Before leaving for Clongowes Wood to make his annual eight-day retreat, he writes Patmore to thank him for his hospitality. During one of their private talks, Patmore, always fascinated by the mystical and the erotic, had asked him what he thought about religious contemplation leading to sexual intercourse, a subject Hopkins's training has taught him to find suspect—hideous, in fact—and which he does not at all feel comfortable discussing, so that he had put off Patmore by promising to write him on the subject once he knew something more. It is a sad fact of the human condition, he tells Patmore now, that "anything however high and innocent may happen to suggest anything however low and loathsome." But, as he is on the subject, he will mention

> among the abuses high contemplation is liable to three things which have come under my notice—(1) Molinos was condemned for saying . . . that during contemplation acts of unnatural vice might take place without the subject's fault, being due to the malice of the devil and he innocent; (2) Fr. Gagliardi S.J. (early in the history of our Society) found a congregation of nuns somewhere in Italy who imagined that such acts were acts of divine union; (3) such practices appear widely in the Brahmanic mystic literature, though naturally the admirers of the Vedas and their commentators have kept dark about it. Even St. Jude seems to allude to such practices in his Epistle.

He is sorry to disgust Patmore "with these horrors; but such is man and such is Satanic craft."

Ah, the havoc and the glory of mortal beauty and of our complex responses to it. It is a topic Hopkins finds himself once more wrestling with during his retreat. There is of course Patmore's preoccupation with sexuality and Christianity. But there is another thing that has come to his attention, which is even more troubling. During his stay at Sydenham, Addis had told him in strict confidence that he had been seeing a woman, one of his parishioners. They have been very discreet—for surely if the disgruntled female parishioner who has been watching him like a hawk had even suspected a liaison, there would be no need to take notes of Father Addis's sermons, for the other would be reason enough for his immediate dismissal.

No doubt Hopkins has urged Addis, who has—like all parish priests—made a solemn promise of chastity, to end the relationship at once. But Addis is too deeply involved, and—whatever he may have promised Hopkins—he will continue to see the woman until at last he leaves the priesthood (and the Church) and subsequently marries her. And so now, in meditating on the Ignatian Foundation and Creation that Sunday, August 23, Hopkins composes a new sonnet, beginning with the question: "To what serves Mortal Beauty?" It is a poem that directly addresses God's purpose in creating physical beauty and our desire to possess it. But how possess it? He knows too well—as everyone learns sooner or later—that physical beauty has a deeply erotic charge, is dangerous, unsettling, and can set the blood dancing. That, as charged as music can be, a beautiful or handsome face will throw us out of gaze and unbalance us in an instant, the image of the desired replaying itself over and over in the mind's eye until caution itself comes to count as nothing.

Of course, that is what mortal beauty is meant to do, Hopkins knows: keep "warm / Men's wits to the things that are," to the power and wonder of the Creator who fans fresh our imaginations with so many possibilities. But, he insists, we are meant merely to meet it, acknowledge it, rather than stare it out of countenance until we begin to idolize it. For we *will* turn our attention to something, whether to the sacred or "block or barren stone" or calf or erotic image. Consider our own history, Hopkins says, English boys brought as slaves to Rome to be sold on the block, and all that entailed: "lovely lads once, wet-fresh windfalls of war's storm," and how Pope Gregory, catching sight of them in the Forum, was stirred to send missionaries to Britain to lift such a people from slavery into freedom. It is for us, then, to "merely meet" beauty, own it, "Home at heart, as heaven's sweet gift," and then leave it alone, to wish instead for that better beauty, God's life in us. So he has warned himself many times over, maintaining a strict chastity of the eyes as he winds his way through the siren call of life's temptations.

A few days later, as he meditates now on Christ's suffering, he composes yet another powerful sonnet: this one on refusing to give in to the temptation to despair, whether as Geldart and Nash had, or as Addis seems destined to do. Yes, he can feel his exhausted self going slacker and slacker, like a rope unraveling strand by strand. How easy to just let go the oar and go under, feasting on the carrion comfort of despair, to cry out, "I can no more," as Newman's Gerontius had once cried out. Gerontius Manley, indeed! But no, there *is* something he can do: hope, wish the long night over and a beacon light shine his way. What in God's name *is* this crippling force, this thing that plays him as a cat plays a mouse or a lion its crippled prey? Why rude (rood) on him, helpless as he is, his all-powerful wring-world right foot rock? Why toss him about like some winnower tossing grain into the air in order to separate it from the chaff, if not that the grain that makes the bread might lie "sheer and clear"?

> Not, I'll not, carrion comfort, Despair, not feast on thee;
> Not untwist—slack they may be—these last strands of man
> In me ór, most weary, cry *I can no more*. I can;
> Can something, hope, wish day come, not choose not to be.
> But ah, but O thou terrible, why wouldst thou rude on me
> Thy wring-world right foot rock? lay a lionlimb against me? scan
> With darksome devouring eyes my bruisèd bones? and fan,
> O in turns of tempest, me heaped there; me frantic to avoíd thee
> > and flee?

And now, in the midst of his retreat, he glimpses into the heart of the matter to see what has been going on all these many months. It is nothing less than his having wrestled with his own dark angel, and this his crucifixion. More, it is God he has been wrestling with all these years, breaking that stubborn will of his that would say yes, but always with a yet, and yet, and a yet. On retreat at Beaumont exactly two years before, he had asked Christ and his mother to lift him up so that he might enter more completely into Christ's total emptying of himself on the cross. And now here he is, uttering the very words Christ spoke as he hung there, looking about, thirsting, uttering the opening lines of the 42nd Psalm, the very words misunderstood by those below watching him die. *Eli eli lama sabbachthani: My God, my God, why hast thou forsaken me?*:

> Why? That my chaff might fly; my grain lie, sheer and clear.
> Nay in all that toil, that coil, since (seems) I kissed the rod,
> Hand rather, my heart lo! lapped strength, stole joy, would laugh,
> > cheer.
> Cheer whóm though? the hero whose héaven-handling flúng me,
> > fóot tród

Me? or mé that fóught him? O whích one? is it éach one? That
       night, that yéar
Of now done darkness I wretch lay wrestling with (my God!) my
       God.

To soldier on, then, regardless of what others do, including his fellow
priests falling along the wayside. He has been given his orders and, in the
spirit of his Order, he will do his duty to the best of his failing abilities. And
since his orders have called for him to be in Ireland when he would rather
be anywhere else, and to do the work (useless as it might seem) of examining and instructing a nation, many of whom resent his presence among
them, why then, so be it. Soldiers. Why is it we feel a surge of pride when we
see our soldiers parade smartly past in their uniforms, even when we know
that among them must be the occasional rapist or slacker or thief or cold-
eyed killer?

Surely he has spent enough time now reading the papers or giving counsel in the confessional box to know that even these men—Britain's finest—
are, like everyone, frail clay. No, worse: foul clay. Still, it is the heart calls the
calling manly, guesses, hopes, even makes believe the soldier or sailor is
there to protect the innocent, the women and children, to go into a situation where most of us would rather not find ourselves, to do the right thing.
Just so, when we see a noble piece of art, a poem, say, we want to believe the
artist or poet is no less, even though we know better, that indeed the uniform (or habit)—red (or black)—at best can only approximate the complexity of the one who wears it, and so "deems; déars the ártist áfter his árt;
/ So feigns it finds as sterling | all as all is smart."

And so with Christ, who likewise knew war and rumors of war, who
slogged his way through, faced Herod, faced the Pharisees, faced the crowds
who followed him when it suited themselves, then turned away. Faced cen-
turions, faced the Temple police sent out to take him in the middle of the
night there by the olive press, protected his followers, who then turned and
fled like shot dogs, leaving even their clothes behind in the scramble under
the feverish torchlights. Faced the High Priest Caiaphas finally, and Caesar's own man, the steely-eyed Pilate and the playboy Herod, faced his tor-
turers and the conscripts who nailed him to the cross.

Christ, who can reeve a rope best, hold it together, keep those last
strands of a man from coming apart, who watches us now in company with
his Father, having served his time, Christ playing, but playing for keeps,
and—seeing one of us do all we can—leans forward, this Paraclete and

Comforter, this good captain, to embrace and kiss our cheek, and call it what it is: a Christ-done deed, Christ acting here, now, in this time and place, at Clongowes Wood College outside Dublin, in the summer of 1885, as in ten thousand places, *anno domini.*

"Let him who is in desolation strive to remain in patience," the *Spiritual Exercises* counsel, "which is the virtue contrary to the troubles which harass him." "Patience, hard thing!" Hopkins returns now, in this sequel to his curtal sonnet "Peace" written six years earlier. "O surely," he had written then, "reaving Peace, my Lord should leave in lieu / Some good! And so he leaves Patience exquisite, / That plumes to Peace thereafter." But that was then, and hard experience has taught him that patience has other qualities than exquisiteness. Hard it is even to ask for patience, or even deem it worth having, especially when deep anxiety verging on madness seems the order of each day.

Patience means war within, means wounds. Patience means weariness, means time's taskings, to be passed over, do without, be tossed about. Means hard obedience, doing what your superiors tell you to do, even when your heart flinches from the doing. Means having friends who seem never to understand the value of what you have done, whether with one's life or one's work. But how else learn patience, except through testing it? Otherwise patience remains a virtue in name only:

> the hard thing but to pray,
> But bid for, patience is! Patience who asks
> Wants war, wants wounds; weary his times, his tasks;
> To do without, take tosses, and obey.
> Rare patience roots in these, and, these away,
> Nowhere.

Isn't patience what his Master had to learn? Not only with the crowds who turned away, or with the authorities who would trap him, but even with his own disciples, including Peter, the one he had chosen to establish his community when he should be taken from them? Patience is there to cover the human wreck to which it roots itself, the way purple ivy covers the walls of old monasteries and bare ruined choirs or buildings along St. Stephen's Green, the wrecks of things long past any purpose they might ever have had. Patience shows itself in purple-crimson flowers and seas of liquid leaves riffling in the breeze and sun all day, so that no one can count how great the cost to the ruined edifice within. How good and kind the patient man is, they say, without any idea of what he has suffered. And we? We who have been there? "We hear our hearts grate on themselves: it kills / To bruise them dearer."

But so it is: our rebellious wills must be broken, so that—and he can barely get the words out between his clenched teeth—"we do bid God bend to him even so." And what is the sweet reward for patience, then? What can we hope for? Human kindness and a deeper understanding of others, even if one is misread and misunderstood. Cell by cell, drop by drop, "Patience fills / His crisp combs" the way bees collect the pollen from the ivy flowers, transforming it into honey, gathering itself to a greatness, like that other metaphor of olive oil pressed and gathering, or like Andromeda waiting patiently for her Perseus to rescue her:

> And where is he who more and more distils
> Delicious kindness?—He is patient. Patience fills
> His crisp combs, and that comes those ways we know.

Time then, to tell himself (again) to rest, to realize that it is not up to him to grant himself the spiritual consolation and peace he so desires and needs, that that must come in God's own time, when the work of forging the soul has been deemed at least begun. "My own heart let me more have pity on," Hopkins tells himself, "let / Me live to my sad self hereafter kind, / Charitable" and not, he says pointedly of himself what he had said of Nash and Geldart, "live this tormented mind / With this tormented mind tormenting yet." "Comforter, where is your comforting?" he had asked earlier. One thing he does know now: that where he finds himself, here in Ireland in the late summer of 1885, he can no more find comfort

> By groping round my comfortless, than blind
> Eyes in their dark can day or thirst can find
> Thirst's all-in-all in all a world of wet.

There is a profound spiritual insight here, and it is this: That one may be surrounded by God's daylight and yet be blind to it. Just so, there are times when thirst can never be satisfied, though we be surrounded with a world of wet, as Coleridge's Ancient Mariner surely knew, and as those shipwrecked at sea know all too well. It is not for us to unlock God's consolation, especially when our self-will, our dogged determination to do it our way, insists on blocking the light. And so, he advises his "Soul, self . . . poor

Jackself," jaded as it is, to "call off thoughts awhile / Elsewhere; leave comfort root-room; let joy size / At God knows when to God knows what." And you can hear the exasperation—"God knows when" this is going to happen, and only "God knows what" he has in store for him. In any case, God's "smile / 'S not wrung, see you," not forced, for if it is his consolation we seek, we will have to realize sooner or later that we are not God. It is in fact a sign of God's consolation that it should come "unforeseen times rather— as skies / Betweenpie mountains—lights a lovely mile," the way, after a long day of rough weather, the setting sun suddenly pies between two mountains and lights up the way ahead.

Tuesday, September 1, and back at St. Stephen's Green: "I have just returned from an absurd adventure," he writes Bridges in a lighter tone, having tasted a new sense of lightness and freedom in ways he had not foreseen. It is an adventure, "which when I resigned myself to it I could not help enjoying." Like some colossal smile, lighting a lovely mile of our journey at the end of a retreat, and in an instant putting things in their proper perspective, a smile miles wider, in fact, than that stormfowl's "colossal smile" he had sung of six years earlier in "Henry Purcell" as its pelted plumage faced into the wind to begin its ascent. "A hairbrained [sic] fellow [named Sweetman] took me down to Kingstown and on board his yacht and, whereas I meant to return to town by six that evening, would not let me go either that night or this morning till past midday. I was afraid it would be compromising, but it was fun while it lasted."

He has been to England and back, he tells Bridges now, and managed to see his family, Patmore, and several other old friends (Addis among them) and even make some new ones, among them W. H. Cummings, "the tenor singer and composer, who wrote the *Life of Purcell*," and who showed him "some of his Purcell treasures and others" and has promised to send him several things. The truth is, he confesses, that he did not try to see Bridges, for he was not sure if he would be welcome just now. Of course he is sorry "to hear of Mrs. Bridges' disappointment: somehow I had feared that would happen."

He has a new batch of sonnets he wants to send Bridges: "five or more," four of which "came like inspirations unbidden and against my will," as if he would just as soon not have written them, they have cost him so much. If only he could produce something of value—he adds, still not understanding what he has forged in the fire of his trials—he "should not mind its being buried, silenced, and going no further." What kills him is "to be time's eunuch and never to beget." And while his holiday has given him "some buoyancy," he fears he shall soon "be ground down to a state like this last spring's and summer's, when my spirits were so crushed that madness seemed to be making approaches—and nobody was to blame, except myself partly for not managing myself better and contriving a change."

But the demons are back soon enough. September and October are taken up with grading Greek exams with great scrupulosity, knowing that a low mark will mean someone's not being able to attend one of Ireland's universities. And so he has devised a point and half-point and quarter-point and eighth-point system for hundreds on hundreds of candidates, staying up late in his room, a wet towel about his head to ease the migraines, reading and rereading mediocre papers to be as fair as he possibly can. It is killing work, and it takes a further toll on his eyes and his health. In early November, he meets Father John Conmee by chance in O'Connell Street, who invites him out to Clongowes Wood to take his rest. And suddenly Hopkins takes his hand there in broad daylight and kisses it, he is so thankful, thankful, like that kitten lapping Hopkins's own hand years before, though his colleague's extravagant gesture of course quite disconcerts Conmee.

From Clongowes Wood, Hopkins writes Everard, now twenty-five, who has recently read his *Eurydice*. Looking back at the poem, Hopkins wonders if he may not have gone too far with his run-over rhymes. But what can he do about that now, how paint over his own complex rhymes? Rhymes like "electric" with "wrecked her? He / C," which he insists have to be read in a startling and rash manner, and only after adequate preparation. Still, he is "sweetly soothed" by his brother's saying he could make anyone understand the poem by reciting it well. "That," Hopkins says, "is what I always hoped, thought, and said; it is my precise aim," for poetry is meant to be spoken, and until "it is spoken it is not performed, it does not perform, it is not itself."

As for sprung rhythm, that "gives back to poetry its true soul and self." It gives poetry its living voice, makes verse stressy, refines it "to an emphasis as much brighter, livelier, more lustrous than the regular but commonplace emphasis of common rhythm as poetry in general is brighter than common speech," though he admits that performing his poems "is not at all easy." In fact, he is not sure he himself could do it, though that no more matters than a composer not being able "to play his violin music or sing his songs. In fact, the higher wrought the art, clearly the wider severance between the parts of the author and the performer."

As with all true poetry, his must first be studied and prepared for as one would read music before it is recited. For this reason—that he did not prepare himself to read it properly—Patmore never learned to admire the *Eurydice* or any of his work, except some in common rhythm. The same is true of plainchant, Hopkins explains, which people dismiss because, though they have heard it murdered, they have never heard it rightly performed. In fact, he has come to believe that just as prose is capable of effects "more beautiful than any verse can attain, so perhaps the inflections and intonations of the speaking voice may give effects more beautiful than any attainable by the fixed pitches of music." And because that "depends entirely on living tradition," it is now possible, with the recent invention of the phonograph, to have a living record "of fine spoken utterance," for "the natural performance and delivery belonging properly to lyric poetry," which after all is speech, "has not been enough cultivated, and should be. When performers were trained to do it (it needs the rarest gifts) and audiences to appreciate it it would be . . . a lovely art." Then "each phrase could be fixed and learnt by heart like a song." In retrospect, the letter reads like his last will and testament as to how he should like his poetry read, if it should ever reach the public's eye.

Friday, November 13: With the grading of exams for the moment over, he writes his mother. He is completely worn out with the grinding repetition of the work, he tells her, and—worse—annoyed with having to also deal with university officials whose behavior he finds "overbearing and ungentlemanly." Were he free to act, and not under the constraints of religious obedience, he "should have taken steps" on his own and others' accounts. How unpleasant to watch one of his colleagues, "a great scholar, one of the old school of fine and laborious scholars . . . very ill treated. It was a painful scene; he was censured by the Standing Committee of the Senate and he replied fiercely and defiantly." And though Hopkins feels it was a mistake on the fellow's part to respond as he did, he can't help but sympathize with him. Such is the world of university politics here. Considering such things, how can the Royal University last much longer? he wonders. No, it must "suffer a sea change into something rich and strange." Add to the mix the current leader of the Irish Party, Charles Stewart Parnell, Ireland's uncrowned king and ally of his old enemy, Gladstone, and one can see why he feels as he does. And though Parnell has found that "he cannot shape the destinies of the country without my cooperation at the Pillar Room of the Rotunda on Monday," Hopkins plans to spend the evening "in unsphering the spirit of Plato or something of the sort."

And then there is Dixon, still trying to get Hopkins's name before the public in the oddest ways. This time it has been a published footnote, thanking his "gifted friend, Fr. Hopkins," for helping him gather information on the Jesuits in Ireland for his study of Reformation England. But even this, he is afraid, is bound to backfire, as with that notice Andrew Lang wrote several years earlier concerning a certain "Gifted Hopkins" who "died of the consequences of his own jocosity." All Dixon's praise can do is bring about "the frame of mind with which one reads . . . of the effects of Mother Seigel's Soothing Syrup which lately burst (or oozed) upon the universe."

On December 23, he writes Everard again. How sad that Matthew Arnold and others like him who one might once have been trusted to defend England's good name should now "drift . . . upon the tide of atheism, where all true guiding principle is lost. Unhappy country . . . its foreign policy [administered] by Gladstone; its speculation by Matthew Arnold—not to speak of what is to befall from Ireland." Still, there is some hope in Leo XIII's "beautiful letter to the English bishops speaking in terms of such heartfelt affection for England that I kiss the words when I read them." He will miss being at Oak Hill for the holidays, especially as his parents and two younger, unmarried sisters are moving to smaller, more rural quarters now, and so it will be the family's last Christmas in Hampstead. Worse, his own holiday will be clouded, for he has just been asked to prepare a supplementary matriculation examination to be held in January, as well as the already-scheduled scholarship exam.

But at least he has friends in Donnybrook, "so hearty and kind that nothing can be more so," and he plans to visit there on Christmas Eve. The hearties are Francis Xavier MacCabe, fifty-two, and his wife and children, all of whom Hopkins dearly loves. These are the sorts of people he finds himself attracted to: the Anglo-Irish Catholic gentry, people of whom none are nicer, he confesses, but a class fast disappearing in Ireland, and who are now being persecuted by two of Ireland's Nationalist archbishops, who in turn will "shortly have a crow to pick with the Holy See."

Several years earlier, when Hopkins was teaching at Stonyhurst, MacCabe had heard him preach and remembered it as the "most beautiful sermon he ever heard on the Blessed Sacrament." And sixty years on, the three older MacCabe children will remember Father Hopkins from this time, fishing in a punt with them in the stone quarry across from their home, and singing ("I make a cheerful noise," he used to joke about himself), as if he were intoning plainchant for a Mass for the Dead. And once, out on the water with the boys, he pulled off his priest's collar, and fairly mimicked in stage Irish, "Goodbye to Rome . . . and to hell with the Pope." Another time, walking down to Donnybrook for a visit, he got to thinking how well he would be treated there, no doubt being offered a glass of champagne to give him stamina, as he had been offered on a previous visit, and with that he had turned and walked back to St. Stephen's Green rather than be well treated for his efforts. Later, when MacCabe asked him *why* he had not visited when he was expected, Hopkins had told him. In fact, when he did visit next, he refused any refreshment, thus once again effectively squashing his affective will with his elective. Abstemious, wary of pleasure, holding himself tightly in rein, he has reneged on what would have given him some pleasure, having forgotten what he had told his heart: how he meant to have more pity on the poor thing.

Another time, when he'd shown up at the MacCabes' late, he explained that he'd gone into a farrier's forge nearby and could not tear himself away from the mesmerizing boom of the anvil. And once, when ten-year-old Jack MacCabe came to St. Stephen's Green to deliver a message, he was awed by how high up Hopkins's room on the upper floor seemed. Just how high was it here? he had asked Father Hopkins.

Well, Hopkins did not know for sure, but he did have a way of finding out. And with that he had begun taking lumps of coal from the firebox in his room and had young Jack drop them from the window while he counted off the seconds and quarter seconds on his watch before the coal hit the ground, trying to determine by an Edward Lear–like mathematical formula how high they must be. Again and again they had tried the experiment, the wide-eyed boy at the window dutifully dropping lumps of coal, and the priest intently eyeing the second hand on his watch, then splitting the differences between the drops. How he'd laughed at Jack's reactions as they tried again and again, until all the coal was gone. *Thirty-four feet it is, Jack. No. Thirty-five. Or is it fifty-one now? Or ten?*

There is an unfinished hymn dating from late this fall. It is songlike, in quatrains of four-stress lines, and it rhymes *aab/ba*. It is the sort of thing any popular Christian hymnal might include, though it quietly instresses many of Hopkins's own theological preoccupations. "Thee, God, I come from, to thee go," it begins, echoing the more peaceable kingdom of some of Hopkins's early Oxford lyrics:

> All dáy long I like fountain flow
> From thy hand out, swayed about
> Mote-like in thy mighty glow . . .

> Once I turned from thee and hid,
> Bound on what thou hadst forbid;
> Sow the wind I would; I sinned:
> I repent of what I did.
>
> Bad I am, but yet thy child.
> Father, be thou reconciled.
> Spare thou me, since I see
> With thy might that thou art mild . . .

It is an uncharacteristically quiet piece (at least on the surface) and it seems to have been written at the close of the most turbulent year of his life, the year that began with the creation of "Spelt from Sybil's Leaves" and Caradoc's soliloquy, before moving on to "I wake and feel the fell of dark," "To seem the stranger," "No worst, there is none," and "Carrion Comfort." It recalls too the great *De Processu* out and back from the Father, and contains these lines:

> I have life left with me still
> And thy purpose to fulfill;
> Yea a debt to pay thee yet:
> Help me, sir, and so I will.

But just how much time has he? And how much of God's purpose is there left for him to fulfill? And, if there is a debt still unpaid, what more is it going to cost him?

Chapter 17

Cloud Puffballs, Torn Tufts:
Dublin, 1886–1887

Mid-February 1886: Hopkins writes Baillie about a proposed study of Homer's language he has undertaken, which will mean retracing Greece's late second millennium B.C. contacts with Egyptian culture, religion, and language. There seems a treasure trove there, if he can just unearth it. So, for example, he has learned from Maspero's *Histoire des Peuples d'Orient*, 1884, that the Greek word for Egypt—*Aigyptos*—derives from the Egyptian Ha-ka-phtah/Abode of Phtah = Memphis. And that the name of the Greek god *Hephaistos* also includes the word "Phtah." Even *Aphrodite* seems to derive from the Egyptian Ha–Phra. What he needs Baillie to tell him is "if among Egyptologists this is either agreed or suspected and if so," he wants "to be oriented on the matter." He has here in the house the second volume of Rawlinson's *History of Egypt,* though the first (of course) is missing. In addition, he also wants Baillie to fast-forward four thousand years and give him "some on-the-spot account of the late [labor] riots" in London, "as witnessed by yourself or friends and informants, also London political gossip in general." News, tidbits of knowledge: anything to keep his flagging interests up.

But even as he writes Baillie about things Egyptian and Greek, he has also been querying Professor John Rhys—now at Oxford—about the old gods of Gaul. "It is the ancient Ogam stones Hopkins should interest himself in now," Rhys explains. That and editing the *Confessions* of St. Patrick Hopkins once spoke of doing. But even in that field partisanship prevails with things Welsh as with things Irish. And of course there are those who are always championing the Anglo-Saxon race.

On Wednesday in Easter Week, April 21, Hopkins is back at Oak Hill to witness his parents' closing up of their old house, in preparation for the move to Haslemere in Surrey come June. He stays a week, then goes up to Oxford and St. Aloysius' for another week. On May 6, he spends the day with the Bridgeses at Yattendon before returning to Oxford that night. He and Mrs. Waterhouse especially hit it off this time round, and a few days later she sends him a copy of the *Book of Simple Prayers* she had asked him to contribute to the year before. "You will think it sadly undogmatic," she writes, "and perhaps when I was gathering it together I was a little too much afraid of dogma." Hopkins could not agree more, but as usual he keeps his own counsel.

Back in Dublin, his chameleon interests turn to things musical, and he asks the bantering, dismissive Sir Robert Stewart to look over his choral arrangement for "Who is Sylvia?" "Now dear Padre," Stewart answers on May 22, tweaking Hopkins, "I saw, ere we had conversed ten minutes on our first meeting, that you are one of those special pleaders who never believe yourself wrong in any respect. You always excuse yourself for anything I object to in your writing or music so I think it a pity to disturb you in your happy dreams of perfectibility," when in fact Hopkins's music is all wrong. Hopkins fires back, calling Stewart's remarks outrageous, even as he sends along a corrected version of his composition.

"Darling Padre!" Stewart jokingly retorts, twitting Hopkins. "*I* never said anything outrageous to you. Don't think so, pray! but you are impatient of correction, when you have previously made up your mind on any point, & I . . . being an 'Expert,' you seem to me to err, often times, very much." In sum, the whole piece seems to him "wanting in coherent plan." After having had his "Sylvia" "mauled" by Stewart, and then having "corrected and simplified" the piece, Hopkins writes his mother that it is finally going to be performed "at a concert or speechday at Belvedere House, a school of ours here in Dublin." That is the good news. The bad news is that he is still mired in the endless round of grading exams. And though he really was greatly improved by his holiday—"Sweetman (the irrepressible, the yachtsman) said he never saw anyone so changed in so short a time. My spirits rose fifty per cent"—he is once again at his alluvial mudflat lows.

A month later, he writes Baillie to tell him that Egyptian inquiries are now off "because examination work is on, that is setting, comparing, revising, and correcting proof of [the printed examination] papers," with the exams themselves to follow. Still, he has hopes of someday making out a case for Greek-Egyptian cross-cultural fertilization, which will have been enough. He likes Matthew Arnold's take on the Home Rule Bill in his recent essay "The Nadir of Liberalism," which he finds "a temperate but strong condemnation" of Gladstone, though Hopkins himself has now come fully round to seeing the need for Home Rule here in Ireland. Yes, it will be a blow for his beloved England, with more to follow, but better that than "re-bellion, bloodshed, and dishonour," which would be "a greater and irre-trievable blow—or have to be refused at a cost it is not worth."

In June, Patmore sends him a copy of his new book of poems. How beautiful it looks, he tells Patmore. And in truth the poems are "a good deed done" both for the Catholic Church and for the British Empire, "which now trembles in the balance held in the hand of [Gladstone's] unwisdom." England's real mission, he believes, should be "to extend freedom and civi-lisation in India and elsewhere," for "we speak of spreading 'Freedom' to the world, and—while it is perfectly true that British freedom is the best, the only successful freedom" is that which has been built on a system of laws. So the cry should be "Law and Freedom, Freedom and Law. But that does not please: it must be Freedom only. And to that cry there is the telling answer: No freedom you can give us is equal to the freedom of letting us alone: take yourselves out of India, let us first be free of you."

Still, the "great end of Empires before God" is "to be Catholic and draw nations into their Catholicism." But the truth is that the British Empire has become "less and less Christian as it grows." And while the best of the un-derpinnings of a true Christian vision for justice are gone, still, something worth having remains. Of course the English praise English civilization. "It is not hard, as Socrates said, among the Athenians to praise the Athenians; but how will [the British Empire] be represented by critics bent on making the worst of it?" He has been in Ireland two years now, and it is bracing to hear how England's enemies here "treat the things that are unquestioned at home." After all, "what marked and striking excellence" has England to show to make her attractive to others? One thing she has to offer is her lit-erature, and good literary criticism will "make this more and more felt." But there will have to be "more of that literature, a continued supply and in quality excellent," even though his own work should have no part in that resurgence.

Dixon writes back to say he has been employed by Routledge (George Routledge being his father-in-law) "to edit a Bible Birthday Book: a collec-tion of texts & verses of poetry," and wants to include the opening stanza of Hopkins's "Morning Midday, and Evening Sacrifice," which Bridges has shown him in manuscript. The following year it will be printed, with minor changes, under the date May 25, with a text from Leviticus: *As for the obla-tion of the first-fruits, ye shall offer them unto the Lord.* Dixon also asks if he can dedicate his new book of poems to him. Nine days later, emerging slowly from the miasma of grading papers just long enough to reply, he tells

Dixon it should be his call. If Dixon wants to dedicate his new book to him—though he dreads his name coming before the public—he will acquiesce. It is, after all, a great honor. And if Dixon wants to publish his lines, he may do so, as long as they do not appear with his name. In any case, he will have to get formal leave for both requests.

Like Dixon, he too saw the Academy exhibit in London, and was particularly taken by Hamo Thorneycroft's statue of the *Sower*. It was "a truly noble work and to me a new light," he adds. "Like Frederick Walker's pictures put into stone." Walker's genius, after all, was amazing, though like Keats he was "cut off by death." In fact, he doubts "if a man with purer genius for painting ever lived. The sense of beauty was so exquisite; it was to other painters' work as poetry is to prose," so that "his loss was irretrievable." True, Whistler's work also has about it "a striking genius of feeling" for "inscape (the very soul of art)." But his execution is sloppy, "negligent, unpardonably so sometimes," so that he remains one of those artists whose genius has yet to come to maturity.

Swinburne, he sees, has just published an ode in *The Times* called *The Commonweal, a Song for Unionists,* an attack on Gladstone's administration for the current political unrest in London. "Somebody called it a rigmarole and I cd. not say it was not: on the contrary everything he writes is rigmarole. But I wonder how he finds it suits him to be clerical, as this ode with appeals to conscience and declaiming against assassination is." And how can Swinburne square what he has written here with his earlier ode in support of the Fenian prisoners condemned to death for their terrorist activities? He is, in fine, just one more modern Liberal who "has changed as much as Gladstone," though as "neither of them have any principles it is no wonder." On the other hand, the passage in Swinburne's new poem about Gordon at Khartoum is very much to the point: "Let but England trust as Gordon trusted, soon shall come upon her / Such deliverance as our daring brought on him." Trust in Gladstone, and your head too may one day grace the tip of a spear, carried through the streets of some foreign city.

On July 3, he adds a postscript. His *"Sylvia"* was not performed after all. Even so, he could not have heard it, for he was busy marking papers, thus "helping to save and damn the studious youth of Ireland." How he wishes Dixon might have been elected to Oxford's Chair of Poetry. But he knows too well that "'life is a short blanket' and it is much if we get something, a spell, an innings at all." So with Christ, he adds, whose "career was cut short and, whereas he would have wished to succeed by success . . . he was doomed to succeed by failure; his plans were baffled, his hopes dashed, and his work was done by being broken off undone."

This is the incredible, mystifying paradox at the heart of it all: that one should keep on, in spite of whatever difficulties, believing that God will somehow make sense of it all. That, when one gives oneself over to Christ, Christ provides the victory as well, and in such a way that we know—if we know anything—that it is God's working in and through us. Still, like Christ, however much Hopkins understands all this, he is finding it "an intolerable grief to submit to it." Yes, he "left the example," and that "is very strengthening," but, he has to admit, "it is not consoling."

July gives way to August, and once again he finds himself being pulled under by work. "Six or seven weeks of it without any break," he tells Dixon, "Sundays and weekdays," but there is "no use talking of it." As for his poetry, he can commit to nothing bigger than a sonnet, "and that rarely," what "with a fagged mind and a continual anxiety." Still, there are things he might work at, if only at odd moments. Just now, for example, he is trying to write a "popular account of Light and the Ether." It is "not meant to be easy reading, for such a difficult subject can only be made easy by a very summary and sketchy treatment." He means it, rather, for those who will "read carefully so long as there are no mathematics and all technicalities are explained." People, he finds, are becoming too theoretical and abstract in their perceptions, unaware of the splendid variety of life's inscapes available to them each blessed day for the asking.

Even literary scholarship is going down the same dead-end road as theory, he believes. So, for instance, "some learned lady having shewn by the flora that the season of the action in *Hamlet* is from March to May, a difficulty is raised about the glowworm's ineffectual fire in the first act, since glowworms glow chiefly from May to September." In turn, F. J. Furnival, compiler of early English texts, has learned "that the grub, though not so easily found, shines nearly as bright as the fullgrown worm, that is beetle, and begins in March, and so all is saved." But is not scholarship of this sort mere trifling? Shakespeare "had the finest faculty of observation of all men that ever breathed, but it is ordinary untechnical observation, neither scientific nor even, like a farmer's, professional, and he might overlook that point of season." In fact, there are "notorious and insoluble inconsistencies in *Hamlet*," as in his having "recast the play expressly for [the actor] Burbage, who was elderly, 'short, stout, and scant of breath' . . . without taking the trouble to correct throughout accordingly."

Then, in mid-September, he takes his annual holiday, accompanied by Brother Curtis, over to North Wales, dear wild Wales, to spend a week in Caernavon and another at Tremadoc. And though it rains almost continuously, he and Curtis manage to climb Mount Snowdon, hike up Pont Abeglaslyn, and take the miniature railway to Blaenau Ffestiniog, a pleasant enough trip, though the thick sulfur smoke from the small engine chuffing up the mountain makes them both sick. And when Curtis is recalled to Dublin to administer an unexpected exam, Hopkins stays on by himself to hike the Pass of Llanberis and Beddgelert. On September 30, he writes Dixon from Mrs. Evans's boardinghouse, 11 Church Street, in Tremadoc. He is here in a "remote and beautiful spot," finishing up his Welsh holiday. As always, Wales breathes poetry, and his landlady serves up the heartiest breakfasts. Guided by a tourist book, he is this morning thinking "of taking a hard-boiled egg with me and rhapsodising either the Vale of Ffestiniog or for a second time Pont Aberglaslyn, which not to have seen, as till a few days ago I never had, is a dreadful underbred ignorance." Once more he has been able to relax, and has even gotten on a little with his play.

And then his time is up. His "delightful holiday comes to an end to-day," he writes Bridges on October 2, but he is going to "take duty"—say Sunday mass—"at Pwllheli tomorrow and start for Holyhead in the evening." But he will "back Tremadoc for beauty against Fishguard" where the Bridgeses have been vacationing in South Wales, any time. Looming right over the village is a magnificent "cliff of massive selfhewn rock, all overrun with a riot of vegetation which the rainy climate seems to breathe here." Portmadoc is only half a mile off, and blessedly not yet discovered by tourists. "Bretons come here in jerseys, earrings, and wooden shoes to sell vegetables," and the place seems to "live upon slate," as the quarrying away of mountains makes plain. The result is that they vanish, "but in the process they take a certain beauty midway between wildness and art."

Hopkins has not written of scenery with this kind of passion since his time here in Wales ten years before, and the vibrant instress of the landscape on him is palpable. He has even been sketching again—Welsh landscapes and running water, to try to capture something of their inner energy and inscape. Mountains everywhere, yes, and sea sand along the coast and two estuaries going down to the sea, "commanded by Moelwyn and other mountains and by Criccieth and Harlech Castles." A "long walk skirting one of these and discovering Snowdon and other grand mountain views leads to Pont Aberglaslyn and into the Pass which from that leads to the valley where Beddgelert is." And the pass itself: how beautiful it is. And the

River Glaslyn, "a torrent of notably green water," of which he made "a drawing (its ruins enclosed) of one fall of it over a rock." And, as always, how hard to capture the inscape of water in motion, which "needs the most sympathetic pencils," of which he has none.

He has even been able to get on a little with his ode to Campion, thanks to his being in a place that has always been for him "a mother of Muses." Even better, he and Curtis "fell upon honest people and lived cheap, too cheap, so that nearly £8 is left out of £20, and that is mismanagement." But why complain, he adds, "when I have seen such lovely things and met such good people, unless that I always complain?" But, then, no one is as hard on himself as Hopkins is, aware that he has set himself a standard of perfection—Christ's, if the truth be told—so that it is no wonder he finds himself always falling short.

A wonderful holiday, he writes his mother on his return to Dublin, though poor Curtis "was dogged from the University with letters (including his own returned from the dead letter office; for he sent off four without addresses, besides other feats). . . ." One batch of papers had to be set three times over, "and that in Wild Wales and on a holiday." And when "day after day these afflictions fell in I used to do the cursing; he bore all with the greatest meekness." Truly, he has been taught a lesson in patience, that hard thing, by Curtis's example, as well as by their landlady at Caernavon, who did her duty each day patiently, without complaining, and who, "poor soul, had great troubles, as by her history appeared."

Degree Day: Examinations are over, he tells Bridges in late October, at least "till the next attack of the plague," and his lectures—"to call them by that grand name"—have begun again. Wales set him up for a time, but all those "accounts of the First Punic War with trimmings, have sweated me down to nearer my lees and usual alluvial low water mudflats, yearnings, groans, and despair." First off, then, he wants to remonstrate with Bridges for disparaging Robert Louis Stevenson, that "master of a consummate style," whose *Jekyll and Hyde* is nothing less than a work of genius. "You are certainly wrong," he tells him, about Hyde "being overdrawn," for if Bridges knew the whole story, he would know that Hopkins's Hyde is even "worse." The truth is that the "amount of . . . genius which goes into novels in the English literature of this generation is perhaps not much inferior to what made the Elizabethan drama." Take Thomas Hardy, whose merits have been "eclipsed by the overdone reputation of the Evans—Eliot—Lewis [sic]—Cross woman . . . half real power, half imposition," and consider the bonfire scene in *Return of the Native* or the sword exercise scene in *Far from the Madding Crowd,* "breathing epic," or the wife sale in *The Mayor of Casterbridge.* No, Hardy is that rare thing: a first-rate novelist.

A week later, Father Matt Russell brings Hopkins along with him to the art studio of John Butler Yeats at No. 7, St. Stephen's Green, to introduce him to Yeats senior and his son, William Butler Yeats, a shy, introspective youth of twenty-one who has set his sights on being a poet, and who already seems to carry the destiny of Ireland on his thin shoulders. With Willie is another poet, Kate Tynan, six years his senior. She is nearsighted, vivacious, and garrulous, and enjoys cultivating literary and political relationships. Along with Lionel Johnson, in fact, young Yeats sees her as the third in the triumvirate now reforming Irish poetry.

Hopkins, sensing an opportunity to make Bridges's name further known here in Ireland, sends three of Bridges's hard-to-find books not to Yeats, but to Tynan at her farmhouse in Clondalkin. "The books came safely this morning," she writes Hopkins on November 6. "You are abundantly generous," though she wishes he had written something in them, "for it would have given them double value in my eyes." When she left Jack Yeats's studio, she remembers, Hopkins and Willie were in the midst of an intense discussion on the nature of finish or non-finish in Irish poetry.

"I seem to have been among odds and ends of poets and poetesses of late," he writes Patmore the following day. One "was Miss Kate Tynan, who lately published a volume of chiefly devotional poems, highly spoken of by reviews. She is a simple brightlooking Biddy with glossy very pretty red hair, a farmer's daughter in the County Dublin. She knows and deeply admires your Muse [but complained] that you are sometimes austere or bare or something like that: 'HOW is it, Fr. Hopkins, that however bare it is it is always poetry?'" And now he is to read Miss Tynan herself, "to say of her what one might say of any writer."

And then, more pointedly, he mentions "young Mr. Yeats" who has in a recent number of the *Dublin University Review* "some striking verses and who has been perhaps unduly pushed by the late Sir Samuel Ferguson." When he called on Yeats senior the other day, he was presented "with some emphasis of manner" a copy of *Mosada: a Dramatic Poem by W. B. Yeats,* with Jack Yeats's portrait of his son. Still, Hopkins adds, "for a young man's pamphlet this was something too much." Of the pamphlet itself he does not think much, but then he was "happily not required . . . to praise what presumably I had not then read, and I had read and could praise another piece." He means *The Island of Statues,* which he has found "a strained and unworkable allegory about a young man and a sphinx on a rock in the sea (how did they get there? what did they eat? and so on: people think such criticisms very prosaic; but commonsense is never out of place anywhere)." Still, there were some "fine lines and vivid imagery" he might praise to a proud father.

In 1932, by which time Yeats will have established himself as Ireland's most important poet, and Hopkins and Bridges—who will come to befriend Yeats—are both gone from the scene, Yeats will write his young cousin, Monk Gibson, whose poetry owes much to Hopkins. "You have gained greatly in intensity of diction from Gerard Hopkins but lost in naturalism," he will tell him. Now, "Gerard Hopkins, whom I knew, was an excitable man—unfitted for active life and his speech is always sedentary, the reverse of that of his friend Bridges when Bridges was at his best." And because Hopkins was a priest and a scholar, he was "the way out of life," while Bridges was "the way into life." And literature is nothing if not "a life-long war against the sedentary element in speech." All of which would seem to be an essential misreading of what Hopkins himself insisted on again and again: that poetry is meant to be spoken, and until then "it is not performed, it does not perform, it is not itself." For, as poetry is emphatically speech, "speech purged of dross like gold in the furnace, so it must have emphatically the essential elements of speech." But to this element in Hopkins Yeats, brilliant as he was, seems to have remained quite deaf.

In mid-November, Hopkins sends Bridges his "completed but not quite finished . . . longest sonnet ever made" what with its eight-stress lines, "and no doubt the longest making," "Spelt from Sybil's Leaves," noting that it is the "longest by its own proper length, namely by the length of its lines; for anything can be made long by eking, by tacking, by trains, tails, and flounces." Still, since Bridges has mentioned caudated sonnets—sonnets with tails—he wants to know "what a *coda* is and how employed." Once again, he reminds Bridges how he is to read his new poem. That it is "made for performance" with a "loud, leisurely, poetical (not rhetorical) recitation, with long rests, long dwells on the rhyme and other marked syllables, and so on." It should, in fact, "be almost sung" and has been "most carefully timed in *tempo rubato.*"

As for his work on rhythm and Dorian measure, that too is proceeding, "but may easily either wreck (by external difficulties, examinations and other ones) or founder (of its own). For in fact it needs mathematics," which he does not have. What he wants to do is write "a philosophy of art" using the Dorian measure as his focal point and, if he can get it published, expand it in a second edition. He is sorry to hear about Lang's depression. Better, though, to conceal such a state rather than broadcast it as Lang has in print. True, Lang can still write amusing verses for the *Saturday Review,* but then Hopkins knows too well that some people "can joke in the deepest gloom."

As for those books of Bridges he has distributed: "Tyrrell expresses his deep admiration of your muse, his conversion, so to speak." But Dowden of Trinity, another recipient, though he said nothing to Hopkins at the time, would years later, ironically in a favorable article on Bridges's poetry for the *Fortnightly Review,* belatedly acknowledging Hopkins's gesture. Hopkins and he were strangers back then "and might have been friends," except that he had thought Hopkins belonged to the Nationalist camp in Irish politics. But the truth was that "Father Hopkins was a lover of literature, and himself a poet. Perhaps he did in many quarters missionary work on behalf of the poetry of his favourite, Robert Bridges. He certainly left, a good many years since, at my door two volumes by Mr. Bridges, and with them a note begging that I would make no acknowledgement of the gift. I did not acknowledge it then; but, with sorrow for a fine spirit lost, I acknowledge it now."

Christmastide, 1886: A portrait painting in velvety yellow tones in the Georgian hallway of Miss Cassidy's home at Monasterevan, forty miles southwest of Dublin, catches Hopkins's eye. It shows two of Miss Cassidy's cousins as children: a young boy and girl, brother and sister, with a basket of fruit and bluebells in vine leaves about the borders. The portrait, done in the mid-Victorian sentimental style, shows the delicate face of a dark-haired boy on the left gazing at his fair-haired sister, who herself gazes into the distance. Both seem more types than individuals in their features, and yet for Hopkins the portrait captures something, and he begins a poem in the chastened neo-classic style of Thomas Gray's *Elegy Written in a Country Churchyard.* To smooth Bridges's feathers, he admits now that he has probably "gone far enough in oddities and running rhymes (as even in some late sonnets you have not seen) into the next line," but this poem, this elegy to his own lost youth, is far plainer.

It is called "On the Portrait of Two Beautiful Young People," and it begins: "O I admire and sorrow!" praising the innocence and beauty of children once again, and sorrowing too—as he had in those poems written at Oxford and Liverpool—for what he too well knows time does to such innocence. Did not his aunt Annie paint him twice in that summer of 1859 when he was just fourteen: the delicate hazel-eyed, fair-haired boy in tie and vest and jacket and wide white open collar? And to see him now, "Bran Maenefa," thirty years on, the anonymous crow-poet aging in his black soutane. What the lying portrait has captured, really, are two children who long ago ceased being such. Perhaps there are tears for such things. Still, it is not the children he focuses on, but tyrant time, time the Heraclitean river, which first sours and then at its ease devours its prey:

> The heart's eye grieves
> Discovering you, dark tramplers, tyrant years.
> A juice rides rich through bluebells, in vine leaves,
> And beauty's dearest veriest vein is tears. . . .
>
> And are they thus? The fine, the fingering beams
> Their young delightful hour do feature down
> That fleeted else like day-dissolvèd dreams
> Or ringlet-race on burling Barrow brown . . .
>
> Enough: corruption was the world's first woe.
> What need I strain my heart beyond my ken?
> O but I bear my burning witness though
> Against the wild and wanton work of men.

All he can do is add his witness to the depths of degradation men and women seem so capable of. And then he puts the poem aside, unfinished (as it will remain, though he will come back to it again and again), as now he prepares to take the train back to Dublin and his never-ending, numbing work. And where *now* is that sweet boy of fourteen his aunt Annie painted once?

Monday evening, January 24, 1887: While he waits for a student, a young Scots Protestant by the name of Robertson, to show up for his tutoring session, he begins a letter to his mother. Robertson is "the best and brightest of all my pupils," he tells her, and "takes a most visible pleasure in learning and being taught," so that teaching him "is correspondingly a pleasure." Still, he "does not tonight appear to be coming," and so he has a few minutes to send some news from dreary Dublin. And though there has been little snow and frost thus far, the weather has still taken its toll on him. "Not that I took a cold, I never do to speak of in winter (I am too cold for it), but it exhausted me every morning and I felt as if kept on long it would kill me." Forty-two now, and already his good eyesight ruined, so that he shall have to get glasses. "The focus is unchanged and objects at all distances as clear as ever," he explains, "but they ache at any exertion."

Worse, "any want of sleep makes havoc of them," and sleep is what he cannot seem to get.

Still, he did have "some very pleasant days down at Monasterevan . . . at Xmas and again at New Year and it was a happy acquaintance to make, for [the Cassidys] made no secret of liking me and want me to go down again." But a month later he tells his mother he wishes he had "never written that silly letter about the people at Monasterevan liking me," for it reminds him of that fellow in Dickens's *Edwin Drood,* the "purest Jackass in Cloisterham," who had written on his wife's tombstone "how in the course of a life of 50 years he had not met a woman who appreciated him as she did." And now Miss Cassidy has asked when he might be "going down again," and God knows he needs the rest.

"Tomorrow morning," he writes Bridges on February 17, 1887, "I shall have been three years in Ireland, three hard wearying wasting wasted years." To top it all, and to show what the effects of living here in Dublin have been, he just that afternoon saw the "blooming Miss Tynan again," who told him that when she first saw him, she took him "for 20 and some friend of hers for 15." But there's no use fooling himself. "They should see my heart and vitals, all shaggy with the whitest hair." In his time in Ireland, he has "done God's will (in the main) and many many examination papers." He knows that as a Professor of Classics at a university—even one as ramshackle as his—he has a duty to write something on classical study. He even feels he could do such a subject justice and so advance the available stock of reality. And the thing is, "there is such a subject; I do try to write at it."

But he feels so helpless, so without that vital energy everyone needs, so that he "cannot get on" and will be "even less able hereafter than now." Wales did help for a while, but the effect of that time long ago wore off. Worse, even if he were out of Ireland and elsewhere, he "shd. be no better, rather worse probably." If only he had a working strength. "With that any employment is tolerable or pleasant, enough for human nature; without it, things are liable to go" very hard. Acedia: a sense of struggling to move upward and outward in a place without exits and the air running out.

And then there is the worsening political situation. Archbishop Walsh, that unabashed Nationalist, has just published a letter in *The Freeman,* defending those "on trial for preaching the Plan of Campaign and saying that the jury was packed and a fair trial impossible." And this, Hopkins wonders, this is the prelate's "contribution to the cause of concord and civil order"? And just today, Archbishop Croke of Cashel, like Walsh a vehement supporter of Home Rule, also published a letter in *The Freeman*, this one "proposing to pay no taxes."

In effect, Hopkins sums up, "one archbishop backs robbery, the other rebellion; the people in good faith believe and will follow them." And so, he fears, it is "the beginning of the end: either Home Rule or [Ireland's] separation [from England] is near." Better to let them come, for "anything is better than the attempt to rule a people who own no principle of civil obedience at all, not only to the existing government but to none at all." He would be "glad to see Ireland happy, even though it involved a serious setback for England, if that could come about without shame and guilt. But Ireland will not be happy: a people without a principle of allegiance cannot be." As for the college, the very ship he is sailing on, no doubt it too will "go down in the approaching gale," and if it does he will probably find himself "cast up on the English coast."

Home Rule, he tells Baillie, is the only viable solution, something Baillie would understand if he lived here. "I do not say things are as bad as they were during the horrors of Irish rebellions or the greater horrors of their putting down," he explains. "I only say that we are approaching a state of things which must be put an end to either by the sword or by Home Rule." Surely the English constitution is strong enough to get the nation through "a crisis of which the natural end is war / without war; for now for the first time the Irish are using the constitution against England."

Yes, "the Irish had and have deep wrongs to complain of in the past and wrongs and abuses to amend which are still felt in the present." But ameliorating these injustices has only inflamed the Irish the more. They have had a taste of better conditions, and now want more. They demand independence and a nation of their own, so that even Home Rule will prove "a disappointment . . . like the rest." But at least "it will have some good effects and it will deliver England from . . . the task of attempting to govern a people who own no principle of civil allegiance."

At the beginning of March, he writes his mother for her sixty-sixth birthday, and then sends his letter off to her new address at Haslemere, "which soon will begin to put on . . . those bright looks" of spring. Dublin remains as dull as dishwater, but an old Stonyhurst pupil—and dear friend—Bernard O'Flaherty, who has just passed his final law exams, is going into partnership with his father, an influential Wexford solicitor, and is leaving Dublin. "He has constantly called on me and taken walks with me ever since I have been here," he adds. Another good friend is the twenty-seven-year-old Irishman Terence Woulfe-Flanagan, who was an Oxford undergraduate when Hopkins was curate there. The son of a retired judge here, he lives at home and is studying medicine. At least these "two young men are not Nationalists," Hopkins adds, which, as things go, is a relief.

He writes Newman for his birthday, reiterating much of what he has said to his mother and Baillie, and Newman writes back, pointedly, that there is one consideration Hopkins has omitted from his account: "The Irish Patriots hold that they never have yielded themselves by the sway of England and therefore have never been under her laws, and have never been rebels. This does not diminish the force of your picture, but it suggests that there is no help, no remedy. If I were an Irishman, I should be (in heart) a rebel." Much of which by this time Hopkins has come to learn for himself from his vantage point here at ground zero.

Friday, March 25. Lady Day: From Monasterevan, where he has come for a few days' rest, he writes his young Irish colleague, Michael Cox, a letter defending the English against charges that they purposely crippled the Irish woolen trade two centuries before. Then, back at St. Stephen's Green, he writes Cox a follow-up letter. Yes, he sees that there was English self-interest in these matters, but he also sees "that it goes but a very little way to explaining the poverty of Ireland," for the Irish peasantry of the seventeenth century was better clothed even than the French, or indeed most of the world, in home-manufactured cloth. But the truth is that it was the Irish Protestant woolen manufacturers in Dublin who petitioned the Irish Parliament to keep Irish Catholics out of the woolen manufacture, so that the real struggle was between "English Protestants jealous for English commercial ascendance versus Irish Protestants jealous for their own commercial (and religious . . .) ascendancy." So the Irish themselves must take the blame for those laws. Yes, he knows this is a bone of contention with the Irish today, and wishes some statesman "both powerful and unselfish," would "apply himself to this matter" and set the record straight. But, alas, that seems highly unlikely now, given the charged political atmosphere here. It is an attempt to reason, Hopkins sees, where reason has little appeal. The Irish sense of having been wronged for so long and so grievously goes too deep at this point for reason to prevail. And to Baillie a few days later, he writes more pointedly that England is no longer capable of dealing effectively with the Irish. To make matters worse, there is the passionate intensity of the Irish Nationalists themselves, both here and in America, who are "more bent on outrage, as dynamite and laying London in ruins, than when the Irish were without power and without redress."

Bridges's friend, H. E. Wooldridge, has undertaken to do a watercolor of

Hopkins, using the 1879 *carte de visite* photograph taken at Oxford, and so Bridges writes him for details to turn the black-and-white photograph into living color. "The irises of the present writer's eyes are small and dull," Hopkins writes back, and "of a greenish brown; hazel I suppose. . . . His hair (see enclosed sample, carriage paid) is lightish brown, but not equable nor the same in all lights; being quite fair near the roots and upon the temples, elsewhere darker . . . and shewing quite fair in the sun and even a little tawny. It has a gloss. On the temples it sometimes appears to me white. I have a few white hairs, but not there." The truth is that he has "of late become much wrinkled round the eyes and generally haggard-looking," and so Bridges is relieved Wooldridge is using that particular photograph.

Rest is what he needs more than ever. And so, for Easter Week, he goes down to Enniscorthy and the Wexford countryside to stay with Bernard O'Flaherty's family. The weather, he tells his mother, was "cold but bright, country beautiful, and the people very kind and homely." Miss Cassidy also invites him to spend more time with her family at Monasterevan, though, he adds ruefully, "it cannot be." Morning mass in the chapel, followed by meals in the community dining room, then back to his room to prepare or read exams, or write notes for his lectures on the Roman historians, the saying of the breviary each day, walks, tending to the small array of herbs and flowers in the greenhouse behind the school, prayer in the small chapel, the daily examination of conscience, the rosary, Benediction with his fellow Jesuits and his students: this is the daily round of his existence, at least as others see it. But, too, there is the rich interior world, so hard to capture and record, his daily commerce with his Lord, fiery particles to candesce a darkness visible.

In mid-May, he writes to thank Patmore for the National Library three-penny edition of his *Angel in the House*. "These cheap issues are a great boon," he tells Patmore, and it is time they came, if literature is "not to be buried under litter," for there is a "kind of smoldering fame a writer may have, which on being fuelled with a cheap supply breaks into flame." He is still at work on his book on meter, and has been "subjecting the terms of geometry, line, surface, and solid and so on . . . to a searching examination. Most therefore of what I have written is metaphysics and stiff reading, though written by me with a flowing pen." But it will all have to be rewritten, for he now sees more clearly what he must do to make his argument clear. But at least he finds "writing prose easy and pleasant. Not so verse (though indeed such verse as I do compose is oral, made away from paper, and I put it down with repugnance)."

In late June, Pope Leo sends his Apostolic Delegate, Monsignor Persico, to Ireland because, as *The Times* of London reports, he "is not satisfied with the attitude of the Irish clergy." Persico's task will be "to furnish his holiness with a report, founded on information and observation obtained on the spot, with regard to the state of affairs" there. The visit is to coincide with the visit of Prince Albert and Prince George to Ireland for their mother's Diamond Jubilee. On the evening of June 27, the two princes attend a garden party at the Royal Hospital in Dublin, at which Ireland's power broker, Lord Emly, is present. And though the Jesuit community has been warned to stay away for fear of mixing religion with British, Irish, and Vatican politics, Hopkins's colleague Father Martial Klein, S.J., Professor of Biology at University College, and an acquaintance of Emly's, attends, in spite of pointedly being told not to by his (and Hopkins's) superior, Father Purbrick. Worse, the headstrong, garrulous Klein insists on talking up politics, to the embarrassment of the Jesuit presence in Dublin.

As a result, Purbrick recalls Klein to London, where he can see that he is facing a man suffering from delusions of grandeur. Klein, believing he has the support of Lord Emly, insists that he has done nothing wrong, and then, seeing he is to be remonstrated with, pulls his trump card. He has never been baptized, he informs Purbrick, and so has never been validly ordained. As a result, he is relieved of all duties and ordered to remain at Farm Street while his claims are investigated. Come November, he will finally leave the order. And though Hopkins will remain silent about the affair, it is precisely the kind of political situation he has carefully avoided, though he seems to have been asked by Purbrick to meet with Klein while in London to see if he might talk some sense into him. The meeting will come to nothing, except that Hopkins will weep openly over Klein's loss when at last he reports back to Purbrick.

July 30: He has been reading Aeschylus' *Choephoroi—The Libation Bearers*—and tells Bridges that he has now "restored the text and sense almost completely in the corrupted choral odes. Much has been done in this way by dint of successive effort: the recovery, from the 'pie' of the MSS." It is a great pity that the choruses have for so long been misunderstood, he explains, for therein lies Aeschylus' "own interpretation of the play." What nobility and genius are there. What manly tenderness! More, he has come to feel the man's inscape: his "earnestness of spirit and would-be piety," qualities he finds neither in Sophocles, "who is only the learned and sympathetic dramatist," nor in Euripides. Two days later, he travels down to London and then on to Haslemere. Once settled there, he invites Bridges down, where the talk once again seems to turn to prosody and the impact of Milton's work on their own.

Later, he travels to Yattendon to visit the Bridgeses, including Mrs. Waterhouse and Mary Plow, the daughter of Bridges's sister, the victim of that horrible multiple murder years before, and now engaged to the Reverend Beeching, Rector of Yattendon. The discussion here turns to Bridges's newest play, *The Feast of Bacchus*, which he has situated in the Menandrian period of Greek history, which Hopkins thinks—rightly—is "the dullest and narrowest world that one could choose to lay an action in, a jaded and faded civilization." He wants "more brilliancy" and "local colour" from *Bacchus,* and so once again can offer only the faintest praise: "In its kind . . . which has for me no attraction, and in its metre, which has to me no beauty," he explains, it is indeed a masterpiece. The language, as in Racine, Hopkins finds both strong and chaste, though "the continual determination to be smooth and lucid" has given the play a "childish effect." He begs Bridges never to repeat the experiment.

On August 19, he returns to Dublin via London and Manchester, staying with the Jesuits there, and taking in the Royal Jubilee Exhibition. Then it is back to preparing a new set of exams. This time, it takes just three weeks before he is once again worn down by work and eczema. It is "a fashionable complaint," he tells Baillie, "to use a consideration which is like the flower upon the nettle." How he wishes he were back again in the Highlands. He must also report the sad news that the son of Baillie's old friend, D'Arcy Thompson, and two companions were drowned on Lough Corrib near Galway. "They landed on an island, I am told, where an old man begged them not again to put out, foreseeing . . . a squall. But they would not heed him, not realising . . . the danger. Their watches were found stopped at about ten minutes after the man's warning." "Mortal my mate," he had addressed his own watch just two years before, "shall I / Earlier or you fail at our force?" Or both together at the same time?

Because he has had to return to Dublin early, he is given permission to stay at the Irish Jesuit novitiate at Loyola House—the former estate of Bishop Thomas Percy—in Dromore, outside Belfast, for a week in late September. During his time there, he watches a ploughman out in the fields working behind a plough, and then tries his hand at it. And so Hopkins conceives "Harry Ploughman," a caudated sonnet, that is, a sonnet with tails. It celebrates what he himself would love to have again—that physical agility and prowess such as he sees in this laborer moving easily behind his plough horse. "Hard as hurdle arms," the poem begins, as the figure he inscapes takes motion, as in a cinematic film conceived by Edison, moving from a still photograph into something far more dynamic. It is another new departure for him, both in the sonnet's form and in its subject: the physical activity he so admires in Hamo Thorneycroft's *Sower* and in Fred Walker's painting of an English ploughman turning the earth to make sillion shine. Like a corps of well-trained troops, the body politic working in unison, the body of Christ, strong and fit for the task to be done, unlike the man writing the lines:

> with a broth of goldish flue
> Breathed round; the rack of ribs; the scooped flank; lank
> Rope-over thigh; knee-nave; and barrelled shank—
> Héad and fóot, shóulder and shánk—
> By a grey eye's heed steered well, one crew, fall to;
> Stand at stress. Each limb's barrowy brawn, his thew
> That onewhere curded, onewhere sucked or sánk—
> Sóared or sánk—,
> Though as a beechbole firm, finds his, as at a roll-call, rank
> And features, ín flesh, whát deed he each must do—
> His sínew-sérvice whére dó.
> He leans to it, Harry bends, look. Back, elbow, and liquid waist
> In him, all quail to the wallowing o' the plough: 'S cheek crimsons;
> curls
> Wag or crossbridle, in a wind liftéd, windláced—
> See his wínd- lílylócks-láced;
> Churlsgrace too, child of Amansstrength, how it hangs or hurls
> Them—broad in bluff hide his frówning féet láshed! ráced
> With, along them, cragiron under and cold furls—
> With-a-fountain's shining-shot furls.

At the same time, he begins a second caudated sonnet, "Tom's Garland," of which he manages to get down the first ten lines. And then another—in two versions, the first a curtal sonnet, the other a caudated curtal sonnet—unnamed, about the inscape of ash boughs seen as they are in winter, bare against the blue winter sky.

> Not of all my eyes see, wándering upón the wórld,
> Is anything a mílk to the mínd so, só sighs déep
> Poetry tó it, as a tree whose boughs break in the sky.

Say it is áshboughs: whéther on a Décember dáy and furled
Fast ór they in clammyish lashtender combs créep
Apárt wide and they néstle at héaven most high.
They touch: their wíldweathér-swung tálons swéep
The smóuldering enórmous wínter-wélkin. May
Mells blúe and snówwhite thróugh them a fringe and fray
Of greenery: it is óld earth's gróping tówards the stéep
　　　　Heaven whom she childs us bý.

Thousand-fingered branches, as if reaching, clawing, for the very heavens they were once childed by, the inscape of the trees in winter or in early spring, showing themselves as they are: part of fallen nature's great procession out from and back to their Creator, old earth groping and pining, like himself, after his heavenly Father.

On his way back to Dublin on September 28, he stays overnight at the Mourne Hotel in Rostrevor, County Down. "Lovely country" this is, he writes Bridges, adding that Bridges's *Bacchus* is still in his box and "will go to Dublin by goods train from Dromore, from a house once Bishop Percy's, and grounds and groves by him very tastily planted then and haunted now." His judgment about *Bacchus* is still the same, but his feelings for it have deepened as he has learned how to enjoy it more. "In its own kind I believe it could not be bettered," its real value "like [the Roman playwright] Terence's" being in its "understanding of human nature." But, like Terence, the comedy is not very comic. Still, he admits, there were moments when he found himself laughing out loud. And for someone like Hopkins who loves the play of language and sorely needs to laugh, as Shakespeare has often made him laugh, that is as essential as rain to parched soil.

He has also been touching up those sonnets written in blood two years before—and has finished a new one, which he thinks highly of, and most of another, which is still looking for an ending. The finished one "is a direct picture of a ploughman, without afterthought." But, he adds, aware of how nakedly he has celebrated the body here, he fears Bridges will see Whitman all over it, "as perhaps there may be, and I should be sorry for that." Two weeks later, he sends Bridges a copy of the poem, replete with its burden lines. These last, he explains, are freely used and might in fact "be recited by a chorus." So his long study of the Dorian mode has paid some poetic dividends, after all. The poem is "very heavily loaded" with sprung rhythm, which is why the lighter refrain or burden lines seemed called for. The rhythm is meant "altogether for recital," and has been "very highly studied."

But after working on it for so long, he "can no longer gather any impression of it," and thinks it may strike Bridges "as intolerably violent and artificial." Which it does, Bridges telling Muirhead shortly after that this last poem "is even less intelligible than usual." It is the same message he conveys to Hopkins himself.

For "Harry Ploughman" to succeed, Hopkins knows, the ploughman must be first and foremost "a vivid figure before the mind's eye." If he is not, then the poem fails. "The difficulties are of syntax no doubt. Dividing a compound word by a clause sandwiched into it was a desperate deed . . . and I do not feel that it was an unquestionable success." What "an immense advance in notation . . . in writing as the record of speech," he explains in his defense, "to distinguish the subject, verb, object, and in general to express the construction to the eye. . . . And I daresay it will come." So, while his meaning "surely *ought* to appear of itself . . . in a language like English, and in an age of it like the present, written words are really matter open and indifferent to the receiving of different and alternative verse-forms, some of which the reader cannot possibly be sure are meant unless they are marked for him."

Actually, he thinks, it might help to underscore the meaning of some of his poems by prefixing "short prose arguments" to them. For if it is "possible to express a subtle and recondite thought on a subtle and recondite subject in a subtle and recondite way and with great felicity and perfection, in the end, something must be sacrificed, with so trying a task, in the process, and this may be the being at once . . . intelligible." Nor should it matter "that the argument should be even longer than the piece; for the merit of the work may lie for one thing in its terseness. It is like a mate [in chess] which may be given, one way only, in three moves; otherwise, various ways, in many." But, with so much defending, he realizes he may have now lost his audience of one.

And he still has "Tom's Garland" to finish. "Please," he asks Bridges in early November, "tell me how correctly to make codas to sonnets; with the most approved order of rhymes and so on. And do not say that I know and that I can find for myself and that there is one in Milton (that one is not enough), but do what I ask you. And soon: a sonnet is hot on the anvil and wants the coda. It is the only time I have felt forced to exceed the beaten bounds." The poem itself comes out of the current labor unrest in England, the infamous Bloody Sunday in Trafalgar Square that same month being one symptom of a deeper social malaise.

In the summer of '87, hundreds of unemployed workers began camping out in the square to make their plight more visible, and soon the area became a center for political agitation for the Socialists. By September, the Police Commissioner, fearing a takeover of London center by mob rule, petitioned the Home Secretary to ban all meetings in the area. And so, through September and October, the Police Commissioner, preparing for the worst, posted two thousand policemen around the square each weekend, when the crowds were largest. Then all meetings there were forbidden. When a meeting challenging the shutdown was called for, all groups were kept from entering. In spite of which, huge crowds converged on the area to protest both unemployment and the use of repressive force in Ireland and were in turn met by police armed with truncheons, reinforced as the day wore on by four hundred of Her Majesty's troops, who were ordered to fix bayonets. John Burns, the dockers' union leader, was arrested, along with the Radical MP R. B. Cunninghame Graham, who was smashed over the head with a truncheon, then dragged through the square by his hair. By evening, Charing Cross Hospital was filled with casualties, and at least two demonstrators were dead.

It is against this backdrop that Hopkins draws his portrait of the English and Irish laborer, his poem subtitled "Upon the Unemployed." Following St. Paul's metaphor for Christ as the head and the Church as the body, Hopkins draws an image of the Commonwealth as the body politic, in which all—high and low—have a rightful place. Most men, he believes, if they have job security, a home, food, and a bed, are satisfied. For Tom's garland does not shine out from his brow, Hopkins explains, but like sparks from his hobnailed boots striking off the cobblestoned streets as he heads for home and his supper. The stars above his head, the earth beneath his feet: let others do the heavy thinking, let them work through those tongue-twisting "thick / Thousands of thorns, thoughts"—as long as Tom has his pick and shovel and a job.

But take away those things that make up his world, undenizen him, and then, as despair makes its inroads, he becomes Hangdog sullen, despairing of ever finding a way out. Add rage to the mix and you have that terrifying new species, Manwolf, whose packs are all too willing to take down a commonweal of which they no longer feel any part:

> Undenizened, beyond bound
> Of earth's glory, earth's ease, all; noone, nowhere,
> In wide the world's weal; ráre gold, bóld steel, báre
> In both; care, but share cáre—

This, by Despair, bred Hangdog dull; by Rage,
Manwolf, worse; and their packs infest the age.

But there is another thing that seems to be at work here, something below the surface, yet present for all that: the sense Hopkins feels of not having the working strength he needs to get him through each long and killing day, himself "undenizened" in Ireland, the odd man out, feeling over again despair and sullen rage he knows he must keep in check by turning to his own model of the suffering Christ. In that sense, Tom turned Manwolf shares something with Caradoc, as Caradoc with Hopkins. Hold such things cheap may who never hung there.

The same day he writes Bridges he also returns a long paper Patmore has sent him called "Thoughts on Knowledge, Opinion, and Inequality" without comment. Instead, he tells Patmore something which he knows "will probably amaze and indeed incense" him: that when he reads Patmore's—or even Newman's prose for that matter—he realizes that "no matter how beautiful the thought," Patmore does not know what writing prose is. At bottom, what both he and Newman do is merely "think aloud . . . with pen to paper." And what such a style lacks is the eloquence proper to written prose. "Each thought is told off singly and there follows a pause and this breaks the continuity . . . which writing should usually have." But the real beauty "of good prose cannot come wholly from the thought. With [Edmund] Burke it does and varies with the thought." But then Burke's style "was colourlessly to transmit his thought," sublime or otherwise.

Newman, on the other hand, follows the tradition of highly educated conversation, the very "flower of the best Oxford life." It is his own tradition Hopkins is speaking of here, his own life before he entered the Jesuits, before his way of speaking changed under the stress of working in the slums of Bedford Leigh and Liverpool, or teaching sixth-formers at Stonyhurst, or hearing confessions, or trying to reach the masses at mass, before coming to Wales and Scotland and Dublin. And this Oxford speech, which Newman never lost, though it may give his writing "a charm of unaffected and personal sincerity that nothing else could," still, Oxford is not England or Ireland or Shakespeare, and Newman has shunned the great "tradition of written English." But "the style of prose is a positive thing." It is not a matter of "single hits," but of a continuity of rhythm from first to last, a form—like poetry—with its own inscape and music.

On December 6, the twelfth anniversary of the wreck of the *Deutschland*, the Bridgeses' first child—Elizabeth—is born, though it takes Hopkins two weeks to send word of congratulations, trusting that "the little nymph" and her mother are well. On the 22nd, he is off again to Monastere-van, "the scene," he tells Dixon, "of the poisoning of the hounds, which threatens to put an end altogether to hunting in all that neighbourhood and with it to Punchestown races," which would mean "the withdrawal of a great deal of money from the country." But "that is how we live now and with fervour cut off our nose to revenge ourselves on our face." He encloses both "Tom's Garland" and "Harry Ploughman," "works of infinite, of over great contrivance," he fears, "to the annulling in the end of the right effect." Both are of a "'robustious' sort and perhaps 'Tom's Garland' approaches bluster and will remind you of [Dickens's] Mr. Podsnap with his back to the fire."

On Christmas Day he writes his mother from Monasterevan, to thank her for her gift and his sisters for their letters. That morning he helped out the parish priest, now recovering from a dangerous sickness, in distribut-ing communion. "Many hundreds came to the rail," he tells her, all "with the unfailing devotion of the Irish." But that devotion, he sees, seems to hang "suspended over their politics as the blue sky over the earth." It is an image he has used to evoke several widely different meanings, from Mary's and nature's maternal presence to a sense of deep isolation, as here, where prayer and politics make up the landscape while remaining "immeasurably remote and without contact or interference." Remote and without contact, alas, like himself.

Chapter 18

The War Within:
Dublin, 1888

December 16, 1887: "We have had to stay already more than a month in London," Bridges writes Muirhead from New Cavendish Street, "and expect to have quite two months of it altogether.—It is rather hard to know what to do with oneself—the dirt is so dreadfully filthy and the reading room at the British Museum has in the interest of the lower classes been made impossible for gentlemen. . . . However there is a concert now and then and there are old friends whom I am glad to see." Worse, it has been raining heavily and he has "got wet through once, and splashed with mud past identification twice," and here in the house—which he and Monica and the baby are sharing with two other families—there is "no room in which I can smoke except my bedroom which is at the top of the house and cheerless."

"My dear Bridges," Hopkins writes from an equally cheerless Dublin on January 12, 1888, "I am glad that you will be back at pastoral Yattendon, but do not understand why you should be unhappy in London. Unless indeed one thing explains it, the new enemies you have made." Among those Bridges has managed to argue with in his essay on Milton's prosody is Patmore. "I am sorry, I must say, for the tussle with Patmore," Hopkins the peacemaker goes on, and Bridges's "cynical remark about forgetting that people believed in their own theories" does not please him. Better to "never make an enemy," he reminds Bridges, "except for duty's sake; try not, even then."

During his time at Monasterevan, Hopkins did try "to get some outstanding and accumulated sonnets ready for hanging on the line, that is in my book of MS, the one you wrote most of, and so for sending to you. All however are not ready yet, but they will soon be." In any case, it is now years that he has "had no inspiration of longer jet than makes a sonnet," except for those two weeks in Wales two years earlier, when he worked on his play and his ode. And so, once again, he will not send those terrifying dark son-nets of his on to Bridges or Dixon or for that matter to anyone. Instead, he is now at work on "a quasi-philosophical paper on the Greek Negatives," but will he ever finish that either? "Or if finished will it pass the censors? or if it does will the *Classical Review* or any magazine take it? All impulse fails me: I can give myself no sufficient reason for going on. Nothing comes: I am a eunuch—but it is for the kingdom of heaven's sake." Time's eunuch: it is a new and darker image he offers Bridges now, in the winter of '88, one that will come to haunt his last poems.

And did Bridges, he wonders, go to see Jem Smith while he was in Lon-don, all five eight and a half, two hundred pounds of him, a brawler from the Shoreditch slums of London with a good knockout punch, who has just won England's heavyweight championship? But there is also a note of deep disappointment as he acknowledges the fact that Bridges has asked Beech-ing rather than him to christen Bridges's daughter. But, then, he is a sus-pect Catholic priest and a Jesuit to boot, and Bridges has made it clear that he would prefer a fellow Anglican to do the baptism.

"I laughed outright and often, but very sardonically," he also tells Bridges, "to think you and the Canon could not construe ['Tom's Garland']; that he had to write to you for a crib. It is plain I must go no farther on this road: if you and he cannot understand me who will? Yet, declaimed, the strange constructions would be dramatic and effective." Must he really in-terpret his own poem for two of his closest readers? Very well, then. The thought, actually, is not that far from Carlyle's and Ruskin's on the body politic, but the expression is unmistakably his. And so he begins. Just as "St. Paul and Plato and Hobbes and everybody says, the commonwealth . . . is like . . . a body with many members and each its function; some higher, some lower, but all honourable. . . . The head is the sovereign [covered] . . . only with the sun and stars." On the other hand, "the foot is the daylabourer . . . armed with hobnail boots," for it is "daylabourers who, on the great scale or in gangs and millions, mainly trench, tunnel, blast, and in others ways dis-figure, 'mammock' the earth and . . . superficially stamp it with their foot-prints." And though they fill the lowest place in the Commonwealth, they still share in "the common honour." And if they lack "glory or public fame," they make up for it by "ease of mind, absence of care . . . symbolized by the gold and the iron garlands." O, he adds, "once explained, how clear it all is!"

He has set the scene at evening, "when they are giving over work and one after another pile their picks, with which they earn their living, and swing off home, knocking sparks out of mother earth not now by labour and of choice but by the mere footing, being strongshod and making no hardship of hardness, taking all easy. And so to supper and bed." And just here he has employed "a violent but effective hyperbaton or suspension, in which the action of the mind mimics that of the labourer—that treads through, prickproof, thick / Thousands of thorns, thoughts"—and then has Tom go on to survey "his lot, low but free from care."

All this people like Tom have learned to shrug off, "the witnessing of which lightheartedness makes me indignant with the fools of Radical Levellers." But then he is reminded that this is all "very well for those who are in, however low in, the Commonwealth and share in any way the Common weal; but that the curse of our times is that many do not share it, that they are outcasts from it and have neither security nor splendour; that they share care with the high and obscurity with the low, but wealth or comfort with neither. And this . . . is the origin of Loafers, Tramps, Cornerboys, Roughs, Socialists and other pests of society." It is, he believes, "a very pregnant sonnet and in point of execution very highly wrought," but then adds, defensively, "Too much so, I am afraid."

"Your Eminence and dearest Father, Pax Christi," he writes Newman on February 20 for the Cardinal's eighty-seventh birthday. "This . . . somehow-or-other manned wreck of the Catholic University," he explains, "is afloat and not sinking; rather making a very little way than losing any." Still, there is no longer any public interest here in Newman's grand idea of a university, though "this does not prevent good and really patriotic people in a quiet but not ineffective way doing what can be done to advance it." He mentions "the resignation (followed by the withdrawal from our Society)" of Klein, "an able, learned, and amiable man; who nevertheless took this step to our and his own injury." At least the all-crucial "money loss of his salary was almost at once made up by the appointment of a learned Father of our Community," John J. O'Carroll, S.J., for the current academic year at the same rate of £400. "In this and in other respects," he is relieved, "the Senate of the Royal University is very friendly to us and to Catholic interests, thank God." As for the political situation here, he daily lives "in an air most painful to breathe and this comes home to me more . . . with time." In fact, he can see only one ray of hope, and that has come out of Rome, with Pope Leo "acting very much as I thought he would" in condemning both the Plan of Campaign and the boycotting, so that "the effect of what he does, though slowly and guardedly, is likely to be powerful."

Finally, he mentions the good fortune—"if it is not cruel to say it"—of his having their mutual friend George Teeling "lodged a few doors down on our side of the Green," where he is being treated by specialists for his lameness, and where Hopkins can see him on a daily basis. George Teeling, forty, more and more incapacitated by spinal disease, nephew by marriage to Judge Thomas O'Hagan of Howth, late Lord Chancellor of Ireland, and once a novice at Newman's Oratory, who left without being ordained. Afterward Teeling taught at the Oratory, then at a Benedictine school in Scotland. Still later, he became private secretary to O'Hagan here in Dublin and—when the Judge died in '85—edited his speeches for publication.

"His doctor now operates on him by cauterising the spine," Hopkins adds, "and today he was lifted higher on his couch than before . . . so that a gradual recovery may be hoped for. He is as winning as ever. I commonly find him in good spirits, neither buoyant nor dejected." But to Bridges he puts Teeling's case more familiarly: "I have a poor, very charming friend on his back with spinal disease," he tells him. "When he complains of rheumatic pains his doctor rubs his hands with joy and says nothing cd. be better." But there is a kindness about Hopkins, a deep concern for people like Teeling, forced by circumstances to be one more good fellow well met, living off his relatives as they are inclined, raconteur and dispenser of the *mot juste* and dabbler in literature, like Hopkins himself one more marginalized presence, one more "lonely began" here in crumbling Dublin.

April, and still wintry: He sits at his desk in one of the small makeshift classrooms, administering an examination to his second-year Latin students. The subject is Virgil's *Georgics*. He thrums his fingers on the desk, then—after a while—picks up one of the unused exam booklets lying near at hand and begins a wedding poem—his "Epithalamion"—for Everard and his fiancée, Amy. He is thinking of Virgil's pastoral world, and perhaps of Edmund Spenser's *Epithalamion,* and of the flowing Thames and then of the swimming places he used to frequent on the Hodder near Stonyhurst, and of the rivers along the Devonshire in the Long Vacation, and perhaps of Fred Walker's painting of boys shouting and swimming in summer. He thinks he will make of the image an allegory of that welcoming new element in which a man and a woman move and have their being when they enter into marriage. "Make believe / We are leafwhelmed somewhere with the hood / Of some branchy bunchy bushybowered wood," he daydreams now, the language rivering and bubbling to the surface:

Southern dean or Lancashire clough or Devon cleave,
That leans along the loins of hills, where a candycoloured, where a
        gluegold-brown
Marbled river, boisterously beautiful, between
Roots and rocks is danced and dandled, all in froth and waterblow-
        balls, down. . . .

And then he is there with them, rather than here in this modest classroom facing St. Stephen's Green, and suddenly there is a shout "That the
hanging honeysuck, the dogeared hazels in the cover / Makes dither, makes
hover," yes, as he recalls a world of riot and rout, "boys from the town /
Bathing: it is summer's sovereign good." Another kind of composition of
place altogether this, and one closer to Whitman, for now "there comes a
listless stranger: beckoned by the noise"—Everard, perhaps, or Hopkins
himself, or anyone exhausted with the plodding workaday world, who
wants to loosen his necktie or Roman collar:

He drops towards the river: unseen
Sees the bevy of them, how the boys
With dare and with downdolphinry and bellbright bodies huddling
        out,
Are earthworld, airworld, waterworld thorough hurled, all by turn
        and turn about. . . .

He listens carefully, watching from a distance as the boys gambol. No
doubt he would love to share in their world as well, as he did long ago on
the Isle of Wight and in Wales and at Stonyhurst. But modestly, apart, at a
remove, yes, like and unlike, where he can splash in that element, the all-
mothering world of it, the male and the female of it. And so

    he hies to a pool neighbouring; sees it is the best
There; sweetest, freshest, shadowiest;
Fairyland; silk-beech, scrolled ash, packed sycamore, wild wychelm,
        hornbeam fretty overstood
By. Rafts and rafts of flake-leaves light, dealt so, painted on the air,
Hang as still as hawk or hawkmoth, as the stars or as the angels
        there,
Like the thing that never knew the earth . . .

A place like and unlike, a place where "flake-leaves light," as if an angel hung there. And now he throws off his collar and soutane, "his bleachèd both and woolwoven wear: / Careless these in coloured wisp / All lie tumbled-to." Then off with his heavy boots, tossing them away with abandon, glad to be rid of a world of hard duty for the moment, like Tom, that he too might once again touch the earth, electric, charged, alive,

> Till walk the world he can with bare his feet
> And come where lies a coffer, burly all of blocks
> Built of chancequarrièd, selfquainèd, hoar-huskèd rocks
> And the water warbles over into, filleted with glassy grassy quick-
>   silvery shivès and shoots
> And with heavenfallen freshness down from moorland still brims,
> Dark or daylight on and on. Here he will then, here he will the fleet
> Flinty kindcold element let break across his limbs
> Long. Where we leave him, froliclavish, while he looks about him,
>   laughs, swims.

He looks up at the heads bent down over their books, forelocks falling forward, and thinks. Thinks about the marriage he should be celebrating, his sacred matter floating on "this only gambolling and echoing-of-earth note," and begins now to explicate his own wedding allegory: What is . . . the delightful dean? / Wedlock. What the water? Spousal love. And those trees he has catalogued—"silk-beech, scrolled ash, packed sycamore, wild wychelm, hornbeam fretty"—what are they but "Father, mother, brothers, sisters, friends," well-wishers, morphed for the moment "Into fairy trees, wildflowers, woodferns / Rankèd round the bower. . . ." And then a look at the clock on the wall, and a bell hardly a wedding bell to remind him that class is over, and the trees turn back into second-year students again, and there is a bustle of boys getting up to leave, and like Coleridge with his *Kubla Khan,* the spell is broken and the poem put aside and all but forgotten.

Once, one of his students will recall—long after Father Hopkins is gone—how Hopkins, while lecturing on Homer's Helen, suddenly looked up from his text and said something like, "You know, I never saw a naked woman." And then, after a moment, "I wish I had." This is Hopkins's world, strict Victorian decorum and modesty at home, then an all-boys' school, followed by Oxford, with its all-male faculty and students, followed by his entry into the Jesuits. Is it any wonder, then, that—evoking a sense of sensual freedom in his daydreaming prologue to his epithalamion—he should have focused on a group of boys gamboling at a Lancashire river spot, though he sees himself even here as modestly holding back from the others? Or that, focusing on mortal beauty, he should have pictured those young, blond, blue-eyed Anglos on the slave block in Gregory's Rome, and seen the chance to save a nation, his rare-dear own? What he will never be able to stomach is the souring of innocence, or the philandering of a priest who has committed himself to a life of chastity. As for the rest—adulteries, rapes, incest, self-abuse, seductions of all kinds—of these he has had his fill and more from men and women both, in the confessional boxes of London, Oxford, Liverpool, Manchester, Glasgow, and Dublin.

"Mayday, a stormy one," he writes Baillie. "Your letter has just come in [and] helps to cheer my very gloomy mind." He thanks Baillie for the photograph of himself and tells him that he may be able to send him one soon in return. This one is "not shopdone," he explains, but "artistically better," taken "the other day as I was walking in our backyard or catswing . . . somebody"—no doubt Father Mallac—"did me instantaneous; for the laboratory, now used for photography." It shows an older and more mature Hopkins than the face in the Oxford photograph, more the Jesuit, hair close-cropped, eyes a bit sunken, as if caught in the midst of some deep reverie, against a backdrop of shadow only.

What he cannot understand is Baillie's saying that—like Bridges—he finds London life intolerable these days. Now he too loves country life and dislikes "any town and that especially for its bad and smokefoul air." But London is another story. London he prefers to any large town in these islands. True, "in fog it is dreadful, but it has many fine days, and in summer. . . . Its air is a balmy air, certainly in the West End [which is] cheerful and quietly handsome, with many fine trees." Besides, he adds wistfully, "there are so many resources, things to go to and hear and see and do. Everything is there. No, I think that very much may be said for life in London," though his first choice, if he could have it, would be "a farm in the Western counties, glowworms, new milk."

But the fact is that he wakes up each morning in Dublin. What he most dislikes about Dublin, as about any of Britain's cities, "is the misery of the poor; the dirt, squalor, and the illshapen degraded physical (putting aside moral) type of so many of the people, with the deeply dejecting, unbearable thought that by degrees almost all our population will become a town population and a puny unhealthy and cowardly one." Yes, cowardly, he insists, recalling Majuba Hill, which still rankles, when "500 British troops after 8 hours' firing, on the Dutch reaching the top, ran without offering hand to hand resistance before, it is said, 80 men. Such a thing was never heard in history." Add to the mix Gladstone, who showed himself equal even to that disgrace by professing that "the Queen's honour was by this dishonour vindicated . . . and stamped the memory of Majuba in the minds of all African colonists forever. What one man could do to throw away a continent and weaken the bonds of a worldwide empire he did." And "may do more in that kind yet." It is Hopkins's duty—as it is Baillie's—to somehow keep "this fatal and baleful influence . . . out of political power. . . . Strange being! He is, without foresight, insight, or resolution himself, the bright form of the thoughts and wishes of the Liberal masses."

Months earlier, Patmore had written Hopkins to say that, after "much meditating on the effect" which the manuscript of his *Sponsa Dei* had had on Hopkins, he had decided not to "take the responsibility of being the first to expound the truths therein contained." And so, on Christmas Day, he "committed the work to the flames without reserve of a single paragraph," though now he has second thoughts about having done so. It takes Hopkins three months to respond. "This . . . is the second letter begun, and the other ran some length, but is cancelled," he answers on May 6 from the Jesuit theologate at Milltown Park. "Your news was that you had burnt . . . *Sponsa Dei,* and that on reflexion upon remarks of mine." How he wishes he had been more guarded in his remarks, for when one takes a step such as Patmore has, one condemns oneself. "Either our work shd. never have been done or never undone, and either way our time and toil are wasted—a sad thought; though the intention may at both times have been good." But, then, it is just one more misunderstanding for which he is to take the blame.

Late May: "Not a low, not a crow, not a bark, not a bray from either of us has crossed the Channel this long while," he complains to Bridges. He wants his friend to send his play, *Nero,* to Judge John O'Hagan, Glenaveena, Howth, Co. Dublin, along with a copy of Bridges's paper on Milton's verse. "O'Hagan is an interesting and able man," he explains, "but old fashioned in his notions of poetry, especially rhythm; he thought, without a suspicion, that Shakespeare's verse was often very rough, had never heard of the doctrine of equivalence, and so on." And there it is, he adds. "I understand these things so much better than you . . . but I have the passion for explanation and you have not."

May gives way to June, then June to July, and once more the busiest time of the year is upon him. The setting of questions in conjunction with other Royal University examiners, then the going over each exam to be as scrupulously fair as he can, hour after hour after hour of it, past midnight there in his room facing the back of the house, his eyes bleeding, plagued with diarrhea, the chamberpot filling, a small smoky coal fire, his haggard face reflected in the window above his desk, migraines, a physical malaise he has no name for, and—all the while—the fate of thousands of students in his hands.

Examinations "began last month," he writes his mother in early July, "and will outlast this one. It is great, very great drudgery" and "a burden which crushes me and does little to help any good end." The Royal University in the main "does the work of examining well," but then "the work is not worth much." Moreover, his entire salary is given over to the university, which—alas—has turned out to be a failure, and "in doing this almost fruitless work I use up all opportunity of doing any other." It is the most candid assessment of his situation he has yet given her.

"What a preposterous summer!" he writes Dixon on the 29th, still in the midst of marking Latin examinations. "It is raining now: when is it not? However there was one windy bright day between floods last week: fearing for my eyes, with my other rain of papers, I put work aside and went out for the day, and conceived a sonnet. Otherwise my muse has long put down her carriage and now for years 'takes in washing.' The laundry is driving a great trade now." All that miserable laundry he has had to take in like Dame Jane Nightwork: those endless translations of bad Latin and worse Greek. He still fears he may go mad at any time, as he counts up the casualties among his classmates who have left the Church and the priesthood for greener pastures or—worse, despairing—leapt off the sterns of ferries in the straits between Dover and Calais, down, down, and down. . . .

July 26, 1888: The sonnet he conceives on this Dublin afternoon between showers is "That Nature is a Heraclitean Fire and of the comfort of the Resurrection." Begin at the beginning with Heraclitus, the pre-Socratic philosopher who flourished half a millennium before Christ and who flourishes even now under a different name. Nature: springing from fire and returning to fire, in which everything and everyone will dissolve and disappear. A world calculated in millions upon millions of years, a world in constant metamorphosis, evolving and devolving, a marvelous brouhaha of chance, with no one it seems at the helm. Enter Lyell, enter Darwin, enter Huxley and the Victorian scientific mind. Enter the whole shebang in the form of a drunken bevy of clouds high over Dublin in the interstices between one summer squall and another, July 26, 1888.

"Cloud-puffballs," he begins, his bleeding eyes following the cloud formations above him, this perennial star-gazer and sunset–painter and cloud-watcher, who years before had studied the heavens as he had bluebells, looking for any least sign of God's presence and beauty and order to be found there. And now, two days shy of his forty-fourth birthday, he realizes with a terrible start that the intense hard looking he had given to searching the heavens for signs of God's presence no longer yields what it had so abundantly twenty or even ten years before. Cloud-gleaning is a young man's game, he sees now, and now those bright eyes with which he used to watch are burned out with grading all those sophomoric renderings of his beloved Greek masterpieces.

"Clouds growing in beauty at [the] end of the day," he had written one Sunday night twenty-two years before. In the afternoon there had been "a white rack of two parallel spines, vertebrated as so often." Then, "at sunset, when the sky had charm and beauty, very level clouds . . . with gold-colour splashed sunset-spot . . . scud-like, rising." The very meadows about him, "yellow with buttercups . . . containing white of oxeyes and puff-balls." And, on the very day that he clearly saw "the impossibility of staying in the Church of England," he had begun by noting the shapes of clouds. "Dull," he had reported that day. "Curds-and-whey clouds faintly at times."

But here, now, on this damp summer's day, he has walked out from St. Stephen's Green to look up at the skies again, only to find the clouds flaunting themselves, chevying down the heavens like hounds at harriers after their prey. Heaven-roisterers, he calls them, swaggering drunkards thronging overhead, the seeming masters of the skies. And between them: shivelights—shards of glassy light deepening the shadows along the roughcast façades of the cottages, brightening and dimming as sunlight burns through the clouds, defining the damask-sharp shadows of elm branches along the walls, marking them, then disappearing. It is all a speeding up, a fast-forwarding, a kind of time-lapse photography: here, there, and then gone.

And the wind—noisy and boisterous and rude as the clouds themselves—scattering the standing pools of water in the unpaved roads before him, beating earth bare, then baking the mud and clay created by the heavy rains and winds in this Heraclitean first day of Creation, as the soft doughy imprint of thousands of hoofmarks and wheel tracks and bootprints turns to ooze, then crust, then dust, as if they themselves were the fuel feeding the clouds above, and which he sees now were never really clouds at all but rather smoke from the things of this world burning, burning, as Augustine said of the streets of Carthage. It is all nature's bonfire—bonefire—we are witnessing, the holocaust of the world, fire returning to fire, and we mortals willy-nilly feeding those same flames. Clouds in their crazed Ovidian meta-morphoses "flaunting," "chevying," "thronging," "glittering," lacing and lancing and pairing. And the wind—that other bully-boy—roping, wres-tling, beating earth bare. It is all a plethora of verbs denoting ongoing, ceaseless action, violent action, in a grand, unending, tumbling cycle—over and over and over, world without end.

And deeper yet into his meditation on death and loss, even as the *Exer-cises* for the Third Week have encouraged him to do. Yes, and what else? What more? In a cruel pun, he notes how the idiot winds likewise snuff and quench the observer observing all of this, and we—who stood apart as na-ture's "clearest-selvèd spark," we, with our abrupt, distinctive, not-to-be-reduplicated selves, we, the so-called pinnacle of all Creation, we, nature's "bonniest, dearest to her"selves—we too go up in smoke in the great bonfire of Creation as it burns drunkenly, merrily on. All is unselved, untuned, and—just as violin or catgut strings go slack, all clear vowelling lost—so do we, like our words, until "all is an enormous dark / Drowned." How his sibilants capture that distinctiveness, piling up in the inscaping of that sheer-off shivelight: "Manshape, that shone / Sheer off, disseveral, a star": inevitably beat level just like the drying mudmarks here on drab Dub-lin's streets on this July afternoon toward the close of the nineteenth century.

But there is something even more sobering: the fact that even man's name will go the same way, and all—*all*—the names in the portraits be lost. Ten thousand more years—a blink in Chthonic time—and even the names of Michelangelo and Mozart and Dante and Milton and Shakespeare will join Callimachus and the lost works of the ancients. An older Yeats of course will find some bitter consolation in the great return, the consolation of the Gyres, the sense of things falling apart and beginning again. And thus far Hopkins would agree, cold consolation that such a vision of nihilistic gaiety is to each of us individually. But in the longer apocalyptic perspec-tive of vasty time, even that gelid consolation pales, and

> áll is in an enórmous dárk
> Drowned. O pity and indig'nation! Manshape, that shone
> Sheer off, disseveral, a star, ' death blots black out; nor mark

> Is ány of him at áll so stárk
> But vastness blurs and time ' beats level . . .

But there is another answer, and it comes midway in the sixteenth of the sonnet's twenty-four lines. And when it comes, it comes unexpectedly, with the clarion cry of abrupt exclamation. It is like God's time cutting instantaneously across the vastness of Darwinian and Lyellian time, which is itself but a wink in God's eternal eye. In a letter to Patmore written four years earlier, Hopkins had remonstrated with him about the nature of the Second Coming. It was an event, he said, as far as he understood the matter, that would be "sudden, surprising, and unforeseen," and when it came, it would be "utterly unmistakeable; in that differing from [Christ's] first coming and all other tokens of himself." Like the sudden electric shock of the resurrection on that first Easter morning, when the women had gone out early to dress their beloved Master's corpse and had witnessed a turning of everything on its head, an event whose reality still had the power to shake one to the core.

No mistaking it, then, the sheer temporal hyperbaton of it. It is the lesson of the nun on the doomed *Deutschland*, seeing something in an insane storm, as she perished on a smother of sand in the winter of '75, herself become the heart's-clarion calling out after her Master and his. Well, no matter now, he still has something he can hold on to: Christ's promise, his consolation, the very thing that had driven a wedge between Hopkins and his own family, and that had once pushed him to the extreme of telling his brother Lionel—who in his eighty-plus years would never understand why his brother had had to become a Catholic and, worse, go over to those despised Jesuits—to stop writing him, though they had managed to call a truce on that one and agree to disagree.

Twenty years before, he had turned his own hand to the plough, and he would not look back. Something out there kept beckoning, most days only faintly, like the light from a winter star or a distant beacon. Still, it was something as certain to him as anything he cared for, and for which he had paid the price. "How to keep," he had written years earlier, crisping the voices of Winefred's maidens,

> is there ány any, is there none such, nowhere known some, bow
> or brooch or braid or brace, láce, latch or catch or key to keep
> Back beauty, keep it, beauty, beauty, béauty, . . . from vanishing
>   away?

Then too he had edged close to despair, until—in an instant—the solution had come home to him. No human answer, but Christ's, manifested in the miracle of his rising. "O why are we so haggard at the heart," he'd asked then. Why

> só cáre-cóiled, cáre-kílled, só fágged, só fáshed, só cógged, só
>   cűmbéred,
> When the thing we freely fórfeit is kept with fónder a care,
> Fonder a cáre kept than we could have kept it . . .

And so here again, in the great Mosaic/Pauline / Johannine *Deus ex machina* resolution of this last hurrah. Who are you? the shepherd fronting forked lightning had asked the figure in the burning bush, and the answer had come back: "I am I am." And again: who *are* you? they had demanded of Christ, and he had answered: "I am." And Paul, addressing the community at Corinth, having seen that one time at least into the core of the great mystery, the once that had flattened him on the road to Damascus, naked lightning instantaneously, unequivocally striking, as Hopkins himself had been struck all those years before on a reading holiday with two Oxford companions in a backwater called Horsham, the realization of what he had to do coming home to him—as he kept insisting—"all in a minute."

"Now I am going to tell you a mystery," St. Paul had told his little congregation in the seaport city of Corinth with the certitude of the mystic who has come up against the shock and brilliance of the resurrected Christ. "We are not all going to fall asleep," meaning not everyone would die as they might have expected. "But we *are* all going to be changed. Instantly. In the wink of an eye, when the last trumpet sounds. For the trumpet IS going to sound," Paul had assured them, "and then the dead will be raised imperishable, and we shall be changed, because this perishable nature of ours must put on imperishability. This *mortal* nature *must* put on immortality."

"In a flash, at a trumpet crash," Hopkins has it, all those scurrying verbs giving way to the central shimmering verb *to be,* as now—in a nanosecond—we take on God's own life. No evolution or devolution, no waiting in groaning expectation. Suddenly, finally, unmistakably, the self of self, what we mean when we say, "I am," will see that it is suddenly at one with the great I AM: "I am all at once what Christ is." And why? Because of the incredible gift of the Incarnation we have been offered: of God's breaking in upon the world—betweenpied mountains—to share His life with us, in the incredible condescension of His becoming "what I am": a human being. And so, yes, "this Jack, joke, poor potsherd," this eccentric, this failure by any standards of the world, this clown, this make-do, this patched-up Jesuit sent to mend this or that or the other in one parish or school or university as best he could, this throwaway, this matchwood flaring up for a moment before going out, careful to match in his own life the life of his ever downwardly mobile master:

> Enough! the Resurrection,
> A héart's-clarion! Awáy grief's gásping, ' joyless days, dejection.
>   Across my foundering deck shone
> A beacon, an eternal beam. ' Flesh fade, and mortal trash
> Fáll to the resíduary worm; ' world's wildfire, leave but ash:
>   In a flash, at a trumpet crash,
> I am all at once what Christ is, ' since he was what I am, and
> Thís Jack, jóke, poor pótsherd, ' patch, matchwood, immortal
>   diamond,
>   Is immortal diamond.

Two years before, thinking of the impact Wordsworth's *Intimations of Immortality* had had on him, he had confessed to Dixon that there were only a handful of poets who had actually ever seen something, whatever that was. That ode was in fact the best thing Wordsworth ever wrote, for here "his insight was at its very deepest." Surely "St. George and St. Thomas of Canterbury wore roses in heaven for England's sake on the day that ode, not without their intercession, was penned." So, too, heaven must still be applauding that day Hopkins penned this poem with its extraordinary linguistic insight into the adamantine inscape of mankind's immortal spirit.

Early August: He and Curtis finally get away from Dublin to spend two weeks in Scotland, taking in the Glasgow Exhibition and hiking the mountains around Fort William. "Six weeks of examination are lately over," he writes Bridges from Monzie Villa on Saturday evening, the 18th, "and I am now bringing a fortnight's holiday to an end." At the moment he and Curtis are in Lochaber, "and have been to the top of Ben Nevis [4,400 feet] and up Glencoe on the most brilliant days, but in spite of the exertions or because of them I cannot sleep ... and we have got no bathing (it is close at hand but close also to the highroad) nor boating and I am feeling very old and looking very wrinkled." Besides, there are no books here, "except the farce" of Curtis reading Minchin's *Uniplanar Kinematics of Solids and Fluids,* as "he is doing so now and dozing and shd. be in bed."

And then, a sardonic note before retiring for the night, commenting on Bridges's and Dixon's misreading of "Heraclitean Fire" along with so much else of his, even though he has been at pains to simplify his syntax. Ah well, there it is, his explanation of what sustains him in his darkest moments: the reality of Christ risen, Christ alive somehow in these islands. Tomorrow being a Sunday, he will try to "put plainly to a Highland congregation of MacDonalds, MacIntoshes, MacKillops, and the rest what I am putting not at all so plainly to the rest of the world, or rather to you and Canon Dixon."

Friday night, September 7: Back in Dublin, he writes Bridges again. After Fort William, he went down to Whitby in Yorkshire to spend a few days with his brothers Arthur and Everard before returning here, to begin setting another "Examination Paper, in a distress of mind difficult both to understand and to explain." He knows now that he "cannot always last like this: in mind or body or both I shall give way—and all I really need is a certain degree of relief and change." But he does not think that what he needs he is going to get in time to save him. Which reminds him "of a shocking thing that has just happened to a young man well known to some of our community. He put his eyes out. He was a medical student and probably understood how to proceed, which was nevertheless barbarously done with a stick and some wire. The eyes were found among nettles in a field." He mentions the case "because it is extraordinary: suicide is common." It is a chilling story, and the horror of it hits eerily close to home.

He also has the words now for "the first verse of a patriotic song for soldiers," since "heaven knows it is needed." He wants to compose "5 verses, but 3 would do for singing." The tune—"very flowing and spirited"—came to him while he was walking in Phoenix Park the day before. The difficulty, he realizes, is that such songs must "breathe true feeling without spoon or brag." And though he hates both, he feels himself "half blundering or sinking into them in several of my pieces, a thought that makes me not greatly regret their likelihood of perishing." But is it not his own soldiering on as a Jesuit he celebrates here? And at what cost? Certainly more than the single shilling recruiting officers offer enlistees when they sign on the dotted line to serve in Afghanistan or South Africa or the Sudan. And what can bring out the diamond brilliance of the self if not duty, duty to the death, if need be? What he in fact hopes himself to do in going where he is told, and serving as best as his aging body can under the banner of his Lord and King. And if it is hard to imagine some sergeant in a pub in Gibraltar singing the words "Call me England's fame's fond lover," not so Hopkins, who had said as much—and more—in the final rousing stanza of the *Deutschland* a dozen years before. And so he sends Bridges four stanzas, together with a tune in G major, and asks Bridges to add a fifth stanza of his own, as a way of England's poets celebrating England's soldiers:

> What shall I do for the land that bred me,
> Her homes and fields that folded and fed me?
> Be under her banner and live for her honour:
> Under her banner I'll live for her honour.
> > *Chorus.* Under her banner we live for her honour.
>
> Call me England's fame's fond lover,
> Her fame to keep, her fame to recover.
> Spend me or end me what God shall send me,
> But under her banner I live for her honour.
> > *Chorus.* Under her banner we march for her honour.

If the piece suffers from spooniness—Hopkins is not after all Kipling—in another month he will effectively write the palinode to these lyrics in a poem to one of his fellow Jesuits just canonized.

Then news from Bridges that the composer W. S. Rockstro, who has been staying with Bridges at Yattendon, has set Hopkins's patriotic piece to music. "I am very glad you like the tune and greatly honoured by Mr. Rockstro's setting an accompaniment to it," he writes. Only for want of a piano here at the college has he not yet heard it. And though Rockstro does not think the piece can be counterpointed, Hopkins thinks otherwise. "Indeed, with some improvements I have since yesterday made, it may be accompanied in canon at the octave two bars off." He will of course transpose the piece to F, for "all keys are the same to me and to everyone who thinks that music was before instruments and angels before tortoises and cats."

Late summer, and the dank, filthy streets of the city. Ah, to go unshod, as he had daydreamed of doing in his unfinished epithalamion. On September 17, he sends a mock-scholarly letter to the editor of *Stonyhurst Magazine,* his friend and colleague from his Stonyhurst days, Father John Gerard, S.J., on the subject of playing football barefoot, a letter which will appear in the November issue. "Sir," he begins in his best mock-serious manner—for he has always loved mimicking others, from his own father to strangers glimpsed in his travels to birdcalls—"Football is sometimes played barefoot in Ireland."

A friend here in Dublin (the irrepressible Sweetman?) has told him that "the club he belongs to challenged some village clubs in his neighborhood; when the game came to be played their opponents stripped their feet and took the field barefoot. He [was] surprised, and thought the bare feet would need to be tenderly dealt with, both by their wearers and by those who, like him, had reared three storeys of wool, leather, and iron between themselves and the county Tipperary." But the men "told them they could not play with any ease, unless unshod." In strictness, the game of hurley "ought to be played with the feet bare," as it is in Phoenix Park. Indeed, with the rise of Irish Nationalism, Hopkins has noticed that the ancient game has undergone a revival, so that it follows that, "as antiquaries discover more and more, advanced players will wear less and less."

More and more he feels the distance between Bridges and himself growing now, not only in terms of the geographical and religious abyss, but even in their ideas of what poetry should be. Hopkins, the Olympian competitor taking on Tennyson and the entire English poetic tradition, but without an audience, pushing the limits of syntax and music in his poems to his audience of three, only to be met with incomprehension. But Bridges? Bridges, except for Christ his dearest, his closest reader? "I am sorry to hear of our differing so much in taste," he writes him on the 25th. The truth is that he was hardly aware of the rift there. Still, he adds, that is "not nearly so sad as differing in religion." For his part, Bridges, with his growing reputation as a poet, along with his friends and critics in increasingly high places, has had to finally point out to his unread Jesuit friend the vast difference between the way he and others approach Greek and Roman literature and the odd way Hopkins does.

What Hopkins really needs is to read the classics in greater depth, and then he would come at them with a better sense of what they have to offer in creating a viable modern poetic style. Don't argue, Hopkins reminds himself. Don't argue, though Bridges just cannot see what he sees. And so he responds to Bridges that, yes, he feels "how great the loss is of not reading, as you say." But if he did read more, he does not believe the effect on him would be what Bridges thinks it would be, on either his poems or his method of composition. "I *must* read something of Greek and Latin letters"—as if this professor of Greek and Latin has not—"and lately I sent you a sonnet, on the Heraclitean Fire, in which a great deal of early Greek philosophical thought was distilled; but the liquor of the distillation did not taste very Greek, did it?" The fact is that the "effect of studying master-pieces" on him is to make Hopkins "admire and do otherwise."

A week later, while strolling through the vast open expanses of Phoenix Park to get some air, he conceives the first part of a sonnet he has promised Father Goldie. Goldie had written asking him to compose a poem in honor of the newly canonized Alphonsus Rodriguez, a Jesuit lay brother who had served as a porter at the Jesuit house in Majorca for over forty years. Now he sends a draft of the new piece, "In honour of St. Alphonsus Rodriguez," off to Bridges for his opinion. Rodriguez was a Jesuit lay brother, Hopkins explains, "who for 40 years acted as hall-porter to the College of Palma in Majorca: he was, it is believed, much favoured by God with heavenly lights and much persecuted by evil spirits." This sonnet—and he says it "snorting"—"aims at being intelligible," so "do not put it aside 'for further neglect' but answer smart. It has to go to Majorca. Call in the Canon, have a consultation, sit, and send result by return—or soon."

"Honour is flashed off exploit, so we say," the new sonnet begins,

> And those strokes once that gashed flesh or galled shield
> Should tongue that time now, trumpet now that field,
> And, on the fighter, forge his glorious day.

This was certainly the way Christ led, and there are many who followed Christ with the examples of their own blood-soaked witnessing. But what of those who experience the war as raging all within, where earth itself "hears no hurtle then from fiercest fray"?

And what of the bedridden, crippled, house- or prison-bound, who suffer with silent courage from depression or migraines, or who have been given the task of reading thousands on thousands of examination papers and whose salary they never see? Cannot the God who over millennia and with infinite patience shaped the very continents, melting mountains along with glaciers, or each spring for untold ages has veined violets cell by cell, who watches with infinite patience over the slow growth of cedars and oaks and maples, cannot this same God "crowd career with conquest" when nothing seems to happen, while the self is honeycombed cell by cell into a saint, as with Alfonso, whose life consisted in large part of greeting whoever knocked, then opening the door in expectation of greeting Christ himself, as indeed he did?

"I am obliged for your criticisms," he tells Bridges on October 19, mentioning that he has now improved the poem's ending. But he can neither understand nor agree with Bridges's strictures against God's hewing or sculpting whole mountain ranges and continents. After all, shape itself— that cognate of inscape—means "in old English to hew and the Hebrew *bara* / to create, even, properly means to hew. But life and living things are not naturally said to be hewn: they grow, and their growth is by trickling increment." Whether hewn or growing, things—and we—are shaped and inscaped by the subtle Master and Creator who bodes and abides.

With a sense of relief, Hopkins adds that he has just turned "the last batch of examination-work for this autumn (and if all were seen, fallen leaves of my poor life between all the leaves of it)." He has finally had to get eyeglasses and is happy neither with nor without them. "The oculist says my sight is very good and my eyes perfectly healthy but that like Jane Night-work I am old." In spite of which, he has taken up sketching again, and wonders why he did not do so sooner. His father has recently written "a little book on *[The Cardinal] Numbers,* the numbers one to ten," to which he has contributed something of his own. Admittedly, the book is "a sketchy thing," playful, and raises "points of interest in a vast, an infinite subject." In fact, the *Saturday Review* had a few laughs at the work's expense, "making great game of it . . . including something I had contributed to it," though at least he was not named.

"Honour is flashed off exploit," he had begun his tribute to St. Alphonsus Rodriguez. But now he is warming himself "at the flame of a little exploit of my own done last night," and cannot believe he has had such "success nor that life had this pleasure to bestow. Somebody"—most likely Curtis—"had tried to take me in and I warned him I wd. take him in at our next meeting." And so, in the spirit of horseplay, he "wrote him a letter from 'the son of a respected livery and bait stables in Parteen [a suburb of Limerick] oftentimes employed by your Honoured Father' asking for an introduction to one of the Dublin newspapers 'as Reporter, occasional paregraphs [sic] or sporting inteligence' [sic]."

It is an example of that inimitable ability to mimic others, and he has been rubbing his hands with delight ever since. "The sentence I think best of was one in which I said I (or he) could 'give any color which may be desired to reports of speeches or Proceedings subject to the Interests of truth which must always be the paremount [sic] consideration.' It succeeded beyond my wildest hopes and action is going to be taken. The letter is even to be printed in the *Nation* as a warning to those who are continually applying in the like strain." But before Hopkins can let it go that far, he will have to step in.

Yet there is also that jarring note embedded in his friendship with Bridges. It has always had its fraught moments, this friendship, but now he is hurt, and hurt deeply, by the delight Bridges takes in telling him news that he dreads to hear. Addis, his fellow comforter and convert in his time at Oxford, has at last left the priesthood and abandoned his parish at Sydenham to go off with one of his female parishioners, and Bridges could not be more delighted. It is as if all these years Bridges had been tallying up the losses of this fiasco of an Oxford Movement—several down, and now just one more to go. "But why should you be glad?" Hopkins remonstrates with him. "Why at any rate should you burst upon me that you are glad, when you know that I cannot be glad?" What is it with Bridges that he should torment him so? "Did you hear of Addis's leaving the R.C. Communion?" Bridges will write Muirhead shortly after, rubbing his hands in the knowledge that he was right all along, that it was just a matter of waiting for these men to return to their senses. He has already met with Addis in London, "and had a long talk with him. It is a great delight to me that he should have relinquished the untenable. He is as zealous as ever but now very much on my lines, but would not come under any formularies—so is not a member of our [Anglican] communion. He saw the reasonableness of becoming one, but could not after his experience burden his conscience again and I think he was wise." Ah, but give him time. Give him time.

"It seems," Hopkins has it out with Bridges, "there is something in you interposed between what shall we say? the Christian and the man of the world which hurts, which is to me like biting on a cinder in bread. Take the simplest view of this matter: [Addis] has made shipwreck, I am afraid he must even be in straits: he cannot support himself by his learned writings; I suppose he will have to teach. But this is the least. I hope at all events he will not pretend to marry, and especially no one he has known in his priestly life." But of course this is exactly what he knows will happen.

Marriage, Hopkins explains, is "honourable and so is the courtship that leads to marriage but the philanderings of men vowed to God are not honourable nor the marriages they end in. I feel the same deep affection for him as ever, but the respect is gone. I would write to him if I had his address, which, I am sorry to say, is still or was lately somewhere at Sydenham; for after bidding farewell to his flock he had not the grace to go away." Still, troubled as he is, he chooses to remain faithful to Bridges, seeing something in him that Bridges himself does not see: that beneath the gruff exterior of a man who has been deeply wounded by life, there is someone worth loving.

The war within, the war without. "My dearest mother," he writes on November 10, "it is not convenient to my time or eyesight or memory or anything to read the long reports of the Parnell trial at breakfast and nevertheless I ought to read them." And so he asks her to send him *The Times,* if the reports are published there. He has written Lionel "to tap his liquor" on China and other things, but is afraid that his letter, "which had a certain soreness," has only succeeded in upsetting Lionel the more. Two weeks later, he writes Arthur in London, offering him some advice on the ideal of feminine beauty. "I hope your exhibition has turned out a great success and sold your pictures and led to commissions," he begins. Someone has just mailed him a copy of his Number 18. "Not that this is my first sight of it by a great deal," he adds, for the three resident students here at the college have hung it in their reading room. And in fact, the pinup "is admired, and it is a sweet and pretty face."

But it is too unfinished, too much like one of Gustave Doré's thrown-off sketches. Worse, the girl's breasts are dwarfed, "and much too high up and probably too flat." After all, a finely proportioned female figure should be "divided in half exactly at the groin and into quarters at the nipples and lowest point of the kneecap respectively," but "these proportions will not suit your girl at all." On the other hand, the head is beautiful "and grows on one, as people have said." The truth is that "the number of really and regularly beautiful faces" is very small. Ancient female sculptures, for instance, "are perfectly regular, but wanting in grace." Even da Vinci's *La Giaconda,* "perhaps the greatest achievement of modern art in the ideal treatment of the human face, is not quite regular." He asks Arthur to send him some drawing chalk or charcoal and a *portecrayon* to hold it, because he wants to follow up on Father Mallac's suggestion and get back to drawing again, though he has no money for supplies. He encloses some sketches so Arthur can see what he has been up to. As for that drawing of the copse he did at Shanklin twenty years before when Arthur was with him, it has "gone to be photographed, that it may not perish." What a pity he never finished it, for it would have taken "only a few days' more work."

Christmas Eve, 1888: A note to his mother, thanking her for the Japanese pocketbook and picture. "I seem to be altogether in Japan," he tells her, for "a generous doctor of this city lent me four or five splendid volumes" on the *Ornamental Arts of Japan.* His great friend Dr. MacCabe has lent him "two little Japanese fairytales," and he finds that "the humour and lifelikeness of the illustrations beats everything that was ever done for fairy-tales." Almost overnight, then, he has become "a little knowledgeable in things Japanese." He is leaving shortly to spend Christmas at Monastere-van, where the parish priest "has just been made Coadjutor Bishop . . . of Kildare and has asked me to his consecration," though Hopkins will have to miss that event because of work. His appointment is of "some importance," he points out, for the man "is no campaigner, would take no part in the [Land] League (presided over by his hotheaded curates), and had the un-usual courage . . . to forbid boycotting." He is portentously silent "for an Irishman," he has noticed, but amiable for all that.

Come New Year's, Hopkins explains, he will unhappily have to make up his retreat for the year. Unhappily, for it "is a severe tax on my short holi-days." He encloses a Christmas card for Lionel, "the only one suitable," by which he means something inoffensively secular. The weather so far has been unseasonably warm, pleasant enough by day, but by night robs him of sleep, and now he is looking forward to the chill bog air of Monasterevan. After all, he sighs, "man like vegetation needs cold and a close season once a year."

Chapter 19

Patch, Matchwood, Immortal Diamond:
Dublin, 1889, and After

New Year's Day, 1889: Once more he finds himself exhausted by the work of examining a nation. And so, at the beginning of the new year, he leaves behind the domestic comforts of Miss Cassidy's home to travel the thirty miles by trap and train and trap into the midlands and bog country of Tullabeg, to St. Stanislaus' College, to make his retreat for the previous year. Before him looms the grim, isolated three-story utilitarian stone building of the theologate. No matter, he is not here for aesthetic reasons, but to come away to listen to the promptings of the heart. His retreat—as usual—does not begin well. He knows how soul-weary he is from five years in Ireland doing work in which he can find no purpose. And so he replays the Ignatian overture of the Principle and Foundation again, trying to see a purpose in his life here. *Homo creatus est ut laudet.* Man was made to praise the Creator. All man's good, he reminds himself, lies in just two things: "in being on the right side, on the side of good, and [then] of doing good," for doing good but being "on the wrong side, promoting a bad cause, means doing wrong." And "doing good but in no good cause" is likewise meaningless. His life, then, his dilemma.

But don't we humans fool ourselves? Consider the Irish, who "think it enough to be Catholics or on the right side and that it is no matter what they say and do to advance it; practically so, but what they think is that all they and their leaders do to advance the right side is and must be right." On the other side, there are his own countrymen, who think, as Alexander Pope says for them, "that he can't be wrong whose life is in the right. So, the philosopher king Marcus Aurelius seems in his *Meditations* to be leading the purest and most unselfish life of virtue," believing that "Reason governs the Universe and [so] ranks himself on the side of . . . Reason." The trouble is that this Roman Emperor, living in the third century A.D., had no standard to rally to. And yet "that standard was then raised in the world and the Word . . . was then made flesh and he persecuted it. And in any case his principles are principles of despair."

So much for nations and for history, then. But what of himself? "I was a Christian from birth or baptism," he sums his life up. "Later I was converted to the Catholic faith, and am enlisted 20 years in the Society of Jesus. I am now 44. I do not waver in my allegiance, I never have since my conversion to the Church." But how does he advance the side he serves on? Looked at from the one angle, what he does is "of little or no use." Yes, he can think of other things he might busy himself in doing. Still, "it is an advantage for there to be a course of higher studies for Catholics in Ireland and that that should be partly in Jesuit hands; and my work and my salary keep that up."

But it is also true that the Catholic Church in Ireland as well as the Jesuits of the Irish Province—including the college—are "greatly given over to a partly unlawful cause, promoted by partly unlawful means, and against my will my pains, laborious and distasteful, like prisoners made to serve the enemies' gunners, go to help on this cause." There it is, then, an Englishman in love with England, aware that Ireland has just cause to want its freedom from an Empire which has subjected it to its will for three centuries and more. A terrible quandary, this mournful life he leads. True, he might "divide the good from the evil and live for the one, not the other," which might justify him, but can never alter the facts.

And yet, even that life might be enough if he just "had bodily energy and cheerful spirits." But these God will not give him. Worse, the more he goes down this road of thought, returning to "that course of loathing and hopelessness" he has replayed so often, the more Hopkins fears he may go mad, a realization which has forced him to "give up the practice of meditation except, as now, in retreat and here it is again." All he can do then is repeat over and over again Jeremiah's words: *Justus es, Domine, et rectum judicium tuum. Thou art indeed just, Lord, and Thy judgments just.*

Exhausted, he falls asleep at his desk, only to awaken with a start. Then he returns to the very place he had left off in his meditations. "What is my wretched life?" What does it all come down to, if not "five wasted years" here in Ireland? He is "ashamed of the little I have done, of my waste of time," although—given his "helplessness and weakness"—how could he be expected to have done otherwise? And what is "life without aim, without spur," live and lancing, without the Spirit's help? "All my undertakings miscarry. I am like a straining eunuch. I wish then for death." But if he died now, he would die imperfectly, "no master of myself," which is "the worst failure of all." As if any but the Master were master over themselves.

The following morning, early, he meditates on the Three Sins—the Sin of the Angels, the Sin of Adam and Eve, and then his own sins. And what has been the fruit of that meditation, as far as he can see? Nothing. Nothing "but loathing of my life and a barren submission to God's will. The body cannot rest when it is in pain nor the mind be at peace as long as something bitter distills in it and it aches." But what *is* this dull dough that sours everything in him? How, for someone like himself, pretend there is "anything worth calling happiness in this world?" O, there must be happiness somewhere, hope, "the anticipation of happiness hereafter." Something even "better than happiness," though there is no happiness now. "It is as if one were dazzled by a spark or star in the dark, seeing it but not seeing by it," when what is needed is "a light shed on our way and a happiness spread over our life."

In the afternoon, more of the same, "more loathing and only this thought, that I can do my spiritual and other duties better with God's help." Better to make his examination of conscience in the early afternoon "and then say vespers and compline." Better, in other words, not to wait for the demons of nightfall. The following day, more of the same, as he repeats the same exercises, feeling once more that sense of self-loathing. He goes for a walk about the boglands in the raw air to clear his head and to say a *Te Deum* in praise of God. And yet, perhaps what is needed now, he thinks, is not praising God but getting down to the harder work of mending his own sorry life.

On Saturday, January 5, he meditates on Christ's coming into a fallen world. All that happens, he writes, is "affected, marked, as a great seal, and like any other historical event . . . by Christ's life and death, whom we by faith hold to be God made man." And while one's life might be said to be affected "by the events of Roman history, by Caesar's victory and murder for instance," this far down the centuries "individuals could not find a difference" in their own lives, "except in what was set down in books of history and works of art, if Pompey instead of Caesar had founded the Empire or Caesar had lived 20 years longer." Like distant starlight, then: there, but making no appreciable difference on anyone.

On the other hand, the lives of Christians, especially of religious, like his own, "are in their whole direction . . . visibly and outwardly shaped by Christ's. Without that even outwardly the world would be so different that we cannot even guess it." And his life has been by its very nature "determined by the Incarnation down to most of the details of the day." This being the case, why push against the inevitable? Why not "make the cause that determines my life . . . determine it in greater detail still and to the greater efficiency of what I in any case should do, and to my greater happiness in doing it?"

After all, Christ's coming was for his "salvation and that of the world," and goes on "in a great system and machinery which even drags me on with the collar round my neck," much as he has chafed against it at times. And how often has he told himself that he is "only too willing to do God's work and help on the knowledge of the Incarnation"? But the truth is that he has been "unwilling enough for the piece of work assigned me, the only work I am given to do, though I could do others if they were given." Thinks: the Royal University was to him what Augustus' census demands were to Joseph: something "inconvenient and painful." But isn't he bound in justice, and paid a good salary besides?

Sunday, January 6. The Feast of the Epiphany: "Yesterday," he notes, "I had ever so much light on [the Epiphany] and the historical interpretation of the gospel and last night on the Baptism and today on that and the calling of Nathanael and so on, more than I can easily put down. However I had better have at least some notes." He begins with a meditation on the Wise Men, "either Zoroastrians or at least of a religion or sect of philosophy (Sabaeism) in which astrology played a part." Then a meditation on the Baptist's remark that Christ baptizes "with breath and fire, as wheat is winnowed in the wind and sun, and uses . . . a fan that thoroughly and forever parts the wheat from the chaff." It is the very image he had used with such terrible force in "Carrion Comfort" three years before. Everything about John, he sees, "is weak and ineffective . . . everything about Christ strong." Christ the hero, Christ the giant, and he—John—childlike, thinking: "All sorts of men come to me and I know the difference between a light sandal and the soldier's heavy *caliga*: I tell you my fingers have not the force to wring open this man's laces, though I stoop and bend my body to the task." Christ King, whose tread can "grind to powder."

Later, a meditation on the Wedding at Cana. Christ's arrival in company with his new disciples must have "overburdened the house," he thinks. "It was not provided for so many," and Mary can see how they stand "and warns Christ in time." And Jesus? My hour has not come, he tells her. Mary "knew he did not need reminding, but she did not know he might not need requesting. . . . She took the side of charity and exposed herself to rebuke.

Do whatever he tells you." Mary's words to the servers reveal just how deeply she understands her son. But even now "Christ makes the supply seem to come from the hosts," six forty-gallon water jars filled to the brim. And when the wine is brought to the head servingman, he notices at once that "there has been no stint," only "an unwise order in the serving."

And with that, the notes come to an end. In his own life too, he suddenly realizes, there has likewise been "an unwise order in the serving." Too duty-bound, too hard on himself, he has given too much of his life's blood perhaps to what was not essential, putting everything aside time after time, resentfully, for the killing work of judging a nation in the name of duty. Well, the work has been done. But has there been, perhaps, an unwise order in the serving?

Mid-February: Back from his Italian adventure, a disgusted Bridges writes Hopkins that he finds the Italians "dirtier than ever," spitting to the side as one passes them on the streets. Worse are the monks, who go about unshaven and in rags. "I am sorry the monks were dirty," Hopkins answers him on the 23rd. "The extreme poverty they have been reduced to does not excuse them; but I offer the following remarks. Shaving is conventional cleanliness: if it were otherwise, the longer the beard the dirtier wd. the wearer be." And besides, Cambridge undergraduates keep their rooms, as Bridges himself once told him, "'dirty, yea filthy,' and they are not poor." As for spitting, he knows from his time in Liverpool that it is "very, very common with the lower classes." He remembers how he used to go up Brunswick Road on a frosty morning, disgusted "to see the pavement regularly starred with the spit of the workmen going to their work" without even bothering to turn aside, spitting "straight before them as you approach, as a Frenchman"—no doubt Father Mallac—"remarked to me with abhorrence and I cd. only blush."

No, the British are not—generally speaking—"a clean people." They are not the worst offenders, of course, and at least they "know what cleanliness means, as they know the moral virtues," though they do not always practice them. The truth is, he has come to see, that English civilization in general "is dirty, yea filthy, and especially in the north; for is it not dirty, yea filthy, to pollute the air as Blackburn and Widnes and St. Helen's are polluted and the water as the Thames and the Clyde and the Irwell are polluted? The ancients with their immense public baths would have thought even our cleanest towns dirty." And then he moves on to the case of Richard Piggott, an Irish Nationalist and a journalist, charged with forging letters in Parnell's name to falsely implicate him in the Phoenix Park murders. "What boobies your countrymen are!" he tells Bridges, "making merry because a traitor to government and then a traitor to rebellion, both in a small way, has not succeeded in injuring an enemy of their own [Parnell] who is a traitor to government in a great way."

March 1: At last, a letter to Lionel, answering his queries about classical history. "Of good histories of Greece there are plenty," he begins—and it is a safe enough topic for the two brothers to engage in. Ernst Curtius's *History of Greece* in translation in five volumes Gerard knows only a little, but thinks very good. Then there is Duncker's *History of Antiquity,* translated by Alleyne, which supplements Curtius, though the reasoning there is both loose and difficult to follow. Also Reinach's *Manuel de Philologie Classique* and Daremberg and Saglio's *Dictionaire des antiquités grecques et romaines,* which he would get if he dared, "illustrated galore, but each *fascicule* is 5 francs and the whole is calculated to consist of about 20 of these." As for Roman antiquities, there is Brugmann, "the great authority on Indoeuropean Philology," and "fugleman of the Young Grammarian school," who has succeeded "in ousting the Old Lights from their stools, to be themselves shortly, perhaps very shortly (for philological views chase one another like cloud shadows among mountains) ousted by still younger men; for youth is a very very bad horse to back in the race for permanence."

Finally, he adds, "as a tooth ceases aching so will my lectures intermit after tomorrow for Shrovetide," so that he can get back to a paper he is writing on the Argei. It is an examination into the ancient Roman practice each May 14 of twenty-seven bundles of rushes "resembling men bound hand & foot" being "thrown by Vestals, pontiffs, and others" from a bridge into the River Tiber. And so another form of ancient human sacrifice ordered by the Sibyl. The part on the Pontiffs is "only half written and the subject touched on is vast, and difficult therefore to treat sufficiently." There remain, too, like burnt embers smoldering, his old interests in Chaldea and Egypt.

Hopkins moves on then to Piggott, over whose suicide in a Madrid hotel three days earlier his Nationalist friends are now "wild with triumph and joy." Only the week before Piggott had confessed to forging Parnell's name. And then, underlining the words for emphasis, Hopkins adds that he wants *"Mr. Tom Burke to know when his successor O'Brien is going to confess to the falsehood of his charge against Mr. Balfour of planning in general and then carrying out in particular the murder of John Mandeville."* Mandeville, a Munsterman imprisoned with O'Brien, had died the previous July owing, it was alleged, to ill treatment. But Hopkins believes the charges of police brutality are false and "far more hideous" than the charges against Piggott. "I do not ask the Irish to see this," he adds, "but I should like the English dupes and dullards to see it. If you knew the world I live in!"

Sunday, March 17: St. Patrick's and the wearing o' the green. He has come once again to Monasterevan for a few days' rest, and once more spring is in the air, greening everything in this land of the green. After mass, he borrows a sheet of Miss Cassidy's embossed paper and one of her pens, and sits down at a desk to compose a sonnet based on the text from Jeremiah XII which he has thought deeply about since his retreat. *Justus quidem tu es, Domine, si disputem tecum: verumtamen justa loquar ad te: quare via impiorum prosperatur? etc.* "Thou art indeed just, Lord, if I contend / With thee," he begins, translating the Latin,

> but, sir, so what I plead is just.
> Whý do sinners' ways prosper? and why must
> Dísappoíntment all I endeavour end?
> Wert thou my enemy, O thou my friend,
> How wouldst thou worse, I wonder, than thou dost
> Defeat, thwart me? Oh, the sots and thralls of lust
> Do in spare hours more thrive than I that spend,
> Sir, life upon thy cause.

It is a brilliant turn in the sonnet, spilling over and coming to a belated halt midway through the ninth line. God knows he is tired, frustrated, and—like the prophets and the Psalmist—takes it upon himself as solicitor to ask his Lord in the heavenly court what his life has come to. Every human being, like every living thing—birds nesting, bushes and trees coming into life again, even the abundant, elbowing weeds like the fretty chervil—needs nourishment, hope, rain, fresh wind, a turning again toward the light. Look around, he frets, and see for yourself. Only he of all he sees about him seems unable to build, but strains, rather, Time's eunuch, breeding nothing:

> but not I build; no, but strain,
> Time's eunuch, and not breed one work that wakes.
> Mine, O thou lord of life, send my roots rain.

Mine. My Lord who gives life. "Giver of breath and bread," he had sung in Wales, but now he begs to be able to bring *something* to fruition, even if only some single work. *Mine:* send *my* roots rain. "All my undertakings miscarry," he had greeted the New Year. "I am like a straining eunuch. I wish then for death." But the irony here is that he has just managed one of those rare poems about the failure of inspiration which turns out after all to be inspired. There is, too, another text behind the poem, another sonnet, this one by the one Romantic he must surely feel now that his own life has followed: the brilliant, ill-fated Coleridge, great-uncle of the first Jesuit he ever met: the same who had rejected his *Deutschland* and then his *Eurydice* and so effectively stopped his own work from waking. "Work without Hope," Coleridge's sonnet is called, and it begins very much like Hopkins's:

> All Nature seems at work. Slugs leave their lair—
> The bees are stirring—birds are on the wing—
> And Winter, slumbering in the open air,
> Wears on his smiling face a dream of Spring!
> And I, the while, the sole unbusy thing ...

And it ends this way: "Work without Hope draws nectar in a sieve / And Hope without an object cannot live." So too with Hopkins in this, his own version of Holy Saturday, with Jesus still in the tomb, helpless, waiting upon the Father, his one hope, to fill him with His own life.

Wednesday night, March 20: Back in Dublin, he writes Bridges a few lines for the "ungracious reason" that he "cannot do anything needing a greater effort." He has been thinking what a fine subject Bridges has chosen for his new play in writing about Achilles, and hopes Bridges will eventually write a sequel to his *Nero*. "It is such a rich picture of life, indeed of our life as it would be without Christianity," Hopkins notes. Just yesterday, he learned it was Nero who "choked the oracular chasm at Delphi with carcasses because the oracle rebuked him for killing his mother." And so Nero "did literally for some time stop the mouth of the god."

He is "flattered and dismayed" that Bridges likes his patriotic song. "It was only a sketch, a rough-hew of a song," he admits, and he is still working on it, but the task "is so extremely difficult that I have not yet succeeded in it and have to put it aside at intervals, especially as I am languishing." Once again, examinations have to be prepared and printed up over the coming weeks. He encloses a copy of "Thou art indeed just," then mentions once more that he has "a good few sonnets more you have never seen." This new sonnet, he fears, will fade over time, for "Miss Cassidy's ink is ... shocking." And observe, he adds, that the poem must be read "*adagio molto* [very slowly] and with great stress." He is delighted too that Daniel is about to reprint a shorter version of Bridges's first volume of sonnets, *Growth of Love,* though in an edition limited to twenty-four copies. So Bridges ought not grudge sending him a copy "that will be after my time unread. For consider: you aim at oblivion." As Anaxagoras once said, he jokes, it is as easy to be forgotten in Dublin as anywhere else. And the barb hits its intended mark.

Monday, April 1: In *The Times* of London, Hopkins reads news of the completion of the Eiffel Tower, which has now reached its final height of 300 meters, dwarfing Paris' medieval jewel, Notre Dame. It is the Centennial of the glorious French Revolution, and a colossal flag has been hoisted atop the looming tower to celebrate a hundred years of "progress in science and humanity." More, Gustave Eiffel has just congratulated himself that "it is a great satisfaction" to have flown the French tricolor from "the highest monument man has yet constructed." Ah yes, Hopkins remembers: a century of progress, auspiciously begun with the Reign of Terror and leading up through the experiment of the French Communard and the executions of untold thousands, including five of his fellow Jesuits.

As for the broken tower of himself: even he can see that the migraines are back with a vengeance, accompanied by diarrhea and sleeplessness and the rest. A room with a bed and his worn, shiny black cassock, a pair of boots and a *prie-dieu* and breviary. These and a table with a cluster of medicine bottles, a towel for his head, a wash bowl, a pitcher of tepid water, a small ceramic bedwarmer, and a chamberpot with which to make his own chamber music. He thinks of Moses, leading his people out of slavery, atop Mount Sinai, fronting the Lord Yahweh Himself in the forked lightning. Thinks too of Christ's heroic passion and crucifixion, of Satan and his angels falling from the heavens in a terrible vertical swoon, a cacophonous groaning and sweeping of a third of the heavens with them. *Ah, these,* M. Eiffel, are towers to dwarf yours.

Thirteen years earlier, in Wales, he had begun writing again, feeling called to it, the magnificent opening round resulting in *The Wreck of Deutschland,* his response to Milton's *Lycidas* and *Paradise Lost.* Like Milton, he too would explain the ways of God to man, explain the meaning of the terrible disaster, and show God's feathery finger at work in the midst of the terrible shock night of history. Or would he? He, a wreck himself now, and cast up on the distant shores of a foreign country?

> The shepherd's brow, fronting forked lightning, owns
> The horror and the havoc and the glory

> Of it. Angels fall, they are towers, from heaven—a story
> Of just, majestical, and giant groans.

But what is man, after all? This groundling tied inevitably to earth, this "scaffold of score brittle bones," drawing each breath "from groundlong babyhood to hoary / Age gasp," whose each breath is "our *memento mori*"? What Grand Guignol, what grand Wagnerian theme, what music shall we evoke? he asks. What bass shall be our viol—what bottom to our vileness? What tragic tones? Like those homiletic tones he had practiced at St. Beuno's, preparing to speak to a world intent on going its own appetitive ways. What in God's name are we, after all, he asks, cast down as he is with fever and stomach trouble and the rest of it? In God's name, in strict justice, what *are* we, after all, but Man Jack the mere thing only, with a hussy masquerading as a princess for a mate?

There: he has said it. He has seen too much, listened to too many confessions, read too many self-congratulatory lies in too many papers. AND WHAT DOES ANYTHING AT ALL MATTER?, he had challenged Bridges in a letter asking him to quit publishing in those de luxe editions reserved for the well-to-do, when people were begging on St. Stephen's Green below.

> He! Hand to mouth he lives, and voids with shame;
> And, blazoned in however bold the name,
> Man Jack the man is, just; his mate a hussy.
> And I that die these deaths, that feed this flame,
> That . . .

And I that . . . that . . . It is a brilliant rhetorical rise, the pleasing modern author—as Bridges had called him—witnessing to the world as it is, the self-proclaimed just man justicing. But even justice, it seems, has been emptied of meaning for him now. And even the best of them, like Addis, gone over to the enemy. Where, he wants to know, where are you now, Lord?

And then the poem takes a sudden turn downward, as his eye catches a reflection in his teaspoon and he spies "life's masque mirrored" there: distended, grotesque, inverted, his aging, tired mask of a face hiding a skeleton as it plays out life's incomprehensible masque. And doesn't *that* after all put things in their proper light? "Even Milton, looking for his portrait in a spoon," George Eliot had written years before in *Middlemarch,* a book he must surely have read, "must submit to have the facial angle of a bumpkin."

Precisely, he sees now, and if the great Milton, on whom he had modeled so much of his own work, then surely himself. And so—sick as he is—he catches his poor, pathetic, self-pitying self, and prays a final time for patience, that hard thing, pleading with his Lord to help him "tame / My tempests there, my fire and fever fussy." Hussy, fussy. Hussy, fussy. . . . That is what this is really all about, isn't it? The flame within, the divine fire no more than some "fever fussy." And the poem tells us what Hopkins has only now begun to realize: that he is far more tired than he suspects.

By late April, in fact, his friends and family and Jesuit brothers can see how ill he is. In mid-April, his brother Lionel, back from China, visits him in Dublin to see how his Jesuit brother is faring, making it amply clear that he dislikes Dublin and Irish Catholics *and* the Jesuits, so that on his departure things are worse rather than better between the two. Then, a week before Easter, Paravicini calls on him several times. All the old banter and friendship is still there, Paravicini feels. But he can also see—in spite of his friend's trying to make light of it—that Hopkins is more wasted than ever, so much so that, on his return to Oxford, he feels he must alert the new English Provincial as to Gerard's deterioration. It is time to bring Gerard home to England when the new assignments are posted in late July, and—even before that—have him return to Oxford for the summer. He is "so lovable—so singularly gifted—&, in his saintliness, so apart from, & different to, all others," Mrs. Paravicini will write Hopkins's mother six weeks later, by which point it will be too late to do anything.

In April, Hopkins sends two bantering letters to Bridges, joking at his friend's insistence on publishing in near-nonexistent editions. Bridges, in no mood to be chided by a man—no matter how "gifted"—who has published nothing, while he at least has been noticed and favorably reviewed, mostly by friends, feeds both of Hopkins's letters to the flames. After the second missive, Bridges returns fire. On Good Friday or thereabouts, he writes Hopkins that at least *he* has a publisher, adding that as of yet he has not been able to find a mainstream publisher. "Very strangely it happened that the only two letters of [Gerard's] which I ever destroyed were the two which he wrote me preceding [his last]," he will tell Dixon later. "It was very like a sort of quarrel. He said . . . he had been joking, and he added a sonnet (very sad) in 'explanation' but it did not read like joking, and the letters were rather bitter, so that I put them in the fire—of course I wish now that I had not done so."

On April 22, the day after Easter, Hopkins takes a short break from work to go down to Rathfarnham, south of Dublin, and stroll about Lord Massey's estate, Killakee, where he charcoals a rough sketch of dark flowing water. How freely it flows on, this life source, in spite of whatever would obstruct it, the rough sketch seems to say. Later that day, he conceives a sonnet—his last—addressing it to Bridges, in which he tries to explain that argumentative tone Bridges has found so offensive. A week later, he encloses it in what will be his last letter to his old friend and sometime adversary.

"Dearest Bridges," he begins, "I am ill to-day, but no matter for that as my spirits are good. And I want you too to 'buck up,' as we used to say at school, about those jokes over which you write in so dudgeonous a spirit." He has it, he adds, quoting Hamlet, "now down in my tablets that a man may joke and joke and be offensive." In truth, he adds, to keep the peace, "I have had several warnings lately leading me to make the entry, tho' goodness knows the joke that gave most offence was harmless enough and even kind." What he had meant to say was that Bridges is far too good a poet to be hidden from the larger public he deserves, and that he must find some way to get his work out to that public, much as Patmore has done.

"You I treated to the same sort of irony as I do myself," he explains, "but it is true it makes all the world of difference whose hand administers." Yes, he was wrong about Daniel, for if "he pays you more than and sells you as much as other publishers (which however is saddening to think of: how many copies is it? five and twenty?) my objections do not apply." Moreover, Hopkins himself has tried to make Bridges's poetry better known here in Dublin, and in this he has had some success, though Dowden he will never forgive. "Could you not kill Mrs. Bridges?" he jokes because he must. "Then he might take an interest in you." And then another joke. Hasn't he already placed Bridges at the very "pinnacle of fame; for it is the pinnacle of fame to become educational and be set for translation into [Greek] iambics, as you are at Trinity." This, he adds, this is what it is "to be a classic; 'this,' as Lord Beaconsfield said to a friend who told him he found his young daughter reading *Lothair,* 'O this is fame indeed.' And Horace and Juvenal say the same thing. And here I stop, for fear of it ripening into some kind of joke."

He is also enclosing a new sonnet. "But we greatly differ in feeling about copying one's verses out: I find it repulsive, and let them lie months and years in rough copy untransferred to my book. Still I hope soon to send you my accumulation." It is his last reference to those dark sonnets he wrote years before. As for this new sonnet, Bridges may be surprised to find it addressed to him. And then it is on to Swinburne, who has a new book of poems out, comically reviewed in their own style: "The rush and the rampage, the pause and the pullup of these lustrous and lumpophorous lines." Is this fame, then? A half dozen poets beckoning to another half dozen: words uttered for their own self's sake?

Later, he gets up from his bed to return to his desk. Who is this Miss Cassidy Bridges wants to know about? "She is an elderly lady"—an *elderly* lady, Bridges—"who by often asking me down to Monasterevan and by the change and holiday her kind hospitality provides is become one of the props and struts of my existence." The town itself is named for the monastery founded there centuries before by St. Ernin. Then came Henry VIII, who confiscated the lands, giving them to Lord Drogheda. "The usual curse on abbey lands attends it and it never passes down in the direct line. . . . Outside Moore Abbey, which is a beautiful park, the country is flat, bogs and river and canals. The river is the Barrow, which the old Irish poets call the dumb Barrow. I call it the burling Barrow Brown."

"The fine delight that fathers thought," his last poem begins, evoking the life force,

> the strong
> Spur, live and lancing like the blowpipe flame,
> Breathes once and, quenchèd faster than it came,
> Leaves yet the mind a mother of immortal song.

It is a poem, ostensibly, about the loss of inspiration which makes it so difficult for him to write, an explanation of what he once felt back then at his starting out in Wales, "the disproportion . . . between the momentary conception of an air and the long long gestation of its setting," as he had explained to Dixon years before. Consider the love of a man and a woman, the conjoining, and the nine months' pregnancy. Consider too the Roman poet, Horace's, injunction to let the poem ripen in the mind's womb for nine years before publishing. Consider too the word "combs," over which Bridges will fret for so long, wondering if it is in fact the right word, forgetting what Hopkins had written him the year before—"Grant in the honey bee some principle of symmetry and uniformity and you have passed beyond mechanical necessity" to the specialized instinct that seems to determine the shape of these cells. It is like "the specific songs of cuckoo and thrush" he has listened to all these years: all things parts of some great design of which we are—if we are fortunate—at least by moments aware:

> Nine months she then, nay years, nine years she long
> Within her wears, bears, cares and combs the same:

> The widow of an insight lost she lives, with aim
> Now known and hand at work now never wrong.

What he misses now is that "Sweet fire the sire of muse," the one Word upon which he waits, so that his mind might become, like Mary's fiat at the annunciation, fruitful again. It is all he wants and all he needs: that one "rapture of an inspiration."

And then, suddenly, as the poem rounds to its close, it begins to lift and lilt: "O then if in my lagging lines you miss / The roll, the rise, the carol, the creation." Look, he can still fly, still soar like that stormfowl with its pelted plumage. Then he settles back, taking the form once more of his Jackself, joke-self:

> My winter world, that scarcely breathes that bliss
> Now, yields you, with some sighs, our explanation.

But whose explanation? Is it his and his winter world yielding—giving up—with some sighs, their explanation? Or do the lines quiver with another meaning altogether? Isn't it, rather, the male and the female of it? The Holy Spirit as Father/Creator offering His and his beloved's explanation together? And what of that other meaning of "yield," as in a final harvest yielding its hundredfold? And aren't those sighs, then, love sighs, God and Hopkins whispering together like some old married couple, "inspiration" chiming in inspired fashion with his penchant for—and the comic flatness of—the very idea of trying yet one more time to explain to Bridges what he has tried telling him now for the past twenty years? It is all there, in these final lines sent off like some dead letter, though it will take years, decades, for Bridges or anyone to unwrap the gift of himself he quietly, patiently, offers up here at the end.

Somewhere, a player-piano rolls out one of those popular sheet music hits of the day, rather like John of the Cross hearing a popular love song from the streets below, locked in some small cell:

> On the grass of the cliff,
> At the edge of the steep,
> God planted a garden,
> A garden of sleep!
>
> Neath the blue of the sky,
> In the green of the corn,

> It is there that the regal
> Red poppies are born.
>
> Brief days of desire,
> And long dreams of delight,
> They are mine when my poppyland
> Cometh in sight.

Toward evening on the first day of May, he sends his mother a short note. "You have not heard from me for very long and now before going early to bed I write a line to say I am in some rheumatic fever, which comes very inconveniently when I shd. be and am setting my Papers for the examinations." He hopes "to be better tomorrow. If I am worse I may see the doctor. I am your loving son." Two days later, he writes his father. He is now laid up in bed with some fever, though he is still able to get around. This is the first day he has taken to bed "altogether," he confesses, and wishes now he had done so before. "The pains are only slight, but I wish that [Clement] Scott and Isidore de Lara"—the song's lyricist and composer—"would agree to plant a garden, a garden of sleep in my bed, as I am sleepy by day and sleepless by night and do not rightly sleep at all." Yesterday he did see Dr. Redmond, "who treated my complaint as a fleabite, a treatment which begets confidence but not gratitude." He remains "your affectionate son Gerard." On the envelope, Manley will later write: "Gerard's last letter."

> In the garden of sleep,
> Where the poppies are spread,
> I wait for the living,
> alone with the dead!
>
> O! Life of my life!
> on the cliffs by the sea,
> By the graves in the grass,
> I am waiting for thee!

A fleabite carrying the dreaded typhus. "My dearest mother," he manages to write two days later, "I am grieved that you should be in such anxiety about me and I am afraid my letter to my father, which you must now have seen and ought, it seems to me, to have had before this morning's letter was sent, can not much have relieved you." Still, he wants to reassure her that he is "now in careful hands." Yesterday, Redmond visited him again and gave him a thorough examination. What is known is that he does have "some fever," but what exactly "has not declared itself." In the meantime, he is "to have perfect rest and to take only liquid food" until the suspended digestion which has given him so much distress has been cured. "There is," he assures her, "no hesitation or difficulty about the nurses, with which Dublin is provided, I dare say, better than any place."

Alas, about Lionel, he adds, "I am and I long have been sad . . . feeling that his visits must be few and far between and that I had so little good of this one, though he and I have so many interests in common and shd. find many more in company." And then he tries to buck up his worried parents. "It is an ill wind that blows nobody good. My sickness falling at the most pressing time of the University work, there will be the devil to pay. Only there is no harm in saying, that gives me no trouble but an unlooked for relief. At many such a time I have been in a sort of extremity of mind, now I am the placidest soul in the world. And you will see, when I come round, I shall be the better for this." But he is "writing uncomfortably" now, "and this is enough for a sick man."

Three days later, having been moved downstairs to a makeshift infirmary on the first floor of No. 85, which has better light and air, Gerard sends another letter to his mother, thanking her for the flowers, and trying once again to reassure her. Too weak now to hold a pen, he dictates the letter to Father Tom Wheeler, forty-two, vice president and minister at the university, who has taken over the task of nursing him. "My fever," he has finally learned, "is a sort of typhoid: it is not severe, and my mind has never for a moment wandered. It would give me little pain were it not that while it was incubating I exposed my head to a cold wind, and took neuralgia which torments me now." Last night he slept well. And the nurse assigned to him from St. Vincent's Hospital down the road "is first rate and every condition is present that could make a serious thing trifling. The only complaint I have to make is that food and medicine keep coming in like cricket balls."

On May 14, Father Wheeler writes to reassure Hopkins's mother. "I think he is now well round the corner and on the high road to mending." Two days later, he signals a worried Bridges that his friend really does seem to be growing stronger now. And with that news, Bridges writes Hopkins. "Dearest Gerard," he begins, "I am sorry to get a letter from one of your people telling me that you were ill with fever. And yesterday I sent you off a budget of notes on Milton's prosody. And when I last wrote I never mentioned your ailing though you told me in your letter that you interrupted it to lie down." What is this fever he has? "F. Wheeler says that you are mending. . . . Let me have a line." If only he could look in on him for himself. Meanwhile, he will just have to be patient. On the other hand, if Gerard is "really mending Miltonic prosody will be just the sort of light amusement for your mind."

But there will be no more letters. Hopkins has been diagnosed with typhoid, a fact which will prompt the Jesuit minister to have the sewage drains inspected a few weeks later. The staff cook has already reported seeing two rats in one of the stewpots, and Mr. McGarvey the plumber will submit a bill for a hefty £250—or Hopkins's salary for seven months—for cleaning the college drains. It is work that should have been done when the Jesuits took over in 1883, but the price then seemed too steep for a college surviving on little in the way of hard cash.

For the next three weeks Hopkins seems to rally a bit, and is visited by several of his Dublin friends. One of them is Margaret MacCabe, who will remember long afterward Hopkins's innocence, humor, and saintliness. Others too visit—among them his colleagues and fellow Jesuits. Bedridden, he is given the last rites of the Church, makes his confession, receives the Blessed Sacrament, and is anointed. And while the official diagnosis is typhoid, it is quite possible that the illness has been made worse by another complaint, which will not even be named until 1932: Crohn's, a disease marked by constant fatigue. For years, Hopkins has complained of indigestion and diarrhea as well as of exhaustion and the inability to work, though when younger he could walk and swim and run and climb with the best of them. But the symptoms look like typhoid, and typhoid in Dublin is as common as measles or smallpox or heart failure, and so typhoid is what he has been told he has. Whatever it is, it is killing him. He sleeps, tries to keep a sense of humor, and jokes with friends. But by Wednesday evening, June 5, Father Wheeler, making his rounds, notices in the flickering gaslight a turn in Gerard for the worse, and immediately he sends off a letter to Hopkins's parents to come to Dublin as soon as they can.

The following day, they are by his side, in a Jesuit setting for the only time in their lives. He can see by their faces and by the fact that they are here how worried they must be, and it hurts him. Strangely, though, what he feels is a deep calm. He has done in this life what he could, and now—six weeks short of his forty-fifth birthday—he is leaving. The days are long now, the sun rising at five and setting at ten each night. But all is shadow, and at times he can hear the muffled sound of distant waters whelming this wreck of himself, the darkness broken now and again by a beaconlike light candescing in the distance.

Around noon on Saturday, June 8, exactly halfway round the solar year from that December day when the nuns called out to the only One, *Ipse—Per ipsum, et cum ipso, et in ipso*—and with his mother and father there in the room with him, the dark waves finally wash over his bed and his fingers loosen and he slips quietly away. Earlier that day, Father Wheeler, making his rounds, has heard Gerard talking to himself. He comes closer to try and make out what he is saying. "I am so happy," he hears him whispering over and over. "I am so happy. I am so happy."

Coda

On Tuesday morning, June 11, a bustling market morning in Dublin, there is a Funeral Mass at the Jesuits' large, baroque church on Upper Gardiner Street, celebrated by several Jesuits of the Irish Province, followed by a procession and burial in the common Jesuit plot in Prospect Cemetery, Glasnevin, where the words P[ATER] GERARDUS HOPKINS OBIIT JUN. 8 1889 AETAT. 44 will in time be chiseled to the base of the large granite crucifix overlooking the vast dead.

Friday Evening, June 14: A letter from Frances Paravicini to Father Hopkins's parents at Court's Hill Lodge, Haslemere, Surrey: "His beautifully gentle & generous nature made him one with his friends," she writes, "and led us to love & to value him,—feeling that our lives were better, & the world richer, because of him." But one thought especially gives her comfort now: that, although Father Gerard's "work in the world, so to speak,—his literary work—was always, for him, mixed with a certain sense of failure & incompleteness, yet he had the life he chose for himself. And, in his religious life, he was *very happy.* My Husband remembers how he would speak of his enjoyment in the saying his office, & in the quiet completeness of his religion. . . ."

Saturday, June 15: Among the letters on Alexander Mowbray Baillie's table when he returns to his London office is one from Mrs. Hopkins. He opens it, only to learn that his friend of twenty-six years is gone. It takes him two days to absorb the news, and then he writes back. He is grieved, deeply grieved to learn of the death of his dear friend, he writes, visibly shaken. In fact, he did not even know Gerard was ill. "It is impossible to say how much I owe to him," he confesses, for "he is the one figure which fills my whole memory of my Oxford life." All of his intellectual growth, Baillie confesses, he "owes to Gerard's companionship," and—except for his own family—he "never had so strong an affection for any one."

"How can I tell you," Bridges breaks the news to Canon Dixon, "the terribly mournful tidings of Gerard's death?" He had been assured his illness was nothing to worry about. But thinking about it, Gerard's "last letters to me and the two last poems are if not a foreboding of it, yet full of a strange fitness for the end. The last poem but one was an address to God [*"Justus quidem tu est"*], most powerful and plaintive. The last was a sonnet to me, explaining some misunderstanding which he thought existed." Ah well. "That dear Gerard was overworked, unhappy and would never have done anything great seems to give no solace. But how much worse it would have been had his promise or performance been more splendid. He seems to have been entirely lost and destroyed," Bridges adds bitterly, "by those Jesuits."

Five days later, he writes Hopkins's mother. "I have thought that I may possess writings of his which you wd like to have copies of: and that it [may] particularly interest you to see his last letters to me." He has already written Father Wheeler asking him "to return to me any of my letters to Gerard which might still be kept among his papers: and he in his reply promised to do so, & said that Gerard had given instructions about his papers."

Six weeks later, he writes Dixon again to say that he has "proposed to edit some of [Gerard's] verse—Daniel to print them—*with a short memorial life of him.* I have after some delay succeeded in getting back from his friends in Dublin the majority of my letters to him—which he had kept." When he has these letters back he will read through them and—seeing in retrospect how much he has revealed of himself there—burn them, though Hopkins's he will mercifully save.

A year later, Bridges is still planning to issue a private edition of Hopkins's poems. "Mr. Daniel says that he will print a selection [of the poems] at any time," he writes Mrs. Hopkins, "free of charge—up to 150 copies. Yourselves and friends to take a certain number, and the rest for private sale among interested outsiders." Because of the pressures of time, he has had to abandon the idea of a memoir, although "a short 'preface' might be written which should put the poems out of the reach of criticism." Then too there are other difficulties.

He should "prefer the postponement of the poems till the memoir is written," Bridges explains, "or till I have got my own method of prosody recognized separately from Gerard's." For, though the two methods of sprung rhythm are the same, Gerard naturally "has the greater claim than I to the origination of it." But, then, he "used it so as to discredit it: and it would be a bad start in favour for the practice we both advocated and wished to be used. Readers would not see that the peculiarities of his versification were not part of his metrical system, but a freakishness corresponding to his odd choice of words etc. in which also his theories were as sound as his practice was strange."

Incredibly, he adds: "In this I am not considering myself, but the prospect of introducing this new way of writing, in which if there is any reputation to come to him, it will be from the recognition of the principles which I think his own verse would damage. I have no doubt of the adoption of the system, and when once it is recognized his verses will establish his claim to foreseeing (not to say outgoing) the limits of it." This preparation, he assures her, will mean a delay of only "a year or 18 months."

And the years go by, the poems yellowing in Bridges's study at Yattendon. On January 21, 1909, nearly twenty years after Hopkins's death, Bridges writes Mrs. Hopkins from his new home at Boar's Hill, Chiswell, outside Oxford. "Thank you," he begins, "for returning that Roman Catholic Magazine [*The Catholic World*]." He does not know who wrote the article on Gerard, nor has he ever heard of the magazine. But the Catholics, being "very hard up for any literary interests . . . are glad enough to make something of Gerard's work." He still plans to do something with Gerard's poems, and in the meantime hopes she will like his references to him in his memoir of Dixon, which should be out soon.

Two months later, he writes her again. He is glad she liked Dixon's poems, insofar as she understood them. "As for the difficulty of appreciating the poems," he adds, "I myself experienced it in the most humiliating degree . . . I am therefore astonished that *all* the reviewers now accept [Dixon's] poetry, and advertise their surprise at its not having been generally received before." On the other hand, Lang has written to say "how much better Bridges' memoir is than Dixon's verse!" At least Lang is being honest, he adds, and doubts "if the reviewers are." Besides, he has noticed that his memoir "has wakened a good deal of interest in Gerard."

For one, Edmund Gosse has been thinking of editing Hopkins's poems. But how, Bridges wonders, can Gosse even consider undertaking such a task? After all, there are no copies of Gerard's work in existence but hers and Bridges's, and he is sure she would tell him if Gosse had approached her. But the truth is that Gosse is "incompetent of undertaking this particular work." In fact, once, when Gosse had visited the Waterhouses at Yattendon back in the 1870s, Bridges had "tried to make him recognise the merits of Gerard's verse," only to find that Gosse wasn't interested. Gerard's work *will* eventually find an audience, he still believes, but only when the time is right. To do so now would only "boom Roman Catholic pretensions to artistic eminence," in the same way that "they pull all the strings to glorify Francis Thompson." When the time does come, he assures her, he means to publish "a selection of Gerard's letters to accompany his poems. In a limited edition, with Roman-Catholic patronage such a book would be sufficiently well received, and it would I think be valuable, and take its place among 'dappled things.'"

Soon after, Bridges sends Mrs. Hopkins her son's letters to Dixon. "I am afraid that you will find the [manuscript] book very awkward to handle," he explains, "but Gerard's way of writing one page at right angles to another makes it difficult to arrange them in any way that is convenient." How he should love to see her again. His own mother "lived to be 90: but you must have outdone that, and I am glad to think you are spared the troubles which burdened the last three years of her life. Indeed when I think of your longevity I hope that you may have a good many more years still to encourage my generation. It helps us to think that we are young."

May 7, 1909: Again Bridges writes Mrs. Hopkins, enclosing a letter from a Father Keating, S.J., asking Bridges about the status of Father Hopkins's poems. "I wonder what your wishes will be," he asks. "My reply to Mr. Keating [sic] was merely that I had always regarded Gerard's family as his literary executors, and that Mr. Keating's letter implied that the Society was." He warns her that if Keating should learn that she has "a copy of all the poems he may bother you." Better, perhaps, to turn the poems over to her son Everard. He himself promises to send Keating absolutely nothing, for he is sure those Jesuits "would make a dreadful mess of the whole thing." He cannot even imagine Gerard wanting "his poems . . . edited by a committee of those fellows." In any case, he reminds her, she will be sure to write him "before taking any steps. I have not mentioned your name to Reverend K. I think he is pretty cheeky." But in fact the poems have belonged to the Society since 1878, when Hopkins turned all his possessions over to his order, though it will take decades more to iron all this out.

October 11, 1909: "I had a very pleasant time at 7 Pembroke Road," Bridges writes Mrs. Hopkins once again, "and Everard told me that Father Keating had been to lunch with him," and could see that "the little society of Jesuit dons at Farm Street was very much what Gerard described them in his day, and had nothing much to do, and suffered from a weak form of literary ambition, so that the notion of editing Gerard's poems was attractive to them." In fact, Everard thinks Keating hardly competent to edit the poems, and would certainly not trust him "with anything of importance."

July 1913: A quarter of a century since Hopkins's death, and still no edition of his poems has appeared. In the meantime, Bridges's own fame has continued to grow, so much so that, at sixty-nine, he has just been chosen England's poet laureate. Kate Hopkins, now ninety-three, writes to congratulate him on this singular honor. "Dear Mrs. Hopkins," he writes back. "When Gerard first saw my first book of poems,—it was in my house in London—he took it up with some curiosity. You can imagine his quiet deliberate examination of it. When he had dipped into it in several places, he looked up and said 'I say, what fun, Bridges, if you were to be a classic!'" Not of course that he thinks he deserves the honor. Well, he must run now, as he has many letters to answer to thank those who have taken the time to congratulate him. He sees Everard's boy occasionally, named Gerard in honor of his uncle.

In late 1918, two years before Kate Hopkins succumbs in her one hundredth year, *The Poems of Gerard Manley Hopkins,* in an edition of 750 copies, edited and with an introduction by Robert Bridges, and published by Oxford University Press, appears. It will take twelve years for the edition to sell out, a single copy of which will eventually cost more than $7,000 to own.

Thursday, July 1, 1926: Virginia Woolf, daughter of Sir Leslie Stephen, the physician who had helped Hopkins's friend Bond at the foot of Mont Blanc sixty years before, visits Bridges, now eighty-two, at Boar's Hill. "He sprang from a rhododendron bush," she notes in her journal, "a very lean tall old man. . . . He is direct and spry, very quick in all his movements, racing me down the garden to look at pinks, then into his library, where I asked to see the Hopkins manuscripts; and sat looking at them with that gigantic grasshopper Aldous [Huxley] folded up in a chair close by." It is Hopkins's poems this brilliant novelist has asked to read in the laureate's home, and not the laureate's. Even the self-contented Bridges must see a certain irony in all of this.

February 28, 1927: Father Joe Rickaby, now eighty-one, writes to his fellow Jesuit, Father Gerald Lahey, Hopkins's first biographer, from what he jokingly calls the *Hotel des Invalides* at St. Beuno's. "Pax Christi," he begins in typical Jesuit fashion. "Fr Gerard Hopkins and myself were together in theology for three years, and were ordained together," and used to go on "long walks . . . and converse intimately." Hopkins was undoubtedly a genius, he adds, which makes him a "difficult man to describe. He was highly original, even whimsical, and said and did odd things. But he was an excellent Religious and thorough Catholic. He was perhaps the most popular man in the house. Superiors and equals, everybody liked him. We laughed at him a good deal, but he took it good-humouredly, and joined in the amusement."

And yet "he was anything but silly. He had a good solid judgment, and was accounted the best moral theologian in the class. In speculative theology he was a strong Scotist, and read Scotus assiduously," which "led to his being plucked at the end of his third year," for he was "too Scotist for his examiners." Later, Father Gallwey "took him with him to Farm Street to preach, having been much struck by the originality of a sermon he gave in the Refectory. I cannot say he was a success either as a teacher or a missioner. He was too whimsical, and too tender-hearted towards the miseries of the poor. His place would have been at Oxford, had Campion Hall been then started."

Rickaby himself was sent to Campion Hall in 1896, when it first opened, seven years after Gerard's death. He is sure that if Gerard had been in his place there, "he would have been a great success, and made a name in the University, for he was still remembered at Balliol. But he was too delicate a mind for a good deal of the rough work that we have to do in the Society." At University College he was "not happy and never took root there. . . . All Ireland was hot about Home Rule then, and Gerard was no politician. He died before his time, for as I knew him, he was robust and strong."

January 1928. Pasadena, California: Hart Crane, twenty-eight, in the midst of composing his epic, *The Bridge,* has been reading Hopkins in Yvor Winters's copy of the *Poems.* He cannot get enough of these extraordinary poems, he tells his friends, and begins copying out as many of them as he can before returning the volume to Winters. He even writes his friend and bookseller in New York, Sam Loveman, to say he is willing to pay a month's rent for a copy of the book, for rarely, if ever, has he come across language like this man's, where words "come so near a transfiguration into pure musical notation—at the same [time] retaining every minute literal signification! . . . What daring!" It is like a new discovery. But of course this is genius speaking to genius.

April 21, 1930: And Robert Bridges, eighty-six, who has managed to outlive Hopkins by over forty years to become one of England's most respected poets, at last dies quietly in his bed.

December 8, 1975. Westminster Cathedral: The Feast of the Immaculate Conception and the centenary of *The Wreck of the Deutschland.* Bearded Lionel Handley-Derry, Hopkins's great-nephew, walks slowly over to the spot in Poets' Corner where a stone plaque memorializing his great-uncle has been set between one commemorating T. S. Eliot and another commemorating W. H. Auden. Besides Hopkins's birth and death dates are emblazoned the words: "Immortal Diamond."

Back in May a committee was formed, consisting of England's reigning poet laureate, Sir John Betjeman, the critic Dame Helen Gardner, Father Martin D'Arcy, S.J., a staunch supporter of Hopkins's poetry ever since Bridges published his edition of the *Poems* fifty-seven years before, and the Duke of Norfolk, whose Catholic roots go back to a time before the Reformation. In his splendid and dramatic voice, Sir John Gielgud reads from Hopkins's poetry, and the Jesuit poet Father Peter Levi gives a moving talk. Hopkins is the first Catholic poet to be recognized in Westminster Abbey since John Dryden, dead now these three hundred years, and the first Roman Catholic priest ever to be so honored.

At the same time, *The Month* issues an apology for not having published the now famous *Deutschland* ode when it had the chance to do so a century earlier, though Hopkins long ago gave up worrying about such things. That "one unwise blunder," the apology notes, "has gained for the *Month* more notoriety than all the distinguished articles it has wisely published."

Notes

Abbreviations used in the Notes

MAJOR MANUSCRIPT COLLECTIONS

Balliol Balliol College, Oxford

BC Boston College, Chestnut Hill, Massachusetts

Bodleian Bodleian Library, Oxford

Campion Hall Campion Hall, Oxford, as catalogued inj. 529–35

Gonzaga Gonzaga University, Washington

Texas Humanities Research Center, Austin, Texas, as catalogued in Jerome Bump, Catalogue of the Hopkins Collection in the Humanities Research Center of the University of Texas, *HQ* 5 (1979), 141–50

BOOKS

AMES *All My Eyes See: The Visual World of Gerard Manley Hopkins,* ed. by R. K. R. Thornton (Sunderland, London, 1975)

Dunne Tom Dunne, *Gerard Manley Hopkins: A Comprehensive Bibliography* (Oxford, 1976)

J *The Journals and Papers of Gerard Manley Hopkins,* ed. Humphry House and Graham Storey (1959)

L1 *The Letters of Gerard Manley Hopkins to Robert Bridges,* ed. C. C. Abbott (1935, 1955)

L2 *The Correspondence of Gerard Manley Hopkins and R. W. Dixon,* ed. C. C. Abbott (1935, 1955)

L3 *The Further Letters of Gerard Manley Hopkins,* ed. C. C. Abbott, 2nd ed. (1956)

OEN *The Collected Works of Gerard Manley Hopkins.* Vol. IV: *Oxford Essays and Notes,* ed. Lesley Higgins (Oxford, 2006)

P *The Poetical Works of Gerard Manley Hopkins* (The Oxford Authors), ed. Norman H. MacKenzie (Oxford, 1990)

S *The Sermons and Devotional Writings of Gerard Manley Hopkins,* ed. Christopher Devlin, S. J. (1959)

RBSL *The Selected Letters of Robert Bridges,* ed. Donald E. Stanford, 2 vols. (1983)

Thomas Alfred Thomas, S. J., *Hopkins the Jesuit: The Years of Training* (1969)

JOURNALS

HQ *The Hopkins Quarterly*
HRB *The Hopkins Research Bulletin*
LN *Letters and Notices (privately published by the Society of Jesus, English Province)*

NB: Oxford University Press is in the process of publishing the eight-volume *Collected Works of Gerard Manley Hopkins,* which will significantly update the familiar five volumes published in matching orange-tan covers back in the 1950s. The first volume (No. IV), Hopkins's early *Oxford Essays and Notes,* edited by Lesley Higgins, appeared in 2006, and includes forty-five of Hopkins's essays, as opposed to the seven in the House/Storey edition of the *Journals and Papers.* The final volume in the series (VIII), *The Poems,* edited by Catherine Phillips, is scheduled to appear in 2012. The co–general editors for the *Collected Works* are Lesley Higgins of York University, Toronto, and Michael F. Suarez, S.J., of Fordham University and Campion Hall, Oxford University. Vols. I and II, *The Letters,* edited by Catherine Phillips and R. K. R. Thornton, will include all the extant letters, both to and from Hopkins, arranged chronologically, as well as some 30 letters not contained in the 1950s edition, plus 127 letters sent to him. Vol. III, edited by Lesley Higgins, will include Hopkins's *Diaries, Journals, and Notebooks,* all uncensored, and arranged chronologically, from 1864 up through his Dublin years. Some fifty of his illustrations will also be included.

Vol. V, *Sermons and Spiritual Writings,* is being edited by Jude Nixon and Philip Endean, S.J., and will make available all of Hopkins's sermons, his commentaries on the *Spiritual Exercises* of St. Ignatius, and his personal meditations on his biblical readings. Vol. VI, *Sketches, Notes, and Studies,* is being edited by R. K. R. Thornton, and will include Hopkins's artwork, musical compositions, translations from Greek and Latin, and his letters to *Nature* magazine on such phenomena as sunspots and the effects on England's climate as a result of the devastating 1883 eruption of Krakatoa. Vol. VII, edited by Lesley Higgins and Michael Suarez, will be a much needed fascimile edition of Hopkins's *Dublin Notebook* into which he poured whatever was on his mind, from grades to drafts of "Spelt from Sibyl's Leaves" and *St. Winefred's Well.* This large black book will vividly capture the complex, near-despairing mind of Hopkins as he encountered an alien city in an unfamiliar world, lecturing, grading, praying, and—when he could—composing some of his most extrordinary poems. Finally, Vol. VIII, the *Poems* themselves, edited by Catherine Phillips, of course create their own set of problems and opportunities for seeing into the poet's mind, since Hopkins left them, like his contemporary Emily Dickinson, in manuscript, often in multiple kaleidoscopic versions.

ABBREVIATIONS FOR NAMES AND TITLES USED

AB Alexander William Mowbray Baillie
CNL C. N. Luxmoore
CP Coventry Patmore
EB Edward Bond
EBP E. B. Pusey
EHC Ernest Hartley Coleridge
EWU E. W. Urquhart
GMH Gerard Manley Hopkins
HPL H. P. Liddon
JHN John Henry Newman
KH Kate Hopkins
MH Manley Hopkins
RB Robert Bridges
RWD Richard Watson Dixon
WD *The Wreck of the Deutschland*
WM W. A. Comyn Macfarlane

Chapter 1: **In the Breaking of the Bread: Horsham & Home, 1866, and the Early Years**

    3 "The world is chárged wíth the grándeur of God": P 139.

    3 "bold and bolder": P 149.

    4 "Oh, / We lash with the best or worst / Word last!" and ff.: *WD*, St. 8, P 121.

    4 "I did say yes" and ff.: *WD*, St. 2, P 119.

    6 "My window shews the travelling clouds" and ff.: "Alchemist," P 75.

    6 "perversion": A widely-used term for Anglican converts to Rome. Cf., e.g., Dr. Pusey's letter to **GMH**, dated Saturday, October 20, 1866. "My dear Sir. . . . What I declined doing was to see you simply 'to satisfy relations.' I know too well what that means. It is simply to enable a pervert to say to his relations 'I have seen Dr. P., and he has failed to satisfy me,' whereas they know very well that they meant not to be satisfied, that they came with a fixed purpose not to be satisfied." L3, 400.

    7 "great aid to belief and object of belief" and ff.: **GMH** to **EHC**, June 1, 1864, L3, 16–17.

    8 "snap-dragon growing on the walls" and ff.: **JHN**, *Apologia Pro Vita Sua*, Penguin, 1994, p. 191.

    8 "on anything so trivial" and ff.: **GMH** to **EHC**, January 22, 1866, and ff. L3, 19–20.

    9 "pied with clouds": May 6, 1866, J 135.

    9 "playing over Christ Church meadows": May 2, 1866, J 133.

    9 "vivid green slanting away" and ff.: May 3, 1866, J 134.

10 "That landscape the charm of Oxford": **GMH** to **RWD**, February 27, 1879, **L2**, 20.

10 "the want of the canon": May 15, 1866, J 136.

11 "in a fit of generous impulse": May 14, 1866, J 136.

11 "beautiful blackness": May 20, 1866, J 137.

11 "beak-leaved boughs dragonish": *Spelt from Sybil's Leaves*, **P** 191.

11 Pater, who goes on for two hours: May 31, 1866, J 138.

11 "and under-reddened with sorrel": June 3, 1866, J 138.

11 "as the subject is disagreeable": June 13, 1866, J 139.

12 "black coats relieved" and ff.: June 13, 1866, J 139. The word "inscape" does not yet appear, and will not appear in his journals until the early spring of 1868, while teaching fifth- and sixth-formers at Newman's Oratory. But ontologically and epistemologically, this is what Hopkins is already searching for. Cf. **OEN**, *Parmenides*, 311 ff.

13 "I have desired to go": *Heaven-Haven*, **P** 29–30.

13 "typical English work": June 18, 1866, J 140.

13 "blue sprays of wych-elm": June 19, 1866, J 140.

13 "flush, swift, and oily" and ff.: June 19, 1866, J 141.

14 "probably the first Catholic priest Hopkins ever spoke to" and ff.: as Addis would tell Father Keating, Hopkins's early (posthumous) champion in a letter dated December 20, 1909. Quoted in J 358.

14 "soft round curdled clouds": June 21, 1866, J 141.

15 "their tongue-shaped petals" and ff.: July 6, 1866, J 143.

15 Seductive country, that Sussex, Pater has called it: **GMH** to **WM**, June 30, 1866, **L3**, 20–21.

15 "To think that a rag of popery" and ff.: **GMH** to **WM**, July 10, 1866, from Oak Hill. "Three new Letters from G. M. Hopkins to W. A. Comyn Macfarlane," **HRB** 6 (1975), p. 4.

15 "Love I was shown upon the mountain-side" and ff.: Late October 1865, **P** 85.

17 "Platter-shaped stars" and ff.: July 19, 1866, J 146.

17 "roughed with lichen" and ff.: July 20, 1866, J 146.

17 "I did not attempt to argue with him": Macfarlane's diary, July 24, 1866. **L3**, p. 397.

17 "Spoke to Macfarlane, foolishly": July 24, 1866, J 147.

18 It is the white-beam: the cross: July 24, 1866, J 147.

Chapter 2: **The Dense and the Driven Passion: Oxford & Hampstead, 1866**

25 "Reverend Sir . . . I address you" and ff.: **GMH** to **JHN**, August 28, 1866, **L3**, 21–22.

26 "some business . . . to do at some time" and ff.: **GMH** to **RB**, August 28, 1866, **L1**, 4–5.

26 "see no way out" and ff.: **GMH** to **RB**, September 22–24, 1866, **L1**, 5.

27 "a penitent waiting for admission" and ff.: **GMH** to **EWU**, September 20, 1866, **L3**, 23.

27 "almost ceased to feel anxiety" and ff.: **GMH** to **RB**, September 22–24, 1866, **L1**, 6–7.

28 "perpetually thank God" and ff.: **GMH** to **EWU**, September 24, 1866, **L3**, 26–27.

28 "TRUMPERY, / MUMMERY, AND G.M." and ff.: **GMH** to **RB**, September 28, 1866, **L1**, 10.

29 "cannot read them twice": **GMH** to **JHN**, October 15, 1866, **L3**, 29.

29 "Among those who listened" and ff.: **MH** to **HPL**, October 15, 1866, **L3**, 434–35.

30 "depend upon the Truth of the Supremacy" and ff.: **HPL** to **GMH**, October 16, 1866, **L3**, 401.

30 "strictly forbids all communion" and ff.: **GMH** to **MH**, October 16, 1866, **L3**, 91–94.

32 "What none would have known of it" and ff.: *WD,* Sts. 7–8, **P** 121.

32 "lighter-hearted" and ff.: **GMH** to **MH**, October 16, 1866, **L3**, 95.

32 "I wish you could get hold of Hopkins" and ff.: William Bright to **HPL**, October 17, 1866, **L3**, 436.

33 "in absolute ignorance of all": **MH** to **GMH**, October 18, 1866, **L3**, 96–97.

33 *"O Gerard my darling boy are you indeed gone"* and ff.: **MH** to **GMH**, October 18, 1866, **L3**, 97.

33 "My dear Mr. Hopkins, It is not wonderful" and ff.: **JHN** to **GMH**, October 18, 1866, **L3**, 404.

34 "Dr. Pusey has not been in Oxford" and ff.: **GMH** to **KH**, October 20, 1866, **L3**, 97ff.

35 "know very well that they meant *not* to" and ff.: **EBP** to **GMH**, October 20, 1866, **L3**, 400.

36 "to prevent my reception" and ff.: **GMH** to **HPL**, November 7, 1866, **L3**, 31.

37 "Remember, God desires us" and ff.: **GMH** to **WM**, **HRB** 6 (1975), p. 7.

37 "Suffer yourself" and ff.: **JHN** to **GMH**, December 6, 1866, **L3**, 405–6.

Chapter 3: **Towery City and Branchy Between Towers: Highgate & Oxford, 1861–1865**

38 "to only one of the pleasures" and ff.: **GMH** to Müncke, May 8, 1861, **HRB** 4 (1973), 3–6.

39 "most trivial subjects" and ff.: April 13, 1862, **J**, 3.

40 "still cock of the walk at Elgin" and ff.: **GMH** to **CNL**, May 7, 1862, **L3**, 1–5.

41 "coming down the narrow staircase" and ff.: **CNL** to Arthur Hopkins, Eton College, June 13, 1890, **L3**, 394–96.

42 "Dear poet" and ff.: **GMH** to **EHC**, September 3, 1862, **L3**, 5–13.

43 "Long beds I see of violets" and ff.: "Winter with the Gulf Stream," **P** 15.

43 "Patriarch of the Old Dispensation": **GMH** to **EHC**, March 22, 1863, **L3**, 15.

43 "palm of ugliness" and ff.: **GMH** to **KH**, April 22, 1863, **L3**, 70–74.

45 "Pusey's great *protégé*" and ff.: **GMH** to **KH**, May 4, 1863, **L3**, 77.

46 "not quite firmly convinced": **GMH** to **KH**, June 8, 1863, **L3**, 81.

46 "It is impossible to say how much I owe to him" and ff.: **AB** to **KH**, June 17, 1889, **L3**, 449.

46 "Yes. You are a Fool" and ff.: **GMH** to **AB**, July 10–13, 1863, **L3**, 199–202.

47 *Shanklin, Manor Farm, July 19* [1863], *Buds of the white lily:* **AMES** *All My Eyes See: The Visual World of Gerard Manley Hopkins*, Ceolfrith Press, Sunderland Arts Center, 1975, p. 118.

47 "The sea is brilliantly coloured" and ff.: **GMH** to **AB**, July 10–13, 1863, **L3**, 200–206.

47 "without climbing a flight of stairs": and ff. **GMH** to **KH**, October 19, 1863, **L3**, 82–83.

48 "with the old signboard of the bear" and ff.: **GMH** to **KH**, January 23, 1863, **L3**, 88.

48 "as if it were Samarkand" and ff.: **GMH** to **AB**, March 1864, **L3**, 207.

49 "Canaletto with genius" and ff.: **GMH** to **AB**, July 20–August 14, 1864, **L3**, 211–14.

50 "a mood of great . . . mental acuteness" and ff.: **GMH** to **AB**, September 10, 1864, **L3**, 216–21.

51 "wretched . . . the only person in history" and ff.: **GMH** to **EWU**, January 6, 1865, **L3**, 18.

51 "most interesting parts" and ff.: "Poetic Diction," D.II.3, *OEN*, 120–22. Hopkins quotes here at the beginning from the preface to the second edition of the *Lyrical Ballads* (1800).

51 "complexity and profusion of thought" and ff.: "The Position of Plato to the Greek World," D.II.5, *OEN*, 127–30.

52 Cf. **GMH**'s long essay, "On the Origin of Beauty: A Platonic Dialogue," D.IV.1, *OEN*, 136–72.

53 "an old man driving a donkey-cart" and ff.: **GMH** to **CH**, July 28, 1865, **L3**, 89–90.

53 "You will no doubt understand" and ff.: **GMH** to **AB**, September 10–12, 1865, **L3**, 226.

54 "At morn we found the heavenly Bread" and ff.: Barnfloor and Winepress, **P** 26.

***Chapter 4:* Fresh-Firecoal Chestnut-Falls: Oxford, the Oratory, London, Abroad, 1867–1868**

55 "Since this severe frost" and ff.: **JHN** to **GMH**, January 14, 1867, **L3**, 406.

55 "on the score of morality": **GMH** to **EWU**, January 16, 1867, **L3**, 36.

55 "When you said you disliked schooling" and ff.: **JHN** to **GMH**, February 22, 1867, **L3**, 406.

56 "The Probable Future of Metaphysics": D.IX.3. *OEN,* 287–91.

58 "a most trying thing" and ff.: **GMH** to **KH,** April 13, 1867, **L3,** 100–101.

59 "versemaking": **GMH** to **EWU,** July 7, 1867, **L3,** 38.

59 "scarcely expressing form": July 10, 1867, **J** 147.

59 "silver bright fish-scale-bespattered sunset": July 11, 1867, **J** 147.

60 "the thinness of French foliage": July 14, 1867, **J** 148.

60 "green-blue, flinty sharp, and rucked in" and ff.: July 17, 1867, **J** 148.

60 "very good, especially the way in which a tree" and ff.: July 27, 1867, **J** 149.

60 "ghastly candid" and ff.: **GMH** to **EWU,** August 15, 1867, **L3,** 40.

61 "the curves in the clusters": August 22, 1867, **J** 152.

61 "if it is better": August 23, 1867, **J** 152.

61 *"shadow-modified . . .* as in tapestries" and ff.: August 24, 1867, **J** 152–53.

61 "copses with slim bare stems": August 26, 1867, **J** 153.

61 "richness and beauty in the blue" and ff.: August 30, 1867, **J** 154.

61 "being a Catholic more than to anything" and ff.: **GMH** to **RB,** August 30, 1867, **L1,** 16.

62 "He had not given up the idea" and ff.: **JHN** to **GMH,** August 19, 1867, **L3,** 407.

62 "kind people offer him breakfast afterwards": September 1, 1867, **J** 154.

62 "twice dead": **GMH** to **KH,** September 4, 1867, **L3,** 102.

62 "in a little mule-cart to the Augustinian" and ff.: September 8, 1867, **J** 157.

63 "Without my prolonging" and ff.: **RB** to **GMH,** September 12, 1867, **RBSL** I, 87–88.

63 "to read almost every thing" and ff.: **GMH** to **AB,** September 15, 1867, **L3,** 228.

63 "Fancy me getting up at" and ff.: **GMH** to **EWU,** September 30, 1867, **L3,** 43–44.

64 "the fattest and biggest": **GMH** to **EHC,** October 26, 1867, **L3,** 45.

64 "a millstone . . . a great want of strength" and ff.: **GMH** to **RB,** November 1, 1867, **L1,** 18.

65 "A 2nd is the class I have always imagined" and ff.: **GMH** to **RB,** November 12, 1867, **L1,** 20.

65 "I am glad you go to confession" and ff.: **GMH** to **EHC,** December 31, 1867, **L3,** 48.

66 "make a great difference in my position" and ff.: **GMH** to **RB,** January 9, 1868, **L1,** 22.

66 "To every word meaning a thing . . . belongs" and ff.: Notes on Greek Philosophy, D.XII.5 (February 9, 1868), *OEN,* 306–8.

67 "very burdensome" and ff.: **GMH** to **AB,** February 12, 1868, **L3,** 230–32.

68 "like an apple of light": March 15, 1868, **J** 162.

69 "a flash of lightning": April 27, 1868, **J** 164.

69 "overhanging the sunk fence into the Park": May 4, 1868, **J** 165.

69 "resolved to be a religious": May 5, 1868, **J** 165.

69 "Slaughter of the Innocents": May 11, 1868, J 165.

69 "I am both surprised" and ff.: JHN to GMH, May 14, 1868, L3, 408.

70 "All I can positively tell you" and ff.: *London Times,* May 23, 1868.

70 "I came a good many times" and ff.: GMH to HPL, June 5, 1868, L3, 49.

71 "Faces, streets, and sunlight" and ff.: GMH to EWU, June 13, 1868, L3, 51–52.

72 "I did say yes / O at lightning and lashed" and ff.: *WD,* P 119.

72 "You see . . . I do not apologise for this" and ff.: GMH to EWU, June 13, 1868, L3, 52.

72 "Honeysuckle at the hedge on the big bank" and ff.: June 16, 1868, J 166–67.

73 "chromatically more perfect than the violin" and ff.: June 20, 1868, J 167.

73 "that Being is and Not-being is not" and ff.: "Parmenides," D.XII.7 , *OEN,* 311 ff.:

73 "I shall be glad to have seen it": GMH to IR, July 2, 1868, L3, 53–54.

74 "noble dead Christ": July 7, 1868, J 170.

74 "noble scape of stars": July 9, 1868, J 170.

74 "gentians in two rows above like double" and ff.: July 11, 1868, J 172.

74 "wax gutterings on a candle" and ff.: July 12, 1868, J 173.

74 "shaped and nippled like the sand" and ff.: July 15, 1868, J 174.

74 "standing like a high-gabled steeple": July 18, 1868, J 176.

74 "like milk chasing round blocks of coal" and ff.: July 19, 1868, J 178.

75 "cut away at the jaws; the eyes . . . big, shallow-set" and ff.: July 20, 1868, J 179.

75 "a Greek galley stranded . . . reared-up rostrum": July 21, 1868, J 180.

75 "a sea-lion couchant or a sphinx" and ff.: July 22, 1868, J 180–81.

75 "Taurus up . . . the colour changing through" and ff.: July 25, 1868, J 181.

75 "a country of pale grey rocky hills" and ff.: July 31, 1868, J 184.

75 "burnt with my other verses" and ff.: GMH to RB, August 7, 1868, L1, 24.

76 "deep doubts about the Anglican way" and ff.: J, 185, 394n.

76 "great massive Norman tower now impoverished": September 1, 1868, J 187–88.

Chapter 5: Owner of the Skies & Stars & Everything Wild: Roehampton, 1868–1870

79 "There are five novices besides myself" and ff.: GMH to KH, September 10, 1868, L3, 104–5.

81 "Chestnuts as bright as coals or spots of vermilion": September 17, 1868, J 189.

81 "Fresh-firecoal chestnut-falls": "Pied Beauty," P 144.

81 "water . . . clouded by milk or soda": September 27, 1868, J 189.

81 "Spiritual Exercises . . . we mean every method" and ff.: Cf. George E. Ganss, Loyola University Press, 1992, pp. 21–22.

81 "black, white, right, wrong": Cf. *Spelt from Sybil's Leaves*, P 190–91.

82 "trees in the river flat below inscaped" and ff.: October 21, 1868, J 189.

82 "brownish paste in the library": November 4, 1868, J 189.

82 "warm wet winds": December 6, 1868, J 189.

82 "and catkins hanging in the thickets": December 9, 1868, J 189.

83 "the most violent gale": December 6, 1868, J 189.

83 "I am glad that you and Nettleship saw" and ff.: Green.

83 "At Cadiz the Admiral" and ff.: **GMH** to **KH**, February 7, 1869, **L3**, 106.

84 "The elms have long been in red bloom" and ff.: January 24, 1869, J 190.

84 "It is nearly a fortnight since my mother" and ff.: **GMH** to **RB**, April 29, 1869, **L1**, 25.

84 "one another without losing their inscape": May 14, 1870, J 199.

85 "fine Spanish oak at the head of the path" and ff.: July 8–9, 1869, J 192.

85 "Shivelights and shadowtackle": Cf. "That Nature is a Heraclitean Fire," P 197–98.

85 "He was . . . a great friend of mine" and ff.: **GMH** to **KH**, October 20, 1869, **L3**, 107.

86 "and was considering how to get away in time" and ff.: December 23, 1869, J 193.

86 "meet George Simcox constantly" and ff.: **GMH** to **KH**, October 20, 1869, **L3**, 108.

86 "as if pressed against by a piece of wood" and ff.: December 23, 1869, J 193–96.

87 "The dense and the driven Passion" and ff.: *WD*, St. 7, P 120–21.

88 "Who's the Fool Now?": December 28, 1869. Cf. Alfred Thomas, *Hopkins: The Jesuit Years.*

88 "very absurd things" and ff.: **GMH** to **KH**, December 30, 1869, **L3**, 108–9.

89 "very jolly old gentleman" and ff.: **GMH** to **CH**, March 1, 1870, **L3**, 110.

89 "little leaves": Cf. Thomas.

89 "I practise at present the evangelical" and ff.: **GMH** to **KH**, March 1, 1870, **L3**, 111.

90 "Grass cloud . . . brassy light" and ff.: March 12, 1870, J 196.

90 "At Norris's market gardens by Sion Lane" and ff.: March 26, 1870, J 197–99.

92 "entered into retreat in the evening" and ff.: Thomas.

92 "appointed to attend Fr. Baron": February 13, 1870, Thomas.

92 "I do not think I have ever seen anything" and ff.: May 18, 1870, J 199.

Chapter 6: **The Fine Delight That Fathers Thought: Stonyhurst, 1870–1873**

94 "a little place in a valley of the moors" and ff.: September 10, 1870, **GMH** to **KH**, **L3**, 111–13.

97 "obligation of not attacking the frontiers" and ff.: August 19, 1870, J 203.

97 "think of nothing at all" and ff.: **GMH** to **KH**, March 2, 1871, **L3**, 113.

98 "Bright morning, pied skies" and ff.: March 14, 1871, J 205.

98 "And the azurous hung hills": "Hurrahing in Harvest," **P** 148–49.

98 "This is the time to study inscape" and ff.: "End of March and beginning of April," 1871, J 205.

98 "A strange one, that Mr. 'Opkins": TK

98 "Take *a few* primroses in a glass" and ff.: "End of March and beginning of April," 1871, J 206.

98 "I have not the right word . . . so simple a flower" and ff.: Early April, 1871, J 206.

98 "dappled with tufted shadow": April 16, 1871, J 206.

99 "bare and bleak but the rivers are beautiful": **GMH** to **RB**, April 2, 1871, **L1**, 26–27.

99 "Your letters are always welcome" and ff.: **GMH** to **AB**, April 10, 1871, **L3**, 234.

100 "there was such a youngladyship" and ff.: **GMH** to his sister Kate, April 25, 1871, **L3**, 114.

101 "the abiding offscape of the hand grasping" and ff.: April 27, 1871, J 207.

101 "across the sky in regular rank" and ff.: May 9, 1871, J 208–9.

101 "alternately when the train is shut" and ff.: May 17, etc., 1871, J 209.

101 "glowing yellow sunset" and ff.: May 24, 1871, J 210.

102 "Fr. Olivain [sic] with four other of our Fathers": May 29, 1871, J 210–11.

102 "I suppose you are trying" and ff.: **GMH** to **KH**, June 17, 1871, **L3**, 116–17.

103 "ropes and hills of melting candy" and ff.: July 8, 1871, J 212.

103 "whether you are secretary" and ff.: **GMH** to **RB**, August 2, 1871, **L1**, 27–28.

105 "over the low-water sands of Holy Loch": August 21, 1871, J 213.

105 "The so-called Chapel Royal . . . is beautiful" and ff.: August 24, 1871, J 214.

105 pleases Hopkins very much: August 30, 1871, J 214.

105 "the bright pieces of evening light": September 15, 1871, J 215.

106 "through the stubble fields and wood": September 17, 1871, J 216.

106 "perched in the sill of the round window" and ff.: December 17–18, 1871, J 217.

106 "lapped strength, stole joy, would laugh, cheer": **P** 183.

106 "For one thing . . . I was sorry to get it" and ff.: **GMH** to **AB**, January 4, 1872, **L3**, 235–37.

107 "the odd instress of . . . the moon leaning on" and ff.: February 23, 1871, J 218.

107 "firstlings of this mildest of early springs" and ff.: **GMH** to **KH**, March 5, 1872, **L3**, 118–19.

108 "and resolved him to enter his abbey of La Trappe" and ff.: March 13, 1871, J 218.

108 Hopkins writes of this in his journal for March 13, 1871, J 218–19.

108 "Happy you! . . . You are in the land" and ff.: **GMH** to **AWG**, March 22, 1872, L3, 55–57.

109 "Mr. Kennedy left us . . . He offered himself" and ff.: April 9, 1872, J 219.

109–10 "flush with a new stroke of enthusiasm" and ff.: August 3, 1872, J 221.

110 "the steeple is so strongly and boldly designed" and ff.: August 4, 1872, J 221.

110 "a Manx song, though indeed it was but four lines" and ff.: August 5, 1872, J 221.

110 "toes the shore and the inlets" and ff.: August 6, 1872, J 221.

110 "hanging in one of the softly fluted green channels" and ff.: August 7, 1872, J 222.

110 "The water is delivered a little below" and ff.: August 8, 1872, J 222.

111 "fine and beautiful ashes and a wychelm" and ff.: August 12, 1872, J 224.

111 "warm and velvety": August 20, 1872, J 225.

111 "The boy's face is poor in expression" and ff.: **GMH** to **KH**, August 30, 1872, L3, 119–20.

112 "He had been reading a novel of Trollope's" and ff.: September 1–8, 1872, J 226.

112 "black scalped places on it" and ff.: September 17, 1872, J 226–27.

112 "dazzled by the gaslight on the white ceiling" and ff.: October 5, 1872, J 227.

112 "a great fall of stars" and ff.: November 27, 1872, J 227–28.

113 "They are having at me with ethics" and ff.: **GMH** to **AB**, December 3, 1872, L3, 238–39.

113 "Lovely-felicitous Providence / Finger of a . . . delicacy" and ff.: *WD*, St. 31, P 127.

113 A blandyke or blandike: the Stonyhurst name for a Jesuit Scholastic's holiday. Stonyhurst was an offshoot of St. Omers, the Jesuit-founded school at Liége, Belgium, by Friar Robert Persons in 1593 to circumvent the penal laws that prohibited Roman Catholics from establishing schools in England. Blandyke is an anglicization of Blendecques, a village on the river Aa in Flanders, an hour's walk from St. Omers. In 1626 the English Jesuits at St. Omers purchased a property there to provide a place where the students could spend their monthly holidays. The custom of calling such monthly holidays blandykes was kept even after the school was transferred to Stonyhurst.

113 "Hard frost, bright sun": December 12, 1872, J 228.

114 "Under a dark sky walking by the river" and ff.: December 19, 1872, J 228–29.

114 "Remainders of snow on the hills" and ff.: December 23, 1872, J 229.

114 "because of the inequality of rank" and ff.: December 30, 1872, J 229–30.

115 "hung and beaded with round buds" and ff.: December 30, 1872–January 12, 1873, J 229–30.

115 "flat-topped hillocks and shoulders" and ff.: February 24, 1873, J 230.

115 "we feel wind colder" and ff.: **GMH** to **KH**, March 2, 1873, L3, 121–22.

116 "there came at that moment a great pang" and ff.: April 8, 1873, J 230.

116 "a thick flesh-coloured ooze" and ff.: April 17, 1873, J 230.

116 "Bluebells in Hodder wood" and ff.: May 11, 1873, J 231.

116 "a two-handed letter": May 15, 1873, J 231.

116 "shadows sharp in the quarry" and ff.: June 16, 1873, J 231–32.

116 "A high wind . . . blowing the crests" and ff.: July 18, 1873, J 233.

117 "Very hot, though the wind" and ff.: July 22, 1873, J 233.

117 "Mr. Colley and I crossed the river" and ff.: July 24, 1873, J 234.

117 "beautiful long outlook" and ff.: **GMH** to **KH**, August 2, 1873, L3, 122–23.

117 "In the night he had a great struggle" and ff.: July 30, 1873, J 234.

117 "one of the higher classes" and ff.: **GMH** to **KH**, August 2, 1873, L3, 122–23.

118 "with more interest than rapture" and ff.: **GMH** to Edward Bond, August 4, 1873, L3, 58–59.

118 "trailing hoods of white" and ff.: August 16, 1873, J 235–36.

119 "They were kind, amiable, and edifying" and ff.: August 27, 1873, J 236.

119 "fresh woods and pastures new": Milton's *Lycidas*.

Chapter 7: **Of Reality the Rarest-Veinèd Unraveller: Roehampton, 1873–1874**

120 "most kindly and encouragingly" and ff.: Journal entry for August 27–28, 1873, J 236.

120 "a great mercy" about . . . Dolben: Journal entry for August 30–September 8, 1873, J 236.

120 "the cross, side-plate, muzzle, regulator" and ff.: Journal entry for September 8, 1873, J 237.

121 "toadstool rings in the big pasture" and ff.: Journal entry for September 14, 1873, J 237.

121 "bold masterly rudeness" and ff.: Journal entry for September 18, 1873, J 237–38.

121 "But ah, but O thou terrible" and ff.: P 183.

122 "I have paid a good deal of attention" and ff.: **GMH** to **RWD**, October 5–10, 1878, L3, 13–14.

122 "The accent of a word means its strongest accent" and ff.: Cf. Hopkins's notes, "Rhythm and the Other Structural Parts of Rhetoric—Verse," and "Poetry and Verse," J 267–90.

123 "This morning, blue mist breathing" and ff.: Journal entry for September 27, 1873, J 239.

123 "Woodpigeons come in flock" and ff.: Journal entry for October 17, 1873, J 239.

123 "Wonderful downpour of leaf": J 239.

123 "Elmleaves very crisp" and ff.: Journal entry for November 12, 1874, J 240.

123 "frosting on trees" and ff.: Journal entry for December 1, 1874, J 240.

123 "going on sadly at Roehampton": Journal entry for December 18, 1874, J 240.

123 the "sunset sky and boughs" and ff.: Journal entry for Christmas Week, 1874, J 240.

124 "But wé dréam we are rooted in earth—Dust!" and ff.: *WD*, St. 11, **P** 121–22.

124 "My last letter to you was from Stonyhurst" and ff.: **GMH** to **RB**, January 22, 1874, **L1**, 28–30.

124 "to pretend to know what is going on" and ff.: **GMH** to **EB**, February 24, 1874, **L3**, 59–60.

124 "I think . . . to be so much offended" and ff.: **GMH** to **RB**, January 22, 1874, **L1**, 29.

125 "Lenten Festivities" and ff.: **GMH** to **KH**, March 2, 1874, **L3**, 123–24.

125 "bas reliefs of the Parthenon" and ff.: Journal entry for April 6, 1874, J 241–42.

125 "even to Ham common" and ff.: **GMH** to **EB**, **L3** 60–61.

125 "I wanted to see if my old enthusiasm" and ff.: Journal entry for June 12, 1874, J 247–48.

126 "folding and rolling on the wind" and ff.: Journal entry for July 7, 1874, J 249.

126 "preparing to speak and writing fast": Journal entry for July 14, 1874, J 249.

126 "shires-long of pearled cloud" and ff.: Journal entry for July 23, 1874, J 249.

126 "never been so burdened and cast down as this year": J 249–50.

126 "by a place a little girl called . . . Ku-am" and ff.: Journal entry for August 8, 1874, J 250.

127 "you cannot well tell what is old" and ff.: Journal entry for August 15, 1874, J 253.

127 "a deep and beautiful cleave" and ff.: Journal entry for August 17, 1874, J 253.

127 "The fish landed are mostly dead" and ff.: J 254–55.

127 "a convert [and] a simple-minded young lady" and ff.: J 256.

127 "rolling up the valley of the Thames" and ff.: J 256.

128 "beautifully dappled" and ff.: J 257.

Chapter 8: A Pastoral Forehead of Wales: St. Beuno's, 1874–1875

129 "very kind and hospitable" and ff.: Journal entry for August 28, 1874, J 257.

129 "another year's teaching at Roehampton": **GMH** to **MH**, August 29, 1874, **L3**, 124–25.

129 "warm breast and with, ah! bright wings!": **P** 139.

131 "all vowels . . . run off the tongue" and ff.: **GMH** to **KH**, September 1–2, 1874, **L3**, 125–26.

131 "look round the whole country" and ff.: Journal entry for September 6, 1874, J 257–58.

131 "a great resort of hawks and owls" and ff.: Journal entry for September 3, 1874, J 257.

131 "where we went into a pretty little new church": September 3, 1874, J 257.

132 "laboring among the Welsh" and ff.: Journal entry for September 6, 1874, J 258.

133 "received the tonsure and the four minor orders" and ff.: September 20–21, 1874, **GMH** to **KH, L3**, 126–28.

134 "a Maltese, who has an interesting history" and ff.: Journal entry for September 10, 1874, J 258–60.

134 "a beautiful liquid cast of blue" and ff.: Journal entry for September 24, 1874, J 260.

134 "An interesting talk . . . a little amusing" and ff.: Journal entry for October 1, 1874, J 260.

135 "The water in the well . . . as clear as *glass*" and ff.: Journal entry for October 8, 1874, J 261.

135 "I steady as a water in a well" and ff.: *WD*, St. 4, **P** 120.

136 "a young man from Liverpool" and ff.: Journal entry for October 8, 1874, J 261.

136 a "vast multitude of starlings" and ff.: Journal entry for November 8, 1874, J 261.

137 "moulded . . . to give it a Welsh etymology" and ff.: Journal entry for February 7, 1875, J 263.

137 "My dearest Bridges . . . the above address" and ff.: **GMH** to **RB**, February 20, 1875, J 31.

138 "vague and dull": **GMH** to **KH**, April 24–29, 1875, **L3**, 131–33.

139 "which came packed in so much sawdust": **GMH** to **KH**, June 10, 1875, **L3**, 133–34.

139 The poem "Consule Jones" was only recovered and published by Joseph Feeney, S.J., in 2002. Cf. "Gerard Manley Hopkins' 'Consule Jones': A Critical Edition with Introduction and Commentary," **HQ**, 29 (2002), 3–20. It appears in the *Oxford World's Classics* paperback as Appendix C, edited by Catherine Phillips, 2002.

141 "He was perhaps the most popular man in the house": Cf. Joseph Feeney, S.J., "A Jesuit classmate remembers G. M. Hopkins: An unpublished letter of Joseph Rickaby, S.J.," *The Month* (London), 261 (2001), 170–71.

141 "Nid, am I Ti fy ngwared i" and ff.: **P** 136.

142 "O God, I love thee, I love thee" and ff.: **P** 106.

142 "Ad lib[itum] sermon at dinner by Mr. G. Hopkins": **Thomas.**

142 "arch and original Breath": *WD*, St. 25, **P** 125.

142 "strong spur, live and lancing": "To R.B.," **P** 204.

143 "The bodies of the four German nuns" and ff.: *London Times,* December 11, 1875, 12.

144 "You ask, do I write verse myself" and ff.: **GMH to RWD**, October 5–10, 1878, **L2**, 14–15.

145 "would be more generally interesting" and ff.: **GMH to RB**, April 2–3, 1878, **L1**, 49.

146 "Into the snows she sweeps" and ff.: *WD*, **P** 119–28.

154 "the most interesting piece of all" and ff.: **GMH to KH**, December 24, 1875, **L3**, 134–36.

155 "disgracefully felled" and ff.: **GMH to KH**, March 2, 1876, **L3**, 136–38.

155 "lucky for him" and ff.: **GMH to KH**, December 24, 1875, **L3**, 135.

Chapter 9: **The Grandeur of God: Wales, 1876–1877**

156 "the highest of the hills bounding the valley": **GMH to KH**, March 2, 1876, **L3**, 136–38.

156 "morning's minion" a veritable "king/dom of daylight's dauphin," **P** 144.

157 "dark Maenefa the mountain" and ff.: "Moonrise June 19, 1876," **P** 131.

157 "oldest friend in the Society" and ff.: **GMH to KH**, June 26–28. 1876, **L3**, 138–39.

158 "That event came off on my birthday" and ff.: **GMH to MH**, August 6–7, 1876, **L3**, 139–41.

159 "His mihi post tantas, immania saecula, clades" and ff.: *Ad Episcpum Salopiensem*, **P** 129–30.

159 "Not today we need lament" and ff.: "The Silver Jubilee," **P** 128–129.

159 "whether it will be in the September number": **GMH to MH**, August 6–7, 1876, **L3**, 139.

159 "Penmaen Pool": **P** 135–36.

160 "Changes in the Province" and ff.: September 23, 1876, **L3**, 141–42.

161 "the boiler supplying the hot water pipes": St. B.

161 "my blackguardly aunts and other kinsfolk" and ff.: **GMH to AB**, January 6–20, 1877, **L3**, 240–42.

162 "The world is chárged wíth the grandeur of God" and ff.: **P** 139.

164 "Look at the stars! look, look up at the skies!" and ff.: **P** 139–40.

165 "You have forgotten or else you never got a letter I wrote" and ff.: **GMH to RB**, February 24, 1877, **L3**, 31–32.

165 "covers the whole of life" and ff.: **GMH to AB**, January 6–20, 1877, **L3**, 240–42.

166 "the most wearisome work": **GMH to KH**, March 1–2, 1877, **L3**, 143–44.

166 Cf. "Sonnet," an early version of "God's Grandeur," included in letter of March 1–2, 1877, **L3**, 144–45.

167 Cf. this early version of "The Starlight Night," **L3**, 145.

168 "And now, brethren . . . you have heard the Gospel of Christ": Dominical for the Fourth Sunday in Lent, March 11, 1877, **S** 225–33.

170 "a junk of a letter is under weigh" and ff.: **GMH to RB**, April 6, 1877, **L1**, 40.

170 "You have no call to complain" and ff.: **GMH** to **RB**, April 3–8, 1877, **L1**, 32–40.

172 *"Doctus Aquinatis reserare oracular Thomae"*: *"Ad Reverendum Patrem Fratrem Thomam Burke O.P. Collegium S. Beunonis invisentem,"* **P** 141–42.

173 "On the Composition of Place in the Spiritual Exercises": Cf. Alfred Thomas.

173 "Each mortal thing does one thing and the same": **P** 141.

174 "strain of the earth's sweet being in the beginning": "Spring," **P** 142.

175 "this shallow and frail town": "The Sea and the Skylark," **P** 143.

175 "I hope you will long continue to work out yr beautiful and original style": **GMH** to William Butterfield, April 26, 1877, *HRB* 1974, 5.

175 "As a dare-gale skylark scanted in a dull cage": **P** 148.

176 "inmate does not correspond" and ff.: **P** 143.

177 "Where now are the bright keepings of the consulship?" and ff.: S 222–24.

178 "I caught this mórning morning's mínion" and ff.: **P** 144.

180 "Glory be to God for dappled things" and ff.: **P** 144.

180 "Having both work here to do" and ff.: **GMH** to **RB**, June 13, 1877, **L1**, 41.

182 "As a theologian . . . his undoubted brilliance was dimmed" and ff.:

182 "had hoped to be professed" and ff.: To Friars William Shapter, Charles De Lapasture, Francis Goldie, S.J., August 17, 1882, *HQ* XXIII, 1–2, pp. 3–17.

183 "It seems . . . that triolets and rondels": **GMH** to **RB**, August 8, 1877, **L1**, 42–43.

183 "What mystery is there about the Provincial" and ff.: **GMH** to **RB**, August 10, 1877, **L1**, 43–44.

183 "No sooner . . . were we among the Welsh hills" and ff.: **GMH** to **MH**, August 15, 1877, **L3**, 146–47.

184 "on the unfathering deeps outward bound" and ff.: **GMH** to **RB**, August 21, 1877, **L1**, 44–47. Hopkins here condenses two allusions to his *Deutschland* ode: St. 13, "widow-making unchilding unfathering deeps," and St. 12, "American-outward-bound."

185 "the labour spent on this great metrical experiment" and ff.: Cf. Bridges's preface to the first edition of Hopkins's *Poems*, 1918.

185 "of half an hour of extreme enthusiasm" and ff.: **GMH** to **RB**, July 16, 1878, **L1**, 56–57.

185 "Summer ends now" and ff.: "Hurrahing in Harvest," **P** 148–49.

187 "The work is nondescript" and ff.: **GMH** to **KH**, October 9, 1877, **L3**, 147–48.

188 "Men go by me whom either beauty bright" and ff.: "The Lantern out of doors," **P** 140.

Chapter 10: Father Hopkins: Mount St. Mary's, Stonyhurst, & Farm Street, 1877–1878

191 "a well-deserved reputation for scholarship": W. F. Lee.

192 "Their acting . . . was creditable" and ff.: **GMH** to **KH**, January 27–28, 1878,

L3, 148–49 and 142–43, where the end of this letter has been incorrectly transposed.

192 "pleased and flattered to hear" and ff.: **GMH** to **RB**, February 25, 1878, **L1**, 47.

193 "Your faithful Gen'ral, Bombardinion" and ff.: Cf. notes for "Brothers," **P** 422.

193 "How lovely the elder brother's / Life" and ff.: "Brothers," **P** 165–66.

194 "My muse turned utterly sullen in the Sheffield smoke-ridden air" and ff.: **GMH** to **RB**, April 2–3, 1878, **L** 47–49.

194 "It is with deep concern that we have to announce" and ff.: *London Times,* March 25, 1878.

195 "The *Eurydice*—it concerned thee, O Lord": **P** 149–52.

197 "thinner than I ever saw myself" and ff.: **GMH** to **KH**, April 24, 1878, **L3**, 150–51.

198 "It is my only copy" and ff.: **GMH** to **RB**, May 13–21, 1878, **L1**, 49–52.

199 "It gave me . . . great comfort to read" and ff.: **GMH** to **RB**, May 30–31, 1878, **L** 52–55.

199 " How to kéep—is there ány any, is there none such" and ff.: **P** 169–71.

200 "Growth in every thing" and ff.: "The May Magnificat," **P** 153–54. It should be noted that the quatrains here, made up of two couplets each, are a curtailing or shortening of the rhymed quatrains used in "The Loss of the Eurydice."

201 "I take a liberty as a stranger" and ff.: **GMH** to **RWD**, June 4, 1878, **L2**, 1–3.

202 "You cannot but know that I must be deeply moved" and ff.: **RWD** to **GMH**, June 8, 1878, **L2**, 3–5.

203 "Pax Christi" . . . He is very glad and ff.: **GMH** to **RWD**, June 13–15, 1878, **L2**, 5–9.

204–5 "all my real and personal estate and effects" and ff.: Apparently the will itself, dated July 11, 1878, but probably drawn up just before Hopkins left St. Beuno's in October 1877, was sent to Dublin following Hopkins's death. It was destroyed in the fire and explosion of the Four Courts during the Irish Civil War in 1922. Cf. Fredric Schlatter, S.J.'s essay, "Hopkins at the Bar: The Case of the Missing Will," *HQ*, 1–2 (Winter–Spring 2002), 52–64.

205 his work . . . "will soon thicken" and ff.: **GMH** to **RB**, July 13, 1878, **L1**, 55.

205 "You will learn that I have just called" and ff.: **GMH** to **RB**, July 16, 1878, **L1**, 56–57.

205 "he who handles flour will be whitened" and ff.: This is the sermon Hopkins preached again the following August at St. Clement's, Oxford, noting then that he was using the notes he had put together for his Farm Street sermon when he preached on the Parable of the Pharisee and Publican then. This is the essential sermon Bridges would have heard Hopkins deliver in London.

206 "Next Sunday's sermon must be learnt better than last's" and ff.: Postcard from **GMH** to **RB**, August 8, 1878, **L1**, 57.

206 "Gerard Hopkins is in town preaching. . . . He is good" and ff.: **RB** to Muirhead, August 10, 1879. **RBSL** I, 125–27.

206 Christ as "the great critic" and ff.: **RWD** to **GMH**, September 25, 1878, **L2**, 9–12.

206 "A visit to Great Yarmouth" and ff.: **GMH** to **RWD**, October 5–10, 1878, **L2**, 12–16.

208 "I daresay . . . we may not meet again for years": Postcard from **GMH** to **RB**, November 3, 1878, **L1**, 58.

Chapter 11: Quaint Moonmarks, Pelted Plumage: Oxford & Bedford Leigh, 1878–1879

209 "a very sweet good creature": **GMH** to **RB**, January 19, 1879, **L1**, 59–62.

210 "When last I heard of him he was converting Pater at Oxford" and ff.: **RB** to Lionel Muirhead, **RBSL** I, December 27, 1878.

210 "When we met in London" and ff.: **GMH** to **RB**, January 19, 1879, **L1**, 60–62.

211 "You so misunderstand my words" and ff.: **GMH** to **RB**, January 29–30, 1879, **L1**, 62–65.

212 Nazareth House. Thanks to Professor Jude Nixon for his extensive research into Hopkins's connection with the poor of Oxford in Hopkins's capacity as chaplain.

212 "a fine wellmannered set of young men" and ff.: **GMH** to **KH**, February 12, 1879, **L3**, 151–53.

213 "'puff preliminary'" and ff.: **GMH** to **RB**, February 15, 1879, **L1**, 65–67.

214 "Your precious little volume is to hand" and ff.: **GMH** to **RB**, February 22, 1879, **L1**, 67–74.

215 "Towery city and branchy between towers" and ff.: **P** 156.

216 "known and believed by almost all Catholics long before" and ff.: Cf. Hopkins's sermon for December 5, 1879, opening a triduum in honor of the 25th anniversary of the definition of the Immaculate Conception.

217 "And so I used to feel of Duns Scotus" and ff.: **GMH** to **CP**, January 3, 1884, **L3**, 349.

217 "The poet wishes well to the divine genius of Purcell" and ff.: **P** 157.

219 "little-headed willows two and two" and ff.: **GMH** to **RWD**, February 27–March 13, 1879, **L2**, 20. Hopkins quotes here from Dixon's poem *Love's Consolation.*

219 "from remarkably clear speaking he will lapse" and ff.: Postcard from **GMH** to **RB**, March 3, 1879, **L1**, 74.

219 "a mitigated sprung rhythm" and ff.: **GMH** to **RWD**, February 27–March 13, 1879, **L2**, 20–26.

219 "My aspens dear, whose airy cages quelled" and ff.: **P** 156–57.

220 two "almost famous" wreck pieces: thus to **RB** in a postcard dated December 16, 1878, **GMH** to **RB**, **L1**, 59.

220 "which is in plain sprung rhythm" and ff.: **GMH to RWD**, March 29, 1879, **L2**, 26.

220 "delight, astonishment, & admiration" and ff.: **RWD to GMH**, April 5, 1879, **L2**, 26–27.

220 "no thought of publishing" and ff.: **GMH to RWD**, May 12, 1879, **L2**, 27–28.

220 "The reason you have not heard from me sooner" and ff.: Postcard from **GMH to RB**, April 8, 1879, **L1**, 75–76.

221 "I think I have seen nothing of Lang's" and ff.: **GMH to RB**, April 22, 1879, **L1**, 79–81.

222 "since the syllables in sprung rhythm are not counted" and ff.: **GMH to RB**, May 26–31, 1879, **L1**, 81–84.

222 "an irritation due to the remains" and ff.: **GMH to RB**, June 22, 1879, **L** 84–85.

222 "two boys of our congregation" and ff.: **GMH to RB**, August 14–21, 1879, **L1**, 85–89.

222 "But tell me, child, your choice" and ff.: "The Handsome Heart: at a Gracious Answer," **P** 158–59. Hopkins composed multiple versions of the sonnet, employing different rhythms and many changes in language, ultimately satisfied with none of them, and surprised that Bridges should like the poem so much.

223 "Some candle clear burns somewhere I come by" and ff.: **P** 158.

224 "You are the salt of the earth": Matthew 5:13.

224 "the sots and thralls of lust": Cf. "Thou art indeed just, Lord," **P** 201.

224 "best gifts surely" and ff.: "The Bugler's First Communion," **P** 161–62.

225 Christ's blood "beat and sympathised with the feelings of his heart" and ff.: Hopkins's sermon for July 6, 1879, the Feast of the Precious Blood, delivered at St. Clement's, **S** 13–15.

226 "more Miltonic plainness and severity" and ff.: **GMH to RB**, August 14–21, 1879, **L1**, 87.

226 "followed by religious orders and approved by Popes": *London Times*, August 12, 1879.

227 "Now Time's Andromeda" and ff.: "Andromeda," **P** 163.

227 "The man . . . that says to himself" and ff.: Sermon for August 17, 1879, **S** 17–18.

228 "They call him . . . teacher" and ff.: Sermon at Worcester for August 31, 1879, **S** 18–21.

228 "Have, get before it cloy" and ff.: "Spring," **P** 142.

228 "cast himself down on his face" and ff.: **S** 18–21.

228 "Watch someone who 'hastens to be rich'" and ff.: Sermon for September 7, 1879, **S** 21–23.

229 "*This* is the house of God" and ff.: Scrap of sermon for September 14, 1879, at St. Clement's, **S** 235–37.

229 God "calls the infidel, heathen, heretic to his Catholic faith": September 21, 1879, for St. Clement's and St. Giles's both, **S** 23–25.

230 "When will you ever, Peace, wild wooddove" and ff.: **P** 164.

230 *"I have left Oxford"* and ff.: **GMH** to **RB**, October 8–16, 1879, **L1**, 90–93.

231 "wonder wedlock" and ff.: "At the Wedding March," **P** 164.

232 "very least advantage when" and ff.: **GMH** to **RB**, October 22–November 18, 1879, L 93–99.

234 "a line or two of introduction": **RWD** to **GMH**, October 19, 1879, **L2**, 29.

234 "against what others might say" and ff.: **GMH** to **RWD**, October 24, 1879, **L2**, 29–30.

234 "I cannot consent to, I forbid" and ff.: **GMH** to **RWD**, October 31–November 1, 1879, **L2**, 30–31.

234 "You are very welcome to shew my poems" and ff.: **GMH** to **RWD**, November 5, 1879, **L2**, 31–32.

234–5 "There will be black sheep among the white": Sermon for Sunday, November 16, 1879, S 32–34.

235 "You know how books of tales" and ff.: Sermon for Sunday, November 23, 1879, S 34–38.

236 "Life and time are always losing" and ff.: Sermon for Sunday, November 30, 1879, S 39–43.

237 To think . . . "I could ever have called myself a Liberal!" and ff.: **GMH** to **AB**, November 19–December 2, 1879, **L3**, 242–44.

238 "One might say: I am in such want" and ff.: Sermon for Sunday, December 14, 1879, S 46–49.

238 "Many thanks for your kind Christmas boxes": **GMH** to **KH**, December 27, 1879, **L3**, 153.

Chapter 12: **Of All Places the Most Museless: Liverpool & Glasgow, 1880–1881**

240 "and shall have less time than ever": **GMH** to **RB**, January 2, 1880, **L1** 99.

240 Bridges will remember: Cf. his preface to the 1918 edition of Hopkins's *Poems*.

240 "Jenkinson Street and Gomer Street": **GMH** to **RB**, February 15, 1880, **L1**, 99–100.

240 "Thy will be done" and ff.: Hopkins's sermon on Duty, Sunday Evening, January 4, 1880, S 50–53.

240 "*'O Deus, ego amo te'*" and ff.: **P** 106–7.

240 "Do I feel for God love enough" and ff.: **S** 50–53.

241 "we cannot father ourselves on God" and ff.: Hopkins's sermon on the Coming of God's Kingdom, Sunday Evening, January 11, 1880, S 53–58.

241 As Her Majesty . . . "is seen at the opening of Parliament" and ff.: Hopkins's sermon on God's Kingdom, Sunday Evening, January 18, 1880, S 58–62.

242 "all passages speaking of God's kingdom as falling" and ff.: Hopkins's sermon on the Fall of God's First Kingdom, Sunday Evening, January 25, 1880, S 62–67.

243 "Every week one of our community goes to Lydiate" and ff.: **GMH to KH,** March 2, 1880, **L3,** 155–57.

244 "The deities of the parliamentary Olympus intervened": *London Times,* February 6, 1880.

244 "I wrote John Lightbound a letter" and ff.: **GMH to KH,** March 2, 1880, **L3,** 156.

244 "friendly scene of reconciliation between Mr. Musgrove and me" and ff.: **GMH to KH,** April 30, 1880, **L3** 157–58.

245 "By great good luck" and ff.: **GMH to KH,** March 2, 1880, **L3,** 155.

245 "out of their season" and ff.: Hopkins's sermon for the Fourth Sunday after Easter, April 25, 1880, **S** 68–75.

246 "Félix Rándal the fárrier, O is he déad then?": **P** 165.

247 "knocked up" with work and illness and ff.: **GMH to KH,** April 30, 1880, **L3,** 137–38.

248 "many times with the greatest admiration": **RWD to GMH,** March 1, 1880, **L2,** 32–33.

248 "deeply kind and cheering" and ff.: **GMH to RWD,** May 14, 1880, **L2,** 33.

248 "not to love my University" and ff.: **GMH to AB,** May 22–June 18, 1880, **L3,** 244–46.

249 "I wish I could pursue music" and ff.: **GMH to RB,** June 18–23, 1880, **L1,** 102–4.

250 "I thought people must be quite touched": **S** 81.

250 "Bad as she was . . . she would not be blinded" and ff.: Friday evening, July 23, 1880, **S** 81–83.

250 "The reason . . . why you feel it" and ff.: **GMH to RB,** September 5–13, 1880, **L1,** 104–10.

251 "more distinctive and higher pitched" and ff.: Retreat Notes, Liverpool, August 20–28, 1880, **S** 122–28.

252 "counter, original, spare, strange": **P** 144.

252 "languid pen" and ff.: September 5–13, 1880, **GMH to RB, L1,** 104–10.

253 "Spring and Fall: to a Young Child": **P** 166–67.

254 "takes more interest in a merchant's business" and ff.: Monday evening, October 25, 1880, **S** 89–93.

254 "In consequence, I was in a manner suspended" and ff.: **S** 89.

255 "I never could write . . . one is so fagged, so harried" and ff.: **GMH to RB,** October 26–27, 1880, **L1,** 110–14.

256 "First the soul's good looked to" and ff.: Friday evening, December 17, 1880, **S** 93–95.

256 "My parish work has been very wearisome" and ff.: December 22, 1880–January 16, 1881, **GMH to RWD, L2,** 36–42.

257 "by frost and starlight" and ff.: **GMH to RB,** January 20, 1881, **L1,** 114–16. Not sent. Hopkins, not one to waste paper, used the verso of the letter to write down some lines of a first draft of his poem "Brothers."

257 "coated with dirty yellow" and ff.: **GMH** to **RB**, January 26–February 8, 1881, **L1**, 116–24.

258 "truckler to Russia" and ff.: **GMH** to **KH**, March 2, 1881, **L3**, 158–59.

258 "There is an admirable but totally unknown living poet named Dixon": Dante Gabriel Rossetti to Hall Caine, quoted in **L2**, 46.

258 "has written for my consent" and ff.: **RWD** to **GMH**, March 28, 1882, **L2**, 46–47.

258 "Every impulse and spring of art" and ff.: **GMH** to **RB**, April 2–3, 1881, **L1**, 124.

259 "become very musical of late" and ff.: **GMH** to **RB**, April 27–May 1, 1881, **L1**, 125–28.

259 "omnium gatherum" and ff.: **GMH** to **RB**, May 14–15, 1881, **L1**, 128–30.

260 "After they had eaten the Paschal Lamb" and ff.: Sermon for Sunday, May 15, 1881, Fourth Sunday after Easter, **S** 95–100.

260 audacious robbery: *London Times*, May 18, 1881.

261 "the account made the more impression on me" and ff.: **GMH** to **KH**, May 20–22, 1881, **L3**, 159–60.

261 comic verses and begs him to send no more: **RB** to **GMH**, June 15, 1881, **RBSL** I, 130.

261 "unless for a certain blackguardry, but will not defend them" and ff.: **GMH** to **RB**, June 16, 1881, **L1**, 130–32.

261 "full of mention of the heart?" and ff.: Sermon on the Sacred Heart of Jesus, Sunday, June 26, 1881, **S** 100–104.

262 "I am afraid you must be very sick" and ff.: **GMH** to **RB**, June 28–July 3, 1881, **L1**, 132–34. Hopkins had begun the letter leisurely enough, then shifted tone on learning on July 2nd that Bridges was ill.

263 "my Liverpool . . . experience laid upon my mind" and ff.: **GMH** to **RWD**, December 1–16, 1881, **L2**, 97.

263 "How is it you do not know I am here?" and ff.: **GMH** to **RB**, September 16–17, 1881, **L1**, 134–37.

264 "never missed doing so except" and ff.: **GMH** to **RWD**, September 24, 1881, **L2**, 58–59.

264 "This dárksome búrn, hórseback brówn" and ff.: "Inversnaid: Sept. 28, 1881," **P** 167–68.

Chapter 13: **Aeonian Time: Roehampton & Tertianship, 1881–1882**

266 "I am a novice again" and ff.: **GMH** to **RWD**, ca. October 9, 1881, **L2**, 69.

267 "I will say no more" and ff.: **RWD** to **GMH**, October 11, 1881, **L2**, 69–71.

267 Manresa house "is the divine Theodora's" and ff.: **GMH** to **RWD**, October 12–17, 1881, **L2**, 71–76.

268 "I hear . . . that you are mending" and ff.: **GMH** to **RB**, October 22–25, 1881, **L1**, 137–40.

269 *"Ventus dissipat omnem meum laborem"*: Thomas.

269 "cross-fingered" and ff.: **GMH** to **RB**, October 22–25, 1881, **L1,** 138.

269 "I can understand that your present position" and ff.: October 26, 1881, **L2,** 80–82.

269 "for they more than equal the Italian" and ff.: **GMH** to **RWD,** October 29, 1881, **L2,** 82–87.

269 "My vocation puts before me a standard" and ff.: **GMH** to **RWD,** November 2, 1881, **L2,** 88–89.

270 the "first outstress" and ff.: November 8, 1881, S 196–202.

271 Satan, that *kosmokrator* and world wielder: Cf. Hopkins's 1877 sonnet, "Hurrahing in Harvest," **P** 148–49, where Hopkins speaks of capturing a glimpse among the "azurous hung hills" of North Wales Christ's "wórld-wíelding shoulder." I am indebted to the poet Geoffrey Hill for this insight.

271 "left master only of the material world" and ff.: S 198.

271 "The angels, like Adam": Notes for November 14, 1881, and ff.: S 200.

272 "when none but himself could know" and ff.: November 15, 1881, S 161–62.

272 "who have already committed themselves" and ff.: S162–63.

273 "consolation should be our normal state" and ff.: November 14, 1881, S 205. *On the Discernment of Spirits.*

273 Ignatius "speaks of the present condition of the lost" and ff.: S 135 ff.: *Meditation on Hell.*

274 Christ's hidden life . . . in Nazareth "is the great help to faith" and ff.: Meditation Notes for November 19–21, 1881, S 176–77.

274 the going from hotter to colder and ff.: On spiritual tepidity. S 208.

274 "Our retreat is still in hand": **GMH** to Edward Belasis, December 1, 1881, copy in Abbott MSS Box 9, Durham University Library.

275 "everything is of love, the love and duty of a grateful friend": December 8, 1881, S 192–95. Contemplation for Obtaining Love.

275 "all things . . . are charged with love, are charged with God" and ff.: December 8, 1881, S 195.

275 "when a man has given himself to God's service" and ff.: **GMH** to **RWD,** December 1, 1881, **L2,** 93.

276 "Why did you not reply" and ff.: **GMH** to **RB,** December 18, 1881, **L1,** 140.

276 "much diminished," some "called off altogether" and ff.: **GMH** to **KH,** December 24, 1881, **L3,** 160–61.

276 "hourly expecting orders to return to Liverpool" and ff.: **GMH** to **KH,** January 1, 1882, **L3,** 162.

277 "six or seven times round the earth" and ff.: Instructions: *On the Principle or Foundation,* S 238–41.

278 "you will see them no more" and ff.: Instructions: *On Death,* S 244–52.

278 "dens of shame" and ff.: S 249.

279 "shutting our eyes will not do away" and ff.: Instructions: *On Hell,* S 241–44.

280 He is still "like a novice" and ff.: **GMH** to **RB**, February 1–3, 1882, **L1**, 140–43.

280 "Bridges struck the truth long ago" and ff.: **RWD** to **GMH**, January 28, 1882, **L2**, 100–101.

280 "mind is much employed at present on the subject of Sacrifice": **GMH** to **RWD**, February 1–3, 1882, **L2**, 101–3.

281 "I mean to be at Carlisle tomorrow": **GMH** to **RWD**, March 26, 1882, **L2**, 103.

281 time would be "needed for this to wear off" and ff.: April 2, 1882, **L2**, 104.

281 "How very glad I am to have seen you" and ff.: **RWD** to **GMH**, April 13, 1882, **L2**, 104–5.

281 "I hope, my dear heart . . . you are now really better" and ff.: **GMH** to **RB**, April 3, 1882, **L1**, 143–44.

282 Glasgow . . . was "repulsive to live in" and ff.: **GMH** to **AB**, May 6, 1882, **L3**, 248–50.

282 "Come in the afternoon, the earlier the better" and ff.: **GMH** to **RB**, May 15, 1882, **L1**, 144–45.

283 "My heart warmed towards that little Bertie Molesworth" and ff.: **GMH** to **RB**, June 5, 1882, **L1**, 145–46.

283 "It is dithyrambic or what they used to call Pindaric" and ff.: **GMH** to **RB**, June 7, 1882, **L1**, 146–47.

284 "when the young poet my companion in study" and ff.: Robert Bridges, *The Testament of Beauty*, Part IV, *Ethick,* Oxford University Press, 1930, pp. 144–45.

284 "It was a needless and tedious frenzy" and ff.: **GMH** to **RB**, June 10, 1882, **L1**, 147–48.

285 "reverence and service" and ff.: Notes on the Foundation, August 7, 1882, S 129.

286 "Pax Christi. My hearties": and ff.: **GMH** to Fathers Shapter, Lapasteur, and Goldie, August 17, 1882, *HQ* XXIII, 2006, 1–2, pp. 3–17.

Chapter 14: **Metaphysician of Sunsets & Snowflakes: Stonyhurst Again, 1882–1884**

287 "leave to go to any one of our houses" and ff.: **GMH** to **RB**, September 26, 1882, **L1**, 150–52.

288 Hopkins explains his new discovery more fully in a letter to Baillie, dated January 14, 1883, in which he writes that "in any lyric passage of the tragic poets . . . there are [often] . . . two strains of thought running together and like counterpointed; the overthought that which everybody, editors, see (when one does see anything—which in the great corruption of the text and original obscurity of the diction is not everywhere) and which might for instance be abridged or paraphrased in square marginal blocks as in some books carefully written; the other, the underthought, conveyed

chiefly in the choice of metaphors etc used and often only half realised by the poet himself, not necessarily having any connection with the subject in hand but usually having a connection and suggested by some circumstance of the scene or of the story." GMH to AB, January 14, 1883, L3, 252.

289 "Ribblesdale": P 171.

290 "a traction engine twice a day" and ff.: GMH to RB, September 26, 1882, L1, 150–52.

290 "You are in the infinite leisure of Yattendon": GMH to RB, early Oct 1882, L1, 152–53.

290 *The Leaden Echo and the Golden Echo*: P 169–71.

291 "I have read of Whitman's" and ff.: GMH to RB, October 18, 1882, L3, 155–58. This suggests that Hopkins came in contact with Whitman's work through Bridges during Hopkins's time at the Farm Street Church in the summer or fall of 1878, reading Whitman's work in Bridges's Bedford Square apartment. But his first contact was even earlier, when he was teaching Rhetoric at Roehampton four years earlier.

293 "dull and museless" and ff.: GMH to RB, November 4, 1882, L1, 159–61.

293 "[*Domeless*] is not archaeologically right" and ff.: GMH to RB, December 1, 1882, L1, 165–66.

293 why "tell us that those on Olympus are domeless" and ff.: GMH to RB, December 20, 1882, L1, 166–68.

294 getting "into his room publicly through the window" and ff.: Eyre to Purbrick, December 1882, LN.

295 might "happen with regard to us" and ff.: Tuite to Delany, LN.

295 "I think Fr. Purbrick might be induced to let you have Hopkins" and ff.: Porter to Delany, November 5, 1882. Joseph Feeney, S.J., "Hopkins in Community: How His Jesuit Contemporaries Saw Him," in *Saving Beauty: Further Studies in Hopkins,* ed. Michael E. Allsopp and David A. Downes (New York: Garland, 1994), pp. 253–94.

295 "the cream of the [English] province" and ff.: Purbrick to Delany, November 10, 1882, LN.

295 "the injustice to myself I was thinking then" and ff.: GMH to RB, November 26, 1882, L1, 163.

296 "I have been in a wretched state of weakness" and ff.: GMH to RB, January 4, 1883, L1, 168–72.

296 "I cd. not venture to ask" and ff.: GMH to RB, February 3, 1883, L1, 173–76.

297 "Thank you very much" and ff.: JHN to GMH, February 27, 1883, L3, 412.

297 "a very kind compliment" and ff.: JHN to GMH, April 26, 1883, L3, 412.

298 "a conspicuous instance" and ff.: GMH to RB, March 26, 1883, L1, 176–78.

298 "We hang up polyglot poems" and ff.: GMH to RB, May 11, 1883, L1, 179.

298 "Wild air, world-mothering air" and ff.: "The Blessed Virgin compared to the Air we Breathe," P 173–76.

300 "a young man Henry Weber" and ff.: **GMH** to **RB**, August 5, 1883, **L1**, 184–85.

301 "Once more death shows its power" and ff.: **GMH** to Grace Hopkins, June 9, 1883, *Renascence*, Vol. 31 (1979), pp. 196–97.

301 "Almighty and Everlasting God" and ff.: Hopkins's prayer is reproduced in **L2**, 159–60.

302 "likely that I shall be removed" and ff.: July 26, 1883, **GMH** to **RB**, August 3, 1883, **L1**, 183–85.

303 "Bad rhymes; continued obscurity" and ff.: **GMH** to **RB**, May 26–31, 1879, **L1**, 82.

303 "The holidays are come" and ff.: **GMH** to **RB**, August 5, 1883, **L1**, 183–85.

303 "an address to the Reader" and ff.: **GMH** to **CP**, August 16, 1883, **L3**, 295–97.

304 "flitting to & fro, hearing their tiny voices": Kate Hopkins, 1928.

304 "settle down and be happy" and ff.: **GMH** to **RB**, October 24, 1883, **L1**, 189.

304 "an old and terribly afflicting thought and disgust": September 3, 1883. Hopkins at Beaumont Lodge, Private Retreat Notes, September 3–10, 1883, **S** 253–54.

307 "The worst of it" and ff.: Postcard from **GMH** to **RB**, September 11, 1883, **L1**, 186.

307 "a dangerous and an over-honourable one" and ff.: **GMH** to **CP**, September 14, 1883, **L3**, 298–300.

307 "one serious fault to find" and ff.: **GMH** to **CP**, September 23, 1883, **L3**, 300–306.

308 "nature is incapable of producing beautiful evil" and ff.: **GMH** to **CP**, September 24, 1883, **L3**, 306–11.

308 "wilder beast from West": **P** 163.

308 "pernicious doctrines and practice" and ff.: **GMH** to **CP**, September 24, 1883, **L3**, 306–11.

309 "'done it' this time" and ff.: **GMH** to **CP**, September 28, 1883, 1883, **L3**, 312–14.

309 "can no longer be trusted to . . . stomach" and ff.: **GMH** to **RB**, October 24–25, 1883, **L1**, 186–89.

310 "Those who accuse themselves" and ff.: **GMH** to **CP**, October 25–29, 1883, **L3**, 319–24.

310 "the making a thing more" and ff.: **GMH** to **CP**, November 7–10, 1883, **L3**, 325–33.

310 "was beautifully witnessed here today" and ff.: Letter to *Nature*, XXIX, pub. November 15, 1883, p. 55. Written at Stonyhurst, November 12, 1883.

310–11 "This is a hard saying, all politics apart" and ff.: **GMH** to **CP**, December 6, 1883, **L3**, 339–44.

311 "The political action and inaction" and ff.: **CP** to **GMH**, December 9, 1883, **L3**, 344–45.

311 "Father Gerard Hopkins may, at any time, go stark-staring mad" and ff.: Eyre to Purbrick, November 20, 1883.

312 "Fr. Hopkins could be spared" and ff.: Purbrick and consultors at Farm Street Church, November 28, 1883. Delany papers, Irish Jesuit Archives.

312 "I have no objection to your inviting Fr. Gerald [sic] Hopkins" and ff.: Purbrick to Delany, November 29, 1883. Delany papers, Irish Jesuit Archives.

312 "the peculiar illumination which may be seen in studios" and ff.: **GMH** to *Nature*, December 21, 1883, pub. January 3, 1884.

313 "the most qualified of the candidates" and ff.: Delany papers, Irish Jesuit Archives.

313 "I have to wish you a happy and a fruitful new year" and ff.: **GMH** to **CP**, January 3, 1884, **L3**, 346–49.

314 "Fr. Hopkins is going to be a fellow" and ff.: Charnley to Purbrick, January 5, 1884. English Jesuit Archives.

314 Trinity "prides itself on its [Latin and Greek] verse writers" and ff.: Delany to Cardinal McCabe, January 23, 1884. Delany papers, Irish Jesuit Archives.

314 "we had a man of fine classical learning" and ff.: Eyre, February 1884. English Jesuit Archives.

Chapter 15: **Spelt from Sybil's Leaves: Dublin, 1884–1885**

318 "Your Eminence and dearest Father" and ff.: **GMH** to **JHN**, February 20, 1884, **L3**, 63.

319 Dublin itself: I am indebted to Norman White and especially to Mary Daly's impressive essay, "Dublin in the 1880s," for much that I have learned here about Dublin during Hopkins's years there.

321 "over the Jews" and ff.: **GMH**'s meditation points for February 29, 1884. **S** 254–55.

321 "led by the spirit" and ff.: **GMH**'s meditation points for March 2, 1884. **S** 255.

321 "Remark the above address": **GMH** to **RB**, March 7, 1884, **L1**, 189–91.

322 "the thought of [Christ's] mind and genius" and ff.: March 8, 1884, **S** 255.

322 "The dense and the driven Passion, and frightful sweat" and ff.: *WD*, St. 7, **P** 120.

322 "Christ's joy in spite of his sorrows": **GMH**'s meditation notes on Our Lady's Sorrows, April 4, 1884, **S** 255–56.

323 "The thought and feeling" of the poems and ff.: **CP** to **GMH**, March 20, 1884, **L3**, 352–54.

323 Patmore "did not on the whole like my poems" and ff.: **GMH** to **RB**, April 16, 1884, **L1**, 191–92.

324 engaged . . . "on examination papers" and ff.: **GMH** to **RB**, April 30, 1884, **L1**, 192–93.

324 "pure gold imbedded in masses of unpracticable quartz" and ff.: **CP** to **RB**, May 2 and May 7, 1884, quoted in **L3**, 353.

324 Patmore has "seen Gerard's poems and has disliked them": **RB** to **RWD**, June 18, 1884, **RBSL** I, 147–48.

325 "a circular ticket" and ff.: **GMH** to **MH**, July 5, 1884, *The Month*, May 1958, 265–66.

325 "the fine scenery of which is less known": **GMH** to **RB**, July 18, 1884, **L1**, 193–94.

326 "Take it that weakness, ill health" and ff.: Retreat notes, July 22–30, 1884, **S** 256–57.

327 "I am extremely glad to hear from both of you" and ff.: **GMH** to **RB**, August 3, 1884, **L1**, 194–95.

327 for "the piece of a new garment" and ff.: **GMH** to **RB**, August 21–24, 1884, **L1**, 195–97.

328 "the happiest of days tomorrow" and ff.: **GMH** to **RB**, September 2, 1884, **L1**, 197.

328 "Consider the services to God" and ff.: Meditation points for the Feast of St. Michael, September 30, 1884, **S** 257.

328 "The times are nightfall" and ff.: **P** 176.

329 "Spelt from Sybil's Leaves": **P** 190–91.

330 duty is what "we are bound to in conduct" and ff.: For **GMH**'s notes on Cicero's *On Duty* [*De Officiis*], culled from his Dublin Notebook, cf. Fredric W. Schlatter's "Poetic Fragments. Comments on Lucan and Cicero, Essay on Duty," 1–106, esp. 54–57 and ff.:

330 "Only the beak-leaved boughs dragonish": **P** 190–91.

331 *"Scene, a wood, ending in a steep bank over a dry dean"* and ff.: *St. Winefred's Well*, **P** 177–79.

332 "I have been & am distressed" and ff.: **RWD** to **GMH**, July 9, 1884, **L2**, 122.

332 "I am heartily ashamed of myself" and ff.: **GMH** to **RWD**, October 25, 1884, **L2**, 123.

332 "I have had no time for unnecessary letterwriting" and ff.: **GMH** to Grace Hopkins, November 2, 1884, *HQ*, IV: 3–4, 181–83.

333 "a very good religious" and ff.: Letter from Joseph Rickaby, S.J., published in *The Month* (London), 261 (2001), 170–71.

334 "I have a kind of spooniness" and ff.: **GMH** to **RB**, November 11, 1884, **L1**, 198–200.

334 "the broken sleeps are a great trial to me" and ff.: **GMH** to **KH**, November 26, 1884, **L3**, 163–64.

335 "Desire this heavenly wisdom" and ff.: Meditation points for December 20, 1884, **S** 257–58.

335 "Poor, strangers, travellers" and ff.: Meditation points for Christmas Eve, 1884, **S** 258.

335 "would have been the world of pleasant" and ff.: **GMH** to **RB**, January 1, 1885, **L1**, 201–4.

336 "to be on the watch" and ff.: Meditation on the three holy kings, January 5, 1885, **S** 258.

336 pray . . . "for the spirit of love in all your doings" and ff.: **S** 258–59.

336 "Pray . . . not to be tormented" and ff.: Meditation for January 19, 1885, **S** 259.

336 "AN IMPERIAL PRINCE" and ff.: **GMH** to **KH**, January 24, 1885, **L3**, 166–69.

337 a crowd of some eight thousand and ff.: Cf. *London Times* for March 2, 1885.

338 "Yesterday Mr. O'Brien M.P. held his monster meeting" and ff.: **GMH** to **KH**, **L3**, 169–70.

Chapter 16: **We Hear Our Hearts Grate on Themselves: Dublin, 1885**

339 "To seem the stranger": **P** 181.

340 "And there they lie": **GMH** to **AB**, May 8, 1884, **L3**, 255.

340 "To hunger and not have, yét hope ón for" and ff.: *St. Winefred's Well*, Act II, **P** 179.

341 "the best you know of England" and ff.: **S** 259.

341 "on the ground has something to do": March 15, 1885, **S** 259–60.

341 *"every* effort is good": **S** 260.

341 "selfsacrifice and zeal" and ff.: **S** 260.

341 "holiness and his humility" and ff.: **S** 260.

341 "in a low way of health" and ff.: **GMH** to **RB**, **L1**, 208–11.

343 "if the whole world agreed" and ff.: **GMH** to **RB**, April 1, 1885, **L1**, 212–15.

343 "now an accomplished fact" and ff.: *London Times*, April 8, 1885.

343 "The Prince and Princess of Wales have been and gone" and ff.: May 17, 1885, **L3**, 171.

344 Gerontius Manley, Geldart's "ritualistic friend" and ff.: Nitram Tradleg, *A Son of Belial* (1882). Cf. **GMH** to **AB**, April 24, 1885, **L3**, 254–55n.

344 "I wake and feel the fell of dark, not day" and ff.: **P** 181–82.

345 "No worst, there is none" and ff.: **P** 182.

346 "Mortal my mate, bearing my rock-a-heart": **P** 186.

347 "I will this evening begin writing to you" and ff.: **GMH** to **AB**, April 24, 1885, **L3**, 254–55.

347 "accumulations . . . ever since I was at school" and ff.: **GMH** to **AB**, May 8, 1885, **L3**, 255–56.

347 "a lonely began": Cf. "To seem the stranger," **P** 181.

348 his "disease, so to call it": **GMH** to **AB**, May 8, 1885, **L3**, 256.

348 "Strike, churl; hurl, cheerless wind": **P** 182. Hopkins jotted down the opening quatrain for what appears to be yet another sonnet, then abandoned it.

348 "like pailfuls of coarse rice": **GMH** to **KH**, May 17, 1885, **L3**, 171.

348 "to work, worry, and languishment of body and mind" and ff.: **GMH** to **RB**, May 17–29, 1885, **L1**, 216–20.

349 "than other mythologies as Homer's epic is [superior to] other epics" and ff.: **GMH** to **RWD**, October 23, 1886, **L2**, 145–49.

349 "in cold blood write 'fragments of a dramatic poem'": **GMH** to **RB**, May 17–29, 1885, **L1**, 216–20.

350 Addis sends him a short note . . . a bed is at his service there and he will be most welcome: W. E. Addis to **GMH**. Addressed to Hopkins at Milltown Park, July 10, 1885, **L3**, 425.

350 "Two men went to the Temple to pray" and ff.: Sydenham, August 2, 1885, **S** 237.

350 "a very sweet lady" and ff.: **GMH** to **KH**, August 20, 1885, **L3**, 172.

351 "anything however high and innocent" and ff.: **GMH** to **CP**, August 21, 1885, **L3**, 365.

352 "To what serves Mortal Beauty?" and ff.: **P** 182–83.

353 "Not, I'll not, carrion comfort, Despair": **P** 183.

354 To soldier on, then and ff.: **P** 184.

355 "Patience, hard thing!" and ff.: **P** 185.

355 "O surely . . . reaving Peace, my Lord should leave in lieu": **P** 164.

355 "the hard thing but to pray" and ff.: **P** 185.

356 "My own heart let me more have pity on" and ff.: **P** 186.

357 "I have just returned from an absurd adventure" and ff.: **GMH** to **RB**, September 1–8, 1885, **L1**, 220–23.

358 "sweetly soothed" and ff.: **GMH** to Everard Hopkins, November 5–8, 1885, **HRB** 4 (1973), 7–12.

359 "overbearing and ungentlemanly" and ff.: **GMH** to **KH**, November 13, 1885, **L3**, 173–74.

360 "gifted friend, Fr. Hopkins" and ff.: Cf. **GMH** to **RB**, December 14, 1885, **L1**, 223–24. Hopkins's letter to Dixon is lost, but we can infer what Hopkins had said to Dixon from Hopkins's letter to Bridges.

360 "drift . . . upon the tide of atheism" and ff.: **GMH** to Everard Hopkins, December 23, 1885, **HRB** 4 (1973), 12–14.

360 "most beautiful sermon he ever heard on the Blessed Sacrament" and ff.: Cf. Joseph Feeney, S.J., "Hopkins and the MacCabe Family: Three Children who knew Gerard Manley Hopkins," *Studies* (Dublin), 90 (2001), 299–307.

361 "Thee, God, I come from, to thee go" and ff.: **P** 184–85.

Chapter 17: **Cloud Puffballs, Torn Tufts: Dublin, 1886–1887**

363 he has learned from Maspero's *Histoire* and ff.: **GMH** to **AB**, February 11, 1886, **L3**, 257–58.

363 Prof. John Rhys to **GMH**, April 24, 1886. **L3**, 416–19.

364 Mrs. Waterhouse to **GMH**, May 10, 1886, **L3**, 426.

364 "I saw, ere we had conversed ten minutes" and ff.: Sir Robert Stewart to GMH, May 22, 1886, L3, 426–27.

364 "Darling Padre!... *I* never said anything outrageous to you" and ff.: Stewart to GMH, no date, but probably late May or early June 1886, L3, 427–28.

364 having "corrected and simplified" and ff.: GMH to KH, June 11, 1886, L3, 176.

364 Egyptian inquiries are now off "because examination work is on" and ff.: GMH to AB, June 1, 1886, L3, 273–74.

365 "a good deed done" and ff.: GMH to CP, June 4, 1886, L3, 366–68.

365 he has been employed ... "to edit a Bible Birthday Book": RWD to GMH, June 21, 1886, L2, 130–31.

366 "a truly noble work and to me a new light" and ff.: GMH to RWD, June 30, 1886, L2, 132–36.

366 "helping to save and damn the studious youth of Ireland" and ff.: GMH to RWD, L2, 136–38.

367 "Six or seven weeks of it" and ff.: GMH to RWD, August 7, 1886, L2, 138–42.

368 "remote and beautiful spot" and ff.: GMH to RWD, September 30, 1886, L2, 142–43.

368 "delightful holiday comes to an end to-day" and ff.: GMH to RB, October 2, 1886, L1, 226–29.

369 Curtis "was dogged" and ff.: GMH to KH, October 5, 1886, L3, 176–77.

369 Examinations are over ... "till the next attack of the plague" and ff.: GMH to RB, October 21, 1886, L1, 232–35.

370 "The books came safely this morning" and ff.: Kate Tynan to GMH, November 6, 1886, L3, 430.

370 "I seem to have been among odds and ends of poets" and ff.: GMH to CP, November 7, 1886, L3, 372–74.

371 "You have gained greatly in intensity of diction from Gerard Hopkins": W. B. Yeats to Monk Gibbon, March 12, 1932, R. F. Foster, *W.B. Yeats: A Life, II: The Arch Poet* (Oxford University Press, London, 2003), 434.

371 "it is not performed, it does not perform" and ff.: GMH to Everard Hopkins, November 5–8, 1885, HRB 4 (1973), 7–12.

371 "completed but not quite finished ... longest sonnet ever made": GMH to RB, November 26, 1886, L1, 245.

371 "longest by its own proper length" and ff.: GMH to RB, December 11, 1886, L1, 246.

372 "might have been friends" and ff.: Edward Dowden, "The Poetry of Robert Bridges" (*Fortnightly Review*, July 1894).

372 "gone far enough in oddities": GMH to RB, February 17, 1887, L1, 250.

372 "O I admire and sorrow!": "On the Portrait of Two Beautiful Young People," P 191–92.

373 "the best and brightest of all my pupils" and ff.: GMH to KH, L3, 178.

374 "never written that silly letter" and ff.: **GMH** to **KH**, **L3**, 179. Cf. Dickens's last novel, *Edwin Drood*, with its description of Sapsea, "the purest Jackass in Cloisterham."

374 "Tomorrow morning . . . I shall have been three years in Ireland" and ff.: **GMH** to **RB**, February 17, 1887, **L1**, 250–52.

375 "I do not say things are as bad" and ff.: **GMH** to **AB**, February 20, 1887, **L3**, 282–83.

375 "which soon will begin to put on . . . those bright looks" and ff.: **GMH** to **KH,** March 2, 1887, **L3**, 179–81.

376 "The Irish Patriots hold" and ff.: **JHN** to **GMH**, March 3, 1887, **L3**, 413–14.

376 a letter defending the English against charges: **GMH** to Dr. Michael Cox, March 25, 1887 (Lady Day), **HRB** 3 (1972), 6–7.

376 "that it goes but a very little way to explaining the poverty of Ireland" and ff.: **GMH** to Dr. Michael Cox, March 31, 1887, **HRB** 3 (1972), 8–9.

377 "cold but bright" and ff.: **GMH** to **KH**, April 26, 1887, **L3**, 182.

377 "The irises of the present writer's eyes" and ff.: **GMH** to **RB**, March 29, 1887, **L1**, 253–54.

377 "These cheap issues are a great boon" and ff.: **GMH** to **CP**, May 12,1887, **L3**, 378–79.

378 "not satisfied" and ff.: Cf. *London Times* for June 21, 1887: "We are informed that the Pope has decided to send Monsignor Persico as Apostolic Delegate to Ireland. We believe the Pope is not satisfied with the attitude of the Irish clergy."

378 For an informative and detailed essay on Father Klein, cf. Fredric Schlatter's "Martial Klein, Hopkins's Dublin Colleague," **HQ** 29 (2002): 69–105.

378 "restored the text and sense" and ff.: **GMH** to **RB**, July 30, 1887, **L1**, 255–58.

379 "the dullest and narrowest world" and ff.: **GMH** to **RB**, August 25, 1887, **L1**, 258–60.

379 "a fashionable complaint" and ff.: **GMH** to **AB**, September 7, 1887, **L3**, 288.

379 "Mortal my mate": "To His Watch," **P** 186.

379 "Hard as hurdle arms": opening of "Harry Ploughman," **P** 193–94.

380 "Not of all my eyes see" and ff.: ["Ashboughs"], **P** 194.

381 "will go to Dublin by goods train from Dromore" and ff.: **GMH** to **RB**, September 28, 1887, Eve of Michaelmas, **L1**, 260–62.

381 "be recited by a chorus" and ff.: **GMH** to **RB**, October 11, 1887, **L1**, 262–263.

382 "a vivid figure before the mind's eye" and ff.: **GMH** to **RB**, November 6, 1887, **L1**, 265–66.

382 "tell me how correctly to make codas to sonnets": **GMH** to **RB**, November 2, 1887, **L1**, 263–64.

383 "thick / Thousands of thorns, thoughts": from "Tom's Garland: on the Unemployed," **P** 195.

384 "no matter how beautiful the thought" and ff.: **GMH** to **CP**, October 20, 1887, **L3**, 380.

385 "the little nymph": **GMH** to **RB**, December 21, 1887, **L1**, 268.

385 "the scene . . . of the poisoning of the hounds": **GMH** to **RWD**, December 22, 1887, **L2**, 153.

385 "Many hundreds came to the rail" and ff.: **GMH** to **KH**, December 25, 1887, **L3**, 182–83.

Chapter 18: The War Within: Dublin, 1888

386 "We have had to stay already more than a month in London": **RB** to Lionel Muirhead, **RBSL** I, 173.

386 "I am glad that you will be back" and ff.: January 12, 1888, **L1**, 268–69.

387 "I laughed outright and often" and ff.: February 10, 1888, **L1**, 272–74.

388 "Your Eminence and dearest Father" and ff.: **GMH** to **JHN**, February 20, 1888, **HQ** 23 (1996), 24–28.

389 "I have a poor, very charming friend" and ff.: **GMH** to **RB**, February 10, 1888, **L1**, 274.

389 "Make believe / We are leafwhelmed somewhere" and ff.: "Epithalamion," **P** 195–97.

391 "I never saw a naked woman" and ff.:

392 "Mayday, a stormy one" and ff.: **L3**, 290–94.

393 "much-meditating on the effect": **CP** to **GMH**, Hastings, February 10, 1888, **L3**, 385.

393 "This . . . is the second letter begun" and ff.: **GMH** to **CP**, May 6, 1888, **L3**, 385ff.:

393 "Not a low, not a crow" and ff.: **GMH** to **RB**, May 25, 1888, **L1**, 274ff.:

394 Examinations "began last month" and ff.: **GMH** to **KH**, July 5, 1888, **L3**, 184–85.

394 "What a preposterous summer!" and ff.: **GMH** to **RWD**, July 29, 1888, **L2**, 157.

395 "Cloud-puffballs": "That Nature is a Heraclitean Fire and of the comfort of the Resurrection," **P** 197–98.

395 "Clouds growing in beauty": June 3, 1866, **J** 138–39.

395 "the impossibility of staying": July 17, 1866, **J** 146.

397 "How to keep" and ff.: *The Leaden Echo and the Golden Echo,* **P** 169–71.

398 "all in a minute": **GMH** to **EWU**, October 4, 1866, **L1**, 27.

398 "Now I am going to tell you a mystery" and ff.: *I Corinthians* 15:51–54.

399 "his insight was at its very deepest" and ff.: **GMH** to **RWD**, October 23, 1886, **L2**, 148.

399 "Six weeks of examination" and ff.: **GMH** to **RB**, August 18, 1888, **L1**, 278ff.:

400 in a distress of mind: **GMH** to **RB**, **L1**, 280ff.:

401 "Call me England's fame's fond lover": **P** 198–99.

401 "I am very glad you like the tune" and ff.: **GMH** to **RB**, September 13/14, 1888, **L1**, 289–90.

402 "Football is sometimes played barefoot in Ireland" and ff.: **GMH** to editor, "Football Barefoot," *Stonyhurst Magazine,* III, November 1888, pp. 236–37.

402 "I am sorry to hear of our differing so much in taste": **GMH** to **RB**, September 25, 1888, L1, 290ff.:

403 "who for 40 years acted": **GMH** to **RB**, October 3, 1888, L1, 292–93.

403 "Honour is flashed off exploit": P199–200, third of three extant drafts.

403 "I am obliged for your criticisms" and ff.: **GMH** to **RB**, October 19, 1888, L1, 296–98.

405 "Did you hear of Addis's leaving": **RB** to Muirhead, December 13, 1888, **RBSL** I, 182.

405 "Iit seems . . . there is something in you": **GMH** to **RB**, October 19/20, 1888, L1, 298.

406 "it is not convenient to my time or eyesight": **GMH** to **KH**, November 10/11, 1888, L3, 185–86.

406 "I hope your exhibition" and ff.: **GMH** to Arthur Hopkins, November 26, 1888, L3, 186ff.:

406 "I seem to be altogether in Japan" and ff, December 24, 1888, **GMH** to **KH**, L3, 189–91.

Chapter 19: Patch, Matchwood, Immortal Diamond: Dublin, 1889, and After

408 "in being on the right side" and ff.: **S** 261–62. Hopkins initially dates his retreat notes January 1, 1888, rather than 1889, a mistake he often made in dating letters at the beginning of a new year.

409 "I was a Christian from birth" and ff.: **S** 262.

410 "loathing of my life" and ff.: January 2, 1889, **S** 262.

410 "more loathing" and ff.: January 2, 1889, **S** 262–63.

410 "affected, marked, as a great seal" and ff.: January 5, 1889, **S** 263.

411 "Yesterday . . . I had ever so much light" and ff.: January 6, 1889, **S** 263–64.

411 "overburdened the house" and ff.: January 6, 1889, **S** 270–71.

412 "dirtier than ever" and ff.: On February 19, 1889, **RB** had written Lionel Muirhead that they were back home after three weeks in Italy, and that he had come away from the experience disliking the Italians even "more, and thought them dirtier than ever." **RBSL** I, 183. In his letter to **GMH** written at the same time he expressed a similar bias, and **GMH** answered on February 23, 1889, as follows. L1, 299.

412–13 "What boobies your countrymen are!" and ff.: L1, 300.

413 "Of good histories of Greece" and ff.: L3, 191–94.

414 *"Justus quidem tu es, Domine"* and ff.: P 201.

415 "ungracious reason" and ff.: L1, 301–3.

416 "progress in science and humanity" and ff.: *London Times* for April 1, 1889.

416 "The shepherd's brow": P 201.

417 "AND WHAT DOES ANYTHING AT ALL MATTER?": L1, 192. April 16, 1884, from Clongowes-Wood College.

417 "He! Hand to mouth he lives" and ff.: **P** 201 and 204.

417 "Even Milton, looking for his portrait in a spoon": George Eliot, *Middle-march*, Penguin, 2003, p. 84.

418 "so lovable—so singularly gifted": Susan de Paravicini to **KH**, June 1889.

418 "Very strangely it happened" and ff.: **RB** to **RWD**, August 10, 1889. **RBSL** I, 188.

419 "I am ill to-day, but no matter" and ff.: April 29, 1889, **L1**, 303–4.

419 "She is an elderly lady" and ff.: **L1**, 305–6.

420 "The fine delight that fathers thought": **P** 204.

422 "You have not heard from me" and ff.: **L3**, 195.

422 "The pains are only slight" and ff.: May 3, 1889, **L3**, 196.

422 "I am grieved that" and ff.: May 5, 1889, **L3**, 196–97.

423 "My fever is a sort of typhoid": May 8, 1889, **L3**, 197–98.

423 "I think he is now well round the corner": Father Thomas Wheeler to **KH**, May 14, 1889, **L3**, 189n2.

423 "Dearest Gerard . . . I am sorry": **RB** to **GMH**, May 18, 1889, **L3**, 433.

Coda

427 "His beautifully gentle & generous nature": Susan Paravicini to **KH**, June 14, 1889.

427 "It is impossible to say how much I owe to him": **AB** to **KH**, June 17, 1889, **L3**, 449.

428 "How can I tell you": **RB** to **RWD**, June 14, 1889, **RBSL** I, 185–86.

428 "I have thought that I may possess writings of his": **RB** to **KH**, June 19, 1889.

428 "proposed to edit": **RB** to **RWD**, August 10, 1889, **RBSL** I, 188–89.

428 "Mr. Daniel says that he will print a selection" and ff.: August 4, 1890, **RB** to **KH**, **RBSL** I, 203–4.

429 "Thank you . . . for returning that Roman Catholic Magazine" and ff.: **RB** to **KH**, January 21, 1909. **RBSL** II, 561–63. The article, titled "Gerard Hopkins: an Epitaph and an Appreciation," was written by Katharine Brégy, and appeared in *The Catholic World*, January 1909, pp. 433–47.

429 "As for the difficulty of appreciating the poems" and ff.: **RB** to **KH**, March 28, 1909. **RBSL** II, 567.

430 "I am afraid that you will find": **RB** to **KH**, April 2, 1909. **RBSL** II, 568.

430 "I wonder what your wishes will be": **RB** to **KH**, May 7, 1909. **RBSL** II, 570.

430 "I had a very pleasant time at 7 Pembroke Road": **RB** to **KH**, **RBSL** II, 571.

431 "When Gerard first saw my first book of poems": **RB** to **KH**, July 28, 1913, **RBSL** II, 628.

431 June 26, 1926: "He sprang from a rhododendron bush" and ff.: *The Diary of Virginia Woolf,* Vol. 3, 1925–1930, ed. Anne Olivier Bell. Entry for July 1, 1926, pp. 90–92. Lady Ottoline Morel snapped several pictures of Woolf and Bridges together on June 26th. Cf. National Portrait Gallery images.

431 "Pax Christi" and ff.: Father Joseph Rickaby to Father Gerald Leahy, February 28, 1927. Cf. Joseph Feeney, S.J., "A Jesuit classmate remembers G. M. Hopkins: An unpublished letter of Joseph Rickaby, S.J.," *The Month* (London), 261 (2001), 170–71.

432 words "come so near a transfiguration into pure musical notation": Hart Crane to Yvor Winters, January 27, 1927. Quoted in Paul Mariani, *The Broken Tower: The Life of Hart Crane,* p. 292.

433 That "one unwise blunder": *The Month,* 1975.

Selected Hopkins Bibliography

Abbott, Evelyn, and Lewis Campbell. *The Life and Letters of Benjamin Jowett*, 2 vols. (London, 1897).

Allsopp, Michael. "Hopkins at Oxford 1863–1867: His Formal Studies," *HQ,* 4/3–4 (Fall–Winter 1977–78), 161–76.

———. "Hopkins at Highgate: Biographical Fragments," *HQ,* 6/1 (Spring 1979), 3–10.

———. "Gerard Manley Hopkins, Oxford, and Edward Urquhart: Doctrinal Controversy and Religious Conversion," in Michael Allsopp and David Downes, eds., *Saving Beauty: Further Studies in Hopkins* (New York: Garland, 1994).

———, and Michael Sundermeier, eds. *Gerard Manley Hopkins (1844–1880): New Essays on His Life, Writing, and Place in English Literature* (Lewiston, NY: E. Mellen Press, 1989).

Arnold, Matthew. *Complete Prose Works of Matthew Arnold,* ed. R. H. Super, 11 vols. (Ann Arbor: University of Michigan Press, 1960–77).

Arnold, Thomas. *A Manual of English Literature,* 5th ed. (1885).

———. *Passages in a Wandering Life* (1900).

Ball, Patricia M. *The Central Self: A Study in Romantic and Victorian Imagination* (London: Athlone Press, 1968).

———. *The Science of Aspects: The Changing Role of Fact in the Work of Coleridge, Ruskin and Hopkins* (London: Athlone Press, 1971).

Barber, Noel, S.J. "Hopkins and the Irish Jesuits," *HQ,* 33 (2006), 34–54.

Beer, Gillian. "Helmholtz, Tyndall, Gerard Manley Hopkins: Leaps of the Prepared Imagination," *Comparative Literature,* 13 (1992), 117–45.

Bender, Todd. *Gerard Manley Hopkins: The Classical Background and Critical Reception of His Work* (Baltimore: Johns Hopkins University Press, 1966).

Benson, A. C. *Walter Pater* (London: Macmillan, 1906).

Bergonzi, Bernard. *Gerard Manley Hopkins* (New York: Collier Books, 1977).

———. *A Victorian Wanderer: The Life of Thomas Arnold the Younger* (New York: Oxford University Press, 2003).

Bischoff, Anthony, S.J. "Three Uncollected Letters," *HRB,* 4 (1973), 3–14.

Boehnke, Barbara. "The Perceptual Origins of Inscape," *HQ,* 24/3–4 (Summer–Fall 1997), 71–94.

Boyle, Robert, S.J. "Hopkins' Use of 'Fancy,'" *Victorian Poetry,* 10/1 (Spring 1972), 17–28.

Bradley, Bruce, S.J. *James Joyce's Schooldays* (New York: St. Martin's Press, 1982).

Bridges, Robert. "An Account of the Casualty Department," *St. Bartholomew Hospital Report* (1878).

———. *Poems* (1873).

———. *The Growth of Love* (1878).

———. Poems by the author of *The Growth of Love* (1880).

———. *Prometheus the Firegiver* (Oxford, 1883).

———. *The Selected Letters of Robert Bridges,* ed. Donald E. Stanford, 2 vols. (Newark, DE, 1983, 1984).

———. *The Shorter Poems of Robert Bridges* (1890).

———. *The Testament of Beauty* (Oxford, 1929, 1930).

———. *Three Friends: Memoirs of Digby Mackworth Dolben, Richard Watson Dixon, Henry Bradley* (1932).

Brown, Daniel. *Hopkins' Idealism: Philosophy, Physics, Poetry* (Oxford: Clarendon Press, 1997).

———. *Gerard Manley Hopkins* (Oxford: Northcote House, 2004).

Bump, Jerome. *Gerard Manley Hopkins* (Boston: Twayne, 1982).

Burke, Edmund. *A Philosophical Enquiry into the Origin of our Ideas of the Sublime and Beautiful* (London, 1757).

Caine, Hall, ed. *Sonnets of Three Centuries* (1882).

Carlyle, Thomas. *On Heroes, Hero-Worship and the Heroic in History* (London, 1841).

———. *Past and Present,* ed. Richard D. Altick (Boston: New York Unversity Press, 1977).

———. *Selected Writings,* ed. Alan Shelston (Harmondsworth: Penguin, 1971).

Champneys, Basil. *Memoirs and Correspondence of Coventry Patmore,* 2 vols. (1900).

Christ, Carol T. *The Finer Optic: The Aesthetic of Particularity in Victorian Poetry* (New Haven: Yale University Press, 1975).

———. *Victorian and Modern Poetics* (Chicago: Chicago University Press, 1984).

Clark, Kenneth. *Ruskin at Oxford* (Oxford: Clarendon Press, 1947).

———, ed. *Ruskin Today* (1964).

Clayre, Alasdair, ed. *Nature and Industrialization* (Oxford: Oxford University Press, 1977).

Coleridge, Henry James, S.J. *The Prisoners of the King: Thoughts on the Catholic Doctrine of Purgatory* (1889).

Coleridge, Samuel Taylor. *Biographia Literaria,* ed. George Watson (London: Dent, 1965).

Colley, Ann. "Mapping In and Out of the Borders of Time: Ruskin and Hopkins," *Victorian Literature and Culture,* 19 (1991), 107–21.

Cotter, James Finn. *Inscape: The Christology and Poetry of Gerard Manley Hopkins* (Pittsburgh: University of Pittsburgh Press, 1972).

————. "Hopkins and Augustine," *HQ*, 31 (2004), 127–42.

Cox, G. V. *Recollections of Oxford* (London, 1868).

Crehan, Joseph, S.J. "Some Hopkins Memories," *HRB*, 4 (1973), 29–30.

Cruse, Amy. *The Victorians and Their Books* (1935).

Dale, Peter Allan. *In Pursuit of a Scientific Culture: Science, Art, and Society in the Victorian Age* (Madison: University of Wisconsin Press, 1989).

Dana, R. H. *Two Years Before the Mast* (1840).

Darwin, Charles. *The Origin of Species By Means of Natural Selection . . .* , ed. J. W. Burrow (Harmondsworth: Penguin, 1968).

————. "Poetry and the Scientization of Language: 'Geist' Son of Waldmann," *Victorian Newsletter*, 79 (Spring 1991), 4–9.

De Laura, David J. *Hebrew and Hellene in Victorian England* (Austin: University of Texas Press, 1969).

————. "Hopkins and Carlyle: My Hero, My Chevalier," *HQ*, 2/2 (July 1975), 67–76.

Dessain, Stephen. *John Henry Newman* (1980).

Dixon, Richard Watson. *Poems by the Late Rev. Dr. Richard Watson Dixon: A Selection with Portrait and A Memoir by Robert Bridges* (1909).

————. *Songs and Odes* (1896).

————. *The Last Poems of Richard Watson Dixon D.D.*, ed. Robert Bridges (1905).

Dolben, Digby Mackworth. *Lyrics of Light and Life XLIII* (1875).

————. *The Poems of Digby Mackworth Dolben*, ed. Robert Bridges (1911; 2nd ed. 1915).

————. *The Poems and Letters of Digby Mackworth Dolben, 1848–1867*, ed. Martin Cohen (Avebury, Wilts: Earls Barton, 1981).

Dowden, Edward. *New Studies in Literature* (1895).

Downes, David A. *Gerard Manley Hopkins: A Study of His Ignatian Spirit* (1960).

————. *Victorian Portraits: Hopkins and Pater* (New York: Bookman Associates, 1965).

Eliot, George. *Middlemarch: A Study of Provincial Life*, ed. Gordon S. Haight (Boston: Houghton Mifflin, 1968).

Ellmann, Richard. *Oscar Wilde at Oxford* (Washington, DC: Library of Congress, 1984).

Engel, A. J. *From Clergyman to Don: The Rise of the Academic Profession in Nineteenth-Century Oxford* (Oxford: Clarendon Press, 1984).

Faber, Geoffrey. *Jowett: A Portrait with Background* (London: Faber & Faber, 1957).

Feeney, Joseph J., S.J. *The Playfulness of Gerard Manley Hopkins* (Aldershot, Hants: Ashgate, 2008).

————. "Grades, Academic Reform, and Manpower: Why Hopkins Never Completed His Course in Theology," *HQ*, 9 (1982), 21–31.

————. "Hopkins' Frequent Reassignments as a Priest," *HQ*, 11 (1985), 101–18.

————. "Hopkins' 'Failure' in Theology: Some New Archival Data and a Reevaluation," *HQ*, 13 (1986–87), 99–114.

————. "Hopkins's Closest Friend in Ireland: Robert Curtis, S.J.," in *Hopkins and*

Dublin: The Man and the City, ed. Richard F. Giles (Hamilton, ONT.: International Hopkins Ass., 1988), 211–38.

———. "The Collapse of Hopkins' Jesuit Worldview: A Conflict Between Moralism and Incarnationalism," *Gerard Manley Hopkins Annual* (1992), 105–26.

———. "Hopkins in Community: How His Jesuit Contemporaries Saw Him," in *Saving Beauty: Further Studies in Hopkins,* ed. Michael E. Allsopp and David A. Downes (New York: Garland, 1994), 253–94.

———. "My dearest Father: Some unpublished letters of Gerard Manley Hopkins," *TLS,* No. 4,838, Dec. 22, 1995, 13–14.

———. "Four Newfound Hopkins Letters: An Annotated Edition, with a Fragment of Another Letter," *HQ,* 23 (1996), 3–4.

———. "At St Beuno's: Newly discovered work by Gerard Manley Hopkins," *TLS,* No. 5,000, Jan. 29, 1999, 13–14.

———. "A New-Found Poem by Gerard Manley Hopkins," *The Month* (London), 260 (1999), 249–51.

———. "A Jesuit Classmate Remembers G. M. Hopkins: An unpublished letter of Joseph Rickaby, S.J.," *The Month,* 261 (2001), 170–71.

———. "Hopkins and the MacCabe Family: Three children who knew Gerard Manley Hopkins," *Studies* (Dublin), 90 (2001), 299–307.

———. "Gerard Manley Hopkins' 'Consule Jones': A Critical Edition with Introduction and Commentary," *HQ,* 29 (2002), 3–20.

———. "An Unpublished Hopkins Couplet, 'To Jesus on my bed I sue': A Critical Edition," *HQ,* 29/1–2 (Winter–Spring 2002), 21–24.

———. "Scarlet Geraniums and the Mother of Muses: Gerard Manley Hopkins in Wales, 1874–1877," *HQ,* 31 (2004), 181–93.

———, with Joaquin Kuhn, eds. *Hopkins Variations: Standing Round a Waterfall* (New York and Philadelphia: Fordham University Press and St. Joseph's University Press, 2002).

Fennell, Francis, ed. *Rereading Hopkins: Selected New Essays* (Victoria, BC: University of Victoria Press, 1996).

Foster, R. F. *W. B. Yeats: A Life,* 2 vols. (London: Oxford University Press, 2003).

Gardner, Helen. *Religion and Literature* (1971).

Gardner, W. H. *Gerard Manley Hopkins, 1844–89: A Study of Poetic Idiosyncrasy in Relation to Poetic Tradition,* 2 vols. rev. ed. (London: Oxford University Press, 1966).

[Geldart, Martin—see Tradleg, Nitram]

Giles, Richard F., ed. *Hopkins Among the Poets: Studies in Modern Responses to Gerard Manley Hopkins* (Hamilton, ONT.: International Hopkins Ass., 1985).

Gilmour, Robin. *The Idea of a Gentleman in the Victorian Novel* (London: Allen & Unwin, 1981).

Gladstone, Right Hon. W. E., MP. *Rome and the Newest Fashions in Religion* (1875).

Goldie, Francis, S.J. *The Life of St. Alfonso Rodriguez* (1889).

Goodwin, Michael, ed. *Nineteenth-Century Opinion* (Harmondsworth: Penguin, 1951).

Gosse, Edmund. *Critical Kit-Kats* (New York, 1896).

———. *Father and Son: A Study of Two Temperaments* (1907).

Green, T. H. *Prolegomena to Ethics,* ed. A. C. Bradley (Oxford, 1883).

———. *Works of Thomas Hill Green,* ed. R. L. Nettleship, 3 vols. (London, 1888).

Grigson, Geoffrey. *Gerard Manley Hopkins* (London: Longmans, Green & Co., 1955).

Grimm, Herman. *The Life of Michelangelo,* trans. Fanny Elizabeth Burnett (London, 1865).

Grosskurth, Phyllis. *John Addington Symonds: A Biography* (New York: Arno Press, 1975).

Grote, George. *A History of Greece,* 12 vols. (London, 1846–69).

———. *Plato, and the Other Companions of Sokrates,* 3 vols. (London, 1865).

Groves, Peter. "Gerard Among the Puseyites: New Light from Old Archives on Hopkins' Undergraduate Religion," *HQ,* 30 (2003), 83–97.

Guerard, Albert, Jr. *Robert Bridges: A Study of Traditionalism in Poetry* (Cambridge, MA, 1942).

Hansen, Ron. *Exiles: A Novel* (New York: Farrar, Straus & Giroux, 2008).

Harries-Jenkins, Gwynn. *The Army in Victorian Society* (1977).

Hartman, Geoffrey, ed. *Hopkins: A Collection of Critical Essays* (Englewood Cliffs, NJ: Prentice-Hall, 1966).

Hayter, William. *Spooner, A Biography* (London: W. H. Allen, 1977).

Heuser, Alan. *The Shaping Vision of Gerard Manley Hopkins* (London: Oxford University Press, 1958).

Hewison, Robert. *John Ruskin: The Argument of the Eye* (1976).

Higgins, Lesley. "Hopkins and 'The Jowler,'" *Texas Studies in Literature and Language,* 31/1 (Spring 1989), 143–67.

———. "A New Catalogue of the Hopkins Collection at Campion Hall," *HQ,* 18/1–2 (April–July 1991), 9–44.

———. "Essaying 'W H. Pater Esq.': New Perspectives on the Tutor/Student Relationship Between Pater and Hopkins," in Laurel Brake and Ian Small, eds., *Pater in the 1990s* (Greensboro, NC: ELT Press, 1991), 77–94.

———. "Jowett and Pater: Trafficking in Platonic Wares," *Victorian Studies,* 37/1 (Autumn 1993), 43–72.

———. "The 'piecemeal peace' of Hopkins's Return to Oxford, 1878–1879," in Eugene Hollahan, ed., *Gerard Manley Hopkins and Critical Discourse,* Georgia State Literary Series (New York: AMS Press, 1993), 167–82.

———. "Hopkins and Friends at Oxford: A New Perspective," *HQ,* 21/1–2 (Winter-Spring 1994; pub. 1996), 3–22.

———. "Uncommon Lives: Fr. Hopkins and Fr. Bacon," *HQ,* 21/3–4 (Summer–Fall 1994; pub. 1996), 77–96.

———. "'Bone-house' or 'Lovescape': Writing the Body in Hopkins's Poetry," in Frank Fennell, ed., *Rereading Hopkins: Selected New Essays, English Literary Studies Series* (Victoria, BC: University of Victoria Press, 1996), 11–35.

Hillier, Bevis. "Portraits of Hopkins," in R. K. R. Thornton, ed., *All My Eyes See: The Visual World of Gerard Manley Hopkins* (Sunderland: Ceolfrith Press, 1975), 3–9.

Hilton, Tim. *John Ruskin: The Later Years* (New Haven: Yale University Press, 2000).

Hopkins, Arthur. *Sketches and Skits* (1901).

Hopkins, Gerard Manley. *The Collected Works of Gerard Manley Hopkins.* Vol. IV: *Oxford Essays and Notes,* ed. Lesley Higgins (London: Oxford University Press, 2006).

———. *The Correspondence of Gerard Manley Hopkins and Richard Watson Dixon,* ed. Claude Colleer Abbott, rev. ed. (London: Oxford University Press, 1955).

———. *The Letters of Gerard Manley Hopkins to Robert Bridges,* ed. Claude Colleer Abbott (London: Oxford University Press, 1955).

———. *Further Letters of Gerard Manley Hopkins, Including His Correspondence with Coventry Patmore,* ed. Claude Colleer Abbott (London: Oxford University Press, 1957).

———. *The Journals and Papers of Gerard Manley Hopkins,* ed. Humphry House and Graham Storey (Oxford: Oxford University Press, 1959).

———. *The Sermons and Devotional Writings of Gerard Manley Hopkins,* ed. Christopher Devlin, S.J. (London: Oxford University Press, 1959).

———. *The Poems of Gerard Manley Hopkins,* ed. W. H. Gardner and Norman H. MacKenzie, 4th ed. (London: Oxford University Press, 1970).

———. *The Early Poetic Manuscripts and Note-Books of Gerard Manley Hopkins,* ed. Norman H. MacKenzie (New York: Garland Press, 1989).

———. *The Poetical Works of Gerard Manley Hopkins,* ed. Norman H. MacKenzie (Oxford: Clarendon Press, 1990).

———. *The Later Poetic Manuscripts of Gerard Manley Hopkins,* ed. Norman H. MacKenzie (New York: Garland Press, 1991).

———. "The Dublin Notes on Homer," ed. Warren Anderson, *HQ,* 19/1–4, special issue (Winter–Fall 1992; pub. 1995), iii–xii, 1–126.

———. "The Dublin Notes on Homer: Part II," ed. Fredric Schlatter, S.J., *HQ,* 24/3–4 (Summer–Fall 1997), 95–127.

———. "Poetic Fragments, Comments on Lucan and Cicero, Essay on Duty," ed. Fredric Schlatter, S.J., *HQ,* 27/3–4 (Summer–Fall 2000), 1–106.

Hopkins, Gerard M. uncollected letters:

To the Bishop of Liverpool, 12 Aug. 1881, *HRB,* 2 (1971), 3–5.

To William Butterfield, 26 Apr. 1877, *HRB,* 5 (1974), 3–5.

To W. A. Comyn Macfarlane, 10 July [1866], *HRB,* 6 (1975), 4.

To W. A. Comyn Macfarlane, 15 July 1866, *HRB,* 6 (1975), 4–5.

To W. A. Comyn Macfarlane [Nov. or Dec. 1866], *HRB,* 6 (1975), 5–7.

To Dr. M. F. Cox, 26 Mar. 1887, *HRB,* 3 (1972), 6–7.

To Dr. M. F. Cox, 31 Mar. 1887, *HRB,* 3 (1972), 8–9.

To Everard Hopkins, 5–8 Nov. 1885, *HRB,* 4 (1973), 7–12.

To Everard Hopkins, 23 Dec. 1885, *HRB,* 4 (1973), 12–14.

To Herr-Doktor Müncke, 8 May [1861], *HRB,* 4 (1973), 3–6.

Hopkins, Lionel C. "Dragon and Alligator, being Notes on some Ancient Inscribed Bone Carvings," "Where the Rainbow Ends," "Archaic Chinese Characters": 3 articles in the *Journal of the Royal Asiatic Society* (July 1913, July 1931, and January 1937).

——. *The Guide to Kuan Hua. A Translation of the "Kuan Hua Chih Nan"* (Shanghai, 1889).

——. *The Six Scripts of the Principles of Chinese Writing by Tai T'ung, a Translation by L. C. Hopkins, with a Memoir of the Translator by W. Perceval Yetts* (Cambridge, 1954).

Hopkins, Manley. *Hawaii: The Past, Present, and Future of its Island Kingdom* (1862).

——. "Politics in the Sandwich Islands," *Cornhill Magazine,* 2 (December 1864), 109–17.

——. *Spicilegium Poeticum* (1892).

——. *The Cardinal Numbers* (1887).

——. "The Dodo non-extinct," letter to *Long Ago,* 11(13) (January 1874), repr in *HRB,* 1 (1970), 17.

——, and Marsland Hopkins. *Pietas Metrica; or. Nature Suggestive of God and Godliness,* by the Brothers Theophilus and Theophylact (1849).

House, Madeline. "Books Belonging to Hopkins and His Family," *HRB,* 5 (1974), 26–41, and "Books Hopkins Had Access To," *HRB,* 6 (1975), 17–21.

Housman, A. E. *Letters of A. E. Housman,* ed. Henry Maas (1971).

——. Extract from unpublished letter of Housman to Sidney Cockerell, mentioning Hopkins, in "Items of Interest," *HRB,* 4 (1973), 40.

Humphrey, William, S.J. *The Religious State. A Digest of the Doctrine of Suarez,* 3 vols. (1888).

Jenkyns, Richard. *The Victorians and Ancient Greece* (Cambridge, MA: Harvard University Press, 1980).

Johnson, Wendell Stacy. *Gerard Manley Hopkins: The Poet as Victorian* (Ithaca: Cornell University Press, 1968).

——. "From Ruskin to Hopkins: Landscape and Inscape," *HQ,* 8 (Fall 1981), 89–106.

Johnston, John Octavius. *Life and Letters of Henry Parry Liddon* (1905).

Jowett, Benjamin. *Dear Miss Nightingale: A Selection of Benjamin Jowett's Letters to Florence Nightingale,* ed. Vincent Quinn and John Prest (Oxford: Clarendon Press, 1987).

Joyce, James. *A Portrait of the Artist as a Young Man* (1916; 1977 ed.).

Kenyon Critics, The. *Gerard Manley Hopkins* (1949).

Kirk, G., S.J., E. Raven, and M. Schofield. *The Presocratic Philosophers: A Critical History with a Selection of Texts,* 2nd ed. (Cambridge: Cambridge University Press, 1995).

Kitchen, Paddy. *Gerard Manley Hopkins* (London: H. Hamilton, 1978).

Lahey, G. F., S.J. *Gerard Manley Hopkins* (London: Oxford University Press, 1930).

Landow, George P. *Victorian Types, Victorian Shadows: Biblical Typology in Victorian Literature, Art, and Thought* (1980).

Lawler, Justus George. *Hopkins Re-Constructed: Life, Poetry and the Tradition* (New York: Continuum, 1998).

Lees, Francis Noel. *Gerard Manley Hopkins* (1966).

Levey, Michael. *The Case of Walter Pater* (London: Thames & Hudson, 1978).

Lewes, George Henry. *The Life and Works of Goethe* (London, 1855).

Liddon, Henry Parry. *The Divinity of Our Lord and Saviour Jesus Christ: Eight Lectures Preached Before the University of Oxford in the Year 1866*, 14th ed. (London, 1890).

Lilly, Gweneth. "Welsh Influence in the Poetry of Gerard Manley Hopkins," *MLR*, 38 (July 1943), 192–205.

Mackenzie, Norman H. *Hopkins* (Edinburgh: Oliver & Boyd, 1968).

———. *A Reader's Guide to Gerard Manley Hopkins* (Ithaca: Cornell University Press, 1981).

———, ed. *The Poetical Works of Gerard Manley Hopkins* (Oxford: Clarendon Press, 1990).

———, ed. *The Early Poetic Manuscripts and Note-books of Gerard Manley Hopkins in Facsimile* (New York: Garland, 1989).

———, ed. *The Later Poetic Manuscripts of Gerard Manley Hopkins in Facsimile* (New York: Garland, 1991).

———. "Gerard Manley Hopkins' 'Spelt from Sibyl's Leaves,'" *Malahat Review*, 26 (April 1973), 218–28.

———. "The Making of a Hopkins Sonnet," in A. A. Macdonald, P. A. O'Flaherty, and G. M. Story, eds., *A Festschrift for Edgar Ronald Seary* (St. John's, Newfoundland: Memorial University Press, 1975), 151–69.

———. "The Imperative Voice: An Unpublished Lecture by Hopkins," *HQ*, 2/3 (October 1975), 101–16.

———. "An Unpublished Hopkins Manuscript," *HRB*, 7 (1976), 3–7.

———. "Hopkins and St. Dorothea," in John North and Michael Moore, eds., *Vital Candle* (Waterloo, ONT: University of Waterloo Press, 1984), 21–39.

———. "From Manuscript to Printed Text: The Hazardous Transmission of the Hopkins Canon," in Dave Oliphant, ed., *Hopkins Lives: An Exhibition and Catalogue*, comp. Carl Sutton (Austin, TX: Harry Ransom Humanities Research Center, 1989), 51–73.

Mahoney, John, S.J. *The Making of Moral Theology: A Study of the Roman Catholic Tradition* (Oxford: Clarendon Press, 1989).

Mallock, W. H. *The New Republic; or, Culture, faith, and philosophy in an English country house* (London, 1877).

Mariani, Paul. *A Commentary on the Complete Poems of Gerard Manley Hopkins* (Ithaca: Cornell University Press, 1970).

———. "Hopkins' 'Felix Randal' as Sacramental Vision," *Renascence*, XIX/4 (Summer 1967), 217–20.

———. "The Artistic and Tonal Integrity of Hopkins' 'The Shepherd's Brow,'" *Victorian Poetry,* VI/1 (Spring 1968), 63–68.

———. "Hopkins' 'Harry Ploughman' and Frederick Walker's 'The Plough,'" *The Month,* n.s. 40, 1 & 2 (July–August 1968), 37–45.

———. "Hopkins' 'Andromeda' and the New Aestheticism," *Victorian Poetry,* XI/1 (Spring 1973), 39–54.

———. "The Sounds of One's Self Breathing: The Burden of Theological Metaphor in Hopkins," *HQ,* 4/1 (Spring 1977), 17–26. Repr. in *Critical Essays on Gerard Manley Hopkins,* ed. Alison G. Sulloway (Boston: G. K. Hall & Co., 1990), 53–59.

———. "Paddy Kitchen's *Gerard Manley Hopkins: A Biography,*" review in *HQ,* 7/3 (Fall 1980), 125–28.

———. "Hopkins and Williams: Too Little, Too Late," in *Hopkins Among the Poets: Studies in Modern Responses to Gerard Manley Hopkins,* ed. Richard F. Giles, International Hopkins Ass., Monograph #3 (1985), 21–23.

———. "The Dark Night of the Soul," in Harold Bloom, ed., *Modern Critical Views: Gerard Manley Hopkins* (New York: Chelsea House: 1986), 51–76.

———. Milton J. Bates' *Wallace Stevens: A Mythology of Self,* David LaGuardia's *Advance on Chaos: The Sanctifying Imagination of Wallace Stevens,* and Mary Lou Motto's *Mined with a Motion: The Poetry of Gerard Manley Hopkins,* reviewed in *Literature & Religion,* 18/1 (Notre Dame, Spring 1986), 73–78.

———. "Walter Ong's *Hopkins, the Self, and God,*" *Hopkins Review,* 13, nos. 1 & 2 (April–July 1986), 55–59.

———. "The Consoling, Terrifying Presence of Hopkins," *Renascence,* special Hopkins issue, vol. XLII, nos. 1–2 (Fall 1989–Winter 1990), 13–20.

———. "Robert Martin's biography of *Gerard Manley Hopkins: A Very Private Life,*" *Nineteenth Century Literature,* 48/1 (June 1993), 121–24.

———. "Hopkins as Lifeline," *HQ,* 25/1–2 (Winter–Spring 1998), 17–18.

———. "Philip A. Ballinger's *The Poem as Sacrament: The Theological Aesthetic of Gerard Manley Hopkins,*" Louvain Theological and Pastoral Monographs, 26, reviewed in *Theological Studies,* 62/2 (June 2001), 415–16.

———. "Hopkins' Late Poetics: The Christ-Saturated Thing Itself," *Image,* 56 (Winter 2007), 100–11.

Marks, John George. *Life and Letters of Frederick Walker, A.R.A.* (1896).

Martin, Robert Bernard. *Gerard Manley Hopkins: A Very Private Life* (New York: G. P. Putnam's Sons, 1991).

———. *Tennyson: The Unquiet Heart* (London: Oxford University Press, 1980).

Masheck, J. D. C. "Art by a Poet: Notes on Published Drawings by Gerard Manley Hopkins," *Hermathena,* 108 (1969), 24–37.

Maxwell-Scott, M. M. C. *Henry Schomberg Kerr: Sailor and Jesuit* (1901).

Mill, John Stuart. *Utilitarianism* (London, 1863).

Miller, J. Hillis. *The Disappearance of God* (Cambridge, MA: Harvard University Press, 1963).

Milroy, James. *The Language of Gerard Manley Hopkins* (London: Deutsch, 1977).

Monsman, Gerald. *Walter Pater* (Boston: Twayne, 1977).

Moore, Michael. "Dangerous Beauty: Hopkins and Newman," in Michael Allsopp and Michael Sundermeier, eds., *Gerard Manley Hopkins (1844–1889): New Essays on His Life, Writing, and Place in English Literature* (Lewiston, NY: E. Mellen Press, 1989), 85–112.

Morrissey, Thomas J., S.J. *Towards a National University: William Delaney, SJ, An Era of Initiative in Irish Education* (Dublin: Wolfhound Press, 1983).

Motto, Marylou. *"Mined with a Motion": The Poetry of Gerard Manley Hopkins* (New Brunswick, NJ: Rutgers University Press, 1984).

Myers, Joanna Shaw. "Hopkins and Mrs. Humphry Ward's Helbeck of Bannisdale," in Francis Fennell, ed., *Rereading Hopkins: Selected New Essays* (Victoria, BC: University of Victoria Press, 1996), 63–83.

Myerscough, John A., S.J. *A Procession of Lancashire Martyrs and Confessors* (Glasgow, 1958).

Nettleship, Richard Lewis. *Lectures on the Republic of Plato* (London: Macmillan, 1901, 1951).

———. *The Theory of Education in Plato's Republic* (1935).

Nichols, Aidan, O. P. *Hopkins: Theologian's Poet* (Ann Arbor: Sapientia Press, 2006).

Nixon, Jude. "'Sweet especial rural scene': Rivisiting Binsey," *HQ*, 16/1–2 (April–July 1989), 39–60.

———. "The Kindly Light: A Reappraisal of the Influence of Newman on Hopkins," *Texas Studies in Literature and Language*, 31/1 (1989), 105–42.

———. "Gerard Manley Hopkins and Henry Parry Liddon: An Unacknowledged Influence," *Resascence*, 42/1–2 (Fall 1989–Winter 1990), 87–110.

———. *Gerard Manley Hopkins and His Contemporaries: Liddon, Newman, Darwin, and Pater* (New York: Garland, 1994).

O'Flynn, Grainne. "Hopkins's Teaching," *HQ*, 14 (1987–88), 163–78.

O'Leary, Sean. *The Alchemist: Gerard Manley Hopkins/Poems in Musical Adaptations.* Two-disc CD set: EarthSweet Earth Productions (2005).

Oliphant, Dave, ed. *Hopkins Lives: An Exhibition and Catalogue*, comp. Carl Sutton (Austin, TX: Harry Ransom Humanities Research Center, 1989).

Ong, Walter J., S.J. *Hopkins, the Self, and God* (Toronto: University of Toronto Press, 1986).

Pater, Walter. *Letters of Walter Pater*, ed. Lawrence Evans (Oxford: Oxford University Press, 1970).

———. *The Renaissance: Studies in Art and Poetry*, ed. Donald L. Hill (Berkeley: University of California Press, 1980).

Patmore, Coventry. *Poems*, ed. F. Page (1959).

Patmore, Derek. *The Life and Times of Coventry Patmore* (1949).

Patmore, Henry. *Poems* (Oxford, 1884).

Phillips, Catherine L. *Robert Bridges, A Biography* (London: Oxford University Press, 1992).

——. "'Believe me very sincerely your': Gerard Manley Hopkins as Letter-Writer," *HQ,* 31 (2004), 157–66.

——, and R. K. R. Thornton. "Two Unpublished Letters of Gerard Manley Hopkins [to Charles Kent, both 27 Aug. 1877]," *HQ,* 33, 1/2 (Winter 2005), 8–14.

Pick, John. *Gerard Manley Hopkins, Priest and Poet,* 2nd ed. (London: Oxford University Press, 1966).

Piper, David. *The Treasures of Oxford* (London: Paddington Press, 1977).

Plato. *The Dialogues of Plato: Translated into English with Analyses and Introductions,* ed. Benjamin Jowett, 5 vols. (Oxford, 1871).

Plotkin, Cary. *The Tenth Muse: Victorian Philology and the Genesis of the Poetic Language of Gerard Manley Hopkins* (Carbondale, IL: Southern Illinois University Press, 1989).

Praz, Mario. *Mnemosyne: The Parallel Between Literature and the Visual Arts* (Washington, DC: 1974).

Pugin, Augustus Welby (cont.). *Contrasts; or a Parallel between the Architecture of the Fifteenth and Nineteenth Centuries* (1836).

Pusey, E. B. *The Church of England A Portion of Christ's One Holy Catholic Church, and a Means of Restoring Visible Unity. An Eirenicon* (1865).

Rickaby, Joseph, S.J. *The Spiritual Exercises of St. Ignatius Loyola* (1923).

——. *Moral Philosophy, Ethics, Deontology and Natural Law* (1929).

Ricks, Christopher. *Tennyson* (London: Collier, 1972).

Ritz, Jean-Georges. *Robert Bridges and Gerard Hopkins, 1863–1889: A Literary Friendship* (London: Oxford University Press, 1960).

——. *Le Poète Gerard Hopkins SJ* (Paris, 1963).

Roberts, Gerald, ed. *Gerard Manley Hopkins: The Critical Heritage* (London: Routledge & Kegan Paul, 1987).

Robinson, John. *In Extremity: A Study of Gerard Manley Hopkins* (Cambridge: Cambridge University Press, 1978).

Rockstro, W. S. *A History of Music,* 3rd ed. (n.d.).

Rossetti, Christina. *The Prince's Progress* (1866).

Ruggles, Eleanor. *Gerard Manley Hopkins* (New York: W. W. Norton & Company, 1944).

Ruskin, John. *The Elements of Drawing,* ed. Bernard Dunstan (London: Herbert, 1991).

Saintsbury, George. *A History of English Prosody,* 2 vols. (1906).

——. *A History of Nineteenth Century Literature* (1910).

Salmon, Rachel. "Poetry and Religious Work: Defamiliarizing Hopkins's *The Wreck of the Deutschland,*" *HQ,* 31 (2004).

Sambrook, J. *A Poet Hidden: The Life of Richard Watson Dixon* (1962).

Saville, Julia F. *A Queer Chivalry: The Homoerotic Asceticism of Gerard Manley Hopkins.* Victorian Literature and Culture Series (Charlottesville: University Press of Virginia, 2000).

Schlatter, Fredric W., S.J. "Hopkins at the Bar: The Case of the Missing Will," *HQ*, 29 (2002), 53–64.

———. "Martial Klein, Hopkins' Dublin Colleague," *HQ*, 29 (2002), 69–105.

———. "Hopkins' Dublin Critic, Joseph Darlington, S.J.," *HQ*, 30 (2003), 98–126.

———. "George Teeling: Mutual Friend of Newman and Hopkins," *HQ*, 32 (2005), 112–28.

———. "William Addis: Hopkins' Friend," *HQ*, 33 (2006), 3–27.

Schmidt, Carl. "Classical Studies at Balliol in the 1860's: The Undergraduate Essays of Gerard Manley Hopkins," in John Prest, ed., *Balliol Studies* (London: Leopard's Head Press, 1982), 161–84.

Schneider, Elisabeth W. *The Dragon in the Gate: Studies in the Poetry of G. M. Hopkins* (Berkeley and Los Angeles: University of California Press, 1968).

Seelhammer, Ruth. *Hopkins Collected at Gonzaga* (Chicago: University of Chicago Press, 1970).

Seller, Robert, ed. *Walter Pater: A Life Remembered* (Calgary, ALB: University of Calgary Press, 1987).

Shimane, Kunio. *The Poetry of G. M. Hopkins: The Fusing Point of Sound and Sense* (Tokyo: Hokuseido Press, 1983).

Sieveking, Lance. *The Eye of the Beholder* (1957).

Sonstroem, David. "John Ruskin and the Nature of Manliness," *The Victorian Newsletter*, 40 (1971), 14–17.

Sprinker, Michael. *"A Counterpoint of Dissonance": The Aesthetics and Poetry of Gerard Manley Hopkins* (Baltimore: Johns Hopkins University Press, 1980).

Staley, Allen. *The Pre-Raphaelite Landscape*, 2nd ed. (New Haven: Yale University Press, 2001).

Starkey, R. L. "Library Register, Highgate School, March 1860–November 1862," *HRB*, 6 (1975), 22–26.

Storey, Graham. *A Preface to Hopkins* (London: Longman, 1981).

———. *A Preface to Hopkins*, 2nd ed. (London: Longman, 1992).

———. *Gerard Manley Hopkins* (Windsor: Profile Books, 1984).

Street, Sean. *The Wreck of the Deutschland* (London: Souvenir Press, 1992).

Sulloway, Alison G. *Gerard Manley Hopkins and the Victorian Temper* (New York: Columbia University Press, 1972).

———, ed. *Critical Essays on Gerard Manley Hopkins* (Boston: G. K. Hall & Co., 1990).

Sussman, Herbert. *Victorian Masculinities: Manhood and Masculine Poetics in Early Victorian Literature and Art* (Cambridge: Cambridge University Press, 1995).

Swinburne, Algernon. *Poems and Ballads and Atalanta in Calydon*, ed. Morse Peckham (Indianapolis: Bobbs-Merrill, 1970).

Tanner, John. "When God Is Hero: Worshipping God as Hero in Carlyle and Hopkins," *HQ*, 10/4 (Winter 1984), 145–63.

Tennyson, Alfred. *Poems*, ed. Christopher Ricks (London: Longmans, 1969).

Thomas, Alfred, S.J. *Hopkins the Jesuit: The Years of Training* (London: Oxford University Press, 1969).

Thornton, R. K. R., ed. *All My Eyes See: The Visual World of Gerard Manley Hopkins* (Sunderland: Ceolfrith Press, 1975), 3–9.

———. *G. M. Hopkins: The Poems* (London: Edward Arnold, 1973).

Tillotson, Geoffrey. *A View of Victorian Literature* (Oxford: Clarendon Press, 1978).

Tradleg, Nitram [Edmund Martin Geldart], *A Son of Belial: Autobiographical Sketches* (London: 1882).

Tynan, Katharine. *Shamrocks* (1887).

———. *Twenty-five Years: Reminiscences* (1913).

Walton, Paul H. *The Drawings of John Ruskin* (Oxford, 1972).

Ward, Bernadette Waterman. *World as Word: Philosophical Theology in Gerard Manley Hopkins* (Washington, DC: Catholic University of America Press, 2002).

Ward, Mrs. Humphry. *Helbeck of Bannisdale* (1898).

Waterhouse, Elizabeth, ed. A *Book of Simple Prayers* (Reading, 1893).

Weyand, Norman, S.J., ed. *Immortal Diamond: Studies in Gerard Manley Hopkins* (1949).

White, Norman. *Hopkins: A Literary Biography* (London: Oxford University Press, 1992).

———. "The Parents and Early Background of Gerard Hopkins," *HQ*, 20/3–4 (Summer–Fall 1993), 63–114.

———. "Gerard Manley Hopkins and the Irish Row," *HQ*, 9/3 (1982), 91–107.

———. "G. M. Hopkins's Contributions to the English Dialect Dictionary," *English Studies*, 68/4 (1987), 325–35.

———. *Gerard Manley Hopkins in Wales* (Bridgend: Poetry Wales Press, 1998).

———. *Hopkins in Ireland* (Dublin: University College Press, 2002).

Williams, Raymond. *Culture and Society, 1780–1950* (Harmondsworth: Penguin, 1963).

Wimsatt, James I. *Hopkins's Poetics of Speech Sounds: Sprung Rhythm, Lettering, Inscape* (Toronto: University of Toronto Press, 2006).

Winters, Yvor. *The Function of Criticism* (1962).

Yeats, W. B. *Letters to Katharine Tynan*, ed. Roger McHugh (Dublin, 1953).

Zaniello, Thomas. "An Early Example of the Musical Analogy in Hopkins," *HRB*, 7 (1976), 15–16.

———. "The Sources of Hopkins's Inscape: Epistemology at Oxford, 1864–1868," *The Victorian Newsletter*, 52 (Fall 1977), 18–24.

———. "The Tonic of Platonism: The Origins and Use of Hopkins's 'Scrape,'" *HQ*, 5/1 (Spring 1978), 5–16.

———. *Hopkins in the Age of Darwin* (Iowa City: University of Iowa Press, 1988).

Zonneveld, Sjaak. "A Note on Spooner and Hopkins," *HQ*, 11/1–2 (Spring–Summer 1984), 43–44.

———. *The Random Grim Forge: A Study of Social Ideas in the Works of Gerard Manley Hopkins* (Maastricht: Van Gorcum, 1992).

Index